WILEY NAUTICAL

THE IONIAN

CRUISING COMPANION

A yachtsman's guide to
the Ionian

VANESSA BIRD

BICENTENNIAL 1807 WILEY 2007 BICENTENNIAL

Copyright © 2007 Vanessa Bird
Published by John Wiley & Sons Ltd, The Atrium, Southern Gate, Chichester,
West Sussex PO19 8SQ, England
Telephone (+44) 1243 779777
Email (for orders and customer service enquiries): cs-books@wiley.co.uk
Visit our Home Page on www.wileynautical.com

Photographs by Vanessa Bird
Aerial photography ©Robert JA Buttress/OTH

Additional photography:
Pages 233, 253 ©Greek National Tourism Organisation (GNTO); Pages 101, 102, 103, 105, 110, 112, 116, 117, 118 (top), 120, 122, 124, 128, 131 (bottom), 132 (bottom), 134, 135 (top), 138, 145 (top), 146, 149 (bottom) ©Prefecture of Lefkada; Page 159 by Richard Neall ©Sunsail; Page 268 ©Amanda Parkinson; Pages 5, 11, 14, 16, 18, 153, 160, 161, 195, 197 by Johnathan Smith ©Sunsail; Pages 6, 7 (bottom) ©Lynn Smith

For Wiley Nautical
Executive Editor: David Palmer
Project Editor: Lynette James
Assistant Editor: Drew Kennerley

For Nautical Data
Cartography: Jamie Russell
Art Direction: Vanessa Bird and Jamie Russell
Cruising Companion series editors: Vanessa Bird and Lucinda Roch
Consultant editor: Elizabeth Watson
Research: Amanda Parkinson and Emma Watson

ISBN-13: 978-1-904358-27-5

IMPORTANT NOTICE

This Companion is intended as an aid to navigation only. The information contained within should not solely be relied on for navigational use, rather it should be used in conjunction with official hydrographic data. Whilst every care has been taken in compiling the information contained in this Companion, the publishers, author, editors and their agents accept no responsibility for any errors or omissions, or for any accidents or mishaps which may arise from its use.

Neither the publisher nor the author can accept responsibility for errors, omissions or alterations in this book. They will be grateful for any information from readers to assist in the update and accuracy of the publication.

Readers are advised at all times to refer to official charts, publications and notices. The charts contained in this book are sketch plans and are not to be used for navigation. Some details are omitted for the sake of clarity and the scales have been chosen to allow best coverage in relation to page size.

Correctional supplements are available at www.wileynautical.com and on request from the publishers.

Printed by PrinterTrento in Trento, Italy

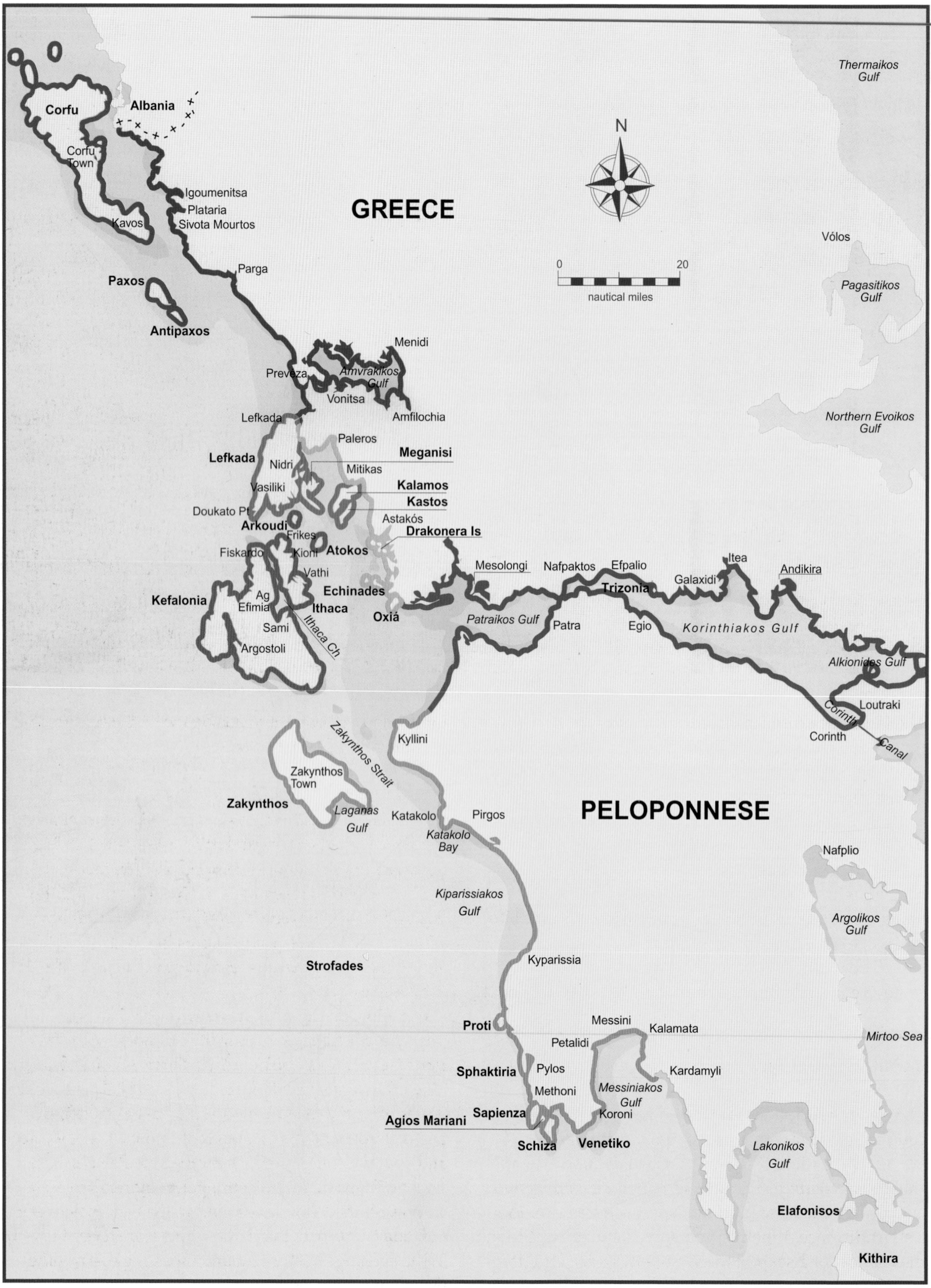
Corfu
Albania
Corfu Town
Igoumenitsa
Plataria
Sivota Mourtos
Kavos
GREECE
N
0
20
nautical miles
Thermaikos Gulf
Vólos
Pagasitikos Gulf
Parga
Paxos
Antipaxos
Menidi
Preveza
Amvrakikos Gulf
Vonitsa
Amfilochia
Lefkada
Northern Evoikos Gulf
Paleros
Meganisi
Lefkada
Nidri
Mitikas
Vasiliki
Kalamos
Kastos
Doukato Pt
Astakós
Arkoudi
Drakonera Is
Frikes
Fiskardo
Kioni
Atokos
Vathi
Mesolongi
Nafpaktos
Efpalio
Itea
Andikira
Galaxidi
Trizonia
Echinades
Kefalonia
Ag Efimia
Ithaca
Oxiá
Sami
Ithaca Ch
Patraikos Gulf
Patra
Egio
Korinthiakos Gulf
Argostoli
Alkionides Gulf
Loutraki
Corinth
Corinth Canal
Kyllini
Zakynthos Strait
Zakynthos Town
Zakynthos
Laganas Gulf
Katakolo
Pirgos
PELOPONNESE
Katakolo Bay
Nafplio
Kiparissiakos Gulf
Argolikos Gulf
Kyparissia
Strofades
Messini
Proti
Kalamata
Mirtoo Sea
Petalidi
Pylos
Kardamyli
Sphaktiria
Methoni
Messiniakos Gulf
Sapienza
Koroni
Agios Mariani
Schiza
Venetiko
Lakonikos Gulf
Elafonisos
Kithira

Introduction

The Ionian Sea forms part of the Mediterranean and lies to the south of the Adriatic, between Italy and the west coast of Greece. It is home to an archipelago called the Ionian islands or *Ionioi Nisoi*, which together cover 892 square miles (2,310km^2) of land. Primarily mountainous, the seven major islands and their many satellites create a dramatic landscape. Their west coasts are typically rugged, with exposed, vertiginous cliffs, and offer few harbours or places of refuge. Their east coasts are softer and more developed, with gentler hills and protected bays. The islands' interiors differ greatly. Most have extensive mountain ranges but there are also pockets of low-lying plains and tracts of agricultural land.

The scenery is varied on the mainland coast. High mountains are juxtaposed with river valleys and marshy wetlands. Bays bordered by craggy rocks combine with salt lagoons and sandy shores, and village harbours contrast with industrial ports and tourist resorts.

As a destination, the Ionian is hard to beat. The sailing is superb: predictable weather, easy navigation and a huge choice of harbours and anchorages within a short distance. Whether you spend a week exploring the islands, or a season, there's plenty to see and do and, despite the steady march of commercialisation and tourism, there are still parts that are relatively unspoilt. Tiny villages backed by vast olive groves peppered with cypress trees are a major characteristic of the Ionian and, if you visit at either end of the season, you'll find uncrowded waters too.

WEATHER & CLIMATE

The Ionian generally enjoys a stable Mediterranean climate of hot summers and mild winters with a high average rainfall. Summer temperatures in this part of Greece tend to reach 28-32°C (82-90°F) during the day and range between 22-26°C (72-79°F) at night. Winter temperatures may drop as low as 15°C (59°F) and higher mountainous regions of the mainland will occasionally see snow.

The winds in this area are usually predictable. The summer months will see little or no wind in the morning, before a northwesterly Force 3-5 picks up after lunch. This *maistro* will normally last until sunset, when it dies off completely. Expect winds to be stronger in mid-summer and for them to blow from a more westerly and southwesterly direction around the Peloponnese. They will also be slightly stronger in more open areas, such as off the Peloponnese and in the waters between Lefkada and Corfu. Katabatic winds sometimes blow up in the evenings in more mountainous regions but they usually only last a couple of hours.

During the winter months and sometimes during July and August the Ionian experiences more southerly winds, which can cause heavy swell. The area is also affected by the *sirocco* – a warm southeasterly or southwesterly wind originating over Libya and Egypt. It is often strong in spring.

The Ionian sees some storms, particularly in the winter and spring. In the summer months they can be brief but torrential, but these normally clear as quickly as they arrive so are not much of a problem. If conditions deteriorate significantly, consider weathering the blow on the water rather than trying to berth in a crowded harbour while the wind is at its worst.

WEATHER FORECASTS

Predicting the weather among the Ionian islands is a tricky business. Most of the reports that are issued relate to open waters, but the geography of the islands and their location can affect wind strength and direction, creating localised weather systems that are different from the forecast. Daily forecasts from the Hellenic National Meteorological Service (HNMS) are broadcast in both Greek and English and can be obtained in various ways. All times listed below are in Universal Time (UT) or Greenwich Mean Time (GMT). Local time in the Ionian is +3 hours in summer and +2 hours in winter.

VHF Radio: Forecasts are broadcast four times a day at 0600, 1000, 1600 and 2200 on the following VHF Channels: Corfu Ch02; Kefalonia Ch27; Kythira Ch85; Petalidi Ch83. Gale warnings are often broadcast on Ch16.

SSB Radio: Corfu Radio issues forecasts on 2830kHz at 0703, 0903, 1533, 2133.

Navtex: Forecasts issued by the HNMS are transmitted daily on 518kHz. The Corfu Radio Coastal Station broadcasts forecasts at 0140, 0540, 0940, 1340, 1740 and 2140.

Telephone: The HNMS operates a 24-hour telephone line on which you can talk to a meteorologist and get an up-to-date forecast for your area. Tel: 21096 29316/17/18/19. To hear a general pre-recorded weather forecast, telephone 1448.

Websites: For the latest forecast and satellite imagery, see www.hnms.gr, www.poseidon.ncmr.gr or www.weatheronline.co.uk/Greece

Television: Weather forecasts are broadcast at the end of all major news bulletins.

SMS: To receive forecasts on your mobile, firstly you need a Greek SIM card, which you can buy for around €15. Secondly, type in W (leave a space), the first four digits of your latitude (leave a space), the first four digits of your longitude (i.e. W GPS 3937 1955), then send to 4264. Within a minute you will receive an SMS with the wind direction and the force for that particular area for the next 24 hours until 0600.

The area covered in this book is divided into five shipping areas:

North Ionio – covers the area from Corfu south to Kefalonia, incorporating the Epirus and Etolo-Akarnanian coast.

South Ionio – south of Kefalonia to Koroni on the south coast of the Peloponnese.

Patraikos Gulf – the Patraikos Gulf between mainland Greece and the Peloponnese.

Korinthiakos Gulf – the Korinthiakos Gulf, from where it meets the Patraikos Gulf to the entrance to the Corinth Canal.

Kythera – sea area along the south coast of the Peloponnese, from Koroni to the start of the Aegean Sea.

IONIAN WILDLIFE

Flora

The Ionian islands have a reputation for being lush and fertile. They're among the greenest of the Greek islands with a diverse range of habitats that produce several thousand species of plants and trees. Mild winters, a high average rainfall and hot summers combined with varied habitats create an area that is one of the richest in flora in Europe. The spring is the best time to visit for flowering plants and it is then that the hillsides, meadows and wetlands explode with colour. Wild flowers are particularly good in April and May, before the harsh summer sun takes its toll, though private gardens still bloom forth with their endless terracotta pots and great swathes of bougainvillaea and oleander.

In the summer months, most of the islands remain green, their hillsides covered in garrigue and maquis,

Terracota pots bursting with colour are a feature in most villages

The Hermanns tortoise

punctuated by the tall spikes of cypress trees. The olive tree is ubiquitous and there are literally millions in the Ionian, many of them centuries old with wonderfully gnarled trunks. Grape and currant vines, citrus fruits, melons and cotton are among the crops grown in this part of Greece and large parts of the islands and coastline have been cultivated for their production since Venetian times. It's an area that is rich in diversity and really quite stunning.

Birds

Wetlands such as the Kalamos Delta, Amvrakikos Gulf and Gialova Lagoon on the mainland coast are an ornithologist's paradise, well known for their large populations of migratory birds. The Amvrakikos Gulf, in particular, sees an annual invasion of 250,000 water birds from 250 species – the highest concentration of its kind in Greece and one of the largest in Europe.

The islands, too, see a vast array of birds, from the common buzzard (*Buteo buteo*) to the Sardinian warbler (*Sylvia melanocephala*), Golden oriole (*Oriolus oriolus*) and the house martin (*Delichon urbica*). Look out for seabirds such as the yellow-legged gull (*Larus cachinnans*) and Cory's or Mediterranean shearwater (*Caloyectris diomedea*), and ashore for flycatchers and finches.

Fauna

On land

The most common sight in and around Ionian harbours is the domestic cat. In some places, such as Kioni on Ithaca, there are so many that you'll be tripping over them as they beg for scraps from the fishermen and people eating at tavernas. Other creatures you might see are the Moorish gecko (*Tarantola mauritanica*) and the Hermanns tortoise (*Testudo hermanni*), as well as goats, sheep, donkeys and, on Mount Enos on Kefalonia, wild horses.

At sea

The Ionian was once home to a great diversity of marine life. Dolphins, whales, turtles and seals thrived in its warm waters and were regularly seen by visitors to the area. Now, however, with intensive fishing, depleted fish stocks and mass tourist developments along great swathes of coastline, many of the area's native species are endangered. According to the Earth, Sea & Sky organisation in Zakynthos, the Mediterranean monk seal (*Monachus monachus*) is one of the most 'critically endangered marine mammals in the world'. Fewer than 20 are now thought to inhabit the whole Ionian, an area that once would have seen hundreds. However, loss of habitat to tourism and killing by fishermen who saw them as a threat to their livelihoods has seriously depleted these numbers.

The loggerhead turtle (*Caretta caretta*) is also facing extinction. One of just three species found in the Mediterranean, the loggerhead is the only one to nest in Greece and can occasionally be spotted in the Ionian. Although they mainly live in the sea, every two to four years females come ashore briefly to nest and lay their eggs. Unfortunately, mass tourism and beach developments have destroyed many of the turtles' nesting grounds resulting in a significant impact on their numbers. The Laganas Gulf, on the south coast of Zakynthos, is one of the few places where they still breed and is now a protected area, with the movements of leisure craft strictly limited (see p237).

Lastly, the short-beaked common dolphin (*Delphinus delphis)* and common bottlenose dolphin (*Tursiops truncates*). Both species were abundant in the Ionian during the 1960s, but since the 1980s scientists have noticed a rapid decline. Fish stocks in this part of Greece are now so depleted that the dolphins have no ready supply of food and increased pollution has also had disastrous consequences.

A BRIEF HISTORY OF GREECE & THE IONIAN

5000BC Archaeologists think Kefalonia was one of the first Ionian islands to be inhabited and have found evidence of human life that dates to the Palaeolithic era (early Stone Age).

10000-3000BC The Neolithic Period, or New Stone Age, sees the cultivation of land and livestock, evidence of which has been found on the Ionian islands. Ancient Corinth is set up.

3000BC The Bronze Age supersedes the Neolithic Period, with cultures developing on the Cyclades and islands in the Aegean. Inter-island trade begins.

2500-1,400BC The Minoan civilisation establishes itself on Crete. Cretan pottery has been found throughout Greece, and it is thought that the Bronze Age Cretans travelled extensively and were a dominant, but peaceful, society. Kefalonia is thought to have traded with the Minoans, as part of the Knossos palace on Crete was built using Kefalonia's native fir tree, *Abies cephalonica*.

1500BC The eruption of a volcano on the island of Santorini destroys much of Crete and, consequently, the Minoan civilisation. Settlers on mainland Greece start to gain in power.

1600-1200BC The Mycenaean Age sees the development of the Greek language. Based on mainland Greece, principally at Mycenae in the Peloponnese, the Mycenaeans soon establish themselves as the dominant culture. This period is infused with myths, many of which Homer used in *The Iliad* and *The Odyssey*. The Tzanata Tombs, near Poros, on Kefalonia are just one example of Mycenaean existence on the Ionian islands.

1200BC The Mycenaean culture collapses.

1050BC The Dorians, a Greek-speaking culture, emerge as the dominant class, migrating across eastern Greece. This period is often referred to as the Dark Age.

800-450BC The Greek culture is restored and trade begins to flourish again. The Greek alphabet is developed and chicken is introduced to the Greek diet. City-states (*polis*) are set up, which divide Greece into autonomous regions, including Athens, Sparta and Corinth. Several of the Ionian islands are inhabited by the city-states and are involved in on-going wars between them. Corinth is particularly influential over the islands.

776BC The first Olympic Games are held at Olympia.

750-700BC Homer writes *The Iliad* and *The Odyssey* (see p10).

650BC Corinthians dig a canal between Lefkada and the mainland.

500-448BC The Persian Wars – a series of battles between Greece and the Persian Empire. The Persians were eventually beaten by the city-states.

447BC Work starts on the Parthenon, one of the most famous buildings of Ancient Greece.

431-404BC The city-states Athens and Sparta become embroiled in the bitter Peloponnesian Wars. Inhabitants from the Ionian islands are drawn into the battles.

404BC Sparta wins the Peloponnesian Wars and dominates Greece for the next 30 years.

338BC The Macedonian Empire, led by Philip II, rises to power and takes control of Greece. Following his assassination in 336BC, Philip II is succeeded by his son, Alexander the Great.

229BC The Romans conquer Corfu and, over the next 40 years or so, gain control over the rest of the Ionians.

197BC Romans defeat the Macedonian Empire, liberating Greece.

146BC Greece becomes part of the Roman Empire, which lasts until the empire's fall in AD323.

31BC The Battle of Actium takes place off Preveza, on the west coast of Greece. Part of the Roman Civil War, the naval battle is between Octavian and the combined forces of Mark Anthony and Cleopatra. Part-way through, Cleopatra withdraws

A BRIEF HISTORY OF GREECE & THE IONIAN

her troops and flees. Mark Anthony follows in her wake and his soldiers are defeated, leaving Octavian to claim victory and become the first Roman Emperor.

AD52 St Paul brings Christianity to Greece.

66 Emperor Nero instigates the digging of a canal between the Korinthiakos and Saronic Gulfs.

323 Constantine I becomes emperor and Constantinople is made capital of the empire.

381 Christianity is made the state religion.

393 Emperor Theodosius I bans all pagan rituals, including the Olympic Games.

39 The Roman Empire is divided into two parts – east and west. The eastern part forms the Byzantine Empire and takes control of Greece.

400-700 During Byzantine rule, Greece and, in particular, the Ionian islands are besieged with attacks from the Goths, Huns, Slavs, Bulgars, Patzinaks and Avars, though none takes overall control.

1081 The Normans, under the leadership of Robert Guiscard, capture Corfu and much of western Greece from the Byzantines. Guiscard dies in 1085 of a fever before he can liberate Constantinople.

1204 The Fourth Crusade sees the Normans and Venetians occupy Constantinople and break up the Byzantine Empire. By 1389 the Venetians have control of the Ionian islands and much of Greece.

1453 The Ottoman Turks capture Constantinople and establish it as the capital of the Ottoman Empire. The Turks and the Venetians fight over the Ionian islands.

1483 The S Ionians fall to the Turks.

1499 All the islands are recaptured by the Venetians and flourish under their rule, despite constant attack from the Turks.

1503 The Turks capture the Peloponnese and much of mainland Greece.

1571 The Battle of Lepanto is fought off the Patraikos Gulf. The battle between the Ottoman Turks and the combined Christian forces of the Venetian, Spanish and Genoese is considered to be one of the greatest naval battles in history and sees the Turks defeated.

1684 The Venetians recapture the Peloponnese, only to lose it to the Turks again in the early part of the 18th century.

1788 Ali Pasha, the 'Lion of Ioannina', is made Pasha of Epirus. A ruthless tyrant, he controls much of north-west Greece and sets his sights on controlling the Ionian islands too.

1797 Napoleon Bonaparte invades Italy. He takes control of Venice and, by default, the Ionian islands.

1814 Following the Battle of Waterloo and the defeat of the French, the British take possession of the Ionian islands. During this year, the Greek liberation movement (*Filiki Etaireia*) is also set up to try to regain control of Greece from the Turks.

1815 The Ionian State is set up.

1815-1864 British rule of the Ionian islands sees the development of trade and industry and the building of roads, schools and educational projects. However, British rule is unpopular with the Greeks.

1821 The Greek flag is hoisted at the monastery of Agia Lavra near Kalavrita in the Peloponnese, heralding the start of the War of Independence.

1827 The Battle of Navarino, probably the most significant event of the War of Independence, is fought off the south-west coast of the Peloponnese. Turkish and Egyptian forces are destroyed by the combined British, French and Russian fleets.

1828 As Greece celebrates its independence, Ioannis Kapodistrias is elected as the first president of Greece. Three years later he is assassinated.

1832 King Otho I of Greece's rule lasts 30 years after which he is

A BRIEF HISTORY OF GREECE & THE IONIAN

	forced to flee the country.
1864	The Ionian islands are unified with Greece and the country is made into a Crowned Democracy.
1870s	The site of Ancient Olympia is discovered by archaeologists.
1893	The Corinth Canal opens, which creates a significant trade link between the Western and Eastern Mediterranean.
1896	The Olympic Games are revived in Athens.
1912	Preveza on the Epirus coast is finally liberated from Turkish rule.
1912-1913	During the Balkan Wars, Greece expands its territory to include Epirus and the N Aegean islands.
1917	Greece joins the Allied forces in the First World War.
1940-1945	Italian troops occupy the Ionian islands during the Second World War. Following the removal from power of Mussolini, Italy surrenders to the Allied forces. The Ionians come under attack from the Germans and Kefalonia, in particular, is hit hard. Five thousand Italian soldiers on the island are killed by the Nazis.
1946-1949	Civil War erupts in Greece between the government and the Communist Resistance party.
1948	A massive earthquake affects most of the southern Ionians. Lefkada is worst hit.
1951	Greece enters NATO.
1953	An earthquake measuring 7.3 on the Richter Scale destroys 80 per cent of Kefalonia and Ithaca. Lefkada and Zakynthos and the nearby smaller islands are also hit.
1981	PASOK, a left-wing political party, is elected as the first Socialist government in Greece. In the same year Greece enters the EU.
2001	Greece adopts the Euro as its national currency, replacing the Drachma.
2004	The Olympics return to Greece and, for the first time since the original games, to Ancient Olympia for the shot-put competition.

For more detailed accounts of Greek history, see under Further Reading on page 19.

HOMER'S IONIAN ODYSSEY

Myths and legends abound in Greece. Every island has tales to tell, some of which are rooted firmly in historical fact, while others are rich in romanticism, worn and tarnished by the passage of time and the embellishment of storytellers. Perhaps the greatest of all these stories is *The Odyssey,* written by Homer around 750-700BC. The book is an epic tale. It gives an account of Odysseus' journey back to his kingdom on Ithaki, 10 years after leaving to fight in the Trojan War. It's packed with action and adventure, monsters, gods and goddesses and a romantic hero or two and, while much sits firmly within the realms of mythology, there are parts that closely resemble historical fact.

Archaeologists and historians have for years argued over the location of Homer's Greece and attempted to match his descriptions with the geography of the Ionian islands. Much attention has been focused on Ithaca, which many believe is Homer's Ithaki, not just for its almost identical name, but for its similarities in terrain. However, Zakynthos, Kefalonia, Lefkada and Corfu have also been linked to *The Odyssey,* and it's a story that the Ionian tourist industry has heavily played upon.

GETTING TO THE IONIAN

By air

The quickest and cheapest way to get to the Ionian is by air. Three of the major islands – Corfu, Kefalonia and Zakynthos – have their own airports, so during the summer months these, and the airports at Preveza (Aktio) and Kalamata on the mainland, are served by regular flights from Europe. Most of these are charter flights and not scheduled international flights, and during peak-season they fill up very quickly. An alternative route is to fly on a scheduled flight to Athens and then get a connecting domestic flight to Preveza, Kalamata, Corfu, Kefalonia or Zakynthos, which are served by regular flights from May to October. The flight from Athens lasts between 1 and 1¼ hours and is usually handled by Olympic Airways, Greece's national airline (www.olympicairlines.com). Air Sea Lines/Pegasus Aviation offer daily inter-island flights between Corfu and Paxos, Patra, Ioannina, Lefkada, Kefalonia, Ithaca and Zakynthos on an 18-seater seaplane. Prices vary considerably throughout the year. For more information, contact Air Sea Lines on Tel: 26610 99316 or www.airsealines.com.

By sea

Inter-island and international ferry links with the Ionian islands and mainland are good. There are major ports at Corfu, Igoumenitsa, Patra and Kyllini and regular services from these to Venice, Ancona, Bari and Brindisi on Italy. See www.greekferries.gr for timetable and ticket details. Information on inter-island ferries is listed in the Island travel section on p11.

By road

Bus: From Athens you can travel by KTEL bus to Corfu, Paxos, Lefkada, Kefalonia, Patra and Zakynthos. Several services operate each day to the major towns and islands and journey times range between 3 and 12 hours. Ticket prices are reasonable.
Car: The most common way to travel to the Ionian by car from the UK, France and Germany is to drive to a major port on the Adriatic side of Italy and catch a ferry to Corfu, Igoumenitsa or Patra (see above). Private EU-registered cars can enter Greece and there is no time limit on how long they can stay.

By rail

Greece's train service is not as widespread as in the rest of Europe and is non-existent in the Ionian islands. If you are travelling to the Peloponnese from Athens, though, you can catch a train to most big towns, such as Patra, Kyparissia and Kalamata. See the Hellenic Railways Organisation's website (www.ose.gr) for information.

ISLAND TRAVEL

By sea

Peak season most of the Ionian is served by regular inter-island ferries. See www.greekferries.gr.

MAINLAND PORTS

Igoumenitsa: Daily car and foot-passenger ferries to Corfu, Paxos and Patra as well as to Italy.
Parga: A seasonal *caique* service to Gaios on Paxos.
Astakos: Daily ferries in season to Sami on Kefalonia and Piso Aetos on Ithaca.
Patra: Regular services go to Igoumenitsa, Corfu, Kefalonia, Ithaca and Italy.
Kyllini: Services to Zakynthos, Poros and Argostoli on Kefalonia.

ISLAND PORTS

Corfu

Corfu Town: Daily car ferry to Gaios on Paxos and hydrofoil services via Igoumenitsa for foot passengers. Weekly service to Sagiada on the mainland.
Ag Stephanos (NW coast) and Sidari: Seasonal and infrequent services to the outlying islands of Othoni and Erikoussa.

Lefkada

Nidri: Car ferry between Porto Spilia and Vathi on Meganisi, Fiskardo on Kefalonia and Frikes on Ithaca.
Vasiliki: Car and foot-passenger ferry to Fiskardo on Kefalonia, Frikes, Sami and Piso Aetos on Ithaca during the summer.

Meganisi

From Spilia Bay (Spartohori) and Vathi you can travel to Nidri, several times a day.

Kefalonia

Argostoli: Regular service between the town and Lixouri, on the other side of the Argostoli Gulf. Daily services to Kyllini on the mainland.
Pesada: Seasonal service between Pesada and Ag Nikolaos on Zakynthos.
Poros: Daily services to Kyllini.
Sami: Car and foot-passenger ferries to Vathy and Piso

Aetos on Ithaca and Astakos and Patra on the mainland.
Fiskardo: Ferry sails to Vasiliki on Lefkada and Frikes on Ithaca.

Ithaca

Piso Aetos: Daily services to Vasiliki on Lefkada, Astakos and Kyllini on the mainland.
Vathy: Weekly ferries to Sami on Kefalonia and Patra on the mainland.
Frikes: Seasonal services between Frikes and Vasiliki on Lefkada and Fiskardo on Kefalonia.

Kalamos & Kastos

A small *caique* links the islands with Mitikas on the mainland. Intermittent service.

Zakynthos

Pesada: Seasonal ferry runs between Pesada and Ag Nikolaos on the north-east coast.
Zakynthos town: There are daily services to Kyllini on the mainland.

By road

Expect the unexpected when driving on Greek roads. Greek drivers are not at all predictable: they tend to drive very fast and often overtake round blind bends or make random manoeuvres, regardless of what the rest of the traffic is doing. If a vehicle flashes its lights at you, it generally means 'get out of the way, I'm coming through'. Driving in Greece is not for the faint-hearted and it's no coincidence that the accident rate is one of the highest in Europe. It is, however, the best way to travel, particularly on the islands. The condition of roads varies considerably from island to island: in some places they will be good, in others they deteriorate to rough tracks pitted with potholes and subject to regular avalanches of rocks off the hills. Signposting also varies, and expect to see signs using the Greek alphabet.

Petrol stations selling unleaded and diesel are everywhere in Greece and you will often find several within a couple of miles. Opening times vary, but in rural areas they usually close around 1830. Most of the major stations take credit cards. For a receipt, the word is *apothixi*.

RULES OF THE ROAD

- Here you drive on the right/overtake on the left.
- The speed limit in built-up areas is 31mph (50km per hour) for cars and 24mph (40kph) for motorcycles. On main roads outside built-up areas, the speed limit is 55mph (90kph) or 68mph (110kph) for cars and 43mph (70kph) for motorcycles, and on motorways it is 74mph (120kph) for cars and 55mph (90kph) for motorcycles.
- Children under the age of 12 must not travel in the front seat.
- Driving any vehicle over the alcohol limit is severely penalised.
- It is compulsory to carry a warning triangle, first-aid kit and fire extinguisher.

Car hire: Car hire is easy to arrange in Greece. Most of the larger villages and towns will have at least one hire car company and travel agents will usually organise it for you too. All driving licences are accepted but you must have held one for at least a year. The minimum age is 18.
Scooter/motorbike hire: Greeks use scooters and motorbikes like the Dutch use bicycles. They're widely available and generally cheaper to hire than cars. You must be in possession of a valid driving licence, which has category A1, 'light motorcycle' on it. Wear a crash helmet at all times. Failure to do so may invalidate your insurance and is also against the law, although this rule is regularly flouted by the Greeks. Prices usually include third-party insurance.
Taxis: Taxis are relatively easy to find. In bigger harbours, particularly those visited by ferries, you'll normally find them near the quay or at least a sign with telephone numbers. Alternatively, ask at a taverna for a local number. Fares for local journeys are reasonable, although taxis hired at airports can be slightly more expensive.
Bus: Bus services on the islands are reasonable but do vary. Most are operated by KTEL and travel regularly between the major villages and towns. Finding a correct timetable can be difficult, particularly as they are frequently not adhered to. Enquire at the nearest travel agent or KTEL office. Bus stations are often nothing more than a large shed and bus stops are not always easy to identify.

ARRIVING BY BOAT

Navigation

The beauty of the Ionian is that navigating around it is relatively unchallenging. The tides and currents are so minimal that you don't have to worry about them; the weather in the summer months is predictable and reassuringly consistent, and the sailing ground is littered with conspicuous landmarks, so it is easy to pinpoint your location. Having said that, it is very important not to become complacent. There are hazards to watch out for (see below), and it's a good idea to check your charts regularly and plot your position, just to make sure you're not going to put yourself on a rock or a sandbank.

Beware!

Rocks and reefs: These are probably the biggest danger in the Ionian, although they are relatively easy to avoid. Watch out for those fringing the islands' coasts and, in places such as the North Corfu Channel, between

Skorpios and Meganisi and off the coast of Paxos, for isolated rocks lying immediately below the surface of the water. On a clear, calm day, you should be able to spot them without difficulty, but in breezy conditions, when it is choppy, they can easily be hidden. Check your charts and keep a good look-out when sailing close inshore.

Sandbanks: While much of the Ionian is rocky, there are patches of the mainland bordered by sandbanks. The north shore of the Amvrakikos Gulf and the waters surrounding Mesolongi on the Patraikos Gulf are both areas needing care. These sandbanks shift constantly and although charts illustrate their general position, be alert when sailing in the area.

Fog: True fog is unusual in the Ionian. You'll often see an early morning mist around the islands but this usually burns off by lunchtime. Haze can be more of a problem, though, as it is a regular occurrence here and can reduce visibility considerably on open stretches of water.

Ferries and day-tripper boats: The Ionian waters are usually busy with ferry traffic during the summer months. Inter-island ferries nip in and out of most major harbours on the islands, as do day-tripper boats. International ferries travelling between Italy, the north Ionian and the south, can be a hazard too, particularly as many travel at high speed. Care should be taken along the north and east coasts of Corfu, in the channel between Lefkada and Kefalonia and along the east coast of Ithaca, which are the main ferry routes. Although in theory power must give way to sail, the reality is that many ferries are loath to change course for small leisure craft.

Fish farms and fishing boats: Fishing is still a big industry in the Ionian and there are few bays on the mainland coast south of Preveza that aren't blighted by fish farms. While most are easy to spot by day, by night many are unlit, so care is needed. Watch out for nets run out behind fishing boats and lobster pots too.

SAFETY AT SEA

All port authorities in the Ionian monitor VHF Ch16 for distress calls. There are several dedicated Coastguard stations around the Ionian (listed below) and Olympia-Radio monitors GMDSS, VHF Ch16 and MF 2182KHz frequencies. It also helps to co-ordinate support for emergencies at sea. The authority responsible for maritime Search and Rescue (SAR) is the Hellenic Mercantile Maritime Ministry, based at Piraeus.

Coastguard station	VHF channels
Kerkira (Corfu)	16, 02, 03, 64
Kefalonia	16, 26, 27, 28
Patra	16, 85
Pylos	16
Petalidi	16, 23, 83, 84

Olympia-Radio	
MMSI	00237100
Call sign	SVO
VHF Channel	16
MF	2182KHz
Tel: (24 hours)	210 6001799 & 210 6060120

Hellenic Mercantile Maritime Ministry	
MMSI	237673000
Call sign	SXE
VHF voice call sign	Piraeus RCC
VHF Channel	16
MF	2182KHz
Tel: (emergency landline)	210 4112500 & 210 4220772

ARRIVING AND ASHORE

Berthing Med-style

Unlike Britain and much of northern Europe, usual procedure in the Med is to berth bows- or stern-to the quay, either to an anchor or on lazylines. There are only a handful of places in the Ionian where you can lie alongside, so be prepared for this. It can be a daunting prospect, particularly if you are unfamiliar with the port, but should become relatively easy with practice.

There is no definite rule about whether you should berth bows- or stern-to a quay. It depends on a number of factors: how shallow the harbour is; whether there is debris at the base of the quay, which a boat berthed stern-to might squat on; weather conditions; and how busy the quay is – you might not want to be stared at by passers-by.

Most marinas use lazylines. These are permanent lines that run from the quay to a mooring block on the seabed, which can be used in place of an anchor to keep the boat off the quay. You'll also find pontoons rigged with lazylines at some popular harbours, such as Spilia Bay on Meganisi, where space is at a premium. Not only do lazylines take the hassle out of berthing stern- or bows-to but they also allow more boats to use a smaller quay.

When berthing bows- or stern-to, it is very important to check and double check that everything is set up correctly before heading towards the quay.

- Make sure you have plenty of fenders out and that they are set at the right height. Ideally, the top of the fender should be level with the toerail and they should be spaced evenly on both sides around the beamiest part of the boat. If you have to squeeze stern-first into a tight berth, though, set them slightly further back.
- If you are berthing stern-to, your dinghy should be tied to a cleat either amidships or at the bow, in order to make sure that you don't run

over it when reversing towards the quay.

- If there are no lazylines, make sure your anchor is untied and that the windlass clutch is freed off. Check that the anchor chain is free to run.
- Check all your lines are ready. They should be neatly coiled, so they don't tangle, and should also be correctly fed, so they don't get caught around the pushpit or pulpit.

Berthing stern-to with lazylines

- Once you have decided where to berth and your lines and fenders are ready, motor slowly in reverse towards the quay, using the throttle to control your speed.
- Watch out for other lazylines lying in the water and be careful not to snag them on your prop.
- As soon as you are close enough to the quay, a crewmember should step ashore and secure both sternlines, tying the windward one first to prevent the bow being blown off.
- Pick up the end of the lazyline from the quay and walk it forward to the bow. Secure it on a bow cleat so that the stern of your boat is kept off the quay. The lazyline may be weighted so that it sinks to the seabed, so it might feel quite heavy.

Berthing stern-to without lazylines

- Prepare your lines and fenders and check that the clutch on your anchor windlass is slack and the chain free to run. This done, motor slowly towards the quay.
- Drop your anchor about three boat-lengths from the quay, letting it run out smoothly and at a controlled pace.
- As soon as you are about one boat-length from the quay, tighten the clutch on your windlass to prevent any more chain running out. The chain will then snub and, hopefully, the anchor will dig in to the seabed to prevent your boat from hitting the quay. Always keep an eye on your helmsman, who will be able to tell you whether you need to let more chain out or take up on the windlass if you are too close to the quay.
- Secure your sternlines as soon as possible, or your bowlines if you are berthed bows-to.
- If anchoring bows-to, set a kedge anchor over your stern. You should also take two bow lines ashore.

PROCEDURES FOR ENTRY INTO GREEK WATERS

Any yacht arriving in Greek waters is required by law to clear in at a port of entry. A Greek courtesy ensign should be flown from the starboard spreader and, if you are arriving from a non-EU country, flag Q (a plain yellow flag symbolising quarantine) should be hoisted at the 12-mile limit. On arrival at a harbour, you should immediately visit the port authorities and/or Customs. The following paperwork/procedures are required for EU and non-EU registered yachts:

EU-registered yachts

- Vessels owned by EU residents are not required to go through customs unless you have anything to declare (firearms, drugs or scuba-diving equipment) or have non-EU nationals on board. All yachts entering Greece are subject to passport control. Valid passports for all the crew should be presented to the port authorities.
- Yachts cruising Greek waters must obtain a DEKPA – a Private Pleasure Maritime Traffic Document. This costs €30 and is obtainable from your first port of entry. It must be presented and stamped at each port you visit, on entry and departure. It is valid for 50 harbours and Greek-flagged yachts should also purchase one.
- The following ship's papers are required and may need to be presented at each port:

1. Yacht Registration Document. Part 1 or SSR (Small Ships Register).
2. Insurance documents for the yacht. Insurance is compulsory, so check your policy is valid before entering Greek waters. The Greek authorities require third party insurance to cover the following: liability for death or injury of any person on board or third party for at least €293,470; liability for damage for a minimum of €146,735; and liability for sea pollution for at least €88,041. A copy of the policy document in Greek must be provided too.
3. Ship's radio licence. All vessels with a VHF radio installed on board must have a valid Radio

Telephone Ships Licence for that boat.
4. A VAT receipt for the yacht. All yachts sailing between countries in the EU must carry details of the yacht's VAT status. Rulings made in 1993 stated that all EU-registered yachts may only be used within the EU if VAT has been paid on them. Customs in Greece may ask you to provide evidence of your boat's VAT status, so it is essential you have either the original VAT receipt, which was issued on buying the boat, or a receipt for VAT paid subsequently. Yachts built pre-1985 and which were based in an EU country on 1 January 1993 are exempt but evidence of this must be produced. For more information, see www.rya.org.uk/cruising.

- The following personal papers are required and may need to be produced:

1. A valid passport.
2. Radio-Telephone Certificate of Competence. At least one crew member on board must be in possession of a valid radio user's certificate. To use GMDSS equipment, a Short Range Certificate or Long Range Certificate is required.
3. International Certificate of Competence. The yacht's skipper must hold an ICC, which is an internationally recognised measure of competence.
4. Health insurance. Visitors to Greece are recommended to have health insurance and to have the relevant documents on board. A European Health Insurance Card, the replacement of the E111 form, can be obtained from the post office. For more information go to www.ehicard.org or call 0907 707 8370.

All the documents listed above should be the originals. Photocopies, particularly of the yacht's registration documents, are often not accepted.

Non EU-registered yachts

- All non-EU registered vessels should contact the customs authorities on arrival at port. The Q flag should be left hoisted until you have been cleared through Customs.
- Valid passports for all the crew must be presented. Visas may be required.
- In addition to the papers listed under EU yachts above, non-EU registered vessels must obtain a Transit Log Book from Customs. This logbook gives temporary permission for yachts to stay in Greek waters and is compulsory for private non-EU leisure craft with at least two cabins for sleeping and dining. Transit Logs are valid for six months from date of issue, although extensions may be granted by Customs. If the skipper,whose name the Transit Log is in, leaves Greece without the boat, the Transit Log must be handed into Customs or the Port Police in the harbour where the boat is laid up.
- While EU-registered yachts are no longer charged a 'cruising tax', non-EU boats may be.
- VAT – Non-EU residents with non-EU-registered yachts are allowed into Greece under a Temporary Importation rule, which enables them to spend 18 out of 24 months in EU countries. If the boat is sold or chartered during this time, VAT applies. Extensions may be granted if the boat is laid up or undergoing repair.

- For further details on procedures for cruising in Greece, see *Foreign Cruising, Volume 2: Mediterranean & the Black Sea*, the RYA and Cruising Association (www.rya.org.uk).

Ports of entry

Island	Port
Corfu	Corfu Town
Paxos	Gaios
Lefkada	Lefkada Town
Kefalonia	Argostoli, Sami
Ithaca	Vathi
Zakynthos	Zakynthos Town
Mainland coast	**Port**
Epirus coast	Igoumenitsa, Preveza
Gulf of Corinth	Itea, Corinth
Peloponnese	Patra, Katakolo, Pylos & Kalamata

Berthing & mooring fees

Paying for an overnight berth or mooring is still relatively unusual in the Ionian. Unlike much of Europe, it is only the larger harbours or marinas that charge per night. Of those mentioned in this book, I've found only a handful that do. Inevitably, as cruising destinations get more popular and more money is invested in developing harbours, more places will start charging. In the meantime, it makes a pleasant change not to be hounded for money as soon as your lines are secured.

Commercial marinas, such as Gouvia, Lefkada, Patra and Kalamata, charge around €38 for a 35-footer. Harbours such as Fiskardo on Kefalonia and Gaios on Paxos, which are extremely popular with yachts peak season, will also demand a small fee. Where known, these have been included under the harbour details, but note that prices are likely to increase slightly each year.

Harbour dues should be paid at the Port Police office, which is usually nearby and identified by a sign showing two crossed anchors, displayed below a large Greek flag. Most Port Police will speak some English.

Smaller harbours often share port authorities and you can usually berth here free. However, the jetties in many places, such as Spilia Bay on Meganisi, or Agni Bay on

Corfu, are owned by local tavernas and if you use them, it is common courtesy at least to have a drink there.

AMENITIES

The size of the harbour and its popularity dictates the range of facilities available to cruising yachts. Many harbours in the Ionian have, at the very least, a quay for visiting yachts, a taverna, a mini-market and a bus or taxi service. But you will also find larger ports and marinas with more comprehensive amenities and/or fishing boat harbours that provide little more than a rough breakwater off which to berth.

Water: Most harbours have taps nearby or are serviced by a local water truck. Expect to pay a few euros to fill your tanks. Water is in short supply on some of the smaller islands, such as Kalamos and Kastos, so try to replenish your tanks elsewhere. It is safe to drink tap water in Greece, although most people prefer mineral water, which is widely available.

Fuel: The majority of marinas and a handful of local harbours have fuel pontoons. Smaller harbours that are popular with yachts are usually visited by mini diesel-tankers, from which you can fill up. Alternatively, if you just need a small amount of fuel, take jerry cans to one of the many local petrol stations.

Gas: Gas is generally used in Greece, so locating a supply of bottles shouldn't be a problem.

Shorepower: Mains electricity is not widely available. Marinas and larger harbours usually have it and, although many small ports often have junction boxes, don't rely on them being connected. 50Hz 220v electricity is most commonly supplied.

Boat maintenance: Boatyards can be found on the larger islands and mainland. Some cater specifically for yachts, offering a range of services from antifouling to engine servicing and GRP or woodwork, while others are used by the local fishing boats. Chandlers are often situated in boatyards or near the harbours in bigger towns, such as Preveza, Lefkada and Zakynthos. Some spares can be hard to find, so it may be worth keeping a small stock.

Rubbish: Waste is becoming a big problem in the Ionian, so please dispose of your rubbish sensibly. Some of the smaller islands, such as the Diapondias, Kalamos and Kastos, do not have rubbish-processing facilities so, if possible, dispose of it elsewhere. Marinas such as Gouvia, Lefkada and Kalamata all have facilities to deal with your waste oil and lubricants.

PROVISIONING

Mini-markets can be found everywhere and larger towns will have several supermarkets. You'll also find bakers, butchers and fruit and veg shops and, in tiny harbour villages, tavernas may stock limited products for visiting yachts. Local markets are good for fresh produce and there is usually a wide range of seasonal fruit and veg to choose from.

Opening hours

Opening hours in Greece can, at best, be described as vague. They vary considerably from place to place and often depend on the shop's owner and/or the season. As a rough guide, clothes and general shops are usually open between 0900-1400, Mon-Sat. Some will reopen in the late afternoon, from 1700 or 1800-2030; others, such as butchers and fishmongers, won't. Supermarkets and food shops open for longer, particularly in touristy areas, and occasionally on Sundays too. Souvenir shops and kiosks are generally open all day and late.

Most banks are open between 0800-1400, Mon-Thurs and from 0800-1330 on Fri. They are all shut on national holidays. ATMs, which are found everywhere, dispense cash 24-hours a day. The post office is usually open from 0730-1400, Mon-Fri, although smaller branches may open less frequently. Pharmacies open between 0830-1400 and 1730-2200, but in larger towns some may stay open later and/or operate a rota system so that there is always a chemist open throughout the day.

Major museums and archaeological sites open from 0800-1500, Tues-Sun, and peak season in the early evenings too. The opening times of smaller museums vary but are similar to those listed above.

Peak season in the Ionian is from May to October. Outside these months, many harbours shut down almost completely as taverna owners head back to the mainland for the winter. While you may find yourself sailing in idyllic, uncrowded waters out of season, finding somewhere to eat could prove hard.

GREEK NATIONAL HOLIDAYS

1 January	Agios Vasileios or Protokronia (New Year's Day) celebrates the arrival of the new year and is the feast day of the saint Agios Vasileios.
6 January	Theofania (Epiphany) is held to celebrate Christ's baptism. At harbours, a priest usually throws a cross into the water, which local men then dive for.
25 March	Greek Independence Day celebrates the rebellion of 1821 against the Ottoman Empire.
1 May	Protomagia (Spring Festival/ May Day).
21 May	Ionian Day celebrates the unification of the Ionian Islands with Greece in 1864.
15 August	Koimisis tis Theotokou (Feast of the Assumption) marks the Assumption of the Virgin Mary.
8 September	Gennisis tis Theotokou marks the birth of the Virgin Mary.
28 October	Ochi Day celebrates the day that the Greek Prime Minister Metaxa refused Mussolini's request to let Italy occupy Greece during the Second World War.
6 December	Agios Nikolaos Day. Many churches throughout the Ionian are named after Agios Nikolaos, patron saint of sailors.
12 December	Agios Spyridon's Day (Corfu) is one of several days that celebrates the patron saint of Corfu, St Spyridon.
25 December	Christougenna (Christmas Day).
26 December	Synaxis tis Theotokou (St Stephen's Day).

National holidays are also held on the First Sunday in Lent, Good Friday and Easter Sunday. All shops, banks and museums are closed on public holidays.

MONEY

Greece's national currency is the Euro, which replaced the Drachma on 1 January 2001. Most of the towns and larger villages in the Ionian have at least one bank or ATM. If not, you'll often find post offices and/or travel agencies that will exchange currency or cash travellers' cheques. Some of the hotels in bigger resorts offer a similar service. Remember to take your passport with you as identification. Cashpoint machines, or ATMs, open 24 hours a day and are multilingual. Most cards are accepted with a pin number but expect your bank to charge you a handling fee.

Credit cards (Visa, Delta, Mastercard, Switch, Maestro, Barclaycard and American Express) are now widely accepted for payment, although in smaller villages and tavernas you should check before purchase.

COMMUNICATIONS

Telephone: There is no shortage of phone boxes in Greece. The majority of villages and towns have at least a handful for both local and international calls and they generally work. The national telephone service, OTE, has offices in most towns and you can make metered calls from them. In larger towns they are usually open daily (0700-2200). Phone cards are sold at kiosks, post offices, souvenir shops and newsagents.
Mobile phone: Reception in the Ionian islands is generally good, although there are a couple of places, such as Sivota on Lefkada and Kioni on Ithaca, where it is notoriously bad. Be aware that phone calls made and received from a UK mobile are usually expensive and you may need to contact your service provider to set up an international 'roaming' service on your phone. If you are cruising in Greece for an extended amount of time, consider buying a SIM card for a Greek network or renting a Greek mobile as the cost of calls will be much cheaper. Twelve-volt chargers are sold for nearly all makes of mobile phone, and most boats are now fitted with 12v sockets, so you can charge yours on board.
Fax: Faxing services are not often advertised in Greece but most travel agencies will provide it for a modest fee.
Internet & email: Internet access is readily available in Greece. In big towns, you'll usually find a handful of internet cafes offering various facilities, and some tavernas in smaller villages are beginning to provide internet access too. Charges vary, depending on how touristy the village or town is, and you will probably be charged by the hour, with printing costs added.
Post: The postal service in Greece is operated by ELTA Hellenic Post. It is usually very fast and reliable on the mainland and the larger islands, but less so on the smaller islands if something is urgent. Most villages and towns have a post office, open Monday-Friday, 0700-1400, identifiable by its blue and yellow sign and bright yellow post boxes. Stamps are sold at souvenir and gift shops and some kiosks. Parcels can be sent via couriers such as ACS Couriers.

FOOD AND DRINK

'Wholesome', 'hearty' and 'traditional' best describe Greek cuisine. Heavily influenced by Italy, the Balkans and the Eastern Mediterranean, Greek food is simple and homely. With hearty stews and oven-baked dishes combined with masses of fresh fish and appetisers, the menu is fairly varied, although changes little from place to place. Ingredients tend to be seasonal and, due to the Ionian's mild climate, fruit and vegetables are usually plentiful. Tomatoes, onions, garlic, peppers and aubergines are all staple foods, richly seasoned with herbs and spices, and pasta is widely found – a legacy from Venetian occupation.

Meal times are a very social, relaxed affair with families and friends sitting down at the table together, sharing their food around. A typical Greek meal consists of a selection of *mezedes* – appetizers such as *hummus* (chickpea dip), *tzatziki* (yoghurt, garlic and cucumber dip), *dolmades* (stuffed vineleaves) and the ubiquitous *horiatiki salata* (a tomato, cucumber, onion, olive and feta salad) – followed by a main meal such as *stifado* (a meat and onion stew), *moussaka* (layers of aubergine, lamb mince and cheese sauce), *souvlaki* (skewered chunks of lamb and vegetables) or grilled fish. The Greeks have an incredibly sweet tooth too, favouring sticky sugary puddings such as *baklava* (layers of filo pastry filled with a nut and honey mix) or *rizogalo* (rice pudding), although these are often eaten independently of the main meal.

The main meal of the day is lunch, so you'll frequently find oven-baked dishes served at tavernas in the evenings that have been reheated rather than cooked afresh. The Greeks also tend to eat late, which means tavernas usually serve well past 10pm. Look for local specialities, such as Kefalonian meat pie on Kefalonia or onion pie on Ithaca, or dishes containing local produce such as olives or honey. Home-produced wine is also worth trying (see opposite), although there are some particularly potent blends on offer.

Where to eat and drink

Taverna: A traditional restaurant serving simple but wholesome Greek cuisine. They are an important part of Greek culture: informal places to dine and socialise.

Estiatorio: A restaurant that is slightly more formal than a taverna.

Psistaries: A taverna specialising in grilled meats.

Psarotaverna: A taverna specialising in fish dishes.

Kafenia: A coffee shop that is usually frequented by Greek men.

Ouzeri: A bar that serves ouzo. *Mezedes* (appetisers) may also be sold here.

Drink

The Ionian islands have a long history of wine production, dating back over 3,000 years. Vineyards cover more than 8,700 hectares of land in the Ionian, producing 21 million litres of wine annually. It is only relatively recently, however, that Greek wine has increased in popularity and gained a good reputation.

Corfu, Lefkada and Zakynthos all have extensive vineyards, but it is Kefalonia that is the most important island for wine production. Some of the best Greek wines originate here. Its vineyards are dominated by the Robola cultivar, and wines to try include Robola of Kefalonia and muscat. Others to sample are Ropa Theotokis, produced on Corfu from the white *kakotriyis* grape, the white Zakynthian Verdea and any of the red wines produced on Lefkada from the *Vertzami* grape.

Another drink advertised everywhere is *ouzo*, a grape skin-based aperitif flavoured with, among other things, star anise, coriander, mint and cloves. It's distinctive for its aniseed flavour and for turning milky white on contact with water or ice.

ABOUT THIS BOOK

Charts and maps

Charts: For detailed information of the harbours in this book, refer to the charts listed under each entry. Where applicable, I have listed those from the Admiralty, Imray and the Hellenic Navy Hydrographic Service (HNHS), whose charts are sold in Greece. The last are comprehensive and detailed, but all the text is in Greek.

The chartlets in this book are for reference only and should not be used for navigation as many have been simplified. For an explanation of the abbreviations and symbols used, see p20. All the marked depths are shown as metres and tenths of metres. The light blue shading indicates where there are depths of over 5m and the dark blue shading where there is less than 5m of water.

The chart information in this product is reproduced with the permission of the Hellenic Navy Hydrographic Service (Licence No 171.7/12/07 S.40). WARNING: The Hellenic Navy Hydrographic Service has not verified the information in this product and does not accept any liability for the accuracy of reproduction or any modifications made thereafter. The Hellenic Navy Hydrographic Service does not warrant that this product satisfies national or international regulations regarding the use of the appropriate products for navigation. Chart information for this book is also reproduced with the permission of the UKHO.

Maps: Michelin produces a good map of Greece (737) for travelling around ashore, but by far the best road maps of Greece and the Ionian islands are published by Road Editions (www.road.gr). They are based on surveys by the Greek Army and contain extensive details and town plans of some of the larger cities. There are individual editions for each major island in the Ionian and three large-scale maps covering the mainland coast included in this book.

Road Editions		
307	Ionian islands	1:150,000
301	Corfu	1:70,000
302	Paxos & Antipaxos	1:30,000
303	Lefkada & Meganisi	1:50,000
304	Kefalonia & Ithaca	1:70,000
305	Zakynthos	1:70,000
3	Epiros/Thessaly	1:250,000
4	Central Greece	1:250,000
5	Peloponnese	1:250,000
Michelin		
737	Greece	1:700,000

Waypoints

All the waypoints listed are referenced to the WGS84 datum, so positions must be adjusted before plotting on charts referenced to the ED50 datum. These waypoints should serve as a guide only and should therefore be plotted on a chart before they are used to check their accuracy and relevance to your passage plan.

Bearings

All the bearings and courses mentioned are True. The magnetic variation should be applied before they are used. Check the compass rose on up-to-date charts for the latest variation.

Lights and frequencies

Distances between the harbours in the Ionian are so small that night-time arrival is rarely necessary. In other cases, where there are shoals and reefs near the harbour entrance, a night-time approach is not advised unless you know the area well. Details of major lighthouses and buoys have been included in the text where appropriate and, while most harbours are lit, these lights do not always work, so should not be relied upon.

REFERENCE

Further reading

Travel guides to the Ionian islands

- *Frommer's Greek Islands,* 4th edition, by John S Bowman, Sherry Marker & Rebecca Tobin, Frommer's (www.frommers.com), 2005.
- *The Greek Islands,* an Eyewitness travel guide, published by Dorling Kindersley (www.dk.com), 2007.
- *Corfu & the Ionians* by Carolyn Bain & Sally Webb, Lonely Planet (www.lonelyplanet.com), 2002.
- *The Rough Guide to the Ionian Islands* by Nick Edwards & John Gill, Rough Guides (www.roughguides.com), 2006.

Travel guides to Greece

- *Frommer's Greece,* 5th edition, by John S Bowman, Sherry Marker & Rebecca Tobin, Frommer's (www.frommers.com), 2005.
- *The Rough Guide to Greece,* 10th edition, published by Rough Guides (www.roughguides.com), 2006.
- *Greece, Athens & the Mainland,* an Eyewitness travel guide, Dorling Kindersley (www.dk.com), 2007.
- *The Peloponnese* by David Willett, Lonely Planet (www.lonelyplanet.com), 2002.

Greek history & mythology

- *A Traveller's History of Greece* by Tim Boatswain & Colin Nicholson, Windrush Press, 2003.
- The *Complete World of Greek Mythology* by Richard Buxton, Thames & Hudson, 2004.

Recommended websites

General sites

- The Prefecture of Lefkada – www.lefkada-monuments.gr
- The Prefecture of Zakynthos – www.zakynthos.gr
- General guide to the Ionian islands – www.ionian-islands.com
- Friends of the Ionian – www.foi.org.uk
- Information for cruising sailors – www.noonsite.com
- Information for cruising yachts world-wide – www.onpassage.com
- Greece & the Greek islands – www.greeka.com
- Greek National Tourism Organisation – www.gnto.gr

Travel companies

- Details of ferry times and how to book tickets can be found at: www.greekferries.gr
- The Association of Bus Operators in Greece – www.ktel.org
- Olympic Airways – www.olympicairlines.com

Weather websites

- Hellenic National Meteorological Service – www.hnms.gr
- Greek weather – www.poseidon.ncmr.gr
- Weather Online – www.weatheronline.co.uk/Greece.htm

SYMBOLS AND ABBREVIATIONS

	Airport		Ferry terminal	PHM	Port-hand mark
	Anchoring		Fishing boats	PA	Position approx.
	Anchoring prohibited		Fishing harbour/quay		Post office
	Anchoring stern/bows-to		Fish farm		Public telephone
	Berthing stern/bows- to	FV(s)	Fishing vessel(s)		Railway station
	Boat hoist		Fuel berth		Restaurant
	Boatyard		Harbourmaster	SWM	Safe water mark
Ca	Cable(s)		Heliport		Shore power
	Car park		Holding tank pump-out		Showers
	Chandlery		Hospital		Slipway
	Chemist		Information bureau	SCM	South cardinal mark
	Church	IDM	Isolated danger mark	SHM	Starboard-hand mark
H24	Continuous		Launderette		Supermarket
	Crane	Ldg	Leading	SS	Traffic signals
	Customs office		Lifeboat		Visitors' berth/buoy
	Direction of buoyage		Marina	WPT	Waypoint
	Flying dolphin		Mooring stern/bows-to buoy	WCM	West cardinal mark
ECM	East cardinal mark	NCM	North cardinal mark		Yacht berthing facilities

LIGHTS AND FREQUENCIES

FR	Fixed red light
FG	Fixed green light
Fl	Flashing light, period of darkness longer than light. A number indicates a group of flashes, eg: Fl (2). Most lights are white unless a colour follows the number of flashes, eg: Fl (2) G. The timing of the sequence, including light and darkness, is shown by the number of seconds, eg: Fl (2) G 10s. The range of the more powerful lights is given in nautical miles (M), eg: Fl (2) G 10s 20M
L Fl	Long flash, of not less than two seconds
Oc	Occulting light, period of light longer than darkness
Iso	Isophase light, equal periods of light and darkness
Q	Quick flashing light, up to 50/60 flashes per minute
VQ	Very quick flashing, up to 120 flashes per minute
Mo	Light flashing a (dot/dash) Morse single letter sequences, eg: Mo (S)
Dir	A light, usually sectored, RWG or RG, usually giving a safe approach within the W sector. Either fixed or displaying some kind of flashing characteristic

Chapter one

Corfu, Paxos, Antipaxos and the Diapondia Islands

This chapter covers Corfu and its satellite islands: Paxos and Antipaxos to the south and the Diapondia islands, Othoni, Erikoussa and Mathraki, to the north-west. These islands mark the northwesternmost part of Greece and the start of the Ionian Sea.

On approach from the Adriatic, Corfu is identifiable from some distance as the northern half of the island is mountainous. The Diapondia islands, however, while conspicuous close-to, are often shrouded in haze so are not readily identifiable. On approach from the south, Paxos and Antipaxos should be spotted without difficulty.

The Northern Ionian offers slightly more challenging sailing than the southern. With fewer islands and mountains to protect the waters, you'll often find stiffer and more prolonged breezes here than in the Southern Ionian, although they tend to follow exactly the same pattern. From May to September the prevailing winds are from the north-west. The mornings are usually calm with next to no wind, but in the afternoons a decent Force 3 to 5 will build before it fades away to nothing again in the evenings.

As with all of the Ionians, a good look-out should be maintained when navigating the waters around the islands. Rocks and shoal patches fringe all of the islands mentioned in this chapter and particular care should be taken around the low-lying southern tip of Corfu as a reef extends offshore for about 2nm. There are also isolated reefs off Corfu's west, north and east coasts, so keep a close eye on your charts and echosounder. Care should be taken in the North Corfu Channel too. Not only is the channel's close proximity to Albania a reason to exercise caution, but this stretch of water is often busy with commercial shipping and ferries. The political situation in Albania is currently settled, but there have been reports of attacks on yachts in the past and it is prudent to stay on the west coast of the channel, near Corfu.

Corfu Nisos Kerkyra

Corfu is the second largest Ionian island and lies off the north-west coast of Greece. Covering 248 square miles (641km^2) of land, the island is the northernmost of the group and marks the start of the Ionian Sea. For many sailors it is the first port of call in this archipelago and, with 136 miles (217km) of coastline, it offers plenty of variation and choice of destination.

Firmly routed within the tourist industry since the 1970s, Corfu has a long-established reputation as a party island. During the season it is descended on by hundreds of thousands of holidaymaking tourists, who congregate at the many resorts that flank the

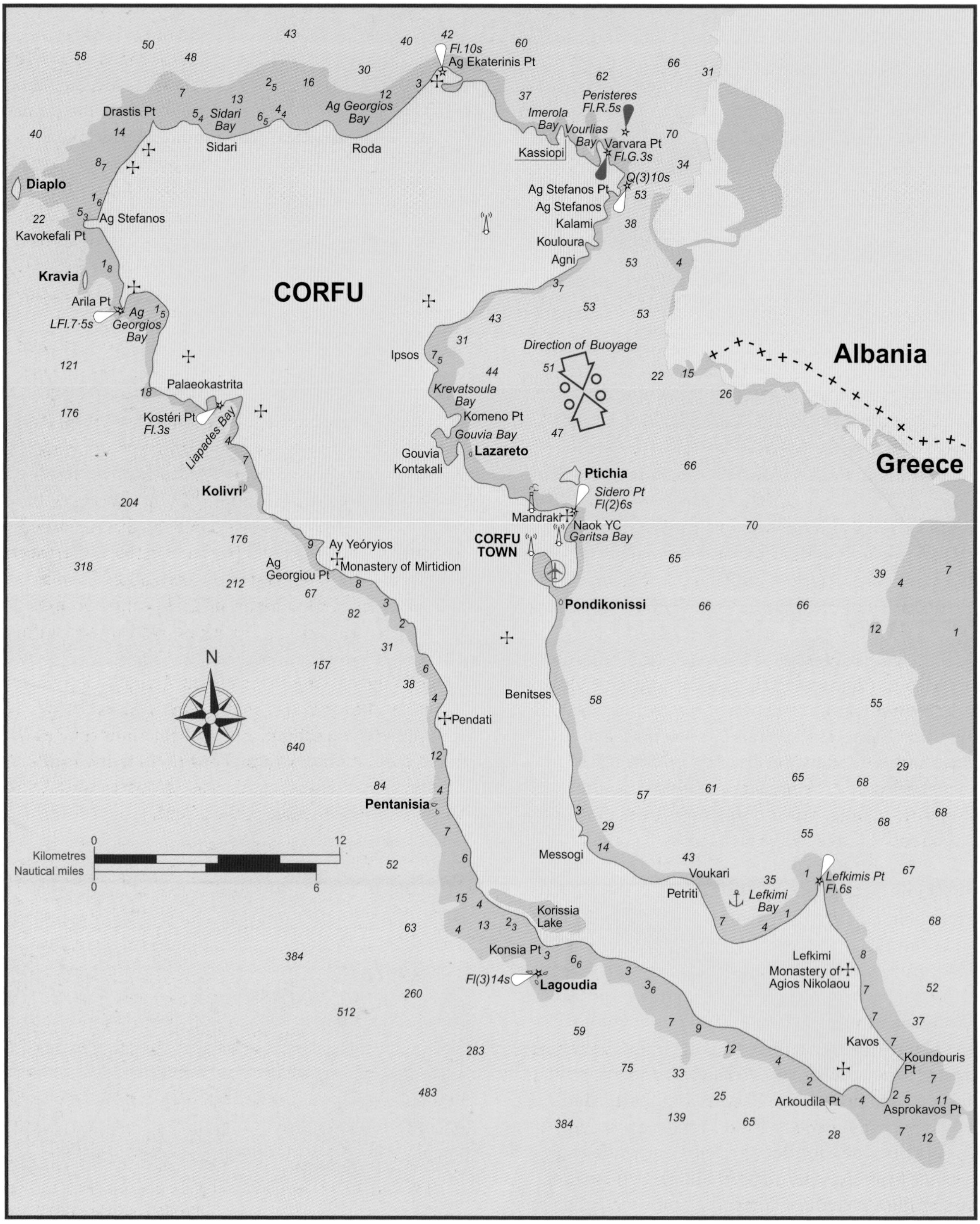

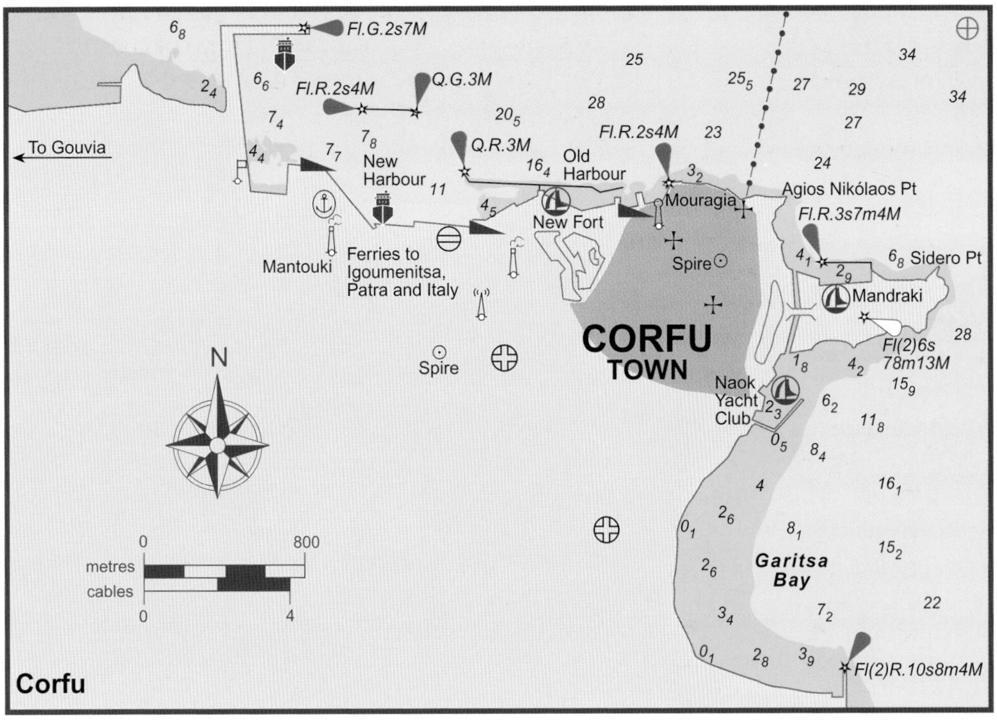

island's coastline. It's by far the most popular of the seven major Ionians and, for many, an acquired taste. While there are some quiet anchorages and traditional villages set in rural countryside, much of the island throbs with tacky tourism. It's a place where draught beer is found on tap, hamburgers and chips are served instead of *mezédhes* and *stifadho* and more English is heard than Greek.

Having said that, though, there are parts of Corfu which are lovely: several of the anchorages on the north-east tip of the island are surprisingly secluded and offer backdrops of lush, green hillsides and idyllic bays. Corfu town, too, is a beautiful place. Its cosmopolitan atmosphere and striking architecture make it, in my mind, one of the most attractive large towns in Greece, and Gouvia Marina, to the north of the harbour, offers the best facilities in the area. If you can escape inland you may even discover some wild countryside and rolling hills that are reminiscent of the Corfu that authors Gerald and Lawrence Durrell and Henry Miller described in the early to mid-20th century. It's not all spoilt, although it can seem that way if you just cruise along the island's north and east coasts.

Historically, Corfu has always been a very important island. Its location, lying so close to Italy, has made it a significant trading centre and a vital link with this part of the Mediterranean. Archaeological finds date Corfu's first settlers to the Palaeolithic Age (c10,000BC) and it is thought that the Phoenicians, an ancient civilisation from Lebanon and Syria, were among the first to inhabit the island. The first Greek settlers moved to Corfu from Euboea, an island in eastern Greece, around the 8th century and they were soon joined by refugees from Corinth. Political unrest between the Corinthians and Corfiats, who wanted independence, eventually led to a series of conflicts and, after the Corfiats gained support from the Athenians, they became embroiled in the bitter Peloponnesian Wars.

The Romans conquered Corfu in 229BC but, after the collapse of the Roman Empire, it was taken over by the Byzantines in 337AD. Under the Romans it had operated as a semi-autonomous state and had prospered, but under the Byzantines it suffered continual attack from pirates, including the Goths, Saracens and Normans. After a short period of Norman rule, Corfu, along with the rest of the Ionian, was taken over by the Venetians who eventually restored it to its former glory, re-establishing it as a key trading centre with towns along the Adriatic coast. Although it suffered from the occasional pirate attack, Corfu was the only island in the Ionian to resist assaults by the Turks and has never succumbed to their rule. Venetian occupation lasted until 1797 when Napoleon conquered Venice, and French rule lasted for around 10 years until the British took over in 1815. The island was unified with Greece in 1864.

Despite the onslaught of tourism, Corfu is rich in history and has some fascinating areas. The nearby waters offer good sailing, and with the quieter islands of Paxos and Antipaxos just a few miles to the south, you don't have to go far to find an effective antidote to counteract the worst bits of the island.

Corfu Town, on the north-east coast of the island, is one of the most attractive large towns in Greece

Corfu Town Kerkyra

East of Corfu Harbour, to the north of Sideros Pt: 39°37'.94N 19°55'.96E
Old Harbour entrance: 39°37'.67N 19°55'.14E

Corfu Town, midway down Corfu's east coast, is the island's capital and commercial centre. It is arguably the most beautiful large town in the Ionian, if not in Greece, and home to half the island's population. During the summer months it can be extremely busy and hectic but it is well worth a visit. The cosmopolitan town has a great vitality and much to offer visitors. The large marina at Gouvia (see p27), 5nm to the north-west, also provides the best facilities in this part of the Ionian.

Corfu Town has had a much more constant and settled history than others in this part of Greece, despite being passed from one occupier to the next. The original town stood on the Kanoni peninsula, about a mile south of its current location, but in the 6th century it was destroyed by the Goths, an East Germanic tribe who had conquered much of the Roman Empire at this time. Forced from their homes, citizens fled north to the rocky Sideros Pt, on which they built a fortified settlement. When the Venetians conquered Corfu in the 14th century, they rebuilt much of the settlement and cut it off from the rest of the island with a moat. They built a compact town to the west of Sideros Pt and then, in the 15th century, another fortress to the west to protect it from enemy attack. Strategically, at the southern end of the Adriatic Sea, Corfu was very important but, despite frequent attempts by the Turks, it remained under Venetian control for four centuries. It eventually fell to the French in the late 18th century and then to the British in 1815.

Gouvia Marina, 5nm to the north-west of Corfu Town

Evidence of Corfu's various occupiers can be seen in the architecture. Narrow, cobble-stoned alleys, tall shuttered buildings and pretty squares in the Old Town hint of Venice and Naples and the Venetians' legacy, while the arcaded streets and Georgian mansions reflect the French and British influence.

For the cruising sailor, Corfu has much to offer. While the town's harbour has little to attract, there are plenty of good alternatives nearby and as somewhere to provision or do routine boatwork it is on a par with Lefkada.

NAVIGATION

Charts: Admiralty 2407, 206, 188, SC5771; Imray G11, G1; Hellenic Navy Hydrographic Service 212/1, 21

Corfu Town is easy to identify from some distance. Continual ferry traffic will help you pinpoint it and, on approach from the south, the old Venetian fortress on Sideros Pt and the expanse of town behind it are conspicuous. There are two commercial harbours, both to the west of Sideros Pt, on Corfu Town's north shore. The New Harbour, westernmost of the pair, is used by ferries and ships, and the Old Harbour, to the east, by local boats. Visiting leisure craft should use the Old Harbour, which is entered via the eastern end of the breakwater. Maintain a good look-out at all times as traffic around Corfu is usually heavy.

At night, Sideros Pt is lit (Fl(2)6s78m13M) and a light (Fl G 3s12m4M), ¾nm north of Sideros Pt, marks the southern tip of the islet of Ptichia. If approaching from the north, watch out for the small above-water rock Kalogiros (Nafsika), ½-mile west-north-west of the islet, as it is unmarked. While it is possible to sail between Kalogiros and Ptichia in daylight, it is not advised at night when you should pass well to the west or east of the islet.

BERTHING

Visiting craft can berth temporarily, to refuel and water, in the New Harbour's eastern corner. However, there is nowhere to berth for any length of time, so head to the Old Harbour, to the east, if you want to stay longer. It is usually busy with local boats but there may be room alongside the breakwater. Depths are between 3-4m and the holding is fair. While the harbour offers reasonable shelter, it is usually rolly with swell from passing

The old Venetian fortress, Palaio Froúrio, is conspicuous on Sidero Pt

ferries; it is also noisy, so head elsewhere if you seek a quiet refuge. Gouvia Marina to the north-west offers a good, secure alternative and is just a short bus/car journey from the town. See p27.

ANCHORING

The nearest anchorage to Corfu Town is in Garitsa Bay, to the south of Sideros Pt (see p34). Alternatively Komeno Bay, to the north of Corfu Town and the islet of Lazareto, offers good shelter from the north-west (see p49).

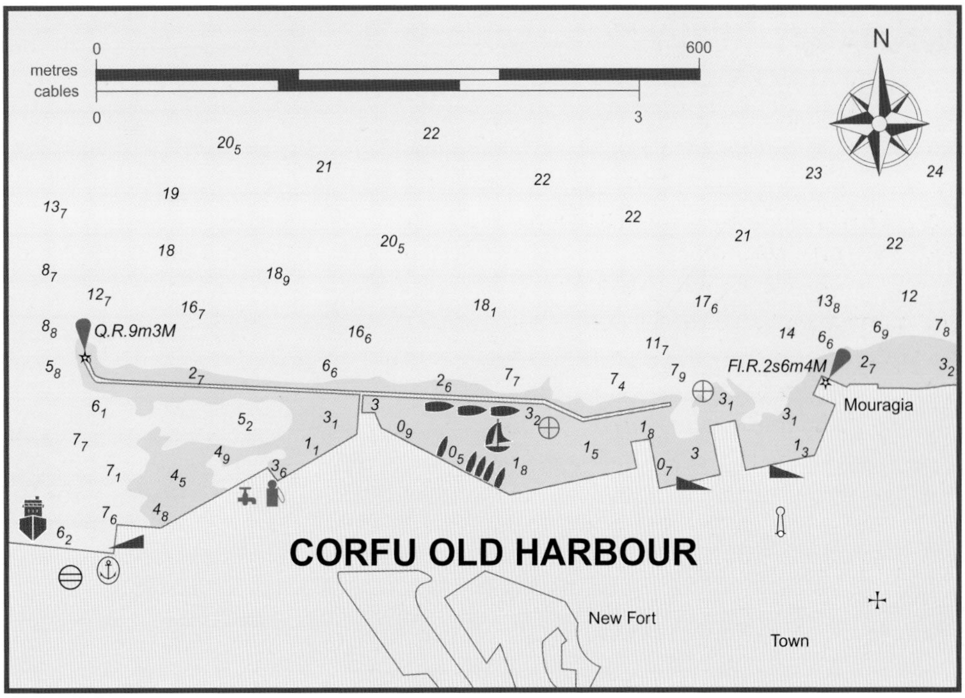

Useful information – Corfu Town

FACILITIES

Water: Taps are on the eastern side of the New Port, near Customs.
Fuel: Diesel and petrol pumps on the eastern side of the New Port, near Customs. There is also a fuel quay at Gouvia Marina.
Ice: Try the larger supermarkets on the outskirts of town.
Laundry: Near the New Port.
Gas: From Gouvia Marina.
Rubbish: Bins along the quay. Waste products such as oil and lubricants can be disposed of at Gouvia Marina. Ask at the marina office for information.
Yacht services/chandlery: Chandlers in the centre of Corfu Town. Gouvia Marina (Tel: 26610 91900/91376) offers a comprehensive range of services as well as a chandler.
Telephone: There are several phone boxes near the Old Harbour and more in the centre of town. Phone cards are sold at kiosks and supermarkets. Mobile reception is good.
Internet: Several internet cafes near the centre and the Liston. Prices from €6 per hour.

PROVISIONING

The main shopping centre of Corfu is to the west of the Esplanade (*Spianádha*), in the Old Town.
Grocery shops: Many mini-markets within the main shopping area – a couple of them near G Theotoki Square (Plateia Sanocco), to the south of the New Fortress. A daily morning market near the New Fortress is very good for fresh produce. For a major shop, head for Gouvia Marina as there is a large AB Supermarket near the main road entrance.
Bakery: Several, on the side-streets to the west of the Esplanade.
Butcher: Several in the town centre.
Banks: Emporiki Bank ATM kiosk on G Theotoki Square, plus a branch of the Alpha Bank and a Piraeus Bank branch and ATM. On Voulgareos St, a side-street of Kapodistria, the road that runs past the western side of the Esplanade, you'll find The Agricultural Bank of Greece (Tel: 26610 39404), another branch of the Alpha Bank and The National Bank of Greece (Tel: 26610 38597). Most travel agents offer currency exchange.
Pharmacy: Lots of pharmacies in the centre of Corfu, plus a couple on side-streets near the port.
Post: Post office to the south of G Theotoki Sq, on Alexandras St. Open 0900-1400, Monday-Friday. Several post boxes in the centre. The postal service in Corfu is good.
Opening times: 0900-1400 and 1800-2200 or later.

EATING OUT

Corfu Town is packed with cafés and bars, particularly around the Liston, an arcaded street on the eastern side of the town. It can be a delightful place to while away a few hours and is the hub of the old part of Corfu. There is also a good selection of tavernas in the old town, behind the Old Harbour. Prices range from very reasonable to very expensive, particularly at the Garitsa end of the town.

ASHORE

Corfu Town is dominated by the two forts – the Old Fort, Palaio Froúrio, on Sideros Pt, and the New Fort, Neo Froúrio, to the west, built by the Venetians and said to be connected via a network of tunnels beneath the city. The Old Fort was erected between 1550-1559, although it is thought that the headland has been fortified since the 8th century. A small but now unused canal bisects the fort from the island and also links Mandraki Harbour with Garitsa Bay to the south. Open to the public daily: Monday, 0830-1500; Tuesday-Sunday, 0830-1600. Admission €4.

The New Fort was built between 1576-1589 to strengthen the city's defences, but many of the buildings inside its walls date to the British occupation in the 19th century. Open daily, 0900-1800; admission €1.50.

The Palace of St Michael & St George, to the north of the Cricket Ground, is the oldest official building in Greece. Built between 1819 and 1824 of Maltese marble, it was used as the residence of the British Lord High Commissioner and was at one time the home of the Greek Royal Family. It fell into disrepair in the late 19th century but was restored in the 1950s by the British Ambassador to Greece, Sir Charles Peake. It is now home to the Museum of Asiatic Art (Tel: 26610 30443), a fascinating collection

Useful information – continued

of artefacts from the Far East. Assembled over many years by a Corfiat diplomat, Grigorios Manos, it was given to the government in the 1920s and includes silks, ceramics, statues, screens and costumes. The museum is open Tuesday-Sunday, 0830-1500; admission €2. The palace is also home to the Municipal Art Gallery (Tel: 26610 39553), which features a collection of 19th and 20th century artwork. Open seven days a week, 0900-2100.

The Cricket Ground, part of the Esplanade (Spianádha), immediately to the south of the palace, was originally a Venetian firing range. The first cricket match was held here in 1823 between the Royal Navy and the British Garrison and it is one of the only cricket pitches in Greece. Overlooking the Esplanade is the Liston, an arcaded street lined with cafes and bars. Designed by the Frenchman Mathieu de Lesseps in 1807 to resemble the Rue de Rivoli in Paris, it's a very cosmopolitan place and a really lovely spot to sit and watch the world go by. In the early evenings it can be quite lively.

Towering over the rest of the buildings, the Church of Agios Spyridon in the centre of the old town is dominated by a large ochre-coloured domed belfry. Built in 1589, it is named after St Spyridon, whose mummified body lies in a silver casket in the church. He is said to have performed many miracles on the island.

Twelve miles south of Corfu is the fascinating Achilleion Palace, named after the Ancient Greek Achilles and built in 1890 for the Empress Elizabeth of Austria. Its architecture embraces a range of styles and it is surrounded by lush gardens commanding spectacular views and filled with statues of the Achilles. Following the Empress's assassination in 1898, the palace was taken over by Kaiser Wilhelm II, who lived there until the outbreak of the First World War. Today it is better known for the James Bond film *For Your Eyes Only*, in which its casino, set up in the 1960s, was used. Open daily, 0900-1600; admission €6.

TRANSPORT

Car hire: Branches of Hertz, Avis, Europcar and Sixt at Corfu Airport. Near the New Harbour, on El Venizelou St, you'll find Budget Rent a Car (Tel: 26610 28590) and a branch of Sixt (Tel: 26610 81287). There are also a couple of scooter places nearby. Most car-rental offices are open 0800-2100, seven days a week. Travel agents in the centre of Corfu can also organise car hire.

Taxis: Taxi rank near the New Harbour.

Bus: The main KTEL bus station (Tel: 26610 39985) is to the west of the New Fortress, off Avramiou St. Travel from here to towns and villages around Corfu, such as Ag Stefanos, on the north-east coast, Kavos and Palaeokastritsa, or Athens on the mainland (12-hour journey). A local service (all dark blue buses) leaves from G Theotoki Square, to the south of the New Fortress, and calls at Gouvia and Kontokali or Benitses, plus other resorts on the island.

Ferry: Corfu's New Harbour is a major ferry terminal. From here you can travel to Igoumenitsa (hourly, seven days a week, journey time 2 hours), Gaios on Paxos (several times a week, 3½ hours), Patra (8-hour journey) and Italy (daily to Ancona, Bari and Brindisi). There are also high-speed catamaran services between Corfu and Italy and a daily foot-passenger hydrofoil between Paxos, Corfu and Igoumenitsa in the summer season. For timetables and/or to book tickets, visit one of the shipping agencies on El Venizelou St, the road past the New Harbour, or see www.greekferries.gr

Air travel: Corfu Airport (Olympic Airways office: Tel: 26610 30180) is just to the south of the town, near Garitsa. Regular daily flights from Athens during the summer and several flights a week to international destinations, such as the UK. Olympic Airways has an office on the road to the west of the Esplanade.

OTHER INFORMATION

Local Tel code: 26610.

Port authority: Port Police office (Tel: 26610 32655/40002/VHF Ch12) can be found near the New Port.

Tourist Office: On Rizospaston Voulefton, south of G Theotoki Square (Tel: 26610 37638). Open 0800-1400, Monday-Friday.

Police: On Samartzi St, south of the market. Tel: 26610 39503.

Doctor: On Rizopaston Voulefton St.

Hospital: Corfu Hospital to the west of the town (Tel: 26610 88200).

Yacht repairs/services: **Gouvia Marina** (Tel: 26610 91900/91376), to the north-west, offers a comprehensive range of services. See p27 for more details.

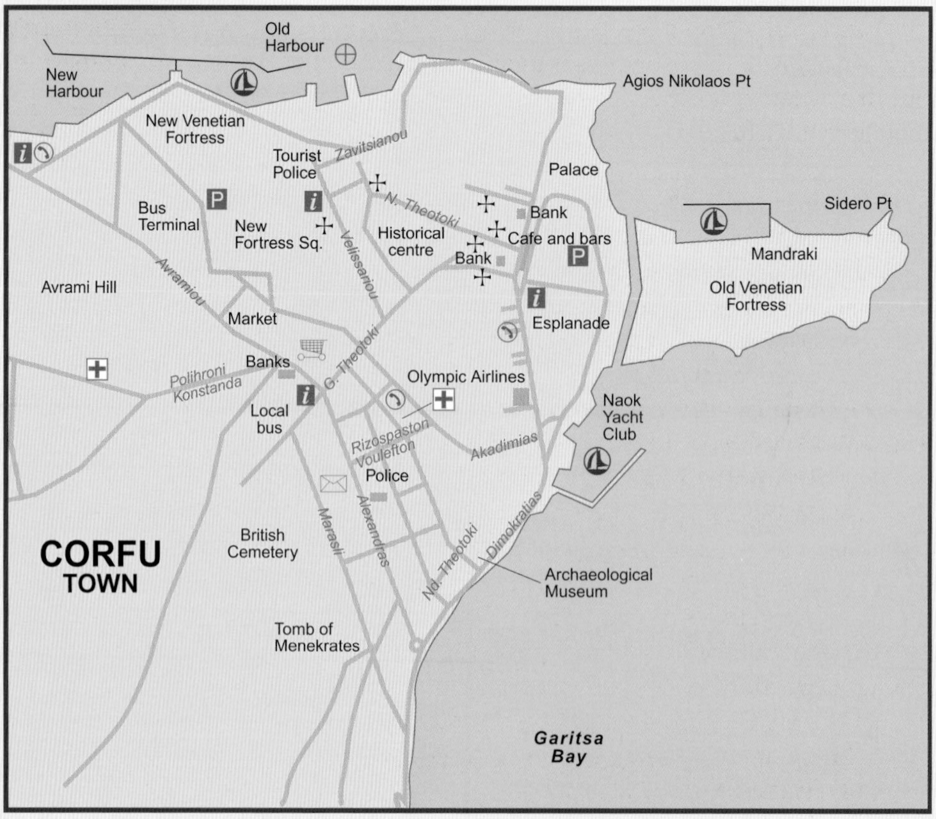

Gouvia Marina Ormos Gouvion

Gouvia Bay: 39°39'.24N 19°51'.06E
Gouvia Marina: 39°39'.04N 19°51'.06E

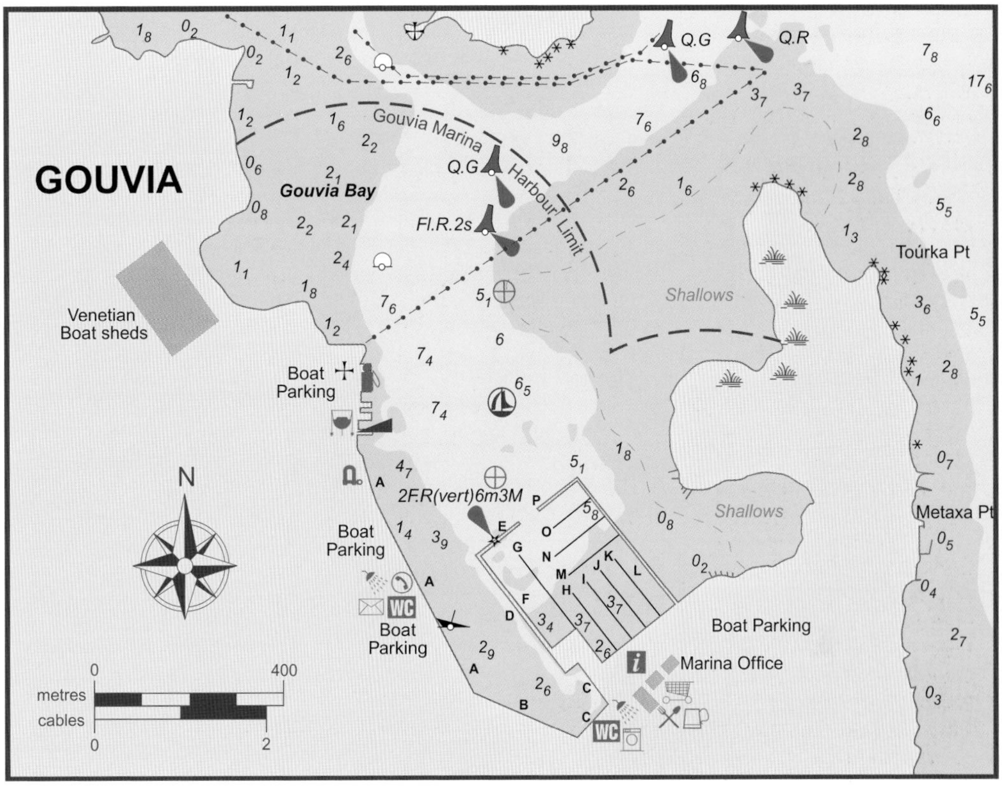

Take care to follow the channel into Gouvia as it is very shallow to the east of the marina

Gouvia Marina is Corfu's main marina and the best equipped on the island. Situated to the north-west of Corfu Town, it stands on the site of an old Venetian harbour and offers good protection from all directions. It is said to be the first privately owned marina in Greece and its extensive range of facilities and services makes it a good place to work on your boat or victual. Corfu Town is a 15-minute drive away, and many of the island's sites of interest are within easy reach.

Immediately behind the marina are the twin villages of Kontokali and Gouvia. Kontokali is the first of many fishing villages-turned-mini-resorts along this stretch of coast, and you won't find tiny backwater tavernas and olive groves here. They've all been replaced with English-style pubs and souvenir shops. It's certainly not the nicest place on Corfu, but as somewhere to victual it serves its purpose very well.

NAVIGATION

Charts: Admiralty 2407, 206, 188, SC5771; Imray G11, G1; Hellenic Navy Hydrographic Service 212/1, 21

The entrance to Gouvia Marina lies north-west of the islet of Lazareto and is identifiable from some distance. A large sandbank extends north of Tourka Point, the entrance's southern headland, so when approaching from the south, head past Lazareto and almost to Komeno Bay before turning to the west and entering the buoyed channel. Once inside the channel, follow it round and into the marina. Don't be tempted to cut the corner or enter the marina too soon as you will go aground on the sandbank. When close to, call the marina on VHF Ch69 for berthing instructions.

Yachts leaving Gouvia Marina should head towards a small church on the headland to the north until the first set of channel marks is identified.

BERTHING

Gouvia Marina incorporates 960 berths for boats of up to 80m (262ft) LOA and 6m (19ft 7in) draught. The majority of the berthing is stern- or bows-to on lazylines but there are some alongside berths available (expect to be charged extra). On entering the marina, call the office on VHF Ch69 for details of where to berth. The marina office is situated opposite pontoon H.

Berthing fees: Sample prices for an 11m (36ft) and a 14m (46ft) yacht during high season (1 April-30 September): €38/€54 per day or €424/€578 per month. Low season (1 October-31 March): €20/€27 per day or €266/€327 per month. Fees include 220v electricity. Daily fees are valid from time of arrival until 1400 the next day. Catamarans are not charged extra but alongside berthing is plus 80%. Prices may vary.

ANCHORING

There is nowhere to anchor in the marina. Anchoring is forbidden in the bay immediately to the north of the marina; however, it is permitted in Komeno Bay to the east (see p49).

Useful information – Gouvia Marina

FACILITIES

Marina office: In the administrative building opposite pontoon H. Opening hours: Monday-Saturday, 0800-1900; Sunday, 0800-1530. Tel: 26610 91900/91376. Watchman (when office closed) Tel: 26610 30932; VHF Ch69.
Water: Fresh water at each berth. There are also taps around the hard-standing. Drinking water available at the fuel station (small charge). Hydrants can be accessed using special cards available from the marina office.
Fuel: Fuel station (Tel: 26610 99198) at the north end of the marina, where there are also tanks for biological waste disposal. BP garage in Kontokali.
Showers: Four shower and toilet blocks around the marina. Also disabled toilet facilities.
Ice: At the marina supermarket.
Laundry: Self-service and dry cleaning (Tel: 26610 91418/91759, Mobile: 69773 96635).
Gas: Nautilus Chandlery at the marina, or supermarkets in Kontokali.
Shorepower: 220v electricity points at each berth. Also electricity points around hard-standing. Metered 380v electricity on request. Cables and plugs available from the marina's chandler.
Rubbish: Bins throughout the marina.
Yacht services/chandlery: Gouvia Marina has hard-standing for 520 boats, plus undercover storage. It has a 65-ton travelhoist, a 45-ton and a 5-ton crane and boat transporter. Various services available at the marina, including boat maintenance, repairs, mechanical and electrical engineering, sail repair and refrigeration. Sample prices for 11m (36ft) and 14m (46ft) yachts (prices may vary): crane in/out: €155/€208. Pressure wash: €50/€92. Crane hire: €94 per ½ hour. Sewage pump-out: €0.24/lt.
At the marina you'll also find: Nautilus Chandlery (Tel: 26610 90343/ email: tolis-co@otenet.gr), and DL Sails (Tel: 26610 90069), which offers sailmaking and repairs, cleaning and sail storage. Boatman's World Chandler is in Kontokali.
Telephone: Several phone boxes around the marina. There is also a phone in the marina office and one next to the Port Police.
Internet: Ask at the marina office.
Weather forecast: A forecast is posted daily at the marina office.

PROVISIONING

Grocery shops: Supermarket at the marina, which will deliver to your boat. AB Supermarket in Kontokali, plus several other mini-markets and grocery shops.
Bakery: La Frianderie Bakery (Tel: 26610 99065) at the marina. There are a couple more in Kontokali and Gouvia.
Butcher: In Kontokali. Fishmonger nearby.
Banks: Emporiki ATM in Gouvia village, but the nearest branch is in Corfu (see p25). Banks are open Monday-Friday, 0900-1300. An exchange office, open seven days a week, is available at the Public Services building, opposite pontoon H. Cash machine at the AB Supermarket in Kontokali.
Pharmacy: Kontokali.
Other shops: Souvenir shop at the marina. Surfer shops in Kontokali. Kiosk selling phone cards, drinks and cigarettes near AB Supermarket.
Post: Several post boxes at the marina. Post can also be delivered here for collection. The marina's address is: Gouvia Marina, Post Box 60, 49083 Tzavros, Corfu. Post box in Kontokali next to The Beer Bucket. The postal service on Corfu is good.
Opening times: Most shops are open 0900-1400 and 1700-2100 but times vary. Tavernas and souvenir shops usually stay open later.

EATING OUT

There are several places to eat at the marina: Argo Restaurant (Tel: 26610 99251), Maistro Café (Tel: 26610 90970) or the La Frianderie Café. Alternatively, Kontokali, a 5-10-minute walk from the marina, has plenty of tavernas and bars. Gerekos Taverna has a good reputation for traditional fish dishes, as does Takis Taverna nearby and Zorbas Taverna Grill behind the marina.

ASHORE

The marina has a swimming pool and children's play area. Gouvia Marina Professional Diving Centre (Tel: 26610 91955/69443 17646) runs PADI courses. The most interesting historical site at Gouvia is the Venetian boatsheds at the northern end of the marina. Built around 1716, they were used for the construction and maintenance of naval vessels when the harbour here was operated by the Venetian Navy. Although the roofs have long gone, the pillars and arches still remain.

TRANSPORT

Car hire: Ocean Sixt Car Rental (Tel: 26610 99159) is next to the Port Police office and Nikos Rent-a-Bike (Tel: 26610 99111/ 69326 86664) is nearby and also in Kontokali (Tel: 26610 91157).
Taxis: Radio Taxi (Tel: 26610 33811/34124), or ask at the marina office.
Bus: Every 30 minutes to Corfu from the marina (blue bus No 7). The bus stop is opposite the AB supermarket near the south gate.
Ferry: Services to Igoumenitsa, Paxos, Patra and Italy leave from the New Harbour in Corfu daily. Times and booking details on www.greekferries.gr
Air travel: International charter and domestic services fly from Corfu International Airport, a 15-minute drive from Gouvia. Contact Olympic Airways (Tel: 26610 30180).

OTHER INFORMATION

Local Tel code: 26610.
Gouvia Marina: PO Box 60, 49083 Tzavros, Corfu. Tel: 26610 91900/91376. Fax: 26610 91829. Email: gouvia@medmarinas.com
Website: www.medmarinas.com
Port Police: Situated at the marina office.
Hellenic Tourism Organisation: Next to the marina office.
Tourist Police: In Corfu (Tel: 26610 30265).
Doctor: At the marina (Tel: 26610 91303; 6976 404021).
Dentist: Several in Corfu Town. Ask at the marina office for recommendations.
Hospital: Medical centre (Tel: 26610 88200) at the marina near Nikos Rent-a-Bike. Hospital in Corfu Town.
Yacht repairs/services: A range of services at the marina. Contact the marina office (Tel: 26610 91900/91376).

The Venetian boatsheds at Gouvia Marina were built in 1716

Gouvia Marina is the best equipped boatyard on Corfu. Note the sweeping sandbank that flanks the entrance, to the east of the marina

Ptichia Island

Ptihia, Ptychia, Nisos Vidho, Vido, Vidos

To the north-east of Ptichia Island:
39°38'.94N 19°56'.26E

Charts: Admiralty 2407, 206, 188, SC5771; Imray G11, G1; Hellenic Navy Hydrographic Service 212/1, 21

The small, wooded islet of Ptichia lies 1½nm north of Corfu Town. Fortified by the French in the early 19th century, and destroyed by the British at the end of their occupation in the 1860s, the island has also been the site of a prison and is rumoured to be connected to Corfu via a network of tunnels linking the city's four fortresses. During the First World War, it was a base for wounded Serbian soldiers, over 1,200 of whom never recovered and were buried in the military cemetery on the eastern side of the island. A mausoleum, designed by architect Nikola Knjazev, was erected on Ptichia in 1936. Today, Ptichia is unoccupied, bar a small seasonal taverna which serves the boatloads of tourists that visit each summer from Corfu.

In settled conditions, yachts can anchor off Ptichia's southern shore in about 5-8m. However, it is not suitable in anything other than calm weather and should definitely not be considered in a strong northwesterly. The holding on mud is reasonable.

Right: Ptichia Island, which lies to the north of Corfu Town, was a base for wounded Serbian soldiers during the First World War

The islet is fringed with shoal waters and rocks, so exercise care when approaching, particularly around its north shore and about ½nm west-north-west of its western tip where there is a nasty reef and some above-water rocks (Kalogiros [Nafsika]).

On approach from all directions, keep a good look-out for ferry and ship traffic as the waters surrounding Corfu Town are often busy. At night, the southern tip of the islet is marked with a light (Fl G 3s12m4M). On approach from the north, this can be hard to distinguish against the lights of Corfu Town.

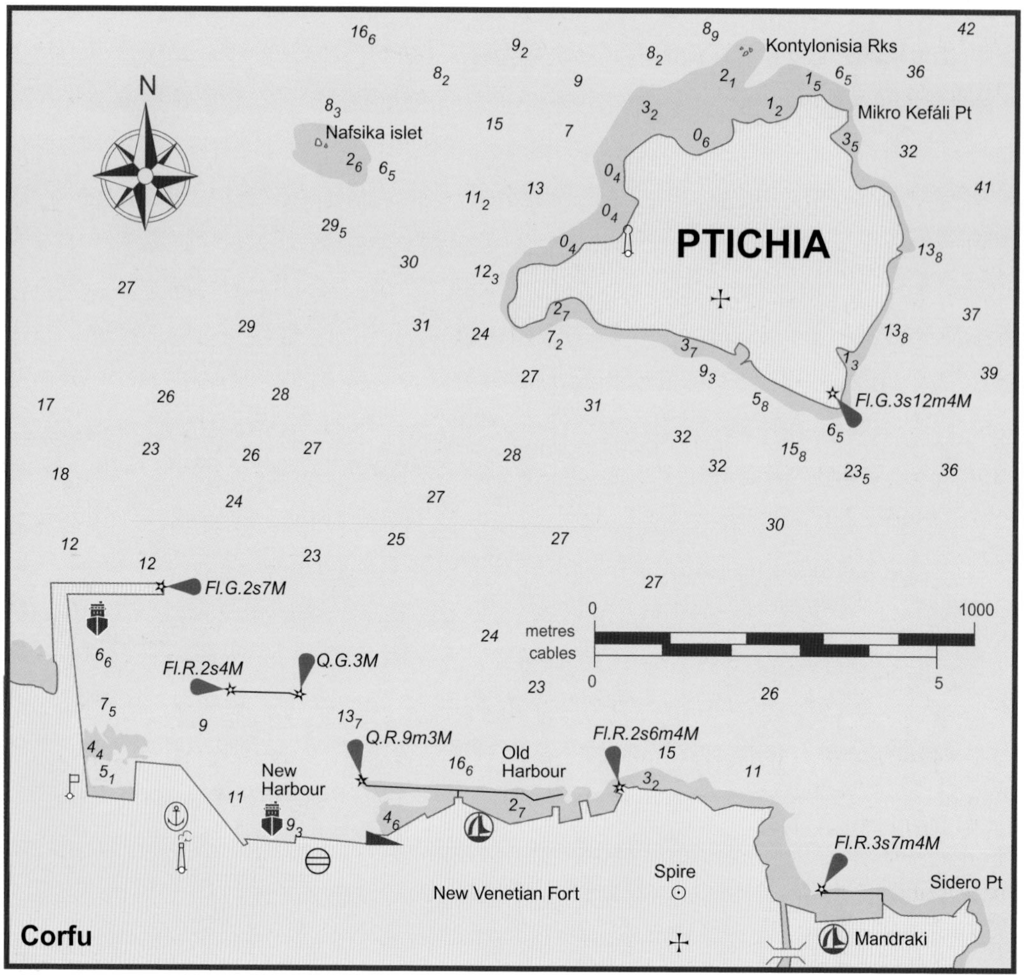

Lazareto Island

Lazaretto, Nisos Gouvinon, Gouvino

To the north of Lazareto Island: 39°39'.24N 19°52'.76E
Charts: Admiralty 2406, 206, 188, SC5771; Imray G11, G1; Hellenic Navy Hydrographic Service 212/1 21

Lazareto is the smaller and westernmost of the two islets to the north of Corfu Town, and lies 1½nm east-south-east of Gouvia Marina. In settled conditions, yachts can anchor off its south coast in less than 6m, but when a strong northwesterly is blowing, shelter should be sought in either Gouvia Marina or Komeno Bay, to the west of Komeno Pt.

The waters surrounding the islet are shallow, particularly off its western shore and in the middle of the south coast, so keep an eye on your echo sounder. On approach from the east, via the channel between Ptichia (Vidho) island and Corfu, keep a good look-out as daytime ferry traffic is heavy.

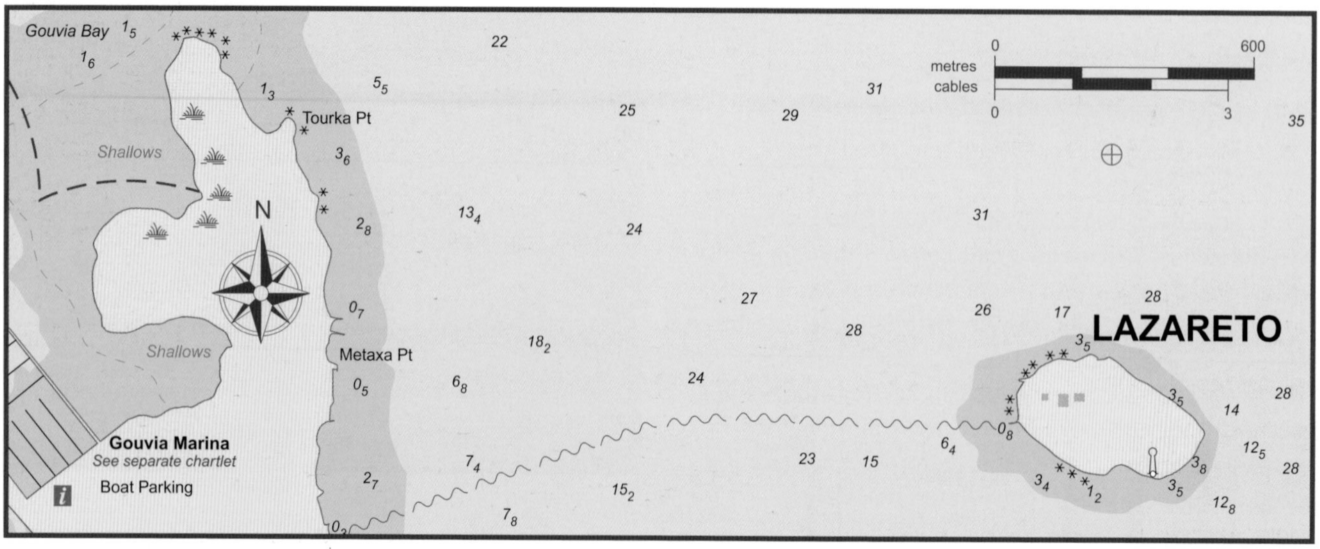

NAOK Yacht Club

To the east of the harbour entrance:
39°37'.24N 19°55'.61E

NAOK Yacht Club's harbour stands just to the south-west of Sideros Pt, tucked in behind the Old Fortress. Home to the Nautical Club of Kerkyra, this harbour, like Mandraki to the north, is not for public use, but a few berths are sometimes available for visitors. Check before arrival. The harbour provides good shelter from the north and west quadrants, but is exposed in a southerly and in poor conditions an alternative berth or anchorage should be sought. The centre of Corfu Town is a 5-minute walk away.

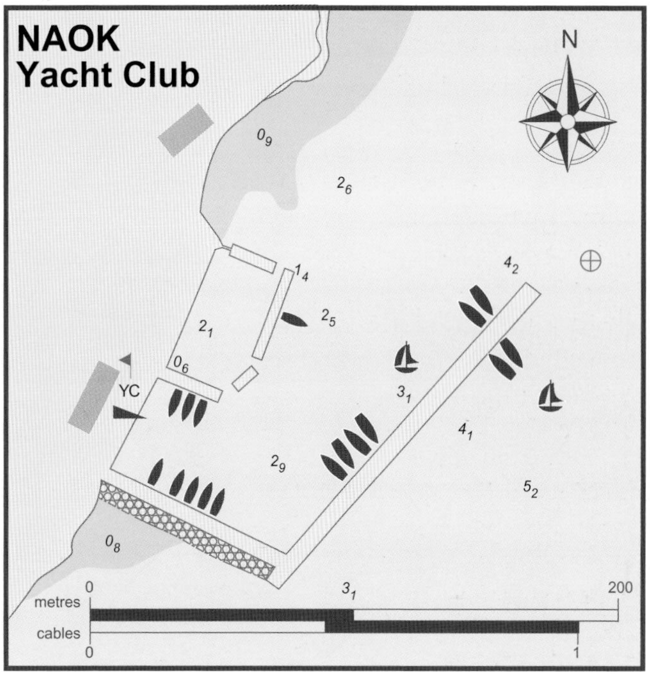

NAVIGATION

Charts: Admiralty 2407, 206, 188, SC5771; Imray G11, G1; Hellenic Navy Hydrographic Service 212/1, 21

The approach to NAOK Yacht Club's harbour is straightforward from all directions. From the north, it will become visible once round Sideros Pt and from the south you should head for Garitsa Bay: the harbour lies in its north-west corner. Watch out for shoals just to the south of the harbour breakwater, close to the shore.

BERTHING

NAOK Yacht Club has limited space for visiting yachts, so check availability before arrival. Most yachts berth stern- or bows-to the inside edge of the outer breakwater, although larger vessels often berth on the outer edge where it is deeper (around 4m).

Depths in the harbour are from 2.5-3m but watch out for the shallow patches just to the north of the western quay and in the south-east corner.

The holding here on mud is good. You can expect to be charged for an overnight stay.

ANCHORING

Yachts often anchor immediately to the north-west of the harbour in 5-8m. The holding here is good and the anchorage is well sheltered from the north and west, although it is not suitable in a southerly. An alternative anchorage can be found in the southern corner of Garitsa Bay (see p34).

NAOK Yacht Club's harbour lies tucked in behind the Old Fortress. It is a private harbour, although berths are occasionally available to visiting boats

Useful information – Naok Yacht Club

FACILITIES

Water: Available from the club.
Fuel: Gouvia Marina, 5nm to the north-west, has a fuel pontoon.
Ice: From supermarkets in the centre of Corfu.
Laundry: In the centre of Corfu.
Gas: Available from supermarkets in Corfu Town, or at Gouvia Marina.
Rubbish: Bins on the quay.
Yacht services/chandlery: The nearest can be found at Gouvia Marina.
Telephone: You will come across several phone boxes on the road behind the club.

PROVISIONING & EATING OUT

The centre of Corfu Town is a 5-minute walk away. Here you will find a wide selection of shops, banks and tavernas. See p25.

USEFUL INFORMATION

NAOK Yacht Club: Tel: 26610 30470.

NAOK Yacht Club is a five-minute walk from the centre of Corfu Town, where all provisions can be found

Mandraki Harbour

(POIATH Yacht Club)

To the north of the harbour: 39°37'.74N 19°55'.76E
Harbour entrance: 39°37'.57N 19°55'.64E

It is thought that there has been a harbour at Mandraki since ancient times but it was the Venetians who, having built the Old Fortress on Sideros Pt in the 1550s, were responsible for the harbour that stands here today. It is not a public harbour, like the Old Harbour to the west, but is operated by the Corfu branch of the Hellenic Offshore Racing Club (HORC) and the Kerkyra Sailing Club. Established in 1961 in Piraeus, near Athens, HORC aims to promote offshore sailing in Greece and has run its own offshore racing school since 1969. The Corfu branch was established in 1976 and now boasts over 150 members.

Situated so close to the centre of Corfu, all the town's amenities are within a 5-minute walk of the harbour and Mandraki offers very good shelter from the prevailing northwesterlies. However, you can't always be guaranteed a berth here, particularly during peak season, so it is best to contact the club beforehand to check availability.

Mandraki Harbour offers good shelter from the north-west

NAVIGATION

Charts: Admiralty 2407, 206, 188, SC5771; Imray G11, G1; Hellenic Navy Hydrographic Service 212/1, 21

Approach Mandraki as you would Corfu's Old Harbour, which lies slightly further to the west. The harbour is tucked into the north face of Corfu's old fortress, and yacht masts and a large white building above the harbour make it conspicuous from some distance. Keep well

Nestled in the north face of Corfu's old fortress, Mandraki harbour was built by the Venetians during the 16th century

offshore until level with the harbour entrance, as depths close to the headland and the fortress decrease to less than 1m; there are also rocks along the outer edge of the breakwater. At night, the entrance end of the breakwater is marked with a red light (Fl R 3s). Maintain a good look-out at all times as traffic is usually heavy in this area.

BERTHING

As there are only a few visitors' berths at Mandraki, you will need to phone ahead to check availability.

If there is a free berth, harbour staff will show you where to tie up stern- or bows-to using the lazylines provided, although note that these lazylines are unreliable. It is also recommended that you try to get as far into the harbour as possible, as the wash from the ferries hits the south wall, causing swell to work its way into the outer part of the harbour, making it uncomfortable.

Depths in the harbour are around 2.5m and the holding on mud is good: be aware, however, that there is a ground chain running along the centre of the harbour from east to west. You can expect to be charged for your berth, with current prices at 0.30¢ per foot.

ANCHORING

There is nowhere to anchor within the vicinity of Mandraki Harbour. The nearest anchorage is in Komeno Bay, 4nm to the north-west (see p49), or Garitsa Bay, to the south (see p34).

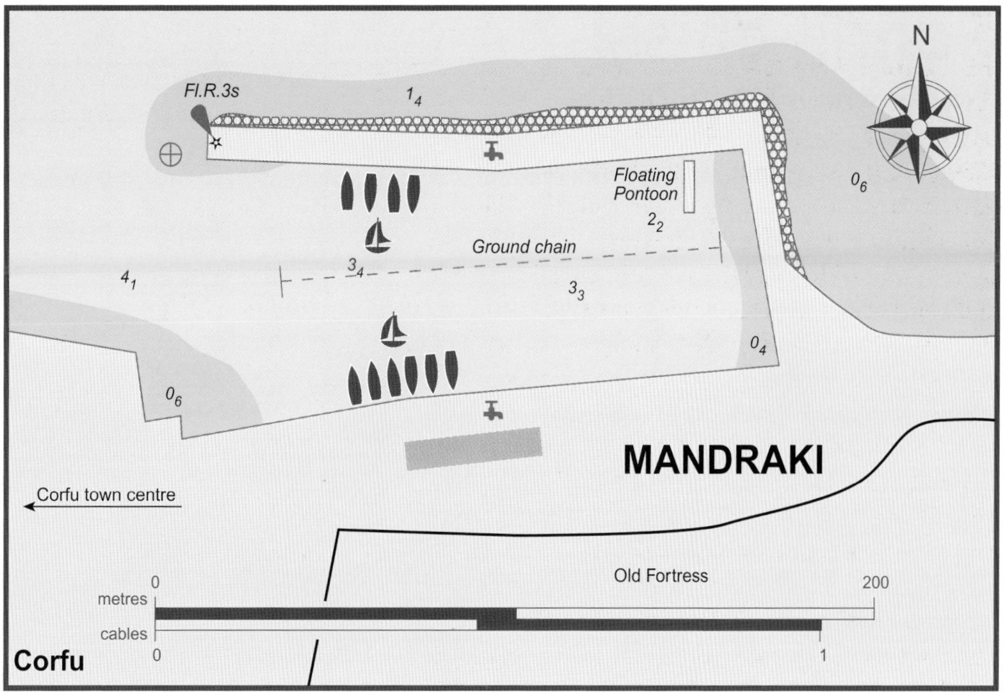

Useful information – Mandraki Harbour

FACILITIES
Water: Taps on the quay.
Fuel: Gouvia Marina, 4nm to the north-west has a fuel pontoon.
Ice: From supermarkets in the centre of Corfu.
Laundry: In the centre of Corfu.
Gas: Available from supermarkets in Corfu Town or at Gouvia Marina.
Rubbish: Bins on the quay.
Yacht services/chandlery: The nearest is at Gouvia Marina.
Telephone: Phone box at the club, others in town.

PROVISIONING & EATING OUT
The centre of Corfu Town is a five-minute walk from Mandraki Harbour. Here you will find a wide selection of grocery shops and places to victual. See p25 for more information.

OTHER INFORMATION
Mandraki Harbour (Corfu branch of Hellenic Offshore Racing Club HORC): Tel: 26610 25759.

Garitsa Bay

Ormos Garitsas

Garitsa Bay, to south of Sideros Pt: 39°36'.94N 19°55'.76E
Charts: Admiralty 2407, 206, 188, SC5771; Imray G11, G1; Hellenic Navy Hydrographic Service 212/1, 21

Garitsa Bay is situated between Sideros Pt and Anemomilos Pt (Fl(2)R 10s). It is a large bay that offers good shelter from the north-west, although it can feel exposed in a southerly.

You can anchor in 6m or less on sand and weed.

Right: Garitsa Bay is near the centre of Corfu

Pondikonissi

Pondikonisi, Pontikonisi

To the north-west of Pondikonissi: 39°35'.24N 19°55'.91E
Charts: Admiralty 2407, 206, 188, SC5771; Imray G11, G1; Hellenic Navy Hydrographic Service 21

Situated to the south-south-west of the Kanoni peninsula, the islet of Pondikonissi and its smaller, flatter sister, Vlaherna, lie in direct line with the runways of Corfu International Airport. Yachts can anchor to the east of the islet in between 5-10m, but to be honest there are much nicer anchorages elsewhere. Not only is it disturbed by the regular roar of aircraft flying incredibly low overhead, but during the summer season it is overrun with tourists and a far cry from the charming place that Gerald Durrell described in 1969 in *Birds, Beasts and Relatives*.

The islet's name translates as 'Mouse Island' but these days tourists outnumber mice. Rocks and shoal patches fringe the island, particularly on its western shore, so be careful when navigating around it.

Its main attraction is its small, white 13th century church, which stands surrounded by cypress trees. During the season there is also a small cafe there. Legend has it that Pondikonissi is the petrified remains of Odysseus' ship, turned to stone by Poseidon. However, the same legend is shared by several rocks and islets around Corfu.

The islet of Vlaherna, lying just to the north of Pondikonissi, is joined to the Kanoni peninsula by a short causeway. Here, too, you'll find bucket-loads of tourists visiting the monastery to Our Lady of Vlaherna, and any charm it may once have had is lost due to its proximity to the airport.

Benitses

Benitsa, Benitsai

East of Benitses: 39°32'.74N 19°55'.56E

Charts: Admiralty 206, 188, SC5771; Imray G11, G1; Hellenic Navy Hydrographic Service 016, 21

About halfway down Corfu's east coast, 6nm south of Corfu Town, is the tiny harbour of Benitses. Since the 1970s it has been known as a tacky package holiday resort that attracts the worst kind of tourist, and it's a reputation it has yet to shake off. While slightly quieter now, the once small fishing village still buzzes with tourists and in the past has not been recommended as a cruising destination. However, at the time of writing, the small fishing boat harbour was being extended. Up until now it has been too small and too crowded for yachts to berth in, but plans have included enlarging capacity to 100 boats and dredging the area to increase depths. These improvements could make Benitses a good destination on an otherwise barren stretch of coastline, as long as you don't mind a few grockles. The harbour was due to reopen in 2006, but hasn't yet done so.

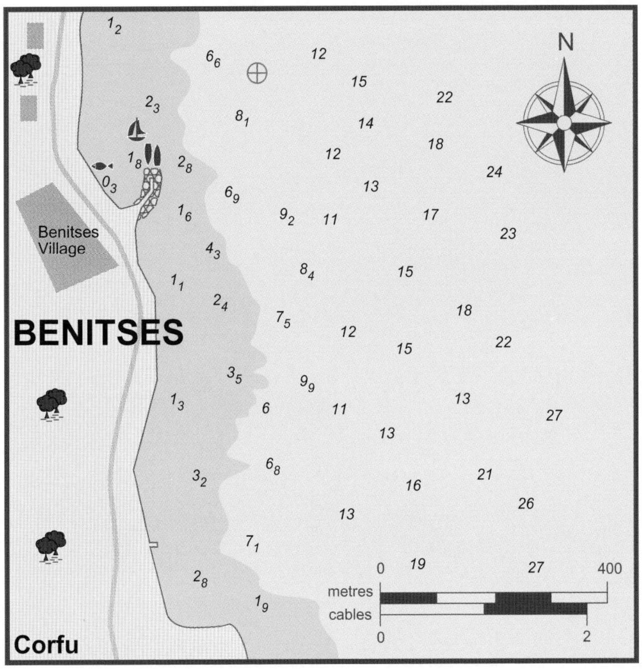

Alternatively, you can still anchor to the north of the harbour, in around 5-10m, although this is not advised in unsettled conditions and should only be considered for short stops.

If you do go ashore, you'll find most amenities among the hotels and bars. There are several mini-markets, tavernas and places to hire a car, and the Corfu Shell Museum houses an extraordinary collection of thousands of shells. The largest of its kind in Europe, it's open seven days a week, 1000-2100.

Petriti **Pentritis**

North-west corner of Lefkimi Bay: 39°27'.74N 20°01'.26E

Charts: Admiralty 206, 188, SC5771; Imray G11, G1; Hellenic Navy Hydrographic Service 21

Petriti lies in the north-west corner of Lefkimi Bay, 12nm south of Corfu Town. It's a small harbour and village relatively untouched by tourism and retaining much of its traditional fishing village feel.

From the north, the approach is straightforward, but from the east, you should stay well offshore off Lefkimi Pt (Ak Levkimmis [Fl 6s9m6M]) as shoals extend to the west and north of it for about ½nm. You should also be aware of rocks immediately to the south of the harbour, some of which are above water.

The harbour itself offers good shelter from all but the south-east, if you can find room on the southern end of the quay. Here you should berth stern- or bows-to in around 2m. Further in it is too shallow for most yachts and the quay is usually busy with fishing boats. Yachts occasionally anchor to the east of the breakwater, taking a line ashore, but you are more exposed here and it is quite shallow.

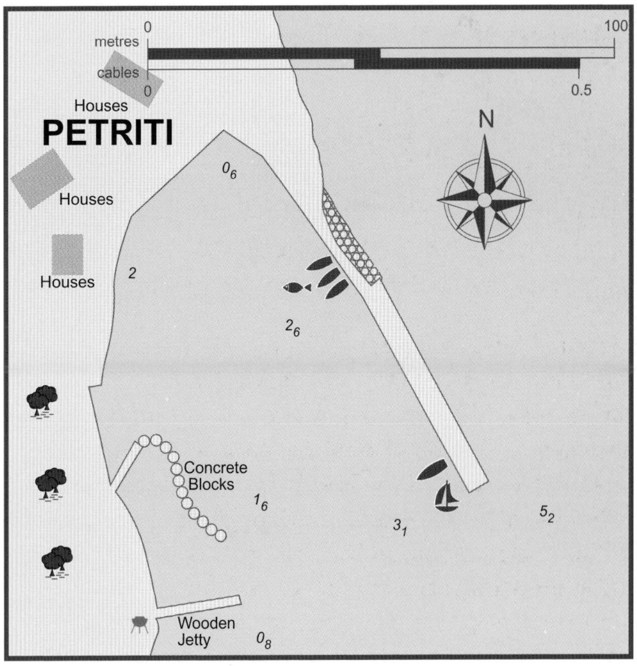

One alternative is to anchor in Lefkimi Bay in around 5-10m, to the south-east of the harbour. The holding on mud is good and the shelter reasonable.

The village of Petriti is a lovely place to spend some time, away from the humdrum of the other harbours on this stretch of coast. It is also home to several very good fish tavernas and a well-stocked mini-market selling fresh fruit and vegetables.

LEFKIMI PT

Lefkimi Pt (Ak Levkimmis) can pose a danger to the unwary. It's extremely low-lying and can be hard to identify even close-to, particularly in poor weather conditions. Sandy shoals extend for around ¾nm to the north and ¾nm to the east of it and, although the headland is marked with a light at night (Fl 6s9m6M), keep your distance from it at all times.

Lefkimi Canal

Potamos Lefkimis, Skala Potamou

East of the entrance to the Lefkimi Canal:
39°26'.14N 20°05'.56E
Charts: Admiralty 206, 188, SC5771; Imray G11, G1; Hellenic Navy Hydrographic Service 21

The entrance to the Lefkimi Canal lies 1½nm south of Lefkimi Pt on the south-east tip of Corfu. Rocky breakwaters extend out on both sides of the entrance and at night the southern breakwater can be identified by its light (Fl R 2s7m3M). Only small boats with a draught of less than 1m can navigate the canal safely, as it is very shallow and often silts up.

The canal runs from the coast inland to Lefkimi, which is renowned for being the largest town in the southern half of Corfu.

The Lefkimi Canal is too shallow for most boats to navigate

Lefkimi Harbour

Lefkimmis, Levkimni, Kavos

East of entrance to Lefkimi Harbour:
39°25'.14N 20°06'.06E

The harbour at Lefkimi, 1½nm south of the entrance to the Lefkimi Canal, is Corfu's second commercial port. It is smaller in size than the one at Corfu Town, but is used by ferries from Igoumenitsa and Paxos. Otherwise there is not much ashore, so when they are not running, it is often deserted and feels very isolated.

Lefkimi is the last harbour on this stretch of coast and is a good place to stop on the way north or south. The harbour has a reasonable amount of room but only moderate shelter as its entrance faces north; with the regular ferry traffic there is often quite a bit of chop.

The town of Lefkimi is a half-hour walk from the port but worth a visit as it is so unlike the others in this part of Corfu and is also good for provisioning.

NAVIGATION

Charts: Admiralty 206, 188, SC5771; Imray G11, G1; Hellenic Navy Hydrographic Service 21

Lefkimi Harbour is easy to identify from some distance due to the regular ferry traffic. The approach from the south is through deep water if you keep in the middle of the South Corfu Strait, which runs between the southern tip of Corfu and the mainland. Don't get too close to Corfu's shore, particularly around Koundouris Pt and Asprokavos Pt where some nasty reefs (Ifalos Aspra Vrakhia) extend to the south-east of the headland for about a mile. Although depths over most of them are around 7m, it is best to avoid the area as not all the rocks are charted.

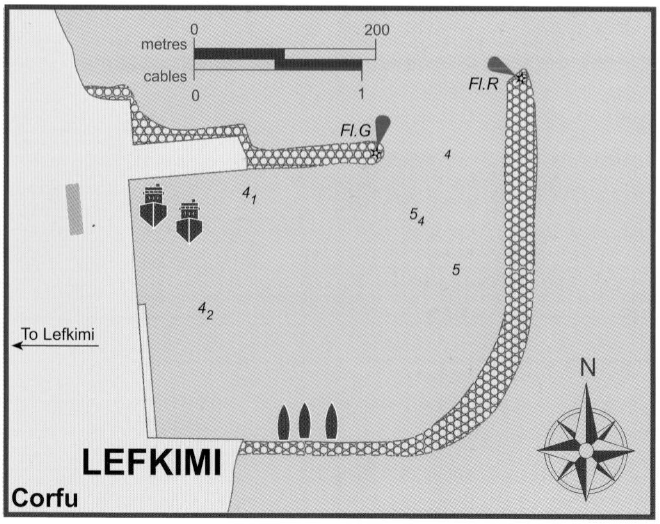

On approach from the north, attention should be paid around Lefkimi Pt. The low-lying headland (see p36) is often hard to identify and shoals extend for about ½nm to the north and east of it.

A pair of lights (Fl G and Fl R) mark the ends of the harbour's breakwaters. Traffic is heavy, so maintain a good look-out at all times.

BERTHING

Visiting yachts should berth stern- or bows-to the south side of the quay, keeping well clear of the ferries, which berth on the north-west side of the harbour. There are usually a few tripper boats on the western quay. Depths in the harbour are between 3-4.5m and the holding on mud is good.

ANCHORING

There are no secure anchorages near Lefkimi Harbour.

ASHORE

There is not much ashore at Lefkimi Harbour, apart from a cafe and a petrol station. However, the town, which is half-an-hour's walk away, has a good selection of tavernas and shops.

The low-lying Lefkimi Pt can be hard to identify until close-to

Lefkimi is a very pleasant market town, with some fine architecture and a pretty little canal running through it. There are branches of the Agricultural Bank of Greece (Tel: 26620 22450) and the National Bank of Greece (Tel: 26620 25274), plus several mini-markets, fruit and veg shops and pharmacies. If you want somewhere to eat, there is a good selection of tavernas and cafes. Useful telephone numbers include the Port Police (Tel: 26620 23277), Police (Tel: 26620 22222) and the Health Centre (Tel: 26620 23100/22800.

Lefkimi Harbour is serviced by ferries from the mainland

Palaeokastritsa

Palaiokastritsa

Inside the entrance to Alipa Bay:
39°40'.34N 19°42'.76E

The dramatic cliffscape that forms the Palaeokastritsa coastline is one of Corfu's finest. Craggy cliffs plunge into azure waters and, though liberally peppered with hotels and apartments, the surrounding hillside is also lush with thick greenery. It is the west coast's primary resort, and what was once a small coastal village now bulges with hotels and holiday homes. The British High Commissioner Sir Frederick Adam helped to popularise it in the early 19th century when he ordered the building of a road to Corfu Town. His favourite place to picnic is now one of the island's major destinations and it's not hard to see why, set as it is among steep, jagged rocks.

The harbour itself offers good shelter from the prevailing winds and is the best place to stock up along this stretch of coast. However, in a southerly, it can be very nasty, so shelter should be sought elsewhere.

NAVIGATION

Charts: Admiralty 2402, 206, 188, SC5771; Imray G11, G1; Hellenic Navy Hydrographic Service 016, 21

Vessels approaching Palaeokastritsa from the south will be able to identify the village from some distance by the numerous buildings on the hillside. Closer-to, on Ag Spiridonos Pt, to the east of the harbour, the large white building of the Palaeokastritsa Monastery will become visible.

From the north, Palaeokastritsa is hidden until you are well round Taxiakis Pt. The fortress Angelokastro on this headland is conspicuous, and as you head further east more of the village appears. Watch out for rocks around the rocky islet of Skialoudi, though, and pass south of it.

Three large bays form this stretch of coast, and the harbour at Palaeokastritsa is in the western corner of the middle one, Alipa Bay. There are lots of rocks just to the north of the harbour entrance, so take great care here and watch out for watersports users.

At night, Alipa Bay is identified by the lighthouse (Fl 3s22m5M) on Kosteri Pt, but be very careful when approaching as there are many rocks and reefs along this stretch of coast.

BERTHING

Depths in the harbour range between 2.5-4m and yachts should berth stern- or bows-to the eastern side of the quay. The holding is good and the harbour is well protected, although in a southerly it can be affected by swell. Day-tripper and fishing boats regularly use the harbour.

The small harbour at Palaeokastritsa is tucked into the western corner of Alipa Bay

ANCHORING

Palaeokastritsa's many bays offer good anchorages in settled conditions. Liapades Bay (Ormos Liapadhes), to the far east of the village, is good in northerly and easterly winds and you can anchor on sand in around 4-5m. The eastern corner of Alipa Bay (Limani Alipa), behind a tiny rocky islet, is also good in these conditions and slightly more protected from the south. However, watch out for rocks in the bay, particularly

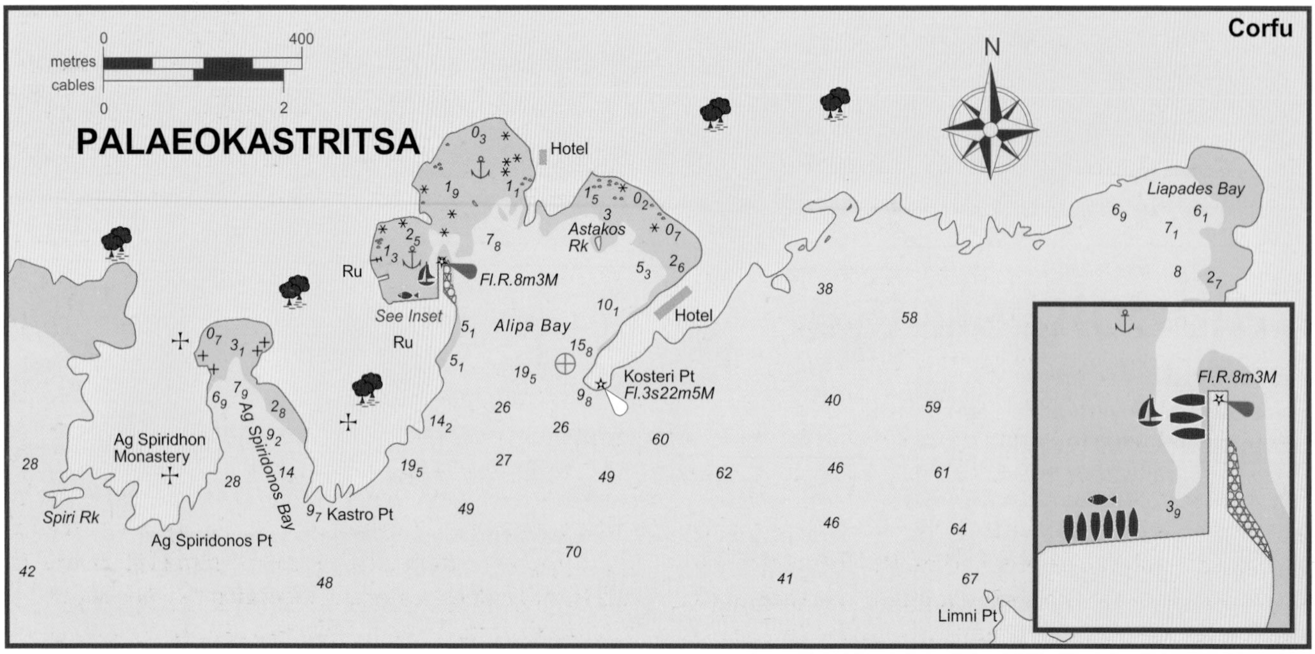

in the northeastern corner and close to the shore. If possible, anchor close to Kosteri Pt in around 5-6m.

Boats sometimes anchor in the inlet to the north of the harbour but it is very rocky, especially near the entrance, so take great care. Anchor in 3-4m.

One other place that offers good shelter from the prevailing winds is to the west of the harbour in Ag Spiridonos Bay. Anchor here in 4-5m. The bay is totally open to the south, however, so should not be used in a southerly.

Useful information – Palaeokastritsa

FACILITIES

Water: Taps are situated on the quay.
Fuel: Petrol station on the road out of Palaeokastritsa.
Ice: Ask at the supermarkets.
Gas: Bottle exchange at the supermarkets.
Rubbish: Large bins on the quay.
Telephone: Phone box near the taverna. More in the centre of town.

PROVISIONING

There are plenty of places to provision in Palaeokastritsa but the village is fairly spread out, so transport will be required.
Grocery shops: Lots of supermarkets – several of them on the road to the harbour.
Bakery: A couple on the main road. Supermarkets also sell limited products.
Butcher: In the centre of Palaeokastritsa.
Banks: 24hr Emporiki ATM in a kiosk on the main road. Some hotels offer currency exchange, as do travel agents.
Pharmacy: Situated on the main road.
Post: Post office can be found in Palaeokastritsa, plus several post boxes. Stamps also sold at souvenir shops. The postal service is good.
Opening times: Most shops are open 0900-1400 and 1730-2100; tavernas, bars and souvenir shops open later.

EATING OUT

Alipa Taverna (Tel: 26630 41614) behind the harbour is good for fish dishes, particularly lobster. Astakos Taverna near the main road is also recommended. Other tavernas of varying quality are situated near the beach and along the main road.

ASHORE

Like most resorts on Corfu there is a good selection of watersports companies in Palaeokastritsa. The Corcyra Diving Center (Tel: 26630 41206) runs a range of diving courses, and companies advertising other sports such as parascending can be found near the beaches.

A steep climb away, on the headland overlooking Ag Spiridonos Bay, is the Moni Theotokon or Palaeokastritsa Monastery. First founded here in 1228, the current 18th century building commands fantastic views over Palaeokastritsa's jagged coastline and it is well worth the very steep walk. It is open to the public and a small museum in one of the courtyards includes a collection of Byzantine and Post-Byzantine icons. Of particular interest is the wooden carving of the Tree of Life. It is open seven days a week, 0700-1300 and 1500-2000. Admission is free, although donations are welcomed; visitors must be appropriately dressed, so no shorts or skimpy tops.

According to legend, one of the rocks you can see from the monastery is the petrified ship of Algerian pirates turned to stone by the Virgin Mary during their attempt to plunder its riches. It is also one of the many rocks around Corfu said to be Odysseus' ship, turned to stone by Neptune.

A four-mile (6km) walk from Palaeokastritsa, near the village of Krini, are the ruins of the 13th century fortress Angelokastro. The castle has sweeping views along Corfu's west coast and for a long time was an important stronghold for Palaeokastritsa's inhabitants during periods of conflict. Although not much remains, it is still one of the most impressive castles on the island.

TRANSPORT

Car hire: Europcar (Tel: 26610 46931) on the main National Road. Most travel agents will also organise car hire.
Taxis: Ask at the tavernas.
Bus: Daily to Corfu. The Bus stop is on the main road.
Ferry: Corfu is the nearest major ferry port. Daily services to Igoumenitsa, Patras, Paxos and Italy.
Air travel: Regular international and domestic services into Corfu International Airport, to the south of the Corfu Town. Contact Olympic Airways (Tel: 26610 30180).

OTHER INFORMATION

Local Tel code: 26630.
Port authority: The Port Police office (Tel: 26630 41297) is situated to the west of the harbour.
Police: The Police Station (Tel: 26630 41203) is in the village.
Hospital: The nearest (Tel: 26610 88200) is in Corfu Town, a 16-mile (26km) drive from Palaeokastritsa.
Yacht repairs/services: The nearest boatyard is at Gouvia Marina, on the east coast of the island (see p27).

Ag Georgios Bay

Ag Georgiou, Ormos Ay Yeoryiou

Anchorage in the north-west corner of Ag Georgios Bay: 39° 43'.24N 19°39'.96E

East of the entrance to Porto Timoni Bay: 39°43'.09N 19°39'.16E

Charts: Admiralty 206, 188, SC5771; Imray G11, G1; Hellenic Navy Hydrographic Service 016, 21

This bay, on the west coast of Corfu, offers good shelter from the prevailing northwesterlies. Its long, crescent-shaped sandy beach makes it popular with tourists but, despite the emergence of a mini-resort along the eastern shore, it can sometimes be a quiet and very pretty haven.

The approach from all directions is straightforward and through deep water. Ag Georgios Bay lies about 3nm north of the town of Palaeokastritsa, to the

Ag Georgios Bay is fringed by a long, sandy beach. Porto Timoni, on the western side of Arilia Pt, offers a good anchorage in a southerly

east of Arila Pt, which at night is lit (L Fl 7.5s29m4M).

There are two anchorages in the bay, one in a little cove on the western shore and a second in the northern part. You can't get very far into the first, as there is a rock just off the shore, so anchor in around 8m. In the northern part of the bay, anchor in 5m or less, but watch out for rocks close to the shore. The area off the beach in the east of the bay is shoal and not really suitable.

Alternatively, if a southerly is blowing, anchor in Porto Timoni, a narrow inlet immediately to the north of Arila Pt. Depths here are between 5-10m and the holding is good, although it is totally exposed to the north-west, so should not be used in bad weather.

Ashore in Ag Georgios Bay, you'll find a collection of tavernas, bars and hotels. There's also a mini-market and some of the hotels offer currency exchange. If you want to stretch your legs, wander along the Alfionas peninsula, where the views are particularly good. This bay is also very popular with windsurfers, so expect to see them whizzing around.

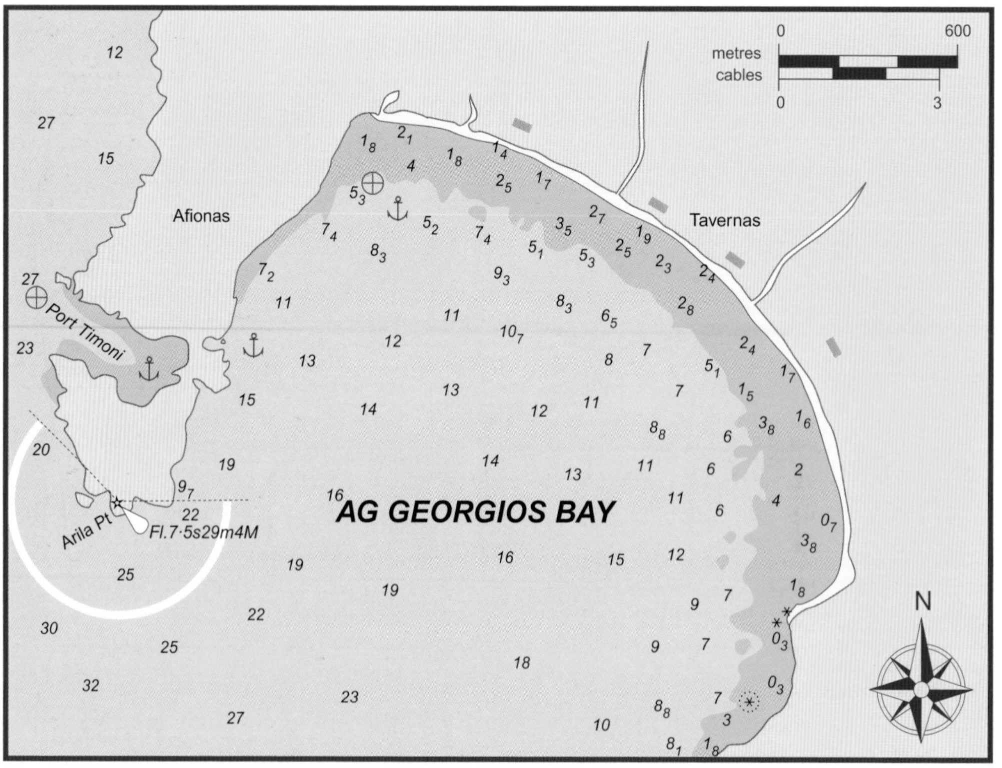

Ag Stephanos

Ayios Stefanos

Ag Stephanos Bay: 39°45'.34N 19°38'.11E
Charts: Admiralty 206, 188, SC5771; Imray G11, G1; Hellenic Navy Hydrographic Service 21

Ag Stephanos lies on the north-west coast of Corfu. It is the northernmost harbour on this stretch of coast and offers good shelter from all directions. However, it is small and often silts up, which makes it inaccessible for most yachts of even average draught.

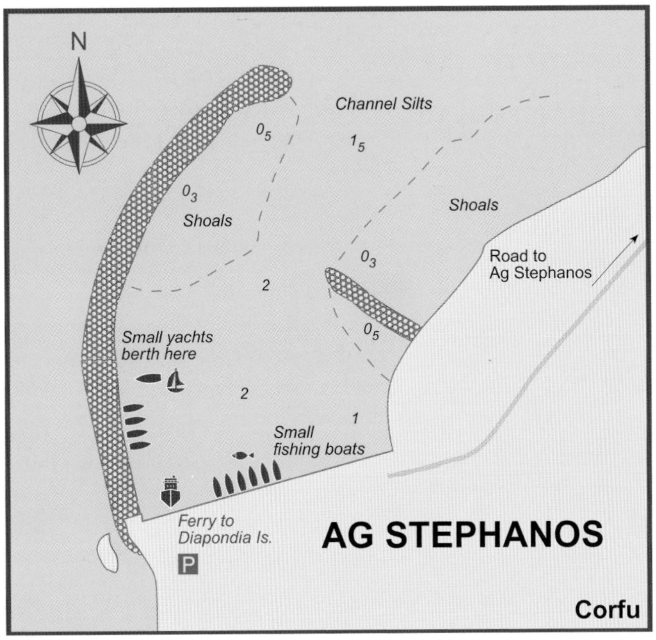

On approach from the south, keep well offshore until you have rounded Kefali Pt (Ak Kavokefali). A shoal extends to the east here and there are rocks nearby. At night, this headland is unlit. Once around Kefali Pt, you should see the harbour's rocky breakwater, with buildings to the north and white cliffs just beyond. From the north, the approach is straightforward but watch your depth as there are shoal patches near the coast and around the islet of Diaplo (Vrak Dhiakopto).

Depths in the harbour at Ag Stephanos are about 1.5m but the channel silts regularly, particularly near the entrance and northern part of the breakwater. Drop a leadline from a dinghy before attempting an approach. If there is enough water, enter the harbour by staying mid-channel, and proceed towards the southern end of the breakwater. If you have a shallow enough draught, berth here bows-to wherever there is room. A small *caique* which ferries people to and from the Diapondia Islands berths on the main quay alongside local fishing boats, so keep clear of this area.

While the harbour offers good shelter from all directions, entering and leaving the harbour can be quite tricky in a strong northwesterly, so only attempt an approach in settled, light-wind conditions.

The village of Ag Stephanos is about 1 mile (1.6km) south-east of the harbour. There are various tavernas here, plus a couple of mini-markets and gift shops. Cars, scooters and boat trips to the Diapondia Islands can be organised by San Stefano Travel (Tel: 26630 51910).

Sidari Bay

Ormos Sidhari, Sidhárion

Anchorage in Sidari Bay: 39°47'.64N 19°43'.06E
Charts: Admiralty 206, 188, SC5771; Imray G11, G1; Hellenic Navy Hydrographic Service 16, 21.

Sidari is one of the north coast of Corfu's primary beach resorts. A popular package holiday destination, during the summer months it heaves with acres of flesh sizzling in the sun. It's tacky and predictable and, like Benitses on Corfu's east coast, could be almost anywhere.

For yachts, Sidari Bay offers a calm weather anchorage but little else. The coast is exposed in all directions and only provides minimal shelter in a southerly. Wash from the ferries that run between Italy, Corfu and Igoumenitsa is also a problem here, so be prepared for it to be quite rolly. It is also very rocky along the shore, and swimmers and watersports create additional hazards.

When approaching from the east, watch out for the reef Ifalos Astrakari, situated 2nm north-east of the resort, where depths are as little as 2.5m.

Anchor off the resort's main beach in 4-5m. Most yachts can't get in very close as the beach is shallow until some distance off. Local fishing and day-trip boats berth off a short mole near the resort, but depths here are less than 1.5m so there is no access for most boats.

Ashore, Sidari has all the facilities of a beach resort, with tavernas, mini-markets, a pharmacy and bank.

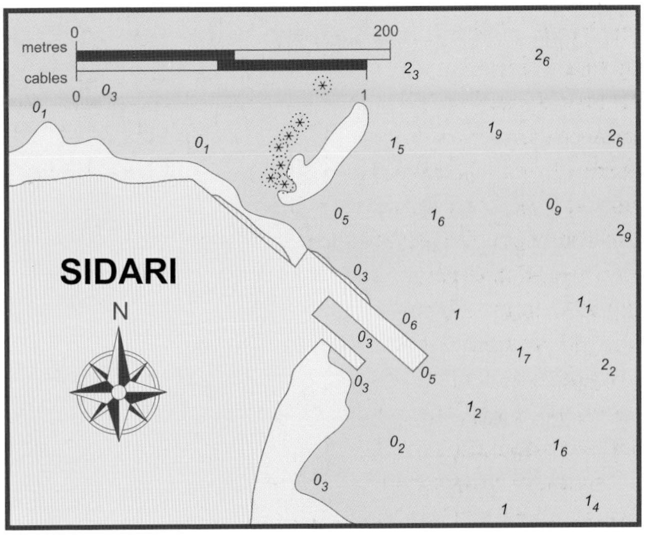

Ag Georgios Bay

Ormos Ay Yeoryiou, Rodas Bay

Anchorage in Ag Georgios Bay, to the north of Roda: 39°47'.64N 19°47'.56E

Charts: Admiralty 206, 188, SC5771; Imray G11, G1; Hellenic Navy Hydrographic Service 21

Ag Georgios Bay lies 4nm east of Sidari on the north coast of Corfu. On its southern shore lies Roda, once a small fishing village and now a major package holiday beach resort. Like Sidari, Ag Georgios Bay offers shelter from the south only and is exposed to wash from ferries travelling between Italy, Corfu and Igoumenitsa. In settled conditions, it can be a good place to stop for lunch, anchoring off the beach in around 5m. However, if the weather becomes more changeable, shelter should be sought elsewhere.

On approach from the west, watch out for the reef Ifalos Astrakari, 2nm north-east of Sidari, and for the rocks along the western shore of Ag Georgios Bay.

In Roda itself you'll find a selection of tavernas, cafes, nightclubs and mini-markets, plus all the other accessories that come with beach resorts. There is also a Citibank ATM at NSK Travel.

Imerola Bay

Ormos Imerolia

To north of entrance to Imerola Bay: 39°47'.49N 19°54'.81E

Charts: Admiralty 206, 188, SC5771; Imray G11, G1; Hellenic Navy Hydrographic Service 016, 21

Imerola Bay, on the north-east tip of Corfu, is within easy striking distance of Kassiopi and a quieter alternative to the resort if you want to spend time in the area. The best anchorage is tucked in the western corner. Here you'll find reasonable shelter from the prevailing northwesterlies and southerlies, although it is not suitable in unsettled conditions. Anchor in 3-4m on mud and sand, making sure your anchor is well dug in to protect yourself from any swell pushed into the bay by passing ferries. A small quay in the south-west corner is used by local fishing boats, so should be kept clear.

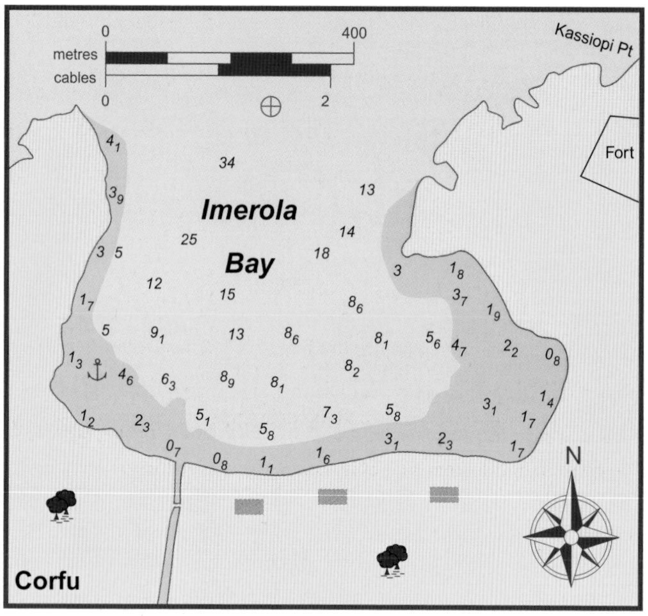

Imerola Bay offers reasonable shelter but can by rolly with swell

Kassiopi

Entrance to Kassiopi Bay: 39°47'.54N 19°55'.41E

If you don't like holiday resorts, Kassiopi is not for you. Once a small fishing village, where Roman emperor Tiberius is reputed to have had a villa, it is now home to more apartments, tacky bars and souvenir shops than ever before and during the summer it can be absolutely heaving. The harbour itself is pretty and, set in a narrow inlet on the north-east coast of Corfu, offers reasonable shelter; in a northerly though, it can become uncomfortable with swell.

The Romans built the first settlement here, recognising Kassiopi's location as strategically very strong. A temple to the god Zeus is thought to have stood on the site of the village's 16th century church; it is said that the temple was visited at one time by the Roman emperor Nero. The castle, on the headland above Kassiopi, was built by the Angevins of Naples in the 13th century, but was later destroyed by the Venetians, fearing capture by the Geonese enemy.

NAVIGATION

Charts: Admiralty 206, 188, SC5771; Imray G11, G1; Hellenic Navy Hydrographic Service 016, 21

On approach to Kassiopi, watch out for day-tripper boats and high-speed ferries travelling between Italy, Corfu and Igoumenitsa. The North Corfu Channel, between the island and mainland Albania, starts to narrow just to the east of Kassiopi, so maintain a good look-out at all times.

If approaching from the south, you must also watch out for If Serpa, a nasty reef to the north of Ag Stephanos (see p45), and Peristeres and Psillos, two rocky reefs 1½nm to the east of Kassiopi. While Peristeres is marked (Fl R 5s30m5M), Psillos is not and is so low-lying that it is often hidden in chop. If heading north towards Kassiopi, go to the west of Peristeres and you will pass through deep water.

Kassiopi itself is easy to identify by its sprawling mass of buildings. The ruins of a Byzantine castle on Kassiopi Pt can also be seen from some distance.

BERTHING

Yachts should berth bows-to the quay on the eastern side of the harbour, just behind the mole. Depths here are around 2-2.5m and the holding is reasonable; however, there are patches of weed in places, so make sure your anchor digs in well. Fishing boats use the mole on the western side of the harbour but there is sometimes room for visitors to berth at the end of it. If so, leave plenty of room between you and the mole to avoid debris at its base, and dinghy ashore if necessary.

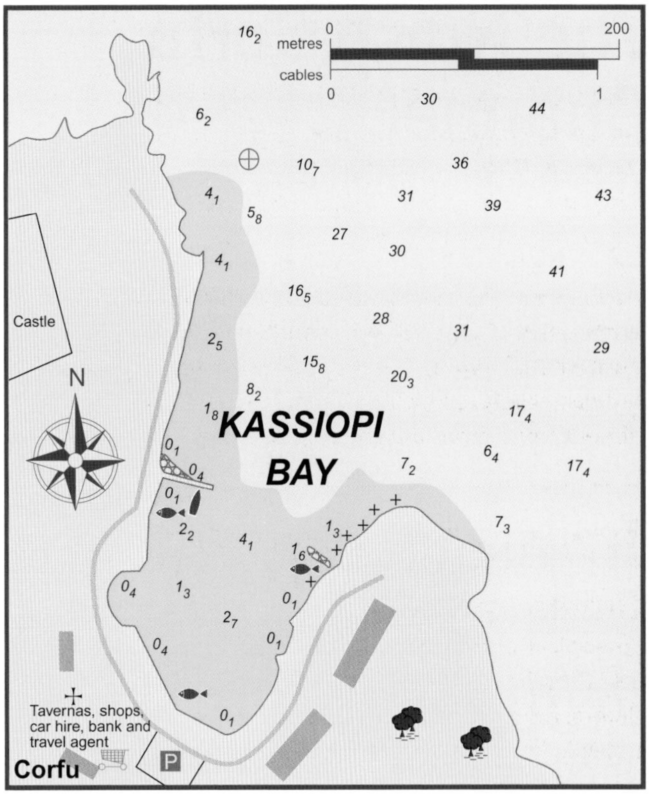

The quay on the western side of Kassiopi Bay is used by visiting boats

ANCHORING

There are several calm weather anchorages within easy reach of Kassiopi. Vroulias Bay, to the west (see p44), offers good shelter in a southerly, as does Arilias Bay to the east. However, neither should be considered in strong northwesterlies.

Useful information – Kassiopi

FACILITIES

Fuel: There are plenty of petrol stations on the Kassiopi-Ipsos road.
Ice: At the Co-op supermarket near the harbour, and at mini-markets.
Gas: Try the Co-op supermarket.
Rubbish: Large bins on the quay near the car park. Smaller ones in the village.
Telephone: Phone box on the quay. Several more in the centre of Kassiopi. Phone cards sold at souvenir shops and kiosks. Mobile reception is good.

PROVISIONING

Grocery shops: Several mini-markets and grocery shops in the centre of Kassiopi.
Bakery: In the centre of Kassiopi.
Butcher: On the main street. Mini-markets also sell a selection of meat products.
Banks: An Emporiki ATM on the main street and Arrow Travel nearby has a Citibank ATM.
Pharmacy: A couple in the village.
Post: Post office at the Co-op supermarket, near the harbour. The postal service on Corfu is good. Stamps sold at souvenir shops and kiosks.
Opening times: Most shops are open all day and until late in the evening.

EATING OUT

There are literally dozens of tavernas, bars, cafes and nightclubs in Kassiopi with average quality and varied choice. Like most resorts, you don't have to look far to find chips and burgers, pizzas, pasta, curry and English beer on tap.

ASHORE

There are some good walks inland of Kassiopi, and to the west of the town the ruins of the castle are worth a visit, though very busy with tourists in season. There are also several watersports companies operating off the beaches and you can rent mountain bikes from a shop in the village.

TRANSPORT

Car hire: Kassiopi Travel Service (Tel: 26630 81388), Yiannis Rent a Car (Tel: 26630 81072) and Travel Corner (Tel: 26630 81220) are all near the main street. Car park just behind the harbour but you have to pay.
Taxis: Often to be found near the harbour or, alternatively, ask at the travel agents.
Bus: Regular service between Kassiopi and Corfu Town, journey around 1½-hours.
Ferry: The nearest terminal is at Corfu Town for travel to Igoumenitsa, Paxos, Patra and Italy. See www.greekferries.gr
Air travel: The nearest airport is just outside Corfu Town. Regular charter and domestic flights. Contact Olympic Airways (Tel: 26610 30180) for flight timetables and prices.

OTHER INFORMATION

Local Tel code: 26630.
Police: Tel: 26630 81240.
Doctor: In the centre of Kassiopi. Tel: 26630 81255.
Hospital: 24-hour medical centre off the main street.

The North Corfu Channel

Vorion Stenon Kerkiras

The North Corfu Channel runs along the north-east tip of Corfu and includes the narrow stretch of water between the island and the Albanian coast. At its narrowest point, the channel measures just 1nm in width and care should be taken throughout its length. Not only is its proximity to Albania a reason for caution, but also there are a couple of major reefs in the area.

The political situation in Albania is, according to the Foreign Office, currently stable and while there are still pockets of unrest, as long as tourists maintain a high level of personal security, the country does not pose too much of a danger. However, there have been reports in recent years of incidents involving yachts being boarded by Albanians and some charter companies now prohibit their clients from sailing along this stretch of coast. This does mean missing one of the nicest parts of the island, but it is important to heed your charter company's advice. If you do use this channel, though, stay on the Greek side and keep a good look-out at all times.

At the northern end of the channel is a small islet – Peristeres (Nsis Peristerai) – and the reef Ifalos Serpa. Peristeres lies just to the west of Varvara Pt, to the south of Kassiopi, and at night is marked by a light (Fl R 5s30m5M). On passage south, keep to the west of Peristeres, as to the east of the islet is a small, unmarked reef. The channel to the west of the islet is through deep water. For details of the Serpa reef, see opposite on page 45.

Vroulias Bay

Ormos Vourlias

Entrance to bay: 39°47'.24N 19°55'.96E
Charts: Admiralty 206, 188, SC5771; Imray G11, G1; Hellenic Navy Hydrographic Service 016, 21

Vroulias Bay, ½nm east of Kassiopi, is a large Y-shaped bay, where several indentations offer reasonable anchorages in settled conditions. The westernmost inlet, Soukia Bay (Ormos Sykia), provides good shelter in a southerly, and you can anchor in around 3-4m on mud and sand. Galiates Bay, in the south-east corner of Vroulias, also offers good shelter from the south but is very exposed in a northwesterly when the wind funnels directly into the bay. The anchorage in the eastern part of Galiates is slightly more protected, but still affected in a strong northwesterly and by swell from passing ferries. Anchor in both parts of the bay in around 5m on sand. There are patches of weed in places but the holding is reasonable once your anchor has dug in.

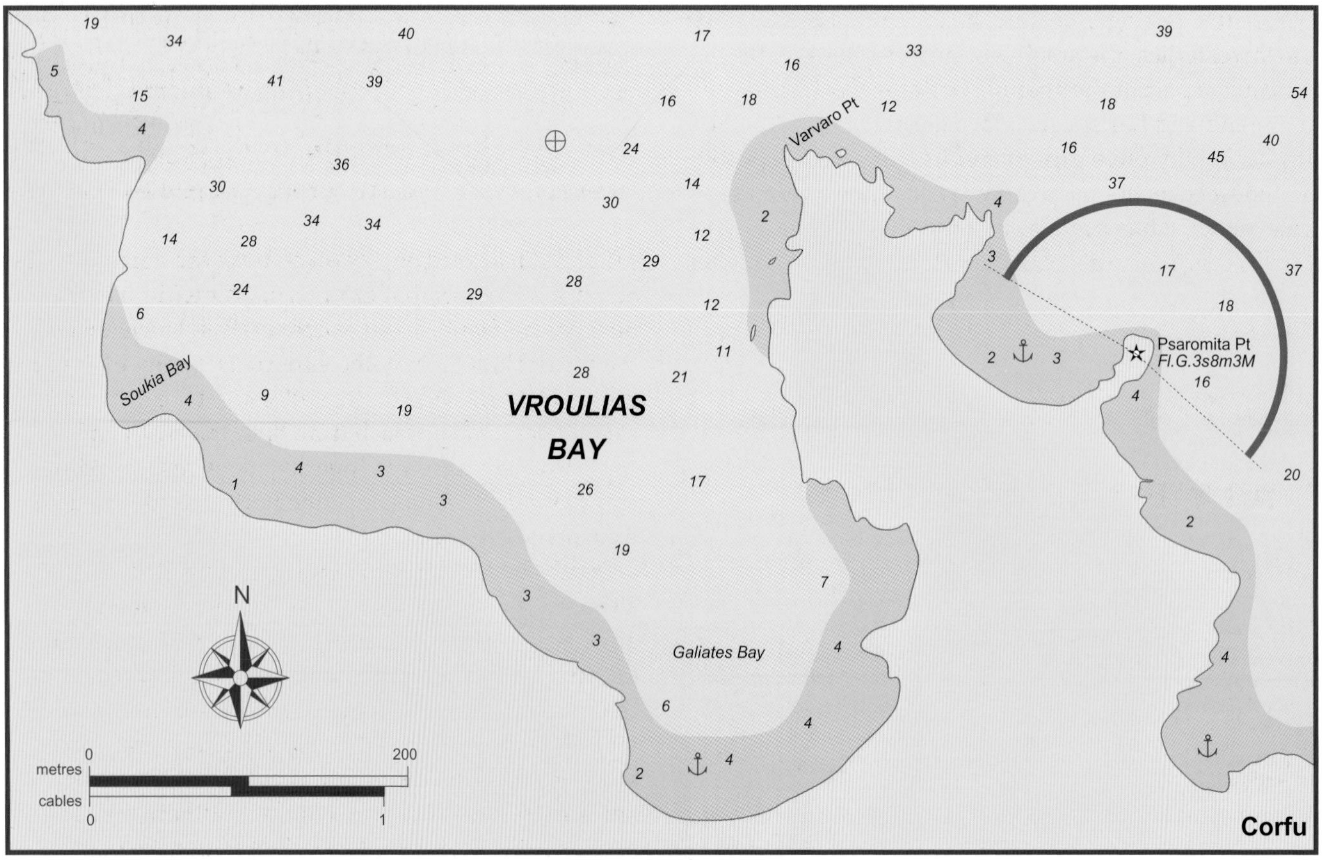

ALTERNATIVE ANCHORAGES

Anchorage to west of Psaromita Pt: 39°47'.19N 19°56'.76E
Entrance to Arilias Bay: 39°46'.84N 19°57'.06E

There are a couple of alternative anchorages to the east of Vroulias Bay. One is in a horseshoe-shaped bay immediately to the west of Psaromita Pt (Fl G 3s8m3M). Tucked in here, and anchored in around 3m, you will find reasonable shelter from the north-west and south, but again this is only really suitable in settled conditions.

A second anchorage lies about 3½ cables south-east of Psaromita Pt in Arilias Bay. Although open to the north-east, this offers better protection from the north-west. However, it is still susceptible to swell from ferries travelling up and down the North Corfu Channel.

On approach to these anchorages from the north, keep well clear of Peristeres and the reef Psillos, both of which lie to the north-east of this stretch of coast. Psillos, in particular, is low-lying and often hidden by chop. The preferred route is to pass to the west of this and Peristeres, which at night is marked with a light (Fl R 5s30m5M).

On approach from the south, watch out for Ifalos Serpa, an infamous and particularly nasty reef that lies to the north of Ag Stephanos (see below).

Ifalos Serpa

Ifalos Serpa is a nasty reef to the north of Ag Stephanos Bay. It extends for about ¼-mile offshore and, while the middle of it is indicated by a marker and its eastern end with a light (Q(3)10s7M), you should keep well to the east and in the middle of the North Corfu Channel. In settled conditions, when the surface of the water is still, you may be able to identify the reef with the naked eye.

Ag Stephanos Bay

Ormos Ay Stefanos

Entrance to Ag Stephanos Bay: 39°45'.92N 19°57'.10E
Charts: Admiralty 206, 188, SC5771; Imray G11, G1; Hellenic Navy Hydrographic Service 016, 21

Ag Stephanos is a delightful bay on the north-east coast of Corfu. Offering excellent shelter from the prevailing northwesterlies, the small wooded bay borders the narrowest part of the channel between Corfu and the mainland and has spectacular views towards Albania. It's backed by olive groves and its eastern shore has a modest collection of tavernas, souvenir shops and bars which, while popular in season, have none of the tawdriness of Corfu's other resorts.

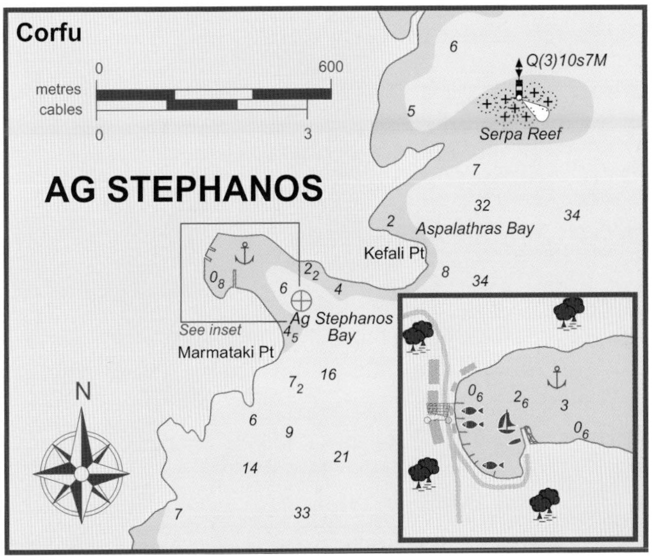

Ag Stephanos Bay is a charming anchorage with good amenities ashore

The main hazard on approach from the north is Ifalos Serpa, a nasty reef that extends offshore, ½nm to the north of Ag Stephanos (see above). Pass to the east of the cardinal that marks the eastern extremity of the reef, giving it a very wide berth, and you will sail through clear water. On approach from both the north and south, the bay is easy to identify and a large building and pylon on the hillside to the north are conspicuous from some distance.

Depths inside the entrance are around 15m, but 200m off the village decrease to 5m. You can anchor anywhere within Ag Stephanos, in 3-5m, but watch out for a shoal patch, which lies in the middle of the bay, immediately to the north-west of the short mole. It is also very shallow close inshore near the wooden jetties. Occasionally yachts berth stern- or bows-to the end of the mole in the southern corner of the bay, but it is usually packed with little boats.

The anchorage, however, offers superb shelter from both the north and south and, while at times it can be rolly with swell from the passing ferries, it doesn't get too uncomfortable.

Ashore you'll find a range of amenities. There are two supermarkets, one at either end of the village, clothes and souvenir shops and a good selection of places to eat and drink. Best known, with an excellent reputation for Greek and international cuisine, is the Eucalyptus Taverna (Tel: 26630 82007) in the old olive press building in the north-west corner of the bay. Taverna Kaparelli (Tel: 26630 81797) is also recommended, or try the village's other tavernas: Taverna Galini and Taverna Kochilli. Although you won't find fuel and water here, Ag Stephanos can be a really charming place to spend a few days. It does get busy peak season with tourists but it's a beautiful spot and there are some good walks nearby.

Kouloura

Ormos Kouloura

Kouloura Bay: 39°44'.73N 19°56'.41E
Charts: Admiralty 206, 188, SC5771; Imray G11, G1; Hellenic Navy Hydrographic Service 016, 21

Kouloura's tiny harbour is usually busy with fishing boats, but some small yachts can squeeze in

Kouloura is a very attractive little bay 1½nm south of Ag Stephanos, where steep-sided cypress-covered hillsides sweep down to a miniature harbour and hamlet of a handful of buildings. It's not as busy as Ag Stephanos or Kalami and in calm weather can be a delightful place to spend the day. The harbour itself is small and shallow but yachts can anchor happily to the west, past a couple of wooden jetties, in about 5m and still be protected from the prevailing northwesterlies. Swell from passing ferries does affect this bay, so expect it to be rolly at times and, if necessary, take a line ashore for extra protection.

The bay is identified by a large white, 16th century Venetian building, right on the water's edge, directly to the south of the harbour. Shoals extend to the east and north of Kouloura Pt and the harbour's breakwater, so give both plenty of clearance when approaching from the south. The harbour is usually full of small dories, but visiting boats drawing less than 1.5m can sometimes find room to squeeze in. If you do decide to enter, approach the bay from its north-east corner and avoid running aground by giving the breakwater as wide a berth as possible. Berth bows-to wherever there is room.

Apart from a handful of houses there's just one taverna ashore at Kouloura. With good views over the bay, Taverna Kouloura's very reasonably priced menu is rather delicious. It gets busy, though, so be early if you want to eat.

Author Lawrence Durrell wrote *Prospero's Cell* at Kalami

Kalami

Ormos Kalami

Kalami Bay: 39°44'.49N 19°56'.06E
Charts: Admiralty 206, 188, SC5771; Imray G11, G1; Hellenic Navy Hydrographic Service 016, 21

Kalami Bay lies about 3½ cables south of Kouloura. Large and horseshoe shaped, it offers good shelter from the prevailing winds and the small resort-cum-village has most basic amenities.

The approach from all directions is hazard free and the bay easy to recognise. From the north a large white house standing on the shoreline in the eastern part of the bay is conspicuous, and from the south,

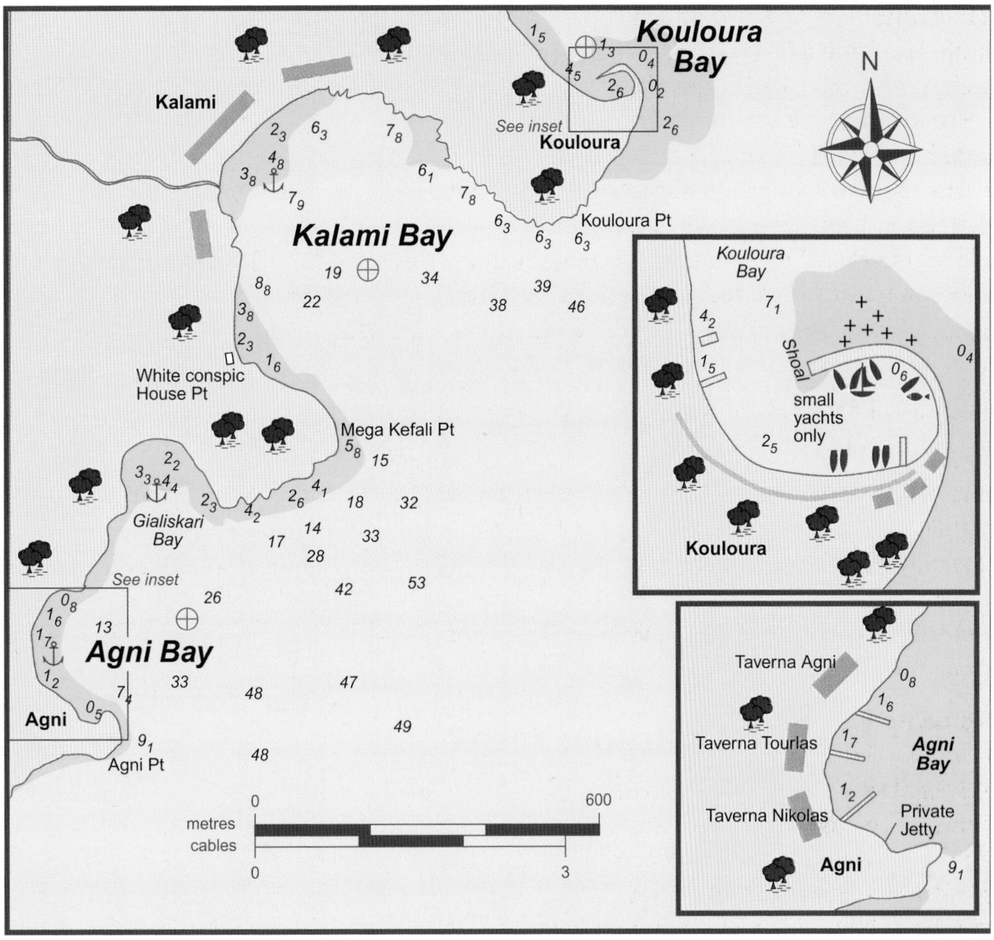

buildings on the olive and cypress-covered hillside above can be seen from some distance. Anchor anywhere in 3-5m. The holding on sand is good, although there are patches of weed, so make sure your anchor digs in well, particularly as gusts often skid in off the hillsides.

Ashore you'll find three well-stocked supermarkets and a couple of tourist agencies offering foreign exchange and car hire. There's a fruit shop, a bakery and plenty of souvenir shops, plus a post box near Georgio's Supermarket and several phones along the main street. Blue Bay Travel (Tel: 26630 91158) will also provide internet services. Along the waterfront are scattered numerous tavernas and cafes of average quality.

Kalami is best known for its connection with writer Lawrence Durrell. He stayed here with his wife, Nancy, and fellow author and friend, Henry Miller, for 18 months prior to the Second World War, and it is here that he started writing *Prospero's Cell*, the first of several travel books. Durrell's former house, the conspicuous white building in the eastern corner of the bay, is now a taverna and holiday home. Durrell describes it in *Prospero's Cell* as being 'set like a dice on a rock already venerable with the scars of wind and water'.

Unlike Agni Bay to the south and Kouloura to the north, Kalami has been swallowed up by a tidal wave of tourism, losing much of its traditional charm.

As an anchorage, it's good, but in peak season look elsewhere for a quiet spot away from the crowds.

Agni Bay Ormos Agni

Agni Bay: 39°44'.17N 19°55'.92E

Charts: Admiralty 206, 188, SC5771; Imray G11, G1; Hellenic Navy Hydrographic Service 016, 21

Agni Bay is delightful and, while busy in summer, is a really pleasant alternative to the mini-resort at Kalami. It lies ½nm south of Kalami, next to a bay called Gialiskari (Ormos Yaliskari). Both Gialiskari and Agni can be used as daytime and overnight anchorages, although the former is more exposed to the south, so wouldn't be as tenable as Agni in a strong southerly. The holding on sand and mud is reasonable, and for extra protection, you could always take a line ashore.

Agni Bay is open to the east but protected from the north and south. There are four wooden jetties in the bay, three of them owned by the tavernas that line the shore. You can either anchor off in 3-5m or, if you

A yacht berthed stern-to off Taverna Tourlas' jetty in Agni Bay

intend to eat at one of the tavernas, berth stern-to the end of one of their jetties. These are usually quite busy with small boats, but it is deep enough for yachts to berth here and the holding is generally good. The heavy ferry traffic along this stretch of coast does send swell into the bay, so it may be more comfortable to anchor off.

Despite being small there is no shortage of good places to eat in Agni Bay. All three of the beachside tavernas have stunning views across the water and towards Albania and serve good, traditional food. Taverna Nikolas (Tel: 26630 91243), the southernmost restaurant, is owned by the very affable Katsaros family and serves simple but delicious fare. It also runs regular ferry services between the taverna and Kalami. Taverna Toulas (Tel: 26630 91350) next door is good for seafood and Taverna Agni (Tel: 26630 91142) serves traditional dishes with a 'Mediterranean twist'. All are recommended.

Taverna Nikolas, one of three excellent restaurants at Agni Bay

Ipsos Ormos Ipsou, Ypsos

Ipsos Bay: 39°41'.89N 19°50'.56E

Ipsos stands on the shore of a wide open bay 3½nm north of Gouvia Marina. It's one of many resorts along this stretch of coast and fairly nondescript. The village itself spans the length of the beach alongside the main, often busy, coastal road. It's a popular destination with the bucket and spade brigade and has a reputation for being loud and rowdy, particularly at night. During the day, however, it's pleasant enough for a short stay and a reasonable alternative to Gouvia. The harbour offers good protection from all directions but is usually busy with small boats, so you can't always be sure of finding a berth.

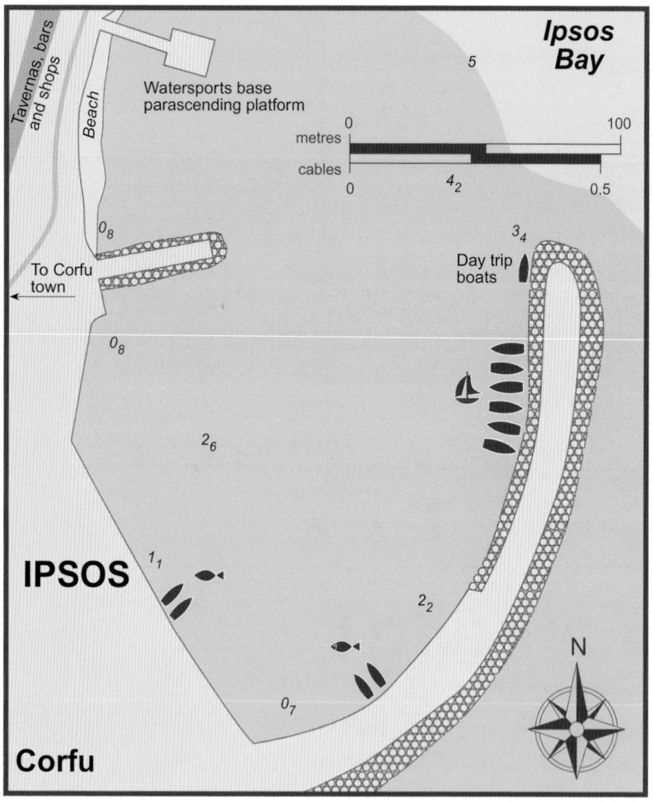

NAVIGATION

Charts: Admiralty 206, 188, SC5771; Imray G11, G1; Hellenic Navy Hydrographic Service 212/2, 21

The approach to Ipsos is through deep water and the village is identified by its long, narrow strip of beach, backed by a sprawling band of buildings. It's favoured by watersports companies and in summer there are usually several motor-boats whizzing around towing parascenders or water-skiers. Closer in you will be able to identify the small harbour in the southern corner of the bay. Immediately to the north of it is a long jetty used by one of the watersports companies.

BERTHING

The harbour at Ipsos is usually busy with small boats, but yachts can sometimes find room to berth towards the end of the rocky breakwater. Depths in this area are around 2-2.5m but it is shallower close to the breakwater, so you will need to berth bows-to. You should also anchor well off as there is debris at the breakwater's base. Use a long boarding plank or passerelle to get ashore. The holding here on mud and sand is good.

ANCHORING

You can anchor in the southern part of Ipsos Bay in around 5m. It's protected from the north-west but more exposed in a southerly, and you may be affected by swell from passing ferries. There are better anchorages to the north (Agni, Kalami and Kouloura), or to the south in Komeno Bay (see p49).

Useful information – Ipsos

FACILITIES
Fuel: There is an Eko petrol station on the north side of Ipsos.
Showers: Open-air showers on the beach.
Ice: Ask at the mini-markets.
Gas: Ask at the mini-markets.
Rubbish: Large bins near the harbour.
Yacht services/chandlery: Gouvia Marina, 3½nm to the south, offers a range of services. See p27.
Telephone: Phone box outside Asteria Taverna on the main road, and several more nearby. Phone cards sold at kiosks. Mobile reception is good.

PROVISIONING
Grocery shops: A couple of supermarkets on the main road.
Bakery: In the centre of Ipsos.
Butcher: Near the centre of Ipsos.
Banks: Emporiki ATM kiosk at the north end of Ipsos. Most travel agencies offer currency exchange.
Pharmacy: At the north end of Ipsos, near Dirty Nellie's Pub.
Post: Post box near Asteria Taverna.
Opening times: Most shops operate to the usual siesta hours but as this is a resort most stay open later than usual.

EATING OUT
For good Greek food, try Asteria Taverna (Tel: 26610 93006) at the south end of Ipsos. Otherwise it is harder to find in Ipsos than curries, burgers, chips, pizza and pasta, of which there is no shortage.

ASHORE
A watersports company on the beach offers a range of activities, including parascending. Corfu Town is a half-hour journey by car.

TRANSPORT
Car hire: Ask at the local travel agents.
Taxis: Usually some near the beach.
Bus: Bus stop near the beach. A regular service runs between Corfu, Ipsos and Kassiopi.
Ferry: Services to Igoumenitsa, Paxos, Patra and Italy operate from the new harbour at Corfu Town. See www.greekferries.gr.
Air travel: International charter and domestic services from Corfu Airport. Contact Olympic Airways (Tel: 26610 30180) for timetable information.

OTHER INFORMATION
Local Tel code: 26610.
Hospital: The nearest is in Corfu Town (Tel: 26610 88200).
Yacht repairs/services: Gouvia Marina (Tel: 26610 91900/91376).

Ipsos provides good shelter from all directions. Yachts should berth bows-to off the end of the breakwater, taking care to avoid debris at its base

Komeno Bay

Kommeno

To the north-east of Komeno Pt: 39°40'.24N 19°52'.16E
Charts: Admiralty 206, 188, SC5771; Imray G11, G1; Hellenic Navy Hydrographic Service 212/2, 21

Komeno Bay is situated immediately to the west of the small islet of Foustanopidima (also known as Komeno) that extends off Komeno Pt. It's a medium-sized, open bay with shelter from the north-west but not from the south.

On approach from the south, you can pass either side of Lazareto Island, and Komeno Pt is identified by a large white hotel on the headland. Anchor in the bay in 6m or less; the holding is reasonable.

Anchoring is prohibited in the shallow bay to the west of Komeno Bay, which lies directly opposite Gouvia Marina.

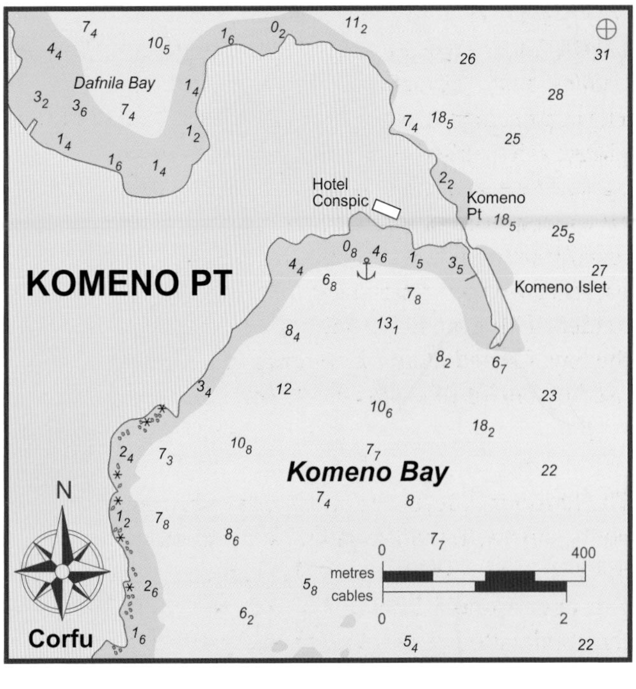

Diapondia Islands

Othoni Island

Nisos Othonoi, Fanos

Othoni is the largest of the Diapondia islands and marks the westernmost tip of Greece. Situated just 12nm north-west of Corfu's north coast, the island covers around 4¼ square miles (10.8km^2) of land and at its highest point rises to 383m (1,256ft) above sea level. It's a rugged island fringed with rocks and reefs and covered in olive trees, said to number around 36,000. Within easy cruising distance of Italy, Othoni is a popular destination with Italian tourists in the summer months. Its climate is well known for being temperate and during the 19th century, when much of the Ionian was under British rule, soldiers were often sent there to recuperate.

The island was first colonised in about 1571 and now has a modest population of approximately 100 permanent inhabitants. Many families have moved away to live on Corfu while others have emigrated to America.

There are several small villages on Othoni but Ammos, on the south coast, is the capital, and the only one with a harbour. This is the main cruising destination, although Fyki Bay, on the north coast of the island, is a beautiful anchorage in the right conditions.

A view towards the Diapondia islands from Corfu

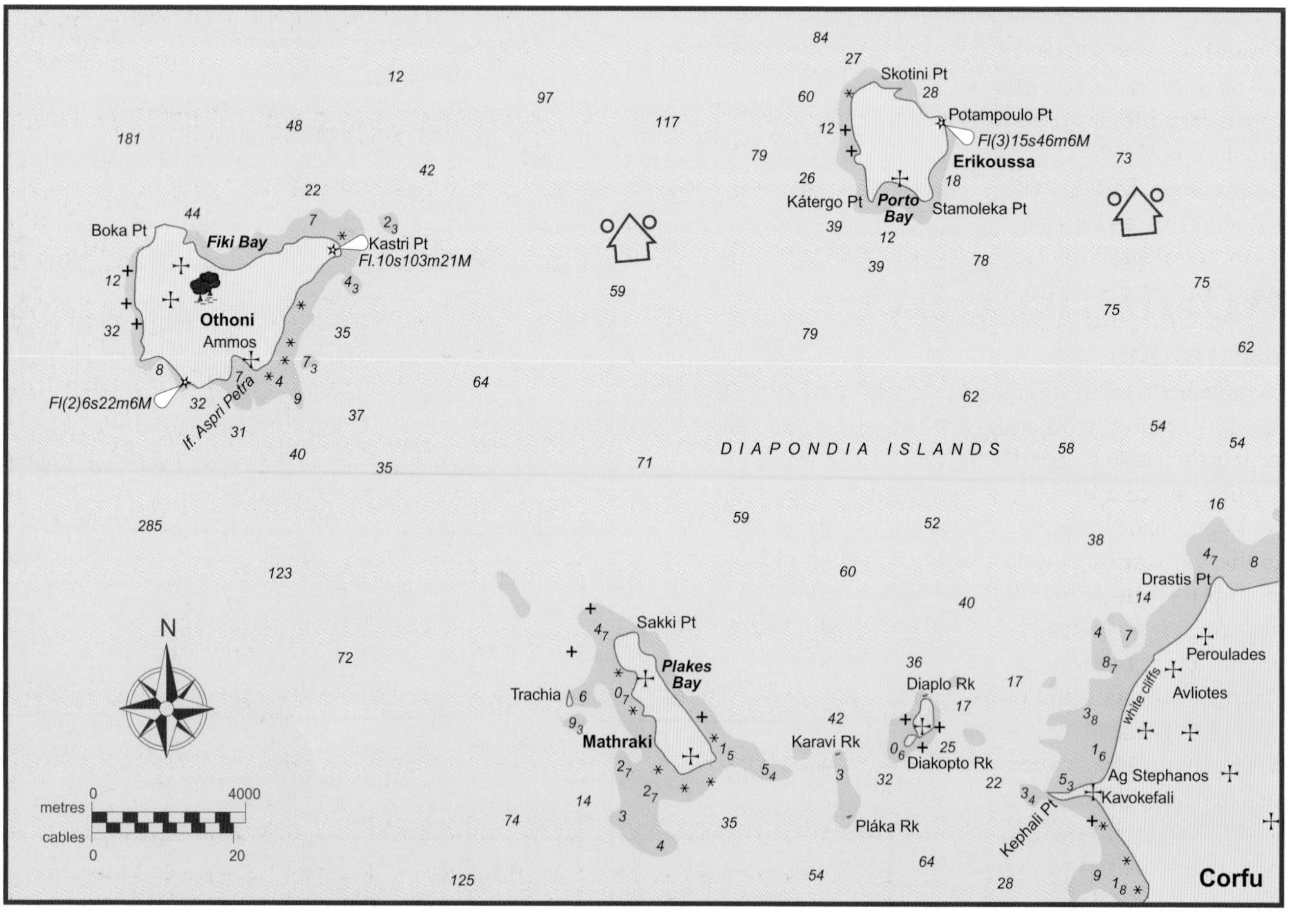

Ammos Bay

Ormos Ammou

Ammos Bay: 39°50'.24N 19°24'.16E

Ammos is the capital of Othoni and lies halfway along its south coast. It's a small village with just a cluster of houses, several seasonal tavernas and a harbour. For yachts this is the island's best anchorage as it offers shelter from the prevailing winds plus the, albeit modest, facilities of the village.

NAVIGATION

Charts: Admiralty 206, 188, SC5771; Imray G11, G1; Hellenic Navy Hydrographic Service 016, 21

The approach to Ammos is tricky and should only be made in daytime. Even in bright, sunny conditions, Othoni can be hidden in haze until close-to, and as reefs and rocks litter the coastline, you need to keep a good look-out at all times.

On approach from the south, follow Corfu's coastline north, staying well offshore. You can pass either side of the island of Mathraki but be aware that there are shoal patches and isolated rocks off its west coast and in the channel between it and the islet of Diaplo, so don't get too close. About 1½nm south of the island you should be able to identify Othoni and its two lighthouses: one on its south-west tip (Fl(2)6s22m6M) and the main one on Kastri Pt (Fl 10s103m21M), to the north-east. Slightly nearer and the houses of Ammos should become visible.

The main hazard, a shoal patch called If Aspri Petra, lies about 3½ cables S of the harbour. Depths over the shoal are as little as 1.8m, so take care to avoid it. Ammos is the western of two harbours on this part of the coast. The eastern harbour, Avlaki, is used by fishing boats and is of little use to yachts. Limited space and the rocks and shoal patches to the south and east of its entrance mean that an approach is not advised. Head for the harbour at Ammos instead. Although depths in Ammos Bay are less than 10m, there is usually enough water for yachts to navigate safely, but keep a keen eye on your echo-sounder.

BERTHING

Berth stern- or bows-to the harbour breakwater, keeping your distance off it as there is debris at its base. Here you will find good shelter from the prevailing winds. However, if a southerly blows up, seek shelter elsewhere as Ammos is very exposed in these conditions. The local ferry and fishing boats use the northern side of the breakwater, but as the area regularly silts you cannot be sure of enough depth to berth here safely.

ANCHORING

You can anchor in the inner harbour in 3-4m, but be sure to keep the area immediately inside the entrance clear as this is where the ferry turns round. Alternatively, anchor to the south-west of the entrance in 8-10m. The holding is reasonable on mud and sand but there are rocks in places, so make sure your anchor is well dug in before leaving your boat unattended.

ASHORE

In the village itself you will find several seasonal tavernas and a small mini-market, which is part of Café Mikros. The mini-market is usually reasonably well stocked with fresh and packaged products and the tavernas are particularly good for fish. There is also a police station, a medical centre and a small post office in the village. During the summer season, when Italian tourists visit the island, the village has a lovely vibrant atmosphere and can be a delightful place to spend a couple of days.

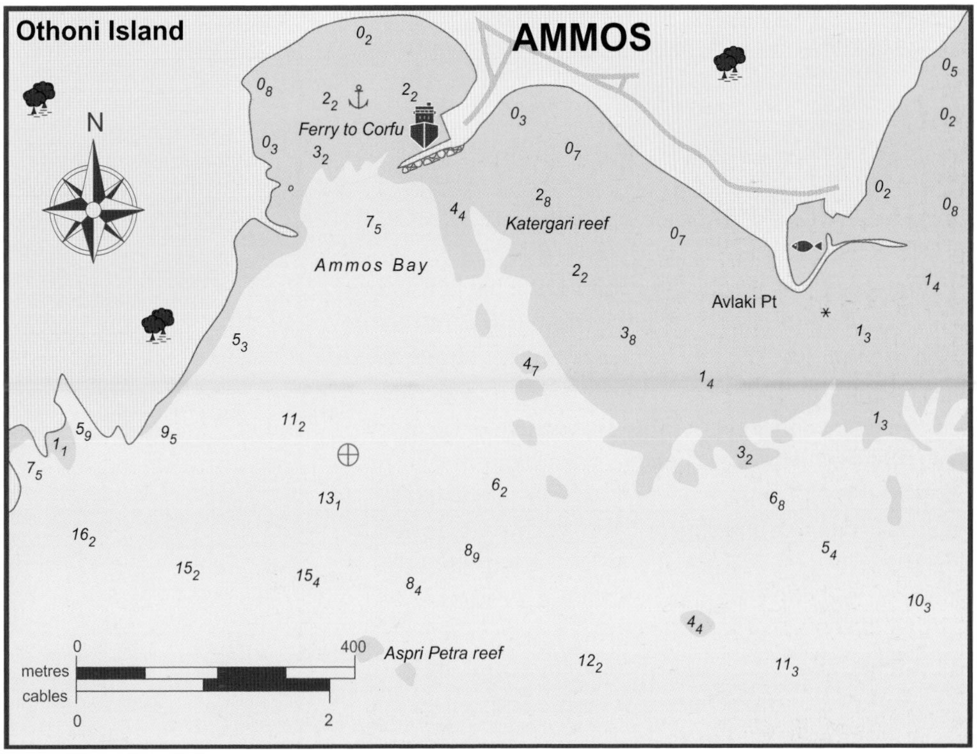

Above: Ammos Bay is the best anchorage on the island for yachts. The harbour is also serviced by a small ferry that brings boat-loads of tourists to the island during the summer months

Fyki Bay Ormos Fyki, Fiki

Anchorage in Fyki Bay: 39°51'.74N 19°23'.86E

Fyki Bay is on Othoni's north coast and is a good anchorage in a southerly. In a northwesterly, though, it is exposed to heavy swell. The approach is straightfoward but keep well offshore when rounding the island, particularly near Kastri Pt, as there are nasty rocks immediately to the south, east and north of it. Depths in Fyki Bay are less than 7m, and keep a good look-out at all times as there are isolated rocks near the shore. Anchor in around 5m on sand.

The sandy beach that fringes Fyki Bay is one of the island's finest and the crystal clear waters are lovely for swimming.

Erikoussa Island

Nisos Erikoysa, Merlera, Merikha

Erikoussa, the second largest Diapondia island, stands to the north-west of Corfu. Lower-lying than its companions, Othoni, to the west, and Mathraki to the south, Erikoussa is a heather-covered island with around 100 inhabitants. Its sandy beaches make it a popular destination with day-tripper tourists from Corfu, but once they've gone home the island is a peaceful retreat and a charming place to spend a couple of days. The main village at Porto Bay offers minimal provisions, so if you intend to visit, you need to come well supplied.

Porto Bay Ormos Porto

Porto Bay: 39°52'.44N 19°34'.96E
Charts: Admiralty 206, 188, SC5771; Imray G11, G1; Hellenic Navy Hydrographic Service 21

Porto Bay, on the south coast of Erikoussa, is the only secure anchorage on the island. It is exposed in a southerly, but in the prevailing northwesterlies offers reasonable shelter and protection. A small harbour in its western corner is used by the island's fishing boats.

The approach to Porto Bay is relatively simple, compared with that of Ammos Bay on Othoni or the harbour at Mathraki. While isolated rocks fringe the coastline, Erikoussa is not as reef strewn as the other Diapondias, and the approach is mostly through clear water. It is often shrouded in haze, however, particularly in the early morning but should become visible about 2nm to the south of the island.

There are reefs around Katergo Pt, the bay's western headland, identified by its high, white cliffs, and to the west of Stamoleka Pt, the bay's eastern headland, so keep a good look-out at all times.

The harbour itself is of little use to yachts. For the most part it is very shallow, with remains of a mole and rocks in the middle, and it is also usually busy with day-tripper boats. Most yachts anchor off the harbour, but occasionally there is room to berth stern- or bows-to the quay behind the western breakwater. This part of the harbour offers the best shelter and is even protected from the south, but you cannot always be sure of a berth. The end of the quay in the eastern part of the harbour is used by the local ferry that travels between the Diapondias and Corfu, so keep clear at all times.

If there isn't room here, anchor in around 5m immediately to the east of the harbour. While this anchorage offers no shelter in a southerly, it is relatively secure in a northwesterly and the holding on sand is reasonable.

In the village you'll find a couple of tavernas and a cafe that sells a limited supply of groceries. There are several beaches on the island, which are good for swimming and snorkelling, and some lovely walks along the coast.

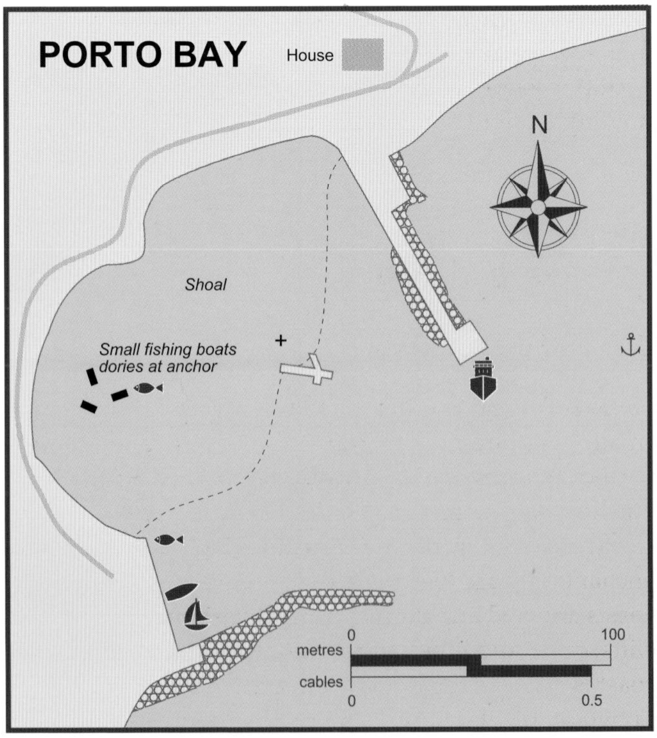

Above: the inner harbour at Porto Bay is shallow and used by fishing boats, although yachts can occasionally find room on the quay

Mathraki Nisos Mathraki

Mathraki is the smallest of the Diapondia Islands. Lying 5nm west of Ag Stephanos on Corfu, the thickly wooded, long narrow island measures one square mile (3km^2) in area and is home to just a handful of people. It's a wonderfully wild place that feels more remote than Othoni and Erikoussa, partly due to its rugged coastline and also because it is less visited than the other Diapondias.

Anyone approaching the island must keep a good look-out at all times and check charts regularly as Mathraki's coastline and neighbouring waters are strewn with rocks and shoals. Just to the east is the tiny uninhabited islet of Diaplo. The channel between Mathraki and Diaplo is navigable, although again extreme caution is advised as there are some nasty reefs nearby. For visiting boats, the only accessible harbour is Plakes Bay, on the island's north-east coast. This is also the only place where you can get ashore, without too much difficulty.

Plakes Bay Ormos Plakes

East of Plakes Bay: 39° 47'.04N 19° 31'.46E
Charts: Admiralty 206, 188, SC5771; Imray G11, G1; Hellenic Navy Hydrographic Service 21

Plakes is the island's sole harbour and the only place you can stop and go ashore. From all directions, approach the island with care as rocks litter the coastline and not all of them are above water. There are some shallows just to the south-east of the harbour entrance, so head in from a northeasterly direction.

The harbour comprises two parts: the outer harbour, protected by two rocky breakwaters, and the inner harbour just beyond. The latter area is very shallow and not suitable for yachts, so visitors should berth in the outer harbour, stern- or bows-to the northerly breakwater or quay. It is deeper off the breakwater (around 5m), but access to the shore is easier if berthed off the quay. Keep its southern end clear, however, as this is where the local ferry berths. The harbour offers reasonable shelter, but can be uncomfortable in a southwesterly when there is a significant swell. The holding on mud and sand is good.

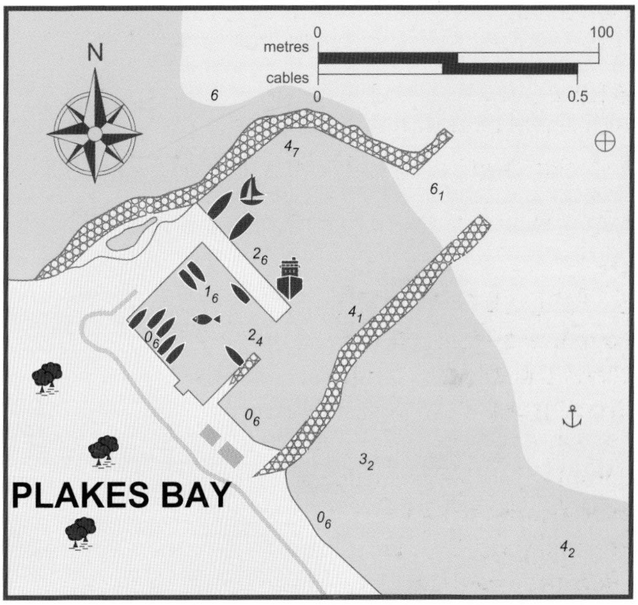

Above: Plakes Bay on Mathraki is the island's sole harbour

If you get a chance to stop at Mathraki, it is worth wandering up the hill. The views from the top towards Corfu and, on a clear day, Othoni and Erikoussa, are stunning. You'll also find several seasonal tavernas on the island, one of which sells basic groceries.

Paxos

Nisos Paxi, Paxoi

Paxos is the real jewel in the Ionian archipelago. The small, 11 square-mile (29km^2)-island is lush and covered in thick terraces of olive groves, intertwined with a patchwork of stone walls. It lies just 7nm south of Corfu and 8nm from the Epirus coast and is an enchanting place to explore over several days. Its west coasts are wild and barren, fringed with precipitous cliffs, caves and limestone arches, while its softer east coast is home to the island's three main villages: Gaios, Longos and Lakka. All three have harbours that offer sheltered anchorages in stunning locations, with good amenities ashore.

Tourism kicked off here in the 1980s and now the diminutive island is one of the most popular destinations in the Ionian. It's an upmarket destination and said to be the most expensive of the islands, but it is still rich in rural beauty. While the summer months can see it drenched in day-trippers from Corfu and yachties from Italy and other parts of the Ionian, it remains an idyllic island that hasn't been spoilt by the ravages of tourism and commercialisation. Lakka and Longos are very traditional and Gaios is a vibrant, bustling type of place that is fronted by some of the most interesting and beautiful Venetian architecture in this part of the country.

Paxos' history is long, but compared with the rest of the Ionian relatively settled. According to Greek mythology it was formed when the god Poseidon struck the southern tip of Corfu with his trident and broke a

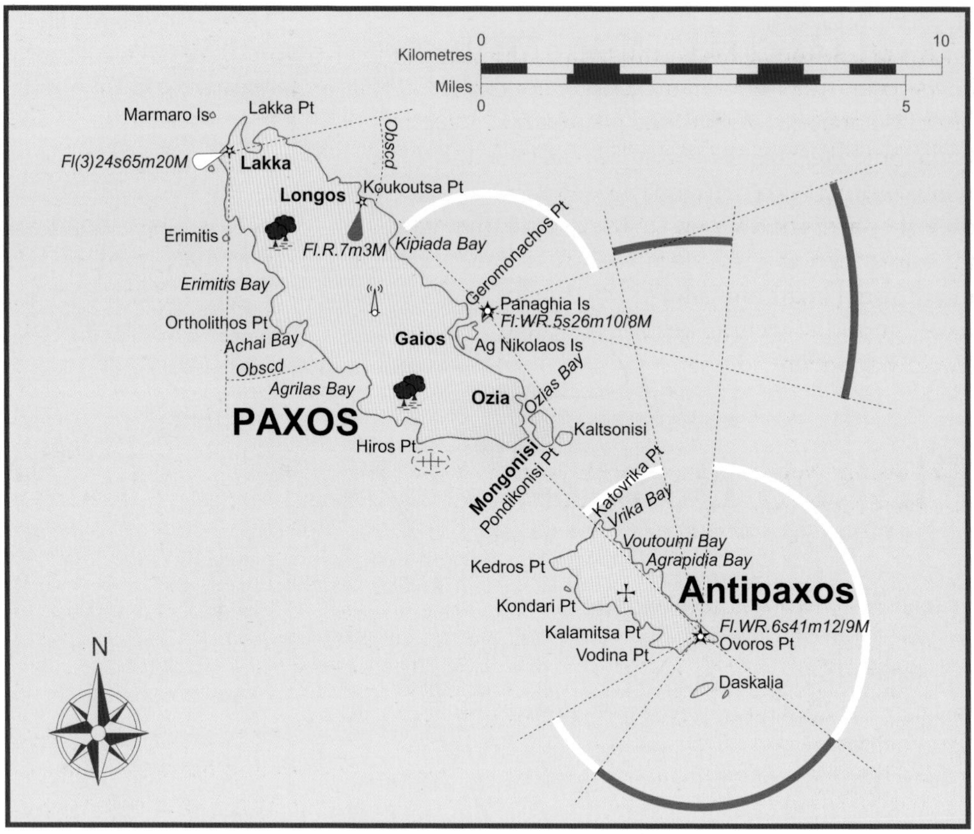

bit of the island off to form a secluded hideaway for his lover Amphitriti. Its earliest settlers are said to date to around the 6th century BC, and it was in the waters off Paxos that part of the Peloponnesian War between the Corinthians and Athenians took place in 433BC. The island saw Venetian occupation from the 14th century onwards, during which time the two fortresses on the island and the main port at Gaios were built, but were devastated by the Turks in 1537 as revenge for their failure in seizing control of Corfu. It too was unified with Greece in 1864 and also occupied by German troops during the Second World War. Indeed, it is even said that the island was used as target practice for German planes.

Whether you stop off here en route north or south, or make the landfall specifically, you won't be disappointed: the surrounding waters offer superb sailing and ashore there are some fabulous walks through olive groves and along the rugged coast.

Lakka Laka

Approach to Lakka: 39°14'.62N 20°08'.38E
Lakka Bay: 39°14'.59N 20°07'.84E
Anchorage in Lakka Bay: 39°14'.40N 20°07'.85E

It is the colour of the water that first catches your attention on entering Lakka Bay, on the north-east tip of Paxos. It's the most incredible shade of cyan mixed with hues of aquamarine and, along with Emerald Bay on Antipaxos, quite different from the rest of the North Ionian.

The narrow but long inlet of Lakka Bay leads to a compact little village which, like Longos and Gaios to the south, is clustered in a tight group around the waterfront. It has more amenities than Longos, so attracts more visitors during July and August, particularly from Corfu where day-trippers come over by the boatload. Yet, despite the daytime tourist invasions, it's a really pleasant place to stop and at night can be very tranquil. The anchorage is large enough to accommodate a fair few boats and it offers good shelter from all but the north-east. Ashore there are numerous tavernas and cafes to swallow most of the visitors and as a place to stretch your legs it couldn't be better – the surrounding ragged coastline is stunning.

NAVIGATION

Charts: Admiralty 2402, 206, 188, SC5771; Imray G11, G1; Hellenic Navy Hydrographic Service 025, 21

Lakka is located on the north-east tip of Paxos, 1½nm north of Longos. The bay can be hard to identify from some distance as the headlands on each side of the entrance merge into one, but close-to it should become visible. Approaching from the north, look for the lighthouse (Fl(3)24s65m20M) on the hill to the west of the harbour. You will soon see buildings and the light beacons (Fl G 2s and Fl R 2s) on either side of the entrance.

The approach from all directions is through deep water, although care should be taken when sailing near Longos as there is a nasty reef (Ifalos Paxoi) just to the east of the harbour (see p57).

Lakka – the most northern village on the island of Paxos

BERTHING

Yachts of less than 35ft (10.7m) can berth stern- or bows-to the quay in the southern corner of the harbour. There is about 2m of water here and the holding is good, but take care not to block the ferry berth, which is at the end of this bit of quay. Occasionally shallow-draught yachts berth bows-to the quay to the east of the main one but it is not advised. This area is used by local fishing boats and, although there is usually room for a handful of visiting boats, depths are relatively shallow at between 1.3-2m.

ANCHORING

Most visiting yachts stop off in Lakka Bay. There is plenty of room to free-swing to your anchor and the village is just a short distance away by tender. It is best to anchor on the north and west sides of the bay in depths of 2.5-3.5m, taking care to keep clear of the buoyed swimming area off the beach in the north-west corner of the bay. It is also advisable to keep your swinging circle fairly small. The holding on mud and sand is good, although it is weedy in places, so make sure your anchor digs in well. There is good shelter from all but the north-east, when it can get quite choppy and in poor conditions may become untenable.

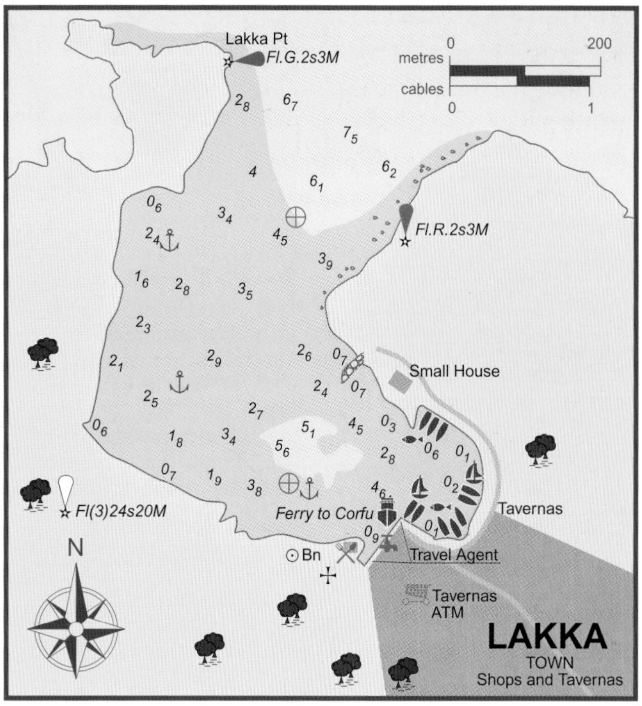

It's the colour of the water that strikes you when you first arrive at Lakka

The large bay at Lakka provides plenty of swinging room, although peak season it can get rather crowded

Useful information – Lakka

FACILITIES

Water: Taps on a timer: €7 for 20 minutes. Minimum charge €7. Ask at Planos Holidays, which can also provide a long hose.
Fuel: A mini-tanker (Tel: 26620 31900) will deliver.
Showers: Ask at Routsis Travel, the travel agent on the quay.
Ice: At the cigarette shop and grocers behind the quay.
Gas: Bottle exchange at Notos Yacht Service & Marine Shop (Tel: 26620 32089/ Mobile: 697 6171719) in Gaios. Ask at travel agent for bottle exchange in Lakka.
Rubbish: Bins in the car park behind the quay.
Yacht services/chandlery: Notos Yacht Service & Marine Shop (Tel: 26620 32089/Mobile: 697 6171719) in Gaios has an extensive range of chandlery as well as offers engine repair and general maintenance. Karabas Services (Tel: 26620 32511; Mobile: 6937 404111), near the square in Gaios, also does engine repair.
Telephone: Telephone and fax at Routsis Travel and Planos Holidays. Phone boxes in the little square towards the rear of the village, near Pounendes Taverna. Both travel agents sell phone cards. Mobile reception is good.
Internet: Available at Akis Bar, in the western corner of the hbr. Up to 30 mins costs €4.50; 1 hr, €7.50; 2hrs, €12; 3 hrs, €16. An A4 print-out costs €2.

PROVISIONING

Grocery shops: A couple of mini-markets set back from the quay. Most basic products available, including fresh fruit and veg.
Bakery: Set back from the quay.
Banks: Citibank ATM behind the quay. The two travel agents on the quay, Routsis Travel (Tel: 26620 31807; open daily 0830-1430 & 1730-2300) and Planos Holidays (Tel: 26620 31821; open daily 0830-1430 & 1730-2200) offer currency exchange.
Pharmacy: The nearest is in Gaios.
Post: Post office in Gaios. Both travel agents on the quay sell stamps. The postal service on Paxos is not speedy, so send urgent mail from Corfu or the mainland.
Opening times: Most shops open 0900-1400 and 1730-2100 but tavernas and souvenir shops stay open later.

EATING OUT

Tavernas, cafés and bars line the waterfront at Lakka. Akis Bar (Tel: 26620 31665), at the W end of the quay, serves excellent breakfasts and has a lovely decked eating area with fabulous views over the water. O Diogenis Taverna (Tel: 26620 31442), near Harbour Lights, is good for simple traditional food; La Rosa di Paxos (Tel: 26620 31471) serves dishes with an international theme and is particularly good for Italian cuisine; Taverna Nautilus at the eastern end of the quay is recommended for seafood and Pounendes, near the square, for pizza.

Most provisions can be found in the pretty village of Lakka

ASHORE

If you can't wait to get back out on the water, there are a couple of watersports companies based in Lakka. Jerry's Watersports Club (Tel: 697700034) organises parascending and water-skiing trips, among other activities, and Oasi Sub-Diving (Tel: 26620 30004; Mobile: 6978167506) runs diving courses. Prices start at around €40 per day, including equipment. PADI and IDIC courses start at €250.

A good way to explore the island and see the countryside is to catch the local bus, which travels between Lakka, Longos and Gaios four times a day. Single tickets costing around €1 can be bought on the bus. Alternatively, explore on foot. There are superb walks from Lakka, around the shore to the lighthouse, or over the hills to the village of Vasilatika, on the west coast of Paxos.

TRANSPORT

Car hire: Nick the Greek (open 0900-1400 and 1800-2200) rents scooters near the car park, as does Siafittano Motorini, near the bakery.
Taxis: Kostas (Tel: 26620 31402); Haris (Tel: 26620 32526); Tasos (Tel: 26620 31613); Vasilis (Tel: 26620 31426); Christos (Tel: 26620 31607).
Bus: Four a day from Lakka to Gaios, Mon-Sat, calling at Longos en route. The journey to Gaios takes 30 mins. Travel agents have the latest timetable. The bus stop is near La Piazza taverna, behind the village.
Ferry: Ferries to the mainland and Corfu leave from Gaios. Kerkyra Lines operates a daily car and foot-passenger service from Corfu's New Port to Paxos, via Igoumenitsa. The journey takes about 3 hrs 15 mins. Foot passengers can also travel via hydrofoil from Corfu's New Port to Gaios, taking 60-90 mins, depending on whether you go via Igoumenitsa. Several services a day, peak season, and a one-way ticket is around €13. Details at the travel agents.
Air travel: The nearest major airport is on Corfu. International and domestic flights leave daily peak season, when there is also a limited seaplane service from Corfu to Paxos.

OTHER INFORMATION

Local Tel code: 26620.
Port authority: In Gaios: Tel: 26620 32533.
Travel agents: Both on the quay, Routsis Travel (Tel: 26620 31807; open daily 0830-1430 and 1730-2300) and Planos Holidays (Tel: 26620 31821) can assist with bus and ferry timetables, car hire, accommodation and information about the island.
Police: In Gaios: Tel: 26620 32222.
Doctor: In Gaios: K Karambouriotis (Tel: 26620 32555).
Dentist: In Gaios: K Veroniki (Tel: 26620 32155).
Hospital: Health centre in Gaios: Tel: 26620 31466.
Yacht repairs/services: Notos Yacht Service & Marine Shop (Tel: 26620 32089/ Mobile: 697 6171719) is in the centre of Gaios, a 30-minute bus journey from Lakka.

Longos Loggos

North-east tip of Ifalos Paxoi shoal: 39°13'.63N 20°10'.14E

Anchorage off Longos, to the south of the outer mole: 39°13'.67N 20°09'.81E

Longos is the smallest of Paxos's three coastal villages. Set between Lakka and Gaios, on the east coast of the island, the tiny fishing village has just a small collection of holiday homes and shops. It's quieter than either of its siblings, but its tavernas offer a reasonable variety and the amenities, while basic, cater for most needs.

The harbour itself offers visiting yachts little more than an anchorage as it is shallow near the quay and usually full of fishing and day-tripper boats. But it is fine as a daytime anchorage or overnight stop in settled conditions.

The harbour at Longos is small, but yachts can anchor off in deep water

NAVIGATION

Charts: Admiralty 2402, 206, 188, 189, SC5771; Imray G11, G1; Hellenic Navy Hydrographic Service 025, 21

The approach from the north and from Lakka is through deep, clear water, but care should be taken if approaching from both the east and south. A reef, Ifalos Paxoi, and a collection of rocks, Vroi Litharia, lie about 3½ cables offshore, east-north-east of the entrance to Longos Bay. In settled conditions, in good visibility and minimal chop, the reef can be identified with the naked eye from some distance as a patch of lighter-coloured water. However, in any kind of chop it is hidden, so exercise extreme caution in the vicinity. While the reef lies some distance offshore, you should pass well to the east of it as there are some nasty rocks between it and Paxos.

The harbour can be identified by the tall chimney of an old soap factory in the western corner of the bay, which is conspicuous from some distance.

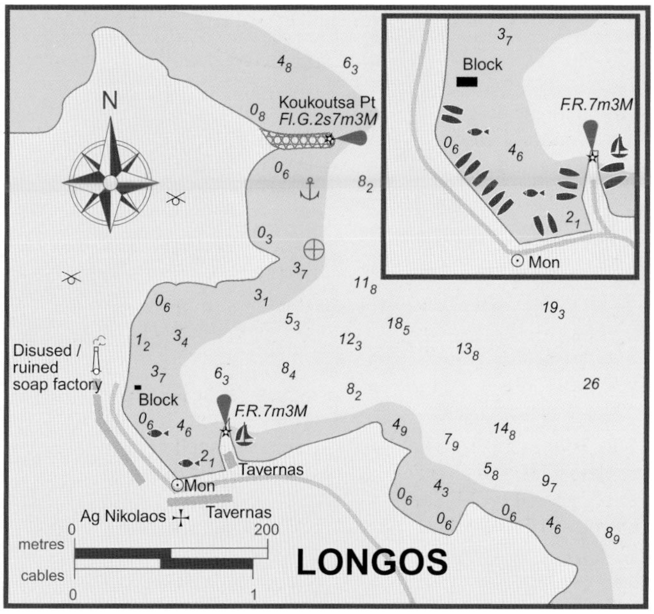

BERTHING

The harbour at Longos is too small and too shallow for most visiting boats to berth comfortably. It is also usually full of local fishing and day-tripper boats, so lie to your anchor in the bay instead.

ANCHORING

Anchor off the outer mole at the entrance to the bay in around 5m. This spot is sheltered from the prevailing winds and the holding is good on mud and sand. However, it is worth taking a line off your stern ashore for extra protection or to stop you swinging if there are lots of boats nearby.

Yachts can also anchor off the coast to the south-west of this mole, with a line ashore. It shelves very quickly, though, so you will not be able to get very close to shore. This bay is affected by swell, so make sure your anchor digs in well before leaving your boat unattended. In poor conditions, it may be too rolly for an overnight stay.

Yachts at anchor in Longos Bay. The village is small but there are some well-stocked grocery shops and several good tavernas

Useful information – Longos

FACILITIES

Fuel: No but you can get fuel delivered to your boat in Lakka and Gaios.
Ice: Ask at the mini-markets.
Gas: Bottle exchange at Notos Yacht Service & Marine Shop (Tel: 26620 32089/ Mobile: 697 6171719) in Gaios.
Rubbish: Small bins behind the village.
Yacht services/chandlery: Notos Yacht Service & Marine Shop (Tel: 26620 32089/ Mobile: 697 6171719) in Gaios can supply most chandlery and also offers a range of maintenance services.
Telephone: Phone box next to Taverna Nasos. Phone cards sold at the mini-markets. Mobile reception is good.

PROVISIONING

Grocery shops: Mastoras supermarket, behind the harbour, is very well stocked. It also has a deli and will deliver. There is a mini-market near the quay.
Bakery: Near Taverna Gios. Fresh bread is also available at Mastoras supermarket.
Butcher: Limited cold meats at Mastoras supermarket.
Banks: There is a Citibank ATM in Lakka and a branch of the Agricultural Bank of Greece (Tel: 26620 31213) in Gaios.
Pharmacy: The nearest is in Gaios.
Post: The nearest post office is in Gaios. There is a post box outside Taverna Nasos and stamps are sold at the souvenir shops. The postal service on Paxos is fairly slow, so send urgent packages from Corfu or the mainland.
Opening times: Most shops open 0900-1400 and 1730-2100, but tavernas and souvenir shops tend to stay open later.

EATING OUT

The traditional cooking at Taverna Nasos (Tel: 26620 31604) is superb and the menu is very reasonably priced. Taverna O Vasilis (Tel: 26620 30062), not far from the mini-market, is usually packed and has a good reputation, so you may have to book ahead, and O Gios (Tel: 26620 31735) near the bakery is good for grilled dishes.

ASHORE

If you have hired a car, it is worth driving out to see Paxos's dramatic west coast: the caves lining Agrilis Bay are particularly impressive. On the way back, stop off at the Olive Press Museum near the village of Magazia. Built in 1865, it was in constant use making olive oil until 1960. Now restored by the daughter of a former owner, it has been turned into a museum and also sells locally produced olive products.

TRANSPORT

Car hire: Julia's Boat & Bike Hire (Tel: 26620 31330) hires motorbikes and scooters. Paxos Thalassa Travel (Tel: 26620 31662) on the quay, to the east of the school, can also organise car rental.
Taxis: Kostas (Tel: 693 2641739; 26620 31402); Haris (Tel: 694 5710899; 26620 32526); Tasos (Tel: 694 5385543; 26620 31613); Vasilis (Tel: 693 2929420; 26620 31426); Christos (Tel: 693 2432485; 26620 31607).
Bus: Three a day from Longos to Lakka and Gaios. The bus stop near the quay is indicated by a Bouas Tours sign on a stick. A timetable is posted here too.
Ferry: Ferries to the mainland and Corfu leave from Gaios. Kerkyra Lines operates a car and foot-passenger service from Corfu's New Port to Paxos, via Igoumenitsa. The journey takes about 3 hours 15 mins and there is one service a day. Foot passengers can also travel via hydrofoil from Corfu's New Port to Gaios. The journey takes 60-90 mins, depending on whether you go via Igoumenitsa, and a one-way ticket costs around €13. There are several services a day peak season. For more details, ask at the travel agents.
Air travel: The nearest major airport is on Corfu. Both international and domestic flights leave daily peak season when there is also a limited seaplane service from Corfu to Paxos.

OTHER INFORMATION

Local Tel code: 26620.
Port authority: In Gaios: Tel: 26620 32533.
Police: In Gaios: Tel: 26620 32222.
Doctor: In Gaios: K Karambouriotis (Tel: 26620 32555).
Dentist: In Gaios: K Veroniki (Tel: 26620 32155).
Hospital: There is a health centre in Gaios: Tel: 26620 31466.
Yacht repairs/services: Notos Yacht Service & Marine Shop (Tel: 26620 32089/Mobile: 697 6171719) is in the centre of Gaios.

Gaios Gai

Approach to Gaios's northern entrance: 39°12'.45N 20°11'.39E • Gaios's northern channel: 39°12'.15N 20°11'.32E
Gaios harbour, off main town: 39°11'.87N 20°11'.33E • Approach to southern entrance: 39°11'.73N 20°11'.75E
Southern entrance to Gaios: 39°11'.85N 20°11'.44E

Gaios is the pocket-sized capital of Paxos and, inevitably, the most popular destination on the island. During the summer months it heaves with tourists of all nationalities, particularly Italians, and has a lively, convivial atmosphere. With its 19th century red-tiled houses, Venetian-style shutters and wrought iron balconies, often festooned with colourful plants, the semicircular waterfront at Gaios is one of the most attractive in the Ionian and draws crowds for just that reason.

The harbour itself is protected to seaward by the islets of Panaghia and Ag Nikolaos and offers good shelter from all directions, particularly the north-west. Occasionally in a southerly, swell is pushed into the harbour through the southern entrance, but most of the time any chop that is found here is generated by passing yachts and day-tripper boats. Expect it to be very busy peak season and be prepared for lots of close-quarters manoeuvring, crossed anchor chains and lively evenings along the waterfront. If you don't mind this, though, then it really is a lovely town to spend a couple of days and a perfect place from which to explore the rest of the island.

NAVIGATION

Charts: Admiralty 2402, 203, 206, 188, 189, SC5771; Imray G11, G1; Hellenic Navy Hydrographic Service 025, 21

There are two entrances to Gaios harbour. The northern one, between Paxos and the tiny islet of Panaghia, is deep and leads directly to the main yacht quay. The southern one, ½nm to the south, is through a narrow and shallow channel between Paxos and the larger islet of Ag Nikolaos, and is nearer the town. Be aware of the unmarked rock, Ifalos Panayia (39°12'.45N 20°11'.39E), which is situated 2.3nm ENE of Panaghia Island.

The northern entrance to Gaios can be hard to identify until close-to, when the lighthouse on Panaghia and the white wall that encloses it will become visible. In peak season there is usually a lot of small boat traffic coming in and out of the entrance, which will also help you to locate it. Maintain a good look-out at all times as this area can get very busy, particularly when the ferry is manoeuvring near its berth, to the west of the entrance. Depths in the entrance are around 40m but shelve quite quickly to 15m and less once past the ferry quay.

The southern entrance is visible from some distance, as buildings in the town can be seen from this direction.

There are two entrances to Gaios: the northern is through deep water, while the southern, between two breakwaters, is shallower

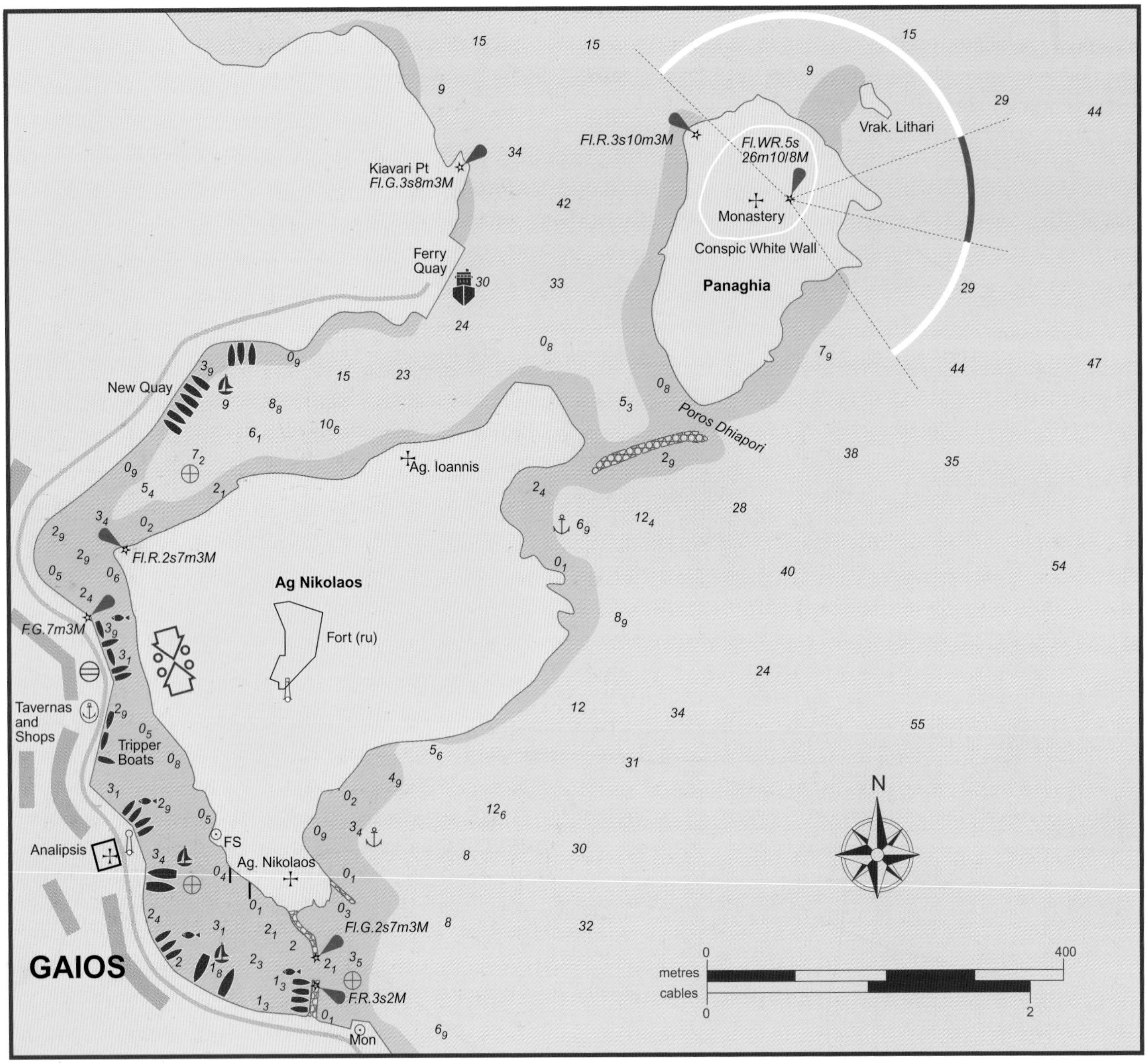

Depths decrease to around 20m once level with the eastern edge of Ag Nikolaos and to around 2m just outside the entrance. If you are in a vessel that draws less than 2m, you should be able to squeeze through, although proceed at a slow speed and stay mid-channel. This entrance is not used as much as the northern one, but keep a good look-out for other vessels as there is only minimal room to manoeuvre should you need to.

The harbour is always a hive of activity, so you need to keep your wits about you and a good look-out when underway in the channel, particularly around the western side of Ag Nikolaos where there is a blind bend and it is hard to see boats approaching.

BERTHING

Visitors can either berth on the new quay towards the harbour's northern entrance or along the quay that flanks the main part of the town. There is normally more space at the new quay and, being away from the main thoroughfare, it is usually quieter. Berth stern- or bows-to wherever there is room, keeping clear of the ferry berth. Depths at the base of the quay are around 2-2.5m, but it is deeper in the channel (5-8m) where you will drop your anchor, so lay plenty of scope. The holding here is good and the berth offers protection from all but the north-east.

The town quay is the first to fill up and is often packed with tripper boats and yachts from 1100-1700. Berth stern- or bows-to wherever there is room, taking care not to lay your anchor over those of your neighbours. Keep clear of the area in front of the town square as this part of the quay is used by local fishing boats. You should also note that depths along the quay immediately to the west of the southern entrance are around 1.5m and therefore not deep enough for a lot of craft, and in a strong southeasterly the swell funnels in through the southern entrance, making it very uncomfortable.

Visiting boats to Gaios will be charged to berth overnight. In 2007 a 42-footer cost €3.48 per night, but prices may vary.

ANCHORING

If there is no room in the harbour, you can anchor off Ag Nikolaos's east coast. Either anchor off the south-east corner in 3-4m or near the breakwater between Ag Nikolaos and Panaghia, in 6-8m. Both anchorages are suitable in settled conditions only as, although they offer shelter from the prevailing northwesterlies, they are exposed in anything from the east or south-east.

Useful information – Gaios

FACILITIES

Water: Can be delivered by mini-tanker – Tel: 69722 78810.
Fuel: Can be very hard to obtain during high season due to the large numbers of Italian motorboats. BP fuel available near the ferry quay. Diesel mini-tanker (Tel: 26620 32488; Mobile: 6972278810).
Showers: Available at the Ionian Fitness Club, near the quay.
Ice: Available from the mini-markets.
Gas: Bottle exchange at Notos Yacht Service & Marine Shop (Tel: 26620 32089/Mobile: 697 6171719).
Rubbish: Bins near the ferry quay and smaller ones throughout the town.
Yacht services/chandlery: Notos Yacht Service & Marine Shop (VHF Ch6; Tel: 26620 32089/Mobile: 697 6171719 [24hr]), on a street to the west of the main square, has an extensive range of chandlery and also offers engine repair and general maintenance. Karabas Services (Tel: 26620 32511; Mobile: 6937 404111) near the square will also do engine repair.
Telephone: Several phone boxes on the quay. More around the square in the centre of Gaios. Phone cards sold at travel agents and mini-markets. Mobile reception is good.

PROVISIONING

Grocery shops: Lots of mini-markets and grocery shops scattered throughout Gaios. The nearest to the new quay is near the Carnayo music bar. Olive oil and Metaxa sold from a small warehouse on the quay. There are also several off-licences near the square.
Bakery: To the west of the main square. Most mini-markets sell limited goods too.
Butcher: Near Taverna Taka Taka, on a street to the west of the main square.
Banks: The Agricultural Bank of Greece (Tel: 26620 31213) branch and ATM is near Zefi Travel on the main quay. There is also a National Bank of Greece ATM to the west of the main square and most of the travel agents offer currency exchange.
Pharmacy: Off the main square.
Post: Post office and post box near the square. Stamps sold at souvenir shops. The postal service on Paxos is okay, but if something is urgent you should post it off the island.
Opening times: Most shops open 0900-1400 and 1700-2100, but tavernas and souvenir shops will stay open later.

EATING OUT

There's an abundance of tavernas, cafés and bars in Gaios. Restaurant Mambo (Tel: 26620 32670) on the waterfront is one of the best and popular with locals. Taverna Pan & Theo (Tel: 26620 32458) next door is good for simple Greek fare, as is Dodo's Taverna (Tel: 26620 32265), on a side-street near the Remego music bar (Tel: 26620 32106). Il Primo (Tel: 26620 32432), to the west of the square, serves excellent pizzas and pasta dishes and, if you have a sweet tooth, you should try the Greek doughnuts served at Genesis Café, near the southern entrance to Gaios, as they are particularly fine.

ASHORE

The Paxos Museum (Tel: 26620 32556), which is housed in the old junior school on the waterfront near the southern entrance to Gaios, contains an eclectic mix of artefacts. Stones from olive presses, tools and pottery are exhibited alongside kitchenware and linens, and several rooms are laid out in the style of an 18th century house. It is open daily 1000-1400 and 1900-2230; entry costs €2. Alternatively, take a watertaxi or your own tender to the islets of Ag Nikolaos and Panaghia. A Venetian fortress, built in the 15th century, stands on Ag Nikolaos, while a small church dedicated to the Virgin Mary is situated on Panaghia.

Yachts can berth stern-to off the town quay, right in the heart of Gaios

TRANSPORT

Car hire: Alfa Car Rentals (Tel: 26620 32505) to the west of the main square; Ionian Rent a Car (Tel: 26620 32553/32373) and Paxos Rent a Car (Tel: 26620 32033). You can also pick cars up from Ita's Cars (Tel: 26620 32007) near the ferry quay. Makis Spyros (Tel: 26620 32031) and Vlahoupoulos Vasilis (Tel: 26620 32598) rent motorcycles.
Taxis: Kostas (Tel: 693 2641739; 26620 31402); Haris (Tel: 694 5710899; 26620 32526); Tasos (Tel: 694 5385543; 26620 31613); Vasilis (Tel: 693 2929420; 26620 31426); Christos (Tel: 693 2432485; 26620 31607).
Bus: Bouas Tours (Tel: 26620 32401) runs four services a day to Lakka, via Longos. The bus stop is to the W of the square, near the Castelo Dancing Club.
Ferry: See Lakka, p56.
Air travel: See under Lakka, p56.

OTHER INFORMATION

Local Tel code: 26620.
Port authority: The Port Police office (Tel: 26620 32259) is near the Alter-Ego café-bar.
Travel agents: Several along the quay: Zefi Travel (Tel: 26620 32114), Gaios Travel, Porto Giaos (Tel: 26620 49082) and Paxos Island Travel (Tel: 26620 30082/32589).
Police: Tel: 26620 32222.
Doctor: K Karambouriotis (Tel: 26620 32555).
Dentist: K Veroniki (Tel: 26620 32155), near the pharmacy.
Hospital: Health centre (Tel: 26620 31466).
Yacht repairs/services: Notos Yacht Service & Marine Shop (VHF Ch 6; Tel: 26620 32089/Mobile: 697 6171719 [24hr]), Karabas Services (Tel: 26620 32511; Mobile: 6937 404111).

Ozia Bay

Ormos Oxia, Mongonisi

Entrance to Mongonisi: 39°11'.16N 20°12'.25E
Mongonisi Bay: 39°10'.92N 20°12'.24E
Charts: Admiralty 2402, 203, 206, 188, 189, SC5771; Imray G11, G1; Hellenic Navy Hydrographic Service 025, 21

Ozia Bay, on the south of the island, is a quieter alternative to Gaios

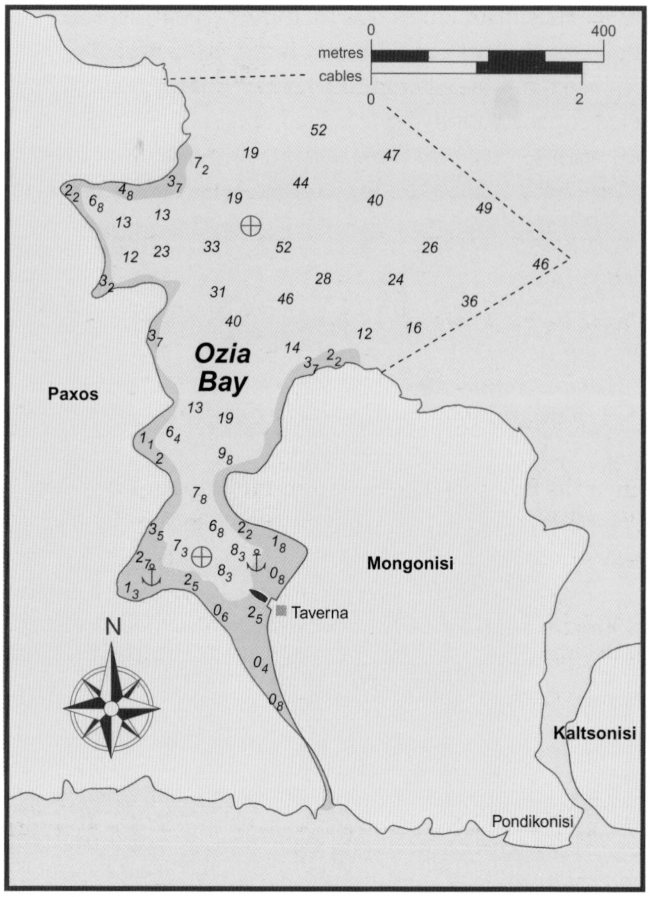

A quieter anchorage, away from the hustle and bustle of Gaios, is 1nm south of the town in Ozia Bay. Enclosed by the coastline of Paxos and the small, olive tree-covered islet of Mongonisi (Mongonissi), Ozia Bay offers good shelter from all directions. From both the north and south, the entrance is hidden until close-to, but lying on the south-west tip of Paxos, it is not difficult to find and the approach is through deep water.

Free-swing to your anchor in the middle of the bay if there is room, or anchor in the northeastern corner off Mongonisi, with a line ashore. The holding on mud is good, although there are patches of weed in places, so make sure your anchor digs in well before going ashore. There is a small quay in front of a building on the eastern shore, off which you can berth stern- or bows-to in depths of around 2.5m. Ashore you'll find the Mongonissi Bay Taverna (Tel: 26620 32140), a seasonal restaurant that has toilets and shower as well as a reputation for lively evenings and tasty cuisine. The islet is also linked to Paxos by a short causeway and Gaios is a 20-minute walk away along the coast if you want to eat there or pick up supplies.

To the east of Mongonisi is the islet of Kaltsonisi. The channel between the two is navigable for most yachts under power and there are depths of around 2.5-3m. It is narrow, though, so transit the channel at a slow speed and in calm weather only. The church on Kaltsonisi's north-west coast is dedicated to St Spiridon and was built in 1686.

WEST COAST

The West Coast of Paxos is wildly rugged and steep-to and there is nowhere for yachts to anchor safely. However, this stretch of coastline is pitted with numerous caves, rock arches and natural stone sculptures and is worth a short detour if you are nearby. The caves in Agrilas Bay (Ormos Prásses) are particularly impressive and can be explored by dinghy.

Antipaxos

Andipaxos

Antipaxos is the island of Paxos' smaller sibling. Lying 1nm to the south, the 1-square-mile ($3km^2$) Antipaxos is one of the most unspoilt of the Ionians and relatively unaffected by tourism. There's only one anchorage on the island – Emerald Bay or Voutoumi – and one harbour, both of which lie on the north-east coast. The harbour is of little use to yachts, being shallow and busy with local fishing boats, but Emerald Bay is a stunning anchorage. Crystal clear azure waters nudge against a brilliant white sandy beach that is fringed with garrigue and lush greenery, and while besieged by tourists from Paxos during the day, peak season, it quietens down considerably in the evenings.

The island itself is rugged but fertile and much of it is used for the cultivation of vines, the grapes from which are used to produce the potent Antipaxos wine.

Great care should be taken when navigating around Antipaxos as the island is surrounded by rocks, particularly at its southern end where a reef extends for approximately 1nm offshore and around the islet of Daskalia (Nsis Dhaskalia). Moreover it is not a good place to linger around if conditions deteriorate significantly.

Emerald Bay Voutoumi

Anchorage in Emerald Bay: 39°09'.58N 20°13'.72E
Charts: Admiralty 203, 206, 188, 189, SC5771; Imray G11, G1; Hellenic Navy Hydrographic Service 21

Emerald Bay gets its name from the colour of its water. It's the most incredible pale turquoise colour, tinged with cobalt and aquamarine. The sandy shore is almost starched white, while in contrast the olive trees behind are lush and green. Situated on the north-east coast of Antipaxos, it's not surprising that it is a popular anchorage and is one of only a few on the island that is suitable for yachts. The approach from all directions is straightforward, although if heading south from Corfu, watch out for the reef Ifalos Panagia, 2½nm east-north-east of Gaios on Paxos. It dries but is often hidden by chop in a northwesterly and there is shoal water to the south and east of it. See p57.

Emerald Bay is the second of two bays on the north-east tip of the island. The first inlet is obscured by a sandbank but you can anchor in Emerald Bay in 5m or less. The holding on sand is reasonable, although if a strong northwesterly is blowing it can get quite rolly so should be considered as a daytime anchorage only. In the summer, Taverna Voutoumi (Tel: 26620 31445) opens on the beach and Taverna Bella Vista on the hill above.

Emerald Bay gets its name from the colour of the water. It's a beautiful anchorage, but expect it to be busy with boats peak season

Agrapidia

To east of Agrapidia: 39°09'.33N 20°13'.99E
Charts: Admiralty: 203, 206, 188, 189; Imray: G11, G1; Hellenic Navy Hydrographic Service: 21

Agrapidia is a tiny fishing boat harbour, about ½nm south of Emerald Bay, on the east coast of Antipaxos. It's a beautiful spot but busy with local fishing boats, so not somewhere that yachts can use. Very occasionally, boats anchor for lunch to the north-east of the breakwater in around 4m with a line ashore, although this should be considered in calm weather only.

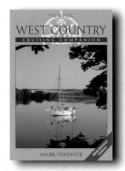

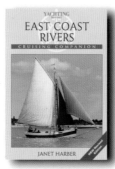

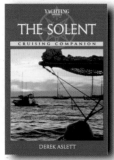

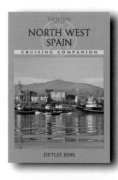

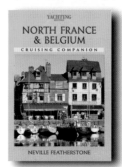

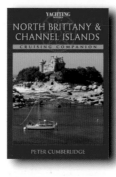

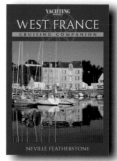

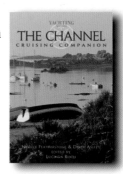

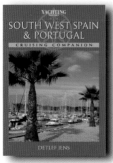

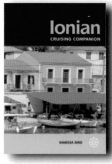

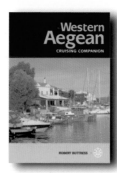

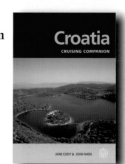

Chapter two

Epirus Coast from Pagania to Preveza, including the Amvrakikos Gulf

High mountain ranges and low valley plains dominate the Epirus coast, which stretches from Greece's border with Albania to Preveza and the Amvrakikos Gulf. It's a dramatic coastline, relatively unspoilt by tourism compared with the Ionian islands and the mainland to the south, but well worth exploring. Landlocked Amvrakikos Gulf is rarely visited by cruising yachts but is a stunning place that contrasts greatly with the jagged cliffscapes of the northern coast. Busy resorts, such as Sivota Mourtos and Parga, are interspersed with tranquil anchorages in quiet backwaters and traditional village harbours, such as Sagiada near the Albanian border.

The sailing in these waters is superb. Largely unobstructed by islands, the prevailing northwesterly winds provide constant breezes which usually blow up to Force 3-6 in the afternoons. When planning your passage, remember that the winds are generally stronger here than among the islands to the south, though they do tend to decrease in early evening. The coastline is mostly hazard free, but as with all lee shores care should be taken in bad weather. While many of the harbours and anchorages mentioned in this chapter provide some sort of refuge, there are others that should be avoided if conditions deteriorate.

As destinations, Preveza, Vonitsa, Plataria and Sivota Mourtos have the best amenities and facilities ashore, but most of the smaller harbours will at least offer basic provisions.

This coastline, and the towns immediately inland, are also rich in heritage, and for those on the cultural trail, there's plenty to see and do. The sanctuary of Dodona, the Necromanteion of Acheron and the city of Nikopoli are among the key ancient Greek sites, while the towns of Arta, Ioannina and Parga are also interesting.

Unlike much of nearby Greece, Epirus remained under Turkish dominance for centuries and although it saw brief periods of Venetian rule it was not influenced to the same degree as Corfu or the Peloponnese. Indeed Parga is one of the few places in Epirus where you can see significant evidence of Venetian occupation; most of the other major towns are dominated by Turkish architecture. Epirus was one of the last places in Greece to be liberated after the War of Independence and that

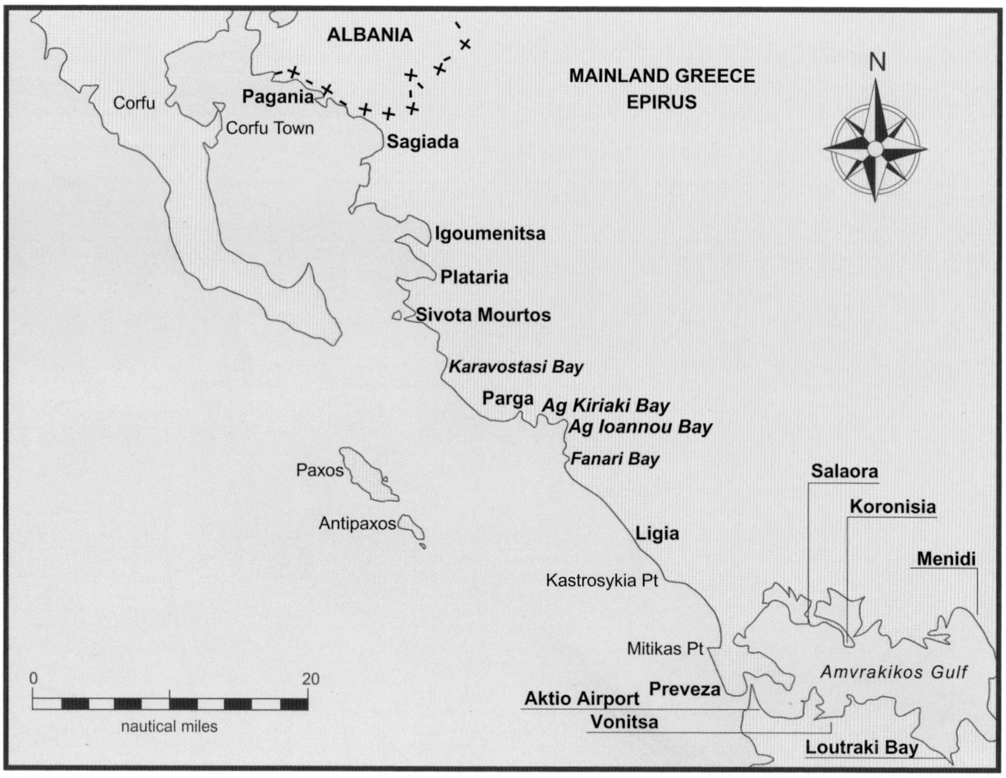

was only as a result of the Balkan Wars of 1912-13.

In previous years, political unrest in Albania has led to harbours on the northern part of this coast being considered unsafe for private yachts and many charter companies have imposed a ban on exploring this area. However, the latest advice from the Foreign Office suggests that the situation is less volatile and that it is now safe for foreigners to travel to places that border the country. There are still pockets of crime and violence in Albania though, and there have also been reports of pirate attacks in this area in recent years. Yachtsmen visiting harbours and anchorages near the border, such as Pagania and Sagiada, are advised to be vigilant about personal security.

However, if you do get to explore the coastline to the south of border, it is well worth it. While Igoumenitsa offers little more than somewhere to change crew, Sagiada is a stunning little spot and Plataria provides a good alternative to the often very busy Sivota Mourtos.

Pagania Paganias

Entrance to Pagania Bay: 39°39'.92N 20°05'.35E

As soon as you enter the boot-shaped bay of Pagania, you are hit by the acrid stench of fish farms. It's not a smell that you can ignore or get used to and it lingers in the air; wherever you anchor in the bay you can't get away from it. It's a shame as Pagania Bay, on the north-west coast of mainland Greece, about a mile from the Albanian border, would otherwise be a delightful anchorage. The enclosed bay offers excellent shelter and

Fish-farms dominate, and rather spoil, the anchorage at Pagania

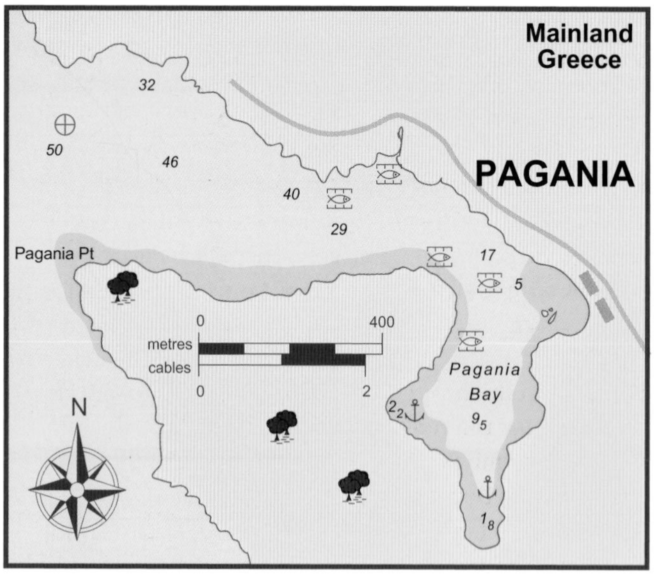

holding is generally good. As a safe retreat in inclement weather, it would serve well, and its remoteness and seclusion has many attractions.

The anchorage's proximity to Albania should put you on your guard though. While the political situation is currently stable, anyone within the vicinity must exercise caution. Cruisers have reported incidents in recent years involving Albanians trying to break into yachts, so stay alert.

NAVIGATION

Charts: Admiralty 206, SC5771; Imray G11, G1; Hellenic Navy Hydrographic Service 010, 21

The entrance to Pagania Bay lies about 5nm north-west of Sagiada. The bay is protected by a dog-legged spit of land and from the south is hard to identify until close in. From the north, the approach is straightforward and the entrance easier to spot. Care should be taken, however, if approaching from the north coast of Corfu. There are several hazards along the North Corfu Channel, such as the islet of Peristeres and the Serpa reef (see p45), just north of Ag Stephanos Bay on Corfu, and you should navigate through here with caution.

I would not recommend entering Pagania Bay at night. While there is plenty of room in the anchorages, the bottleneck at the entrance to the bay is littered with fish farms, one of which lies almost mid-channel. The fish farms are buoyed but rarely lit at night.

ANCHORING

You can anchor in the western and southern corners of the bay, both of which are clear of fish farms, in 2-6m of water. The seabed is mud and the holding generally good. Shelter is superb. Avoid the eastern side of the bay, in front of the buildings, as it is shallower here and there is also some debris under the water.

Entering Pagania at night is not recommended as fish-farms litter the entrance and you cannot rely on them being lit

Sagiada Sayiadha, Ormos Sagiadas

Harbour entrance: 39°37'.46N 20°10'.83E

Sagiada on the north-west coast of mainland Greece, two miles from the Albanian border, was once one of the most prosperous ports in Epirus, with the majority of the area's trade passing through it. It was here, in the 18th century, when much of Greece was under Turkish rule, that the notorious Turkish tyrant Ali Pasha met Napoleon and sought

Sagiada is a pretty little harbour, set amid a sparce and, in places, barren landscape

assistance in his military campaigns (see p71). Today, the tiny harbour, which lies tucked in the north-east corner of Sagiada Bay, is a sleepy place. In fact, it's hard to believe that it played such a significant role in Epirus's history, the size of the harbour bearing little resemblance to the size of its reputation. Yet the harbour has a charm and unspoilt quality that makes it one of the nicest destinations on this stretch of coast. It's a beautiful spot, with stunning views of Corfu to the west and the rugged mountains of Albania to the north.

For yachts, the harbour provides excellent shelter and adequate facilities, and with Corfu town just 12nm away, it's an easy day's sail for lunch or a good place to spend the night.

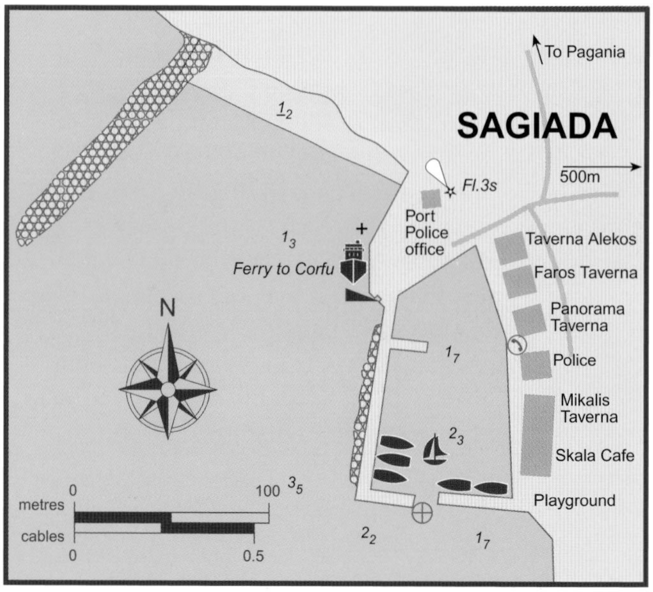

NAVIGATION

Charts: Admiralty 206, SC5771; Imray G11, G1; Hellenic Navy Hydrographic Service 010, 21

The approach to Sagiada from the north is straightforward and through deep water until about 2nm from the harbour. If approaching from the south, you are advised to head north until you are level with Corfu Town, before turning east on a 90° bearing towards Sagiada. The bay to the south of Sagiada is shallow, particularly around the Thiamidos Shoals. Here depths decrease to as little as 1m so don't be tempted to cut across them. The shallowness of Sagiada Bay and its position on a lee shore mean that entry into the harbour is not recommended in heavy weather.

BERTHING

Sagiada harbour is quite small and the entrance particularly narrow, but yachts under 12.2m (40ft) should get in without difficulty. Berth stern- or bows-to on the western wall of the harbour or, alternatively, if there is plenty of room, tie up alongside the southern quay near the entrance. Depths in the harbour are less than 2.5m and the holding is generally good. The breakwater to the north-west of the harbour protects it from the worst of the prevailing winds.

Sagiada's harbour is small, but offers reasonable shelter. There's also a good selection of tavernas here

Useful information – Sagiada

FACILITIES
Water: Tap on the quay.
Fuel: Take a taxi to the Avin fuel station in the village.
Ice: Ask at the tavernas.
Gas: Nearest supply is at Igoumenitsa.
Rubbish: Large bins in the car park behind the tavernas.
Yacht services/chandlery: The nearest services are at Gouvia Marina on Corfu, 12nm to the west.
Telephone: Several phone boxes by the harbour.

PROVISIONING
The village of Sagiada is quite small and spread out. There is a small selection of shops on the main road which leads through the village towards Filiates. For major provisioning, head to Igoumenitsa.
Grocery shops: A couple of mini-markets in the village. Opening times vary, but are usually from 0900-1400 and 1800-2100.
Bakery: Bread available at the mini-markets.
Post: Post box behind Taverna Alekos, in the north-east corner of the harbour. Post office on the main road through the village. Open 0730-1400.

EATING OUT
Sagiada has a well-deserved reputation for its fish cuisine. There are several tavernas and cafés along the eastern side of the harbour (Taverna Alekos, Faros Café, Panorama Taverna, Mikalis Taverna and Skala Café), all of which serve a good selection of simple but very tasty dishes. The grilled fish and shrimp at Panorama Taverna were particularly memorable.

ASHORE
Sagiada is a good place from which to explore the mountainous northern part of Epirus. It's within easy reach of Igoumenitsa, from where you can travel to Corfu, Patra or Italy, and there's also a weekly ferry to Corfu from the harbour. Filiates, about 11 miles (18km) to the east, is a small market village, and about 5 miles (8km) further inland is the Monastery of Giromeri (Tel: 26640 22407).

The monastery, which dates back to the 14th century, is inhabited by just four monks, but in the 16th century it was the most important monastic centre in Epirus and was home to over 300 monks. The building, which perches high on a hillside, is also known for its 'Secret School', a hidden room in which pupils were taught Greek covertly during the Turkish occupation.

TRANSPORT
Car hire: Nearest hire firms are in Igoumenitsa, a 20-minute taxi ride from Sagiada.
Taxis: Ask at the tavernas.
Bus: Several bus stops along the road through Sagiada. Services are erratic though, so it is easier to get a taxi to Igoumenitsa.
Ferry: In season, a ferry (Tel: 26650 26280) runs from Sagiada to Corfu every Friday. The trip takes 45 minutes. Igoumenitsa, to the south, is a major port and ferries to Corfu, Paxos, Italy and Patra run from here. See p71.
Air travel: The nearest airport is on Corfu Island. Domestic and international charter services fly from here several times a week. Alternatively, Aktio airport at Preveza is a 3-hour drive away.

OTHER INFORMATION
Local Tel code: 26640.
Port authority: The port police office (Tel: 26640 51951) is in the building behind the ferry quay; manned in season.
Police: Small police station (Tel: 26640 51287) near Mikalis Taverna.
Doctor: No. Nearest in Igoumenitsa, a 20-minute car journey from Sagiada (see p71).
Dentist: No. Nearest in Igoumenitsa.
Hospital: No. Nearest medical centre is in Filates (Tel: 26640 22203), 11 miles (18km) to the east.

The waterfront at Sagiada has recently been developed

Igoumenitsa

Igoumenitsas, Egoumenitchsa

The start of the Igoumenitsa channel: 39°30'.09N 20°11'.95E

To the NW of Igoumenitsa Bay: 39°30'.74N 20°14'.16E

Igoumenitsa is a great place if you want to go somewhere – Corfu, Patra or even Italy – but as a cruising destination it is poor. In fact, even the Igoumenitsa Port Authority agrees and in 2007 was actively discouraging any yachts from going there. In 2007 there was nowhere within easy reach of the town where yachts could berth, and while an anchorage in the north-west of the bay offers reasonable shelter, the constant comings and goings of ferry traffic make it an undesirable place to spend any length of time.

As somewhere to victual or change crew, Igoumenitsa is good, but it is almost as easy and certainly more pleasant to take the boat to Plataria or Sivota Mourtos (see p72 & 74), hire a car and drive into the town.

Plans for a yacht marina at Igoumenitsa are in the pipeline but, as Greece's third largest ferry port, all building work is currently being concentrated on the commercial docks.

NAVIGATION
Charts: Admiralty 2406, 206, SC5771; Imray G11, G1; Hellenic Navy Hydrographic Service 014, 010; 21

The main hazard on approach to Igoumenitsa is the ferry traffic. With hourly ferries to Corfu and several a day to Italy, there is continual movement within the bay. The New Port at the south-east end of Igoumenitsa Bay is the international ferry port.

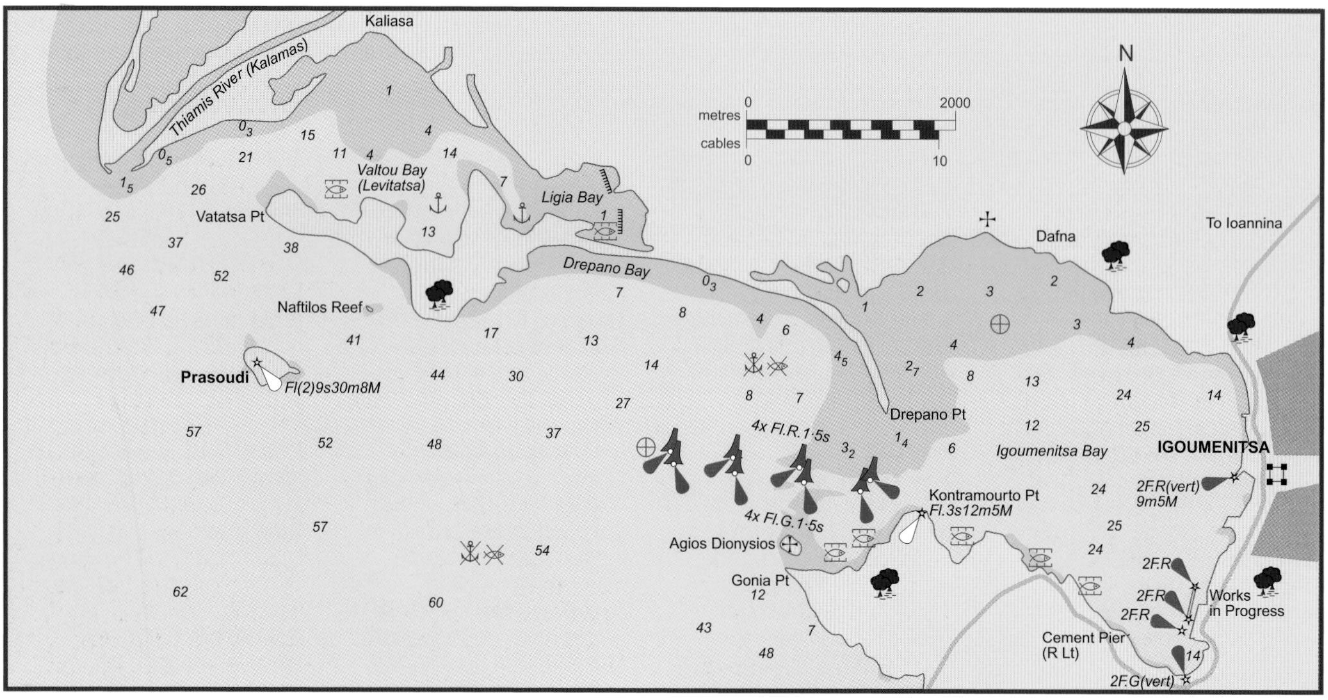

Domestic ferries leave from the Old Port to the north.

The entrance to Igoumenitsa Bay is easy to spot on approach from both the north and south – all you need to do is follow the ferries. Once inside the entrance, a series of flashing port and starboard buoys mark the channel. Regulations within the bay mean that you are not allowed to enter the channel, whatever your size, if another vessel is heading in the opposite direction. Priority is always given to those leaving Igoumenitsa. If there is a boat moving through the channel, then the port authority advises waiting to the south of the entrance.

The Port Police can be contacted on VHF Channel 14 and also operates a VTS (Vessel Traffic Service). You should maintain a good look-out at all times, as traffic within the bay is usually very heavy, both day and night.

BERTHING

In the past, visiting yachts have tended to berth in the old fishing harbour, which is situated to the north of the Old Port. However, in 2007 this was closed until further notice. The chances of a marina being built in the near future are slim.

Igoumenitsa's port is not currently yacht friendly

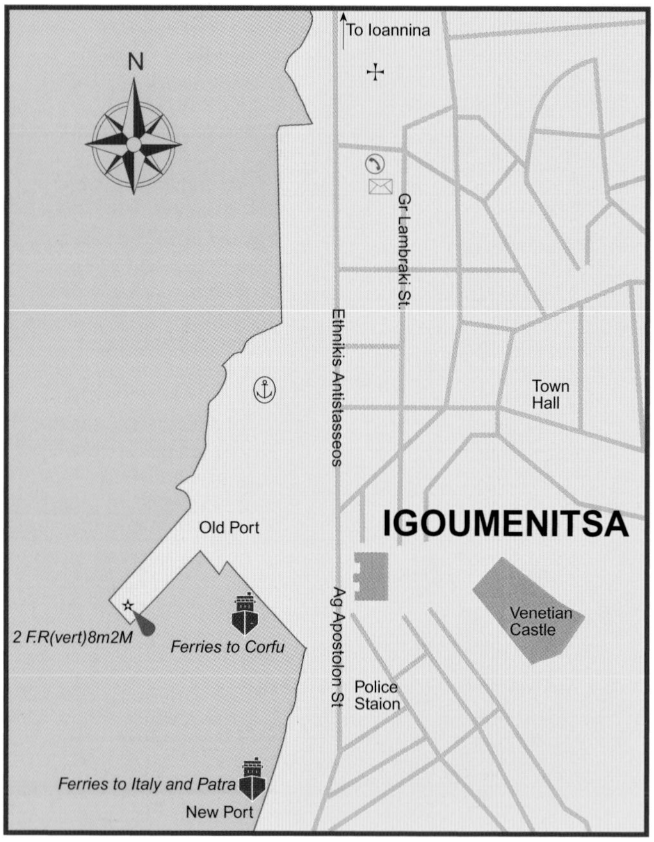

ANCHORING

It is possible for yachts to anchor in the north-west corner of Igoumenitsa Bay. Here depths are less than 5m and the holding and shelter from the prevailing winds are generally good. However, the constant movement of ferry traffic in and out of Igoumenitsa does generate some swell, which can prove uncomfortable. For a better alternative, try the anchorage in Valtou Bay to the east (see p72), which offers good all-round shelter.

Useful information – Igoumenitsa

FACILITIES

Fuel: There are fuel stations on the outskirts of town.
Ice: Try at the supermarkets.
Rubbish: Bins along the waterfront.
Yacht services/chandlery: The nearest boatyard is at Gouvia Marina, on Corfu, about 17nm to the west.
Telephone: Several phoneboxes along Ethnikis Antistasseos St, the main road past the Old Port. Mobile reception is good.

PROVISIONING

Grocery shops: Several supermarkets and mini-markets in Igoumenitsa, all within close proximity to the Old Port.
Bakery: On Gr Lambraki St, which runs parallel to Ethnikis Antistasseos St, the main road past the Old Port.
Butcher: On Gr Lambraki St.
Banks: Branches of Emporiki Bank (Tel: 26650 22403), Agricultural Bank of Greece (Tel: 22650 22310), Alpha Bank (Tel: 26650 27303) and National Bank of Greece (Tel: 26650 22304) are on Ethnikis Antistasseos St. All have ATMs and are usually open between 0900-1400, Monday-Friday.
Pharmacy: Numerous. One is on Ethnikis Antistasseos St, near Emporiki Bank.
Post: Post office on Gr Lambraki St. Open Monday-Friday, 0730-1400.

EATING OUT

You will find plenty of tavernas and cafes along Ethnikis Antistasseos St; but the main trade is people en route to somewhere else, so quality is average and the choice of cuisine minimal. Fast-food cafés abound.

ASHORE

While Igoumenitsa itself has little attraction, its transport links can take you to Corfu, Paxos or mainland Greece very easily. Ferries to Corfu and Paxos run daily in peak season and the crossing takes between 1½ and 2 hours.

Sights of interest in the area include the remains of a Turkish castle, which lie to the east of the Old Port. The castle was captured and destroyed in 1685 by the Venetian Frangisko Morozini.

Further afield, 62 miles (100km) to the north-west, is the town of Ioannina. The capital of Epirus, Ioannina is well known for its connection with the ruthless Ali Pasha. The Turkish tyrant, who was born in Albania in 1741, was known as the Lion of Ioannina after he was installed as the Pasha of Epirus in the town in 1788. Ali Pasha's reputation as a murderer made him a formidable leader, but under his rule, Ioannina flourished and became the most advanced and prosperous town in the Western Ottoman empire. However, his ambitious plans to become an independent ruler of Albania and part of Greece proved to be his downfall. When Sultan Mahmud II of Turkey realised the danger that Ali Pasha posed, he ordered him to be killed. A lengthy siege within the fortress at Ioannina ensued and Ali Pasha was eventually killed on the island of Nisi in 1822. His head was reputedly sent to Constantinople and put on display but his body was buried at Ioannina. Visitors to the island of Nisi, a 15-min boat trip from Ioannina, can visit the Monastery of Agios Pantelimion where Ali Pasha was killed.

Also of interest at Ioannina is the Archaeological Museum (Tel: 26510 33357), which includes artefacts from Dodona (see below); the Museum of Epiros' Folk Art (Tel: 26510 78062), for its examples of local crafts; the Popular Art Museum (Tel: 26510 26356) in the Aslan Pasha mosque; and the Byzantine Museum (Tel: 26510 25989), which has an impressive collection of icons from the 16th-19th centuries.

A couple of miles to the north of Ioannina, in the village of Perama, is the largest network of caves in Greece. The mile-long system, which lies at the foot of Mount Mitsikeli, was discovered during the Second World War by a fugitive hiding from German soldiers. The Perama Caves (Tel: 26510 81521) are open to the public daily. Between Igoumenitsa and Ioannina is the oldest Oracle in Greece. Thought to date back to 1,000BC, the Oracle at Dodona was focused on an ancient oak tree, around which were arranged a collection of bronze cauldrons. Prophecies were said to be divined by the rustling of the tree's leaves and the sounds the cauldrons made when they were chimed.

The most impressive site at Dodona is the theatre, which would have been used for drama and music performances in Ancient Greece. Up to 18,000 spectators could have been seated at the theatre, and when it was taken over by the Romans in the 1st century BC, it was used as a fighting arena. The theatre has since been restored and theatrical performances are still held here. Dodona (Tel: 26510 82287) is open to the public daily.

TRANSPORT

Car hire: Plenty of hire companies in Igoumenitsa: Europcar (Tel: 26650 23477) and Budget Car Rental (Tel: 26650 26226) are both on Ethnikis Antistasseos St. Avis (Tel: 26650 26944) is on Ag Apostolon, the road behind the New Port.
Taxis: Tel: 26650 22500; 23200; 23500. Usually plenty near the ports.
Bus: The Ktel bus station (Tel: 26650 22309) is on Kyprou St, which runs parallel to the northern end of Ethnikis Antistasis St, the road past the Old Port. Bus services to Athens (8 hours away) operate five times a day, Parga (1 hr) five times a day, Ioannina (2 hrs) nine times daily; Preveza (2½ hrs) twice daily.
Ferry: Several ferry companies operate out of Igoumenitsa: Minoan Lines (Tel: 21041 45700) runs domestic services between Patra, Corfu and Igoumenitsa six times a week in high season, three to four times a week low season (no sailings on Mondays). It also runs a service between Patra, Igoumenitsa and Ancona in Italy. Anek (contact Revis Travel Tourism, Tel: 26650 22104) runs daily services between Igoumenitsa and Ancona in Italy, and Igoumenitsa and Patra during the summer. Superfast Ferries (Tel: 26650 292009) runs daily services between Igoumenitsa, Bari and Brindisi in Italy. Ventouris Ferries (contact Barkabas Achilleas Travel, Tel: 26650 23911) runs between Bari, in Italy, and Igoumenitsa, via Corfu. Two departures a day in peak season; two departures a day, three times a week, low season. Kerkyra Lines (contact Nitsas Travel, Tel: 26650 28121) runs a car and passenger ferry service between Corfu, Igoumenitsa and Paxos, once a day, Monday-Friday.
Air travel: The nearest airport is on Corfu. Take a ferry to Corfu Town and then taxi to the airport. Aktio airport at Preveza is about 3 hrs away by car.

OTHER INFORMATION

Local Tel code: 26650.
Port authority: The Port Police office (Tel: 26650 22235/99400) is in the Old Port.
Tourist Information Centre: In the Customs House near the Old Port (Tel: 26650 22227).
Police: The Police Station (Tel: 26650 23228/29665) is on the main road through Igoumenitsa, halfway between the Old Port and the New Port.
Dentist: Nikol D Sarras (Tel: 26650 24250) on Ethnikis Antistasseos St, the main road behind the Old Port; Priovolou (Tel: 26650 21050) on Olympou St.
Hospital: Igoumenitsa medical centre (Tel: 26650 24420) is near the port.

Valtou Bay

Igoumenitsa Creek, Vatatsa

Anchorage waypoint: 39°31'.34N 20°10'.51E

Valtou Bay is a haven away from the commercial port of Igoumenitsa. The anchorage lies at the entrance to Igoumenitsa Bay to the east of the mouth of a branch of the Thiamis (or Kalamas) River. This area and the wetlands of the Kalamas Delta are a real find for wildlife enthusiasts. Here you will often see otters and a variety of important bird species, such as the little egret (*Egretta garzetta*), the glossy ibis (*Plegadis falcinellus*) and the pygmy cormorant (*Phalacrocorax pygmeus*). Wild horses are also a common sight in the area.

There are some good walks along the shore and, although there are no facilities within an easy distance, there is a seasonal taverna situated on the north side of the bay.

NAVIGATION

Charts: Admiralty 2406, 206, SC5771; Imray G11, G1; Hellenic Navy Hydrographic Service 0144, 010, 21

The approach from both the north and south is straightforward. However, the area is often heavy with ferry traffic, so keep a good look-out at all times.

The entrance to Valtou Bay lies between the mouth of the Thiamis River and Vatatsa Pt. Once inside the entrance, follow the channel around to the east, staying as close as possible to the southern side of the peninsula as the northern side of the bay is quite shallow. Two good anchorages can be found in inlets to the east.

ANCHORING

The first inlet, to starboard, has a fish farm in it, but further on you will reach a U-shaped anchorage that offers good, all-round shelter. Anchor in between 15-18m of water. A second anchorage lies in the next inlet, but Ligia Bay, at the far end, is very shallow and a fish farm blocks it from use.

Plataria Ormos Platarias

Plataria Bay: 39°27'.04N 20°16'.21E

Tucked in the far eastern corner of Plataria Bay, on the Greek mainland, is the small fishing village of Plataria. It's a quiet spot, away from the mêlée of Igoumenitsa and the popular resort of Sivota Mourtos. Recent improvements to the harbour have included extending the breakwater and installing new water and electricity points. However, the village is still far enough off the beaten track that it doesn't get too crowded, although it is becoming more popular with charter flotillas and Sailing Holidays turns its yachts around here weekly. As a base for exploration inland, Plataria is excellent and with a good choice of tavernas and facilities ashore, it is also a pleasant place to spend a few days.

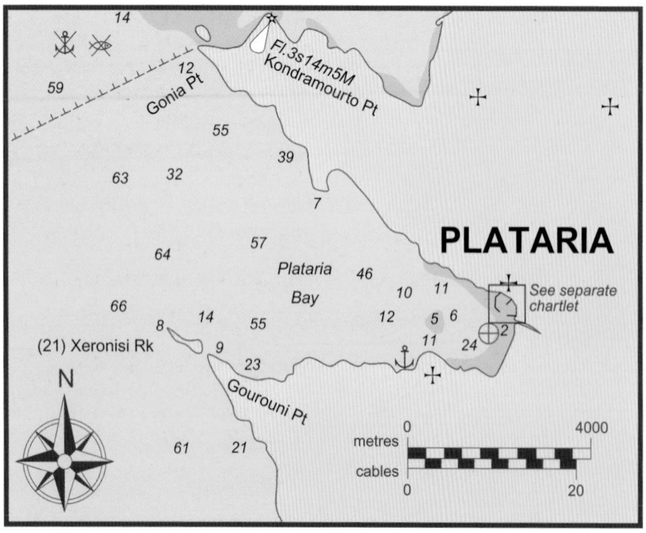

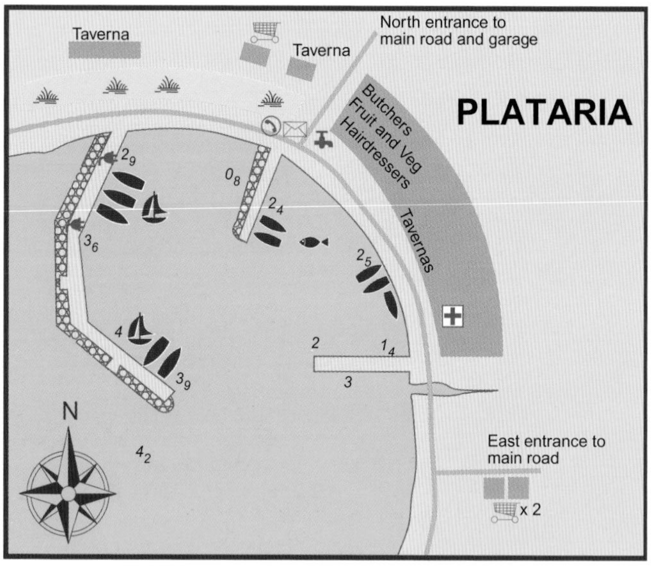

NAVIGATION

Charts: Admiralty 206, 188, SC5771; Imray G11, G1; Hellenic Navy Hydrographic Service 014, 010, 21

The approach to Plataria from all directions is straightforward and hazard free. The bay is situated halfway between Igoumenitsa and the islands off Sivota Mourtos, the peaks of which are identifiable from some distance. If approaching from the south, stay well clear of the islet of Hironisi, which lies off the southern headland of Plataria Bay, as a shoal extends off here. Once inside the entrance to Plataria Bay, travel east and you will see the village and harbour at the head of the bay.

It is very important to maintain a vigilant look-out in the channel between Corfu and the mainland as ferry traffic here is heavy, both night and day.

BERTHING

Most yachts berth on the inside edge of the harbour breakwater, stern- or bows-to. There is also room for boats to tie up on the quay at the north-east end of the harbour but it is quite shallow here so suitable for smaller boats only. The eastern quay, in front of the tavernas, is now deep enough to go side-to. The bollards along this quay, however, are quite far apart, so rope has been tied in between for ease of mooring. The harbour offers good shelter from the prevailing winds, although yachts berthed on the far end of the breakwater, near the harbour entrance, may feel more exposed in a southerly, when gusts tend to blow into the bay. The holding is good on mud.

Plataria is a quieter alternative to Igoumenitsa. It is also a suitable place to base yourself if you want to spend a couple of days exploring ashore

Useful information – Plataria

FACILITIES

Water: Taps on the quay, but they require the local waterman to unlock them. Ask at nearest taverna for his whereabouts.
Fuel: Shell petrol station on main road past Plataria.
Showers: Ask at the tavernas.
Ice: At the supermarkets.
Gas: At the supermarkets.
Shorepower: Metered power points on the quay.
Rubbish: Small rubbish bins along the waterfront. Larger bins on the breakwater.
Yacht services/chandlery: The nearest is at Gouvia Marina on Corfu (about 20nm to the north).
Telephone: Several phone boxes are situated along the waterfront. Mobile reception is good.

PROVISIONING

Grocery shops: Elena supermarket near the breakwater, next to Odysseia Taverna. Also a couple of supermarkets on the eastern road out of Plataria. Spiros fruit and veg, on the northern road, offers a good selection of fresh produce.
Bakery: Next to Taverna Irakilis, on the eastern side of the harbour.
Butcher: On north road out of Plataria (Tel: 26650 71094). A second one next to El Greco, on the eastern side of the harbour.
Banks: Nearest are in Igoumenitsa, 20 minutes' drive away.
Pharmacy: Next to Stefanos Taverna (Tel: 26650 71888).
Post: Post box on the quay. No post office.
Other shops: Hairdresser next to Spiros fruit and veg on north road out of Plataria. Also a couple of kiosks along the main street past the harbour.
Opening times: Most shops are open from 0900-1400 and 1800-2100 but times do vary depending on the season.

EATING OUT

Plataria offers a wide choice of taverna and snack bar. Odysseia Taverna, Restaurant Nik Giannoulis, El Greco, Taverna Heracles, Stefanos Taverna and Petros Grill & Pizzeria line the waterfront, and there are many more cafés and snack-bars in the village. The tavernas serve a range of good Greek cuisine and some of the locally caught fish is particularly worth trying.

ASHORE

Plataria is a good place to base yourself if you want to explore ashore. It's a safe harbour and reasonably secure. Igoumenitsa, 20 minutes' drive away, is an international ferry port and ideal if you need to change crew or want to travel to Corfu or Paxos. Head north-east of Plataria and you will find several sites of historic interest: the Oracle of Zeus at Dodona is about 1½ hours' drive away; the town of Ioannina, capital of Epirus, is about 2 hours away, and the Perama Caves, to the north of Ioannina, are also worth a visit (see p71).

TRANSPORT

Car hire: Cars can be hired in Igoumenitsa, 20 minutes' drive from Plataria.
Taxis: Taxi-rank near the harbour.
Bus: The Igoumenitsa bus travels past Plataria.
Ferry: Domestic and international ferries to Corfu, Paxos, Patra and Italy leave daily from Igoumenitsa (see p71).
Air travel: The nearest airport is on Corfu: take a ferry from Igoumenitsa to Corfu Town and then a taxi to the airport. Aktio airport at Preveza is about 3 hours away by car.

OTHER INFORMATION

Local Tel code: 26650.
Dentist: The nearest are in Igoumenitsa: Nikol D Sarras (Tel: 26650 24250); Priovolou (Tel: 26650 21050).
Hospital: There is a medical centre (Tel: 26650 24420) in Igoumenitsa.

Sivota Mourtos Syvota, Limini Mourtos, Mourto

Southern entrance to Sivota Mourtos: 39°23'.78N 20°13'.70E
Quay at Sivota Mourtos: 39°24'.44N 20°14'.35E
Sivota Harbour: 39°24'.47N 20°14'.22E

The village of Sivota Mourtos is said to get its name from the naval Battle of Sivota, which was fought in the waters off the southern tip of Corfu in 433BC. The eminent Athenian historian Thucydides (460-400BC) wrote extensively about the conflict, part of the Peloponnesian War between the Athenians and the Spartans, and the cluster of craggy islands he describes were thought to be those off Sivota Mourtos. The war was started after Corinth, one of the leading city states of Greece at the time and an ally of Athens, became embroiled in a bitter dispute with Corfu. The Corfiats were eventually defeated but so too was Athens and for the next 30 years Greece was dominated by Sparta.

Known as Volia and later Mourtos (a Turkish name which was adopted when the area was under Ottoman rule), the village was renamed Sivota in the late 1950s, but is now often referred to as Sivota Mourtos.

The harbour itself has seen a lot of redevelopment in recent years, with many of the quiet anchorages overlooked by large concrete hotels and apartments. It's a popular resort with both Greeks, Italians and, increasingly, charter flotillas; but while it can get very busy in high season, it still retains a charm and is worth a visit. The anchorages are fringed with crystal clear waters and tucked in among the islands you can find plenty of all-round shelter. Good road links also make Sivota Mourtos an attractive base from which to explore inland.

Sivota Mourtos is now a popular tourist resort

NAVIGATION

Charts: Admiralty 206, 188, 189, SC5771; Imray G11, G1; Hellenic Navy Hydrographic Service 010, 21

The peaks of Sivota's mini archipelago (Sivota [Mavro Oros] Ag Nikolaos and Megalo Mourtemeno) are distinctive and identifiable from all directions. A lighthouse (Fl(3)20s87m11M), which was built in 1884 by the French Company of Ottoman Lighthouses, stands on the north-west tip of Sivota Island, and a second beacon (Fl R 1.5s6m2M) is located on the end of the ferry quay in the harbour at Sivota Mourtos.

The approach to the islands from all directions is straightforward and through deep water but care must be taken when navigating among the islands. There are a number of shallows and sand bars to be aware of, so check your charts before you start exploring off piste. Do not travel between Sivota island and Ag Nikolaos as there is a reef in between and it is shallow.

If approaching from the south, you should also watch out for the reef which extends off the southern tip of Sivota island. To add a bit more spice to this approach, a sand bar extends right across the channel between the eastern shore of Ag Nikolaos island and the mainland.

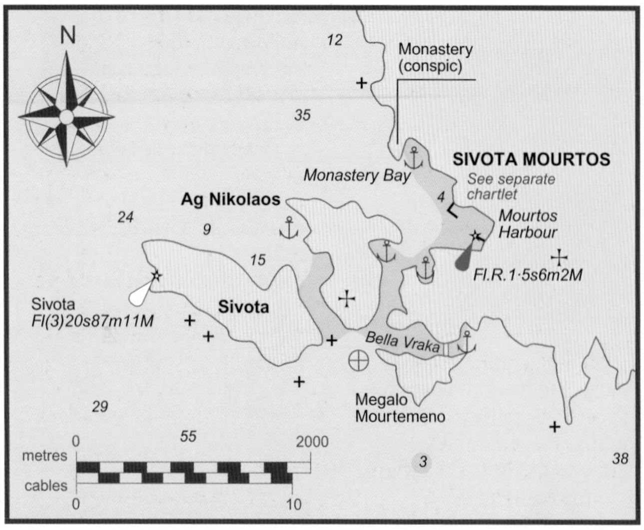

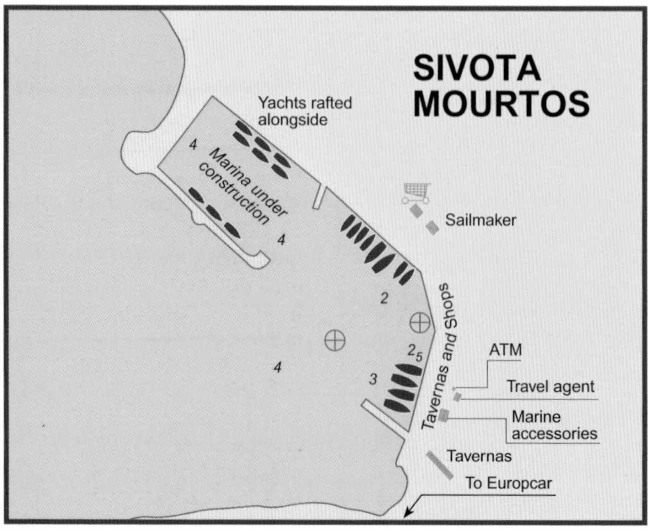

Islands protect Sivota Mourtos and provide several anchorages too

Depths over the sand bar are just over 2m, so yachts drawing less can get over it. However, you should proceed slowly and keep a close eye on your echosounder. A drying sand bar (Bella Vraka) joins Megalo Mourtemeno to the mainland and both sides of this are good anchorages.

With so much development in recent years, the waters surrounding Sivota Mourtos can get busy with dinghies, speedboats and swimmers, so be careful when navigating through the islands. A small ferry service runs from the town quay to the island of Paxos and fishing boats also use the harbour.

BERTHING

There are two places to berth at Sivota Mourtos: the town quay in front of the tavernas or the harbour at the western end of the quay.

Berthing on the town quay is either stern- or bows-to. It's a good place to tie up as you are close to everything, but can get noisy late at night in peak season due to its proximity to the tavernas and bars. The ferries that zip up and down this stretch of coast tend to create quite a swell towards the quay and it is a bit more exposed, particularly in a northwesterly.

The newly enlarged harbour is open for use, although in 2007 it was not finished and completion looks unlikely due to the depletion of EU funding. Some lazylines have already been installed to maximise the number of boats that can berth here, but these are predominantly for fishing boats and generally yachts still tend to moor stern- and bows-to along the harbour's inner perimeter, where port police turn up to collect the berthing fees (€3.94 for a 10m [33ft] yacht).

Shelter in the harbour is very good as the new breakwater has been built slightly further out than the old one and gives better protection. Be aware, however, of mooring outside the mole (on the SE side) as it is uncomfortable due to the swell from the ferry.

ANCHORING

Several anchorages near Sivota Mourtos. See p76-77.

Useful information – Sivota Mourtos

FACILITIES

Water: Taps outside tavernas on the quay, which are unlocked by Makis the waterman usually twice a day.
Fuel: Mini tanker does deliver. The nearest petrol station is on the outskirts of town, on the road to Parga.
Showers: Ask at the tavernas.
Ice: At the supermarkets.
Gas: At the supermarkets.
Shorepower: Power points on the quay.
Rubbish: Bins situated near the quayside.
Yacht services/chandlery: No but Marine Accessories (Tel: 26650 97515) and Giorgos Nasios (Tel: 26650 93052), on the quay, both sell fishing, diving and camping gear. A sailmaker is located on the NE quay.
Telephone: Several phone boxes on the quay. Mobile reception is good.

PROVISIONING

Grocery shops: Sivota Mourtos is a good place to victual. Several well-stocked supermarkets on the quayside and a couple more in the village itself.
Bakery: Soukas (Tel: 26650 93361) and Tsoumanis (Tel: 26650 93225) on a road off the quay.
Butcher: In the village.
Banks: Emporiki Bank ATM behind the quay. Isabella Tours (Tel: 26650 93317) nearby also does currency exchange.
Pharmacy: At the S side of the bay, near to where the fishing boats berth.
Post: Post box in the village.
Opening times: Opening times vary but shops are usually open between 0900-1400 and 1800-2100, depending on time of year. Tavernas open until late.

EATING OUT

The quay at Sivota Mourtos is packed with tavernas, cafés and bars and offers a good selection of cuisine. Tzimas (Pharos) Restaurant (Tel: 26650 93076), Filikas Restaurant (Tel: 26650 93345) and Trehandiri (Tel: 26650 93232) all serve superb fresh fish; George's Family Restaurant is exactly that and very welcoming and Restaurant Dionysos cooks a variety of Greek and international food. If you fancy Italian, Parasole – Italian Ristorante on the quayside and Mediterraneo Ristorante Italiano (Tel: 26650 93060), just before the port, serve excellent and very generously-portioned pizza and pasta dishes. Dotted among these are many more cafes and bars.

ASHORE

Sivota Mourtos is a lovely place to base yourself for

Useful information – Sivota Mourtos

a few days, and there are some delightful anchorages and beaches to explore. The village is just 30 mins drive from Igoumenitsa, so the transport links and the sites of interest near there are all within easy reach. The historic town of Parga (see p78) is a 30-minute drive south along the coast.

TRANSPORT

Car hire: Europcar (Tel: 26450 23581) is located behind the harbour. Sivota Travel (Tel: 26650 93439) and Top Travel International (Tel: 26650 97500) are on the main road just before the harbour and Isabella Tours (Tel: 26650 93317) is on the quay.
Taxis: Tel: 26650 93444; 26650 93229, or ask at the travel agents.
Bus: A limited but daily Ktel bus service operates between Igoumenitsa, Plataria, Sivota Mourtos and Parga. Timetable from travel agents.
Ferry: Domestic and international ferries to Corfu, Paxos, Patra and Italy leave daily from Igoumenitsa, 30 mins' drive from Sivota Mourtos (p69-71).
Air travel: The nearest airport is on Corfu; take a ferry from Igoumenitsa to Corfu Town and then a taxi to the airport. Aktio airport at Preveza is about two hours away by car.

OTHER INFORMATION

Local Tel code: 26650.
Tourist information: Tel: 26650 93197 (summer only).
Port authority: Tel: 26650 93100.
Police: Tel: 26650 93333.
Doctor: Dr Giogakas (Tel: 26650 24727).
Hospital: The nearest hospital is in Igoumenitsa (see p71 - Tel: 26650 24420).

Monastery Bay

Zeri, Zeres

Monastery Bay anchorage: 39°24'.74N 20°13'.96E

Charts: Admiralty 206, 188, 189, SC5771; Imray G11, G1; Hellenic Navy Hydrographic Service 010, 21

A ruined monastery (conspic) watches over this anchorage, which is situated to the north-west of Sivota Mourtos, in the northern entrance to the harbour. Today the bay is also easily identified by the brightly coloured slides of a water park that sit on the hillside above the beach. Anchor in 3-4m of water and take a line ashore.

There is a small, wooden jetty in the bay, where you can berth stern- or bows-to. It is owned by the Pericles Taverna, so if you tie up to it you are obliged to eat there. Keep clear of the buoyed area to the south-east of the anchorage as this is reserved for swimmers.

Passing ferries push swell into Monastery Bay, so you will need to put out plenty of fenders if rafted up and don't get too close to the jetty. Shelter from the wind within the bay, though, is generally good, although the holding isn't that reliable due to the seagrass/weed bottom.

A second taverna, Stavedo Restaurant (Tel: 26650 93544), lies above the beach, and the village of Sivota Moutos is just a 20-minute walk away.

The monastery that gives this bay its name is conspicuous from all directions

Ag Nikolaos Bay

Mid-channel: 39°24'.40N 20°13'.97E
Charts: Admiralty 206, 188, 189, SC5771; Imray G11, G1; Hellenic Navy Hydrographic Service 010, 21

Two anchorages lie to the east of Ag Nikolaos. The first, to the west of the main approach channel to Sivota Mourtos, and closest to the island, is small and a popular spot for over-wintering yachts. It's a shallow bay, with a reef running around its inner perimeter, so there is not much room and most yachts anchor in the entrance. Over-wintering yachts tend to raft up too, so there is often not much free-swinging space.

The second anchorage is on the opposite side of the channel, off the mainland. Again popular with over-wintering boats, this bay is larger and deeper but is overlooked by a packed hillside of villas. The holding is good here, and both anchorages offer reasonable all-round shelter.

Care should be taken when crossing the sand bar to the S of these anchorages as it gets shallow very quickly. The sand bar spans the channel, so proceed with caution at slow speed and watch your echosounder.

Many yachts raft up in Ag Nikolaos Bay long-term, so there is not a lot of room here to free-swing to your anchor

Bella Vraka

East side of Bella Vraka: 39°23'.96N 20°14'.33E
Charts: Admiralty 206, 188, 189, SC5771; Imray G11, G1; Hellenic Navy Hydrographic Service 010, 21

There are two anchorages on the north coast of Megalo Mourtemeno, one either side of the sand spit known as Bella Vraka. The anchorage on the western side of Bella Vraka is overlooked by a Neilson hotel and watersports centre, so is usually packed with dinghies, windsurfers and small speedboats. Visiting yachts are also discouraged from anchoring here.

The small bay to the east of the sand bar is much more pleasant, with plenty of room to swing to your anchor. On approach, watch out for rocks to the south of Mikro Mourtemeno and to the west of the islet of Sariki. Proceed with caution as it gets quite shallow here.

Either anchor in the middle of the bay or take a line ashore. The bottom is fairly weedy, so make sure your anchor is well dug in before leaving the boat unattended. The bay offers good shelter from the prevailing winds, but tends to feel exposed in a strong southerly or southwesterly. Dinghies from the Neilson club also use this area, so it does get busy at times. The village of Sivota Mourtos is a 20-minute walk away.

OTHER ANCHORAGES

Two calm weather anchorages can be found between the north-east coast of Sivota island and the north-west coast of Ag Nikolaos. They are totally exposed to the elements, however, and, with a nasty reef to the south in close proximity, they are not recommended in unsettled weather. Don't be tempted to pass through the gap between the southern ends of the islands either, as it is very shallow here and you will go aground.

The islands of Megalo Mourtemeno, Sivota and Ag Nikolaos off Sivota Mourtos

Karavostasi Bay Ormos Paramythias, Paramithia

Anchorage off Karavostasi beach: 39°20'.32N 20°17'.16E

Charts: Admiralty 206, 188, SC5771; Imray G11, G1; Hellenic Navy Hydrographic Service 010, 21

Lying between Sivota Mourtos and Parga on the Greek mainland is Karavostasi Bay, identifiable on approach by the three large hotels on the hillside above the beach. The sandy beach in Karavostasi Bay is one of the best along the Threspotia coastline and stretches for a third of a mile (500m). At the southern end of it is Elina or Dymokastro – ruins of a walled settlement dating back to 400BC. To the north is the pretty town of Perdika. The coastline in this area is particularly attractive and the area surrounding the Paramithioti River is a wildlife park.

For yachts, the anchorage off the beach is suitable only in calm weather, as it is exposed in all directions. Anchor in 4-6m of water on mud and sand.

Parga Ormos Valtou, Valtos

Valtou Bay: 39°16'.94N 20°23'.46E

The area surrounding Parga is a spectacular stretch of coastline. The town itself perches like an amphitheatre in the heart of a triple-horseshoed bay, clinging for protection from the Venetian castle that stands guard on the middle headland. It's a popular destination with yachtsmen: the town is steeped in history, yet it offers everything that the modern tourist could wish for. Narrow, winding streets are packed with shops selling everything from the tackiest of souvenirs to the most stylish pair of designer boots or jewellery. And for those that want to explore the town's cultural background, the fortress dates back to 1571.

Parga sits on the site of the ancient city of Toryni, which was destroyed in 168BC by the Roman general Emilios Pavlos. Parga itself is older than the town that stands there now. The original, fortified town was situated to the north, but in 1365AD its inhabitants relocated to its current site, which was easier to protect from attack.

Since then Parga has had a turbulent history, being passed from one occupying state to the next, although today little evidence of the town's troubled past remains. The surrounding countryside is fertile and the area boasts a higher percentage of olive trees than in the rest of Epirus. In the evenings, the waterfront to the east of the castle comes alive with bustling cafes, bars and market stalls, and in the height of summer the streets are chock-a-block with visitors of all nationalities.

For the yachtsman, Parga offers an attractive destination for an overnight stay. In a northwesterly, the harbour provides reasonable protection and the holding is generally good. In a southerly, however, it is exposed as the wind funnels in to the bay, and Sivota Mourtos or Plataria, to the north, offer better protection.

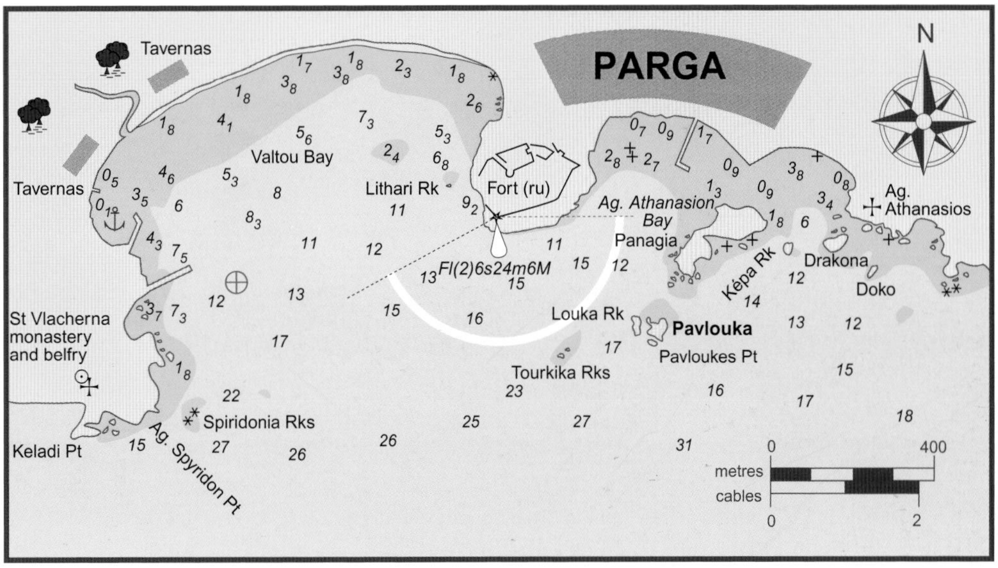

NAVIGATION

Charts: Admiralty 2402, 206, 189, SC5771; Imray G11, G1; Hellenic Navy Hydrographic Service 026, 21

On approach from the south, head north-west up the coast from Preveza. Parga and its outlying small island of Panagia are easily identifiable from the south. Panagia has a white chapel on the middle of it. From the north, head south past Sivota Mourtos. The conspicuous belfry of the Monastery of St Vlacherna on Keladi Pt, the westernmost headland of Parga Bay, indicates the town's location. From Gaios, on Paxos, steer 064° for about 10nm.

Once off Parga Bay, you will see a small harbour to the west of the castle. If heading towards it, stay well clear of the shore off Ag Spyridon Pt as there are a couple of rocky patches that are hard to spot around this headland. Keep an eye out for swimmers and water-skiers in the bay, particularly along the beach close to the harbour.

It is possible to go into Ag Athanasiou Bay, to the east of the castle, but watch out for the rocks around Panagia island and the islet of Pavlouka. There is a particularly nasty reef just to the east of this (Vroi Tourkika). Another nasty one to steer clear of is to the south-east of Doko, at the eastern end of Parga Bay. Do not be tempted to try and circumnavigate Panagia either. A reef connects the island to the mainland and the depth over it is less than 1m.

An approach to Parga should only be made in settled weather and not at night.

The harbour in Valtou Bay, Parga. The breakwater has been extended to provide better protection

BERTHING

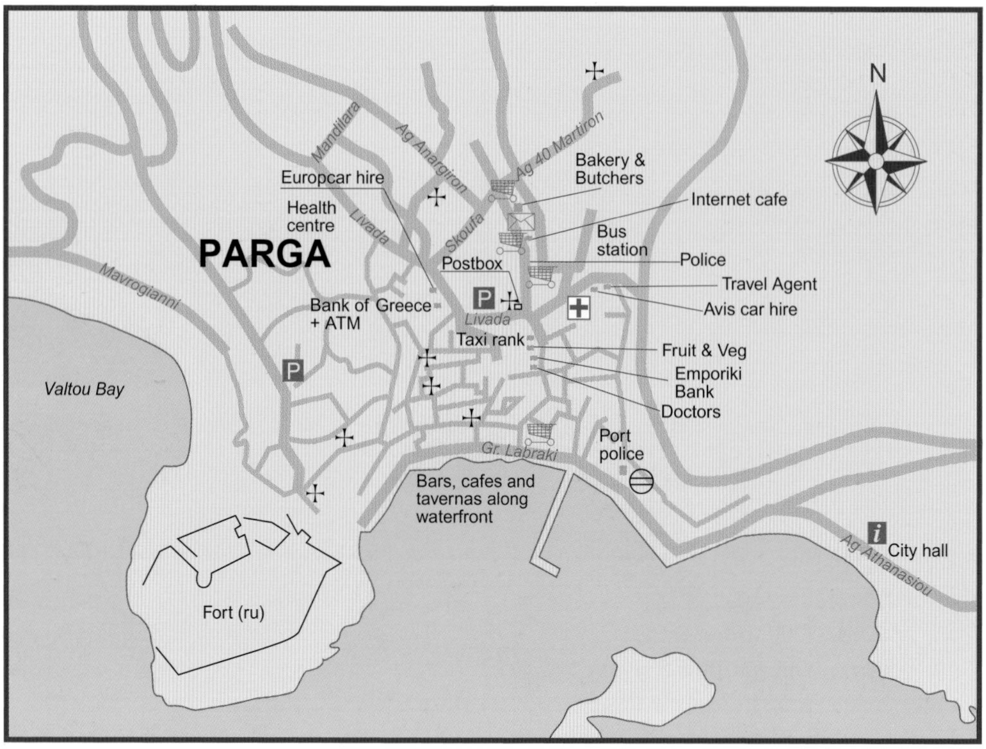

Over the last couple of years improvements have been made to the harbour and the rocky breakwater to the south has been extended to give better protection. It is still quite a rough harbour, though, with a lot of rubble at the base of both sides of the inner mole. If you want to berth here, avoid damaging your rudder by going bows-to, and keep well off the quay.

Most of the charter flotillas that come in here use a unique berthing technique called Parga parking. If there is no room in the harbour, they run their boats bows-to up the soft sand, drop a kedge anchor over the stern, to prevent being blown on to the beach, and then take bow lines ashore to various rocks and trees. The shoreline shelves very steeply at the western side of the bay, so even though it is shallow enough to wade ashore from the bow of your boat, your keel will remain in deep water. But please remember, Parga parking should only be attempted in settled weather.

Occasionally you will find room on the quay in Ag Athanasiou Bay, to the east of the castle, but this tends to be out of season only. During peak season, the quay is usually packed with day-trip boats, ferries and fishing boats. While this quay is protected from the

Parga is a beautiful town that clings for protection from the Venetian castle. It's a vibrant place to visit, particularly at night

prevailing northwesterlies, a lot of swell does get pushed into the bay and it can get quite lumpy here. When this happens, the port police will ask any yacht tied up alongside the quay or anchored nearby to move.

If you intend to leave your boat for the evening, make sure you lock it up and take any valuables with you. There have been break-ins on yachts in Valtou Bay.

In summer, a local boat operates as a water taxi between the harbour and the town quay during the day (€2 one way).

ANCHORING

If the harbour is full, you can anchor just outside it in Valtou Bay. Either free swing to your anchor off the end of the mole or drop your hook to the south of the breakwaters and take a line back to them. This bay is a popular watersports arena, so stay tucked in as close to the western shore as you can. Watch out for the reefs off Ag Spyridon Pt, though.

It is also possible to anchor to the east of Panagia island, in 3-4m on mud and weed. However, the anchorage isn't suitable for an overnight stop as it is not very well protected and northwesterlies push swell into the bay. There are lots of islets and rocks in the vicinity, so take great care when entering the bay. A sand bar runs to the north of Panagia, therefore you can only pass to the south of the island.

The town of Parga sits in the heart of a triple-horseshoed bay

Useful information – Parga

FACILITIES

Water: Taps at the end of the quay and on the beach. No hoses, though, so you will need to use jerrycans.
Fuel: A mini-tanker will deliver. BP fuel station on the road out of Parga.
Showers: Ask at the tavernas.
Ice: Ask at the tavernas.
Laundry: On the road out of Parga.
Gas: At supermarkets in Parga.
Shorepower: There are a couple of connections at the southern end of the harbour in Valtou Bay.
Rubbish: Bins situated near the quayside.
Yacht services/chandlery: Chandlers in Parga.
Telephone: Lots of card phones in Parga. Phone cards available from kiosks and newsagents. Mobile reception good.
Internet: Flamingo Internet Cafe, near the post office, north of the main crossroads. Terra Internet Cafe is near the ferry quay.

PROVISIONING

Grocery shops: A couple of mini-markets behind Valtou Beach, plus several well-stocked supermarkets in Parga itself, near the post office, a 20-minute walk away. Most open from 0800-2200. There are also several fruit and veg shops in the town centre.
Bakery: Numerous bakeries in the centre of Parga. One near the post office.
Butcher: Several, one near the post office.
Banks: National Bank of Greece (Tel: 26840 31525) on Livada Street, to the west of the main crossroads, near Europcar. Emporiki Bank (Tel: 26840 32145) and ATM on side street to the south of the main crossroads. The Agricultural Bank of Greece (Tel: 26840 31208) also has a branch near the centre. The banks are usually open between 0900-1400, Monday-Thursday, and 0900-1300 on Fridays. The majority of the travel agents in Parga will also change travellers' cheques.
Pharmacy: Three in the centre of Parga: Thanasis Kolonis, Dimitrios Lenas and Mantrios Siatonnis (Tel: 26840 31510). All three open 0900-2130 Monday-Saturday and 0900-1400 on Sundays and speak good English. They also run an emergency service rota, so you can always get help from the pharmacies. Details of availability is usually posted on the shop doors.
Post: Post box opposite the Ote building on the main crossroads in Parga. The post office is located further up the street next to the police station. It is open 0800-1300, Monday-Friday.

EATING OUT

There really is no shortage of choice for eating out in Parga. If you feel like treating yourself, try Restaurant Castello (Tel: 26840 31239), next to Hotel Acropol in the old part of town. It serves a cross-section of international dishes and the quality is superb. The cafe-restaurant Kastro (Tel: 26840 31119), at the entrance to the castle, is also good. Its sister bar, The Blue Bar (Tel: 26840 32067), on the waterfront near the ferry quay, has over 100 cocktails on its menu, and they are worth sampling. Glafkos Bar also serves good cocktails. Kineziko (Tel: 26840 32458), near the bus station, is Parga's only Chinese restaurant. Open from 1800, it also does takeaways.

Alternatively, wander along the waterfront; it's packed with cafés, bars and restaurants, and the view over the water and Panagias island is gorgeous, particularly at sunset.

There are also several tavernas behind the beach in Valtou Bay.

ASHORE

There is plenty to do in

Useful information – Parga

and around Parga. Once you've exhausted yourself with shopping and been refreshed with a drink on the waterfront, take a walk up to the Venetian castle. It dates back to 1571, and is the third to have been built there, the previous two having been destroyed by enemy attack. Open to the public daily (free), it commands stunning views of Parga and Valtou Bay.

The islet of Panagia in Ag Athanasiou Bay is also worth a row. There are two churches on the island, one dedicated to the Virgin Mary and a second, smaller one to Ag Nikolaos (St Nicholas); and on the south side of the island are ruins of a French fortress built in 1808.

There's a good walk to the Monastery of St Vlacherna, on the headland to the west of Parga.

George's Watersports on the beach in Valtou Bay offers parasailing and other activities in the summer.

TRANSPORT

Car hire: Europcar (Tel: 26840 32777) is on Livada Street, to the west of the main crossroads, next to Hotel Paradise. Open seven days a week, 0830-1300 & 1730-2100. Avis (Tel: 26840 32732) is on the same street. Open seven days a week, 0800-2100. Hertz (Tel: 26840 32788) is on Ferreou Street, National Car Rental (26840 31700) is on Alex Baba Street. Open seven days a week, 0800-2100. Several travel agents in the centre of Parga will organise car hire for you.
Taxis: Taxi rank outside the Ote building, on the main crosswords in Parga. Tel: 26840 32855.
Bus: The Ktel bus station (Tel: 26840 31218) is on the road out of Parga, to the east of the main crossroads. Four services a day, Monday-Friday, to Igoumenitsa. The journey time is 1½ hours. Also five services a day, Monday-Friday, to Preveza, and three services a day to Athens. The journey takes 3 hours.
Ferry: The ferry to Paxos leaves from the tripper boat quay in Ag Athanasiou Bay. Igoumenitsa to the north is the nearest major ferry terminal (1½ hours by car). Domestic and international ferries to Corfu, Paxos, Patra and Italy leave daily from the port.
Air travel: The nearest airport is Aktio at Preveza, a 1½-hour drive from Parga. International and domestic flights fly from there several times a week.

OTHER INFORMATION

Local Tel code: 26840.
Port authority: Tel: 26840 31227; VHF Ch12 & 18
Tourist Information: Tourist office (Tel: 26840 32107) in the Town Hall, near the ferry quay.
Police: Tel: 26840 31222.
Doctor: Three in Parga: Dr George Christou (Tel: 26840 3100); Dr George Stelios (Tel: 26840 32402) and Dr Spyros Padiotis (Tel: 26840 32450).
Dentist: Two private practices: Yiannis Niras (Tel: 26840 31888) and Dora Georgiadou (Tel: 26840 31613). Open 0900-1300 Monday-Friday.
Hospital: A medical centre on the outskirts to Parga (Tel: 26840 31233). The nearest hospital is in Preveza (Tel: 26820 22871), a 1½-hour drive to the south.

Ag Kiriaki Bay Ay Kyriakis

Ag Kiriaki Bay: 39°16'.64N 20°26'.36E
Charts: Admiralty 206, 188, SC5771; Imray G11, G1; Hellenic Navy Hydrographic Service 21

Ag Kiriaki Bay, situated just over 2nm east of Parga, is a medium-sized anchorage offering good shelter from the prevailing northwesterlies. Yachts can anchor in 3-8m of water on a mixture of mud and sand.

The best place is in the north-west corner of the bay, but you should move elsewhere if anything with a southerly in it starts to blow, as the anchorage is exposed in this direction.

A couple of tavernas near the beach are only open peak season.

Ag Ioannou Bay

Ay Ioannou

Ag Ioannou Bay: 39°16'.51N 20°28'.18E
Charts: Admiralty 206, 188, SC5771; Imray G11, G1; Hellenic Navy Hydrographic Service 026, 21

One mile to the east of Ag Kiriaki Bay is Ag Ioannou Bay. It is the larger of the two bays and the steep-sided hills on both sides offer slightly more shelter. However, it is still exposed to the south and not recommended for a night-time stop.

On entering the bay, you may notice a strange whirlpool off the western headland. This is a fresh water spring, which bubbles continuously. Anchor off either of the beaches in the north-west corner of the bay in less than 8m.

If hopping between the two coves, watch out for rocks along the shoreline.

Ag Ioannou Bay is exposed in a southerly

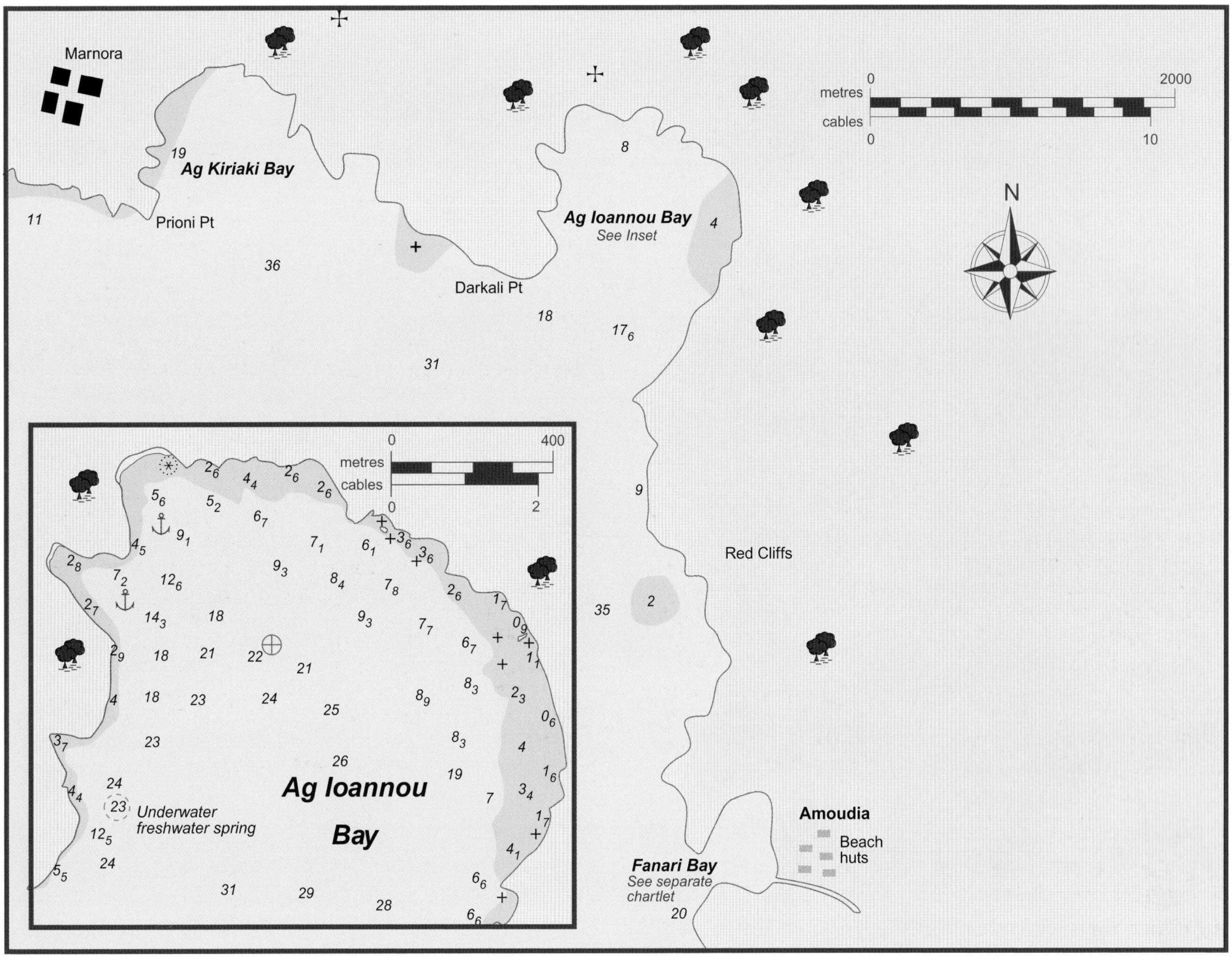

Fanari Bay

Approach to Fanari Bay: 39°14'.14N 20°28'.26E

Fanari Bay, 4½nm south-east of Parga, is a charming and totally unexpected place. With its wide sandy beach, the bay itself is not so unusual, but the river that flows out of its southern side comes as something of a surprise. When you arrive at Fanari and look towards the village of Amoudia, you don't expect to see a river bordered by tall reeds and low-lying marshes, and a quayside with boats berthed alongside. It's such a contrast from the bay, which is protected by high craggy rocks and fringed by beach. Yet it's a particularly lovely spot. Amoudia is fairly spread out, but tavernas line the riverside and even in the height of the summer it has a wonderfully tranquil atmosphere.

As an anchorage, the bay offers reasonable shelter, although is uncomfortable if there is any swell and only suitable for settled conditions. However, shallow-draught vessels will find more shelter berthed alongside the quay in the River Acheron, with the added advantage of being near the centre of the village.

Fanari Bay, the River Acheron and the village of Amoudia

NAVIGATION

Charts: Admiralty 206, 189, SC5771; Imray G11, G1; Hellenic Navy Hydrographic Service 026, 21

From Parga, follow the coast south for about 4½nm, past the bays of Ag Kiriaki and Ag Ioannou (see p82). From off the entrance to Preveza, head north for about 23nm. Fanari Bay lies just to the south of some red cliffs and the entrance is flanked by rocky headlands.

Inside you will see the River Acheron to starboard, its mouth protected by a rocky mole. Fanari Bay itself opens up to port. Depths at the bay's entrance range between 5-8m but closer in, about level with the mole, decrease to less than 5m. The area immediately off the beach shelves to as little as 0.5m. In the summer, it is buoyed off for swimmers.

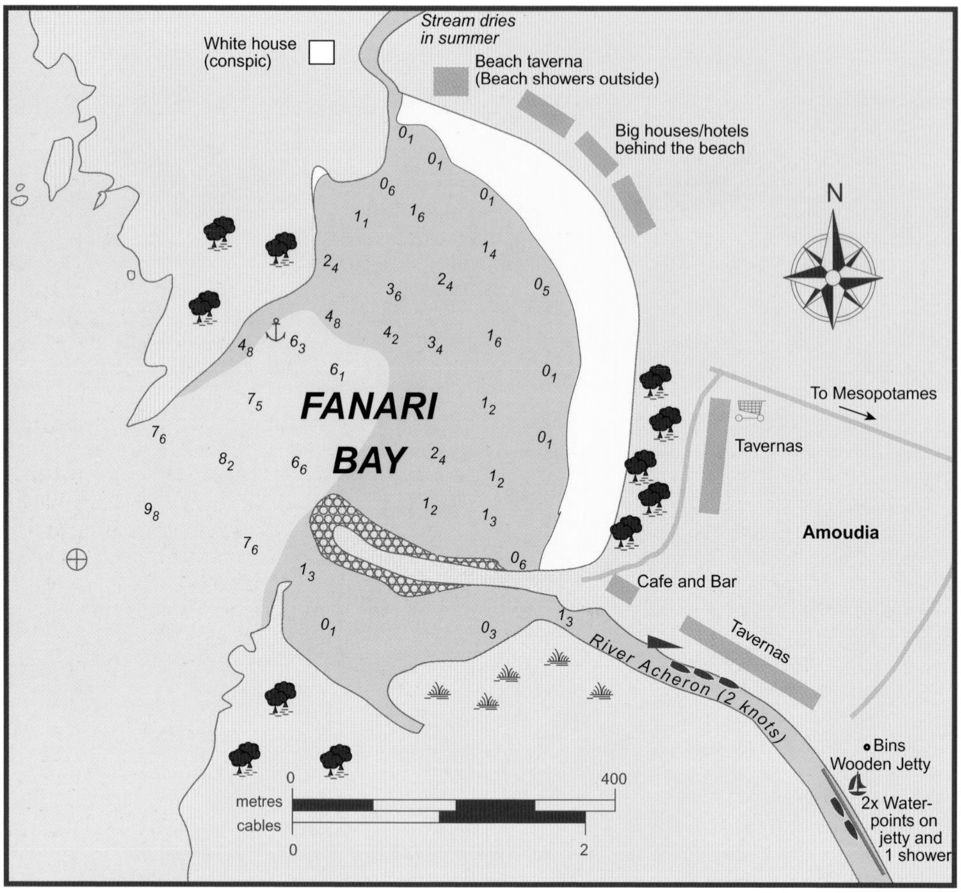

For boats drawing less than 2m it is possible to navigate part of the River Acheron up to the quay. However, there is only about 1.6m at the entrance to the river and although depths increase to just over 2m inside the mole, you should proceed very slowly in case of grounding.

There is a slight current on the river and a speed restriction of 2 knots. Do not attempt an approach in poor conditions.

BERTHING

If you are shallow enough to use the river, berth side-to along the town quay or the wooden jetty to the north of the tavernas, facing upstream. The quay is used by local fishing and tripper boats, and if it is full you should raft alongside another boat. Do not raft more than two boats deep, as the river is not very wide and you will block the channel. The holding on mud and sand is reasonable.

ANCHORING

In settled weather, you can anchor in the western corner of Fanari Bay. Shelter is good from all directions, apart from the south-west. However, swell does get pushed into the bay when the wind is in the north and the anchorage can be quite rolly at times. Stay fairly close to the western headland as the rest of the bay is shallow. Anchor in 6-7m of water on mud and sand.

Useful information – Fanari Bay

FACILITIES

Water: Several taps on the wooden jetty beyond the tavernas.
Fuel: Take a taxi to the nearest petrol station.
Ice: Ask at the tavernas.
Gas: Ask at the mini-markets.
Rubbish: Bins situated behind the quay.
Yacht repairs/services: The nearest are at Preveza. See p87.
Telephone: Several phone boxes along the quay and the road past the beach. Phonecards are sold at the mini-markets and mobile reception is good.

PROVISIONING

Grocery shops: Several mini-markets. One in the side-street next to Hotel Glaros.
Bakery: The mini-markets stock a limited supply of fresh bread.
Butcher: Mini-markets have limited stocks.
Banks: The nearest is in Parga, 30 mins away by car.
Pharmacy: Plenty in Parga.
Post: Post box opposite To Symposio behind the beach. The postal service on the mainland is good.

EATING OUT

The riverfront at Amoudia is lined with a good selection of tavernas. O Pataras (Tel: 26840 41185), halfway along the quay, is popular with the locals and serves delicious traditional cuisine at reasonable prices. Paralia and Akrogiali on the quay have an extensive menu and Roxani, on a side street off the quay, serves very good fish, as does Thomas Restaurant on the road past the beach.

Useful information – Fanari Bay

ASHORE

The River Acheron is well known for its connection with the mythical River Styx. It is said to be a branch of one of the five rivers of the underworld across which Charon ferried dead souls to Hades.

Further upstream, at the confluence of the rivers Kokitos and Acheron, is a marshy plain which was once Lake Acherousia, thought to be the gates to the underworld. It is here, in Homer's *The Odyssey*, that Odysseus enters the underworld to meet Teiresias, the fallen hero from the Battle of Troy. On a rocky hill overlooking the now receded lake stands the Necromanteion of Acheron. This sanctuary, built on a cave, is considered to be one of the most important of its kind in Greece and its location, so close to the River Acheron and the gates to the underworld, is particularly significant.

In ancient times, the sanctuary was visited by pilgrims seeking advice from the spirits of the dead. Following a series of rituals involving fasting, isolation and the unknowing consumption of hallucinogenic drugs, they were lowered into an antechamber to 'communicate' with the spirits. Their sensations were so heightened by the drugs and the lack of food that the sanctuary's priests were able to trick them into believing that they had, indeed, entered the underworld.

The Necromanteion of Acheron

Visitors to the site today can wander through the various rooms of the sanctuary and descend into a rather eerie vaulted chamber, where it is thought the pilgrims 'communed' with the dead. It is open seven days a week, 0830-1500, and admission is free.

Several tripper boats from Fanari run excursions from the quay up the River Acheron during the season.

TRANSPORT

Car hire: Acheron Rent a Car (Tel: 26840 23105). Parga is a 30-minute taxi ride away and Europcar, Avis, Hertz and National Car Rental all have branches there. See p82.
Taxis: Ask at the tavernas.
Bus: Buses to Igoumenitsa, Preveza and Athens leave from Parga's bus station (see p82).
Ferry: A service to Paxos runs from Parga. Igoumenitsa, two hours to the north (see page 71), is a major terminal with daily services to Corfu, Patra and Italy.
Air travel: The nearest airport is Aktio at Preveza, an hour away by road. Charter and domestic flights leave several times a week.

OTHER INFORMATION

Local Tel code: 26840.
Doctor: No, nearest in Parga, a 30-minute taxi ride away. See p82.
Dentist: No, nearest in Parga.
Hospital: Preveza hospital is an hour's taxi ride away. Parga has a medical centre (Tel: 26840 31233).

Shallow-draught yachts can berth alongside on the River Acheron

Ligia Lygia

Off Ligia harbour:
39°08'.84N 20°33'.76E

Anyone considering visiting Ligia should have a good look at the weather before making an approach. The harbour's position on the coast of mainland Greece, halfway between Parga and Preveza, is exposed and the rock-strewn coastline immediately surrounding its entrance is a serious

The coastline surrounding Ligia is rock-strewn and any approach should be made with extreme caution

hazard if conditions are poor. Yet the small fishing harbour is a pleasant retreat from the business of Parga or Preveza and, if the weather is settled, Ligia is a good overnight stop on an otherwise unfriendly stretch of coastline.

NAVIGATION

Charts: Admiralty 203, 206, 189, SC5771; Imray G11, G1; Hellenic Navy Hydrographic Service 21

From Preveza, follow the coast north-west for about 16nm. Ligia lies to the north of Kastrosykia Pt. If approaching from this direction, beware the reefs to the east and north of the headland, as depths over them decrease quite considerably.

On approach from Parga, follow the coast south for approximately 12nm. Stay well offshore and keep an eye on your depth as there are several uncharted rocks close inshore, within a couple of miles of Ligia.

The main danger on approach to Ligia is immediately off the harbour, as rocks lie to the south-east and west of the narrow entrance channel and off the breakwater. There is no room for error when making this approach so only go into Ligia in settled weather and in daylight.

Taking care to keep a good look out for rocks below the water, approach the entrance from the south-west. The channel is shallow (3m), so proceed at a slow speed. At the entrance, watch out for shallows at the western end of the breakwater, before turning to port and heading into the harbour.

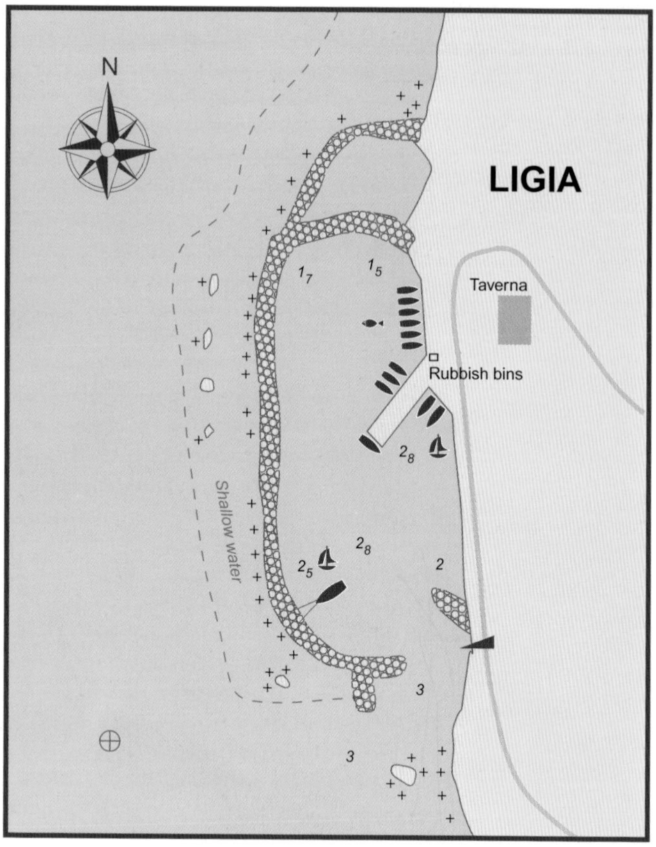

BERTHING

Berth stern- or bows-to off the breakwater, opposite the quay. Yachts can berth off or alongside the quay but it is usually full of fishing boats, which have priority. Swell often gets pushed into the harbour if the wind is in the south; it can get quite roly, so keep a fair distance off the breakwater and put plenty of fenders out if lying alongside. The holding is good on mud and sand.

ANCHORING

There are no safe anchorages near Ligia.

Useful information – Ligia

FACILITIES

Fuel: Take a taxi to nearby petrol station.
Showers: Ask at the taverna behind the harbour.
Rubbish: Rubbish bins on the quay.
Yacht services/chandlery: Nearest facilities are in Preveza, about 15nm to the south. See p88.
Telephone: Phone box outside To Shaloma taverna.

PROVISIONING

Grocery shops: Mini-market in the village, above the harbour.

EATING OUT

To Shaloma (Tel: 26820 56240) is a very good taverna just behind the harbour at Ligia. Popular with the locals, it has a lovely bustling atmosphere and serves a wide selection of Greek cuisine. Worth a visit as the food is delicious, particularly the fish.

ASHORE

The beaches to the north and south of the harbour are a popular spot with surfers and a pleasant place to stretch your legs if you intend to stay in Ligia for a day or two.

TRANSPORT

Car hire: Nearest in Preveza, see p91.
Taxis: Ask at the taverna.
Bus: There's an erratic bus service between Ligia and Preveza. Your best option therefore is to take a taxi to Preveza (20 minutes), from where buses to Athens, Parga and Thessaloniki leave daily.
Ferry: The nearest ferry terminal is at Igoumenitsa (2½ hours away by car). Ferries to Italy, Corfu, Paxos and Patra leave daily. Ferries to Meganisi, Kefalonia and Ithaca leave from Nidri and Vasiliki on Lefkada.
Air travel: The nearest airport is at Aktio, immediately outside Preveza. Domestic and international services fly in and out several times a week.

OTHER INFORMATION

Local Tel code: 26820.
Port authority: Ligia comes under the auspices of Parga's Port Authority (Tel: 26840 31227).
Doctor: The nearest is in Preveza, 15nm to the south. See p91.
Dentist: The nearest is in Preveza.
Hospital: Preveza hospital (Tel: 26820 22871) is 20 minutes away by car. Parga, to the north, also has a medical centre (Tel: 26840 31233).
Yacht repairs/services: There are three boatyards and various chandlers and sailmakers in Preveza. See p89 for more details.

Preveza

Preveza channel: 38°56'.34N 20°44'.76E
Off Preveza: 38°57'.39N 20°45'.46E

Preveza stands at the end of a long, narrow peninsula at the entrance to the Amvrakikos Gulf. A cosmopolitan place, with its myriad back streets and bustling waterfront, it has a vibrant feel and can be a lovely spot to spend a couple of days. As a cruising destination, it has lots to offer. The town is superb for provisions, it has a good, well protected marina and the three boatyards at Aktio, on the peninsula to the south, offer a comprehensive range of services. It's a good base if you want to explore inland, or if you are en route to the north or south Ionian, and

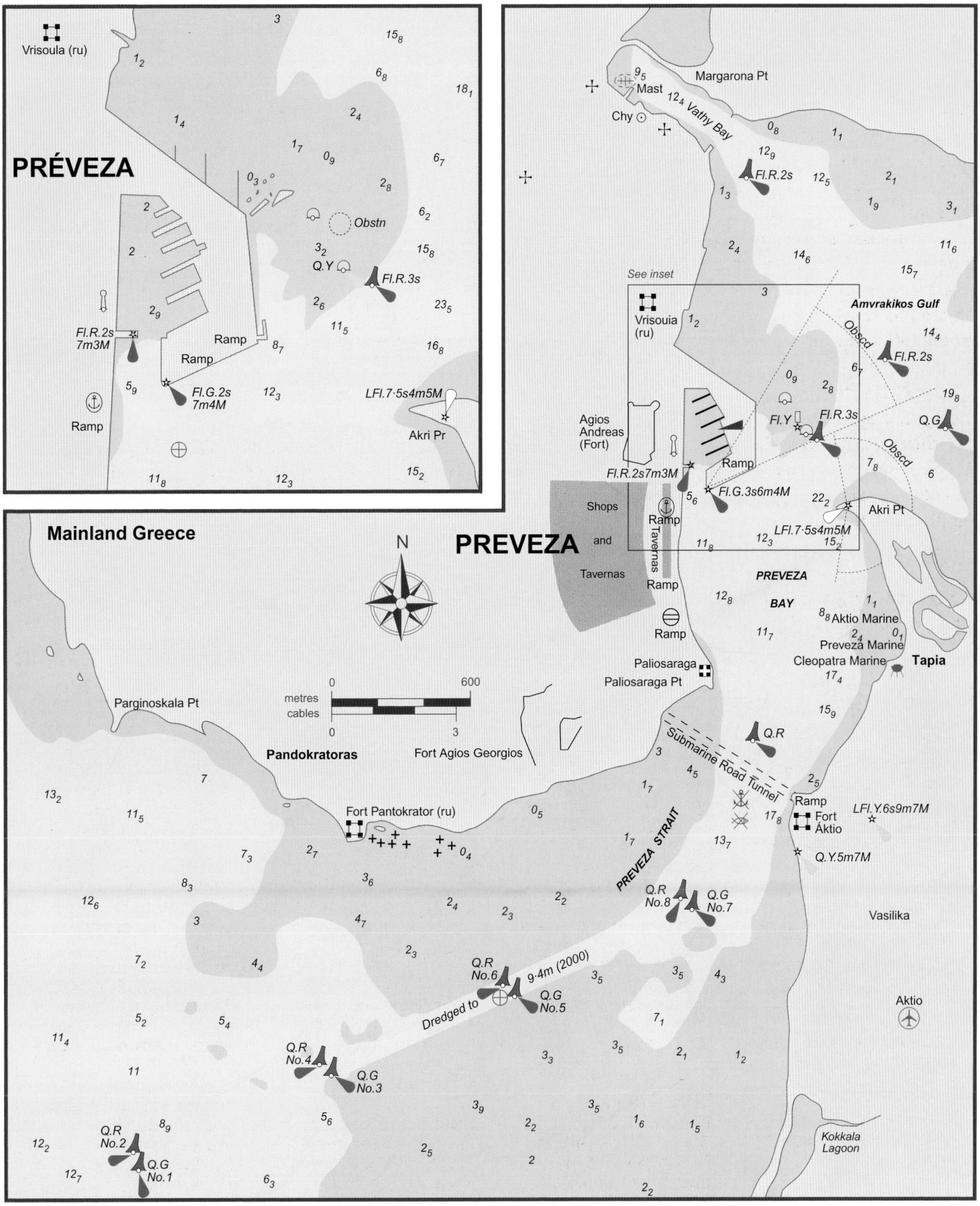

it is also convenient for Preveza airport at Aktio.

Preveza is one of the biggest towns along this stretch of coast and for centuries has been one of the most significant, playing a vital role in trade between Greece and Italy.

NAVIGATION

Charts: Admiralty 2405, 203, 189, SC5771; Imray G1, G11, G12; Hellenic Navy Hydrographic Service 213/1, 21

Approaching from the north, follow the coast south until you see the fort of Pandokratoras. This marks the northern headland of the entrance. From the Lefkada Canal, head due north for about 5nm until the markers at the entrance of the Preveza channel become visible. Keep well off the coast as there are several reefs and shoal patches off Ag Nikolaos Bay and to the east and south-east of Skilla Pt. Planes landing and taking off from the airport at Aktio also mark the channel's position.

It is very important not to stray outside the buoys in the Preveza channel as shallows extend both sides of it. A pair of leading lights on the Aktio peninsula (Q Y 5m7M & LFl Y 6s9m7M) should bear 066° once you are in the channel. Depths at the entrance are about 15m but soon drop to 10m once inside. In a northwesterly, it can be difficult to pick out the buoys against the mainland, so stay in deep water until you are sure you have identified them. There are four pairs of markers (Q R & Q G) in the channel, before you reach Fort Aktio on the Aktio Peninsula, and Fort Ag Georgios on the Preveza side, followed by a single port-hand mark just beyond. From there, the channel widens and you can head north towards the town quay and marina or north-east and on to the Amvrakikos Gulf.

A submerged road tunnel between the two peninsulas has almost eliminated ferry traffic on this stretch, but cargo ships use the commercial dock at Preveza, so maintain a good look-out at all times. A slight current of between 1.5 and 3 knots in the channel increases or decreases depending on wind direction. However, it is not usually a problem once level with the forts.

The marina at Preveza. You'll find good protection from the prevailing winds here and it is within easy walking distance of the town

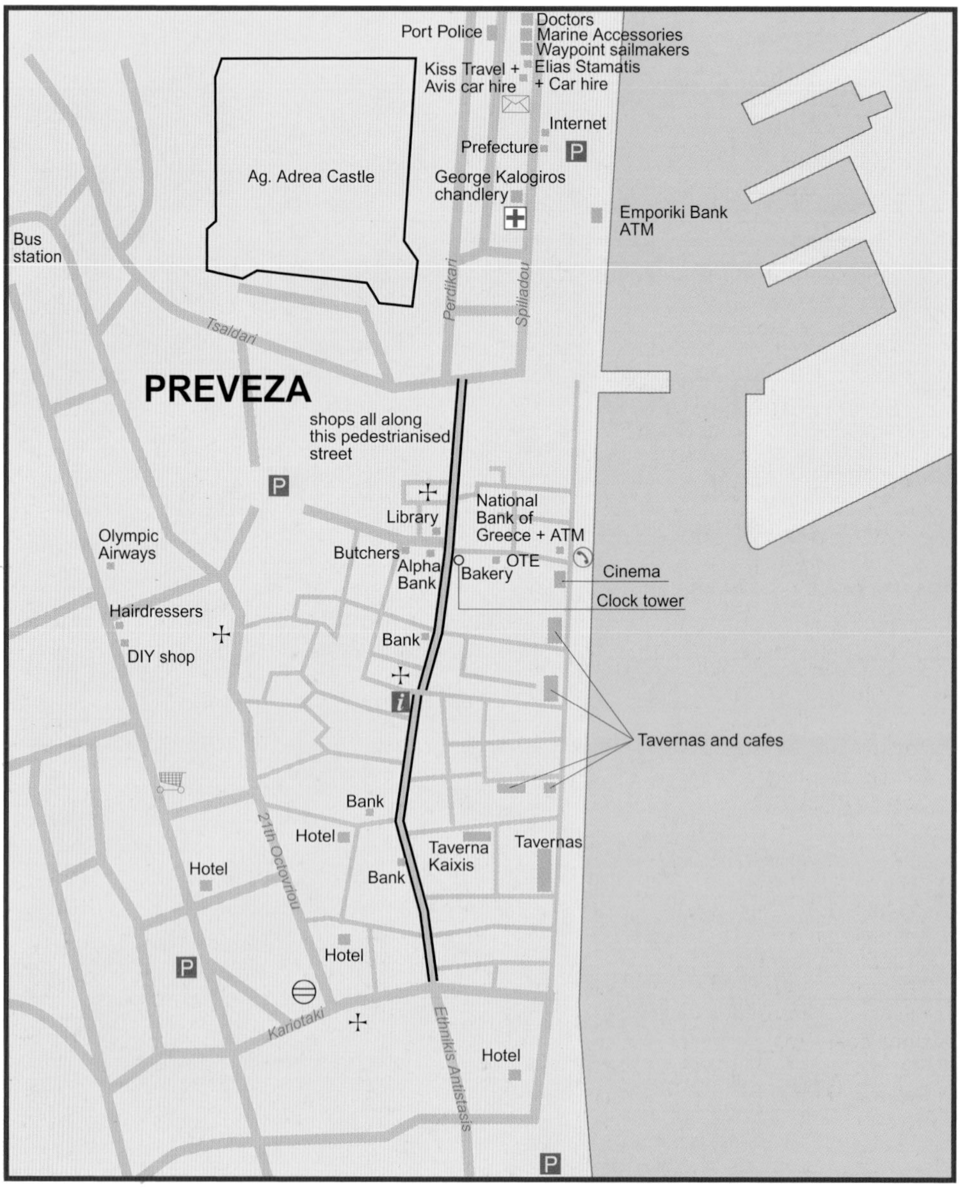

BERTHING

At Preveza you can berth either in the marina or on the town quay.

Preveza Marina: The marina offers the best protection, particularly if you tie up on the pontoons, although the berths in the north-east corner are slightly more exposed to the south. Tie up alongside the finger pontoons or berth stern- or bows-to the quayside. The marina gets busy in the summer, so expect to raft up two or three boats deep. Lazylines are fitted in the marina.

Town Quay: This area to the south of the marina is also popular in summer. Berth side- or stern-to wherever there is space. It can get quite rolly at times as a swell is often pushed on to the town quay, even if there is no wind, so make sure you have plenty of fenders out. The quay is protected from the prevailing northwesterlies but is slightly more exposed in a southerly. It can also be very noisy, especially to the south where all the shops and restaurants are situated. There must be a sewage outlet somewhere near the town quay too, because it can really stink here.

ANCHORING

The nearest anchorage to Preveza is in Vathi Bay, to the north of the marina. From off the town, follow the main Preveza channel until it splits, just beyond Aktio Pt. The channel to Vathi Bay leads off to the north and another to the Amvrakikos Gulf leads to the east. Follow the channel to the north, leaving the red buoys (Fl R 2s) to port. Anchor at the head of the bay, beyond the boatyard, in 6m or less. The holding on mud is good and the shelter all round.

Vathi Bay lies to the north of Preveza and is a good anchorage

Useful information – Preveza

FACILITIES

Water: Taps at the marina and along the quay.
Fuel: A mini fuel tanker will deliver (Tel: 26820 26751), or take a taxi to petrol stations in town.
Ice: Ask at the tavernas.
Gas: Marine Accessories (Tel: 26820 25327) on Spiliadou Street, opposite the marina. Supermarkets in Preveza may also stock gas bottles.
Rubbish: Bins on the main road past the quay, plus on the town quay.
Yacht services/chandlery: Several chandlers on Spiliadou Street: Marine Accessories (Tel: 26820 25327) sells chandlery and Yanmar diesel services; Waypoint (Tel: 26820 26636) is a sailmaker and rigging specialist, and George Kalogiros (Tel: 26820 29197) sells a range of marine accessories and fishing gear. Several charter holiday and yacht management offices near the marina.

Opposite Preveza, at Aktio, at the entrance to the Amvrakikos Gulf, are three boatyards: Cleopatra Marina, Aktio Marine and Preveza Marine.
Cleopatra Marina (Tel: 26820 23015/ VHF Ch67/www.cleopatra-marina.gr) has room for 300 boats ashore. The yard has a 50-ton travel hoist and can provide electrical, mechanical and general boatwork services, as well as facilities for osmosis treatment and steel work. Water and electricity available to all boats. A sailmaker, chandlery, laundry, toilets and showers, weather report and tool hire service also available, plus 24-hour surveillance.

Preveza Marine 'Ionion' (Tel: 26820 24305) next door, has a 65-ton travel hoist, a 20-ton hydraulic lift and capacity for 350 boats. Services include metred mains electricity and water, plus shower, toilet, laundry and internet facilities as well as a daily mini-van to Preveza, which is free of charge. The yard offers general engineering, maintenance and painting, plus a chandler on site. Prices (approximate, including VAT): hauling and launching, €22 per metre; storage (for first seven months) per metre per month, €16.66; storage (after seven months – max 1 year), €8.33; pressure wash, €3.80. Storage prices include use of a steel cradle and the water, shower and toilet facilities. Some surcharges apply to multihulls, boats of ferro-

If you don't mind the smell, you can berth stern-to off the town quay

Lazylines in Preveza Marina make berthing relatively easy

Useful information – Preveza

cement construction, boats over 16m LOA, and owners living aboard between November and March, inclusive. A return launch service runs three times a day to Preveza. Times from Reception.

Aktio Marine (Tel: 26820 61305/ VHF Ch67), next to Preveza Marine, has facilities for laying up ashore, maintenance and repair and sandblasting. It also has a sailmaker, chandler and mini-market on site. The biggest boat it can handle is 65ft (20m) LOA by 26ft (8m) on the beam and 70 tons. Prices (approximate, including VAT): hauling out and launching (including pressure wash), €27.37 per metre; storage for first seven months, €17.70 per metre per month. Multihulls and boats over 15m by special arrangement only. Aktio Marine also organises transport to and from the airport and Preveza town. Shower and toilet facilities.

Telephone: Several on Spiliadou Street, opposite the marina. Others in the centre of Preveza. Phonecards available from the kiosk near Port Police. Mobile reception is good.

Internet: Internet cafe next to DEH (the electricity board) on Spiliadou Street. Prices: €2.40 per hour, 0.20¢ for B&W printed sheet, 0.40¢ for colour print-out. There's another internet cafe (€2.50 per hour) next to News Stand on a side street just off the waterfront, to the left of Prevere Restaurant.

PROVISIONING

There are three main shopping areas in Preveza, joined by a series of small side streets and alleys. El Venizelou Street, behind the town quay, consists mainly of tavernas, cafés and bars. Eth Antistasis is a pedestrianised road packed with clothes, jewellery and shoe shops, plus the odd grocery store. Irinis Street, the main road towards Parga and Igoumenitsa, is more commercial, with bigger, general purpose shops, supermarkets and business units. In the side roads you'll find gift shops, hairdressers, haberdashers, kitchen shops and cafés.

Grocery shops: An Atlantik supermarket can be found at the southern end of Irinis Street. Bigger supermarkets, such as Champion and Lidl, are on the outskirts of town, to the north of the marina.

Bakery: Several in the centre of Preveza. One near the Ote office, another south of the clock tower.

Butcher: Several in the centre of Preveza; the nearest to the town quay is on a side street north of the clock tower.

Banks: Emporiki ATM in the car park behind the marina. Piraeus Bank (Tel: 26820 22454), Eurobank and National Bank of Greece (Tel: 26820 22365) on El Venizelou Street, behind the town quay. Alpha Bank (Tel: 26820 27652) on Theofanou Street, N of the clock tower. Branches of the Agricultural Bank of Greece (Tel: 26820 22203) and Bank of Cyprus (Tel: 26820 89700) are on Irinis St.

Pharmacy: Several in the centre of Preveza. The nearest to the marina is on Spiliadou Street, near Nicopoli Hella Tourism & Travel. Another pharmacy opposite the library, at the N end of Eth Antistasis Street.

Post: Post Office and post boxes on Spiliadou Street. Open 0730-1400, Mon-Fri. Stamps also sold at souvenir shops; the postal service on the mainland is good.

EATING OUT

There are lots of tavernas, cafes and bars along the waterfront (El Venizelou St), and many more in the side streets. Taverna Kaixis (Tel: 26820 24866) on Parthenagogiou St is

Three boatyards at Aktio on the opposite side of the Preveza Channel offer a comprehensive range of services for cruising yachtsmen

Useful information – Preveza

very good, as is Taverna Symposio and the seafood restaurant next door on the waterfront.

ASHORE

Preveza is one of the few towns in the area with a cinema. Behind the town quay, near the National Bank of Greece, it shows Greek and international films (Tel: 26820 25784).

If you've hired a car there are several interesting places within easy driving distance.

The Rodia Wetland Centre (Tel: 26830 41219) at Strongili has an information centre and organises bird-watching trips.

Just to the north of Preveza are the ruins of the ancient city of Nikopoli, dating from 31BC. Following his victory in the Battle of Actium against Mark Antony and Cleopatra (see p8 & p9), Octavian built it on the site of his army's pre-battle encampment. Under Roman rule, Nikopoli flourished and was an important centre of trade but, after various invasions, it was finally destroyed by the Bulgarians in the 9th century AD. The city was subsequently abandoned and Preveza was built nearby as a replacement.

Less than an hour's drive away from Preveza is the town of Arta (see p94), which became the province's capital following the destruction of Nikopoli, and is famous for its Turkish bridge over the Arachthos River.

TRANSPORT

Car hire: Several hire firms on Spiliadou Street, opposite the marina: Europ Rent a Car (Tel: 26820 23003) is at the travel agents Elias Stamatis. Open Monday-Thursday, 0900-1400; Friday, 0900-2000; Saturday, 0900-2000. Avis car hire at Kiss Travel (Tel: 26820 23753) is open daily, 0800-2100.
Taxis: Tel: 26820 23750; 22887; 28470; 28030; 22213; 22478.
Bus: The bus station (Tel: 26820 22213) is just off Irinis Street, the main road through Preveza, near the junction with Bizaniou Street. Regular services to: Athens (five times a day between 0910-1930, journey time 4½ hours); Igoumenitsa (twice a day, 2½ hours) and Thessaloniki (once daily, 8 hours), plus smaller towns in between.
Ferry: Igoumenitsa, 2½ hrs away by car, is a major ferry terminal. Daily services to Corfu, Paxos, Patra and Italy (see p71). Ferries to Kefalonia, Ithaca and Meganisi operate from Nidri and Vasiliki on Lefkada (see p118 & p130).
Air travel: Aktio airport at Preveza (Tel: 26820 22355) is 10 minutes by car from the marina, through the toll tunnel (€3 each way). International and domestic services fly from Preveza several times a week. Kiss Travel (Tel: 26820 23753), Elias Stamatis (Tel: 26820 23003) and Nicopoli Hella Tourist & Travel (Tel: 26820 24810), on Spiliadou Street, for travel information and booking facilities, and Olympic Airways (Tel: 26820 28340) has an office on Irinis Street. Open Monday to Friday, 0800-1530.

OTHER INFORMATION

Local Tel code: 26820.
Tourist Office: Contact on Tel: 26820 21078.
Port authority: The Port Police (Tel: 26820 22226) is above Café Match Ball on Spiliadou St, opposite the marina, and entered from the back of the building. Some English spoken.
Police: Tel: 26820 28090, 22226; Tourist Police: Tel: 26820 89566.
Doctor: Cristos I Matsiras (Tel: 26821 24905), above La Fontana Restaurant & Pizza, on Spiliadou Street. There's another practice (Tel: 26820 23371) on Parthenagogiou Street, a side street off El Venizelou Street (open 0900-1300 & 1800-2000), and a third near the library (Tel: 26820 26378, open 0800-1400 & 1800-2000). Two more can be found on Irinis Street.
Dentist: Dimitros Agathos (Tel: 26820 60272) is situated on Bizaniou St, parallel to Irinis Street, the main road through Preveza. Alternatively, dentist Dimitra Tsoutsi (Tel: 26820 27585) is on Kontou Street, to the west of Irinis Street.
Hospital: Preveza Hospital (Tel: 26820 22871/46200) is to the north of the harbour. English is spoken.

The clock tower in the centre of Preveza. The town is a good place to visit if you need to provision, and transport links are excellent

The Amvrakikos Gulf

Gulf of Amvrakia, Ambracian Gulf

The Amvrakikos Gulf reminded the politician John Cam Hobhouse of Loch Lomond when he visited the area with Lord Byron in 1810, and indeed the 154 square mile (400km^2) gulf is more like a lake than part of the sea. It joins the Ionian Sea via a narrow channel that bisects Preveza and Aktio on the Epirus coast and to a large extent is unexplored by cruising boats. Yachts visiting Preveza tend to bypass the Amvrakikos Gulf in favour of the myriad islands to the north or south, but it's an idyllic spot with superb sailing in unadulterated waters.

Among the most productive coastal areas in Greece, the gulf is also home to one of Europe's most significant wetlands. Its northern coast is a patchwork of shallow lagoons, swamps and salt marshes into which the estuaries of two rivers flow, while to the east and south it is bordered by high mountains. According to the Hellenic Ornithological Society, in winter the Amvrakikos Gulf attracts the largest concentration of waterbirds in Greece, with over 250,000 birds from 250 species using the wetlands either to overwinter or to pause on their journey south. It's an important breeding ground for the Dalmation pelican, little bittern, stone curlew and glossy ibis, and bottlenose dolphins are occasionally seen in the brackish waters that take a year to recirculate.

As well as its complex ecosystem, the gulf also has some pretty harbours. Vonitsa is delightful and very Greek and, while Menidi and Amfilochia can be crowded with tourists at peak season, the harbour at Koronisia is remote and unspoilt though too shallow for most yachts. The sailing is good and you'll usually get the waters to yourself, which is rare in much of the Ionian. Care should be taken around the northern shore of the gulf though; sandbanks and shallows extend some way offshore, particularly around the river entrances. However, with a keen eye on your echosounder you can explore some isolated anchorages quite safely.

The Amvrakikos Gulf is a beautiful place to explore

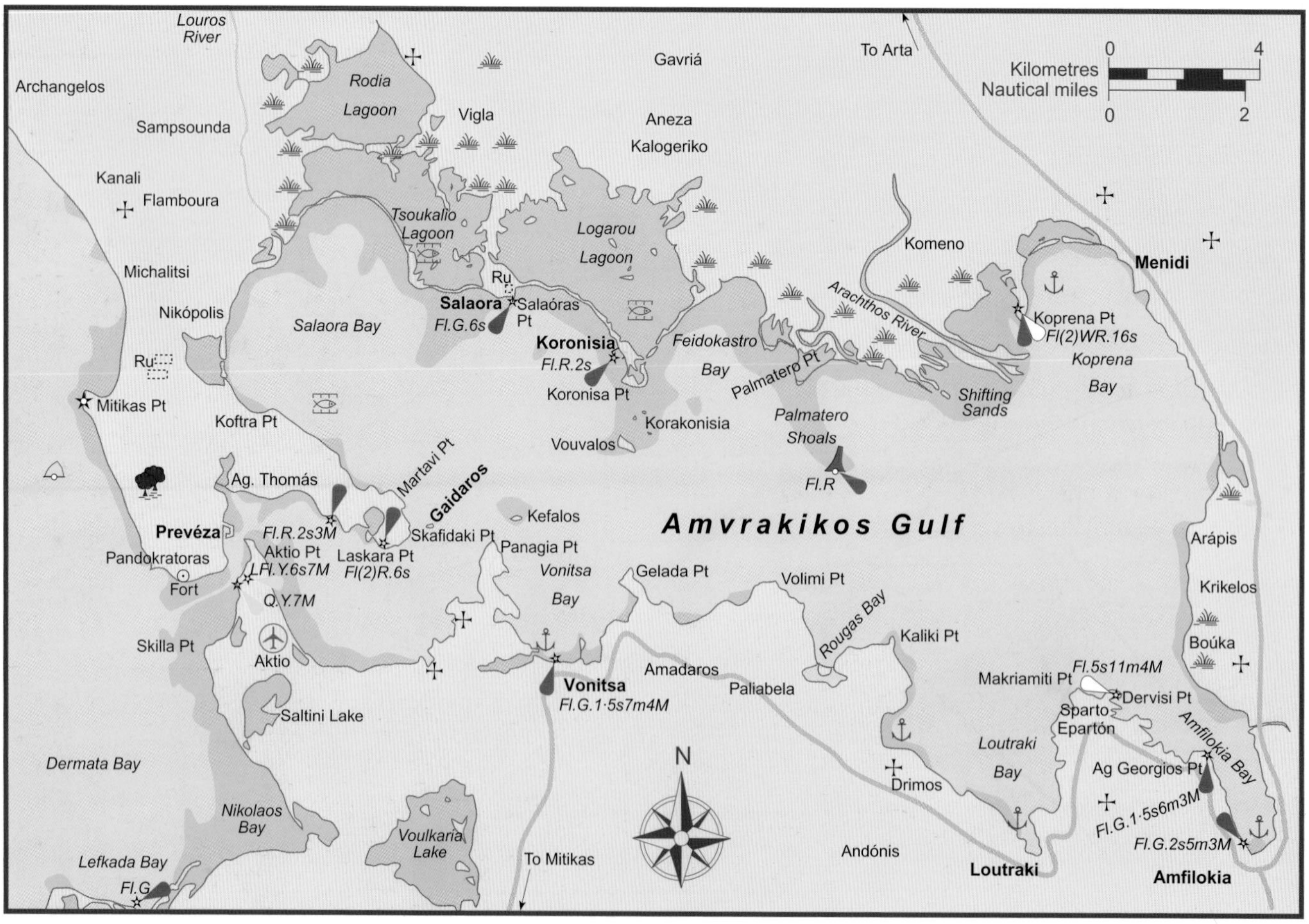

Salaora Ormos Salaoras

Off the harbour at Salaora:
39°01'.64N 20°52'.26E

The English poet Lord Byron and his politician friend John Cam Hobhouse visited Salaora in 1810, en route to meet the evil Turkish tyrant Ali Pasha at Ioannina. Byron commented at the time that there was little more than a single house at Salaora and the same can be said today. The Salaora Information Centre (Tel: 26810 74772) and a couple of run-down buildings are the only signs of life on this part of the causeway between Arta and Koronisia. The harbour was once the port of Arta but now a single mole off the quayside is the only evidence of this.

NAVIGATION

Charts: Admiralty 203, 189, SC5771; Imray G11, G12, G1; Hellenic Navy Hydrographic Service 026, 2131. 21

Enter the Amvrakikos Gulf via the Preveza channel, taking care to avoid the shallows that extend on either side. Once past Preveza, the channel sweeps round to the east and then to the south before heading north-east and opening up into the gulf. There is a small islet (Gaidaros) close to Skafidaki Pt, which you should leave to port, but the main channel into the gulf is through deep water. Salaora is identified by a large, conspicuous mountain, which sits to the north of the harbour. It can be seen from some distance, so it is not difficult to find.

If approaching from the eastern end of the Amvrakikos Gulf, take care to avoid the Palmatero Shoals, which extend S of Palmatero Pt. The southern edge of the shoals is marked by a light (Fl R). There are also several islets off Koronisia to watch out for. If coming from Amfilochia or Loutraki, keep an eye out for If Alexandrou, which lies 1½nm to the east-north-east of Kaliki Pt.

BERTHING

The only place for a yacht to berth at Salaora is stern- or bows-to off the eastern side of the small mole. However, you are advised to anchor well off and take a line ashore by dinghy as there is a lot of debris at the mole's base. Several rusty iron loops in the side of the mole give you something to tie to but as Salaora harbour offers no shelter and there are no facilities ashore, lying to your anchor in Salaora Bay may be a better option. Depths around the mole are between 2-3m.

Salaora is backed by a distinctive mountain

ANCHORING

There are a couple of anchorages in Salaora Bay, to the west of the harbour, which offer reasonable shelter. Tuck yourself up in the north-west corner of the bay and anchor in 4-6m of water. The bottom is a mixture of sand and mud and the holding is generally good.

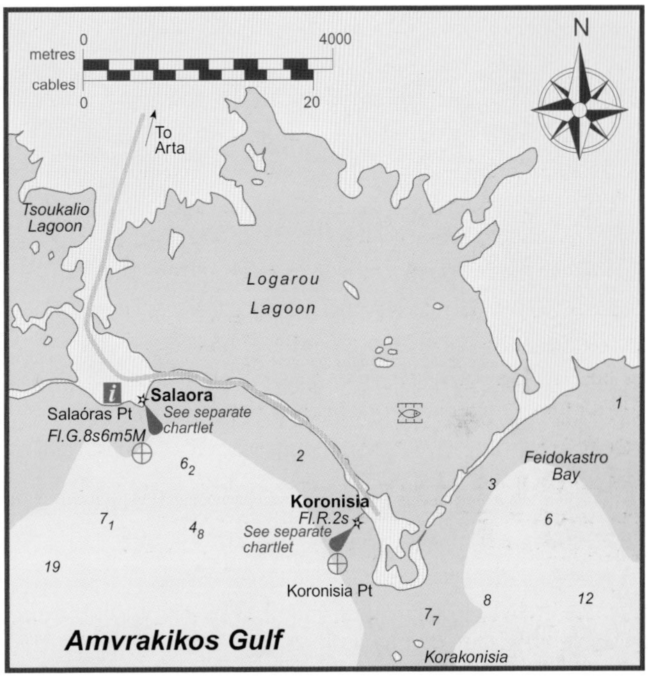

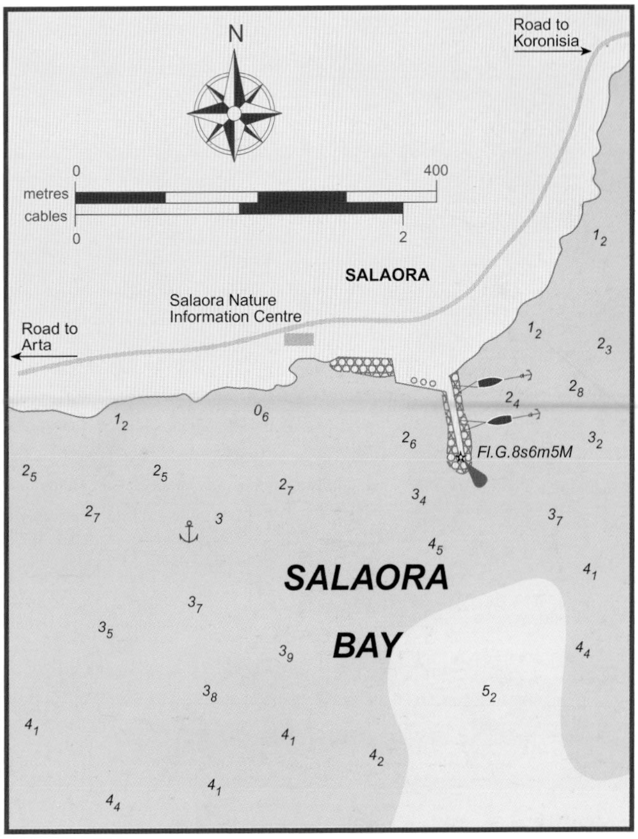

Arta

The small agricultural town of Arta is a useful place to visit for provisions or a day out. Situated inland of the north shore of the Amvrakikos Gulf, it is the second largest town in Epirus and one of the most attractive in the province. Dominated by Turkish and Byzantine architecture, it is a good alternative to Preveza, with plenty of amenities, including banks, supermarkets, grocery shops, a post office, car hire firms and bus services to Athens, Mesolongi, Preveza and Lefkada.

Arta stands on the site of the ancient city of Ambracia, which was ruled by Phyrhus, King of Epirus in the 2nd century BC. It was destroyed by the Romans in 189BC and fell into decline after it was replaced as provincial capital by the new city of Nikopoli to the west. The town that stands there now was later rebuilt and has seen Venetian and French occupation, although from 1449 to 1881 it was ruled principally by the Turks.

Sites of interest include the famed packhorse bridge on the western side of the town. Spanning the Arachthos River, the arched stone bridge is shrouded in folklore. It is said that its builder, annoyed that its foundations were continually being washed away, took the advice of a talking bird and buried his wife alive in the central pier. The advice worked and the foundations held, but it is said that she now haunts the bridge.

Arta's bridge is legendary and said to be haunted

Koronisia Korakonisa

Off Koronisia harbour: 39°00'.74N 20°54'.56E

Koronisia lies to the east of Salaora at the end of a long causeway that stretches out into the Amvrakikos Gulf. It's a quiet little harbour, tucked in to the south of a small hillock on which the village is built. Part of the surrounding marshland and mudflats is slowly being reclaimed and fishing huts have been built at various points along the causeway.

The harbour at Koronisia is small and the entrance particularly shallow, which renders it inaccessible for many yachts. For those that can get in here, though, good all-round shelter is provided. In recent years, money has been spent on smartening up the waterfront, but facilities such as water should not be relied upon as, in 2007, not all the taps in the harbour were working.

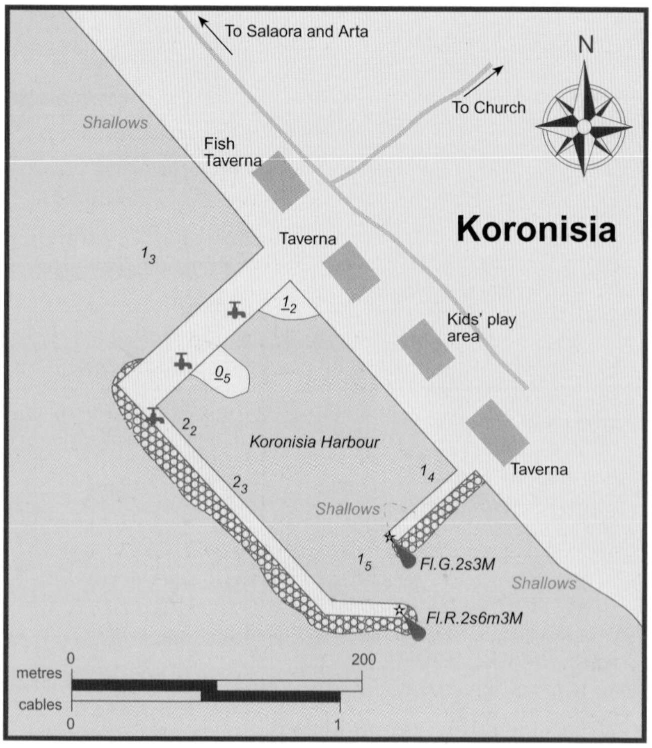

The harbour at Koronisia is small and the entrance shallow

The village itself is small and offers little in the way of amenities, although the tavernas along the waterfront provide good fare for the hungry yachtsman. If you can find transport, Arta, 17 miles (27km) to the north, is an excellent place to provision.

NAVIGATION

Charts: Admiralty 203, 189, SC5771; Imray G11, G12, G1; Hellenic Navy Hydrographic Service 2131, 21

From Preveza, follow the channel round until you enter the Amvrakikos Gulf. Koronisia lies about 5nm north-east of Skafidaki Pt. Watch out for the shallows around the islets of Gaidaros and Kefalos, and off Koronisia, the islets of Vouvalos, Vlachos and Diapori. About 1½nm south-west of the harbour, depths decrease to less than 10m and closer in to less than 3m. Approach the harbour from the south and proceed at a very slow speed. The entrance regularly silts to less than 1.5m so, if in doubt, drop a lead line from a dinghy first before heading in. Keep as close to the end of the western breakwater as possible as it is marginally deeper here.

The entrance to Koronisia regularly silts, so you may need to do a recce first before entering by yacht

BERTHING

Once inside the harbour depths range between 1.3-2.3m. Moor stern- or bows-to the western breakwater as this is the deepest part of the harbour. There are plenty of rings and bollards to tie up to and the holding on sand and mud is good.

ANCHORING

The waters around Koronisia are shallow and suitable for anchoring, but careful use of your echosounder is required. For the best shelter, however, head for Salaora Bay, see p93.

Useful information – Koronisia

FACILITIES

Water: Taps on the quay, although in 2007 only the one in the north-west corner of the harbour worked.
Fuel: No, although there is a petrol station on the road to Arta.
Gas: The nearest supply is in Arta.
Rubbish: Bins on the quay.
Telephone: Phone box outside the fish taverna on the quay. Mobile reception okay.

PROVISIONING

Grocery shops: Small mini-market in the village. Arta, 17 miles (27km) to the north, has several well-stocked supermarkets.
Banks: Arta, to the N, has branches of most banks.
Post: Post box in the village, but if urgent, post in Arta.

EATING OUT

There are three tavernas along the waterfront at Koronisia: a fish taverna, Floiovos Taverna and Amvrakikos Taverna. Shrimp is a speciality of the Amvrakikos Gulf and is served at the tavernas here, along with a good variety of traditional cuisine.

ASHORE

The village of Koronisia is a small but pleasant enough place to wander around. The Byzantine church of the Virgin's Nativity on top of the hill dates back to the 10th century and is said to be one of the oldest churches in Epirus. There is also a children's play area on the waterfront.

TRANSPORT

Car hire: Take a taxi to Arta. There are several travel agents in the town centre that will organise transport for you.
Taxis: Ask at the tavernas.
Ferry: The nearest terminal is at Igoumenitsa (3 hours' drive by car). International and internal services operate from the port.
Air travel: Aktio airport at Preveza is a 1-hour drive from Koronisia, via the toll tunnel (€3 each way). International services to Europe fly to/from Preveza several times a week.

OTHER INFORMATION

Local Tel code: 26810.
Hospital: The nearest hospital is in Arta (Tel: 26810 22222).
Yacht repairs/services: The three boatyards at the entrance to the Amvrakikos Gulf offer a range of services, from hauling out to general maintenance and sailmaking. See p89-90 for details.

Koronisia's church dates to the 10th century

Menidi Menidhion

Off Menidi: 39°02'.34N 21°06'.86E

Menidi is in the north-east corner of the Amvrakikos Gulf. A small village off the main Arta to Mesolongi road, it is packed with tavernas and a popular destination with tourists during the summer months. The harbour offers good all-round shelter but is shallow and usually busy with fishing boats.

If you want to visit the nearby town of Arta (see p94), Menidi is a good place to base yourself as the village has the best transport links along the northern coast of the Amvrakikos Gulf.

NAVIGATION

Charts: Admiralty 203, 189, SC5771; Imray G11, G1; Hellenic Navy Hydrographic Service 2131, 21

The approach to Menidi is straightforward and through deep water. From the entrance to the Amvrakikos Gulf, head east for about 12nm before heading north for about 4nm.

Care should be taken around the islets of Gaidaros and Kefalos, at the entrance to the Gulf, and around the sandbanks to the east of the Palmatero Shoals. While the sandbanks are charted, they are constantly shifting, particularly near the entrance to the Arachthos River, so keep well off the coast in this area and an eye on your echosounder.

BERTHING

Menidi harbour is shallow, so berth bows-to along the outer arm of the breakwater, wherever there is room. This is the deepest part of the harbour, although depths here are still only between 1.8-2.5m. A swell is occasionally pushed into the harbour but the holding is generally good so it should not be a concern.

ANCHORING

There is a pleasant anchorage in Koprena Bay, to the east of Koprena Pt (Fl(2)WR 16s9m5/3M), which provides reasonable shelter from the prevailing northwesterlies. The holding is good, although the bottom is quite weedy, so make sure your anchor is well dug in.

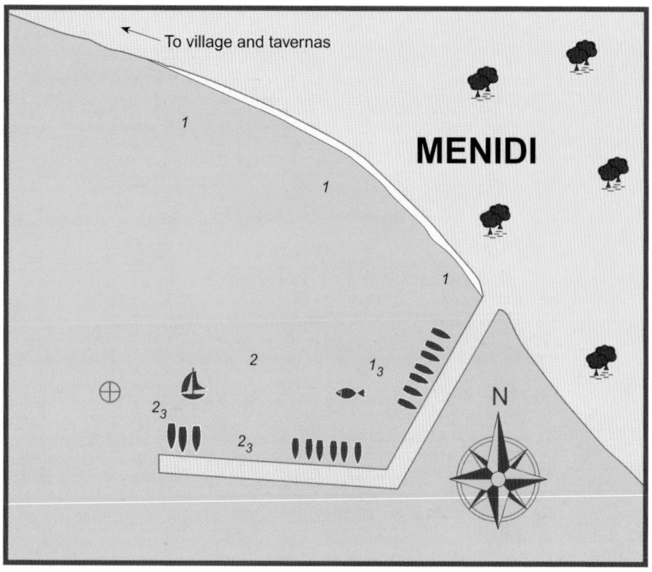

Menidi's harbour is very shallow and usually full of fishing boats and dories. There is, however, a good anchorage to the west in Koprena Bay

Useful information – Menidi

FACILITIES

Fuel: There is a petrol station on the main road.
Ice: Ask at the tavernas.
Gas: The nearest supply is in Arta, 11 miles (18km) from Menidi.
Rubbish: Bins on the quay.
Yacht services/chandlery: There are three boatyards at Aktio, at the entrance to the Gulf of Amvrakikos, which offer comprehensive services. See p89-90.
Telephone: A couple of phone boxes in the village. Mobile reception is good.

PROVISIONING

Grocery shops: Small mini-market in the village.
Banks: The nearest banks are in Arta, 11 miles (18km) to the north-west, or Amfilochia, 15 miles (24km) to the south.
Pharmacy: The nearest is in Arta.
Post: Post box in the village but no post office.

EATING OUT

Menidi is a popular tourist destination, so there are plenty of tavernas near the harbour. The fish and seafood dishes are particularly good but prices are often quite high.

ASHORE

From Menidi, travel by car or bus to the town of Arta, 11 miles (18km) to the north-west (see p94). Alternatively, if you are at anchor in Koprena Bay, take your dinghy to the mouth of the Arachthos River, just to the south. Like the marshland and lagoons to the west, this area teems with wildlife.

TRANSPORT

Car hire: Take a taxi to Arta and hire a car there. The tourist agencies in the town centre will organise transport for you.
Taxis: Ask at the tavernas.
Bus: A bus service to Athens from Arta and vice versa stops at Menidi up to eight times a day, Monday-Friday. The bus also stops at Amfilochia, 15 miles (24km) to the south.
Ferry: The nearest ferry terminal is at Igoumenitsa, 3 hours' drive by car. Domestic and international services leave from the port.
Air travel: Aktio airport at Preveza is 1 hour's drive away, via the toll tunnel (€3 each way). The airport is serviced by charter and internal flights several times a week.

OTHER INFORMATION

Local Tel code: 26810.
Port authority: The Port Police office (Tel: 26810 88616) is to the north-west of the harbour on the road out of Menidi.
Police: Tel: 26810 88222.
Hospital: A health centre (Tel: 26810 88220) is in the village. Arta (Tel: 26810 22222) and Amfilochia (Tel: 26420 23444) also have medical centres.

Menidi is a popular tourist destination during the summer months

Amfilochia

Amphilochia, Amfilokhia

Off the town of Amfilochia: 38°52'.19N 21°10'.06E

Amfilochia is situated at the end of a long, narrow bay in the SE corner of the Amvrakikos Gulf. The small town, which wraps around the head of the bay, was founded by Ali Pasha in the 18th century and until 1907 was known as Karvasaras – a corruption of the Turkish word *caravanserai*, which means, literally, 'caravan palace' or staging post. Ali Pasha used the town as a military station for many years, but now the port is home to just a few fishing boats.

As a destination it offers reasonable shelter, although not from the prevailing northwesterlies that funnel down Amfilochia Bay. It's a place to stop for lunch, but for overnight shelter Vonitsa to the west is a much better option.

NAVIGATION

Charts: Admiralty 203, 189, SC5771; Imray G11, G12, G1; Hellenic Navy Hydrographic Service 2131, 21

From Preveza, follow the channel east until you enter the Amvrakikos Gulf. Then, avoiding the shallows around the islet of Kefalos, head east for about 12nm. Amfilochia lies at the far end of the gulf. The approach is through deep water, although there is a small shoal (If Alexandrou) to the north of Loutraki Bay. Amfilochia harbour is at the head of the bay.

BERTHING

Yachts tend to berth side- or stern-to at Amfilochia, at the northern end of the quay, just to the south of the fishing boat harbour. The prevailing wind is onshore here, so it can get very choppy and uncomfortable in strong winds and you are advised to berth only on the quay in settled weather. There are also a few bollards along the quay to which you can tie up, so lay an anchor to the north-west as extra protection and to prevent yourself being blown onshore if the wind picks up. At the end of 2006, five floating pontoons had been placed just to the NW of the town quay. Lazylines were also being fitted, but there were no other facilities available.

ANCHORING

It is possible to anchor in Amfilochia Bay but it is deep, with depths off the quay increasing quickly to over 15m. Just to the south of the quay is a shoal patch (thought to be an underwater volcano) that should be avoided.

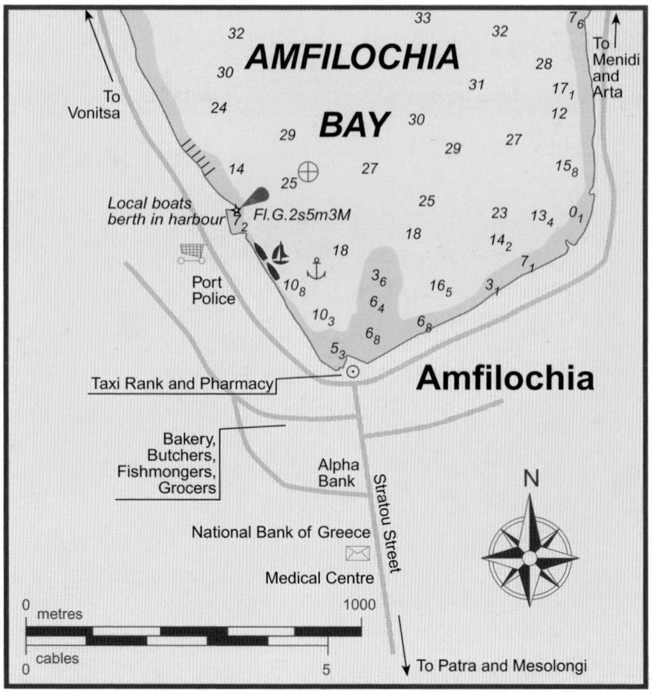

Useful information – Amfilochia

FACILITIES
Water: A water tanker does deliver but finding it can be a problem.
Fuel: Take a taxi to a nearby service station.
Gas: Ask at the Proto supermarket, behind the quay.
Rubbish: Bins situated near the quay.
Yacht services/chandlery: The nearest services are at Preveza, to the west.
Telephone: Several along the waterfront. Kiosks on the quay sell phone cards. Mobile reception is good.

PROVISIONING
Grocery shops: A couple of small supermarkets within easy walking distance of the quay. Near the taxi-rank you'll find a grocer, and another one near the butcher on a side street off Stratou Street, the road to Mesolongi.
Bakery: On a side street off Stratou St, which runs parallel to the waterfront.
Butcher: Near the bakery. There is a fishmonger on the same road.
Banks: Branches of Alpha Bank (Tel: 26420 24392) and National Bank of Greece (Tel: 26420 22067) can be found on Stratou St. The Agricultural Bank of Greece (Tel: 26420 22333) is nearby.
Pharmacy: A couple of pharmacies near the roundabout in the centre of Amfilochia.
Post: The post office is on Stratou St. Opening times: Monday-Friday, 0730-1400. The postal service in Amfilochia is good. Stamps are also available from kiosks.

EATING OUT
Several tavernas near the quay and on Stratou St.

ASHORE
The ruins of the ancient city of Limnaia, on the hillside above the town, is the main site of interest in Amfilochia. Transport links are good and from here you can travel to Arta, Preveza or Mesolongi.

TRANSPORT
Car hire: Ask at Katsoudas Travel (Tel: 26420 23162) on Stratou St, the road to Mesolongi.
Taxis: Taxi rank near the small roundabout at the north end of Stratou St.
Bus: The Ktel bus station (Tel: 26420 22225) is near the Proto supermarket, opposite the quay.
Ferry: Either Igoumenitsa, 3 hrs to the north, or Patra, 3 hrs to the south. Both international and domestic services use these ports. Ferries to Meganisi, Kefalonia and Ithaca leave from Nidri and Vasiliki on Lefkada, 2 hrs away by car.
Air travel: Aktio near Preveza is the nearest airport (¾-hour by car). Charter and domestic services fly from Aktio several times a week in season.

OTHER INFORMATION
Local Tel code: 26420.
Port authority: The Port Police Office (Tel: 26420 22340) is just beyond the quay, near the Proto supermarket. Follow the sign for the shipping agency.
Police: Tel: 26420 22222.
Hospital: The medical centre (Tel: 26420 23444/23914) is on Stratou Street, the main road out of Amfilochia.

Loutraki Bay

Ormos Loutrakiou

Anchorage in Loutraki Bay:
38°52'.44N 21°04'.36E
Charts: Admiralty 203, 189, SC5771; Imray G11, G12, G1; Hellenic Navy Hydrographic Service 2131, 21

You will find a couple of good anchorages in Loutraki Bay, a large bay to the west of Amfilochia. The first is in its southern corner, to the north of the village and fish farm, and provides average shelter in less than 8m of water.

The second, in Paliomilou Bay, affords good protection from the prevailing winds. Watch out for the several fish farms in the area and take care to avoid If Alexandrou, a reef to the north of the bay.

Vonitsa

Ormos Vonitsis

Off Vonitsa: 38°55'.44N 20°53'.36E

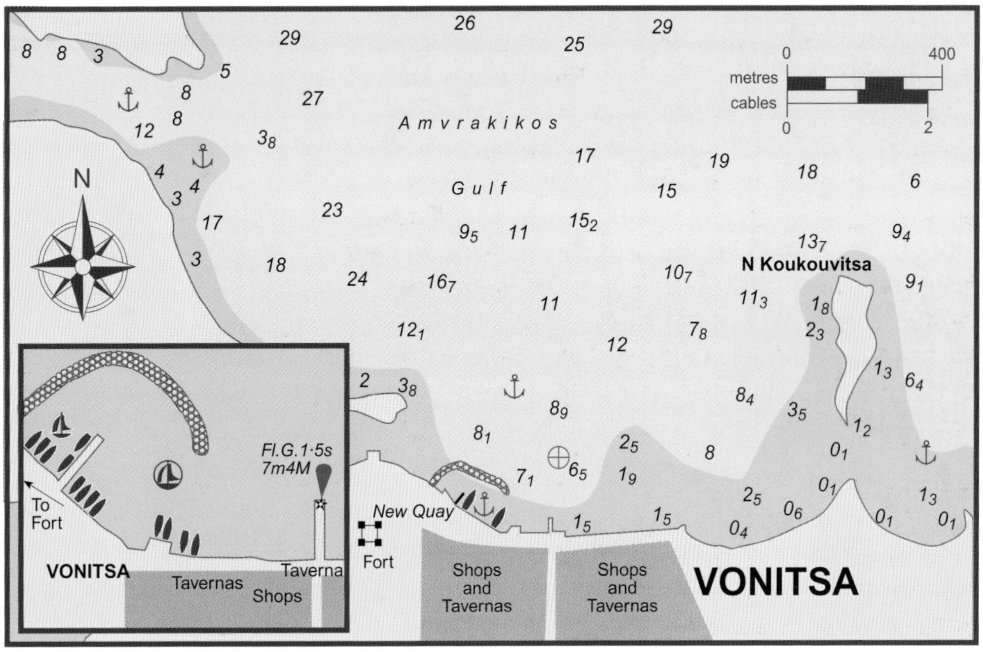

Vonitsa is the first town you reach on entering the Amvrakikos Gulf and is situated about 8nm to the east of Preveza. It's an attractive place that dates back to the 4th century, built on the site of the ancient city of Anactorian. Like many of the towns in this part of Greece, Vonitsa has had a turbulent history, passing from one ruling occupier to another and back again. Twice it was captured by the Turks and twice the Venetians captured it back only to lose it to the French in the late 18th century following the dissolving of the Venetian Republic. In the late 1790s Ali Pasha took control, fortified the castle and stationed troops here to fight against nearby Lefkada.

Today Vonitsa has rural charm. The waterfront, with its commanding views of the Amvrakikos Gulf, is a pleasant place to while away a few hours, and as somewhere to provision, it rates highly. In recent years, the harbour has seen improvements and looks to be developed further, with the addition of pontoons behind a breakwater that gives good all-round shelter.

The harbour at Vonitsa is being developed to make it more yacht-friendly, which is good news as the town is a great place to provision

NAVIGATION

Charts: Admiralty 203, 189, SC5771; Imray G11, G12, G1; Hellenic Navy Hydrographic Service 2131, 21

From Preveza, follow the channel as it sweeps to the east and round into the Amvrakikos Gulf. Two headlands at the entrance to the gulf are marked with lights: Laskara Pt (Fl(2)R 6s12m4M) and Panagia Pt (LFl G 7.5s6m3M). Once in the gulf proper, proceed eastwards, taking care to avoid the shoals around the islet of Kefalos. There's deep water between Kefalos and Panagia Pt, so you can pass on either side of the islet. However, if you do pass between the two stay in the middle of the channel. Vonitsa lies at the southern end of Vonitsa Bay, and the harbour is below the Venetian castle, to the west of a short pier.

BERTHING

Yachts can berth stern- or bows-to the quay, either side of the short jetty opposite the breakwater. There are plans for pontoons to be laid in the harbour, but in 2007 these had not been installed.

ANCHORING

There is a lovely anchorage just to the north-west of Vonitsa in Markou Bay, which offers good all-round shelter. Anchor in 6m or less at the western side of the bay. Alternatively, you can anchor to the east of Koukouvista. The small island is joined to the mainland by a short isthmus and affords reasonable protection.

Yachts also occasionally anchor off the town as depths are less than 10m until level with the northern headland of the salt lagoon. It's a beautiful spot and usually quite quiet too.

Useful information – Vonitsa

FACILITIES
Fuel: There is an Elin petrol station at the southern end of the main road. Also Eko and Jet Oil petrol stations on the outskirts of Vonitsa.
Water: Only available on the E side of the harbour.
Gas: Available from supermarkets.
Rubbish: Rubbish bins on the quay.
Yacht services/chandlery: Papa Stratos near the National Bank of Greece, on the main road through Vonitsa, sells a small range of chandlery, fishing nets and rope.
Telephone: Several telephones on the quay, another outside the Agricultural Bank of Greece.
Internet: Internet cafe on the road behind the waterfront, near the Hotel Bel Mar.

PROVISIONING
Grocery shops: Several mini-markets and fruit and veg shops at the southern end of Vonitsa's main road and near the bus station.
Bakery: Several bakeries on the main road through Vonitsa. The one opposite the Elin petrol station at the southern end of the main road is particularly good.
Butcher: On a side street which is situated between two bakeries off the main road.
Fishmonger: On main road.
Banks: Alpha Bank (Tel: 26430 22235) and Agricultural Bank of Greece (Tel: 26430 22303) have branches and ATMs on El Venizelou St, the main road to the waterfront. The National Bank of Greece (Tel: 26430 22305), on Dem Ragou St, is open 0800-1430, Mon-Thurs, 0800-1400 on Friday, and has a 24-hour ATM.
Pharmacy: Several. One near the National Bank of Greece. There are another couple on the road past the bus station, a 10-minute walk from the waterfront.
Post: The post office is opposite the Alpha Bank on the main road. Open Monday-Friday, 0730-1400.
Hairdresser: English-speaking hairdresser near the dentist, off the main road.
Other shops: Various shoe and clothes shops, a photographic developers and an off-licence on the main road.

EATING OUT
There are numerous tavernas on the waterfront, close to the harbour. The Poseidon Taverna at the eastern end serves good and very reasonably priced traditional dishes. Tzaki cafe and snack bar and Castelo's are also good. There are several more cafés on a side street off the western end of the quay.

ASHORE
If you get the opportunity, and it's a clear day, wander up to the Venetian castle overlooking the harbour at Vonitsa. From the top you get the most magnificent panoramic view of the Amvrakikos Gulf. The hill on which it was built was fortified in Byzantine times but the castle was built later by the Venetians during their occupation of the town.

TRANSPORT
Car hire: Europcar (Tel: 26450 22905) and Hertz both have branches at Aktio airport at Preveza, a 10-minute taxi-ride from Vonitsa. However, the branches are only open when flights are due in or out of the airport, and not every day. Alternatively, there are several car hire firms in Lefkada town, 20 minutes away from Vonitsa.
Taxis: Taxi rank situated on the waterfront.
Bus: The Ktel bus station (Tel: 26430 22500) is to the east of the main road, near the medical centre. Services to Preveza, Parga, Athens and Mitikas run daily.
Ferry: The nearest major ferry port is at Igoumenitsa, a 3-hour drive away. Services to Patra, Corfu, Paxos and Italy operate from there. Ferries to Kefalonia, Ithaca and Meganisi run from Nidri and Vasiliki on Lefkada.
Air travel: Aktio airport at Preveza is a 10-minute car journey from Vonitsa. Domestic and charter flights fly from here weekly.

OTHER INFORMATION
Local Tel code: 26430.
Port authority: Vonitsa is looked after by Preveza Port Authority (Tel: 26820 22226; 28854).
Police: Tel: 26430 22100.
Dentist: Above the DVD club on the main road.
Hospital: Vonitsa Medical Centre (Tel: 26430 22222) is to the east of the bus station.
Yacht repairs/services: The nearest boatyards (Cleopatra Marina, Preveza Marine & Aktio Marine) are at Aktio, about 10nm to the west. See p89-90.

The boatyards at Aktio and the town of Preveza are close to the Amvrakikos Gulf

Chapter three
Lefkada, Meganisi, Kalamos & Kastos

This chapter covers Lefkada and its major satellite islands, including Meganisi, Kalamos and Kastos. Considered by many to be the core of the Ionian, these islands, and the waters between, are packed with harbours and anchorages to explore. It is the most sheltered part of the Ionian, offering good sailing within the confines of a relatively small area. All the ports are easily reached but there is considerable diversity and interest for people of all sailing abilities. The beauty of this part of Greece is that there is so much choice.

Weather conditions tend to follow a regular pattern here: little to no wind in the mornings and a decent Force 3-4 from the north-west in the afternoons. While heavy seas are uncommon, a significant chop can build up with the wind in the afternoons; if there have been storms to the south, there may also be a rolling swell. Some areas, such as the Meganisi Channel, are particularly gusty and conditions can change suddenly and dramatically, although often they don't last very long.

While eyeball navigation around these waters will usually suffice, don't be complacent. There are reefs and shoals near the islands, so study your charts before you hit them.

Lefkada
Nisos Lefkada/Lefkas/Levkas

Lefkada, which lies to the south of Preveza, off the Etolo-Akarnanian coast, is an island of contrasts. The fourth largest of the Ionian islands, over 70 per cent of its terrain is mountainous, yet its coastline is varied and interesting. Long, sandy beaches fringe the north coast, steep craggy rocks dominate the western coast, with pearly white cliffs at its southern end, while the eastern shores are lush with greenery. Its interior and harbours differ greatly too and, although the tourist industry holds sway in many of the villages and towns, the island remains quintessentially Greek. Lefkada town is more popular with Greeks and Italians than the British and is very much an administrative centre rather than a tourist development. In contrast, Nidri is pure package holiday resort, with commercialisation

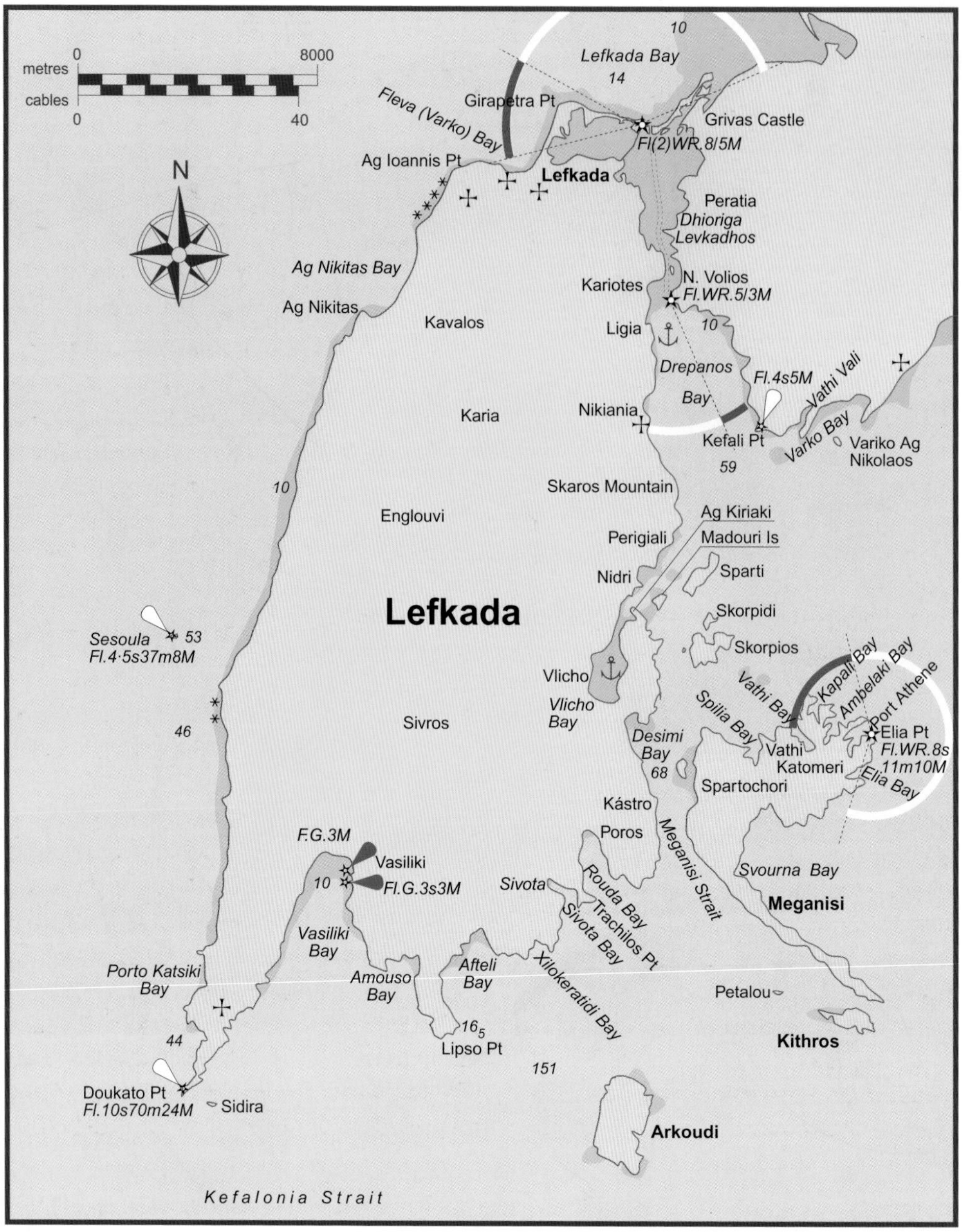

oozing out of every street. Vasiliki is becoming steadily more popular, too, as its reputation for being a world-class windsurfing centre increases. But you can still find traditional fishing communities away from the resorts.

Covering 116 square miles (302km^2), Lefkada is almost an extension of the mainland. The two are connected via a causeway and road bridge across low-lying saltmarsh at the north-east end of the island. The Lefkada Canal separates the two and is opened to seagoing traffic every hour. It's the main thoroughfare for leisure craft heading north or south and a quicker route than going round the outside of the island. A canal was first dug here by the Corinthians in 650BC and although this silted up, the Romans re-excavated it in 198BC when the island was part of the Roman Empire. The present one was built by the Greeks and the British in the late 19th century.

Lefkada's economy has, until quite recently, been mainly tied up with agriculture and the island is well known for its olives, wine, currants and honey.

As a destination for cruising, this island has much to offer. The marina and boatyard at Lefkada town has a wide range of facilities; Nidri, though hideously over-developed, is one of the better places to provision and you can be sure of excellent meals at both Ligia and Sivota. The sailing is not bad either, and Lefkada's position at the head of the main part of the Ionian makes it an ideal starting or finishing point for your cruise.

Lefkada town is the capital of the island. It's compact and has much to offer the cruising yachtsman in terms of provisioning and places to eat

Lefkada Town Lefkas, Levkas, Leucas

Approach to the south entrance of the Lefkada Canal:
38°47'.14N 20°44'.11E
South entrance to Lefkada Canal:
38°47'.50N 20°43'.69E
1st pair of buoys Lefkada Canal:
38°47'.66N 20°43'.59E
2nd set of buoys Lefkada Canal:
38°47'.92N 20°43'.63E
3rd set of buoys Lefkada Canal:
38°48'.16N 20°43'.66E
4th set of buoys Lefkada Canal:
38°48'.32N 20°43'.69E
5th buoy (single green) Lefkada Canal:
38°48'.46N 20°43'.67E
Town Quay at Lefkada:
38°50'.02N 20°42'.71E
Off Town Quay, Lefkada:
38°50'.04N 20°42'.77E
Approach from south to floating bridge:
38°50'.22N 20°42'.81E
Floating swing bridge at Lefkada:
38°50'.63N 20°43'.06E
Northern entrance to canal:
38°50'.76N 20°43'.35E

Lefkada town, on its north-east coast, is the island's capital. Compact and peppered with a maze of streets and alleys, Lefkada is the main yachting centre of this part of the Ionian and the gateway to the islands of the north and south. A short hop from mainland Greece, the town has a cosmopolitan, convivial feel and is popular with Greek and Italian tourists.

Although it was first established in 1684, very little of the original Venetian town still exists. Like Kefalonia, to the south, the island was hit hard by the major earthquakes of 1948 and 1953. Much of the town was destroyed and has been replaced with more modern concrete, wood and corrugated iron buildings, giving it a distinctly unique feel.

For the yachtsman, it's a superb location, with a new, large marina close to the heart of the town and all the facilities and provisions you need nearby. The town quay and marina offer good shelter from the prevailing winds and even in the height of summer there is usually room to berth.

NAVIGATION

Charts: Admiralty 203, 2405, SC5771; Imray G11, G12 & G121; Hellenic Navy Hydrographic Service 213/2

From the south: The southern entrance to the Lefkada Canal is easy to identify on approach. Heading up Drepanos Bay, you will see two buoys (a port and a starboard) marking the entrance, and just to the east a light (Fl WR 5/3M) on the islet of Volios. The castle of Agios Georgios lies on the mainland behind. Pass through the middle of the first pair of buoys and do not stray outside them; remains of a mole are situated to the west while the waters to the east are shallow. Inside the channel, dredged to 5-6m, head north, obeying the canal's speed limit of 4 knots. There are three further pairs of lit marker buoys (Q R & Q S) followed by a

The northern entrance to the Lefkada Canal can be hard to identify from a distance and is guarded by a long sandbank

single starboard buoy, with electricity cables running overhead. The channel then turns to the north-west and is marked by withies. Follow it for about 2nm, past salt lagoons to port and starboard, until you reach Lefkada Town. A breakwater pontoon lies to the west and the entrances to the marina are to the north and south of this. The town quay is just beyond.

From the north: While the mountains of Lefkada are easy to locate from some distance, the northern entrance to the canal is not. There's usually quite a haze here and the sandy spit that protects the entrance blurs with the shoreline behind. On approach, head for Lefkada and a point slightly east of the mountains. Closer in, you'll be able to identify the castle of Agios Mavra, to the south of the entrance.

It can get quite windy here in the afternoons when the prevailing northwesterly has kicked in, so lower your sails early and motor into the canal. Keep your speed to about 3 knots, to maintain wash at a minimum, particularly if there are lots of boats around.

On the western side of the entrance is a long sandbank. Although this area is regularly dredged, watch your depth as it is quite shallow. Once through the entrance, the channel gets deeper and there is more room to manoeuvre. Further up the canal to port you'll see a couple of rusting buoys, marking debris under the water. Vicious gusts often blow through here and there is usually a couple of knots of current running, so be careful not to be blown on to the buoys.

You should now be able to see the bridge. If it's not open, gill around in the channel until it is (see below for details) or, if the canal is busy, lie alongside the quay wall just to the north of the bridge. There aren't many places to tie up and the quay is rough in places, so put out plenty of fenders.

The Lefkada bridge: The bridge that joins Lefkada to the mainland is actually a floating barge, F/B *Ag Maura*, which is anchored mid-channel and has two lifting drawbridges, one each side. Every hour on the hour, between 0600 and 2100, the drawbridges are lifted and the barge swings parallel to the mainland to let boats through. Yachts heading north normally have right of way but, occasionally, if there are not many boats in the canal, only one drawbridge will be raised (usually the western one), and those heading south have priority. It can be tricky when only one is raised, particularly when there is a current running, but if you wait until the bridge is fully lifted and out of reach of your masthead, you should be able to proceed through the gap without difficulty. Do bear in mind that the bridge operator wants to keep it raised for as little time as possible; if you arrive late you may not be able to get through and may have to wait another hour.

If you want to use the canal between 2100 and 0600, call the bridge operator on VHF Ch12 to announce your arrival.

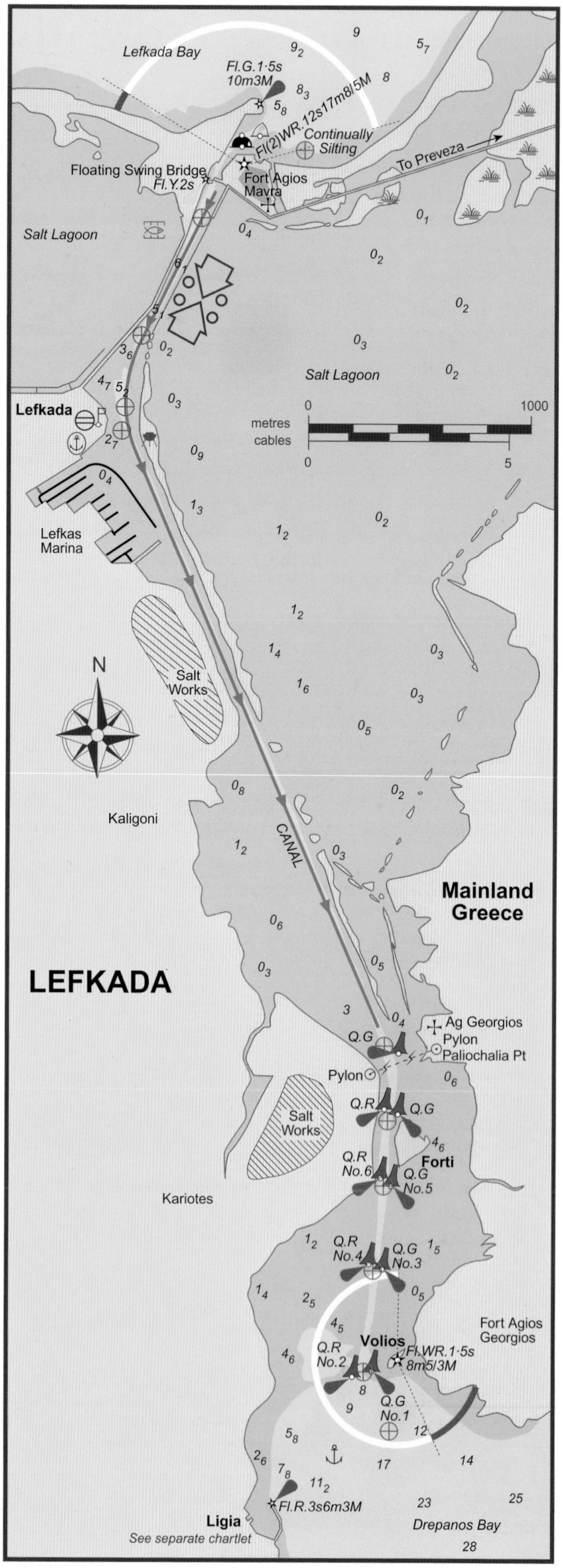

Lefkas Marina

Entrance to marina:
38°49'.82N
20°42'.90E

Lefkas Marina is spacious and offers extensive facilities

BERTHING

Lefkas Marina, situated just to the south of the town quay, has berths for 620 boats of up to 45m (131ft) LOA and 3.5m (11ft 5in) draught. The majority of the berthing is stern or bows-to on lazylines, but there are also some alongside berths (although expect to be charged extra). On entering the marina, you should call the office on VHF Ch69 to get directions.

Berthing fees: Sample prices for an 11m (36ft) and a 14m (46ft) yacht during high season (1 April-30 September): €40/€56 per day or €475/€646 per month. Low season (1 October-31 March): €21/€27 per day or €309/€379 per month. Fees include 220v electricity. Daily fees run from arrival until 1400 the next day. Catamarans are charged an extra 50 per cent and alongside berthing is plus 80 per cent. Prices may vary.

Useful information – Lefkas Marina

FACILITIES

Marina office: In the building that looks like an aircraft control tower, opposite pontoon F. Open: Monday–Saturday,0800-1900; Sunday, 0800-1530. Tel: 26450 26645/26646. Watchman (when office closed) Tel: 69373 90390; VHF Ch69.
Water: Taps at every berth.
Fuel: Fuel jetty (pontoon K) at the S end of the marina.
Showers: Three shower and toilet blocks.
Ice: Ask at the mini-market.
Laundry: At the shower block in the centre of the marina.
Gas: Bottle exchange at the mini-markets.
Shorepower: 220v & 380v electricity plug-in points at every berth; 380v electricity is metered.
Rubbish: Bins near quay.
Yacht services: Lefkas Marina has a 70-ton travelhoist and a 60-ton crane, with hard-standing for 278 boats. Range of services, from engineering to maintenance and repair. Sample prices for 11m (36ft) and 14m (46ft) yachts (prices may vary): crane in/out, €163/€221; pressure wash, €67/€107; crane hire, €94 per ½ hour; sewage pump-out, €0.24/lt.

Waypoint (Tel: 26820 26636), a sailmaker from Preveza, has recently opened a branch here. Services include sail repairs and some chandlery.

A1 Yacht Trade Consortium (Tel: 26450 22177/www.a1yachting.com) chandlery, brokerage, charter and general yacht management.
Telephone: Several around the marina, one in the marina office. Phonecards at the supermarket. Mobile reception is good.
Fax: Ask at marina office.
Internet: Ask at the marina office.
Weather forecast: Posted daily at marina office.

PROVISIONING

Grocery shops: Supermarket to the south of the main road entrance. Also a Champion supermarket a mile south-east of the marina.
Bakery: Some fresh bread at the supermarket. Alternatively, several bakers on Ioannou Mela, the pedestrianised street running through the centre of Lefkada, a 10-minute walk away.
Butcher: The nearest is on Dimitriou Golemi, the main road past the town quay.
Banks: Several in the town centre. See p107 for details.
Pharmacy: On Ioannou Mela St.
Post: Post boxes at the marina, post office in town. Post can be delivered to the marina for collection.
Opening times: The supermarket is open throughout the day. Other shops vary.

EATING OUT

There are several places to eat and drink within the marina complex. Blue café-bar (Tel: 26450 25047) is near the marina office, as is Zorbas café-bar (Tel: 26450 21011); further along the waterfront are Il Porto and Costa Costa restaurant. Lefkada's town centre is a 10-minute walk from the marina and packed with tavernas and cafés. See p107 for details.

TRANSPORT

Car hire: Ask at the marina office. The marina has plenty of car parking and trailer-storage space, including some under cover. Several car hire firms and travel agents in the town. See p107 for details.

Lefkada Marina offers some of the best facilities in this part of the Ionian

Lefkada Town Quay

BERTHING

The town quay lies immediately north of Lefkas Marina. It is a large area that curls round the eastern shore of Lefkada, from the hump-backed bridge at the end of the island's causeway to a small fishing harbour at the north-west end of the marina. It's usually busy as it is convenient for the town and, unlike the marina, berthing overnight is free. Boats can go stern- or bows-to here but deeper draught yachts should watch for underwater debris at the base of the quay at its eastern end. Berth bows-to to avoid grounding your rudder or keep well off the quay. The holding in mud is good and the quay offers adequate shelter except in strong southerlies.

ANCHORING

There is nowhere to anchor off Lefkada Town or in the Lefkada Canal.

Yachts can berth on Lefkada's town quay, which is conveniently situated for the centre of town

Useful information – Lefkada Town Quay

FACILITIES

Water: Taps along the town quay. Man comes round each morning with hoses and a key for the taps.
Fuel: Fuel jetty at the east end of the town quay.
Showers: Ask at tavernas.
Ice: Ask at the tavernas or the Marine Market on Dimitriou Golemi, the main road past the town quay.
Laundry: At the southern end of Dimitriou Golemi.
Gas: Bottle exchange at the mini-markets.
Rubbish: Bins situated on the quayside.
Yacht repairs/services: Contract Yacht Services (Tel: 26450 24490), on the main road opposite the south-east corner of the town quay, provides engineering, guardianage and winterising services. Chandler below the office.

Lefkas Marine Centre (Tel: 26450 25036/Mobile: 693670 8688). Yacht repairs, guardianage, yacht supplies and electronics.
Telephone: Phone boxes on the road behind the quay and plenty in the town itself. Phonecards from kiosks. Mobile reception is good.

PROVISIONING

Lefkada's town centre is compact and easily walkable. Most of the essential shops are along two roads: Ioannou Mela, a part-pedestrianised street, runs through the heart of the town and Dimitriou Golemi is the main road past the town quay.
Grocery shops: Several supermarkets on Dimitriou Golemi, including the Marina Market. Also a Champion supermarket a mile SE of the marina. Greengrocers on sidestreets and on Ioannou Mela.
Bakery: Several on Dimitriou Golemi and Ioannou Mela.
Butcher: Several on Dimitriou Golemi and Ioannou Mela. Also fishmonger.
Banks: Alpha Bank (Tel: 26450 26570) on Agios Mina square, at southern end of 8th Merarchias, a road off the southern end of Dimitriou Golemi; Agricultural Bank of Greece (Tel: 26450 22320) on main square off northern end of Ioannou Mela; Emporiki (Tel: 26450 26551) on 8th Merarchias (see above). National Bank of Greece (Tel: 26450 21141) on Ioannou Mela near the Church of Pantokratoras. All open Monday-Friday, 0800-1400 and all have 24hr ATMs.
Pharmacy: Several on Ioannou Mela.
Other shops: A good selection of clothes, music, photography and souvenir shops; small bazaar area at the northern end of Ioannou Mela.
Post Office: At the south end of Ioannou Mela. Open Monday-Friday, 0700-1430. Post box on Dimitriou Golemi near the Marina Market. The postal service on Lefkada is good. Stamps available at souvenir shops.
Opening times: Shops vary. Most open 0900-1330, close for siesta and reopen between 1800-2000; tavernas and souvenir shops later. Some closed on Sundays.

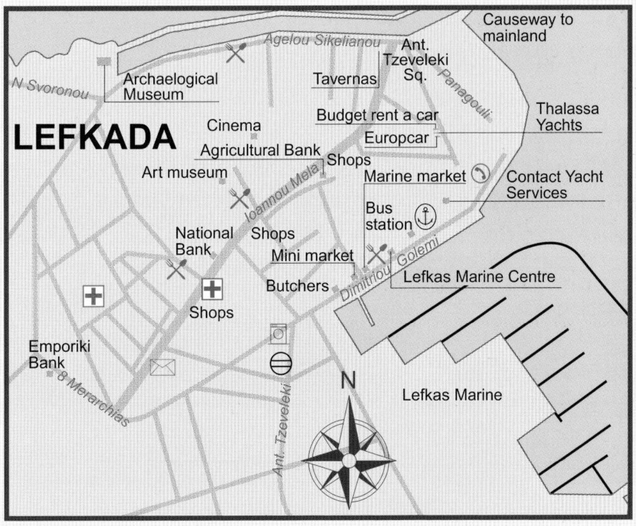

EATING OUT

Most of the tavernas and bars of interest are on Dorpfeld (at the northern end of Ioannou Mela beyond the square) and the seafront at the north of the town. There is plenty of choice in Lefkada, catering for most tastes. Italian restaurants are particularly prevalent and Voglia di Pizza (Tel: 26450 26461) on Agelou Sikelianou, by the beach, serves some of the best pizzas on the island; Roma Ristorante Italiano (Tel: 26450 23455) in the main square, Burano (Tel: 26450 26025) in the east harbour and Gustoso Pizzeria (Tel: 26450 24603) in the west harbour, all have good reputations. For traditional fare, try Taverna Regantos (Tel: 26450 22855) on Verioti St.

ASHORE

There is plenty to see ashore in Lefkada town besides the shops, tavernas and cafes. Ten minutes' walk along the seafront, at the western end of Agelou Sikelianou, is the Archaeological Museum (Tel: 26450 21635). Open Tuesday-Sunday, 0830-1500, it is home to an interesting collection of Ionian antiquities. Entry is €2.

The tiny Phonograph Museum on Konstandinou Kalkani St, just off the east side of the square, is a curious place stuffed with gramophones, records and household objects. Admission is free and it is open most days, mornings and evenings. To the north-west, near Marka Square, is the Post-Byzantine Museum. Situated beneath Lefkada's public library, it incorporates a collection of work by painters from the Ionian School and icons from churches and monasteries on the island. Admission free; open Tuesday-Saturday, 0830-1330.

Just over the bridge, on the mainland side of the Lefkada Canal, are the ruins of the castle of Agios Mavra (Santa Maura), built in the 14th century by Giovanni Orsini. It is said he was given the island of Lefkada as part of a dowry following his marriage to the daughter of Nikiforos I, the Despot of Epirus. It was conquered by the Turks in 1479 who built a large bridge with 360 arches across the salt marshes, over which water was carried to the castle. Remains of it still exist within the lagoons, but most of it was demolished by earthquakes. The castle was enlarged by the Venetians in the 18th century but subsequent earthquakes and bombing during the Second World War caused extensive damage and just the ruins and scattered cannon remain. Open Mon, 0900-1330 and Tues-Sun, 0830-1500, admission free. There are some beautiful walks in the area.

TRANSPORT

Car hire: Europcar (Tel: 26450 23581), 16 Panagou St (side road off the eastern part of town quay); Avis (Tel: 26450 26632), 10 Panagou St. Open Monday-Sunday 0900-2100. Travel Mate (Tel: 26450 22538), 16 Panagou St. Budget, Panagou St.
Bicycle hire: Bikeland (Tel: 26450 26426) on Ioanni Marinou (north-west of the Municipal Arts Gallery) rents out city, mountain and high-performance bikes, plus 50cc scooters. From €6-22 per day.
Taxis: Taxi Lefkada (Tel: 26450 21200/ 24600/21001); or ask at marina office. Taxi rank at Agios Minas square,

Useful information – Lefkada Town Quay

at the southern end of 8th Merarchias.
Bus: KTEL (Tel: 26450 22364) bus station next to the Port Police on Dimitriou Golemi. Four a day to Athens (five-hour journey), and regular services to Preveza on the mainland, Ligia, Nikiana, Nidri and Vasiliki on Lefkada.
Ferry: Car and foot-passenger services between Nidri and Meganisi up to five times a day, peak season. Ferries to Kefalonia and Ithaca leave from Nidri and Vasiliki.
Air travel: The nearest airport is at Preveza on the mainland, which takes 30-minutes to reach by road.

OTHER INFORMATION

Local Tel code: 26450.
Lefkas Marina: East Shore, Lefkada 31100, Greece. Tel: 26450 26645/26646. Fax: 26450 26642. Email: Lefkas@medmarinas.com Website: www.medmarinas.com
Port Police: On main road behind town quay, next to the bus station. Tel: 26450 22322. Additional branch at the marina office.
Police: Tel: 26450 22346/29370.
Doctor: Dr Eleni Skavada (Tel: 26450 26005) at 4 Tzavala St, off Ioannou Mela. English speaking.
Hospital: To the north of the southern end of Ioannou Mela. Tel: 26450 25371/38200. Doctor's surgery at the marina.

Remains of the castle of Agios Mavra near Lefkada

Ligia Lygia, Liyia

Off the harbour entrance: 38°47'.33N 20°43'.30E

The village of Ligia (population 600), on the east coast of Lefkada, lies close to the southern end of the Lefkada Canal. A picturesque harbour, it has beautiful views across to the ruined castle of Agios Georgios and the mainland beyond, and also offers good shelter from the prevailing northwesterly winds.

Ligia is Lefkada's main fishing port and as a working harbour is usually packed with fishing boats on permanent moorings. Consequently, room for yachts is scarce. The south-west side of the harbour is shallow and boats over 30ft may have difficulties finding somewhere to moor. There is normally space for a couple of boats on the northern end of the breakwater but be prepared for an early wake-up call as most of the fishing boats return to port at 0500 to unload their fish.

If you can find room, however, it is worth it. The tavernas in Ligia serve some of the best fresh fish on Lefkada and, being right on the main Lefkada-to-Nidri road, it's also a convenient place from which to explore the island. Please be aware though that in the past year there has been a rise in vandalism on the quay and a couple of attempted thefts on the yachts.

The island's main fishing port, Ligia is usually busy with caiques

NAVIGATION

Charts: Admiralty 203, 2405, SC5771; Imray G11, G12 & 121; Hellenic Navy Hydrographic Service 2131

Ligia is easily spotted from all directions and the approach is straightforward. Keep an eye on your depth, though, as the northern part of Drepanos Bay is relatively shallow.

If heading south from the Lefkada Canal, steer 210°T towards the village. From the south, head north up the Meganisi Channel, passing either side of Skorpios and

If there is room, yachts can berth off the breakwater at Ligia

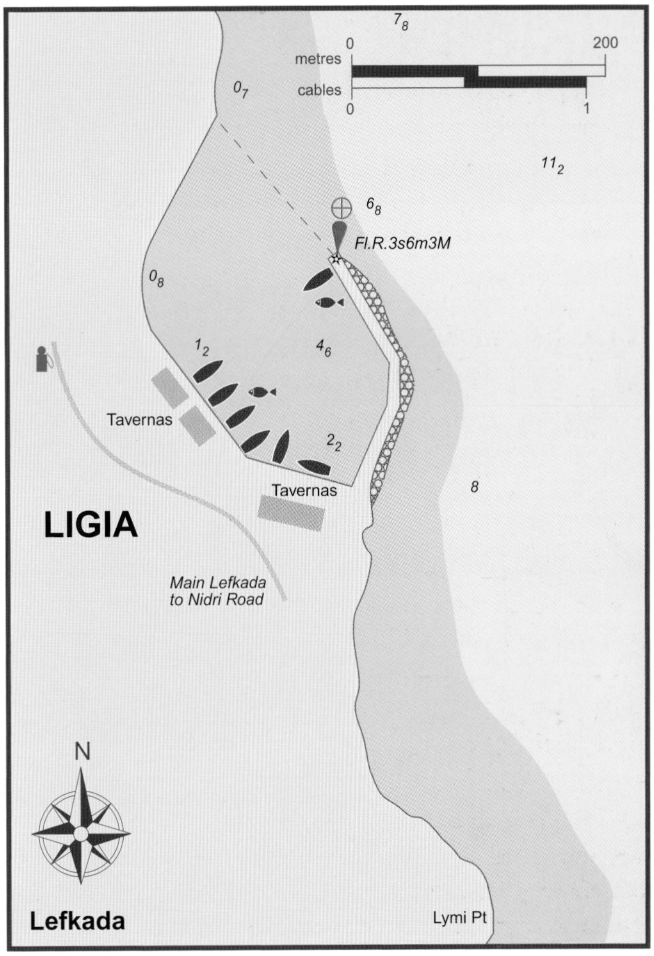

Sparti islands. Watch out for the shoal patch of water off the southwestern tip of Sparti, as depths here decrease to less than 5m.

BERTHING

Space is tight in Ligia, although usually a couple of yachts can squeeze in on the end of the breakwater. Most berth alongside but there is also room to go stern or bows-to. Occasionally boats moor off the end of the mole but watch for underwater debris. You can go further inside the harbour where it is more sheltered; however, the majority of the berths are reserved for local fishing boats so you should be prepared to move if one returns. It is also very shallow on the western side of the quay in front of the tavernas.

Most of the fishing boats lie to lazylines or moorings, so be careful not to get caught up when anchoring. Holding is good.

ANCHORING

If there isn't room to moor within the harbour, then you can anchor close in to the shore either to the N or S of Ligia. It is extremely exposed here, however, and there is no shelter from the prevailing winds, which blow up strongly in the afternoons and funnel down Drepanos Bay. Use in calm conditions, as a lunchtime stop only.

Useful information – Ligia

FACILITIES

Water: Tap at the end of the quay.
Fuel: Service station right on the quay, to the right of the taverna.
Showers: Basic facilities – ask at tavernas.
Ice: Ask at tavernas.
Gas: Bottle exchange at mini-markets.
Rubbish: Bins near the quayside.
Yacht services/chandlery: Nearest in Nidri or Lefkada Town.
Telephone: Card phones in the village. Mobile phone reception is good.
Post: Post boxes in the village. Stamps also at supermarkets and souvenir shops. Postal service is reasonable on Lefkada.

PROVISIONING

Grocery shops: Mini-market. Provisions are basic but good as there are many guest houses in the area. Lidl supermarket is 3.5 miles north of Ligia.
Bakery: In the village.
Butcher: In the village.
Banks: Nearest in Nidri.
Pharmacy: Nearest in Nidri.
Opening times: Shops operate to siesta hours. Closed 1400-1800.

EATING OUT

Giannis (Tel: 26450 71407) on the waterfront is a very good fish taverna. Restaurant Xouras (Tel: 26450 71312), also on the quay, serves delicious fish and traditional Greek meals. Restaurant Nirikos (Tel: 26450 71270) is a pizzeria in Kariotes, a mile north of Ligia.

ASHORE

Ligia is a good place from which to explore Lefkada. Hire a car from Nidri or explore by taxi.

TRANSPORT

Car/scooter hire: Available from Nidri or Lefkada town. Cars can be delivered to Ligia for an extra charge.
Bus: KTEL operates a regular service down the east coast of Lefkada, with up to seven a day between Lefkada town, Ligia and Nikiana. Only a few buses operate during siesta hours (1400-1800), so plan accordingly.
Ferry: Services to Kephalonia, Ithaca and Meganisi from Nidri.
Airport: The nearest is at Preveza on the mainland, 45 minutes by taxi.

OTHER INFORMATION

Local Tel code: 26450.

Nikiana

Off the harbour entrance: 38°45'.68N 20°43'.24E

Nikiana (population 547) lies 1.5nm south of Ligia in Episkopos Bay, on Lefkada's east coast. It's a reasonable-sized harbour with a small, pretty village along its inner perimeter.

Well protected from southerly winds by a breakwater, Nikiana is also sheltered from the prevailing northwesterlies but can feel exposed if a strong northerly blows down the Lefkada Canal.

Despite being smaller, Nikiana is more welcoming to yachts than Ligia, with room for boats to moor and a good selection of facilities ashore. However, it suffers from being a charter base, where much of the space is occupied by crewless yachts, and consequently lacks the atmosphere of similar-sized ports.

It's a good place to base yourself on the island, though, as all the facilities of both Lefkada town and Nidri are within easy reach. It is also rural and without the tourist developments of other harbours on the island.

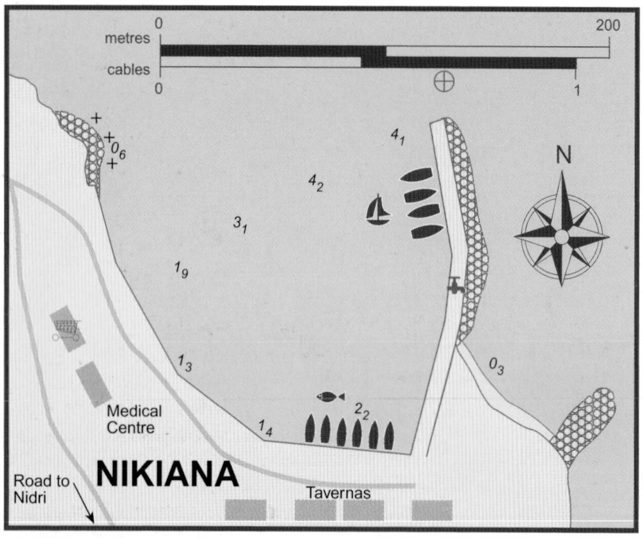

NAVIGATION

Charts: Admiralty 203, 2405, SC5771; Imray G11, G12 & 121; Hellenic Navy Hydrographic Service 2131

From the buoys marking the southern entrance of the Lefkada Canal, head 183°T for about 2nm, following the east coast of the island south. From Kephalonia, Ithaca or the south coast of Lefkada, head north past Skorpios, Nidri and Sparti. There is plenty of water from all directions, but care should be taken around the southwestern end of Sparti where there is a shoal patch and depths decrease considerably. This also applies near Nidri as it is a popular resort and its waters are often busy with pleasure and commercial craft.

From a distance, the entrance to Nikiana is hard to pick out, as boulders on the mole blend in with the surrounding landscape. Immediately south of the village, however, are several large hotels, which are conspicuous from all directions and if you look north

Nikiana lies just south of Ligia and is a good place to base yourself if you want to explore ashore

of them you will find Nikiana. Entry to the harbour is then straightforward.

BERTHING

The S part of the harbour is reserved for fishing boats and a charter company's yachts are moored alongside. The only available space is along the small breakwater at the E side of the harbour, where there is room at the N end for up to 10 yachts to tie up bows- or stern-to. Watch out for underwater debris here, particularly at the very end of the breakwater, which has collapsed and is partially submerged. The 2003 earthquake caused some damage and a lot of rubble lies at the base of the mole.

ANCHORING

If the harbour is full, you will find space to anchor off the western side of the bay, taking a long line ashore. Flotillas often do this as there is rarely room on the mole for a whole group.

A big ground chain runs right across the entrance to the harbour, however, so be careful when anchoring. Make sure you don't drop your anchor too far to the east or it may foul on the chain. The seabed is mud and holding is good.

There is also a good lunch-time anchorage off the beach to the south of Nikiana, but be aware that it can get quite gusty here from the north in the afternoon.

Useful information – Nikiana

FACILITIES

Water: Tap on the quay. Water is free and hoses are provided, although they won't reach to the far end of the breakwater.

Fuel: Take a taxi to a nearby service station.

Showers: Katarina's Taverna (€2-3); ask at other tavernas.

Ice: Ask at tavernas.

Rubbish: Bins at the south end of the quay.

Yacht service/chandlery: The nearest is at Nidri (5-minute taxi ride) or Lefkada (20 minutes).

Telephone: Phone boxes in the village. Phonecards available at supermarkets. Mobile reception is good.

Post: Service is good. Post office and boxes are situated in the village.

PROVISIONING

Grocery shops: Two really good, well-stocked supermarkets on the main road. For major provisioning, go to Nidri.

Bakery: On the main road.

Butcher: On the main road.

Banks: Several in Nidri.

Pharmacy: Several in Nidri.

Opening times: Shops operate to siesta hours (closed 1400-1800) but are open on Sundays.

EATING & DRINKING

Katarina's Taverna (Tel: 26450 71026), overlooking the harbour, is a very good, family-run place. Open seven days a week, it serves breakfast, lunch and dinner. Booking not required.

Pantazis Psistaria (Tel: 26450 71211) on the quay serves good Greek cuisine. Open for lunch and dinner from 1 May to 30 Sep only.

ASHORE

Nikiana is good for children as there are numerous rocks and places for them to play around in. There are also some sites of interest further inland, within walking or driving distance. The Hermitage of the Holy Fathers (Agioi Pateres) lies three miles west of Nikiana. Set in a cave, it is one of the oldest Christian monuments on Lefkada, dating back to 325AD. There are also some good views of the island from the hermitage.

Continue along the road and you will come to the monastery of Agios Georgios. Thought to date pre-1500, it has a remarkable collection of wall paintings, and during the early 18th century was responsible for the cultivation of 273 square miles of land, including the Skares forest, which forms the backdrop to Nikiana.

TRANSPORT

Taxis: Ask at the tavernas. For all other transport, see under Ligia p109.

OTHER INFORMATION

Local Tel code: 26450.

Medical Centre: 72130.

The harbour is used by a charter company and so is often full of boats

Sparti

Off north-west coast of Sparti: 38°43'.14N 20°44'.46E

Sparti is the northernmost of the Prigiponnisia (Prince's Islands), a group of densely wooded islands to the east of Nidri, which also include Madouri, Skorpidi and Skorpios. It's uninhabited and, although a rough road runs round the perimeter, it is rarely visited by yachtsmen.

You can anchor for lunch off the north-west corner of the island but it is an exposed anchorage and would soon become uncomfortable if the wind picked up.

NAVIGATION

Charts: Admiralty 203, 2402, SC5771; Imray G11, G12, G121; Hellenic Navy Hydrographic Service 213/2

From the southern end of the Lefkada Canal, steer 166°T for about 4½nm. Sparti is the first island you come to and lies opposite Perigiali on Lefkada.

From south of the Meganisi Channel, head north, leaving the islands of Thilia and Skorpios to starboard. Sparti is north-west of Madouri island, which is opposite Nidri. If you intend to sail up the west coast of Sparti, watch out for the shoal patch off its south-west tip. Depths decrease here to less than 3m and, although there is deep water just to the west of the shoal, proceed with caution. Watch your depth and stick close to the eastern shore of the islet of Heloni.

ANCHORING

Not many people anchor off Sparti, preferring instead to head south to the more protected anchorages of Vlicho or Tranquil Bay. However, it is possible to drop your hook in the bay off Sparti's north-west coast if conditions are favourable. It is deep, though, so expect to anchor in 10-15m of water.

The Prigiponnisia Islands off the east coast of Lefkada are a group of densely wooded islets. Madouri (pictured nearest) is identified by a large and conspicuous neo-classical mansion on its western shore

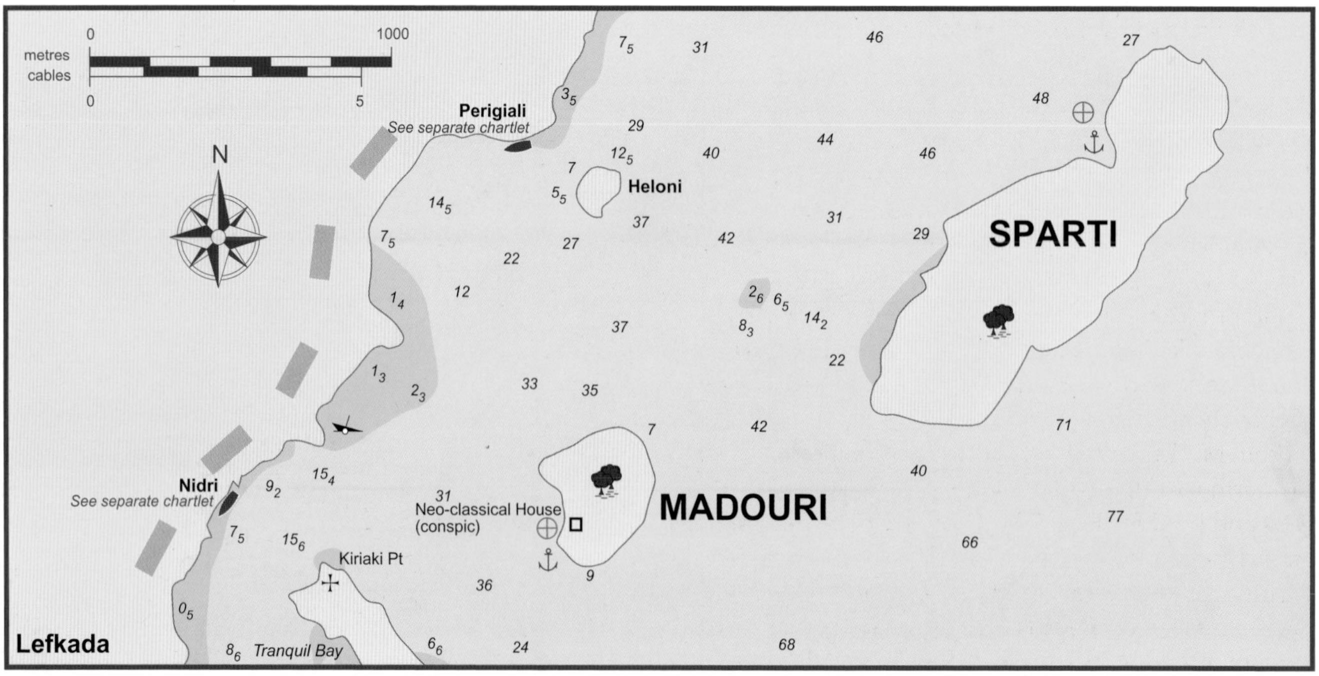

Madouri Island

Nisos Madouri, Madhouri

Off the west side of Madouri: 38°42'.40N 20°43'.36E
Charts: Admiralty 203 & 2402, SC5771; Imray G11, G12 & G121; Hellenic Navy Hydrographic Service 213/2 & 21

Madouri is a small island opposite Nidri. It is easily identified by a grand, neo-classical mansion on its western shore, set against a backdrop of thickly-grown pines. The mansion was built by Aristotle Valaoritis (1824-1879), a renowned poet who wrote the Greek National Anthem. A staunch politician who fought for the union of the Ionian islands with Greece, Valaoritis is said to have found inspiration for his work from Madouri Island.

Still owned by members of the family, the island is private and, although you can anchor to the south-west, you may not go ashore. It is also only suitable as a lunch-time stop as there is no protection from either northerly or southerly winds.

The neo-classical mansion was built by Greek poet Aristotle Valaoritis

Perigiali Periyiali

South end of quay: 38°43'.11N 20°43'.49E

Perigiali is situated on the east coast of Lefkada between Nikiana and Nidri. It's often described as a village (population 284), but in recent years has become more like a suburb of Nidri as the number of hotels and guesthouses has increased and the boundaries between the two have blurred. The harbour is actually a long straight quay with reasonable shelter from the north-west, but is exposed to all other directions and offers little in the way of facilities. Yet it's a good and slightly quieter alternative if the town quay at Nidri is full, as it is rarely busy here. Perigiali is just far enough away to discourage the masses, but it is still within easy walking distance of all of Nidri's facilities.

NAVIGATION

Charts: Admiralty 203, 2402, SC5771; Imray G11, G12, G121; Hellenic Navy Hydrographic Service 213/2

Perigiali is relatively easy to spot from all directions. It is identified by its long, straight concrete quay running parallel with the coast, with a small jetty at either end.

If approaching from Drepanos Bay, follow the east coast of Lefkada south. From Kefali Pt, Perigiali is about 3nm to the south-west and lies just to the north of the islet of Heloni.

From Mitikas or the north coast of Kalamos, head for the north-east tip of Sparti. Once off the island, turn west and head for Perigiali. If you decide to approach via the south-west corner of Sparti, deeper-draught yachts should look for the shoal between the island and the islet of Heloni. Depths here decrease to under 5m, so caution should be exercised.

If approaching from the south, via the Meganisi Channel, head north, leaving the islands of Thilia and Skorpios to starboard. Passing either side of Madouri island, follow the coast north, past Nidri and on to Perigiali. Again, take great care north of Madouri. You can sail either side of Heloni as depths in the

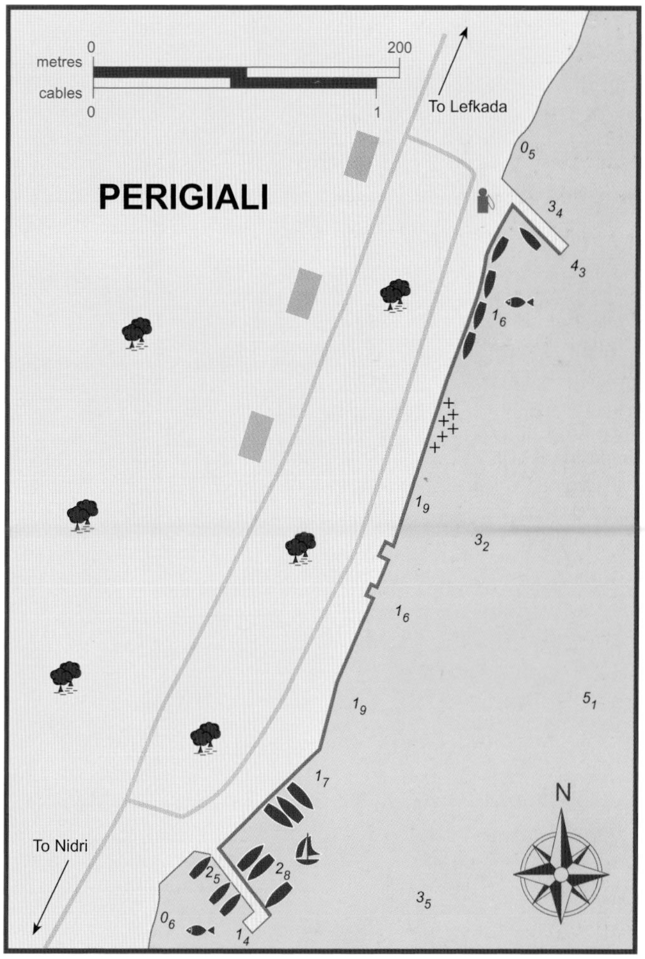

Yachts can berth stern-to off the jetty at the southern end of the quay

channels are around 10m, but proceed with caution as it is shallow in places. Anyone leaving Heloni to port should also be aware of the shoal patch off Sparti where depths decrease to less than 5m. Alternatively, head up the east coast of Sparti and approach Perigiali from the north.

The main hazard in this area is waterborne traffic. Nidri gets very busy, particularly in summer, with recreational craft and ferries coming and going all the time. Anyone approaching Perigiali from this direction should keep a good look-out.

BERTHING

The harbour at Perigiali consists of a long, straight concrete quay, with short, perpendicular jetties at either end. There is a fuel quay at the northern end, where fishing boats usually tie up, but yachts tend to berth at the southern end. Go stern- or bows-to, either on the main part of the quay or off the jetty.

It is frequently busy with traffic in this area, which can produce a nasty chop, so it is advisable to put out plenty of fenders and keep your bow or stern well off the quay.

ANCHORING

The nearest place to Perigiali to anchor is off the islet of Heloni (Cheloni, Kheloni). It's not ideal, however, and if you want to anchor along this stretch of coast you are advised to go to either Tranquil Bay, opposite Nidri, or Vlicho Bay just beyond (see p119).

Useful information – Perigiali

FACILITIES

Fuel: At the north end of the quay.
Ice: Ask at the tavernas.
Gas: Nearest bottle exchange is at the supermarkets on Nidri's main street (5-10-minute walk).
Rubbish: Nearest large bins are in Nidri.
Yacht repairs/services: Nearest is IGR Yacht Services (Tel: 26450 92601/Mobile: 6932 956861), behind the Athos Hotel in Nidri. IGR does yacht repairs, engineering and maintenance. Marina Vliho in Vlicho Bay (Tel: 26450 5218) offers a range of services, including woodwork, painting and engine repair. Georges Chandlery (Tel: 26450 92237) in Nidri sells most spares or will be able to order them for you.
Telephone: On the main Lefkada to Nidri road, which is set back from the quay.

PROVISIONING

Perigiali has basic provisions, but Nidri is only a 5-10-minute walk from the village, along the main road, and is good for stocking up.
Grocery shops: Mini-market on the main road, which is set back from the quay. Nidri has a wide choice of shops.
Bakery, butcher, banks, pharmacy, post office: see Nidri, page 117.
Opening times: Opening times vary, although the mini-market is usually open 0800-1330 and 1830-2100.

EATING OUT

There are several tavernas along the main Lefkada to Nidri road, which runs through Perigiali. The village has at least a dozen hotels and guesthouses, some with restaurants attached. Alternatively, walk into Nidri, where tavernas and bars abound (see p117-118).

ASHORE

Most people who stop at Perigiali prefer it as a quieter alternative to Nidri rather than as a base to explore Lefkada. However, there are some interesting sights nearby. The waterfalls at Dimosari are a pleasant 2½-mile walk from Nidri (see p118) with the mountain village of Vafkeri beyond. Only a handful of people live there now, but the village dates back over 400 years and there are some good views of Nidri and Lefkada's satellite islands (Sparti, Skorpios, Meganisi and Kalamos). You can hire mountain bikes from Athos Travel (Tel: 26450 92185) in Nidri and explore the Geni Peninsula encircling Vlicho Bay. Or visit the 'Red Church' Kokkini Ekklissia, to the north-west of Perigiali. Built in the 16th century, the monastery is considered to be one of the most significant Christian monuments on Lefkada. It is known as the Red Church because it stands on the site of an older church (1478), which was constructed of the local red clay.

Useful information – Perigiali

TRANSPORT
Car hire: Available in Nidri, on the town's main street: Budget (Tel: 26450 92008) open seven days a week, 0800-2100; Europcar (Tel: 26450 92712); Avis (Tel: 26450 92136); Homer Rent a car & Motorbikes (Tel: 26450 92554); Hertz (Tel: 26450 92289); Trident Car Rentals (Tel: 26450 92978). Sixt (Tel: 26450 92623). Nidri is a 5-10-minute walk away but most companies will deliver to Perigiali for a small fee.
Taxis: Taxi Lefkada (Tel: 26450 92000). Or ask at the tavernas or hotels.
Bus: KTEL (Tel: 26450 22364) runs a service from Lefkada Town to Nidri six times a day. The bus does not officially stop at Perigiali, so to catch it you are advised to walk to the bus stop at Nidri.
Ferry: Services to Kefalonia, Ithaca and Meganisi run daily in peak season from Nidri.
Air travel: The nearest is at Preveza on the mainland, an hour away by taxi.

OTHER INFORMATION
Local Tel code: 26450.
Doctor: The nearest is in Nidri. There is also the Vliho Health Centre (Tel: 26450 95204) at Vlicho, which is a 5-minute drive from Nidri.
Hospital: The nearest is in Lefkada (Tel: 26450 25371), about 40 minutes away by road.

Perigiali is near enough to Nidri to take advantage of its amenities, but far enough away that it's quieter and less touristy too

Nidri Nydri, Nydhri, Nidhrion

Off the town quay: 38°42'.39N 20°42'.76E

Nidri is Lefkada's equivalent of Corfu's Kassiopi or Palaeokastritsa. It's the largest resort on the island (population 682) and the once small fishing village is now crammed with tavernas, bars and souvenir shops. Peak season, Nidri positively groans with package holiday tourists from dusk till dawn, and if you're looking for a quiet idyll, it's not for you.

Situated on the east coast of Lefkada, Nidri lies immediately to the north of the entrance to Vlicho Bay, looking out towards the islands of Madouri, Sparti and Skorpios. It was the first harbour on Lefkada to be developed for visiting yachts and is one of the best places for victualling on the island.

Facilities for yachts are also good. There's a chandler, various boat services, water, gas bottle exchange, and fuel is available at Perigiali, just up the coast. So whatever your requirements, they can normally be met in Nidri. And for those who want to enjoy the town's hustle and bustle without being right in the middle of it, the quieter anchorages of Tranquil and Vlicho bays are within easy reach.

Nidri town quay itself is reasonably well protected with good, all-round shelter. Strong northerly winds occasionally blow down from Drepanos Bay but they are infrequent. While there is often chop in the day from the constant movements of all the boats, at night you are more likely to be kept awake by partying holiday-makers than by a nasty swell.

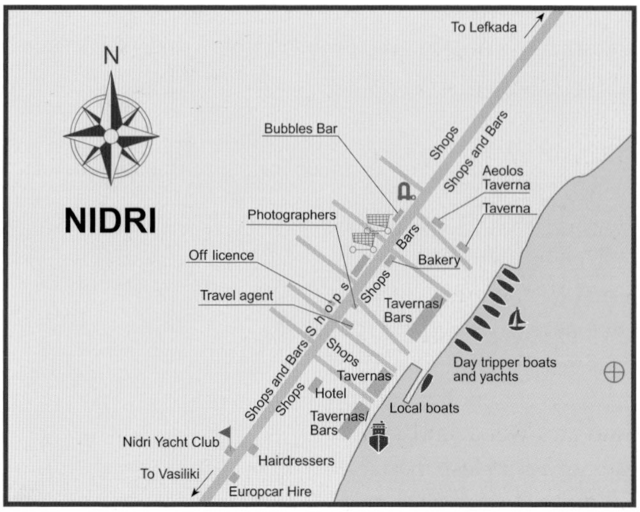

NAVIGATION

Charts: Admiralty 203, 2402, SC5771; Imray G11, G12, G121; Hellenic Navy Hydrographic Service 213/2

Hotels and holiday homes line the shoreline and hills around Nidri, making it conspicuous from all directions. If approaching from the north and Drepanos Bay, follow the east coast of Lefkada south. Nidri lies about 3½nm south of Kefali Pt, past the villages of Ligia, Nikiana and Perigiali. You can pass either side of the islet of Heloni (Cheloni, Kheloni) but deeper draught yachts should watch out for the shoal off the south-west tip of Sparti where depths decrease to less than 5m.

From Vathi on Meganisi head north-west for about 4nm. The main hazard from this direction, and indeed if approaching from the north coast of Kalamos, is the Heiromiti Shoal (If Khiromiti, see p130), between Meganisi and Skorpios. It is about the size of a football pitch and, although it is occasionally marked with a charter company's flag, it is not always visible. Stay well clear and keep an eye on your depth. If you keep in close to the Meganisi coast until Platigiali Bay, then head north-west towards the channel between Lefkada and Skorpios, you will pass through safe water.

From the south, head north up the Meganisi Channel leaving the islands of Thilia, Skorpios and Madouri to starboard. Nidri's town quay lies opposite Kiriaki Pt, just to the south of a small sailing centre.

A good lookout should be maintained at all times when approaching Nidri. The waters immediately off the town are often busy with recreational boats and ferries. Ferries won't get out of your way, so it is up to you to alter course. Several watersports companies are based on the beach too, so watch out for waterskiers, windsurfers and paragliders.

BERTHING

You can berth either stern- or bows-to on Nidri's town quay. The central section, which is marked with yellow and black stripes, is reserved for the Port Police and no berthing is allowed here. Just next to it is where the day-tripper boats tie up and, although this area is often vacant, if you do berth here you will be asked to move. Occasionally you can stop for an hour or so, but it is better if you tie up elsewhere.

If you want to stay overnight in Nidri, choose a spot at the southern or northern ends of the quay. Keep clear of the ferry berth at the southern end, below which is a jetty used by Neilson Yachts. Occasionally the charter company allows people to use this, but you are advised to ask first as it may be about to be used by boats coming back in. There is another rather rickety quay just to the south of this jetty and if there is nowhere else to tie up, you may find room here. Holding is reasonable, but do make sure that your anchor is well dug in as the constant traffic around Nidri can create a considerable chop.

Nidri is a popular destination with cruising yachts, as is Tranquil Bay, on the opposite shore

ANCHORING

Among the advantages of Nidri is that if the town quay is full, which it invariably is in summer, there are several good places to anchor within easy reach. One of the options is just to the south of the ferry berths, before Neilson Yachts' jetty. The holding is reasonably good on sticky mud and weed, and you can anchor in less than 5m quite close in to shore. Alternatively, there is a good anchorage opposite in Tranquil Bay or further to the south in Vlicho Bay; see p119.

The town quay at Nidri is often busy with day-tripper boats

Useful information – Nidri

FACILITIES

Water: Several water points along the town quay. An attendant is usually there morning and evening.
Fuel: Either take a taxi to a nearby service station or motor north to Perigiali where there is a fuel quay.
Showers: Ask at the waterfront tavernas.
Ice: Available from the fish shop on the main street, near George's Chandlery. Or ask at the tavernas.
Laundry: Nidri Yacht Club (€3). Marina Vliho in Vlicho Bay has two commercial washing machines but these are only available to the boatyard's customers.
Gas: Bottle exchange at several of the mini-markets on the main street.
Rubbish: Bins at the southern end and middle of the town quay.
Yacht repairs/services: Tiny Georges Chandlery (Tel: 26450 92237) on the main street is literally crammed with boat spares. There's no room to spend hours browsing but if you have a specific requirement you'll probably find it here. It also stocks fishing equipment. IGR Yacht Services (Tel: 26450 92601/Mobile: 6932 956861), behind the Athos Hotel, does GRP repairs, engineering, yacht management and maintenance. English speaking, IGR also runs an English to Greek translation service.

There are two boatyards in Vlicho Bay, south of Nidri. Marina Vliho (Tel: 26450 95218/95614), in the north-west corner of the bay, offers a range of services from woodwork through painting to sail and engine repair. Reception open from 1000-1330 and 1800-2030.
Telephone: Several phone boxes along the waterfront and in the main street. Phone cards at kiosks and also at some of the mini-markets. Mobile reception is good.
Fax: Infohouse at 265 Tilemahon Sterioti Street (off the main street, just before Georges Chandlery). Also available at several travel agencies in Nidri.
Internet: Nidri Yacht Club (€2 for 30 mins). Infohouse (see above) has seven PCs, internet, email, scanning and printing services. Aeolos Taverna, on a side street at the northern end of the town quay, opposite the post office, also has internet facilities. Alternatively, you can go to Vic's Bar (Tel: 26450 29190) at the northern end of the main street.

PROVISIONING

There are two main streets in Nidri. The first, just behind the quay, is packed with tavernas, cafes and bars, and the second, which runs parallel, is where most of the shops are. For clarity, I've called this the main street.
Grocery shops: Nidri is a great place to stock up, as there is plenty of variety. Walk along the main street and you will find at least six mini-markets, plus other good food shops.
Bakery: Kominatos on the main street is very good and there is another at the north end of Nidri. Most mini-markets sell fresh bread.
Butcher: A couple on the main street; there is also a fishmonger (Tel: 26450 92248) near Georges Chandlery on the main street.
Banks: Most of the banks are at the north end of the main street: Alpha Bank, Citibank, National Bank of Greece and Emporiki all have ATMs. Several travel agents also do currency exchange.
Pharmacy: Several on the main street.
Post: In a side street off the northern end of the town quay, opposite Aeolos Taverna. Stamps at most souvenir shops. The postal service in Nidri is good.
Opening times: These vary depending on the shop. Most open from 0900-1400, close for siesta and reopen again at 1800. As Nidri is a popular late-night resort, many shops stay open for longer than usual in the evenings. Shops are normally open seven days a week.

EATING OUT

There's plenty of choice in Nidri with nearly every taste and cuisine catered for. However, like most resorts of its kind, quality is average. The majority of tavernas are on the waterfront, either behind the town quay or just off the beach, and several bars are situated on the main street. The Catamaran Café serves a decent choice of pizzas and seafood; To Liotrivi (26450 92271) is a traditional Greek restaurant serving good food, as is Ta Kalamia (Tel: 26450 92137) on the main street; there's a Chinese restaurant

Useful information – Nidri

at the Athos Hotel (Tel: 26450 92384); Nic the Greek is one of the oldest tavernas in Nidri and very traditional; Aeolos on a side street at the north end of the quay serves both Greek and Continental meals. There are plenty of bars to choose from too, among which are the Barfly, Saloon Bar, Byblos nightclub, Sail Inn and New Quay Bar. Try Nidri YC for English food, beer and Sky Sports. Also does a free book swap.

ASHORE

Nidri is a good base from which to explore the rest of the island. Transport is easy and most places are within a respectable driving distance. There are also plenty of good walks. One of the most popular is up the Dimosari ravine to the waterfalls. It's about 2½-miles and, apart from the last bit, mostly flat. To get there, take the road off Nidri's main street signposted to Rachi (Rahi), then follow the signs to the waterfalls.

Like Vasiliki, Nidri boasts numerous watersports companies, so if you fancy trying paragliding, waterskiing or being thrown around on an inflatable ring, now is your chance. Nidri Watersports (Tel: 26450 92529) on the beach north of the town quay is open from 1000-2100 and offers a range of activities. Prices start from €3 to hire a canoe up to €30 for a parasailing trip. The Lefkas Diving Centre (Tel: 26450 72105) runs dive and snorkelling trips from Nidri, and several windsurfing companies can be found in Vasiliki, just a 30-minute drive away.

TRANSPORT

Car hire: All the hire car companies are on Nidri's main street: Budget (Tel: 26450 92008) opens seven days a week 0800-2100; Europcar (Tel: 26450 92712); Avis (Tel: 26450 92136); Homer Rent a car & Motorbikes (Tel: 26450 92554); Hertz (Tel: 26450 92289), closed November to March; Sixt (Tel: 26450 92623); Trident Car Rentals (Tel: 26450 92978).
Bicycle hire: Athos Travel (Tel: 26450 92185)
Taxis: Taxi Lefkada (Tel: 26450 92000).
Bus: KTEL (Tel: 26450 22364) operates regular daily bus services between Nidri and Lefkada Town and Nidri and Vasiliki.

The waterfalls at Dimosari

Ferry: Car and foot-passenger services run between Nidri and Porto Spilia and Vathi on Meganisi up to five times a day, peak season. Ferries also sail to Fiskardo on Kefalonia and Frikes on Ithaca.
Air travel: The nearest airport is at Preveza on the mainland – 1hr away by taxi.

OTHER INFORMATION

Local Tel code: 26450.
Port authority: Tel: 26450 92509.
Doctor: Dr Christos Gizelis (Tel: 69454 64613) is an English-speaking doctor in Nidri. A second English-speaking doctor has a surgery on the main street (Tel: 69389 95263). Vliho Health Centre (Tel: 26450 95204), at Vlicho, is a 5-minute drive from Nidri.
Hospital: Nearest is in Lefkada (Tel: 26450 25371), about 45 mins away by road.

Nidri's town centre. You'll find everything here – from butchers, bakers and supermarkets, to banks, bars and chandlers

Tranquil Bay

Wpt in Tranquil Bay: 38°42'.12N 20°42'.80E

Tranquil Bay is to the south-east of Nidri. It may be tranquil by name but certainly not by nature. During the high season it is generally packed with boats, and even out of season it is a popular anchorage for live-aboards and long-term cruisers. Having said that, it is a good spot if you want to be near to, but not on top of, the hustle and bustle of Nidri. The bay faces west and provides good all-round shelter.

NAVIGATION

Charts: Admiralty 203 & 2402, SC5771; Imray G11, G12 & G121; Hellenic Navy Hydrographic Service 213/2

The approach to Tranquil Bay is easy and hazard-free. Head towards Nidri, and turn into the bay once past the church of Agios Kiriaki on the headland directly opposite the town.

ANCHORING

Tranquil Bay gets very busy, so it is good practice to anchor stern-to with a line ashore to stop you swinging around. While you can drop your hook anywhere within the bay where there is room, it is important to dig it well in. The bottom is weedy and holding is only good once you have cut through this. Beware the shoal patch in the south-east corner of the bay. Anchor in 5-10m.

FACILITIES/PROVISIONING

There are no facilities in the bay, but Nidri, with its banks, supermarkets, tavernas and all the supplies you could want, is a short hop by tender across the channel.

ASHORE

The church of Agios Kiriaki on the northern headland of Tranquil Bay is worth a visit. One thought is that the church was built on an ancient temple of the Nymphs. Another site of interest, on the hillside above the church, is the grave of the German archaeologist Wilhelm Dörpfeld, whose theories that Lefkada was Homer's Ithaca in the *Odyssey* (see p10) caused controversy at the turn of the 20th century. Dörpfeld's house is on the peninsula.

Right: The anchorage in Tranquil Bay is very popular with liveaboards

Vlicho Bay Vlycho, Vlikho

Entrance waypoint: 38°41'.56N 20°42'.39E
Quay off Vlicho village: 38°41'.15N 20°42'.01E

Vlicho Bay, to the south of Nidri, on the east coast of Lefkada, is a large, enclosed bay. Entered via a narrow channel, 0.5nm from Nidri, it offers a good alternative anchorage to Tranquil Bay. Shallow and flanked by high, tree-clad mountain ranges to the south and west, it is a good place to anchor if you want the facilities of Nidri but prefer not to be right in the centre of it. The bay offers reasonable shelter from the prevailing winds. However, the surrounding hillside does funnel southerly and northerly winds, which can make the bay very gusty at times, particularly in the early evening.

Yachts can anchor anywhere or berth on either of the small quays at the south-west end of the bay. Like Tranquil Bay, Vlicho attracts liveaboards to its free moorings but despite the tourist developments further up the coast it remains relatively unspoilt. The small village of Vlicho (population 410) lies on the southwestern shore.

NAVIGATION

Charts: Admiralty 203 & 2402, SC5771; Imray G11, G12 & G121; Hellenic Navy Hydrographic Service 213/2

On approach from any direction, head for Nidri, about halfway down the east coast of Lefkada. Once off Nidri, head south, past the town and ferry quays. You will see Tranquil Bay to port and shortly afterwards the channel narrows to a bottleneck before opening up to form Vlicho Bay, easily identified by the two boatyards on the north-west shore. Depths in the channel shelve to about 3m but increase to around 6m in the centre of the bay. The south and south-east parts of the bay are very shallow, at 1m or less, and quite marshy, so it is best to stay near the centre.

All the hazards in the approach to Nidri should be considered when on passage to Vlicho. Watch out in particular for the regular ferry traffic.

BERTHING

At the south-west end of the bay there are two small quays in about 3m of water, next to the main road to Nidri. The older quay is usually packed with boats berthed alongside, some of them looking as if they haven't moved for years; but you can normally find space on the newer quay. Berth either bows- or stern-to but make sure that you are a good distance off the quay and that your anchor is well dug-in. The hillsides in Vlicho Bay often funnel strong gusts along this quay, from the west-north-west, which can create quite a chop. If you are planning to leave your boat here unattended, it is a good idea to put a kedge anchor out as extra protection. The seabed is sticky mud and weed but gives good holding.

In 2007 there were concrete blocks on the foreshore which looked as if they were going to be used to extend the quay. However, harbour improvements take a considerable amount of time in Greece, so it may be some years before the new blocks are in place. A brand new T-shaped pontoon has also been installed on the north-west

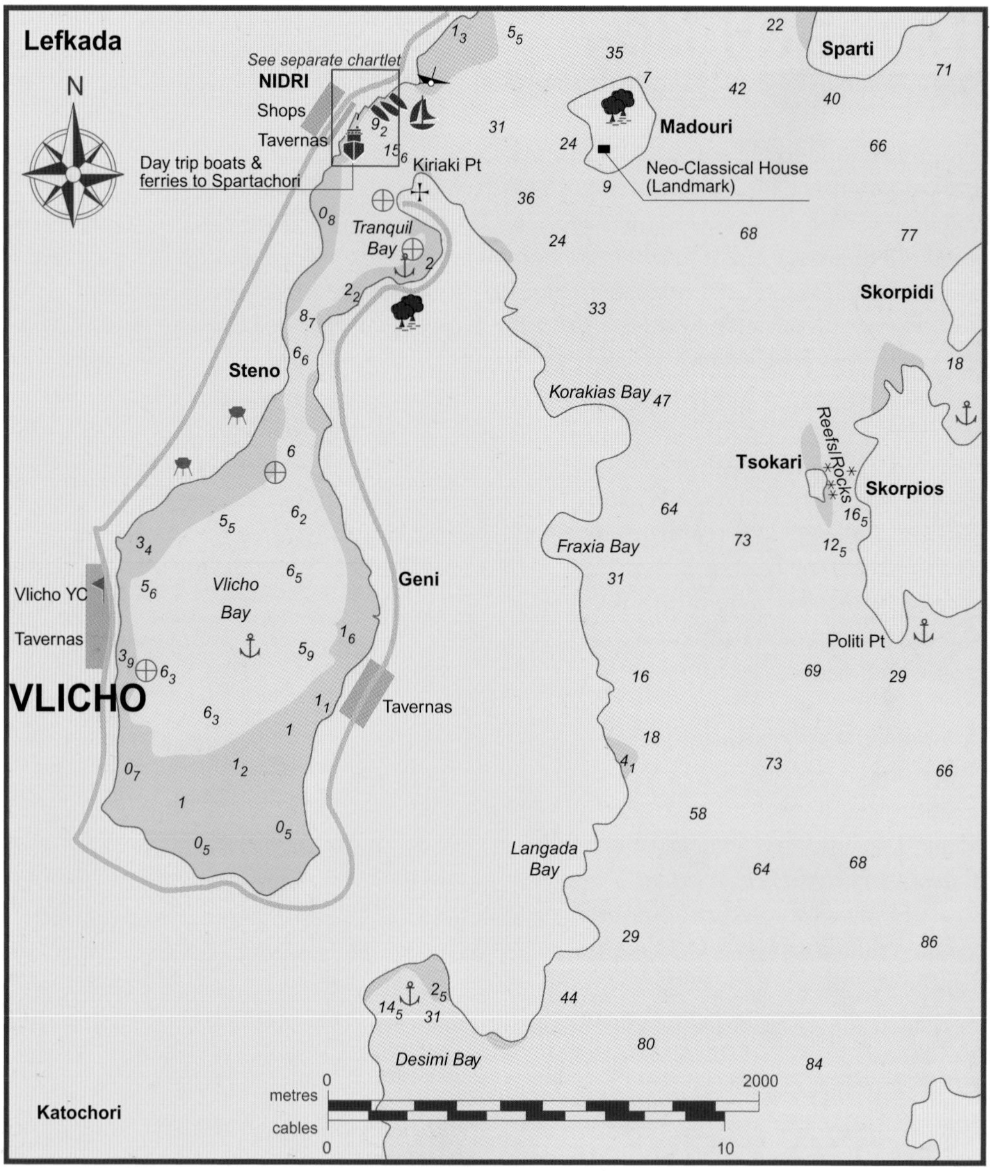

shore. This is reserved for the Sail Ionian charter fleet.

Vlicho Bay is a large, enclosed bay south of Nidri that is flanked by high, tree-clad mountains

ANCHORING

Most of the bay is less than 10m deep so you can anchor almost anywhere, apart from the southern end where depths are around 1m. There is also plenty of room to free-swing so you don't have to worry about taking a line ashore. The eastern side of the bay is usually popular as there are a couple of small tavernas here, and it is possible to anchor off and take a line ashore. The north-west corner, off the boatyard, is also a good spot as it is sheltered from the northwesterly winds. Unless the wind is very strong, Vlicho Bay is usually suitable for overnight anchoring.

Useful information – Vlicho Bay

FACILITIES

Water: On the quayside.
Fuel: Take a taxi and jerrycans to a nearby service station.
Ice: Ask at tavernas.
Gas: Bottle exchange at some supermarkets in Nidri (five minutes by car or 30 minutes on foot).
Telephone: Phone box next to the quay on the main road. Mobile reception is good.
Post: One in Vlicho village. Stamps available at supermarkets and souvenir shops. The postal service on Lefkada is generally good as it is one of the larger islands and closely connected to the mainland.
Yacht services: A small chandlery and yacht management service are situated near the quay. There are also two boatyards in Vlicho Bay, one just to the north of the village and another, Marina Vliho, on the west side of the entrance. Marina Vliho (Tel: 26450 95218/95614) was established in 1960 and offers a range of services, including woodwork, painting, antifouling, electrical engineering and sail repair. Facilities for yard customers include: water, electricity, showers, toilets and a launderette. Reception is open from 1000-1330 and 1800-2030.

The Vliho Yacht Club (Tel: 26450 29282) in the village is a family run club with laundry and internet facilities. Closed Tuesday. Other services are available in Nidri, which is a five-minute drive away.

PROVISIONING

Grocery shops: Supermarket and mini-market in Vlicho village. Nidri is very good for supplies if you need a major shop.
Banks: In Nidri.
Pharmacy: In Nidri.
Opening times: Shops operate to siesta hours (closed 1400-1800).

TRANSPORT

Car/moped hire: In Nidri. Most hire companies will deliver to Vlicho for a small surcharge.
Taxis: Ask at tavernas in Vlicho.
Bus: KTEL operates a regular service down the east coast of Lefkada, with up to seven a day between Nidri and Lefkada town. Services also operate from Nidri to Vasiliki.
Ferry: In Nidri there are daily services to Meganisi, Kephalonia and Ithaca.
Airport: At Preveza on the mainland, an hour by taxi.

EATING OUT

Four tavernas in Vlicho village serve good, wholesome Greek food. There are also a couple of tavernas on the eastern side of the bay. Alternatively, Nidri is a 30-minute walk away and has many eating establishments.

ASHORE

If you don't want to get involved with the hustle and bustle of Nidri, but feel the need to stretch your legs, there are some lovely walks around the southern and eastern sides of Vlicho Bay. Either take the coast road or row your tender ashore. If you have hired a car or would like a good long hike, take the small road uphill behind Vlicho to the village of Haradiatika and the abandoned hamlet of Alatro beyond. On the outskirts of Alatro you will find Agios Ioannis Prodromos, a beautiful little church full of early 17th century wall paintings, one of the only examples of its kind on Levkas. Views from here are spectacular.

OTHER INFORMATION

Local Tel code: 26450.
Doctor: Vlicho Health Centre (Tel: 26450 95204).
Dentist: In Nidri.
Hospital: In Lefkada Town, approximately 25 minutes' drive to the north.

There are several tavernas at Vlicho – a short row from the anchorage

Desimi Bay

Dessimou Bay, Dessimi Bay, Dhessimi Bay, Ormos Desimo

Entrance waypoint : 38°40'.17N 20°42'.89E

Charts: Admiralty 203 & 2402, SC5771; Imray G11, G12 & G121; Hellenic Navy Hydrographic Service 21

Desimi Bay lies about 2½nm south of Nidri on Lefkada's east coast. The large, deep bay on the south-eastern end of the Geni peninsula is a good anchorage in all but southerly and north-easterly winds. Anchor in its north-west corner in 8-12m. There is a taverna (Pirofani) ashore and two campsites, one at either end of the sandy beach. It's a popular anchorage with good views across to Meganisi.

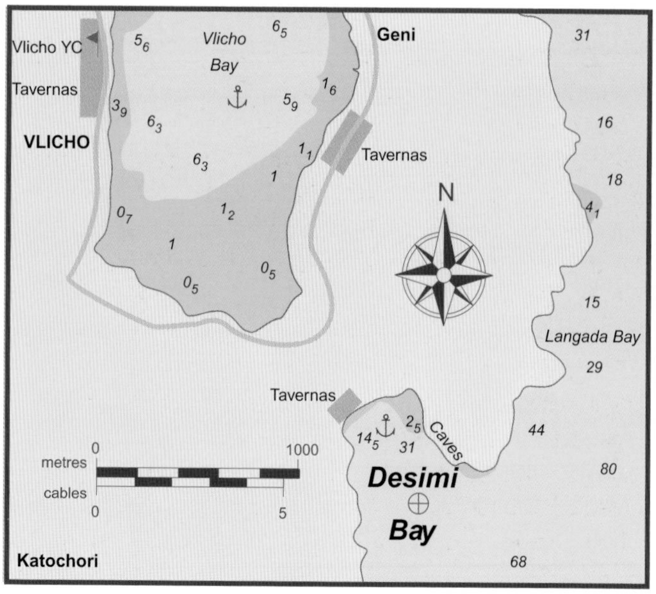

Rouda Bay

Ormos Roudha

Entrance waypoint: 38°37'.45N 20°42'.36E

Bay: 38°37'.99N 20°41'.99E

Anchorage: 38°38'.31N 20°41'.87E

Rouda Bay lies on the south-east coast of Lefkada and is the first you come to when leaving the southern end of the Meganisi Channel. It's a large bay, with the small resort of Mikros Gialos (Mikros Yialos or Ghialos) at its head. This has a couple of hotels, a campsite and basic provisions. The little village of Poros (population 236) overlooks the bay on the hillside to the east.

While there is often some swell at the entrance, Rouda Bay itself is usually very flat and is well protected from all directions but the south. It's a good lunchtime or overnight stop and, should conditions deteriorate suddenly, you will find a safe refuge in the harbour of Sivota, a 20-minute motor to the west.

Rouda Bay. The best anchorage and shelter can be found on the western side of the bay

NAVIGATION

Charts: Admiralty 203, SC5771; Imray G11, G12 & G121; Hellenic Navy Hydrographic Service 21

The approach to Rouda Bay is straightforward. From Nidri, head south down the Meganisi Channel and at the southern tip of Lefkada turn west. The entrance to Rouda Bay is about 1nm further on. From Fiskardo, on the north-east coast of Kefalonia, head 032°T for approximately 11nm. From Frikes, on the north-east corner of Ithaca, head 007°T, passing either side of Arkoudi Island. There are reefs off the south-west, south-east and north-east corners of Arkoudi so stay a safe distance from the island. It is also very important to keep a good look-out while crossing the Kefalonia Strait as shipping lanes run along the north coast of Kefalonia and down the east coast of Ithaca. The same applies if you are on passage from the south.

The entrance to Rouda Bay is through deep water and is free of hazards.

BERTHING

On the eastern side of the bay is a concrete quay and small harbour protected by a short mole. While the harbour is accessible to fishing boats and small motor-boats, it is not suitable for yachts and, consequently, Rouda Bay is recommended as an anchorage only.

ANCHORING

The best and most sheltered place in Rouda Bay is on the western side, in a small inlet to the left of a big house. However, as long as you avoid the buoyed swimming area off the main beach, you can anchor anywhere. The seabed is mud, with patches of weed, and the water is so clear that you can often see your anchor on the bottom. Drop it in 10-15m of water.

Useful information – Rouda Bay

FACILITIES

Basic provisions can be found at the small resort of Mikros Gialos (also known as Poros beach) at the head of bay. The village of Poros, a 2½-mile walk up the hill, also has the essential amenities, but is small. For a major shop, travel to Nidri or Vasiliki.

Water: Nearest is at Sivota (20 minutes' motor to the west).

Fuel: Nearest is at Nidri, about 6nm to the north.

Ice: Ask at the tavernas.

Laundry: At Poros Beach Campsite in the north-east corner of the bay; may not be open to non-campsite clients.

Gas: Nearest supply is at Sivota.

Rubbish: Bins on the beach.

Telephone: In Mikros Gialos and at Poros Beach Campsite, in the north-east corner of the bay.

Internet/Fax: At Poros Beach Campsite.

PROVISIONING

Grocery shops: Small mini-market at Poros Beach Campsite. Another small mini-market in Poros village, a 2½-mile walk up the hill. Better provisions at Sivota (20 minutes' motor to the west) or Nidri (about 6nm north).

Banks: Nearest at Nidri.

Post box: At Poros Beach Campsite. The mini-market has stamps.

Opening hours: Generally 0900-1400 and 1800-2030 but do vary. Siesta hours between 1400-1800.

EATING OUT

O Molos (Tel: 26450 95548) is a good fish taverna on the harbour front at Mikros Gialos, in the north-east corner of Rouda Bay. Zolithros (Tel: 26450 95111), also at Mikros Gialos, serves very good fresh fish and has superb views. There are a couple of tavernas in Poros.

ASHORE

The charming little village of **Poros**, nestled in the hillside above Rouda Bay, remains very traditional and is less touristy than the resort of Mikros Gialos below. It's a 2½-mile walk from the beach but well worth it.

If you want to stretch your legs further, head north from Poros for about half a mile and you will come to the tiny, 17th century church of Analipsi. It's one of the oldest on Lefkada and contains some very faded wall paintings.

Located on the very SE tip of Lefkada are Bat Caves, which aquired their name from the fact that there are bats within and also that they resemble a pair of bat's ears. The cave to explore is in the bottom right hand 'ear': You can take your dinghy inside, although you will have to duck down for the first metre or so until the cave opens up to reveal starfish, coral, sea cucumbers, stalactites, stalagmites and, of course, bats. The best time to visit is first thing in the morning when there is no swell and the sunlight bounces off the water, emphasising the beautiful turquoise and aquamarine colours.

TRANSPORT

Car hire: Ask at Poros Beach Campsite.

Taxis: Ask at the tavernas or Poros Beach Campsite.

Bus: KTEL (Tel: 26450 22364) operates a twice-daily service from Lefkada Town to Poros.

Ferry: A service to Fiskardo on Kefalonia and Frikes on Ithaca runs from Vasiliki, about 9nm west from Rouda Bay. Ferries to Meganisi, Kefalonia and Ithaca run from Nidri, about 6nm to the north.

Air travel: The nearest airport is at Preveza on the mainland, a 1½ hour-drive by taxi.

OTHER INFORMATION

Local Tel code: 26450.

Chandlery/yacht services: Nearest is Sivota Yacht Services (Tel: 02645 031849; Mobile: 06946 580785) in Sivota (a 20-minute motor to the west).

There is a mini resort ashore and basic provisions can be found in the village of Poros nearby

Sivota Syvota, Ormos Sivota

Entrance to Sivota Bay: 38°36'.88N 20°41'.51E
Off flagpoles in Sivota channel: 38°37'.13N 20°41'.39E
Sivota Harbour: 38°37'.35N 20°41'.04E

The fjord-like inlet of Sivota Bay is protected by steep-sided mountains

Sivota is situated on the south coast of Lefkada, immediately to the west of Rouda Bay. It's a little village tucked in a fjord-like inlet that curls around protectively and hides the harbour from the sea.

Over the last couple of years the village has made a conscious effort to improve facilities to attract more yachts and now the harbour is often bustling with activity. It can get crowded, particularly when the Sivota-based charter company has a turnaround day, but there is usually plenty of room for everyone. In September, the village hosts the annual Ionian Regatta's after-race party and if you want to see what the harbour looks like when it's really full, then this is the time to visit. It's not unusual for boats to be rafted three or four deep.

Sivota is a working port, albeit small, and as a result it has some of the finest fish restaurants on the island. For its size (population 113), it has a good selection of shops and most provisions can be bought. Those that can't can be purchased from Nidri or Lefkada Town, both within easy driving distance (30 and 45 minutes respectively). Although the bay can often be quite gusty, Sivota is the safest harbour along this stretch of coast and offers good shelter.

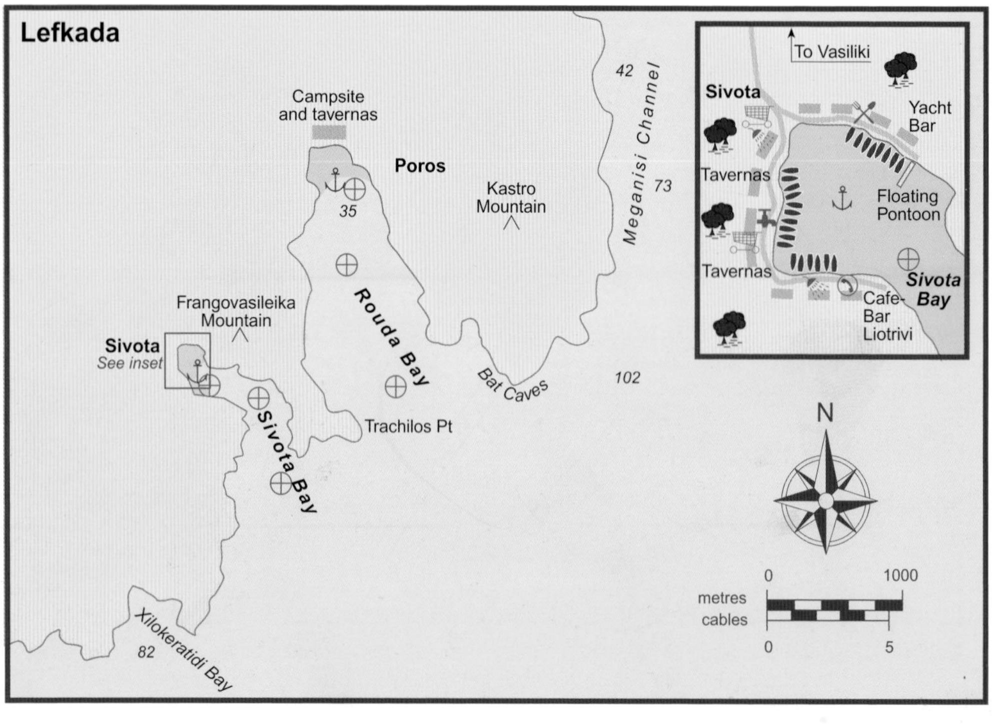

NAVIGATION

Charts: Admiralty 203, SC5771; Imray G11, G12 & G121

From the southern end of the Meganisi Channel, turn west and follow the coastline for approximately 2nm. From Fiskardo on Kefalonia, steer 032°T for 10nm, heading towards the Meganisi Channel. Leave Arkoudi island to starboard, and when Rouda Bay, the easternmost bay on Lefkada, becomes visible, steer to a point slightly west of it. The entrance to Sivota lies almost due north of Arkoudi island.

From the south-east, steer 315°T, passing to the east of the islands of Atokos and Arkoudi and heading towards the Meganisi Channel.

All approaches to Sivota are through deep water and hazard free. However, if on passage from the south, be aware of the shipping lanes which run up the east coast of Ithaca and through the Kefalonia Strait, which divides Kefalonia and Ithaca from Lefkada. Visibility in this area is good 99 per cent of the time but don't linger in the channels as traffic is frequent and it is surprising how quickly it will creep up on you.

The entrance to Sivota can often be difficult to find as the channel forms a dog-leg and the village itself is hidden behind the hills. Look for three houses with pink roofs stepped down the hillside, slightly to the west of Rouda Bay. These are on the eastern headland of the entrance to Sivota. Once inside the bay you will see three flagpoles on the shore to port, flying Greek, Italian and European flags. Follow the channel round to the left and the village of Sivota will become visible. The channel to Sivota is deep on both sides, so you can use the full width of it.

BERTHING

There are four quays within the harbour: the first, on the southern side, is immediately to port as you enter the bay and runs from the Café Bar Liotrivi to a small beach in the south-west corner. A second, on the western side, runs in front of several tavernas and café-bars, while a third, smaller quay is situated to the north-east. The fourth is the floating pontoon outside the Yacht Bar.

The southern quay has the deepest water (2.5-3m) and you can go bows- or stern-to here; but be aware that a ground chain lies approximately 80m from the quay. Also note that the Café Bar Liotrivi is open until late and can be noisy. It's not a good place, therefore, to berth if you want an early night. The same goes for the north-east quay, in front of Restaurant Ionio and the Yacht Bar. It's shallower here (2m), but yachts of up to 40ft should be able to berth stern or bows-to if care is taken. The western quay (2-3m of water) is used by local fishing boats and, although in front of several tavernas, is usually quieter. Go stern-to if possible as the quay is fairly low and bows-to may make disembarking harder. The holding can be dodgy as the seabed is weedy, so drop your anchor further out than usual. Keep clear of the permanent moorings in the south-west corner of the bay. Finally, the floating pontoon: here you will find lazylines installed on its western side, but you will need to drop your anchor if using its eastern side. Costs per night, inclusive of electricity and water, for a 42ft yacht are €8 – pay Andreas at the Yacht Bar.

The charter company Sailing Holidays uses Sivota as its base, so twice a week on turnaround days it can get quite busy. The days vary from season to season but the harbour is large and there is normally room for everyone.

ANCHORING

A popular alternative to tying up on the quays is to free-swing to your anchor in the bay. Depths there are between 8-10m and the seabed is mud and weed. While the bay provides good shelter, it sometimes gets quite windy in the afternoon with northwesterly gusts coming off the hills and down the valleys. It is worth checking that your anchor is dug in well before leaving the boat unattended.

Another good anchorage is on the eastern side of the entrance channel, opposite the three flagpoles.

Sivota is a vibrant place and packed with tavernas and shops. There's usually plenty of room to berth on the quay too

Useful information – Sivota

FACILITIES

Water: Metered taps by Taverna Delfinia (€2 coin for about 40-60 litres of water), to the right of the Café Bar Liotrivi. Hoses provided. None on the north-east quay.
Fuel: Take a taxi to the service station outside the village.
Showers: Available at Taverna Delfinia; Taverna Palia Apothiki (Café Taverna Old Store); Stavros Taverna (€3); in the building to the right of the Café Bar Liotrivi; at Sivota Economy Spar at the north-west corner of the bay and at Restaurant Ionio in the north-east corner.
Ice: Ask at the tavernas.
Gas: Bottle exchange at the supermarket to the right of Taverna Delfinia.
Rubbish: Bins next to Taverna Delfinia, and next to the beaches at the northern and southern ends of the bay.
Telephone: Several along the quay. Phone cards available at both supermarkets. Mobile reception is poor as the hills that flank the village block signals; slightly better on the S side of the harbour, near Café Bar Liotrivi.
Internet: Ask at Sivota Economy Spar and at Restaurant Ionio.

PROVISIONING

Grocery shops: Supermarket set back from the quay to right of Taverna Delfinia. Fresh bread every day, fruit and veg, gas bottle exchange, phone cards and fish bait. There's a second supermarket, Sivota Economy Spar, at the N end of the harbour which sells a wide range of goods, including eggs, English books and newspapers.
Shops: A couple of souvenir shops in the village.
Banks: Nearest in Nidri (a 30-minute taxi ride away).
Bakery: A mobile bakery usually tours the harbour in the morning at about 0900.
Butcher: Nearest in Nidri.
Pharmacy: Nearest in Vasiliki (15 minutes by taxi).
Post: No post office, but post box on quay, below supermarket. Stamps available at souvenir shops and supermarkets.
Opening times: Times vary, but usually open 0900-1400 and 1830-2100, seven days a week.
Fishing and marine shop: On the E side of the harbour.

EATING OUT

Sivota has a good selection of local restaurants compared with many similar-sized towns. The fish is particularly good. Café Bar Liotrivi (The Olive Press, Tel: 26450 31870) is in a restored stone olive press building at the south end of the harbour. A small garden and shaded seating is ideal for daytime drinks; in the evening there's a DJ and late night dancing. Taverna Delfinia (Tel: 26450 31180), on the western quay, is one of the oldest established and largest tavernas in Sivota. Fresh fish caught by the owner, Yannis, is a speciality, and several dishes on the menu are exclusive to Delfinia. Open seven days a week for breakfast, lunch and dinner. Taverna Palia Apothiki (The Old Store), to the right of Delfinia, is in a beautifully converted grain store. It opened in 2002 and has set a high standard. Open seven days a week for breakfast, lunch and dinner. Stavros, to the right of the Old Store, is a good fish taverna with a balcony seating area. Spiradoula (No Problem), next door to Stavros, was established in 1970. It offers good food and a roof garden dining area with views over Sivota Bay. Restaurant Ionio (Ionian Taverna) on the north-east quay is often less crowded but has a very good fresh fish menu. The Yacht Bar (Tel: 26450 031820) on the north-east quay is a modern bar with waterside seating. Open until as late as there are customers, it has a DJ booth and dance floor and is one of the last places in Sivota to get the afternoon sun.

ASHORE

Sivota is a very sheltered harbour, making it a good place to leave your boat for the day and explore Lefkada. You can hire a car and travel inland to see the 1654 monastery of Agios Ioanniou Theologou, south of Vournikas, or the Karoucha cave near Sivros. Or if you don't intend to sail there, head west to Vasiliki, the windsurfers' Mecca. Road links are good. Alternatively, walk/row to the small beaches around Sivota Bay and channel.

TRANSPORT

Car/moped hire: Ask at Sivota Economy Spar. Alternatively, hire from Nidri or Vasiliki; expect a surcharge for delivery.
Taxis: Ask at tavernas.
Bus: KTEL service from Sivota to Lefkada Town runs twice daily.
Ferry: Ferries to Fiskardo on Kephalonia run from Vasiliki (a 15-minute taxi-ride or about 8nm by water), while those to Meganisi, Kefalonia and Ithaca run from Nidri (a 30-minute taxi-ride or about 8nm by water).
Airport: the nearest airport is at Preveza on the mainland, a 1½-hour taxi ride away.

OTHER INFORMATION

Local Tel code: 26450.
Yacht services: Sivota Yacht Services (Tel: 2645 031849; Mobile: 6946 580785) specialises in electronics, hydraulics and engine maintenance. The business is run by an English marine engineer.
Doctor: 24-hour medical centre in Vasiliki (15-minutes by taxi), doctor in Nidri (30-minutes by taxi).
Hospital: In Lefkada Town (1 hour by taxi).

Afteli Bay

Ormos Aphteli, Schidi Bay

Entrance waypoint: 38°35'.63N 20°39'.36E
Charts: Admiralty 203, SC5771; Imray G11, G12 & G121; Hellenic Navy Hydrographic Service 21

Many day-trip boats stop at Afteli, a large bay about 2nm to the west of the entrance to Sivota. It boasts a lovely beach but can be a rather rolly anchorage even when there is no wind. A good place for lunch-time stops, although only in flat calm conditions. Depths are considerable, too, until close in.

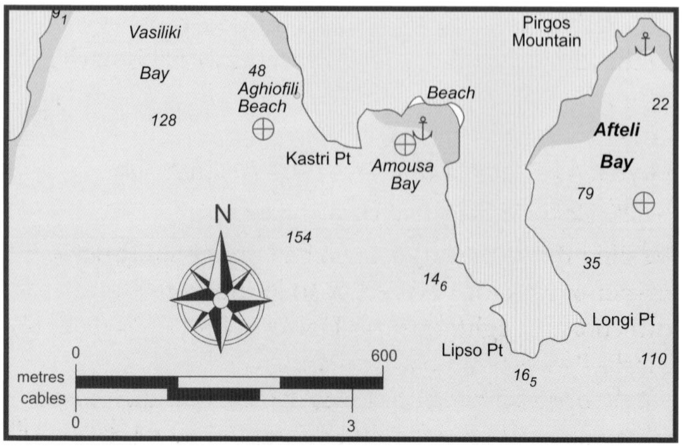

Kastri Bay Ormos Ammouso, Ammousa Bay, Amouso Bay

Entrance waypoint: 38°35'.74N 20°37'.56E

Charts: Admiralty 203, SC5771; Imray G11, G12 & G121; Hellenic Navy Hydrographic Service 21

Further to the west, just before you reach Vasiliki, is Kastri Bay. This large, south-west-facing bay has a white, sandy beach and is tucked behind Lipso Pt. It's a lovely daytime anchorage and less popular than other nearby beaches such as Aghiofili, but not at all protected. Once the prevailing winds get up in the afternoons, swell is pushed in here, so the anchorage should only be used in calm conditions. Should the weather deteriorate suddenly, Sivota, about 6nm to the east, is a good refuge.

Vasiliki

Vassiliki, Ormos Vasilikis

Approach to Vasiliki: 38°35'.82N 20°36'.57E

Outer Harbour entrance waypoint: 38°37'.55N 20°36'.33E

Inner Harbour entrance waypoint: 38°37'.61N 20°36'.38E

Situated on the south-west coast of Lefkada, Vasiliki Bay is a windsurfer's Mecca. It's renowned for being one of Europe's finest windsurfing destinations and during peak season literally hundreds of boards can be seen scorching across the bay. The strong, north-westerly winds within the bay most afternoons attract windsurfers from around the world. Erik, as the wind is known locally, produces particularly good sport. It was named after the British windsurfer Erik Beale, who in 1988 set a record of 40.48 knots at the British Speed & Slalom Championships.

Even if you have no interest in windsurfing, Vasiliki is worth a visit for the yachtsman. The village itself, in the north-east corner of the bay, is small (population 368) yet vibrant and, although it attracts a largely youthful and trendy crowd for its watersports facilities, it has none of the tackiness of other resorts on the island, such as Nidri.

The strong afternoon winds so enjoyed by the windsurfers can make life interesting for anyone entering the bay on a yacht and the chop that builds up is at times particularly unpleasant. However, it generally dies down in the evening and yachts tied up in the inner harbour are assured of reasonable shelter.

NAVIGATION

Charts: Admiralty 203, 2402, SC5771; Imray G11, G12, G121; Hellenic Navy Hydrographic Service 213/2

Vasiliki Bay is the large, open bay on the south-west corner of Lefkada and is easy to locate from all directions. A lighthouse on Doukato Pt (Fl 10s70m24M) marks its westernmost headland.

On approach from the southern end of the Meganisi Channel, head west for about 7nm, following the south coast of Lefkada. Vasiliki Bay lies just beyond Lipso Pt. From Fiskardo, on the north coast of Kefalonia, head north for about 10nm. If approaching from the south-east, leave Atokos and Arkoudi island to starboard and steer slightly west of Lipso Pt – look for the brown diagonal scar running down the east-facing mountain-side. On this passage and from the north coast of Kefalonia and Ithaca, watch out for cargo ships and high-speed ferries. Shipping lanes run through the Kefalonia Strait, between Lefkada and the north coast of Kefalonia, and along the east coast of Ithaca and, while visibility is usually good, these lanes are often busy.

Similarly, when entering or leaving Vasiliki Bay, keep a good look-out for the Vasiliki to Fiskardo ferry, which runs two or three times a day in high season. The western side of the bay is normally alive with windsurfers, so it's important to keep an eye on them, too, especially in the afternoons.

Vasiliki Harbour lies in the north-east corner of the bay, to the east of the beach, and all approaches to it are through deep water. The small village of Pondi (Ponti) lies on the north-west side of the bay.

The outer breakwater at Vasiliki is lit (Fl G 3s7m3M)

BERTHING

There are two places to berth in Vasiliki: in the inner harbour at the northern end of the bay or on the concrete quay between the two moles. Both are marked by lights. Most yachts moor in the inner harbour, which is better protected, but entry can be tricky as a river just to the west of the harbour regularly deposits sand at its narrow entrance, partially blocking it. Consequently, some deeper-draught yachts may experience difficulties passing over the sandbar, particularly if it is breezy as it often is in the afternoons.

If you want to go into the inner harbour, make sure you have all lines, fenders and anchors ready before making your approach. Keep as tight in to the southern mole of the inner harbour as possible, taking care not to run over the anchor lines of yachts already berthed. Keeping an eye on your depth, proceed slowly through the entrance, so that if you do touch on the sandbar you can easily motor off. Once inside the inner harbour, depths increase and there is more room to manoeuvre. Yachts tie up stern- or bows-to the southern mole, while fishing, tripper and motor boats use the rest of the harbour. Although the inner harbour is flanked by tavernas and café-bars, it has a genial atmosphere and doesn't get too rowdy.

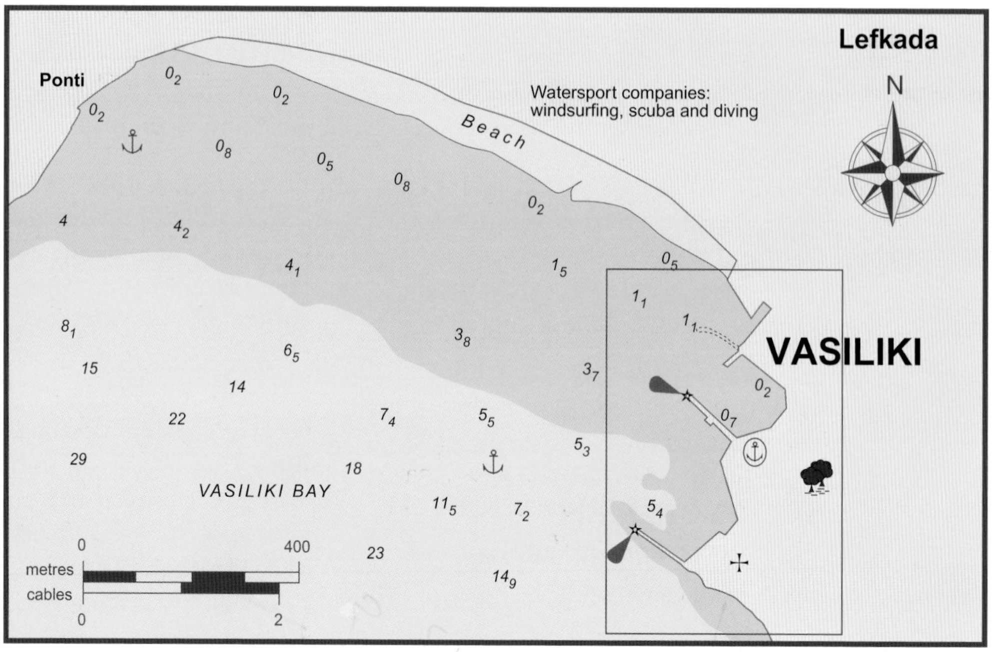

An alternative place to berth is alongside the concrete quay, to the south of the inner harbour, between the two moles. It can be quite rolly here, particularly in the afternoons, as there is no breakwater to protect the quay from any swell; this usually dies down in the evening. Tie up side-to wherever space is available, but avoid the southern end of the quay, next to the mole, as the Vasiliki to Fiskardo ferry comes alongside here. While it is not there overnight, it does enter the harbour two or three times a day in high season.

There are plans to develop this part of the harbour to provide more space for bigger yachts but so far the only improvements have been the installation of rings for tying up along the quay.

There are two harbours at Vasiliki: the outer one is large and susceptible to swell, and the inner one has a sandbar running across its entrance

ANCHORING

You can anchor off the beach in Vasiliki Bay, although it is not advised. The seabed shelves quite gradually, so you can't get very close in, and the waters off the beach are usually very busy with swimmers, windsurfers and dinghy sailors. The risk of collision is therefore high, particularly in the afternoons when the wind picks up. The seabed is sand and mud and the holding is generally good but the bay is exposed.

If you do want to anchor, there are several inlets on the eastern side of Vasiliki Bay. The cove to the west of Kastri Pt, off Aghiofili beach, is a good spot for lunch or a swim, but get here early as it is popular with daytrip boats in the afternoons. It is also an untenable anchorage once the prevailing winds start to curl round Doukato Pt as they push a swell into the bay.

Vasiliki's waterfront is packed with tavernas

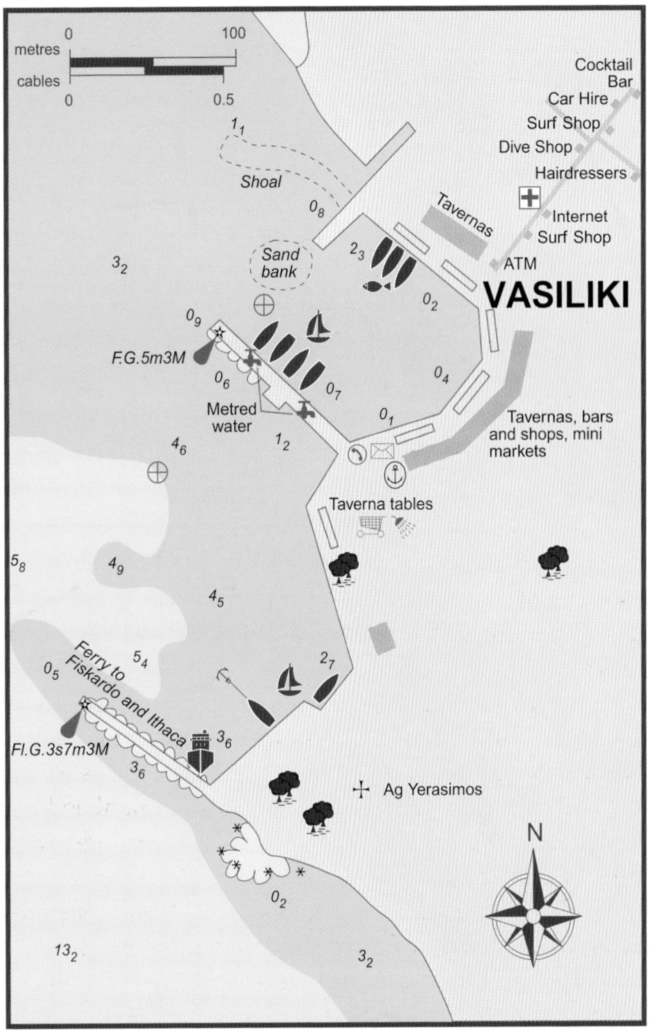

Useful information – Vasiliki

FACILITIES

Water: Several metered water points and hoses on the yacht quay in the inner harbour.

Fuel: Take a taxi to the service station near the medical centre.

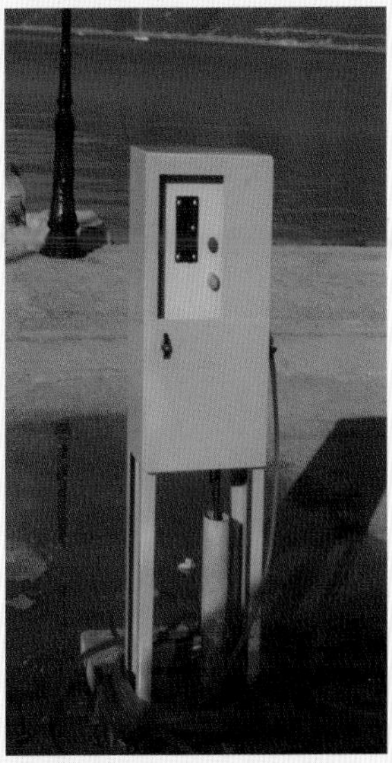

Metered water points can be found on the yacht quay

Showers: At the supermarket to the right of the yacht quay in the inner harbour (€3); also at Vagelaras Taverna next door.

Ice: At Vagelaras Taverna (to the right of the yacht quay in the inner harbour); ask at other tavernas.

Gas: Bottle exchange at several supermarkets.

Rubbish: Bins by the car park on the eastern side of the beach.

Yacht services/chandlery: Nearest is Sivota Yacht Services in Sivota (Tel: 2645 031849; Mobile: 6946 580785), which specialises in electronics, hydraulics and engine maintenance.

Telephone: Telephone box at the end of the yacht quay in the inner harbour; one next to Yannis grillhouse and others on Vasiliki's main street. Mobile reception is good.

Internet: At GM Rent a Car & Bike on the main street. Also at several travel agents in the village.

PROVISIONING

The main shopping area in Vasiliki is arranged along the waterfront and up a long, narrow street leading from the north-west corner of the inner harbour. For clarity, I've called this the main street.

Grocery shops: There are several well-stocked supermarkets and mini-markets along the waterfront, near the inner harbour. On the main street is Melas supermarket; Olivea, which sells a very good selection of olive products; Nikos supermarket and another just beyond.

Bakery: On the main street, just past Abraxas Tunnel Bar. Christina bakery and croissanterie is further along the street.

Butchers: Opposite Vassiliki Divers and Trekking Hellas on the main street. There is another butcher further up, near the post office.

Banks: Emporiki ATM near Penguins on the waterfront. There's no bank but several shops do currency exchange, including: GM Rent a Car & Bike (Tel: 26450 31650) and Samba Tours (Tel: 26450 31555) on the main street.

Pharmacy: On the main street.

Post Office: On the main street beyond Abraxas Tunnel Bar. Post box at the end of the yacht quay in the inner harbour.

Opening times: Vary, but usually 0900-1300, 1800-2100. Mostly seven days a week.

Useful information – Vasiliki

EATING OUT

The waterfront at Vasiliki is packed with tavernas and café-bars offering traditional Greek cuisine, pizzas and snacks. These include, on the north side of the harbour: Alexander (Tel: 26450 31858) – a popular restaurant that serves a good selection of wood oven-baked pizzas as well as fish and Greek dishes – Oceans Seafood, Stelios and the Penguin Restaurant, which is run by an Australian couple. Along the eastern side of the inner harbour is the Ionian café-bar, Yannis grillhouse, Gusto Creperie, Elena café (Tel: 26450 31890), Jomil café, Delfini Taverna and Vagelaras Taverna. So there is plenty of choice within easy walking distance.

ASHORE

The bay is a fine watersports arena, with the beach largely taken up with companies offering windsurfer and dinghy hire and tuition. Windsurfing kit can be hired from several huts along the beach and both Club Vass (www.clubvass.com) and Wildwind (www.wildwind.co.uk) holidays can be found here. If you would prefer to be under the water rather than on it, Vassiliki Divers (Tel: 26450 31130/www.vassiliki.com) runs a range of diving trips and courses around Vasiliki and Kastri Bay. Prices start at €15 for a snorkelling trip and range from €250 for a 10-dive pack to €550 for a DiveMaster course.

Ashore, Trekking Hellas (Tel: 26450 31130/www.vassiliki.com) organises walking trips three times a week. The two- to three-hour treks cost €10 per person and include visits to the nearby natural springs and the deserted village of Roupakias.

Vasiliki is a good base from which to explore the rest of the island. There's a bicycle shop in the village and several car hire firms on the main street. The west coast of Lefkada is worth visiting; it's not recommended by boat as there aren't many places to stop, but it's easy to get to by car. Porto Katsiki, on the south-west coast, and Egremni, just to the north, are two beaches worth going to. You can also drive right up to the lighthouse at Doukato Pt. It's a superbly wild spot and if you're lucky you may see the colony of monk seals that live around the headland.

The lighthouse itself, which dates to 1890, is said to have been built on the site of an old temple to Apollo, the son of Zeus. Legend has it that the Ancient Greeks believed the white cliffs of Leucadian Pt at Doukato, from which Lefkada gets its name, were a gateway to the underworld and that if you leapt off the rocks your sins or ailments would be cured.

TRANSPORT

Car hire: GM Rent a Car & Bike (Tel: 26450 31650) on the main street off the north-west corner of the inner harbour. Nick's Car & Bike Rental (Tel: 26450 32000) at the petrol station in Vasiliki. Alternatively, ask at travel agents.

Taxis: Ask at travel agents or tavernas.

Bus: KTEL (Tel: 26450 22364) operates a service from Lefkada Town to Vasiliki five times a day.

Ferry: During peak season a car and foot-passenger service runs from Vasiliki to Fiskardo on Kefalonia up to three times a day. A ferry also runs from Vasiliki to Frikes, Sami and Pisaetos on Ithaca. Some ferries run out of season but you have more choice from Nidri, about 14nm away by water or 30 minutes by road. For more information, contact Four Islands Ferry on Tel: 26450 31555/31520.

Air travel: The nearest airport is Preveza on the mainland, a two-hour taxi-ride away.

OTHER INFORMATION

Local Tel code: 26450.

Police: Tel: 26450 31012/31218.

Hospital: There is a 24-hour medical centre (Tel: 26450 31065) near the petrol station. Nearest hospital is in Lefkada Town (Tel: 26450 25371), an hour's drive away.

Heiromiti Shoal

If Khiromiti, Cheramidou, Cheiromyti, Keramidou

0.4nm to the south of Heiromiti Shoal:
38°40'.47N 20°45'.93E
Charts: Admiralty 203; Imray G11, G12, G121; Hellenic Navy Hydrographic Service 21

The Heiromiti Shoal lies between Skorpios and Meganisi. It's a large reef, about the size of a football pitch, and while it is reasonably well charted it can often be difficult to spot, particularly in any chop. It is sometimes marked with a stick bearing a charter company's flag, but it is not lit and extreme caution should be exercised in the vicinity.

The reef's location is north of a transit from the entrance to Vathi Bay on Meganisi to Politi Pt on the south-west tip of Skorpios. If travelling from east to west, keep south of this line, hugging the Meganisi coast until Platigiali Bay; then head north-west up the channel between Lefkada and Skorpios. Reverse this procedure if you are heading from west to east. Alternatively, stay close to the south coast of Skorpios before heading south-east once off Kotsilas Pt, on the north-east tip of the island.

Keep an eye on your depth at all times and stay well clear of any boats that appear to be anchored. The chances are they're not anchored in 70m of water, but a lot less. Depths over some parts of the reef are under 1m.

The Heiromiti Shoal is often marked with a charter company's flag

Skorpidi Nisis Skorpidhi

Off the west coast of Skorpidi: 38°42'.14N 20°44'.36E

Charts: Admiralty 203, 2402, SC5771; Imray G11, G12, G121; Hellenic Navy Hydrographic Service 3416

Skorpidi is a small islet to the north of Skorpios which, along with the island of Skorpios, is owned by the Onassis family (see below). The water is fairly deep here, so is not suitable for anchoring off.

Like Skorpios, Skorpidi is private, so landing here is strictly prohibited.

Skorpios

Off north coast of Skorpios: 38°41'.82N 20°44'.66E
Off Jackie Onassis' beach hut on Skorpios: 38°41'.26N 20°44'.47E
Off south side of Skorpios: 38°41'.24N 20°44'.71E
Anchorage off south coast of Skorpios, on east side of isthmus: 38°41'.41N 20°44'.88E

The island of Skorpios off Lefkada's east coast is well known for its famous owner, the Onassis family. The Greek shipping magnate, Aristotle Onassis, bought the island in 1963 and, until his death in 1975, used it as his summer residence. It then passed to his daughter, Christina, but on her death in 1988, at the age of 37, Skorpios was inherited by her daughter, Athina.

Today the island is little used by the Onassis family, but remains a closely guarded secret. While yachtsmen and day-trippers can anchor off its shores and land on one of the beaches on its north-west coast, access above the High Water mark is strictly forbidden. Indeed the whole island is under constant surveillance and trespassers will be found and immediately escorted off.

Aristotle, his son, Alexander, who died in a plane crash aged 25, and Christina are all buried on the island. On its southern shore is a beach hut, the favourite retreat of Aristotle's second wife, Jackie, widow of the US president John F Kennedy.

Four anchorages exist off the island, all of which offer reasonable shelter in good conditions and are pleasant as daytime stops.

There are two anchorages off the island's south coast

NAVIGATION

Charts: Admiralty 203, 2402, SC5771; Imray G11, G12, G121; Hellenic Navy Hydrographic Service 21

Skorpios is situated just over 1nm to the east of Nidri. It's the largest of the Prigiponnisia (Prince's Islands), a group that includes Sparti, Madouri and Skorpidi, and is conspicuous from all directions.

If approaching from the southern entrance to the Lefkada Canal, head south for 6nm. You can pass either side of Sparti, but watch out for the shoal off the island's south-west tip where depths decrease to under 3m (see p112).

Skorpios, off the east coast of Lefkada, is the Onassis family's private island

If approaching from the north coast of Kalamos, head towards the north-east tip of Meganisi, taking care to pass around the outside of Mikro and Makro Nisopoulos as the inside channel is reef-strewn. Do not be tempted, either, to cut across from Makria Pt to the anchorages on the south coast of Skorpios, as you will go straight over the often unmarked Heiromiti Shoal (see p130). Either follow the coast of Meganisi east until Platigiali Bay and then turn north-west to Politi Pt on Skorpios or head north from Makria Pt to Kotsilas Pt on Skorpios. The Heiromiti Shoal lies in the channel between the two islands so it is safe to pass close to the south coast of Skorpios.

From the south, head north up the Meganisi Channel, leaving the island of Thilia to starboard. There's a little islet to the west of Skorpios called Tsokari, which you must also leave to starboard. Keep to the middle of the channel and don't get too close to the islet as there are shoals at both the north and south ends.

ANCHORING

There are four anchorages off Skorpios, the first of which is in a big bay incorporating three smaller coves on the island's north coast. This bay is where Aristotle Onassis often anchored his yacht *Christina*. The 325ft steel ship was built in 1943 as a Canadian convoy escort and bought by Onassis in 1954. He converted her into a luxury floating home at a cost of $4-million and lived aboard a great deal of the time between 1954 and 1975. Indeed it is said that whenever he stayed at Skorpios he never actually spent a night on the island, preferring instead to sleep on his ship. Now owned by a family friend, John Paul Papanicolaou, and renamed *Christina O*, you can charter her for £260,000 per week.

Anchoring is prohibited in the easternmost cove of the bay, identified by a quay in its south-east corner, but you can do so in either of the two to the west. The middle cove tends to attract tripper boats, so is usually busy, while the western cove is quieter. You can swim off the beach at either but do not stray above the High Water mark as you will be politely, but firmly, asked to leave.

On the south coast of Skorpios is Jackie Onassis' beach hut. It is deep here but you can anchor off the beach in about 10-15m. Again, landing is prohibited. Alternatively, you can anchor either side of the narrow isthmus, to the east of the hut. It is still deep on the western side, but on the eastern side it is relatively shallow and you can drop your hook anywhere in 5-10m. While you are protected from the north in both anchorages, they are exposed to the south and unsuitable in blustery conditions. Generally these are recommended as daytime anchorages only, but in the right weather and with care you could overnight off the eastern side of the isthmus.

Jackie Onassis' beach hut, on the south side of the island

Meganisi

Nisos Meganisi/Meganissi

Meganisi is the first island that most people head for when cruising in this part of the Ionian. Lying off Lefkada's east shore, it is the largest of its satellite islands at just under 8 square-miles (20km^2), and one of its prettiest. From the air it looks like a large lamb chop and, although the eastern side of the island's 'tail' offers a few fair-weather anchorages, it is the deeply indented northern coastline that gives good shelter in beautiful surroundings. Numerous bays, coves and inlets litter this shoreline, and cruising yachts will find good amenities in the villages of Spartochori, Vathi and Katomeri, slightly inland.

Meganisi's north coast is dotted with numerous bays and coves

The southern part of the island is rocky and barren and fringed with deep waters, which make it fairly inhospitable. When the prevailing northwesterlies pick up in the afternoons, the western coast, flanking the

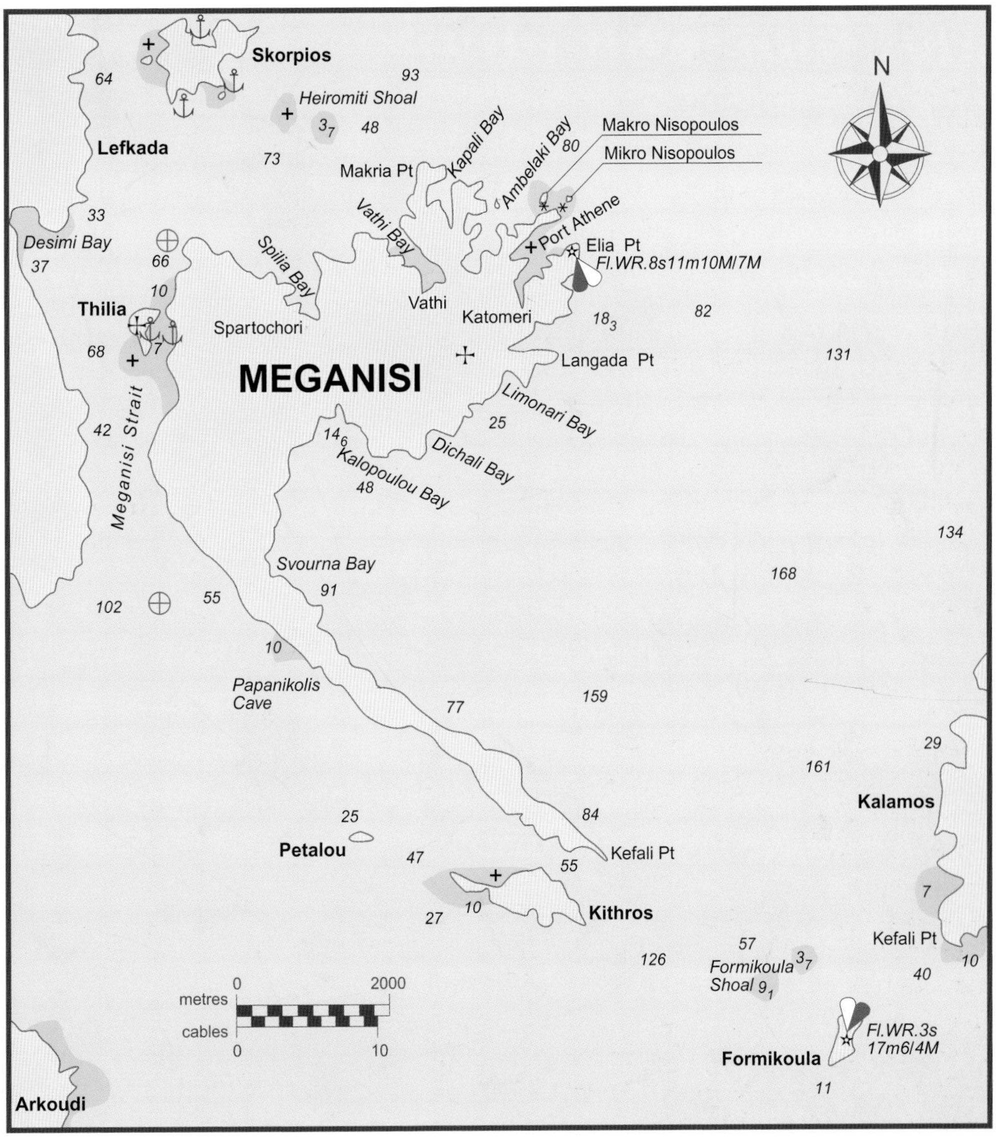

Meganisi Channel, can feel quite exposed.

Its harbours are a delight and it is not hard to see why they are so popular. Spilia Bay offers easy berthing in the form of lazylines, excellent tavernas and a pretty little village perched on the hillside above the harbour, while Vathi is the island's main port – a small fishing community and a vibrant, bustling place providing good amenities. The multi-branched bays on the NE tip of the island are slightly more secluded with good all-round shelter in a striking location, and are a starting point for some great walks around the island.

Meganisi's harbours and anchorages get very busy peak season, notably with charter flotillas whose clients appreciate the simple berthing and large anchorages. At Vathi in the height of summer you may need to forgo some sailing to guarantee a good berth for the evening.

The main hazards on approach are the Heiromiti Shoal (see page 130), midway between the north coast of Meganisi and the island of Skorpios, and the reefs around the eastern tip of the island. Be vigilant, too, as it is usually busy with leisure traffic shuttling between the harbours on Lefkada and Meganisi and visiting the caves along the south-west coast of the island.

Meganisi has a long association with smugglers and is said to have been a favourite haunt of pirates, who hid in the many indented bays before ambushing passing ships. It is also thought that Meganisi is the island of Taphos, which was colonised by Taphius, son of the god Poseidon, and described by Homer in *The Iliad* and *The Odyssey*.

Caves along the south-west coast of the island are said to have been used by smugglers in the past. Today they are popular with tourists

Meganisi Channel

Steno Meganisiou

North-east of the Meganisi Channel:
38°40'.07N 20°44'.33E
South end of the Meganisi Channel:
38°37'.36N 20°44'.24E

The Meganisi Channel, which lies between the east coast of Lefkada and the west coast of Meganisi, is well known for having its own weather system. To the north or south of it, it can be a windless day, with barely a ripple on the water, yet within the channel the chances are there will be a brisk breeze. This is mainly due to the shape of the surrounding hills on the islands of Lefkada and Meganisi, which help funnel the wind through the channel. But what makes it even more interesting is that at the northern end the wind usually blows from the north-west, whereas at the southern end it blows from the south, regardless of the time of day. It is not unusual to enter the channel on a broad reach and leave close-hauled, the wind having swung 180° in just 2½nm.

The channel, which at its widest measures 1½nm and at its narrowest just ½nm, is very deep. Although there is a good anchorage to the east of the islet of Thilia (see p143), at the northern end of the channel, most of the coastline that flanks it is too deep and too flat to offer anywhere decent to anchor, for even a short time. It's the main route south for vessels leaving the Lefkada Canal, so keep a good look-out at all times, particularly at the southern end where there is usually a lot of traffic.

This part of the Ionian offers superb sailing in a beautiful location

Spilia Bay Porto Spiglia

Entrance to Spilia Bay: 38°40'.03N 20°45'.59E
Spilia Bay: 38°39'.74N 20°45'.73E

Lying in the north-west corner of Meganisi, opposite Skorpios island, is Spilia Bay and the village of Spartochori. Spilia Bay is ideal for the first night of your holiday, away from the hustle and bustle of harbours on Lefkada. It's easy to locate, hazard-free and the taverna-owned pontoons are all fitted with lazylines, which makes berthing simple. Overall, the bay offers good shelter from the prevailing winds, although it can feel slightly exposed in a northerly. Even so, you can still find a sheltered berth for the night in Spilia Bay, and in a southerly it offers excellent protection. In summer, katabatic winds blow into the harbour for a couple of hours in the early evening, but these will usually have died down by the time most people finish dinner.

The steep-sided, thickly wooded hills and crystal clear waters make Spilia Bay a magical spot for the evening or a couple of days. Spartochori, perched on the hillside above the bay, is one of the prettiest villages in the Ionian. And despite its popularity with holiday-makers during peak season, it is relatively untouched by tourism and remains very traditional.

NAVIGATION

Charts: Admiralty 203, SC5771; Imray G11, G12 & G121; Hellenic Navy Hydrographic Service 21

All the approaches to Spilia Bay are through deep water. From the Lefkada Canal, head south along the east coast of Lefkada, past the islands of Sparti, Skorpios and Skorpidi. Spilia Bay lies opposite the south coast of Skorpios. Check your charts when approaching from this direction as the very shallow Heiromiti Shoal lies approximately 1nm north of the entrance to Spilia Bay and its location is often unmarked (see p130). Spilia Bay is identified by the village of Spartochori, on the hillside above, and is visible from some distance.

From the south-west, head north up the Meganisi Channel, passing on either side of the islet of Thilia. Spilia Bay is about 1½nm to the east of the northern end of the channel and is the first large bay you come to on the north coast of Meganisi.

Once off Meganisi's north coast keep a good look-out for ferries as regular services run between the island and Nidri on Lefkada. Yachts must keep clear of the ferry when entering or leaving Spilia Bay, particularly near the ferry quay, immediately to the west of the bay's entrance.

Spilia Bay offers reasonable shelter from the prevailing northwesterlies

BERTHING

There are three places to berth in Spilia Bay: off a concrete quay to the west of the ferry berth; off the pontoons in front of the waterfront tavernas in the western corner of the bay; or to the south-east off another concrete quay.

The concrete wall behind the ferry berth in the west of the bay is rigged with lazylines and boats can berth here bows- or stern-to. This is the most sheltered area and is usually full. It is also not suitable for larger boats. Alternatively, you can berth off the outside edge of the L-shaped jetty, although you will have to vacate by 1000 as the day-tripper boats start arriving from Nidri and don't leave until around 1730. This is the last place to fill up in the bay but there are no lazylines and it is very deep, so lay plenty of scope. The inside edge of this jetty has lazylines but is used by local fishing boats.

The pontoons to the south of this jetty belong to two brothers, Panos and Babis Konidaris, who own Asteria taverna and Porto Spilia Taverna. Lazylines are rigged on both pontoons and there is always someone there to catch your lines. Note, however, that the berths can become uncomfortable in a strong north-westerly wind.

The concrete quay in the south-east corner of the bay has 25 lazylines and belongs to Spilia Taverna. The quay is more sheltered from the evening katabatic winds than the jetties on the west side of the bay and there is always plenty of room. Berth bows-to rather than stern-to in order to avoid your rudder squatting on rubble at the base of the wall. There is also a small quay at right angles with space to go alongside.

As with most taverna-owned pontoons, it is good manners to at least have a drink at the

There are several taverna-owned pontoons in Spilia Bay, which are rigged with lazylines

taverna, even if you do not intend to eat there. Taverna owners are often unamused if sailors use their pontoons but not their restaurant, especially if it is quiet. The competition between the taverna owners at Spilia Bay is also particularly fierce.

Four tavernas can be found ashore at Spilia Bay

ANCHORING

Spilia Bay is deep (40m-plus), so there is nowhere within it for a yacht to free-swing at anchor.

There are anchorages to the west of the bay's entrance but these are recommended for calm weather use and should only be used in a southerly as they are totally exposed to the north.

Holding is generally good here but if you do plan to spend the night, dig your anchor in well and take a line ashore to protect yourself against the katabatic winds that pick up in the evenings.

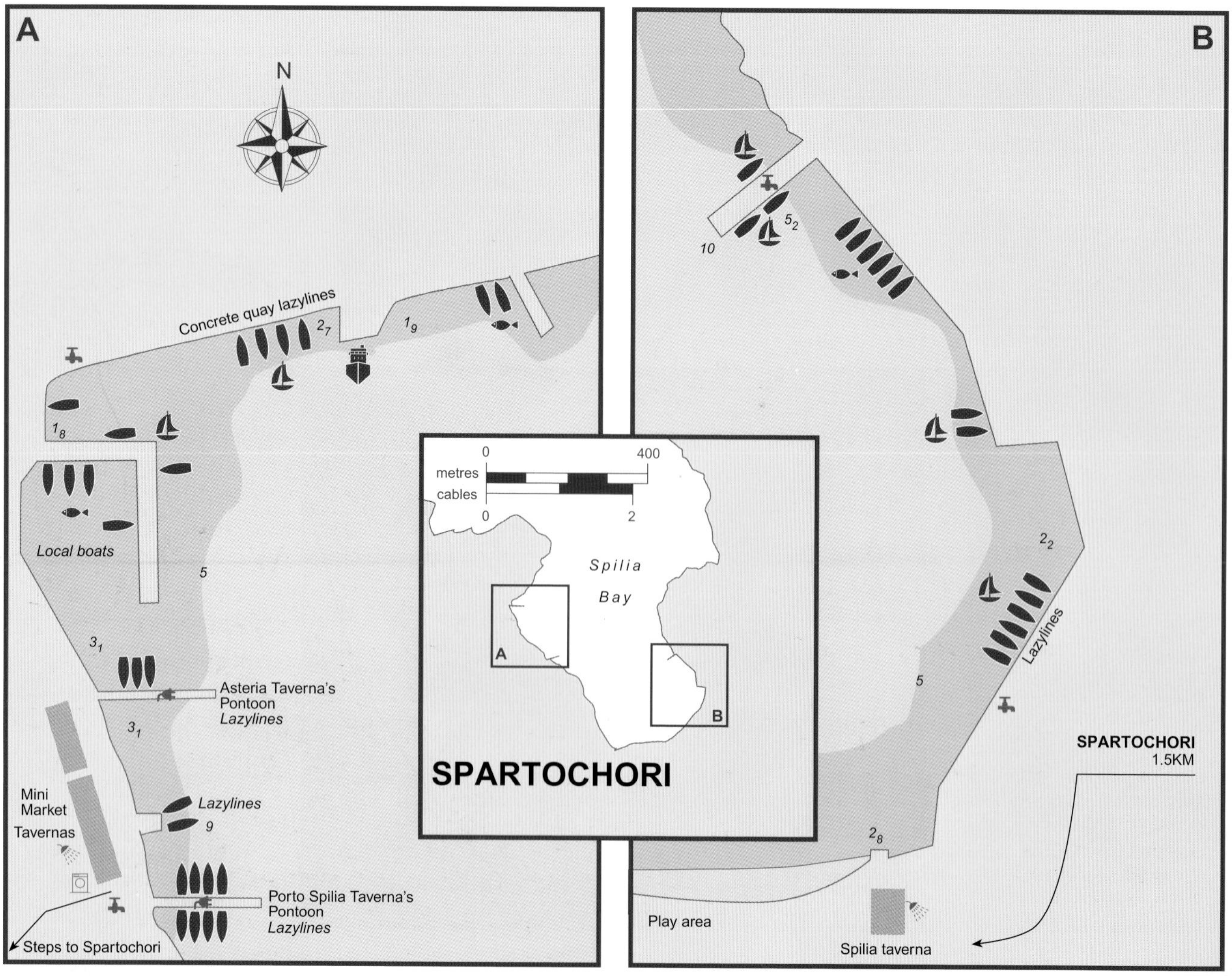

Useful information – Spilia Bay

FACILITIES

Water: At both the fisherman's quay (0800-1030) and near Porto Spilia Taverna, provided by a local who charges €5 per fill. At the south-east corner of the bay there is a hose on the quay.
Showers: Porto Spilia Taverna (€3); Asteria (€3); Spilia (€1.50).
Ice: From Porto Spilia Taverna, Asteria and Spilia Taverna.
Laundry: Porto Spilia Taverna (€5); Spilia (€5). Launderette on the main street in Spartochori.
Shore power: Available on both floating pontoons.
Rubbish: Bins behind Porto Spilia Taverna and Asteria, and at the end of the ferry berth.
Chandlery/yacht services: The nearest is in Nidri.
Telephone: A couple near the tavernas and several more in Spartochori. Phone cards are sold at the tavernas. Mobile reception is okay.

PROVISIONING

Grocery shops: Small mini-markets, which stock the basics, at both Porto Spilia Taverna and Asteria. Steve and Jerry at Spilia Taverna will also supply milk, beer and ice. There's a mini-market and deli beneath the Roof Garden Café in Spartochori, a second below Tropicana Pizza restaurant and a third on the high street, beyond Lakis Taverna.
Bakery: Fresh bread delivered daily to the mini-markets in Spilia Bay.
Banks: The nearest is at Nidri on Lefkada.
Pharmacy: The nearest is in Katomeri, 1½ miles east of Spartochori.
Post: No post office in Spartochori; post box near the Roof Garden Café. Stamps sold at the souvenir shop below Tropicana Pizza restaurant in Spartochori.
Opening hours: Shops open 0900-1400 and 1730-2030, but closed on Sun. Tavernas open all day.

EATING OUT

Spilia Bay: All four tavernas around the edge of the bay offer first-rate food, stunning views and good hospitality. Porto Spilia Taverna (Tel: 26450 51233), is a large, bustling taverna run by brothers Pano and Babis Konidaris, helped by their mother. It is very popular, particularly at lunchtime, and rightly so, as it serves a wide selection of very good meals. Pano is a free-diver and catches fresh lobster and seafood, which is kept in an underwater pen at the end of the jetty. Prices are reasonable and there is no need to book in advance. Asteria taverna (Tel: 26450 51107; www.asteria.gr), to the right, is a similar set-up, again run by Pano and Babis Konidaris, while the rustic-looking taverna next door completes the trio on the west side of the bay. Spilia Taverna (Tel: 26450 51616), in the south-east corner of the bay, has superb views towards Lefkada. Run by the Tsolakis brothers, Steve and Jerry, it has an idyllic vine-covered terrace right on the waterfront.
Spartochori: The Roof Garden Café has arguably the best view in Spartochori: an unbroken panorama of Lefkada, Skorpios and the mainland to the east. The food is a mixture of Greek and international dishes. Tropicana Pizza (Tel: 26450 51486), above the mini-market and souvenir shop, serves good home-made pizzas. Lakis Taverna is a traditional no-frills restaurant in the centre of the village. Food is cooked on an open-air grill and the taverna regularly hosts

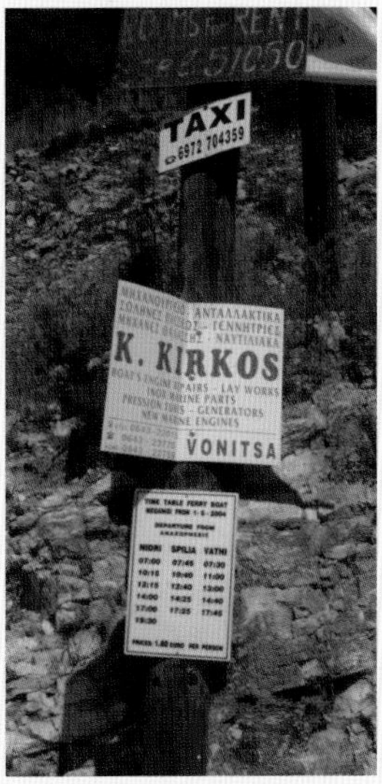

Greek dancing evenings. Popular with flotilla and *caique* parties, it is worth a visit, if only to witness the elderly Mama Lakis's extraordinary party piece: dancing with a table on her head.

ASHORE

Porto Spilia is a beautiful bay with some lovely surrounding walks. The village of Spartochori on the western shore is a steep, 5-10-minute walk up the hill and worth visiting for the view.

TRANSPORT

Car hire: The nearest is in Nidri on Lefkada.
Taxis: Tel: 26450 51671/ Mobile: 6972 704359.
Ferry: A car and foot-passenger service between Nidri on Lefkada and Spilia and Vathi on Meganisi runs five times a day. Journey, 20 minutes; costs around €1.80 per person/ €10 per car. The first ferry leaves Spilia Bay at 0745, the last at 1725.
Air travel: The nearest airport is on the mainland at Aktio, near Preveza, a 1½hr-drive from Nidri.

OTHER INFORMATION

Local Tel code: 26450.
Doctor: The nearest is in Katomeri, 1½ miles from Spartochori.
Hospital: The nearest medical centre is at Vlicho, near Nidri (Tel: 26450 95204). The nearest hospital is at Lefkada, 45 minutes from Nidri.

The pretty village of Spartochori commands fantastic views over the Ionian

Vathi

Little Vathi, Vathy, Ormos Vathi

Approach from west: 38°40'.35N 20°46'.40E
Harbour entrance: 38°39'.89N 20°46'.92E

Vathi, on Meganisi's north coast, is one of the loveliest harbours in the Ionian and is also the capital of Meganisi. Despite being hugely popular peak season, it is remarkably unspoilt and very much a traditional fishing village. It's similar, architecturally, to Fiskardo, on Kefalonia, considered by many to be the epitome of a traditional Greek harbour. However, Vathi does not have the same polished appearance. You'll still see fishermen mending their nets on the quay and the tavernas are frequented by Greeks, not just tourists.

The small village of Vathi fringes the harbour and is surrounded by lush vegetation. It offers excellent all-round shelter, although in a strong northerly chop is sometimes pushed into the bay, which can affect boats berthed at the southern end of the harbour. Ashore, there are some lovely walks around the headlands and up to the village of Katomeri, where you can get the most spectacular views over the bays to the east and the islands to the north. It's an idyllic spot and does get very busy. In peak season, the harbour fills up quickly, so arrive early if you want to spend the night here.

NAVIGATION

Charts: Admiralty 203, SC5771; Imray G11, G12 & G121; Hellenic Navy Hydrographic Service 21

From a distance, Vathi can be hard to identify and it is only once you are inside the entrance to the bay that you will be able to see the village and harbour. Approaching from the south-east, follow the coast of Meganisi north until you reach Makria Pt, the northernmost tip of the island, taking care to pass to the east of Makro and Mikro Nisopoulos, two islets off Ambelaki Bay. The entrance to Vathi Bay lies about ½nm west of Makria Pt.

On approach from the Lefkada Canal, head south, passing on either side of Sparti and Skorpios. Once off the south coast of Skorpios, do not be tempted to head directly for Vathi Bay. The Heiromiti Shoal (see p130), which is about the size of a football pitch, lies between Skorpios and Meganisi, about 1nm north of the entrance to the bay, and the risk of running aground is high. If approaching from the west coast of Skorpios, either hug the coast of the island, only heading south-east for Meganisi once off Kotsilas Pt, or head south for the north-west tip of Meganisi and then follow the coastline east to Vathi Bay. Vathi lies 1nm east of Spilia Bay.

Once inside Vathi Bay, head up the channel to the harbour. It is deep here and you can use the full width of the channel.

Vathi is a popular destination with cruising yachts, but remains relatively unspoilt

BERTHING

Vathi Harbour is rectangular in shape and yachts should berth bows- or stern-to its western and southern sides. Larger yachts should berth on the western side, which is deeper, and avoid the shallow south-east corner, which is suitable for shoal-draught boats only. *Caiques* and motor boats use the eastern side of the harbour, where it is very shallow.

Yachts berthing in the south-west corner of the harbour usually raft up alongside to prevent anchor lines getting crossed. Two or three yachts can also anchor off the mole on the north-west side, but should keep well east to avoid interfering with the ferry quay. Berth bows-to and anchor well off to avoid under-water debris at the end of the mole; then take a long line ashore.

There is a good-sized pontoon with lazylines for up to 38 boats in front of Karnagio Taverna in the bay to the W of the harbour. The depths here vary so have a quick scout around before committing to a stern-to berth. Sheltered from northerly and southerly winds, its facilities include showers, a bar, barbecue area and soon-to-open mini market. It is only a 5-minute walk into Vathi.

Vathi is a very attractive and very Greek village

ANCHORING

As you enter Vathi Bay there are two small inlets to the west where it is possible to anchor. A taverna, Karnagio, is in the southernmost bay. The northern one is used by local fishing boats. Both are good lunch-time stops but can become uncomfortable if a northerly swell develops.

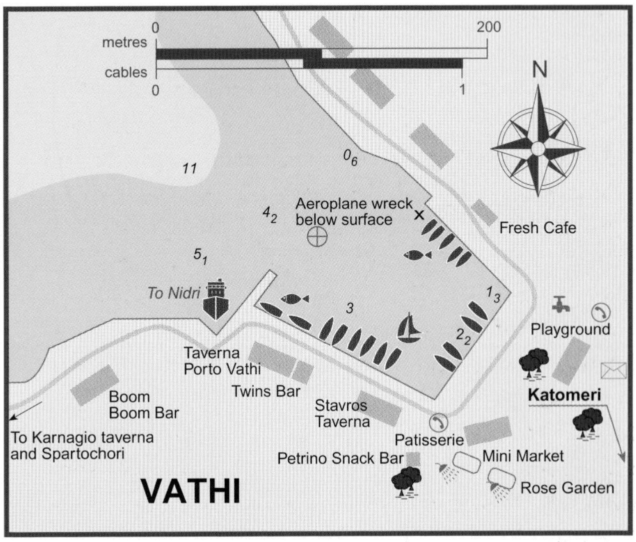

Useful information – Vathi

FACILITIES

Water: A water lady visits the quay morning and evening. The hose reaches right around quay, although not to the end of the mole. Cost: €5 per fill.
Fuel: There is a petrol station in Katomeri, a 5-min taxi-ride from Vathi.
Showers: Rose Garden Taverna (€3); Karnagio (in the bay to the west of Vathi).
Ice: Ask at the tavernas.
Rubbish: Bins at the south end of the quay and beside the ferry berth.
Telephone: One next to Petrino snack bar, another by the playground. Phone cards sold at the mini-markets. Mobile reception is good.
Chandlery/yacht services: The nearest are at Nidri on Lefkada.

PROVISIONING

Grocery shops: Mini-market next to Patisserie.
Bakery: Patisserie next to the Rose Garden taverna. Alternatively, walk past the Rose Garden, take the road on the right and you will see a bakery on the right hand side.
Butcher: The nearest is in Katomeri.
Pharmacy: There is one in Katomeri.
Post: The post office is at the eastern end of the square. Times are irregular but usually open for a few hours each morning. Stamps at the mini-market.
Opening hours: Tavernas open all day but the shops usually shut for a siesta (1400-1730), before reopening in the evening.

EATING OUT

The Rose Garden taverna (Tel: 26450 51216), run by the very affable Efi and Steven Palmos, is situated at the S end of the harbour in the village square. Open seven days a week for breakfast, lunch and dinner, it serves good quality Greek food. Stavros (Tel: 26450 51111) on the quay is a favourite of the locals, as is Taverna Porto Vathi (also known as George's, Tel: 26450 51125) next to the mole.

For light snacks and music, try the Twins Bar, near Taverna Porto Vathi. Run, yes, by twins, it is open late every night and serves lunches and evening snacks. Alternatively, try Petrino Snack Bar, to the E of Stavros taverna, or Fresh Café, NW of the playground. The Boom Boom music bar, just beyond the ferry quay, is a popular spot with local youngsters.

In the bay to the west of Vathi is Karnagio, a café-restaurant serving good Greek fare. And in the village of Katomeri, a 30-minute walk from Vathi, is Hotel Meganisi, the only hotel on the island, which has a bar and restaurant.

ASHORE

There are some lovely walks from Vathi. Either head north to the village of Katomeri or east to the bays of Kapali or Ambelaki. The bays are all good for swimming and surrounded by beautiful countryside. There is also a children's play area just behind the square in Vathi.

TRANSPORT

Car hire: The nearest is in Nidri on Lefkada.
Taxis: Tel: 6972 704359.
Ferry: A car and foot-passenger service between Nidri on Lefkada and Spilia Bay and Vathi on Meganisi runs five times a day. Vathi to Nidri takes 20-30 minutes and costs around €1.80 per person/ €10 per car. The first ferry leaves Vathi at 0730, the last at 1740.
Air travel: See Spilia Bay on page 137.

Kapali Bay

Harbour waypoint: 38°40'.61N 20°47'.17E

The first of three large, multi-branched bays, Kapali Bay lies ¾nm east of the entrance to Vathi on the north-east coast of Meganisi. It's a very pretty anchorage: olive trees line the shore and hillside behind, while its numerous inlets provide plenty of nooks and crannies for anchoring. Sheltered from all directions, Kapali and the bays to the east are particularly popular with charter flotillas which organise crew barbecues here. Do not be surprised, therefore, if your peaceful anchorage is suddenly invaded by a large fleet, although there is normally plenty of room to relocate to a quieter spot.

NAVIGATION

Charts: Admiralty 230, SC5771; Imray G11, G12 & G121; Hellenic Navy Hydrographic Service 21

From Vathi head east, keeping well clear of the shoal off the eastern headland of Vathi Bay and Makria Pt, the western headland of Kapali Bay.

On approach from the north, pass to the east of the islands of Skorpios and Sparti. If sailing from the Lefkada Canal steer 156°T for 8nm towards the east coast of Meganisi. Beware the Heiromiti Shoal (see p130), which is often unmarked and lies NW of the bays between Skorpios island and Vathi on Meganisi.

Yachts approaching from the south can either head north up the Meganisi Channel, before turning east along the north coast of the island, or up the eastern side of Meganisi, following the coast round from the lighthouse at Eliá Pt. Take care to pass outside Mikro and Makro Nisopoulos as the inside channel is reef-strewn.

From all directions, water depth is great, although there are a few rocky patches in this area. All of them are easily visible, so just keep a good look-out. Give Makria Pt, the western headland of Kapali Bay, a wide berth as a shoal extends north for a short distance.

ANCHORING

Kapali Bay has fewer branches than Ambelaki Bay to the east but there are still plenty of nooks and crannies in which to anchor, even in the height of summer. Drop your hook and take a line ashore, rather than swinging freely, so that you occupy as little space as possible, leaving room for other yachts nearby. Depths are deep at 10-15m until quite close in.

FACILITIES & PROVISIONING

Kapali Bay is quiet and unspoilt, with no tavernas or shops. Vathi is a short walk away along the coast road and most provisions can be picked up there. Alternatively, there is a small mini-market at Jimmy & Spiro's taverna at Port Athene, to the south-east.

One of many anchorages on the north coast of Meganisi

Ambelaki Bay

Ormos Ampelakia, Abelike Bay, Ambelakia Bay

Entrance waypoint: 38°40'.42N 20°47'.68E
Far end of the bay: 38°39'.96N 20°47'.41E

Ambelaki Bay, which is located to the east of Kapali Bay, offers slightly more protection from the prevailing winds and consequently can get very busy during the peak season.

Although you can't guarantee to have the whole bay to yourself (the western side in particular proves very popular in summer), Ambelaki has more branches than Kapali and can still be a quiet and pleasant overnight stop.

NAVIGATION

Charts: Admiralty 230, SC5771; Imray G11, G12 & G121; Hellenic Navy Hydrographic Service 21

Follow the same navigation instructions as for Kapali Bay (see above), taking care round the islets of Makro and Mikro Nisopoulos to the east. There are a few rocks on the eastern side of the entrance to the bay, so it is best to stay in the middle of the channel and don't cut the corner.

ANCHORING

This bay offers plenty of nooks and crannies to anchor. You can do so anywhere at the head of the bay, apart from the designated swimming area at the southern end, which is marked with buoys. Anchor off and row ashore. The busiest part of the bay is the western side and in summer it is usually full of motor boats.

All these north coast bays are popular with charter flotillas

Ambelaki offers good holding in mud, with depths of between 8-10m. As this bay gets very busy, it is good practice to anchor and take a line ashore to prevent free swinging.

FACILITIES & PROVISIONING

A small taverna is situated on the eastern side of the bay, which is only open at peak season. There is a small mini-market at Jimmy & Spiro's taverna in Port Athene to the east and Vathi is a 20-minute walk along a track. The village of Katomeri on the hillside to the south is also within easy walking distance.

The small beaches in all three of the bays along this coastline are very popular for barbecues. During the hot, dry months of August and September, however, they are often banned on the islands to prevent accidental fires. If you do intend to barbecue, please keep all flames away from trees and shrubbery and do not leave the fire unattended at any time. Finally, douse the flames with sea water and make sure the embers are well and truly out to prevent rekindling if a breeze picks up in the night. Take all your rubbish away with you too, and be aware that wild foxes roam around this bay – please do not try to hand feed them.

Port Athene

Ormos Atherinos, Port Atheni

Entrance to Port Athene: 38°40'.19N 20°48'.30E
Anchorage on east of the bay:
38°40'.01N 20°48'.17E
New concrete quay on east of bay:
38°39'.76N 20°47'.94E

Port Athene is the third bay of the trio and the furthest east. It is the most developed of the three, in that it has two small quays and a taverna on the eastern side, but is still very peaceful and a good place to spend the night.

Port Athene is particularly good for families as children can play on the beach or swim in the crystal clear waters, and several paths around the bay are fun to explore.

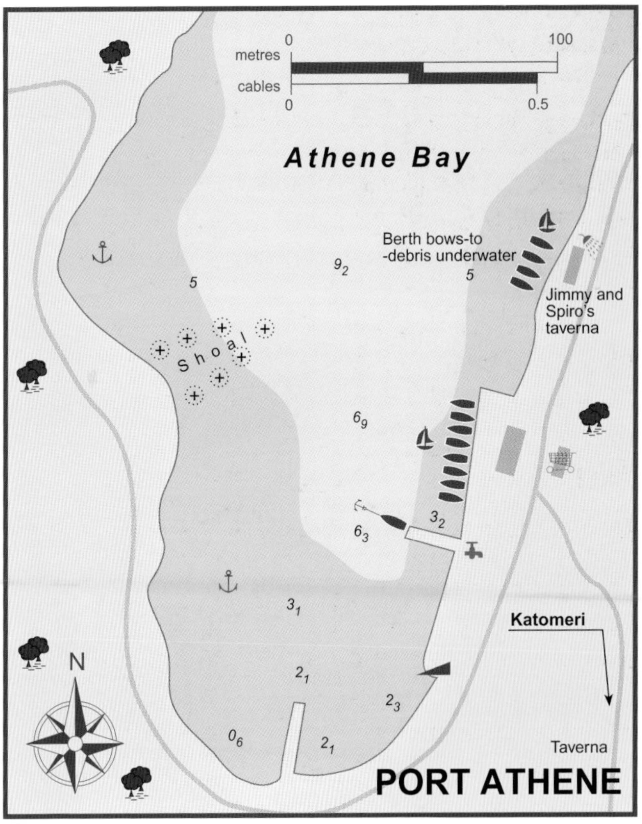

NAVIGATION

Charts: Admiralty 230, SC5771; Imray G11, G12 & G121; Hellenic Navy Hydrographic Service 21

Follow the instructions listed for Kapali and Ambelaki bays. If approaching from the north, leave Makro and Mikro Nisopoulos, two islets off the headland that separates Ambelaki Bay and Port Athene, to starboard. Watch out for rocky patches in this area too. If approaching from the south, up the east coast of Meganisi, keep clear of the shoal off Eliá Pt, the headland marked by a lighthouse (Fl WR 8s11m10/7M).

Port Athene is Y-shaped, and the main hazard is a shoal which separates the bay in two and extends up the middle of the Y towards the entrance. When entering the bay, make sure you know which side you want to go to – the anchorage to the west or the quay and taverna to the south-east – as you cannot change your mind halfway without retracing your steps. The shoal is sometimes marked with a stick and a flag, just like the Heiromiti Shoal, although do not rely on this.

BERTHING

On the eastern side of Port Athene bay are two small quays. The first you come to is a rickety old thing that appears to have been built out of barn doors. It is, however, safe to tie up to, although more suitable for smaller boats. Moor bows-to to avoid squatting your stern on the underwater debris at its base. This wooden jetty is attached to a sturdier stone-built quay equipped with six lazylines. This is also shallow, however, and you can only berth bows-to here. Beyond this is a newer concrete quay where you can moor bows- or stern-to. Let out plenty of scope when anchoring as this part of the bay can be quite gusty in the afternoon and the holding is not always good.

ANCHORING

There are several anchorages in Port Athene bay – on the W side or beyond the small quays on the E side. Don't forget about the shoal that runs down the middle of the bay, though, so stick to one side or the other. Holding in mud and weed is generally good. Depths at the head of the bay are between 5-8m, while further out it's 10-15m.

FACILITIES

Facilities are basic at Port Athene. There is a very small mini-market/cafe situated just behind the south quay, which also sells ice, and a vegetable truck occasionally visits the bay in the evening. The village of Katomeri is a 30-minute walk away, south-west of Port Athene, or you can walk slightly further to Vathi, past the church of Agios Kostantinos.

Two showers are available at Jimmy & Spiro's, plus toilets. In summer, water can be obtained on the southern quay. A man comes round morning and evening with a long hose. Cost €3-5.

EATING & DRINKING

Jimmy & Spiro's taverna is run by two brothers and is a large, very friendly establishment. The food is simple, but very good, and if big parties are in for the evening there is often after-dinner entertainment, such as Greek dancing.

Jimmy & Spiro's taverna in Port Athene Bay

The quay at Port Athene. Here you'll find a taverna and a mini-market that stocks basic supplies

Elia Bay Ormos Elia

To the east of Elia Bay: 38°39'.44N 20°48'.71E

Charts: Admiralty 203, 189, SC5771; Imray G11, G121, G1; Hellenic Navy Hydrographic Service 21

Elia Bay, on the east coast of Meganisi, about 1nm south of Port Athene, offers good all-round shelter. It's a deep, narrow bay, protected from the south by Langada Pt (Ak Langadhá) and good for daytime and/or overnight stays. The beach at its head is often popular with tourists but you will usually get the anchorage to yourself; most yachts preferring the bays of Kapali, Ambelaki and Port Athene to the north. On approach from this direction, watch out for the rocks off Elia Pt (Fl WR 8s11m10/7M) and pass to the east of Mikro and Makro Nisopoulos, as a reef extends between them and Meganisi's shore.

In Elia Bay, anchor in less than 8m, taking a line ashore to prevent you swinging. A road off the beach leads to the village of Katomeri, 1km away, which is good for provisioning.

Kalopoulou Bay

To the south of Kalopoulou Bay: 38°38'.44N 20°46'.11E

Charts: Admiralty 203, 189, SC5771; Imray G11, G121, G1; Hellenic Navy Hydrographic Service 21

Kalopoulou Bay is a good daytime anchorage. Lying tucked up on the east coast of Meganisi, to the west of Elia Bay and directly overland from Spilia Bay, it offers good shelter from the north-west but is exposed in a southerly. Anchor in the north-east corner in 8-10m. The holding on mud is reasonable.

Svourna Bay

Ormos Svarna

To the east of Svourna Bay: 38°37'.64N 20°45'.66E

Charts: Admiralty 203, 189, SC5771; Imray G11, G121, G1; Hellenic Navy Hydrographic Service 21

Svourna Bay is the southernmost anchorage on the east coast of Meganisi, situated just over 1nm south of Kalopoulou Bay. It is very deep here (15m-plus) and does not offer adequate shelter from any direction, so is unsuitable for an overnight stay.

West coast of Meganisi

To the east of the islet of Thilia: 38°39'.46N 20°44'.21E

Papanikolis Cave: 38°36'.77N 20°45'.72E

Charts: Admiralty 203, SC5771; Imray G11, G12 & G121; Hellenic Navy Hydrographic Service 21

Meganisi's steeply-shelving west coast shores are exposed and the changeable winds that blow through the Meganisi Channel quickly make any potential anchorage untenable. However, to the east of Thilia, a small island off the north-west coast of Meganisi, there is one which is good in calm weather. You can anchor off any of the beaches on this part of Meganisi's coast in reasonable depths, but NOT just to the south of the island, where underwater cables are marked by a crossed-out anchor sign on the foreshore.

If approaching from south of the Meganisi Channel, keep a good distance off the southern tip of Thilia as a reef extends off its shore.

Further south, on the west coast of Meganisi's 'tail', is the cave of Papanikolis. The second largest sea cave in Greece, Papanikolis is said to have been named after a Greek submarine that hid in it during the Second World War, when Meganisi was occupied by Nazi troops. It is also said that during Turkish rule, a priest and his students hid here from pirates. These stories have made it a popular tourist attraction and daytrip boats from Lefkada and Meganisi visit regularly. It's a stunning cave and you can take your dinghy right into it.

However, don't attempt to anchor nearby. It's very deep here and there are lots of boulders on the seabed, which could easily snag your anchor. Instead, have someone stay on board to gill the boat around while the rest of your crew explore by tender. The best time of day to visit is in the early morning, when conditions are calm and there is no swell.

Kalamos

Nisos Kalamos

Rising to 2,444ft (745m), the highest peak on Kalamos is conspicuous from all directions. It's the easiest island to identify in this archipelago: its steep and densely wooded hills contrast greatly with its smaller sibling, Kastos, to the south, and the low-lying Meganisi to the north. Thick with pine trees and rich in rural beauty, it, like Kastos, remains relatively unspoilt by tourism.

The island offers three destinations: the capital Port Kalamos, the small hamlet of Episkopi, on the north coast, and the uninhabited village of Port Leone, which was abandoned following the earthquake of 1953. All have their own charm and, while the island offers only basic amenities, its harbours are delightful places to spend a few days.

Care should be taken on approach to the island. Not only do the Formikoula Shoals off the southern tip pose a hazard for yachts approaching from the west, but the channel between Kalamos and Kastos is regularly exposed to violent gusts, which whip off the surrounding hillsides.

Incidentally, in Greek mythology, Kalamos was the son of the god Maiandros and the water-loving plant *Acorus calamus*, or sweet flag, similar to the iris, is said to be named after him.

The islands of Kastos (left) and Kalamos

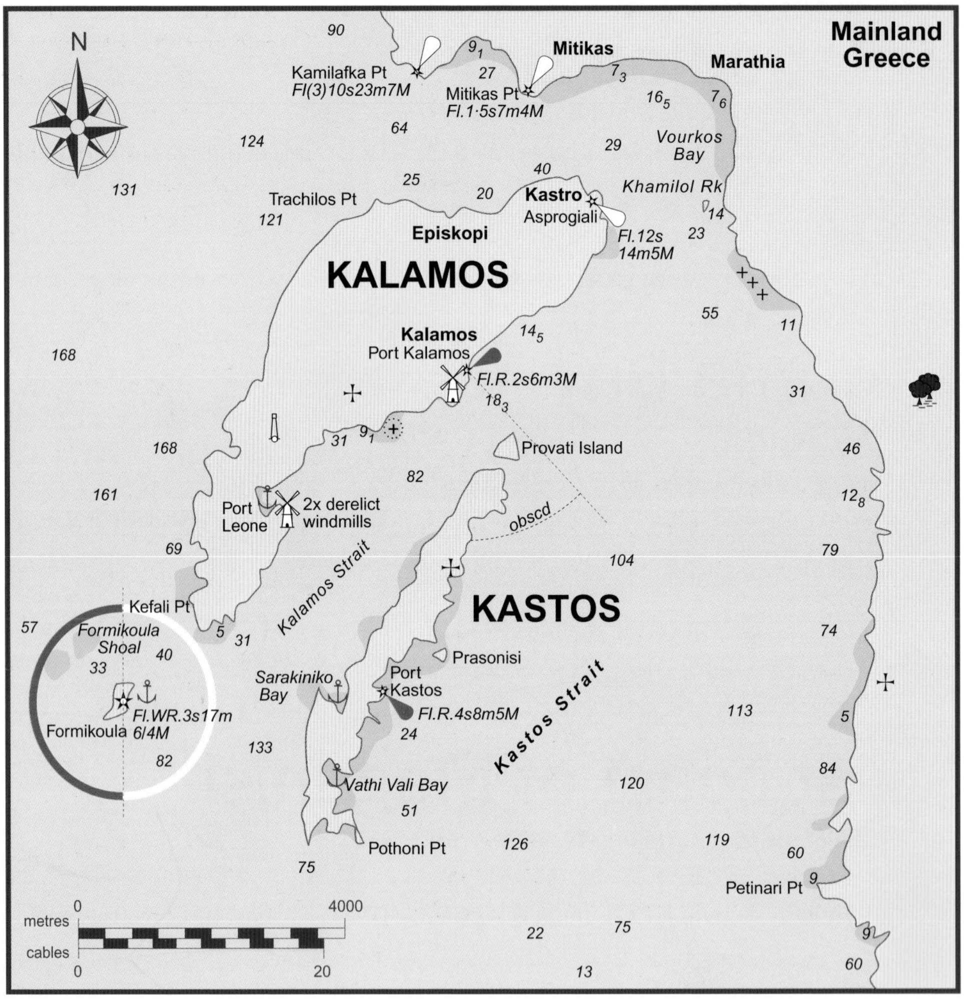

Port Kalamos Kalamou

Approach to Kalamos: 38°36'.95N 20°55'.76E

Alongside quay at Kalamos: 38°37'.35N 20°55'.94E

Port Kalamos is the main harbour on the island and lies on the E coast, slightly N of the northern tip of Kastos. It's a pretty harbour at the base of a steep hillside, on which the village of Kalamos is perched. Offering good protection from southerlies and from the southwesterlies that funnel up the channel between the islands, Port Kalamos is an increasingly popular destination for cruisers. It's a sleepy little place, with narrow lanes that weave up from the harbour to a village of closely-packed stone houses. Tourism is beginning to have its impact, but for the time being Port Kalamos is an enchanting place, devoid of tackiness and rich in rural beauty.

Port Kalamos is the island's main harbour and a delightful place to visit

NAVIGATION

Charts: Admiralty 203, SC5771; Imray G12, G121; Hellenic Navy Hydrographic Service 21

On approach from Port Athene on Meganisi, steer 095°T east for 6nm towards the northern end of Kalamos island. Once past the light on Asprogiali Pt (Fl 12s14m5M), follow the east coast of the island south to Port Kalamos, which at night can be identified by a light on the breakwater (Fl R 2s6m3M).

If on passage from Atokos, steer 030°T for 8nm. Yachts approaching from the west or south can pass either side of the island of Formikoula, which has a sectored light (Fl WR 3s6/4M); but be aware of the shoal patch to the north-west. From Formikoula, head north-east up the channel between Kalamos island and Kastos.

All routes take you through deep water, the only danger being the shoal situated to the north-west of Formikoula island.

Port Kalamos can be identified from the south by three windmills on a headland, one of which perches on a rock right by the water's edge. These windmills lie immediately to the south of Port Kalamos and are conspicuous from all directions. On approach from the north end of the island, the village can be identified from some distance.

When entering the harbour, watch out for the shallow patch slightly to the north of the entrance.

BERTHING

You can moor either stern or bows-to the breakwater, although it is quite high so berthing bows-to makes disembarking easier. The owner of George's Restaurant is often around to take your lines and will also recommend where to go if space is tight.

The southern and western parts of the harbour are shallow (1-2m) and usually occupied by local fishing boats, so should be avoided. However, there is sometimes space to berth bows-to in front of Il Panino café on the north-west side of the harbour, and the owner also often comes to take your lines. The wall to the right of Il Panino is reserved for fishing boats.

Port Kalamos is becoming increasingly popular with flotillas and can fill up quite quickly, so arrive early if you want to spend a night here.

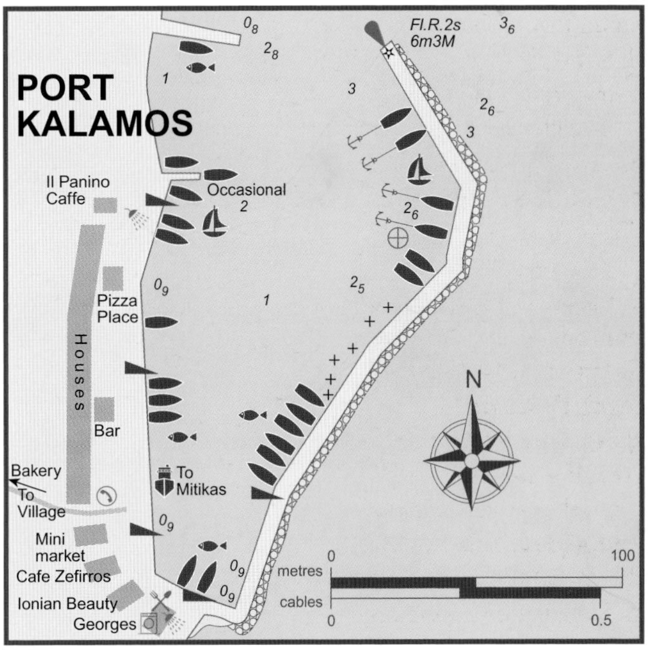

Visiting boats berth stern- or bows-to the harbour breakwater

ANCHORING

Just to the S of the harbour is a small beach, which in calm weather is suitable as an overnight anchorage. Swell does get pushed up the channel between Kalamos and Kastos, though, so it can be uncomfortable and is better for daytime stops only. There is also a small bay to the N of the harbour, but again only anchor here if the weather is settled as the holding is unreliable.

Useful information – Port Kalamos

FACILITIES
Water: Kalamos island has a restricted water supply and, although some water is available to yachts at the southern end of the breakwater, it is better to fill up elsewhere.
Showers: Available at George's Restaurant (€2) as well as Il Panino (€1.50).
Ice: George's Restaurant and Il Panino.
Gas: At the mini-market.
Rubbish: Located north of Il Panino creperie. All rubbish on Kalamos has to be taken off the island for processing, so to help prevent pollution within the harbour take your rubbish with you.
Telephone: Phone box outside the mini-market. Cards sold at the mini-market. Mobile reception is okay.
Post: In the village. The postal service on Kalamos is slow. Stamps sold at the mini-market.

PROVISIONING
Grocery shops: You will find a mini-market on the western side of the quay. However, its opening times are erratic.
Baker: In the village: walk up the hill past the mini-market.
Banks: Nearest at Mitikas on the mainland.
Pharmacy: Nearest at Mitikas on the mainland.
Opening times: Shops operate to siesta hours and are closed on Sundays.

EATING OUT
George's Restaurant – a white building with blue shutters at the southern end of the harbour – is a popular and lively establishment. The menu is limited but the food very good. The fish soup, a speciality on Kalamos island, and 'roasted lamp [lamb] with potatoes' are particularly delicious. Popular with flotillas. Ionian Beauty, just behind George's, is another good taverna, usually slightly quieter. The menu includes traditional Greek fare and lots of fresh fish.

Café Zefirros, to the left of the mini-market, is a good café-bar, while Il Panino Caffé (Tel: 26460 091046), a creperie and bar at the northwestern end of the harbour, can also be recommended.

Port Kalamos (Tel: 26460 91071), next door to the creperie, trades as a pizzeria and bar.

For a totally relaxed feel head to the Beach Bar. It is a 15-minute walk to the old windmill just S of Port Kalamos, and it is here that this bar can be found. Only open in high season, it serves good, cheap Greek Mezze dishes.

ASHORE
There are some lovely walks from Port Kalamos, around the village, hillside and along the beaches to the south. The road out of Port Kalamos leads through some beautiful countryside to Episkopi on the north coast of the island, and there are other good trails from the village.

TRANSPORT
Ferry: Daily *caique* from Port Kalamos to Mitikas on the mainland.
Air travel: The nearest airport is at Preveza on the mainland. Take the *caique* from Kalamos to Mitikas and then a taxi to Preveza (45 minutes).

The windmill to the south of Port Kalamos is a distinctive landmark

Port Leone Kefali

Port Leone bay: 38°35'.93N 20°53'.11E

Port Leone lies on the south-east corner of Kalamos, approximately 2½nm from Port Kalamos. Set in a large, north-east facing bay, the village was abandoned following the earthquake of August 1953. Tremors as high as 7.3 on the Richter Scale were recorded in the area and many of the houses in the village were destroyed. The water supply was cut off and Port Leone was never rebuilt. Now all that remains are some ruined houses and an olive press, although the church is in good condition and still maintained by villagers from Port Kalamos. A small, rather noisy taverna is based on the shore.

Port Leone is special. It has the eeriness of a ghost town but is a very beautiful spot and a good place to anchor overnight. It is well sheltered from the prevailing winds and there are several coves to anchor in, so it doesn't get too crowded.

The village is said to have derived its name from the Venetians, who were the first people to produce maps of the area.

NAVIGATION

Charts: Admiralty 203, SC5771; Imray G12, G121; Hellenic Navy Hydrographic Service 21

The approaches to Port Leone are all straightforward and through deep water. From Port Kalamos steer 248°T for about 2½nm. From the south, head north towards Kastos and then turn north-east into the channel between the islands. It can get quite gusty here during the afternoons, particularly from the north-west, so take care. From the north-east coast of Meganisi, steer 160°T, staying fairly close to the southern tip of Kalamos. Avoid the shoal areas north-west of Formikoula island.

Port Leone is hidden by a headland on approach from the south, but can be identified by two ruined windmills on the eastern side of the bay.

BERTHING

In the west side of the bay are two small stone jetties which a couple of boats can tie up to. It's fairly shallow here, so only smaller boats can berth here and you should go bows-to.

The taverna on the waterside has claimed ownership of these jetties and requests that they are only used by its customers.

ANCHORING

If you don't want to visit the taverna there are plenty of safe anchorages around the bay. Anchor off the beaches to the north, south or west, taking a line ashore if it is busy. It's fairly deep in the bay, at 8-12m, but holding is good.

Port Leone is sheltered, so it is a protected place to spend the night, although gusts sometimes scud off the hills.

EATING OUT

A small taverna is situated on the waterside next to the wall with graffiti on it that says 'No rubbish here'. Open during the summer months only, it serves a small, typically Greek menu.

If you decide to barbecue on the beach, please make sure that you observe the usual fire precautions and take all your rubbish with you. Not everyone has done this in the past and the beach on the west side of the bay has been spoilt by litter.

Two ruined windmills identify the entrance to Port Leone

ASHORE

Port Leone is a beautiful place so it is worth going ashore and wandering around the abandoned village and olive groves. Most of the buildings are unstable though, so take extreme care if you decide to go into any of them. The church is safe to enter, however, and services are held for the islanders on Sundays.

There are several good walks around the foreshore and up into the hills behind the village. It's also a lovely bay in which to swim and snorkel.

Part of the ruined hamlet at Port Leone has been taken over by a taverna. Graffiti on the walls has rather spoilt this otherwise desolate spot

Episkopi

Approach waypoint: 38°39'.24N 20°55'.79E

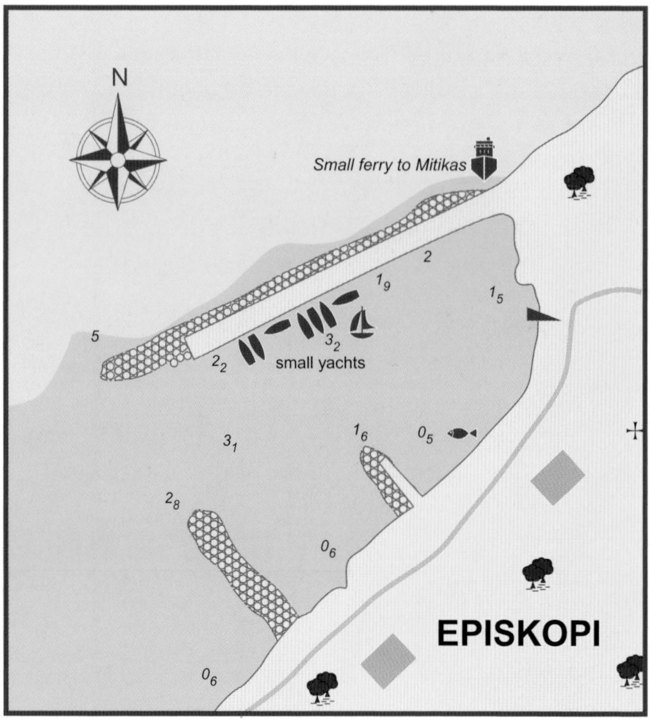

Episkopi is a tiny harbour on the north coast of Kalamos, opposite Mitikas on the mainland. It's a peaceful spot, with a sprinkling of houses and sheltered from the south. Although it offers good holding, the harbour is very shallow and only boats drawing less than 4ft 9in (1.4m) can safely use it. Those that can get into the harbour must take great care when manoeuvring as there is little room for error.

NAVIGATION

Charts: Admiralty 203, SC5771; Imray G12 & G121; Hellenic Navy Hydrographic Service 21

If approaching from Drepanos Bay in the north, steer 126°T, heading directly for the north-east coast of Kalamos. On approach from the south, head north towards the southern tip of Meganisi, taking care around the island of Formikoula where there is a shoal off the north-west corner. Once level with Kefali Pt on Meganisi, head north-east for about 7nm until you see the Episkopi breakwater and entrance, where depths are around 5m. A port-hand light marks the end of the breakwater. From Port Kalamos, head north following the coast round. Episkopi lies slightly south-east of a ruined monastery.

BERTHING

Episkopi harbour is formed by a breakwater and two small stone jetties that jut out from the shore. Yachts of less than 4ft 9in (1.4m) draught can berth alongside or stern- or bows-to the breakwater, where there are rings and bollards at regular intervals. It is too shallow for yachts on the northern shore by the slipway and this area is used by local fishing boats.

ANCHORING

There are several small coves on the north-east coast of Kalamos where you can anchor for the day in calm conditions. However, they do not offer sufficient protection to be good overnight anchorages.

EATING OUT

In the summer months a small taverna opens up in the harbour but this is the only facility in the village. Mitikas on the mainland is a 10-minute trip by motor boat and most provisions can be obtained there.

Episkopi's harbour is tiny and shallow

ASHORE

There are several interesting walks from Episkopi through the rich countryside of Kalamos. Take the road (the only one on the island) out of the village and you can walk to Port Kalamos over the high, volcanic mountains. There are some spectacular views of the Ionian from the top.

To the east of the harbour are the ruins of a monastery where it is said that the mother of Karaiskakis, a leader in the War of Independence, is buried.

Kastos

Nisos Kastos

Kastos is the smaller of the two islands that lie off the Etolo-Akarnanian coast, immediately to the south of Mitikas. Lower lying than its sibling, Kastos measures 2.3 square miles (6km²), and is home to just a handful of residents.

While popular with visitors from the mainland in peak season, it has conceded little to tourism and remains very traditional and unspoilt. As a cruising destination, it excels in its simplicity: there are several anchorages around its limestone-fringed shores but only one harbour and village. This harbour, Port Kastos, on the island's east coast, offers good shelter from the prevailing winds and basic amenities. It's ideal if you are looking for somewhere quieter to spend a day or two.

The island of Kastos and its satellite Provati, viewed from the north

Port Kastos

Approach to Port Kastos: 38°33'.83N 20°54'.82E

Entrance to Port Kastos Bay: 38°34'.07N 20°54'.85E

Inside Port Kastos Harbour: 38°34'.13N 20°54'.73E

Port Kastos, on Kastos's east shore, is a delightful harbour. It's the only village on the island and unusual in this area as it is so under-developed. The harbour itself is small, which has so far restricted the number of visitors to the island and kept it very traditional. Visiting Port Kastos really is like stepping back in time and, with only around 50 permanent residents on the island, it rarely gets too busy.

Port Kastos offers reasonable shelter from the prevailing winds, although it is not so pleasant in a southerly, when it can get quite gusty. From here, however, you are well placed to head south-west to Ithaca or Kefalonia or north to Meganisi and Lefkada.

NAVIGATION

Charts: Admiralty 203, SC5771; Imray G12 & G121; Hellenic Navy Hydrographic Service 030, 21

On all approaches, the steep-sided island of Kalamos, immediately to the north of Kastos, is identifiable from some distance. From the Lefkada Canal, head south-east for the north-east tip of Kalamos and Asprogiali Pt. Kastos will come into view once you are round this headland and you should then proceed towards its east coast. The harbour of Port Kastos lies two-thirds of the way down the island's east coast, and the approach from this direction is hazard free. You can pass either side of the islet of Prasonisi, although if you do use the channel between it and Kastos you should proceed slowly and keep an eye on your echosounder, as depths are around 5m and less. Port Kastos lies just under 1nm south of the islet and from this direction houses in the village can easily be seen.

From the south, the harbour is harder to identify. A windmill on a headland marks the entrance to the bay. The bay itself is relatively deep until near the breakwater, where depths decrease to less than 6m.

BERTHING

There's room for about 10 boats to berth stern- or bows-to the breakwater, which lies to port as you enter the harbour. The bottom is very weedy, so drop your anchor early and let out plenty of scope to give it a chance to dig in. If the breakwater is full, a couple of boats can berth on the small mole to starboard as you enter the bay. There are rings and bollards to tie up to, but there is no access to the shore, so you will have to dinghy across to the main quay.

In calm weather you can anchor on the other side of the mole but it not very well protected and not advised

Port Kastos is the only harbour on the island

in a southerly. Depths in the harbour are less than 5m. The inner harbour on the south-east of the bay is very shallow and usable by fishing boats only.

ANCHORING

If the breakwaters are both full, there is room to anchor off the west and north coasts of Port Kastos Bay, taking a long line ashore. The holding is not good here, though, so make sure your anchor is well set before leaving your boat unattended.

Less than a mile to the north-east of Port Kastos is the islet of Prasonisi. You will find a calm-weather, daytime anchorage immediately to the west of this islet, in a little bay off Kastos.

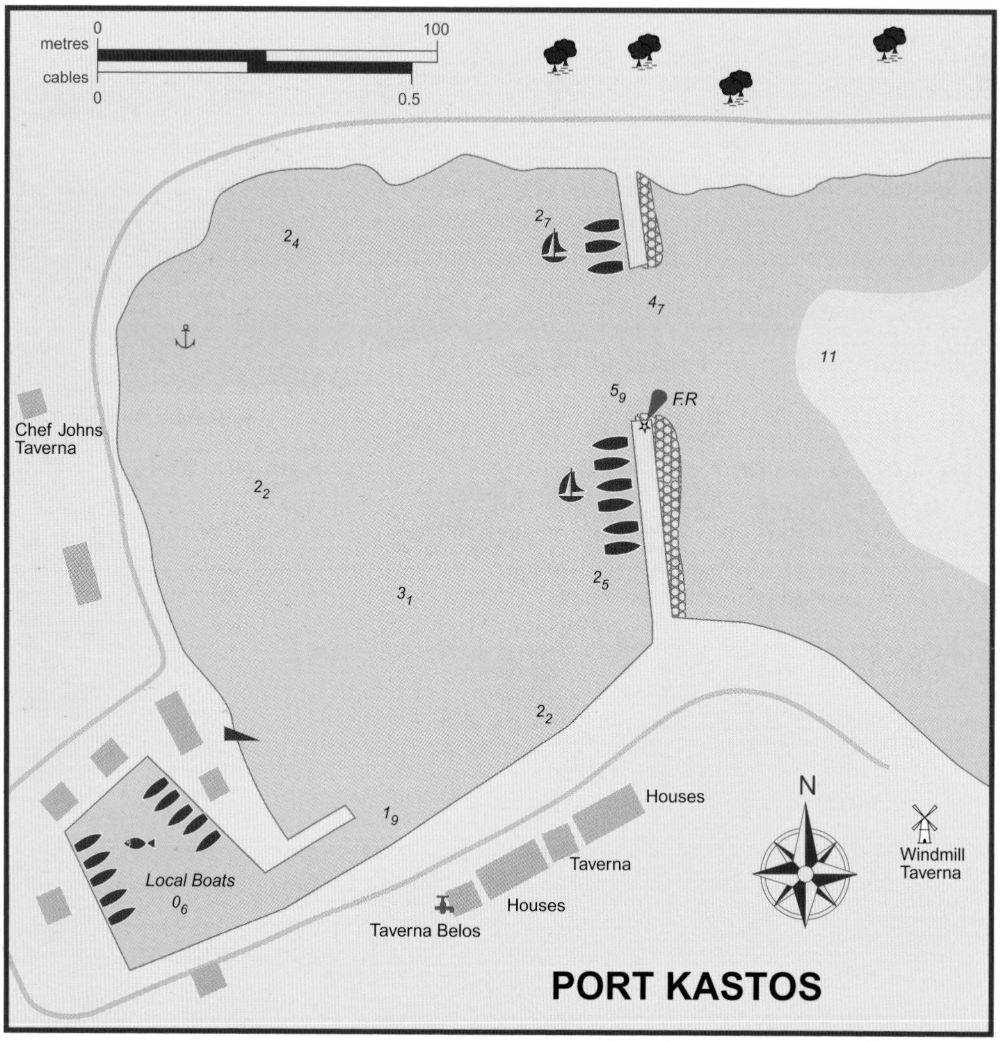

Useful information – Port Kastos

FACILITIES

Water: From Taverna Bellos on the waterfront (€3). Hoses, which reach all the berths close by, are provided.
Ice: Ask at the tavernas.
Rubbish: Bins on the breakwater, but if possible take all your rubbish with you as there is no processing facility on the island.
Telephone: Phone box in the village. May not be able to buy phone cards here. Mobile reception is okay.

PROVISIONING

Grocery shops: There is a very small mini-market in the village, which has erratic opening hours.
Post: Post box in the village. Stamps from the village shop. However, the postal service on the island is very slow.

EATING OUT

There are three tavernas at Port Kastos: Bellos Restaurant in the harbour, the Windmill Restaurant, to the south of the harbour, near the windmill, and Chef John's Restaurant on the hillside above the village. All three serve traditional Greek cuisine. Everything is bought on to the island, so the menus are quite basic, but the seafood cooked here is superb. Chef John's (Tel: 26460 91127) is particularly good for an evening meal as the views are stunning. You can also arrange to be picked up from the village and taken to the restaurant if you don't fancy the walk.

ASHORE

Although there aren't many facilities at Port Kastos, it's a really pleasant and peaceful place to spend a couple of days. There are some lovely walks around the island and the church of Agios Ioannis Prodromos is worth a visit. Built in the mid-19th century, it is decorated inside with the most beautiful oil paintings.

TRANSPORT

Ferry: A small *caique* runs from Port Kastos to Mitikas on the mainland. Ask at the tavernas for details.

Air travel: The nearest airport is near Argostoli on Kefalonia. Charter flights to and from the UK and Athens leave several times a week. See p212.

OTHER INFORMATION

Local Tel code: 26450.
Doctor: No, the nearest is on the mainland, or at Vathi on Ithaca. See p223.
Hospital: There is a medical centre at Astakos on the mainland, or Vathi on Ithaca.

You can berth stern-to the quay in the north-east corner of the bay

About 10 boats can berth off the main breakwater at Port Kastos

Sarakiniko Bay

Ormos Sarakiniko, Saracene

Sarakiniko Bay: 38°34'.04N 20°54'.07E

There are several Sarakiniko bays in the Ionian, reputedly named after the Saracen pirates they sheltered. This Sarakiniko Bay lies on the west coast of Kastos. Largish, with a small islet in the middle of it, Sarakiniko is a well-protected anchorage that is currently being developed. The plan is that the bay will be used as a ferry port for the island in the winter months, when the strong southerly winds force the closure of the main quay at Port Kastos. A small mole has been built in the south-west corner of the bay to protect the ferry quay and there is room on the inside edge for a couple of boats to berth. While the channel between Kalamos and Kastos can be a windy place, the southern end of Sarakiniko Bay is a well-protected and snug anchorage. At the moment it is also a very secluded and charming spot to spend the night.

NAVIGATION

Charts: Admiralty 203, SC5771; Imray G12 & G121; Hellenic Navy Hydrographic Service 030, 21

The approach to the bay is straightforward. From the

Sarakiniko Bay can be a snug anchorage in poor conditions and a couple of yachts can berth off the small mole in the south-west corner of the bay

north coast of Kalamos, head 221°T. Sarakiniko Bay lies opposite the southern tip of Kalamos and can be identified by a small islet in the middle of it. From east of Atokos Island, head 022°T and it's the first large bay you come to. There are some rocks off the small islet, so keep a good look-out and distance from them.

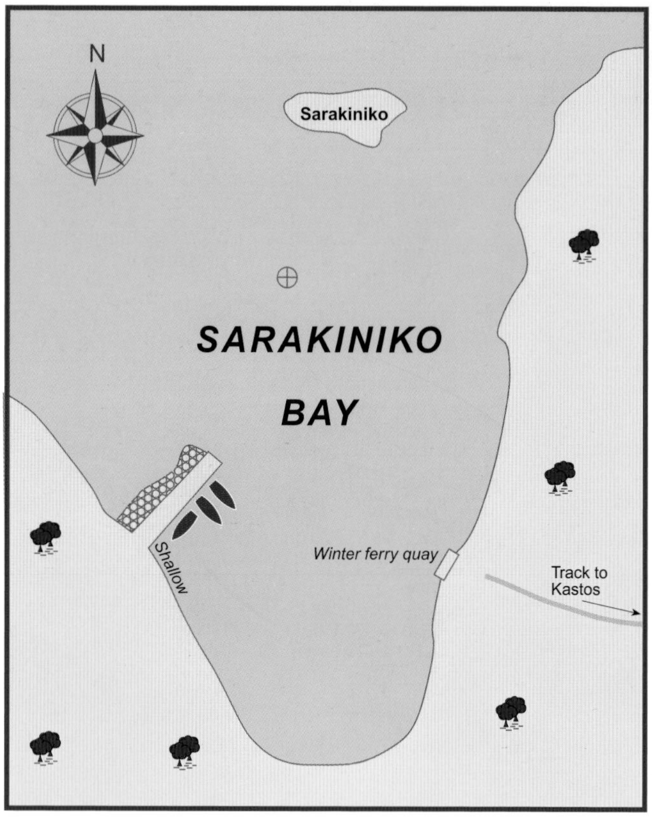

BERTHING

Berth alongside or stern-to the concrete quay behind the mole in the south-west corner of the bay. This is a very well protected berth with space for a couple of boats. There are 12 rings and two bollards to tie up to and a starboard-hand light marks the end of the quay.

The ferry quay on the opposite shore is currently not in use, so it is possible for a couple of boats to berth there.

ANCHORING

The southern corner of the bay is the most protected, and depths are less than 10m throughout so you can anchor almost anywhere. If there is a strong north-westerly blowing in the channel, a small swell can be blown into the bay, but it is not dangerous and provided you tuck yourself in well to the south you should be sheltered enough.

FACILITIES

There are no facilities in Sarakiniko Bay. The nearest place for basic provisions is Port Kastos on the west coast of the island.

ASHORE

A road from the quay in the south-west corner leads around the bay to the ferry quay. From there, follow a rough road that takes you east over the hills to Port Kastos, on the other side of the island. If you walk over for supper, don't forget a torch for the journey back.

Vathi Vali Bay

Ormos Vathy Vali

Vathy Vali Bay: 38°31'.14N 20°54'.13E

Charts: Admiralty 203, SC5771; Imray G12 & G121; Hellenic Navy Hydrographic Service 030, 21

Vathi Vali lies on the SE coast of Kastos. On approach from Ithaca, head for the S coast of the island, passing to the E of Atokos, and Vathi Vali is the first big bay you come to on the E coast. From Port Kastos, steer 208°T for about 1nm. Anchoring depths within the bay are considerable, so take a line ashore for extra protection. The bay is protected from the NW, but offers no shelter in a southerly and should only be used in calm weather.

SOUTH KASTOS ANCHORAGES

South-east tip of Kastos: 38°32'.29N 20°53'.95E

Charts: Admiralty 203, SC5771; Imray G12 & G121; Hellenic Navy Hydrographic Service 030, 21

At the southern end of Kastos, west of Podari Pt, are a couple of large coves suitable for anchoring. They provide sufficient shelter in the morning and early afternoons, but once a southerly breeze has picked up later on they can be uncomfortable due to the swell that is often pushed into them. Suitable as day stops only, you should not overnight here. Beware of some nasty rocks off the westernmost headland of the two bays.

NORTH KASTOS ANCHORAGES

To the north of Kastos: 38°36'.84N 20°57'.36E

Charts: Admiralty 203, SC5771; Imray G12 & G121; Hellenic Navy Hydrographic Service 030, 21

The bay on the north-east coast of Kastos offers an alternative anchorage. It's not at all protected in a southerly but in a northwesterly will give you adequate shelter for a lunch or daytime stop.

Off the north coast of Kastos lies the small islet of Provati. The narrow channel between the two is navigable, although make sure that you proceed with caution.

Chapter four
The Etolo-Akarnanian coast

The Etolo-Akarnanian coast extends from the Lefkada Canal to the entrance of the Patraikos Gulf. It's a distinctive coastline, bordered by high, sparsely vegetated mountains to the north and a low-lying delta to the south, closely guarded by myriad islands and islets just offshore. It's a rather bleak-looking and unpopulated place, but the parched and rocky hillsides form a dramatic backdrop and the waters to the west offer some of the best sailing in the Ionian.

Off the northern part of this coastline, the prevailing northwesterly winds are relatively gentle. Although they usually pick up in the afternoons, they are quite consistent and the waters fairly flat. The shores south of Astakos, however, are more exposed and often affected by the Peloponnese's weather system, which generates southerlies. These, if allowed to build up over several days, can create an unpleasant chop which makes hard going for smaller vessels punching into it. In bad weather this area is best avoided and shelter should be sought elsewhere.

While this lee shore offers fewer safe harbours than the Epirus coast north of Preveza, its deep waters are relatively free from isolated dangers and there is little commercial shipping to dodge. Paleros and Vounaki, on the northern part of this coast, offer the best shelter and both have excellent amenities and provisions for cruising yachts. Mitikas, to the south, is currently being developed, but has the potential to be a good destination. In the right weather conditions, Astakos is away from the rat race of other harbours.

The Dragonera and Echinades islands provide a selection of anchorages but isolated rocks and reefs and little protection mean that this area should be avoided if conditions deteriorate significantly. The coastline to the east forms the mouth of the River Acheloos, the largest river in Greece, and alluvial deposits have littered this area with sandbanks and shoals. In places the marshy coastline is indistinct and care should be taken when navigating here. However, it's a beautiful spot, rich in wildlife, and in the right conditions should be explored.

Kefali Point

0.2nm north of Kefali Pt: 38°45'.60N 20°45'.70E
Charts: Admiralty 2405, 203, SC5771; Imray G121, G11, G12; Hellenic Navy Hydrographic Service 2131, 21

There is a small anchorage tucked in behind the northern shore of Kefali Pt. While the beach is a pleasant place to stop, this anchorage is suitable only in calm weather as there isn't much shelter here.

The northwesterly wind usually funnels down Drepanos Bay, between mainland Greece and Lefkada, and makes any anchorage untenable for more than a couple of hours. The headland is marked with a light (Fl 4s5M).

Kefali Pt lies just south of the Lefkada canal and is lit at night

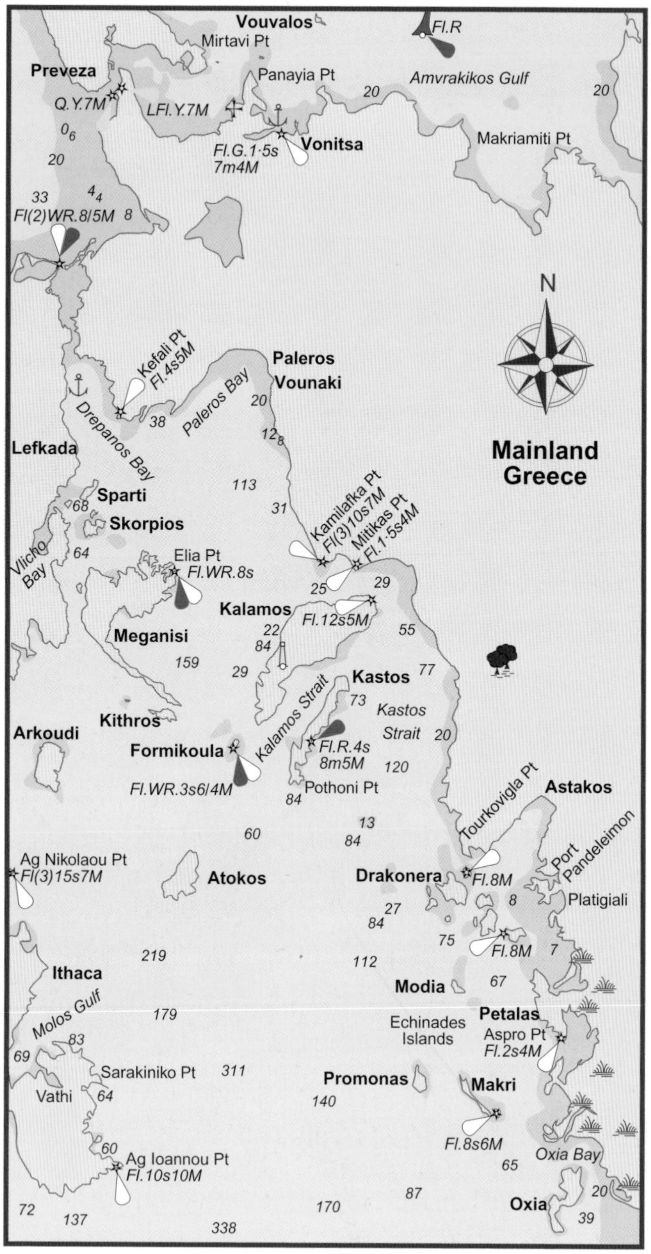

Vathi Vali

Entrance waypoint: 38°45'.26N 20°46'.57E
Charts: Admiralty 2405, 203, SC5771; Imray G121, G11, G12; Hellenic Navy Hydrographic Service 2131, 21

This bay, east of Kefali Pt, would be a very good anchorage if it wasn't for the fish farms up the eastern side of the inlet. There is room to anchor beyond the outer fish farm, but if you want to stop somewhere along this coast there are better places. The anchorage is also open to the south, so it is not good in a southerly. On approach from the west or south be careful of Miaouli, a reef that lies less than half a mile south-east of Kefali Pt.

Immediately west of Vathi Vali, before Kefali Pt, is a small daytime anchorage. Day-trip boats often anchor here while their passengers go for a swim and, although it is okay for a lunch-time stop, it is not at all sheltered if the wind blows up from any direction. If approaching from the east, watch out for the Miaouli reef.

Fish farms take up much of the anchorage in Vathi Vali Bay

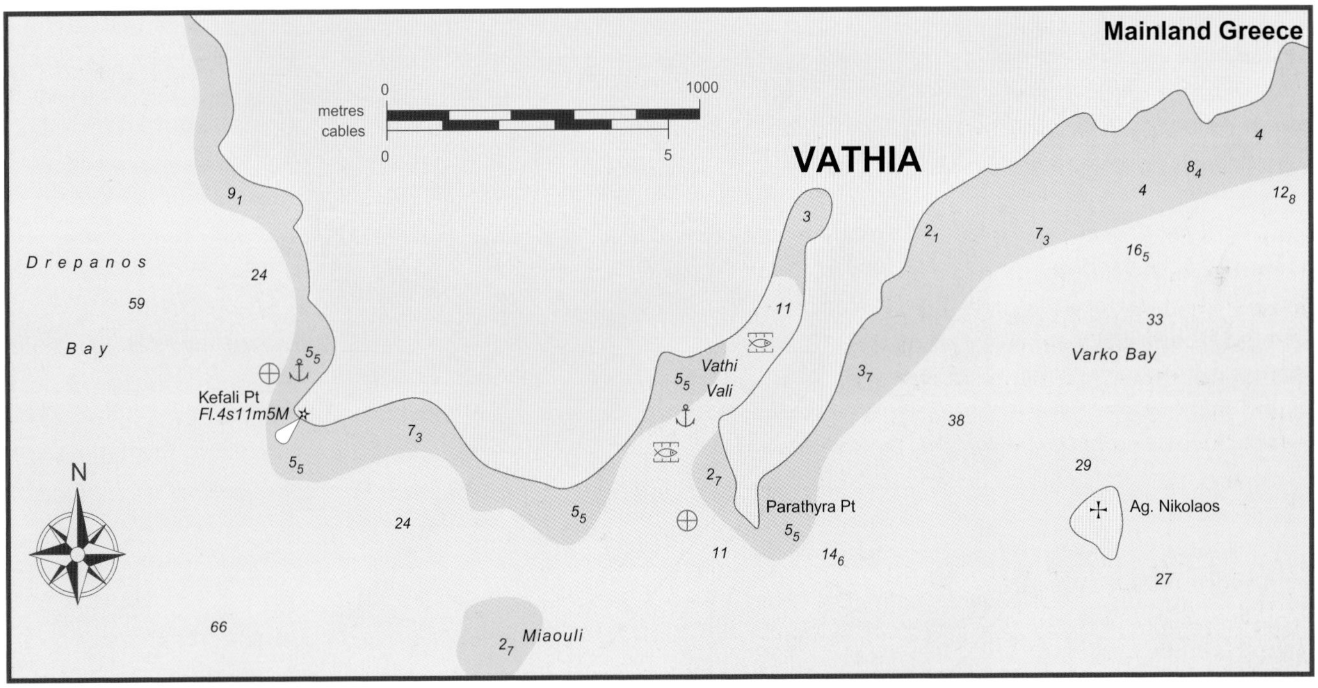

Varko Bay

Nerokratima Bay

0.7nm NE of Vrach Agios Nikolaos:

38°45'.88N 20°47'.81E

Charts: Admiralty 2405, 203, SC5771; Imray G121, G11, G12; Hellenic Navy Hydrographic Service 2131, 21

Varko Bay, sometimes referred to as 'Nerokratima' or 'Cocoa Bay', lies to the east of Vathi Vali on the Greek mainland. It's a big, wide, open bay that is a good overnight anchorage as well as a lunch-time stop. There's a little hotel in the west of the bay but you can anchor anywhere – off the rocks or the shingle beach. Don't get too close to Varko Pt, to the east, though, as it is quite shallow in places. You should also be aware when anchoring of a small area of shoal water just off the shore in the centre of the bay.

The wind normally blows a northwesterly here, although you should be fine swinging to your anchor. The holding is good on weed and shingle and you can anchor in about 5m of water. However, if you intend to spend the night, take a line ashore for extra protection.

Off Varko Bay is the tiny island of Agios Nikolaos. You can pass either side of the island as the water is deep until close in. You can anchor off the island but as it is so deep you will need to lay plenty of scope. There is usually lots of birdlife on the island.

Deep water surrounds the islet of Ag Nikolaos in Varko Bay

Varko Bay is a wide, open bay off the mainland, with plenty of room to anchor

Church Bay

1.5nm NE of Varko Pt: 38°46'.51N 20°49'.47E
Charts: Admiralty 203, SC5771; Imray G121, G11, G12; Hellenic Navy Hydrographic Service 2131, 21

Church Bay is a small anchorage to the east of Varko Bay off the Greek mainland. So called because of the small church that overlooks the beach, this is a good anchorage for a lunch-time stop.

Care should be taken if approaching from the west; it is quite shallow around Varko Pt, so give the point a wide berth. You should also pass to the outside of the rocky islets of Vrak Pogonia. You can't go in between the rocks and, although it is generally deep water here, you should keep an eye on your depth.

Church Bay offers reasonable holding but is not that sheltered, particularly in a southerly as the wind is often strong here. The seabed shelves steeply so you can get quite close in to the beach. Anchor in 5-10m of water.

A small white church (conspic) overlooking the water gives this bay its name

Paleros

Palairos, Zaverda, Ormos Palairou

Off Paleros Harbour: 38°46'.84N 20°52'.31E

Protected by a large, scarred mountain, which turns a beautiful pinky colour in the evening light, the harbour and village at Paleros is a charming place to spend a night or two. An increasingly popular destination for cruising yachts, the village remains very traditional and, despite the heavy presence of holiday companies in the area, has retained much of its rural charm.
Life continues at a very unhurried pace in Paleros and while new businesses are prospering, the village has not been spoilt.

The village itself consists of two settlements which have gradually been interwoven over time. The one in the upper village (Paleros) was originally an agricultural community that cultivated the surrounding hillsides, while the hamlet of Zaverda evolved around the small harbour; its main source of revenue coming from the sea. A distinction is still made today between those that live in the upper and lower parts, although the village is united in every other respect.

The harbour offers good shelter from all directions and as somewhere to victual has got much to offer. It is also within an hour's sail of the Lefkada Canal and is a good starting place for a cruise around the southern Ionian islands.

NAVIGATION

Charts: Admiralty 203, 189, SC5771; Imray G121, G12; Hellenic Navy Hydrographic Service 2131, 21

Paleros is situated in the north-east corner of Paleros Bay (Ormos Palairou). From the southern entrance to the Lefkada Canal, head south until Kefali Pt (Fl 4s 5M), then turn east and follow the coastline around Paleros Bay, taking care to avoid Miaouli, a reef that lies less than half a mile south-east of Kefali Pt. From the south, head north passing either side of Kalamos or Meganisi, depending on the direction from which

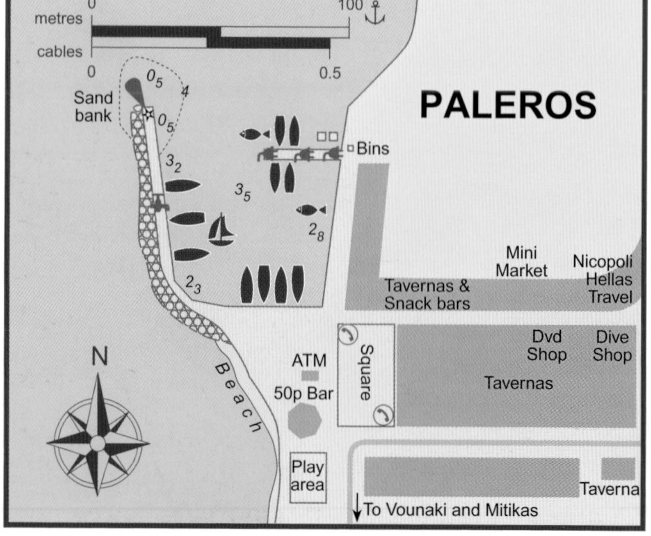

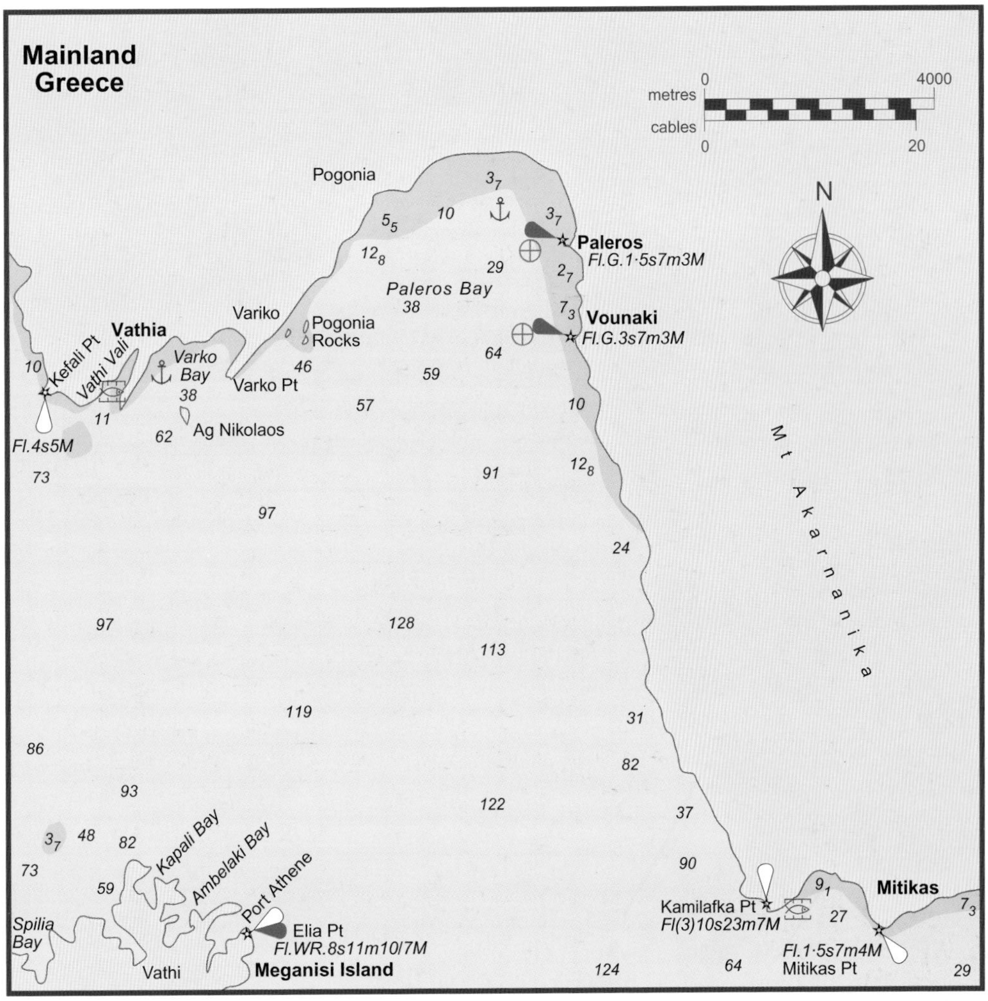

you are approaching. If approaching from the Meganisi Strait, between Meganisi and Lefkada, take care to avoid the Heiromiti Shoal, which lies halfway between Meganisi and Skorpios. Follow the Meganisi coastline closely until Makria Pt and you will pass through clear water.

The final approach to the village and harbour, through Paleros Bay, is straightforward and hazard-free and can be made in the dark. If you do head for Paleros at night, steer for the northernmost of two lights (Fl G 1.5s 7m3M) on the east coast of the bay, as this marks the harbour breakwater. The second light, a mile to the south, indicates the entrance to Vounaki Marina.

The entrance to Paleros is at the northern end between the breakwater and the floating pontoon. Be aware that a sandbank is developing just off the entrance to this harbour (see chart on page 156). It extends for about 20m north and east from the breakwater and for about 30m within the harbour.

BERTHING

Berth either stern- or bows-to the breakwater or the floating pontoon on the east side of the harbour. If possible, berth at the western end of the pontoon as the jetty's large mooring sinkers lie just below the surface near the shore. Yachts can also berth on the quayside in the south-east corner of the harbour. The southern end of the harbour is shallow and used by local fishing boats. Watch out for lazylines when manoeuvring within the harbour to avoid fouling them on your prop.

Paleros is a pretty, traditional village that is good for provisioning

ANCHORING

Small yachts often anchor in the area just to the north of the harbour entrance. The holding here is generally good and depths range between 3-5m. At the northern end of Paleros Bay is another pleasant spot. Anchor off the beach in about 10m on mud. Occasionally yachts anchor off the small beach just below the harbour, but do not be tempted to go any further south of this as there are several rocky reefs near the shore between here and Vounaki Marina.

Useful information – Paleros

FACILITIES

Water: Tap at the southern end of the breakwater. Water points on the floating pontoon.
Fuel: There are a couple of service stations a few minutes' drive from Paleros. Vounaki Marina, 1nm to the south of Paleros, has a fuel pontoon (see p160).
Showers: Available at several of the tavernas in the village. Try Dionysus and the Tomorrow Restaurant on the waterfront.
Ice: Ask at the tavernas.
Gas: Gas bottle exchange at Nico's supermarket in the upper village.
Shorepower: On the floating pontoon at the north-east side of the harbour.
Rubbish: Bins on the quay.
Yacht services/chandlery: Sunsail's base at Vounaki Marina offers various facilities, by prior arrangement only (see p160). Alternatively, there are several boatyards on the east coast of Lefkada and chandlers in Lefkada town.
Telephone: Several phone boxes in the square immediately to the west of the harbour. Phone cards available from kiosks and supermarkets. Mobile reception is good.
Internet: The Old School Cafe at the top of the town next to the Port Police is run by Kosta, Tel: 69763 93900. €2 per hour.

PROVISIONING

Grocery shops: Several supermarkets and grocers in the upper and lower parts of Paleros. Those in the upper part of the village will deliver to the harbour. A Dia supermarket is on the outskirts of the town.There is no market in Paleros but local traders often drive around the village selling goods from their vans.
Bakery: Behind the square, near Nicopoli Hellas Travel. Sells a good selection of cakes, pastries and biscuits. Also three cake shops in the village.
Butcher: A couple in the upper village. The grocery shop near the square also has a limited supply.
Banks: There is a National Bank of Greece ATM on the waterfront by the harbour.
Pharmacy: Two in the upper village near the post office and the church.
Post: The post office is on the high street in the upper village. Open Monday-Friday, 0730-1400. Post box near the National Bank of Greece ATM. Stamps available from the souvenir shops.
Opening times: Most of the shops are open Monday-Saturday to normal siesta hours. The grocer in the lower village is usually open on Sundays. No early closing.

EATING OUT

The waterfront at Paleros is packed with tavernas and cafes and, if none suits, then there are several more in the upper village. Along the beach front, you'll find: Dionysis (Tel: 26430 41988), run by Maki and his German wife, Sylvie. Dionysis serves a good selection of dishes and, although slightly more expensive than other restaurants in Paleros, is definitely worth a visit. Restaurant Tomorrow (Tel: 26430 41611), further along the road past the beach, serves breakfast, lunch and dinner and has an extensive Greek menu. Taverna Anna (Tel: 26430 41569), at the far end of the road, is very traditional and good for seafood. There is also a Chinese and Indian restaurant nearby, which does takeaways (Tel: 26430 41042).

Near the Square you'll find Ta Navtaki Taverna, Restaurant Paleros (Tel: 26430 41674) and Trata Taverna (Tel: 26430 41635), which serves very good fish caught by the restaurant's owners Spiro and Kosta. Taverna Skamnia (Tel: 26430 41809), just beyond the square opposite the bakery, has no sea view but does have a very attractive courtyard. In the upper village, you'll find The New Mill Tavern (Tel: 26430 41634). It's a small and very eccentric place to eat and while the cuisine can sometimes be very good, the choice is often limited. For fast food, try Chicken Nic's behind the kiosk in the square.

A Sou'Wester 18 berthed at Paleros

ASHORE

Paleros is a perfect base if you want to explore the mainland coast and the Gulf of Amvrakikos but not by boat. Preveza, a good place to shop, is just 30 minutes away by car, and all the local sites of interest are within easy reach.

On the peninsula to the west of Paleros is the huge Venetian castle of Plagia, Agios Georgios, which stands guard over the southern approaches to Lefkada Canal. Built in the 17th century, the ruined castle is now protected and commands stunning views over Lefkada and the inland sea towards Meganisi and Kalamos.

TRANSPORT

Car hire: Nikopolis Hellas (Tel: 26430 42114), the travel agent behind the square near the bakers, runs a branch of Sixt car hire. Cars can also be hired from Lefkada.
Taxis: Usually some taxis on the waterfront. If not try: Tsidimas Michalis (Tel: 26430 41501), Achimastos Vagelis (Tel: 26430 41248). Tria/Ntantis Vasilis (Tel: 26430 41410), Kouvaras Kostas (Tel: 26430 41663), Gatsos Christos (Tel: 26430 41790) or Velios Kostas (Tel: 26430 41139).
Bus: Bus stop on the main road through the upper village. The services are limited; one runs at about 0700 to Vonitsa bus station, where you can get buses to Lefkada, Preveza and Athens.
Ferry: The nearest international ferry port is at Patra, a 2½-hour drive to the south. Inter-island ferries operate from Nidri and Vasiliki on Lefkada and run to Frikes on Ithaca, Fiskardo on Kefalonia and Spilia Bay and Vathi on Meganisi.
Air travel: The nearest is Aktio airport at Preveza, about 30 minutes away by car. Direct charter flights from Europe are limited and only run between May and October. However, several internal flights run weekly between Preveza and Athens.

OTHER INFORMATION

Local Tel code: 26430.
Police: To the north of the square. Tel: 26430 41205.
Port Police: Situated in the upper village.
Doctor: Next to the town hall (Tel: 26430 41207), open in the mornings, Mon-Fri. English speaking.
Hospital: There is a 24-hour medical centre in Vonitsa (Tel: 26430 22222), 20 minutes away by car. Lefkada hospital (Tel: 26450 25371) is 30 minutes away.

Vounaki Marina

Approach to Vounaki Marina: 38°46'.00N 20°51'.81E
Vounaki Marina entrance: 38°46'.25N 20°52'.51E

Vounaki Marina is situated on the mainland, opposite the island of Lefkada and about 1nm south of Paleros. The 90-berth marina is Sunsail's main base in the Ionian and forms part of a larger hotel complex run by the company. During the season it is busy with Sunsail yachts for three days of the week, but you will still find visitors' berths available.

The marina itself offers reasonable shelter: a breakwater shields it from the west and south and, although the entrance faces north, it is protected from any northerly swell by a floating pontoon and T-shaped jetty.

Vounaki is a good place to base yourself if you need to victual or change crew. Paleros, a small but well-stocked village, is a 15-minute walk from the marina and Preveza airport is just 30 minutes away by car. The marina also has a small maintenance yard which, by prior arrangement, can carry out most repairs.

Anyone intending to visit Vounaki should note that the marina is closed to private yachts from the end of October until the beginning of May when the Sunsail base is shut and its yachts laid up. During peak season it can get very busy with both private and charter yachts, so if you do intend to stay at Vounaki it is worth contacting the marina office first to book a berth.

NAVIGATION

Charts: Admiralty 203, 189, SC5771; Imray G121, G12; Hellenic Navy Hydrographic Service 2131, 21

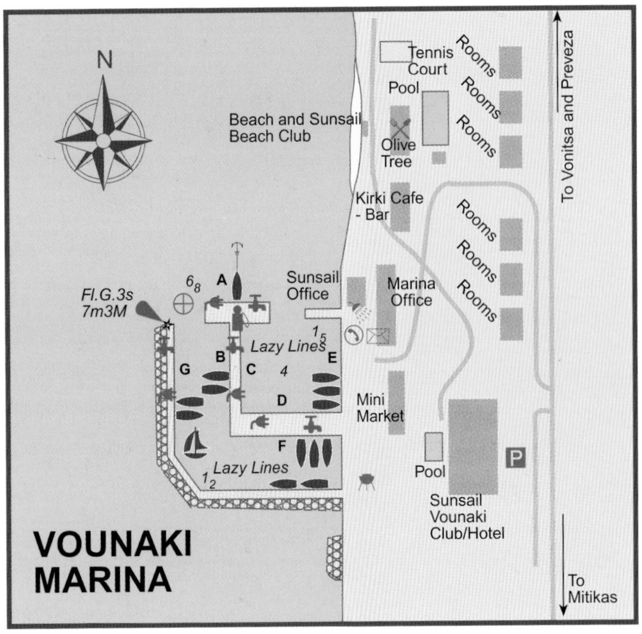

Vounaki does not appear on Admiralty charts, although the light on the marina's breakwater (Fl G 3s3M), the southernmost of two lights on this stretch of coast, is marked. The marina itself stands at the foot of Mount Akarnanika, a distinctive mountain with scars running down its face that is conspicuous from all directions.

On approach from either north or south, head for Paleros Bay, a large bay situated to the east of the southern entrance to the Lefkada Canal. Vounaki lies about 1nm south of the village of Paleros and is identified closer in by a large hotel complex on the hillside above the marina. The approach is through deep water and free of dangers. However, a good look-out should be maintained close to the marina's entrance as the waters in the immediate vicinity are often busy with dinghies and windsurfers from Sunsail's beach club. There are two entrances to the harbour on its northern side, and if you call the marina office you will be given instructions on which to use.

The marina at Vounaki is open to visiting boats during the season

BERTHING

On approach, call up the marina on VHF Ch10 for berthing instructions. Most of the marina staff speak English and the office is manned seven days a week from 0830-1900 May-October. All the berths in Vounaki are rigged with lazylines and on entering the marina you will be directed to a pontoon marked A-G. Boats of up to 15.2m (50ft) LOA can berth within the marina, stern- or bows-to the pontoons, but larger yachts may have to tie up either alongside the fuel jetty or, occasionally, in the outer marina. Sunsail staff will then assist with your lines. Once safely tied up, you should register your boat at the marina office. Berthing fees are valid from the time of arrival until 1400 the next day and must be paid before departure. **Berthing fees per night**: Up to 30ft (9.5m), €24; 30-40ft (9.5-12.5m),€31; 40-50ft (12.5-15.5m), €39. Prices may vary. You pay extra for electricity and water (see below).

ANCHORING

The nearest anchorage is at the head of Paleros Bay, which is about 1½nm north of Paleros. Anchor in 10m or less on mud. The holding here is generally good and the anchorage offers shelter from the prevailing winds. It is not suitable in a southerly.

Useful information – Vounaki Marina

FACILITIES

Water: Water points at all berths on all pontoons. Price per fill is €5.
Fuel: Is available at all berths on A, B, C, F & D pontoons.
Showers: Shower and toilet block next to the marina reception.
Ice: Available at the mini-market.
Laundry: Can be arranged locally. Ask at the marina office for more information. A 5kg load costs €15 for a wash and dry.
Gas: Gas bottle exchange.
Shorepower: 220v sockets on all berths apart from pontoon E. €5 per night.
Rubbish: Bins behind the mini-market.
Yacht services/chandlery: Sunsail's on-site yard offers services such as inboard and outboard engineering, haulage, mast and rigging maintenance and repair, by prior arrangement only. Crane out/launch up to 15 tons. Winterising and guardianage services are also available.
Telephone: Card phone outside marina reception. Mobile reception is good.
Fax: Ask at the marina reception. Small charge.
Internet: Services are available at the hotel reception and the Old School Cafe in Paleros.

PROVISIONING

Grocery shops: The mini-market near the marina reception has limited fresh and packaged products. Open mornings and afternoons for six days a week. Credit cards accepted. The mini-market also sells gifts and souvenirs. Paleros, a four-minute taxi-ride or a 10-15-minute walk away, is good for provisioning.
Bakery: The mini-market has a limited supply but there are a couple of good bakeries in Paleros.
Butcher: In Paleros.
Banks: National Bank of Greece ATM by the harbour at Paleros.
Pharmacy: One near the post office in Paleros.
Post: Post boxes outside the marina office and hotel reception. The post office is in Paleros. Open 0730-1400, Monday-Friday.
Opening times: The marina reception is open between 0900-1700, seven days a week.

EATING OUT

The Olive Tree Restaurant, situated to the north of the marina, beneath the main swimming pool, is open for lunch five days a week and dinner four evenings a week. Its menu features reasonably priced international cuisine, including pizzas, pasta, seafood, steak, salad and traditional Greek food. The restaurant usually hosts at least one flotilla dinner per week, so it can get quite busy and you may need to book. Ask at the marina reception for details.

The Kirki Café-Bar, just behind the beach, has stunning views across to Lefkada and is open daily until 2300. Alternatively there are numerous tavernas in Paleros, which is a 10-15-minute walk from Vounaki, along the beach.

ASHORE

Sunsail operates a beach club at Vounaki, providing a selection of watersports for its customers. Depending on how busy it is, some of these facilities may be available to users of the marina. For details, enquire at the beach.

TRANSPORT

Car hire: Ask at the marina office. Europcar (Tel: 26450 23581), based in Lefkada town, will sometimes deliver to Vounaki for a small surcharge.
Taxis: For information, ask at the marina office.
Bus: The nearest bus station is at Vonitsa (Tel: 26430 22500). Services run daily to Preveza, and from there regular services to Igoumenitsa, Parga and Athens.
Ferry: The nearest terminal is at Patra, a 2½-hour drive from Vounaki. International and inter-island services run from the port daily. Services to Kefalonia, Ithaca and Meganisi leave from Nidri and Vasiliki on Lefkada. See p118 & p130.
Air travel: Aktio airport at Preveza is a 30-minute drive from Vounaki. During high season there are several domestic and charter flights in and out of the airport each week.

OTHER INFORMATION

Local Tel code: 26430.
Marina office: Sunsail Vounaki Marina, Paleros, AK 30012, Etoloacarnania, Greece. Tel: 26430 41944; VHF Ch10 (May-October only). Email: voumarina@ionianbase.gr
Doctor: Doctors' surgery near the town hall in Paleros (Tel: 26430 41207).
Dentist: In Paleros.
Hospital: 24-hour medical centre in Vonitsa (Tel: 26430 22222) and a hospital in Lefkada (Tel: 26450 25371), a 30-minute drive from Vounaki.

Sunsail's staff can carry out maintenance, but book in advance

Vounaki Marina is Sunsail's main base in the Ionian. With room for 90 boats, the marina has good facilities and is close to Paleros

Mitikas Mitika, Mytika

Approach to Mitikas: 38°39'.94N 20°57'.15E
Off Mitikas Pt: 38°39'.74N 20°56'.66E

Mitikas is situated on the mainland coast, 8nm south of Paleros and opposite the island of Kalamos. As a cruising destination, the small town (population 684) has real potential. It's within easy hopping distance of Lefkada, Kefalonia and Ithaca, well stocked with shops and tavernas and, at the moment, thankfully untouched by the tourist industry. Yet until the new harbour is finished, space is at a premium at Mitikas and it remains an infrequent destination for most yachts. In 2005 underwater concrete blocks marking the outer perimeter of the new port were put in place, but in 2006 it was discovered that Mitikas didn't have planning permission to build a harbour, so its future now looks very uncertain.

The town itself is spread along the coastal road. It has a sleepy feel, even in the height of summer and, despite the fact that increasing the size of the harbour will invariably heighten potential for tourist development, I think it highly unlikely that it would ever reach the scale of other ports, such as Nidri on Lefkada. It's very much an agricultural community and a working town, and looks set to remain so.

Although room in the harbour is currently limited, if you can get in you will be protected from all but southwesterly winds and will find the holding generally good.

NAVIGATION

Charts: Admiralty 203, 189, SC5771; Imray G121, G11, G12; Hellenic Navy Hydrographic Service 21

The easiest way to locate Mitikas is by heading for the northern tip of Kalamos island, which lies directly opposite the town. The steep-sided island is visible from all directions, and once close to, the town's harbour and houses will come into view. The approach to Mitikas is through deep water and the only hazards to watch out for in summer are the small inflatables that often zip between the town and the islands of Kalamos and Kastos.

On approach from the south, stay mid-channel at the southern entrance to Vourkos Bay, which lies just to the east of Mitikas's harbour, as there are rocks close to the mainland coast (Kamiloi) and off the northeastern tip of Kalamos.

BERTHING

Until the new harbour is complete (if this ever happens), the only place for yachts at Mitikas is within the fishing boat harbour. Space is usually limited due to the number of fishing boats but it should be possible to find somewhere to berth among them, either stern- or bows-to the harbour walls.

ANCHORING

In settled weather, it is possible to anchor in both Mitikas Bay, to the west of the harbour, and in

Mitikas' harbour is being developed to make it more yacht friendly

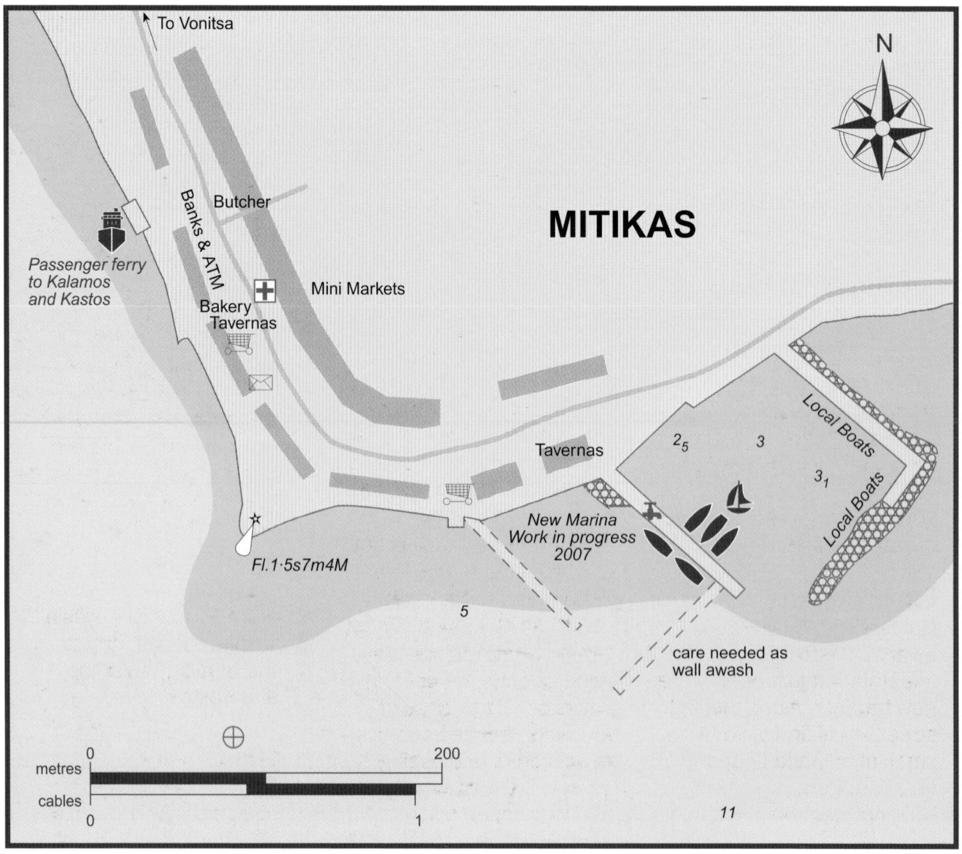

The main harbour at Mitikas is used by fishing boats and has a beautiful backdrop of rugged hills and mountains

Vourkos Bay, to the east. Anchor in Vourkos Bay, about ½nm from Mitikas Pt, in about 10-15m of water. The holding is good on sand and you should be sheltered from all but southerly winds. In Mitikas Bay, anchor off the village, towards the head of the bay, in about 10m. This anchorage is a good lunch-time stop, but in the afternoon, the prevailing winds can whistle in here and produce an uncomfortable swell.

Useful information – Mitikas

FACILITIES

Water: Taps on the mole and on the quayside.
Fuel: Take a taxi to the petrol station on the outskirts of Mitikas.
Ice: Ask at the supermarket nearest the harbour.
Gas: Gas bottles available from the supermarkets.
Rubbish: Large bins near the harbour.
Yacht services/chandlery: No, the nearest services are at Vounaki Marina (see p160) or Lefkas Marina on Lefkada (see p105). Nautiliaka Chandlery (Tel: 26460 42218) in Astakos (about 20 miles [32km] from Mitikas) sells a limited selection of marine equipment and fishing gear.
Telephone: Several card phones along the main road through Mitikas.

PROVISIONING

Grocery shops: There's a very well-stocked supermarket just behind the new harbour. Along the high street, you'll find several small mini-markets and grocery shops.
Bakery: Near the Agricultural Bank on the high street. Mini-markets also stock a limited supply of baked products, and the supermarket near the ferry quay has a bread shop attached.
Butcher: A couple in Mitikas – one on a side street near the Agricultural Bank of Greece, and another near the post office.
Banks: The Agricultural Bank of Greece (Tel: 26420 81322) has a branch and ATM on the high street, near Remezzo Café, and The National Bank of Greece, near Athena mini-market on the high street, has an ATM.
Pharmacy: Several along the high street, one opposite the taxi rank and another at the western end opposite the electronics shop.
Post: The post office is on the high street, next to a supermarket. It is open 0830-1400, Monday-Friday.
Other shops: Mitikas has a good selection of general shops selling a range of products, from electronics to souvenirs and fishing tackle. There is also an ironmonger, two hairdressers and a carpenter's along the high street.

EATING OUT

The fish taverna Mouragio, to the north of the ferry quay, has a good menu and you can eat while watching local children hunting octopus off the quay. There are lots of small tavernas and cafés along the high street, with gorgeous views across the water towards Kalamos and Lefkada. Try Galaros Taverna or Remezzo Café at the northern end of the road or Mytikas Restaurant further down. There's also a good taverna just behind the new harbour, which is often bustling with locals in the height of summer.

ASHORE

From Mitikas it is possible to take a small ferry to the island of Kalamos and Kastos.

TRANSPORT

Car hire: The nearest car hire firm is at Nikopolis Hellas (Tel: 26430 42114) in Paleros, a travel agent which runs a branch of Sixt car hire. Paleros is about 11 miles (18km) to the north.
Taxis: Taxi rank at the S end of the high street.
Bus: The nearest bus station is at Astakos, about 20 miles (32km) to the south.
Ferry: A small ferry to Kalamos runs daily from the quay at the northern end of Mitikas.
Air travel: Aktio airport at Preveza is a 50-minute car journey from Mitikas. Domestic and charter flights fly from here several times a week.

OTHER INFORMATION

Local Tel code: 26420.
Police: Tel: 81231.
Doctor: The nearest doctor is in Paleros, about 11 miles (18km) to the north. See p158.
Dentist: Kaah, situated on the seafront.
Hospital: The closest medical centre is at Astakos, 20 miles (32km) to the south (see p165).

Astakos

Off Astakos harbour:
38°31'.94N 21°04'.96E

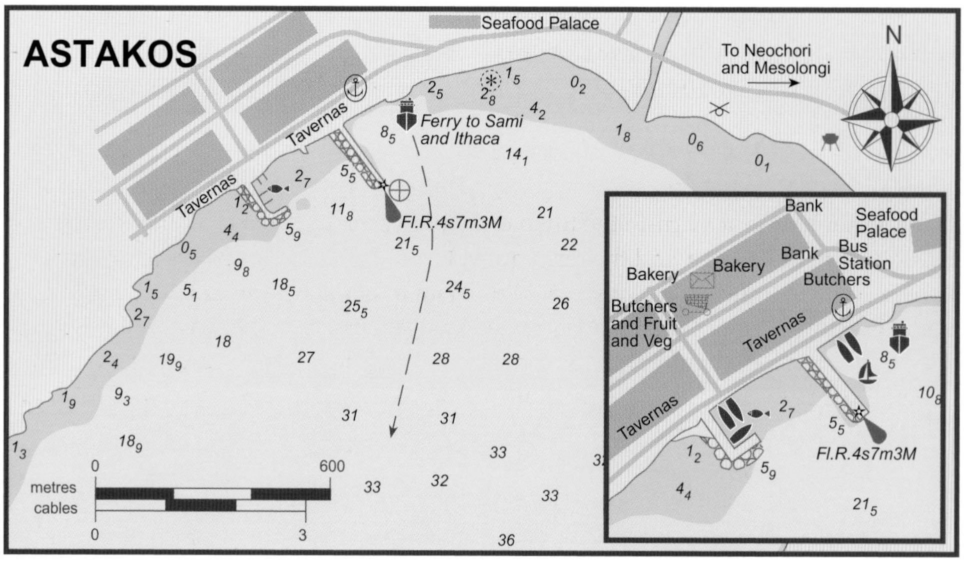

'Astakos' is Greek for lobster, which is rather appropriate for a town that has sustained much of its economy on fishing since ancient times. Flanking the north-west shore of Astakos Bay, 14nm south-west of Mitikas, it is still a thriving, albeit small fishing port. It's mentioned throughout Classical and Byzantine times and, although much of today's town only dates back to the 1800s, remains of an ancient Astakos, formerly known as Dragamestos, lie just to the north-west. It was so prosperous that at one time it even had its own currency.

Greek mythology depicts Alkmeon, son of the King of Argos, as one of the earliest settlers in the area, where some of the oldest evidence of human occupation has been found near to the town. The village of Karaiskakis, 2½-miles to the north of Astakos, is where George

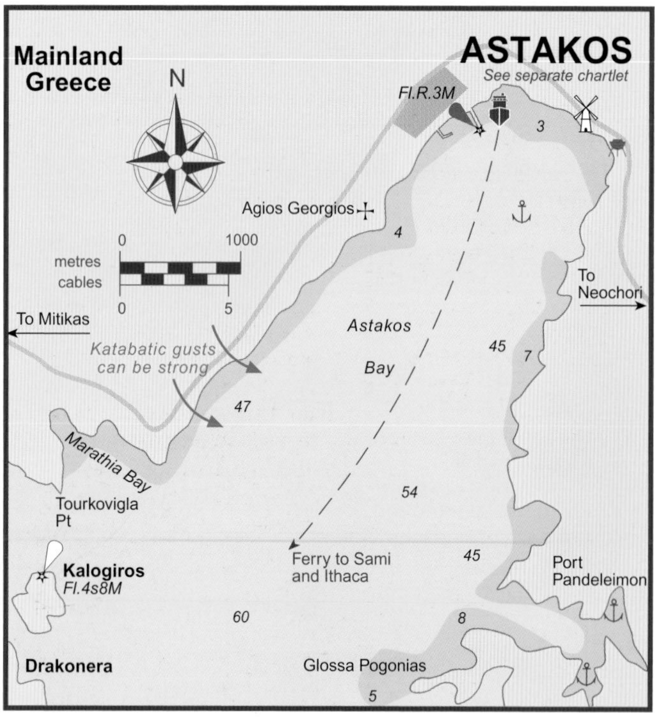

Karaiskakis, one of the country's most important military figures, camped during the 1921 Greek Revolution when Greece fought back against 400 years of slavery under Ottoman rule.

Astakos today is very traditional and very Greek. Tavernas and café-bars line the waterfront, catering for the passing yachting trade and tourists en route to Kefalonia and Ithaca. However, the influence of tourism on Astakos is relatively low-key and is fundamentally an agricultural and fishing port. With butchers, bakers, grocers and supermarkets, it is superb for victualling and a good place to spend the night en route to or from the Patraikos Gulf. Protected from the north-west by the area's natural geography, the quay at Astakos is secure in all but a southerly, when an uncomfortable swell can be pushed into the bay.

NAVIGATION

Charts: Admiralty 203, 189, SC5771; Imray G121, G12, G13; Hellenic Navy Hydrographic Service 213/3, 21

Although the entrance to Astakos Bay is guarded by a tight cluster of islands, the approach from all directions is quite straightforward. From the southern entrance to the Lefkada Canal, head south via the north-east tip of Meganisi and the south-west tips of Kalamos and Kastos, taking care to avoid Fourmikoula and the shoals of that name immediately to the north of the islet. Once level with the northern tip of Atokos island, head east for Tourkovigla Pt, the western headland of Astakos Bay. The channel between the mainland and the islands of Drakonera and Kalogiros is relatively shallow but not a problem for most yachts.

From the south, there are several ways to approach Astakos. You can head north, leaving the islets of Modia, Soros and Gravaris to starboard and passing up the channel between Pistros and Tsakalonisi, Drakonera and Karlonisi. Or head north through the channel between Podikos and Provatio. If you take this route, watch out for the isolated rock Navagio, just to the south-west of Podikos, and the reef Dei, to the east of Karlonisi. It also gets quite shallow near the entrance to Port Pandeleimon, so don't get too close to the shore. If you decide to explore the Northern Echinades, remember that many of the inter-island channels are strewn with rocks and reefs (see p166) and keep a good look-out.

A car ferry runs daily from Astakos to Ithaca and Kefalonia, so watch for this when in the bay itself. It approaches at quite a speed and docks just to the east of the town quay.

BERTHING

Berth either bows- or stern-to the town quay between the fishing boat harbour and the ferry quay. Holding here is good and there is usually plenty of room to tie up. The quay is protected from the prevailing NW'lies, although it can feel slightly more exposed in a S'ly. The fishing boat harbour to the west of the quay offers the most protection but it is very shallow, which makes it unsuitable for yachts. Watch out for buoys and lazylines.

ANCHORING

It is possible to anchor at the head of Astakos Bay in less than 10m of water. Or try Marathia Bay, to the west of Astakos, immediately to the east of Tourkovigla Pt. The bay is a peaceful spot, surrounded by lush countryside, and offers good protection from the north-west. Unfortunately the beach at its head has become popular with travellers and is often marred by the attendant cars, vans, tents and litter. Anchor in less than 10m on mud.

Useful information – Astakos

FACILITIES

Water: There are a couple of taps on the waterfront, to the west of the ferry quay.
Fuel: There are two petrol stations (Revoil and Eko) on the outskirts of Astakos.
Ice: Ask at the supermarkets (see below).
Gas: Available from the supermarkets.
Rubbish: Large rubbish bins near the fishing boat harbour.
Laundry: A washing machine is available at the Poseidon Palace.
Yacht services/chandlery: Nautiliaka Chandlery (Tel: 26460 42218) sells a range of marine products and fishing gear. Nautika Boatyard, to the east of Astakos, builds and repairs fishing boats and may be able to offer some services.
Telephone: Several card phones along the waterfront near the ferry quay, and a couple more on the main street.

PROVISIONING

Grocery shops: A good supermarket on a side street off the main road, plus a couple of fruit and veg shops nearby.
Bakery: Two: one near the post office and a second on the high street just beyond the Agricultural Bank of Greece.
Butcher: Three in Astakos – one on the high street, a second opposite the supermarket, and a third near the National Bank of Greece. There are also two fishmongers nearby.
Banks: The Agricultural Bank of Greece (Tel: 26460 41433) is on the high street, to the north of the bus station; The National Bank of Greece (Tel: 26460 41987) is on a side street nearby.
Pharmacy: Situated near the post office.
Post: The post office is on the road that runs parallel to the main high street; open 0800-1400, Monday-Friday.

EATING OUT

Like Paleros and Mitikas to the north, Astakos has a good selection of waterfront tavernas and bars serving a wide range of Greek cuisine. While you will be lucky to find a lobster here, fish dishes are good. Dionysis (Tel: 26460 41996), near the fishing boat harbour, is particularly recommended and reasonably priced. The Poseidon Palace near the bus station specialises in seafood. It is a very grand establishment and looks slightly out of place alongside the 19th century architecture of the town but its menu is extensive. There are fast food shops on the main street and lots of cafés along the waterfront.

ASHORE

Astakos is a good place to base yourself if you want to explore inland. Although there is no car hire company in the town, the bus service is good, and regular ferries between Kefalonia, Ithaca and Astakos make inter-island travel easy. If you can rent a car, do visit the archaeological site of Oiniadae, to the south of Astakos. Oiniadae was one of the most important ports along this stretch of coast in ancient times and excavations carried out by the American School of Classical Studies in Athens in 1900-1901 found evidence of five boatsheds, quays and slipways

Remains of a small theatre have also been found, with inscriptions on the seats dating it to the third century BC. In the time of Alexander the Great (356-323BC), the port was destroyed by the Aetolians, who were considered some of the most turbulent people in Greece.

TRANSPORT

Car hire: The nearest car hire firm is in Paleros, about 32 miles (51km) to the north. The travel agent Nikopolis Hellas (Tel: 26430 42114) runs a branch of Sixt car hire.
Taxis: Taxi rank near the ferry quay. Or ring Tel: 26460 41000.
Bus: The Ktel bus station (Tel: 26460 41219) is opposite the ferry quay.
Ferry: A daily ferry to Sami on Kefalonia and Ithaca leaves from the quay opposite the bus station. The nearest international ferry port is Patra, 1 hour to the south. Services from Patra travel to Italy, Corfu, Igoumenitsa and several Ionian islands in between.
Air travel: Nearest airport is Aktio at Preveza, 1¼-hrs away by car. Charter and domestic flights leave from here several times a week.

OTHER INFORMATION

Local Tel code: 26460.
Port authority: The Port Police office (Tel: 26460 41052) is in a little hut on the quayside near Spiros Taverna.
Police: Tel: 26460 41206.
Dentist: Xesfingis Konstantinos (Tel: 26460 42491).
Hospital: The Health Centre (Tel: 26460 41101) lies to the east of the town. Follow signs from the quay.

The small harbour at Astakos is shallow and unsuitable for yachts

Echinades Islands

Nisidhes Ekhinades

Charts: Admiralty 203, 189, SC5771; Imray G121, G12, G1; Hellenic Navy Hydrographic Service 030, 21

One of the earliest references to the Echinades islands is in *Metamorphoses* by Ovid, the Roman poet (43BC-AD17). Ovid wrote that the Echinades, a collection of about 20 islands and islets snuggling into the coast of mainland Greece, just to the south of Astakos, were formed as a result of the river god Achelous's revenge against a group of nymphs. The nymphs had slaughtered 10 bullocks in honour of the rural gods but had failed to invite Achelous to the festivities. So enraged was he by this oversight that he swelled with anger, swept the nymphs out into the Ionian sea and turned them into the islands that we now know as the Echinades archipelago.

Thucydides (460-400BC), the Athenian historian, suggests a more conventional cause for their formation – that they were the result of alluvial deposit from the nearby River Acheloos. But whatever their origin, today the Echinades are a tranquil spot away from the hustle and bustle of the main Ionian islands and are only occasionally frequented by cruising yachts. They offer several small anchorages but are suitable for settled weather only. Although surrounded by deep water, you should navigate around them with care as rocks and reefs protrude at regular intervals.

The Echinades at sunrise. This archipelago is a tranquil spot away from the busyness of the main Ionian islands

Drakonera

Anchorage off the north coast of Drakonera Island: 38°29'.54N 21°01'.56E

Drakonera is the largest island of the northern group and, along with its satellite islands and islets, Kalogiros, Sofia, Lamprino, Pistro, Karlonisi, Tsakalonisi and Provatio, lies immediately to the south of Tourkovigla Pt. Bays on its northern coast provide the best anchorages in this area, although they should be considered in calm weather only.

If approaching from Kalamos or Kastos, follow the mainland coast south as far as Tourkovigla Pt. Drakonera is the first and the largest island you will see and the first anchorage lies in a bay directly opposite the small island of Kalogiros. The second anchorage lies just beyond.

From the south, approach Drakonera leaving the islands of Modia, Soros and Gravaris to the east, and passing up the channel between Pistros and Tsakalonisi, Drakonera and Karlonisi. Do not attempt to sail between the north coast of Pistros and the south coast of Drakonera as the channel is reef-strewn.

Provatio

Off the south-east coast of Provatio island: 38°27'.39N 21°03'.31E

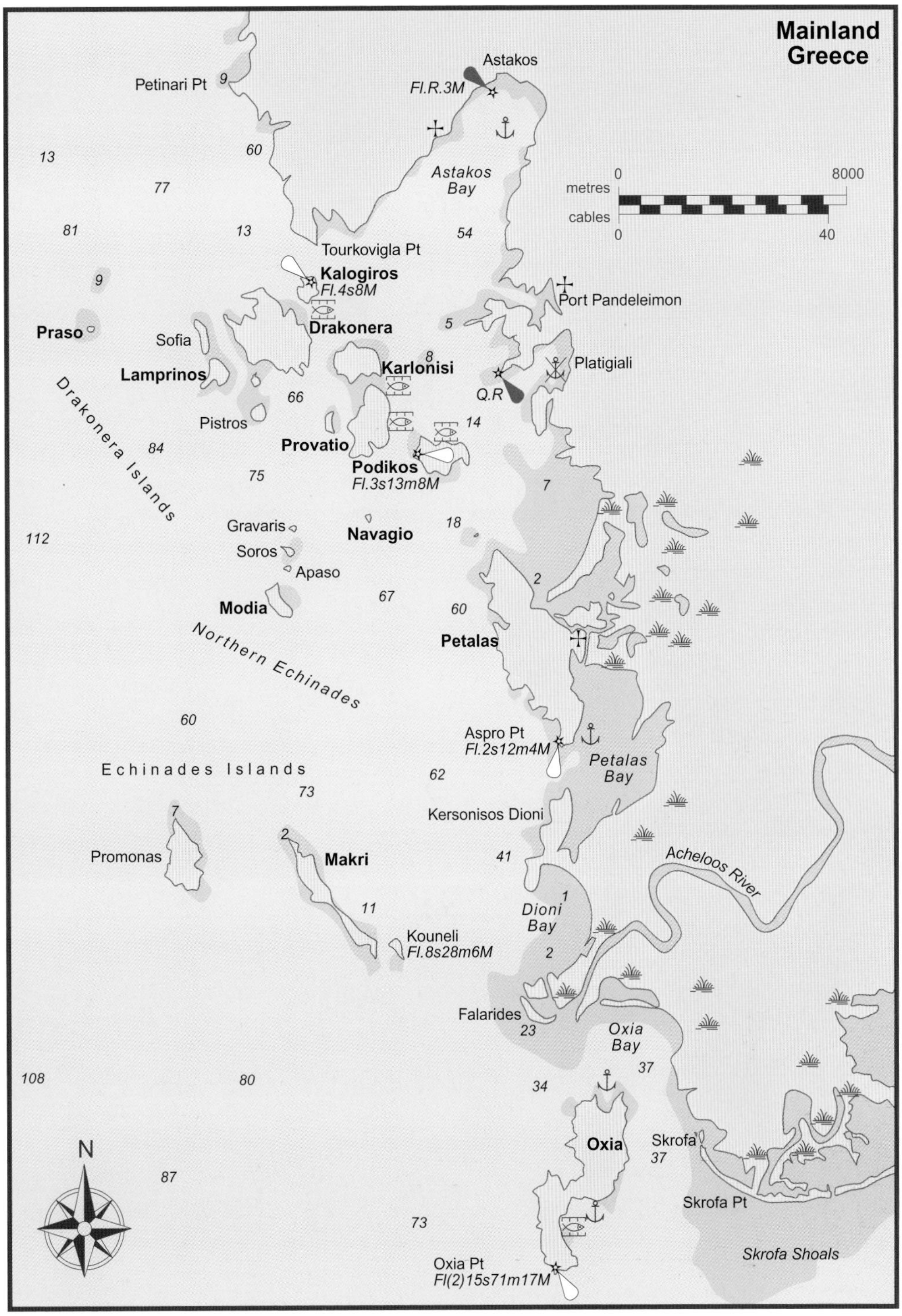

An alternative anchorage to those off Drakonera is a small cove on the south-east coast of Provatio, the 300-acre island which lies to the west of Podikos. Sheltered from the prevailing north-westerlies, the cove can be used overnight, although should only really be chosen in settled weather as it is not at all protected from the south.

Care should be taken around the southern tip of the island as rocks extend out from the shore, and, if approaching from the south, watch out for the rock Navagio, which stands in open water, about ¾-mile from the island.

OTHER ANCHORAGES

The two anchorages mentioned above are the best in the Northern Echinades but are not the only ones within the area. Little coves along the coasts of Karlonisi and Podikos are also suitable for small boats. However, some of the channels between the islands are littered with rocks, so pay close attention to your charts and maintain a good look-out at all times. You should also only navigate among the islands in daylight.

Port Pandeleimon Pandelimon

Entrance to Port Pandeleimon Bay: 38°29'.54N 21°04'.86E

Charts: Admiralty 203, 189, SC5771; Imray G121, G12, G1; Hellenic Navy Hydrographic Service 213/3, 21

Its name suggests a harbour, but Port Pandeleimon is, in fact, just a bay with two branches at its head. Situated about 2½nm south of Astakos, the approach to the bay is through deep water and easy to identify from this direction. From the south, it is harder to spot, but the entrance lies about 1½nm north of the shipbreaker's yard at Platigiali, where huge swages of concrete quay fringe the bay.

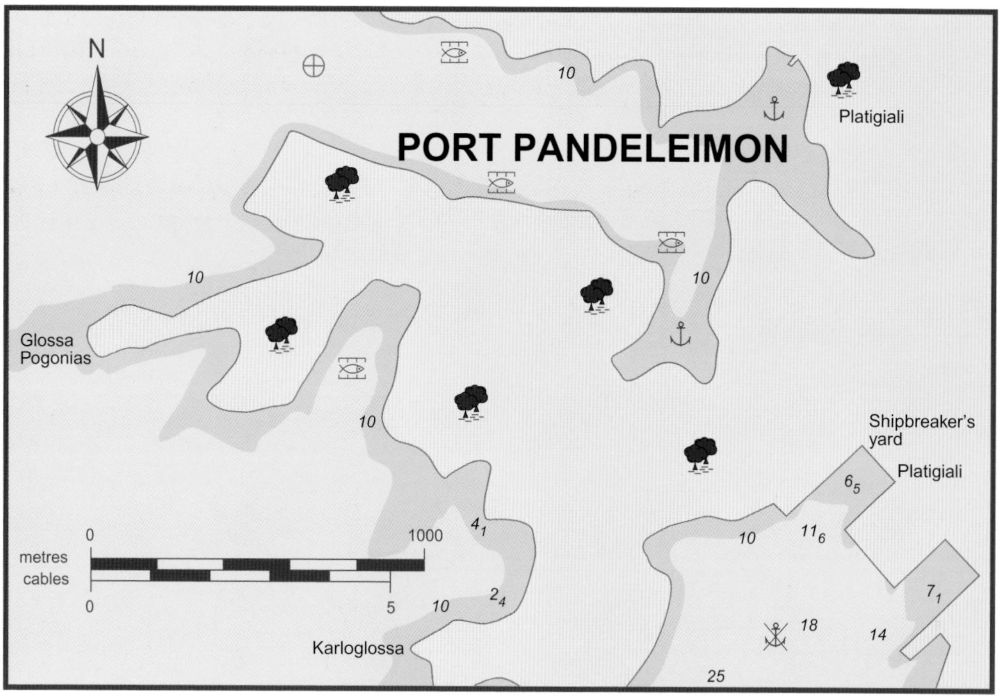

In the last few years, Port Pandeleimon has been taken over by fish farms, so anchoring room is minimal. On a recent visit it was possible to anchor in both the inlets at the head of the bay. However, the fish farms in the vicinity are moved occasionally, so the anchorages may not be clear. If there is room to anchor, both offer reasonable shelter from the prevailing winds, with the one to the south giving slightly more. Anchor in 3-5m on mud.

Care should be taken around the fish farms which, although usually buoyed, are rarely lit at night and often extend into the middle of the bay. As with Pagania, to the north, the stench of fish farms is very strong here, and if you are looking for a quiet, secluded anchorage, Petalas, to the south, is much better.

Platigiali is now home to a ship-breaker's yard

Port Pandeleimon is 2½ miles south of Astakos. Fish-farms block several bays, but it is still possible to find somewhere to anchor

Platigiali

Entrance to Platigiali Bay: 38°28'.36N 21°05'.61N

It was once possible to anchor in Platigiali, the bay to the south of Port Pandeleimon, but its new use as a shipbreaker's yard has meant that anchoring here is now forbidden. While not much shipbreaking appears to happen here (there are rumours of more dubious activities), the security presence is high, as you will soon discover if you try to enter the bay by water. Even road access to Platigiali is now restricted.

Petalas Nisis Petalás

Anchorage off the south-east coast of Petalas: 38°23'.84N 21°06'.46N

Charts: Admiralty 1676, 203, 189, SC5771; Imray G121, G12, G1; Hellenic Navy Hydrographic Service 030, 40, 21

The south-east coast of Petalas offers an idyllic anchorage

Petalas is the largest island in the Echinades archipelago and the closest to the Greek mainland, lying about 5nm south of Astakos. Home to over 4,000 olive trees and a handful of goats and cows, the 2.3m^2 (6km^2) island offers an idyllic anchorage with good all-round shelter, and at its highest point rises to 76.2m (250ft) above sea level. It is almost joined to the mainland on its east coast by an alluvial spit of land created by the River Acheloos, and the surrounding area is very fertile and rich in wildlife.

The anchorage itself is off the south-east coast of Petalas and is reached via a channel between the southern tip of the island and the headland of Kersonisos Dioni. The approach is through deep water until you reach Aspro Pt (Fl 12s12m4M), the entrance to Petalas Bay, where depths decrease to less than 8m. Anchor immediately to the north-west of the entrance in less than 5m of water on mud and sand. The holding is good. Don't be tempted to anchor at the northern end of the bay, though, unless you are in a shoal draught yacht, as it is very shallow here, with depths decreasing to less than 1.5m.

Petalas is a perfect place to spend the night. Remote enough that it attracts few visiting yachts, the anchorage offers shelter from all directions and is a good refuge if you don't want to head to one of the harbours along this stretch of coast.

The River Acheloos

The River Acheloos is Greece's largest river. From its source, high up in the Pindus Mountains, the backbone of mainland Greece, the river flows for 130 miles (209km) before meeting the Ionian Sea just to the north of Oxia island. The god of the river, Achelous, son of Oceanus and Tethys, was regarded as 'ruler and representative of all freshwater in Hellas' and myths surrounding the river god abound. Legend has it that the god, who was able to take the form of any creature, fought Heracles as a bull for the hand of the goddess Deianira and that it was his anger at losing her to Heracles that forced the river to overflow and destroy crops. He is also said to have been the father of the Sirens and responsible for creating the Echinades islands (see p166).

The god Achelous was greatly worshipped in ancient times and today the river is still considered a powerful source. Not only has its flow been harnessed for hydro-electric power but part of the river has been diverted to help irrigate the Thessaly Plain. A protected area under the EU Birds Directive, the Acheloos River is home to a rich source of wildlife and is a beautiful spot to explore by dinghy.

Oxia Island Nisis Oxia

Anchorage off the south-east coast of Oxia: 38°17'.44N 21°06'.56E

Charts: Admiralty 1676, 203, 189, SC5771; Imray G121, G12, G13, G1; Hellenic Navy Hydrographic Service 40, 21

Oxia Island lies immediately north of the entrance to the Patriakos Gulf

Oxia is the southernmost island in the Echinades group and stands the tallest at 1,381ft (421m) above sea level. Lying just to the north of the entrance to the mouth of the Patraikos Gulf, the island has three anchorages: one on the north coast of the island, in Glicha Bay, a second on the west coast and a third on the east coast. Sadly, all three are now marred by fish farms and, although the anchorage in Glicha Bay is now too small to hold most yachts, it is still possible to squeeze into both the western and eastern bays.

Both these bays offer reasonable daytime shelter, although not from all directions. The bay on the west coast is completely open to the prevailing northwesterlies, so will only provide shelter in a southerly. The bay to the east of Oxia offers the reverse and is possibly the preferred of the two. Both anchorages provide good holding on mud but as space is limited within the bays, due to the fish farms, you should take a long line ashore to prevent swinging round your anchor. The anchorages are also deep, so expect to anchor in around 20m of water.

An alternative anchorage is situated to the west of Oxia Island between the islets of Skrofapoula and Skrofa. Careful attention should be paid to your echosounder in this area as the nearby waters are shallow and the shape of the Skrofa Shoals, immediately to the south, is constantly changing due to shifting sands.

Oxia Bay Ormos Oxias

Oxia Bay: 38°19'.84N 21°06'.86E

Charts: Admiralty 1676, 203, 189, SC5771; Imray G121, G12, G13, G1; Hellenic Navy Hydrographic Service 40, 21

Oxia Bay is situated to the north of Oxia Island, just to the east of the mouth of the Acheloos River (Potamos Akheloos), and is a semicircular bay shrouded in sandbanks, with a fish farm in its eastern corner. It offers reasonable shelter and good holding, but should only be used as a daytime stop in settled weather.

On approach from both the west and south, stick close to the coast of Oxia Island before heading into the bay and do not be tempted to cut across the shoals at the river's mouth, or cut in close to the islet of Falarides. The surrounding waters are shallow and the sandbanks constantly change position, so the risk of running aground is high. You should therefore pay close attention to your echosounder and proceed at a slow speed when in the vicinity. Anchor in the middle of the bay on mud and sand in less than 5m.

Chapter five
Approaches to the Corinth Canal

The Patraikos and Korinthiakos Gulfs, which separate mainland Greece from the north coast of the Peloponnese, are beautiful and little used cruising grounds, even in peak season. Yachts navigating their waters tend to be en route to or from the Corinth Canal, in the south-east corner of the Korinthiakos Gulf, and consequently many of the anchorages and small harbours here go unnoticed.

The Patraikos Gulf extends from the Ionian Sea to the Rio-Antirio Strait, where it turns into the Korinthiakos Gulf. Combined, these large expanses of water stretch for 81nm. The gulfs are bounded by very different landscapes: the north coast of the Patraikos Gulf is low-lying and fringed with marshland, sandbanks and shoals, while much of the Korinthiakos Gulf's coastline is characterised by its sparse hillsides with high craggy mountains in places.

The sailing is really good here, particularly in the Korinthiakos Gulf: the winds tend to be steady and, although often strong in the afternoons, are consistent in their direction and speed. In the Patraikos Gulf, the prevailing winds come from the north-west but swing to a more westerly direction where the gulf narrows at the Rio-Antirio Strait. In the winter months easterly winds are common but they also occur during the summer, particularly at the western end of the gulf. Fog is occasionally a feature here too, and some of the larger bays along the north coast can be quite breezy as gusts spin off the hillsides.

The main hazards along this stretch of water are the sandbanks that flank the N coast of the Patraikos Gulf, particularly around Mesolongi. Both the Admiralty and Imray charts warn that the shape of these sandbanks and their positions are constantly shifting and unless you intend to visit Mesolongi, you are advised to stay well clear of this coastline. Even in daylight, the waters just to the S and W of Mesolongi are tricky to negotiate and the harbour should only be approached in settled conditions. Boats run aground quite frequently in this area. Hazards in the Korinthiakos Gulf take the form of rocks and careful study of charts is advised before you head into some of the bays.

As well as remote anchorages, there are some superb little harbours along this stretch of water. The traditional harbours at Galaxidi and Nafpaktos contrast greatly with the commercial centres of Patra and Corinth. The island of Trizoni is a gem, popular with overwintering yachts, and Andikira is usually quite quiet.

There's no shortage of things to see and do in the approaches to the Corinth Canal, and with a handful of decent harbours and large towns for provisioning, there are plenty of safe destinations too.

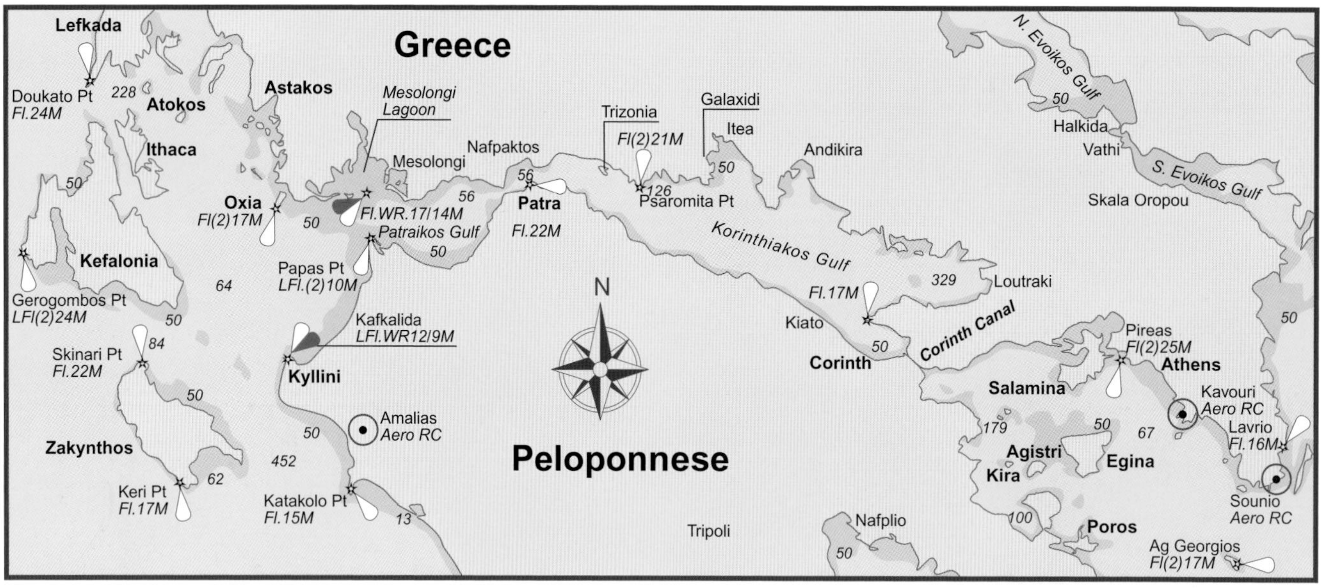

Mesolongi

Messolongi, Messongi

Entrance to the Mesolongi channel:

38°18'.74N 21°24'.76E

The E side of Mesolongi hbr: 38°21'.74N 21°25'.26E

On entering the Patriakos Gulf, the first port you come to is Mesolongi, on the north coast. Lying about 16nm north-west of Patra, it offers excellent shelter from all directions and a large harbour in which to berth. It is reached via a long, 2½nm channel which cuts through the salt pans and lagoons, to a small agricultural town that can supply basic provisions. Mesolongi is quiet and sometimes slightly threadbare, and despite the significant role that it played in the War of Independence in the early 19th century, it's not particularly popular with tourists. But for a cruising yachtsman, en route to Corinth or the Peloponnese, it serves very well.

The low-lying entrance to Mesolongi can be hard to identify

NAVIGATION

Charts: Admiralty 1676, 189, SC5771; Imray G13, G1; Hellenic Navy Hydrographic Service 213/3, 040, 21

The entrance to the channel can be difficult to identify until close to, particularly in poor conditions with reduced visibility. Look for the small cluster of houses on the islet of Tourlis, which lies immediately to the east of the entrance. The lighthouse (Fl WR 5s12m17/14M) on the islet of Agios Sostis, to the west of the entrance, is also conspicuous. On approach from the east, stay well to the south of the sandbanks off Evinos Pt, which are marked by a southerly cardinal (Q(6)+LFl 15s). These shift frequently and the risk of running aground in this area is high if you get too close to them.

The entrance to the Mesolongi Channel is marked by a pair of buoys (Fl R 4.5s/Fl G 4.5s) ½nm south of the islet of Tourlis. A further four pairs of buoys (Q R/Q G) mark the channel at regular intervals along its 2½nm

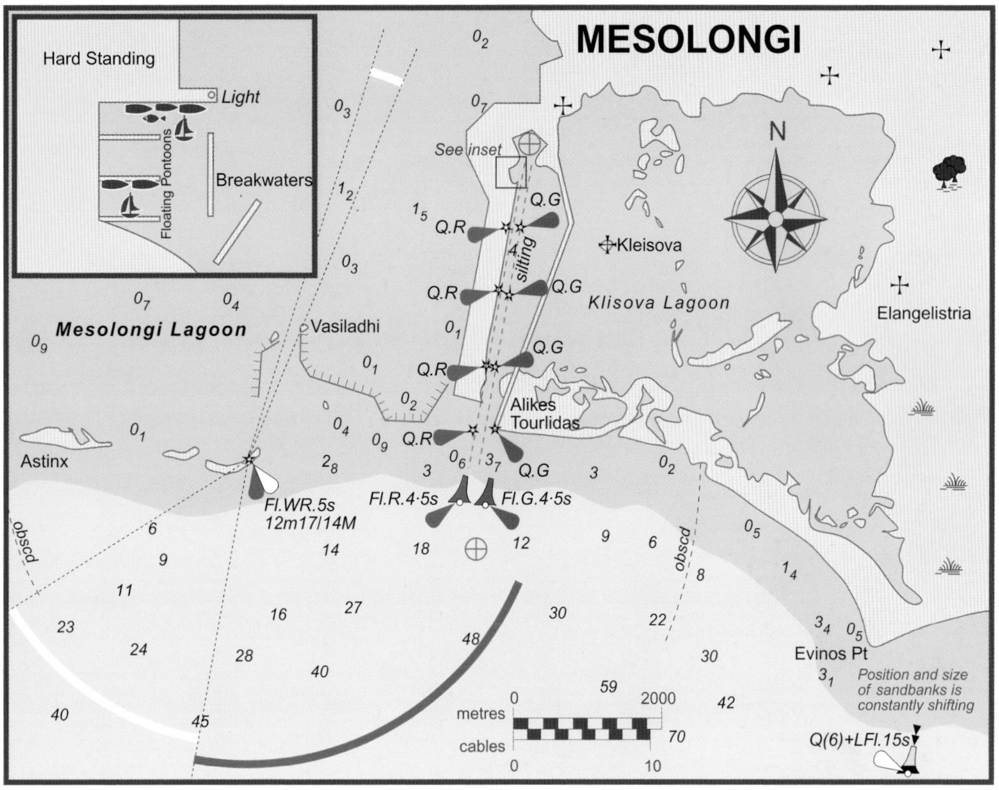

length. It is dredged periodically to 5-6m but is susceptible to silting. Small coasters and other vessels also use it, so maintain a good look-out at all times and keep speed to a minimum.

An approach at night is not advised. Although the channel is usually lit, the buoys are often difficult to identify, especially at the entrance, and the surrounding sandbanks pose a serious hazard. Similarly, an approach in bad weather is not recommended.

BERTHING

Work to develop a new harbour at Mesolongi is in progress. In 2007 pontoons had been installed in the western corner of the harbour, protected by two breakwaters. There were no lazylines and yachts were berthing alongside both the pontoons and the quay. Although the harbour has no facilities, the shelter and holding here is very good.

Alternatively, visitors can berth on the eastern side of the harbour, alongside or bows/stern-to the eastern quay. The northern quay is used by small coasters and workboats, and the shallower southern part by fishing boats. The shelter here is as good as in the harbour to the west but you may find there is a bit more chop.

ANCHORING

There is nowhere to anchor within Mesolongi harbour or channel. The nearest anchorage that offers protection from the prevailing northwesterlies is to the west, to the south-west of the islet of Agios Sostis. Anchor in around 6m on sand and mud. The holding is reasonable but there is no shelter from the south here, so use as a short-term stop in calm weather only.

Useful information – Mesolongi

FACILITIES

Water: Taps in the eastern corner of the harbour.
Fuel: No, but a mini-tanker will deliver (Tel: 26310 22763) and there is an Eldon petrol station on the outskirts of Mesolongi.
Showers: At Theoxenia Hotel on the NE quay.
Ice: Ask at the tavernas.
Rubbish: Large bins on the quay.
Telephone: Card phone near the Port Police office. Phone cards sold at the kiosk nearby. Mobile reception is good.

PROVISIONING

Grocery shops: Lidl supermarket on the outskirts of Mesolongi. Mini-market in the centre, near the church.
Bakery: In centre of town.
Butcher: In the centre of Mesolongi.
Banks: The Alpha Bank (Tel: 26310 24641) and National Bank of Greece (Tel: 26310 22402) are on Lordou Vyronos Street, near the town centre. The Emporiki Bank (Tel: 26310 26411) is on Char Trikaupi Street and the Agricultural Bank of Greece (Tel: 26310 22244) is near the centre.
Pharmacy: There are two pharmacies on the road out of Mesolongi, near the medical centre.
Post: Post box near the centre of Mesolongi. The postal service is good.

EATING OUT

There are a couple of tavernas in the trees behind the eastern part of the harbour, which serve reasonable cuisine. Tourlis, at the entrance to the Mesolongi channel, is also home to a few tavernas, but it's about an hour's walk away along the causeway. Alternatively, the centre of Mesolongi is a 10-minute walk north of the harbour, where you will find a collection of tavernas and cafés on the pedestrianised street near the main square.

ASHORE

The walk along the causeway to Tourlis is a really pleasant way to spend a couple of hours. Although you have to walk along a road, the views over the salt pans are stunning and when you finally reach the hamlet on Tourlis, it is as if you've stepped into another country. The wooden houses on stilts and the people that fish the lagoon in flat-bottomed dories would look equally at home in Malaysia. On a clear day, the views from here south over the Patraikos Gulf are particularly striking. The Museum of Art & History (Tel: 26310 22134) is situated on the main square in Mesolongi itself. This small museum (open daily, 0900-1300 and 1600-1900) houses a collection

Useful information – Mesolongi

of paintings and artefacts from the 1820s when Mesolongi was struggling for independence. There are also a few items on display that belonged to Lord Byron, the English poet who was perhaps the town's most famous resident, moving to Mesolongi in 1824 to help wage war against the Turks. In the NE part of the town is the Garden of Heroes, or O Kipros ton Iroon. Here there are statues to the townspeople who defended Mesolongi from the Turks, including one of Lord Byron, under which his heart is said to rest. Open daily, 0900-1300 and 1800-1900.

For something more adventurous, you could try rockclimbing at the town of Krioneri. Situated 18km from Mesolongi, it lies under Mt Kotaris. Catering for all levels, the Krioneri Climbing Club can be contacted on Tel: 26310 41125 or alternatively call EOS Climbing Club Messologi on Tel: 26310 25503.

TRANSPORT

Taxis: Ask at the tavernas.
Bus: Twice daily service between Thessaloniki and Amfilochia calling at Mesolongi and Agrino, among other towns. Change at Agrino for Lefkada. Bus stop in town.
Ferry: The nearest terminal is at Patra, to the SE. Regular daily services leave from here for Kefalonia, Corfu, Igoumenitsa and Brindisi, Bari and Ancona in Italy. For timetables and tickets, see www.greekferries.gr
Air travel: The nearest airport is at Preveza (Tel: 26820 22355), a 1½-hour car journey from Mesolongi. International and domestic services run several times a week. Athens Airport (Tel: 21035 30000), 3 hours away by car, has flights to more destinations.

OTHER INFORMATION

Local Tel code: 26310.
Port authority: Port Police office (Tel: 26310 51121/ VHF Ch12) on the quay, opposite where the ships moor.
Police: Tourist Police: Tel: 26310 27220.
Hospital: Medical centre (Tel: 26310 57100/ 27411) on the outskirts of Mesolongi.

The east quay at Mesolongi, where yachts can find room to berth alongside

The Rio-Antirio Strait (Stenon Riou Andirriou)

This is the narrowest stretch of water between mainland Greece and the Peloponnese and marks the junction between the Patraikos and Korinthiakos Gulfs. Identified by the cable-stayed bridge that spans the gulf (see opposite), at its narrowest point the strait is just 1nm wide.

Before the bridge was built, the strait was busy with commercial shipping and ro-ro passenger ferries travelling from one side of the mainland to the other and, although it forms a bottleneck between the gulfs, traffic in this area has greatly reduced. However, it is still important to maintain a good look-out at all times when passing through the strait.

There is a slight current in this area of 1.5-2 knots, its direction influenced by the bearing and strength of the wind. At night, the headlands on either side of the strait are lit: Antirio Pt (Akra Andirrion) shows Fl(2)10s16m10M, while Rio Pt (Akra Rion) displays Fl 6s16m6M.

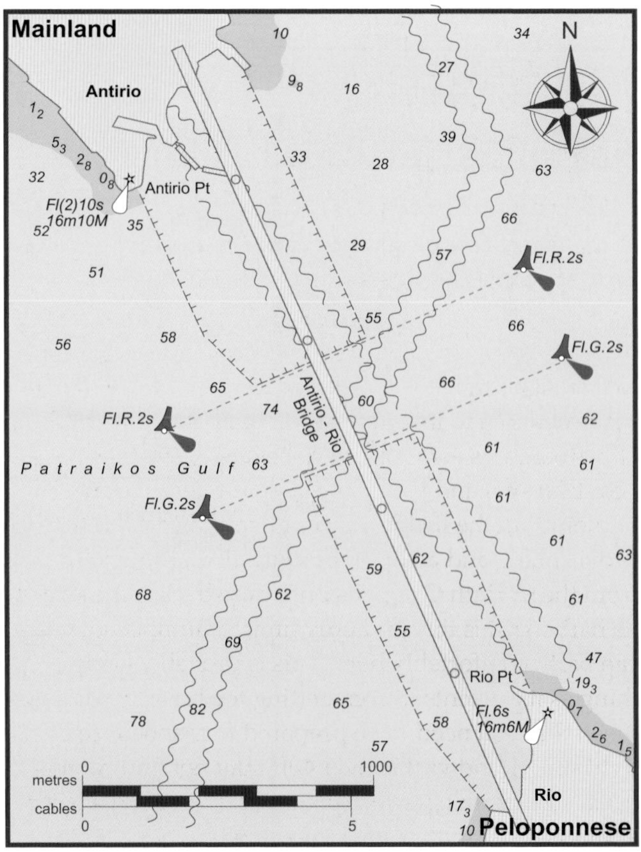

The Rio-Antirio Bridge

The distinctive Rio-Antirio Bridge joins mainland Greece to the Peloponnese

In 2004 the Rio-Antirio bridge was completed. Spanning the Patraikos Gulf between mainland Greece and the Peloponnese, the 9,383ft (2,860m) bridge rises to 525ft (160m) above sea level. It is one of the longest cable-stayed bridges in the world and an impressive sight for anyone entering or leaving the Patraikos and Korinthiakos gulfs.

It's rather beautiful to look at but apparently construction was highly challenging. The bridge crosses an active fault line, straddling two plates, and the scale of the bridge and an unstable seabed created many problems. It was finished, though, in time for the Olympic flame to be carried over it to Athens for the 2004 Olympic Games and now replaces the numerous car ferries that used to shuttle people across the gulf.

A good look-out should be maintained at all times when sailing here, as vessels still travel between Antirio and Rio and the bridge's location marks the narrowest point of the gulf.

PROCEDURE FOR PASSING UNDER THE BRIDGE

Due to the amount of traffic that passes under the bridge daily, you need to contact the Rion Traffic Control on VHF Ch 14/Tel: 26340 32370 when you are 5nm away from the bridge in order to get permission to pass underneath it. You must be prepared to give your vessel's name (spelt phonetically), height, length and from which direction you are heading towards the bridge. Rion Traffic will then inform you as to which part of the bridge to go under and may ask you to contact them again when you are 2nm from the bridge for final permission to proceed.

Nafpaktos

Navpaktos, Ormos Navpaktou, Navpaktos, Naupactos

Immediately off the entrance to Nafpaktos harbour: 38°23'.34N 21°49'.86E

Nafpaktos is a complete contrast to the low-lying Mesolongi. Set against a steep hillside, with a Venetian castle clinging to its upper slopes, the miniature harbour at Nafpaktos is enclosed by castellated walls. It's a beautiful spot and worth the visit, if only to see the harbour, but the lively market town is also good for provisioning and a handy port of call en route to or from the Corinth Canal. Its only drawback is the size of its harbour: it is tiny and only limited numbers of boats can berth comfortably here. This is probably a good thing as it prevents it from getting too busy; but it does mean that you need to be prepared to manoeuvre in tight spaces and yachts over 40ft may not find room to berth. The harbour is well protected with good shelter, although in a southerly it is affected by swell.

The historical significance of Nafpaktos relates to the Battle of Lepanto in 1571. Nafpaktos was originally called Lepanto and it was in the waters to the west of the town that the battle between the Turkish occupiers and the combined Christian forces of the Venetian, Spanish and Genoese took place. It was one of the greatest naval battles in history and the Christian fleet, led by Don John of Austria, successfully fought and defeated the Turks, with comparatively little loss to their own forces. A statue to the Spaniard Miguel de Cervantes overlooks the harbour at Nafpaktos. The author of *Don Quixote* lost his left hand during the battle.

NAVIGATION

Charts: Admiralty 1676, SC5771; Imray G13, G1; Hellenic Navy Hydrographic Service 040, 21

Nafpaktos can be identified from some distance by its imposing Venetian castle, which sits on the hillside above the town. Closer to, the castellated walls of the fortified harbour will become visible. At night, the eastern side of the entrance is marked by a light (Fl G 1.5s15m3M). The approach from all directions is straightforward and through deep water.

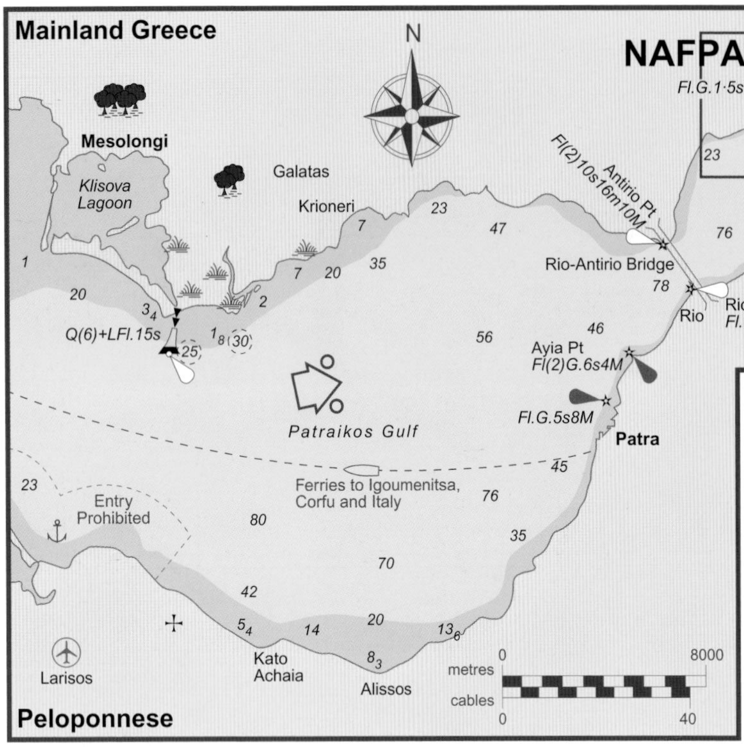

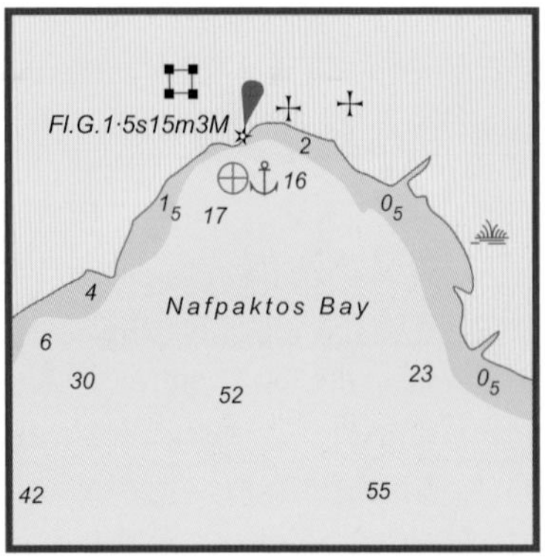

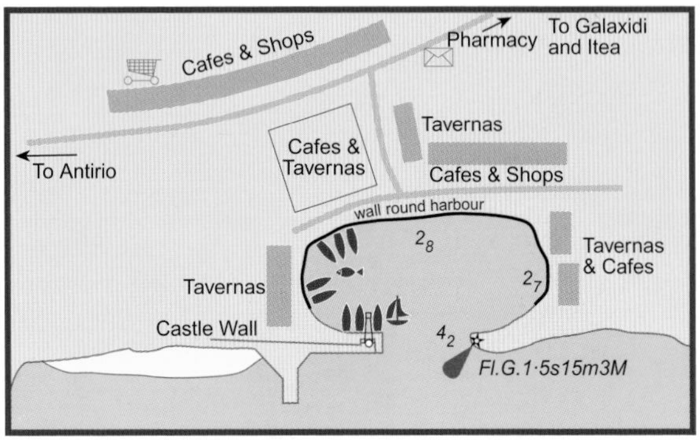

BERTHING

The walled harbour at Nafpaktos is tiny, so you should have all lines and fenders ready before entering. Yachts up to around 40ft (12.2m) can either berth stern or bows-to the quay immediately to the west of the entrance, or to the north of the harbour near the steps. Depths in both areas range between 2.5-3m and the holding is good. Smaller yachts can also berth stern- or bows-to on the western side in around 2m, but the south-west corner should be avoided as this is the shallowest part. Fishing boats and dories use the harbour's eastern corner.

ANCHORING

The harbour is too small to anchor in. However, you can drop your anchor just outside in Nafpaktos Bay. Suitable in calm conditions only when there is no chop, you should anchor off the beach to the south-west of the entrance in about 8-10m of water. The holding on mud is reasonable.

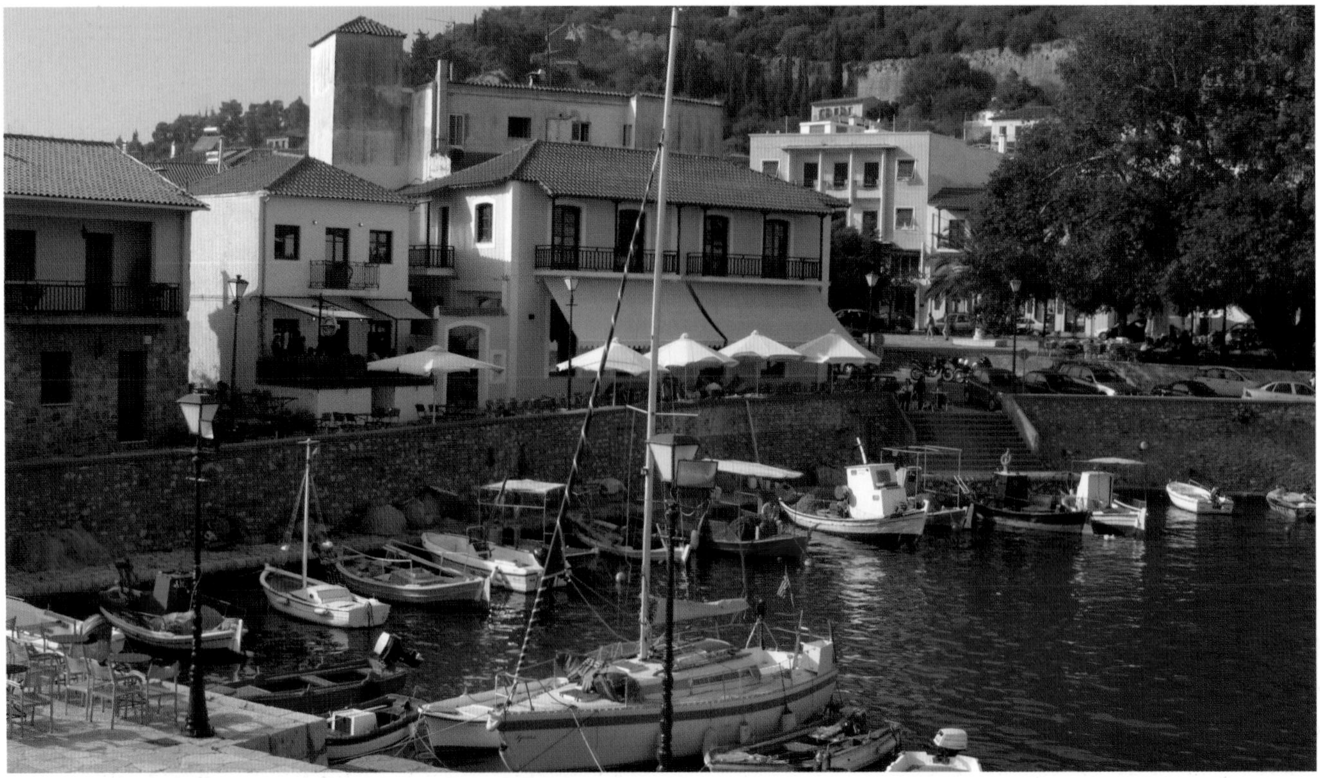

Space is tight in Nafpaktos' harbour, but yachts can berth immediately inside the entrance, bows-to the quay

Useful information – Nafpaktos

FACILITIES

Water: Taps are on the quay but they aren't always connected.
Fuel: Take a taxi to a nearby petrol station. There is a BP garage in the town centre and several more on the outskirts of Nafpaktos.
Ice: From mini-markets.
Laundry: Near the Piraeus Bank on Intze Street.
Gas: From mini-markets and several of the petrol stations stock bottles.
Rubbish: Bins on the quay.
Telephone: Phone box near the square, more scattered throughout the town. Phone cards sold in kiosks and mini-markets. Mobile reception is good.

PROVISIONING

Grocery shops: Several mini-markets and also larger supermarkets: Lidl, Champion and Spar are a mile due west of the harbour. Fruit and veg shops near the centre and a market on Saturday mornings.
Bakery: Several on the main road through Nafpaktos.
Butcher: A couple on the main street, and a fishmonger on the road past the harbour.
Banks: Alpha Bank (Tel: 26340 29291) on Ilarchon Constantinou Street, the main street in Nafpaktos; Piraeus Bank (Tel: 26340 20055) on Intze St; Agricultural Bank of Greece (Tel: 26340 27214); National Bank of Greece (Tel: 26340 27672); Emporiki Bank (Tel: 26340 28311).
Pharmacy: Several. You can find one next to the post office on the main street through Nafpaktos.
Post: The post office is on the main street, north-east of the harbour. The postal service is good. Post box near Emporiki Bank. Stamps from kiosks and souvenir shops.
Other shops: There are several shops and places specialising in gardening equipment and plants. Also clothes and shoe shops can be found along the main street, along with an optician and a hairdresser.
Opening times: 0900-1400 and 1700-2100, although tavernas and supermarkets stay open later.

The tiny harbour of Nafpaktos is enclosed by castellated walls

EATING OUT

Cafés and bars line the western and eastern corners of the harbour, and there are several tavernas in the square to the north. The road past the harbour and to the east is also packed with tavernas, so you will have no difficulty finding somewhere. Steki Restaurant, on the main road behind the square, is one of the best for traditional cuisine.

ASHORE

The Venetian castle that watches over the town is worth the steep climb uphill, and on a clear day you'll get some stunning views from the top across to the Peloponnese. Built in the Middle Ages, the castle is said to stand on the site of an ancient acropolis. It is open daily to visitors.

TRANSPORT

Car hire: Advance Rent a Car (Tel: 26340 26250). Also several travel agents in Nafpaktos can organise car hire.
Taxis: Ask at the tavernas.
Bus: Regular service between Agrinio and Itea. The bus stop is on the main road.
Ferry: The nearest terminal is Patra, 9nm south-west of Nafpaktos. Daily services to Igoumenitsa, Corfu, Kefalonia and Bari, Brindisi and Ancona in Italy. For timetables and tickets, see www.greekferries.gr
Air travel: The nearest airport is at Preveza (Tel:

A statue of Spanish author Miguel de Cervantes

26820 22355), a 1¾-hour car journey from Nafpaktos. International/domestic services run several times a week. Athens airport (Tel: 21035 30000), 3 hours away by car, offers flights to more destinations.

OTHER INFORMATION

Local Tel code: 26340.
Port authority: The Port Police office (Tel: 26340 27909/VHF Ch12) is situated to the east of the harbour.
Police: Tel: 26340 27258.
Dentist: One near the Elle Salon hairdresser, on the main road, not far from the post office (Tel: 26340 22536).
Hospital: The Medical Centre (Tel: 26340 23690/1) is on the outskirts of Nafpaktos on the road to Itea.

Trizonia Island

Nisis Troizonia

East coast of the island, on the approach to Trizonia Harbour: 38°21'.94N 22°05'.21E

Trizonia, the only inhabited island in the Korinthiakos Gulf, is a delightful place. The harbour on its east coast is a real gem and a popular port of call for cruising yachts. Many people choose to over-winter here and with its sheltered bay it's a wise choice. It is protected from all directions and, although there are just a handful of houses ashore, the list of amenities for visitors is long. Expect it to be busy all year round but if you can get in here, you'll find an idyllic spot. There are no cars or motorbikes on the island either, so you are also guaranteed some peace and quiet.

The harbour at Trizonia is an idyllic spot and a popular place for overwintering yachts

NAVIGATION

Charts: Admiralty 1676, SC5771; Imray G13, G1; Hellenic Navy Hydrographic Service 40, 74

Trizonia lies about 11nm east of Nafpaktos and can be hard to identify until close to as it blends in with the surrounding coastline. The harbour is tucked into a deep bay on the east coast of the island and can be approached from all directions. Care should be taken, though, if approaching via the north coast, as a reef extends offshore of its north-east tip for about ¼-mile. Stay mid-channel between the mainland and Trizonia until clear.

BERTHING

Visiting yachts can berth alongside on two pontoons within the harbour breakwaters at Trizonia. When space is limited, you can berth stern- or bows-to the pontoons but be cautious when laying your anchor as there are ground chains on both sides. These chains are to be used for lazylines but at the time of writing these had not been laid.

If the pontoons are full, go alongside the quay in between the jetties or along the inner edge of the western breakwater. Local fishing boats use the eastern side of the harbour.

ANCHORING

Yachts occasionally anchor in the bay to the south of the marina. There is good shelter here from the prevailing northwesterlies and reasonable holding

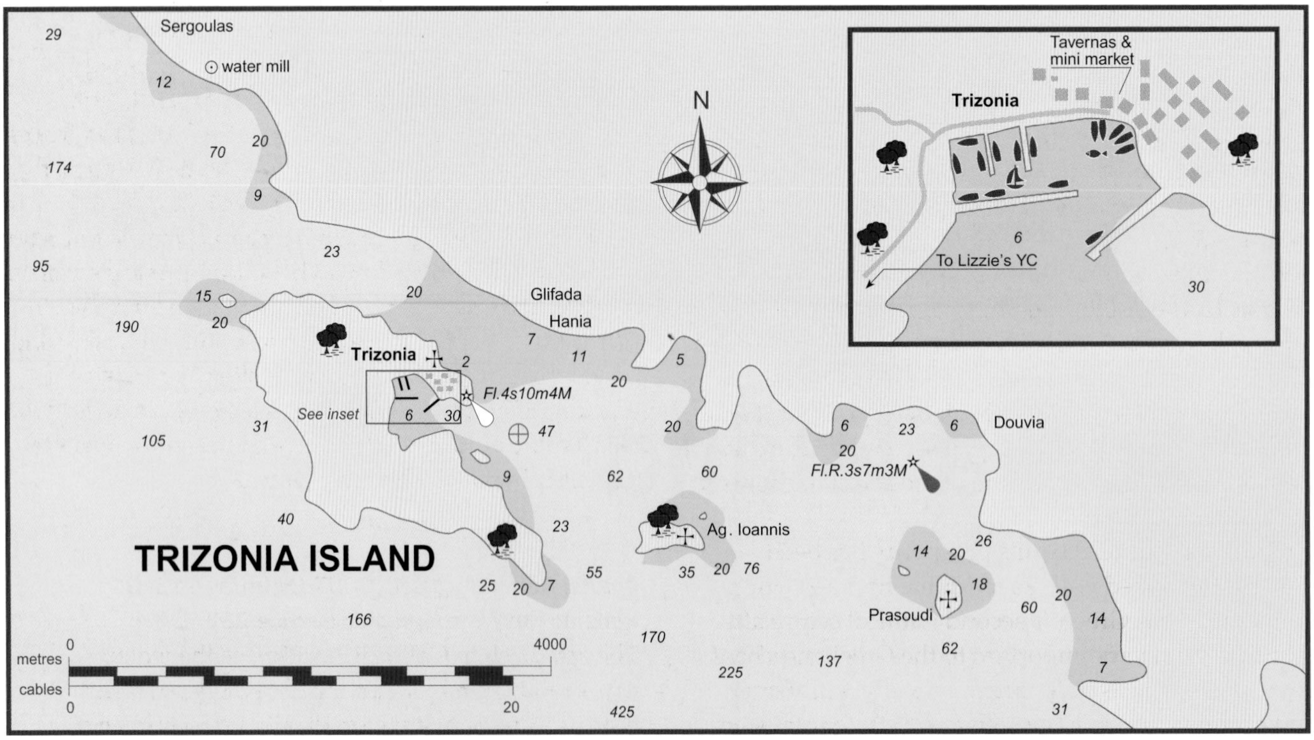

can be found in 2.5-3m on mud and weed once your anchor has taken hold.

Alternatively, you can find a good calm weather anchorage off the north coast of Ag Ioannis (Vrak Ay Ioánnis), a small islet about 3½ cables east of the southern tip of Trizonia. Suitable in settled conditions only, care should be taken round the east and north-east coast of the islet as there are rocks nearby.

Useful information – Trizonia Island

FACILITIES

Water: Metered tap near the harbour.

Showers: At Lizzie's Yacht Club, on the hill to the west of the harbour.

Laundry: At Lizzie's Yacht Club and at Hotel Drymna (Tel: 22660 71204).

Gas: Ask Christos Kalogeropoulous at the harbour.

Rubbish: Small bins near the quay but, if at all possible, please take rubbish with you.

Yacht services/chandlery: Christos Kalogeropoulous (Tel: 22660 71661; Mobile: 69 45568955) offers summer and winter guardianage services and can also do general boat and engine maintenance.

Telephone: Phone box near the tavernas. Mobile reception is good.

Internet: Ask at Hotel Drymna.

PROVISIONING

Grocery shops: Mini-market on the north-east side of the harbour.

Bakery: Some fresh bread sold at the mini-market.

Butcher: Some packaged meat products sold at the mini-market.

Banks: The nearest are at Nafpaktos but Hotel Drymna offers currency exchange.

Opening times: The tavernas are usually open from lunch-time until late, seven days a week.

EATING OUT

Trizonia boasts several tavernas, all very good for fish. There is also a restaurant attached to Lizzie's Yacht Club and Hotel Drymna.

ASHORE

The island lies in a beautiful location and, while there isn't much ashore apart from a handful of houses and tavernas, it's a very pleasant place to wander around, with good views across the Korinthiakos Gulf.

TRANSPORT

Car hire: There are no cars or motorbikes on the island.

Bus: To catch a bus to Athens, travel to Nafpaktos on the mainland.

Ferry: A small boat runs between Trizonia and Hania, near Glifada on the mainland, several times a day. International services leave from Kyllini, a major port south of Patra which is about 2 hours away by car.

Air travel: The nearest airport is Athens, a 3-hour drive from Glifada. Regular services fly to and from Europe.

OTHER INFORMATION

Local Tel code: 22660.

Hospital: The nearest medical centre is at Nafpaktos: Tel: 26340 23690, where there is also a dentist and doctor.

Yacht repairs/services: Christos Kalogeropoulous (Tel: 22660 71661; Mobile: 69 45568955).

Galaxidi

Galaxidhi, Galaxidhiou, Ormos Galaxidhiou, Galaxeidi

Entrance to Galaxidi Harbour: 38°22'.74N 22°23'.32E

Galaxidi is one of the jewels of the Corinth Gulf. Situated 3½nm to the south-west of Itea, it's a quieter and more upmarket version of Kioni on Ithaca, in a really beautiful location. The harbour is sheltered from the prevailing winds, and ashore a modest but good selection of amenities caters for most needs.

Galaxidi was established here in around 300BC but it is thought that the original town, which was known as Oianthi, was built on the hillside behind and that it was founded as early as 1393BC. Its move to the coast and subsequent development helped secure its future and it was long considered to be one of the safest harbours in the Korinthiakos Gulf.

Since that time, Galaxidi's prosperity has been inextricably linked with its maritime heritage. For a long time it was Greece's second nautical centre after Syros and was very important to the Greek merchant navy. Its shipyards built large numbers of schooners and brigs, and during the 18th and 19th centuries the town flourished, with ship owners travelling great distances to recruit crew and buy its ships.

However, the arrival of steam power in the early 1900s signalled the start of a rapid decline for the Galaxidi industry. Shipbuilders and owners were slow to adjust to the new technology and, with higher production costs and different trade routes being followed, the town's significance within the Greek merchant navy diminished. It had serious consequences for the town, too, and with so much local investment tied up in ships, led to Galaxidi's decline.

Today, remnants of Galaxidi's prosperous past can be seen in the large Venetian-style buildings that dominate much of the town, but it is hard to imagine that the harbour was once home to such a bustling industry and a large fleet of ships. It now has a slightly sleepy feel and is a delightful place to spend a couple of days. It is also a more attractive alternative to Itea if you want to visit Delphi in the hills to the north.

NAVIGATION

Charts: Admiralty 1600, SC5771; Imray G13, G1; Hellenic Navy Hydrographic Service 232/1, 74

The approach to Galaxidi is tricky, as the waters surrounding the harbour entrance are strewn with rocks and reefs, and it should only be attempted in

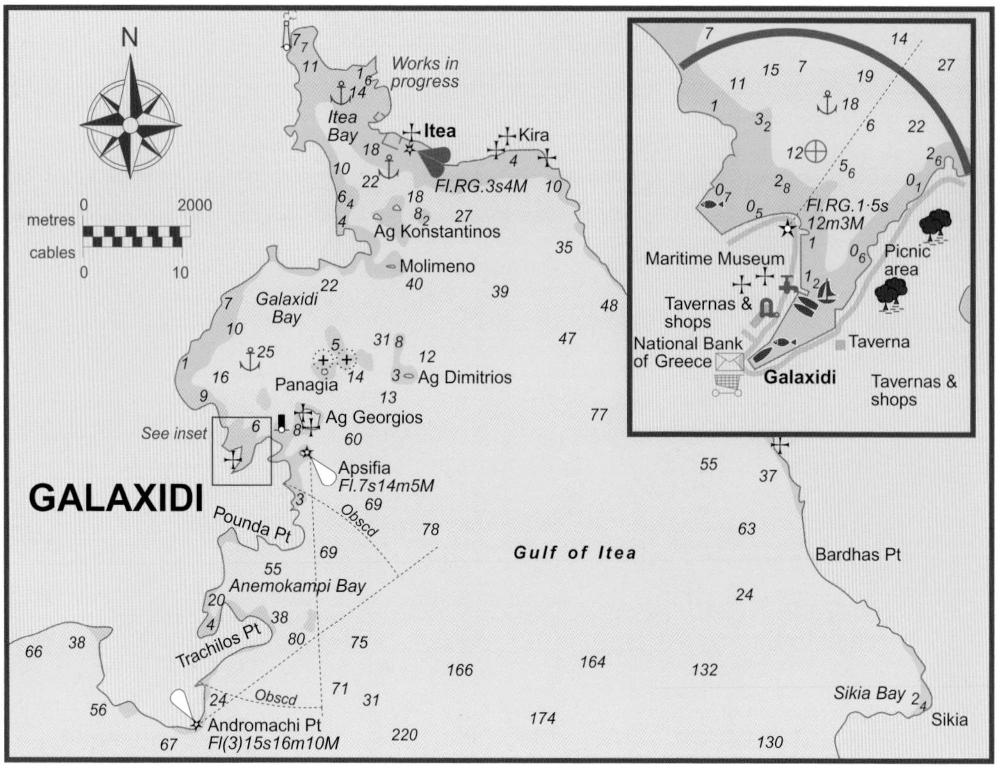

daylight. Study of the charts suggests that the safest route would be to approach Galaxidi via the north-east corner of Galaxidi Bay, skirting round the outside of all the rocks and islets littering its eastern side. However, in calm, settled weather, it is possible to find safe passage through the islets, saving a few miles.

Proceed as follows: off Pounda Pt, in the Itea Gulf, you will see a collection of small islets and rocks to the north. The closest islet, Apsifia (Fl 7s14m5M), is your next point of reference. Once off its east coast (and keeping some distance away as it is fringed with rocks), head north-west on a bearing of 313°T in the channel between Apsifia and the islet of Ag Georgios. Stay in mid-channel as there are reefs around Ag Georgios, and pass to the east of a large rectangular beacon that stands on a reef just offshore of Kentri Pt.

When you are well clear of the reef, identify the entrance to Galaxidi's harbour and the town flanking its northern shore, and then head south-west towards the harbour. Depths in the middle of the harbour are around 10m until you are level with a short pier covered in taverna tables. The depths then decrease steadily to less than 5m and between 2.5-3m off the main quay. It is shallow along the eastern side of the harbour so stay in the middle of the channel at all times.

Vessels approaching from the direction of Itea should check their charts carefully before setting off. There are lots of rocks between Panagia and Dimitrios, two islets to the north and north-east of Ag Georgios, and not all of them show above water. For a safe passage, do not be tempted to sail between the two, but stay well to the west of Panagia when approaching Galaxidi.

BERTHING

Visiting boats should berth stern- or bows-to the quay, to the south of a large square pier with a fixed awning

The waterfront at Galaxidi. The town is an upmarket version of Kioni on Ithaca

over part of it. Depths here are between 2.5-3m and the holding is good on mud and sand. It is not advisable to head too far into the harbour, though, as depths at the western end decrease to 1m and less, and this area is used by local fishing boats. The area to the north of the pier is also shallow and can become uncomfortable in a south-southeasterly swell.

Yachts can berth on the quay and find reasonable shelter here

ANCHORING

You will occasionally see yachts anchoring in the northern part of the harbour, on the eastern side of the town. It is more exposed than the main quay but offers adequate shelter in settled conditions. You can anchor in 2.5-3m on mud and sand.

Alternatively, you can anchor in Galaxidi Bay, to the north-west of the harbour. The majority of the bay is deep (15-20m) and it is also exposed in a northwesterly, so if conditions deteriorate you should seek shelter elsewhere. Watch out for fish farms here.

Useful information – Galaxidi

FACILITIES

Water: Taps on the quay near the Port Police.
Fuel: Take a taxi to a nearby petrol station.
Ice: Ask at the tavernas or mini-markets.
Laundry: To the north of the harbour, on the main road out of Galaxidi.
Rubbish: Bins on the quay.
Yacht services/chandlery: Mouragio on the quay sells fishing tackle and small items of chandlery.
Telephone: Phone box on the quay.

PROVISIONING

Grocery shops: Well-stocked mini-market at the western end of the quay, near the Happy Cloud Taverna.
Bakery: Near the pharmacy at the western end of the harbour.
Butcher: In the centre of Galaxidi.
Banks: National Bank of Greece ATM on side road off the western end of the harbour.
Pharmacy: Near the bakery.
Post: Post office next to the National Bank of Greece. Open 0900-1400, Monday-Friday. Post box next to the Maritime Museum. The postal service is good. Stamps available at souvenir shops.
Opening times: 0900-1400 and 1730-2100. Tavernas are open later.

EATING OUT

One of the best meals I have ever eaten in Greece was at Galaxidi, at Limania taverna on the quay. It was a huge feast, including exquisite mussels and fresh fish, and was very reasonably priced. Omilos (Tel: 22650 42111), the taverna at the far eastern end of the harbour, has beautiful views over Galaxidi Bay and a good menu, as does Maritsa on the quay near Mouragio. Taverna Tassos is good for seafood but quite expensive and The Happy Cloud (Tel: 22650 42430) café-bar at the western end of the quay is good for puddings. This is just a handful of the numerous tavernas and cafes in Galaxidi.

ASHORE

The Nautical Museum (Tel: 22650 41795), on a side street off the quay, is fascinating if you have an hour to spare. Extremely well organised, its exhibits include a collection of nautical paintings from the 19th century, logs and registers from Galaxidi-built ships, navigation instruments, blocks, models, figureheads and copies of the *Galaxidi Chronicle*, which was published in 1865. The museum is open daily and prices comprise €5 per adult and €1 per child.

You will find several good walks around the pine-covered Kentri Pt and some little pebbly beaches where you can swim. If you have hired a car, Delphi (see p183) is a 30-minute drive from Galaxidi.

TRANSPORT

Car hire: Rent a Car Alexis (Tel: 22650 42080).
Taxis: Are often at the W end of the quay. Otherwise, ask at the tavernas.
Bus: Bus stop to the north of the harbour, near the main roundabout.
Ferry: Patra is the nearest terminal. Services to Kefalonia, Corfu, Igoumenitsa and Brindisi, Bari and Arcona in Italy leave daily from Patra. See www.greekferries.gr for tickets and timetables.
Air travel: Preveza Airport (Tel: 26820 22355) is a 3-hour drive from Galaxidi. Several international and domestic flights a week in the season. Athens Airport (Tel: 21035 30000) is a 2-hour drive from Galaxidi and has more flights.

OTHER INFORMATION

Local Tel code: 22650.
Port authority: Small, seasonal Port Police office (Tel: 22650 41390/VHF Ch12) on the quay.
Police: Tel: 22650 41222.
Doctor/Dentist: In Itea.
Hospital: Medical centre (Tel: 22650 41312) in Galaxidi.
Yacht repairs/services: Mouragio on the quay sells basic chandlery.

Itea Iteas

Immediately to the south of the entrance to Itea harbour: 38°25'.74N 22°25'.41E
Entrance to Marathias Bay, an anchorage in Itea Bay: 38°26'.03N 22°24'.21E

The marina at Itea is slowly being developed

Itea is an unremarkable agricultural town on the north shore of the Itea Gulf, 3½nm north-west of Galaxidi. It is relatively new, having only been built in 1830, and the harbour and marina is slowly being developed to accommodate visiting yachts. At present it offers little more than a berth, although electricity points have been set up on the pontoons and lazylines have been fitted throughout. The marina offers good shelter from the north-west, but is exposed in a strong southerly, when swell gets pushed into the basin. The town is good for provisioning and, being just 10 miles (16km) south of Delphi, is an ideal base from which to visit the famous archaeological site.

A view across the Gulf of Itea from the mountains near Delphi

NAVIGATION

Charts: Admiralty 2405, 1600, SC5771; Imray G13, G1; Hellenic Navy Hydrographic Service 232/1, 232, 74

From all directions, head for the Itea Gulf (Krissaios Kólpos/Kólpos Itéas) on the northern shore of the Korinthiakos Gulf. The approach to the bay is through deep water and the passage through it safe until you are north-west of Galaxidi. Here, care must be taken as there are numerous rocks, reefs and mini islets along the west coast of the gulf. Do not attempt a passage between the islets, particularly those immediately to the south of Itea, as there are lots of shoals nearby, with depths dropping to as little as 1.8m. Care should also be taken in windy conditions, as low-lying rocks can be hidden in chop. If at all possible, approach Itea via the eastern coast of the gulf as you will then pass through deep, clear water.

The town of Itea is visible from some distance: the surrounding hillsides are a rich, reddy brown and the town a low-lying swathe of buildings flanking the shore at the head of the gulf. The marina and harbour are to the west of it and easy to identify.

At night, the pier on the eastern side of the harbour

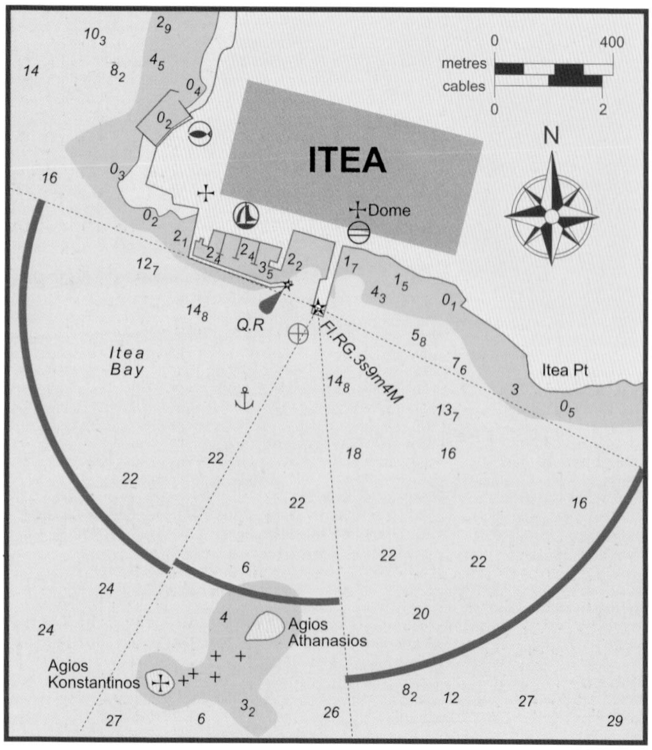

is lit (Fl RG 3s4M), but extreme care should be taken on approach to avoid the rocks and islets to the south.

BERTHING

Yachts visiting Itea berth in the marina. Either go alongside the inner edge of the breakwater or stern- or bows-to the pontoons, wherever there is room, using the lazylines provided. The holding here on mud is good.

ANCHORING

The inlets to the north-west of Itea, in Itea Bay, offer numerous deep-water anchorages. Marathias Bay, to the west, is the best location, but it is very deep, so expect to anchor in around 10m.

Care should be taken around the northern end of the bay, as ore from the surrounding hillsides is loaded into ships here and there are often vessels at anchor nearby.

Useful information – Itea

FACILITIES

Water: Water bottles can be filled from a couple of taps behind the harbour.
Fuel: Plenty of petrol stations on the outskirts of town.
Showers: Toilet block behind the quay, not always open.
Ice: Sold at the supermarkets.
Gas: Sold at the supermarkets or petrol stations.
Shorepower: Several electricity points along the pontoons.
Rubbish: Bins behind the quay.
Telephone: Phone boxes near the harbour and in the centre of Itea. Phone cards sold at the kiosk behind the harbour and the OTE building in the town centre. Mobile reception here is good.

PROVISIONING

Grocery shops: Several supermarkets and general grocery shops in the centre of Itea, to the north of the harbour.
Bakery: In the centre of Itea.
Butcher: Near the town centre.
Banks: Branch of the National Bank of Greece (Tel: 22650 32150) and ATM not far from the harbour, plus branches of the Alpha Bank (Tel: 22650 34162) and the Agricultural Bank of Greece (Tel: 22650 33062) near the centre of Itea.
Pharmacy: Several in the centre of Itea.
Post: Post office near the town centre; stamps sold at souvenir shops. The postal service in Itea is good.
Opening times: Shops operate to usual opening times: 0900-1400 and 1730-2030. Few shops open on Sundays.

EATING OUT

There are lots of tavernas and cafés to the east of the harbour. Most serve simple traditional fare and are reasonably priced.

ASHORE

Delphi is a 10-mile (16km) drive from Itea, up a winding and at times precarious road to the north of the town. Sitting high on the mountain tops, Delphi is one of the most significant archaeological sites in Greece. According to legend, it was here that the paths crossed of two eagles released by the god Zeus from opposite ends of the Earth, pinpointing Delphi as the centre of the world. The site was consequently made into an important sanctuary and, during the Geometric Period (11th-8th century BC), people would travel great distances to consult the oracle Apollo. The Cult of Apollo became known world-wide and for a long time Delphi was an important religious and political centre. It is also here that the Pythian Games were established; held every four years to commemorate Apollo's victory over Python, they included athletic and cultural activities and competitions. Under the Byzantine Empire, however, all worship of the Cult of Apollo was strictly forbidden and Delphi's significance soon diminished.

The site was eventually rediscovered in the 19th century by the Athens-based French Archaeological School and is now a major tourist attraction. Monuments of interest include the Sacred Way, a paved path lined with statues that leads to some of the most important features at Delphi; the grand Temple of Apollo, dating to the 6th century BC; the theatre, and the stadium where the Pythian Games were held – one of the best preserved in Greece.
You need plenty of time to explore Delphi; if possible, get here early, before the coach-loads of tourists descend. There's also a museum, which includes artefacts found during excavation, and on a clear day the panoramic views from Delphi and the road leading to it are breathtaking.
The site is open daily, from 0830-1800; admission costs €6.

Itea is a good base from which to explore Delphi

TRANSPORT

Car hire: Rent a Car (Tel: 22650 34395) near the harbour has a range of cars at reasonable prices.
Taxis: Ask nearby tavernas for recommendations.
Bus: The bus station is near the town centre. From here you can travel to Athens, or along the coast to Galaxidi, Nafpaxtos and Antirio.
Ferry: The nearest terminal is at Patra, on the north-west tip of the Peloponnese. From here you can travel to Kefalonia, Ithaca or Zakynthos, or further afield to Italy.
Air travel: Athens International Airport (Tel: 21035 30000) is a 2-hour drive from Itea. Lots of services daily to and from Europe.

OTHER INFORMATION

Local Tel code: 22650.
Port authority: Port Police office (VHF Ch12; Tel: 22650 32345) behind the harbour.
Police: Tourist police station (Tel: 22650 33333) in the centre of Itea.
Hospital: Medical centre (Tel: 22650 32224/32222) on the western side of the town.

Andikira Gulf

Kolpos Andikiron, Antikyron

Approach to Andikira, to the east of the islet of Tsarouchi (Nisidha Tsarokhi): 38°18'.44N 22°38'.71E
Andikira Bay: 38°22'.54N 22°38'.06E

Andikira is a pretty little village set against a backdrop of dramatic, steep-sided mountains. Although the bay it sits in is affected by gusts that skid off the surrounding hills, the harbour offers good shelter from all directions and the village has most of the amenities a cruising yacht requires. The Andikira Gulf has numerous deep-water anchorages and is within a short distance of Itea, Delphi and Corinth.

NAVIGATION

Charts: Admiralty 2405, 1600, SC5771; Imray G13, G1; Hellenic Navy Hydrographic Service 232/1, 232

From all directions, head towards the Andikira Gulf (Kolpos Andikiron), a large bay 36nm north-west of Corinth and to the east of Itea. The village and harbour lie tucked in the western corner of Andikira Bay at the head of the gulf and cannot be seen until close to. However, a large bauxite ore factory, where aluminium is extracted, stands on the opposite shore and is conspicuous from some distance.

The approach to Andikira is through very deep water and it only gets shallow close to shore. There are often big ships near the factory, though, so maintain a good look-out at all times. At night there is a light on Kefali Pt (Fl 3s19m4M), Andikira Bay's western headland, and the group of buoys to the south of the harbour are also lit (Q R).

BERTHING

Berth stern- or bows-to the mole, either on its inside or outside edge. It is fairly deep here, with depths of 3m near the quay and 5.5m at the end of the mole. The harbour offers good protection from all directions and the holding is good. Local boats use the quay.

ANCHORING

You can anchor immediately off the harbour but should steer clear of the south-west corner of the bay where there are several large buoys. Alternatively, there is a good place to the south of Andikira in Ag Isidoros Bay. It offers all-round shelter and ashore you'll find a pleasant little beach and a seasonal cafe. Local boats use this bay, though, so watch out for the permanent moorings when manoeuvring. Anchor in around 5m on sand.

Vereses Bay to the south offers good shelter from all directions except the south-west and, like Ag Isidoros, is deep. Anchor in 5-10m on sand and mud. Avoid Grammatikou Bay, on the opposite shore, south of the aluminium factory. It's rather spoilt by the backdrop of unsightly industrial buildings and also severely affected by gusts that whip off the surrounding hillsides. Note that anchoring is prohibited in the bay to the south of Mounda Pt (Ak Mounta).

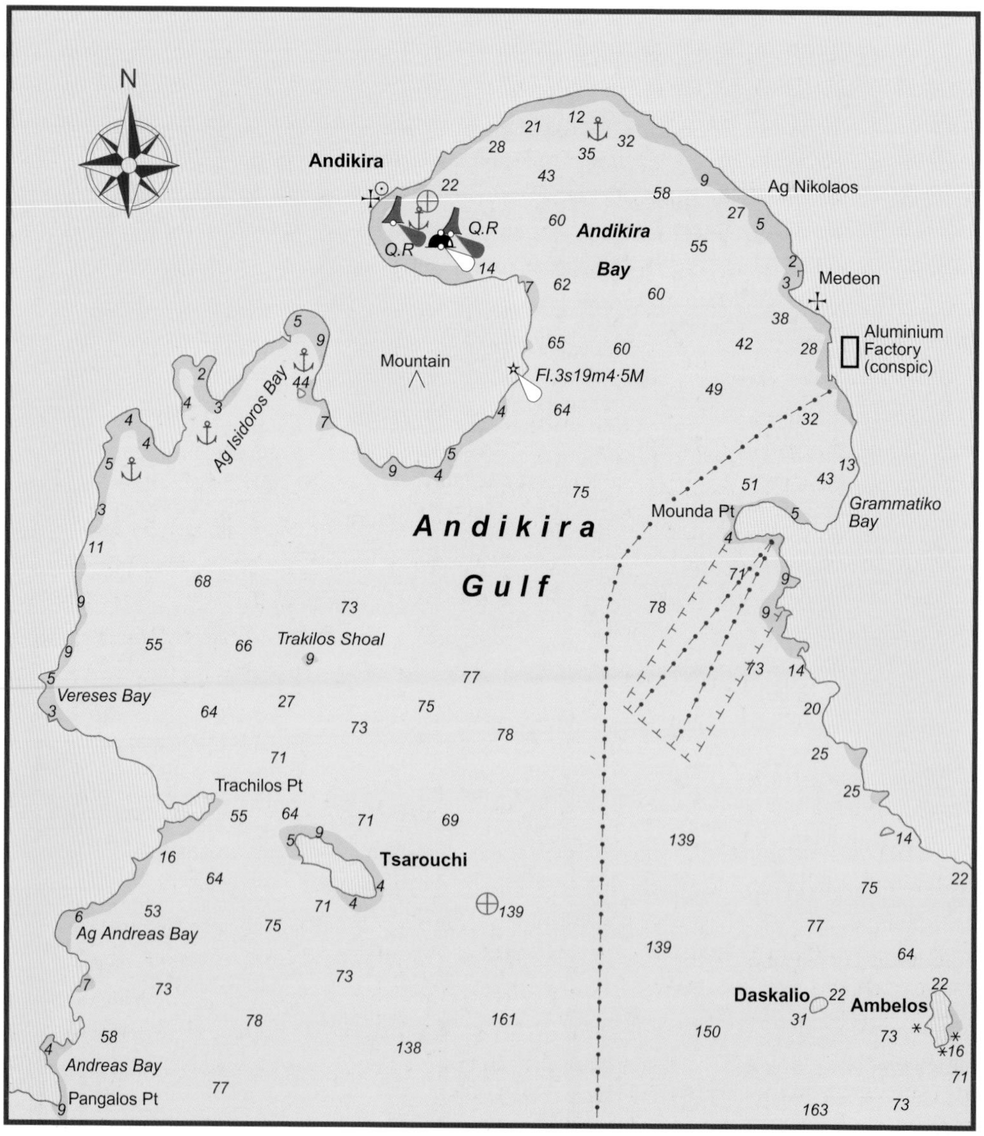

Useful information – Andikira

FACILITIES
Water: Yes.
Fuel: No but there is a petrol station nearby.
Gas: Ask at the mini-markets.
Shorepower: Yes.
Rubbish: Bins behind the quay.
Telephone: Phone box on the quay. Others in Andikira. Mobile reception is good.

PROVISIONING
Grocery shops: There are a couple of mini-markets back from the waterfront.
Bakery: In Andikira.
Butcher: In Andikira.
Banks: ATM in the village.
Pharmacy: In the village.
Post: Post office in the village. Open Monday-Friday, 0800-1300. The postal service is good.
Opening times: 0900-1400 and 1730-2030; tavernas and cafes are open until later.

EATING OUT
Andikira is good for fish tavernas. Take your pick from the handful along the quay or those in the village. Delfinia fish taverna (Tel: 22670 41489), Akteon Taverna (Tel: 22670 41280) and Castello Pizzaria (Tel: 22670 43200), among many others, all have a good reputation. There are also several café-bars situated not far from the waterfront.

ASHORE
The historic site of Ancient Delphi is about 10 miles from Andikira. See p183.

TRANSPORT
Taxis: Ask at the tavernas.
Bus: Contact the KTEL office in Andikira (Tel: 26670 41279) for details of services.
Ferry: International and inter-island ferries leave from Patra, at the eastern end of the Korinthiakos Gulf. See p194 for details.
Air travel: The nearest airport is at Athens (Tel: 21035 30000), a 2-hour drive from Andikira. International charter and domestic flights several times a day.

OTHER INFORMATION
Local Tel code: 22670.
Port authority: Near the quay. VHF Ch12 or Tel: 22670 41205.
Police: Police station (Tel: 26670 41220) in the village.
Doctor: Ask at the medical centre for recommendations.
Hospital: Medical centre (Tel: 22670 22790/22791) in the village.

Loutraki Ormos Loutrakiou

Off the beach in Loutraki Bay: 37°58'.53N 22°58'.46E
Charts: Admiralty 2404, 1600, SC5771; Imray G13, G1, G2, G3; Hellenic Navy Hydrographic Service 232

Loutraki, 2½nm to the east of Corinth, is little more than an anchorage. While the resort-town offers numerous amenities and is bustling with life, there is nowhere for visiting yachts to berth comfortably. A short mole at the northern end of the beach provides only minimal room and is usually busy with fishing and day-tripper boats. Anchoring off in the bay is your best bet, but it is very deep here (25m-plus) until close to and offers no shelter from the prevailing northwesterlies. Consider it as a short-term, calm-weather anchorage only.

The small quay at Loutraki is of little use to yachts

If you do decide to stop here, anchor in 4-5m off the beach, keeping a good look-out for swimmers as the area is full of tourists in peak season. The holding on sand is reasonable, although there are patches of weed, so make sure your anchor digs in well.

Ashore, you'll find an exhaustive selection of shops, including mini-markets, pharmacies and clothes boutiques. There are branches of the National Bank of Greece (Tel: 27440 63563), Agricultural Bank of Greece (Tel: 27440 63404), Alpha Bank (Tel: 27440 62942) and Piraeus Bank (Tel: 27440 62857). A post office, Tourist Information Centre and train and bus terminals are all at the south end of the main road through the town. There's also a medical centre (Tel: 27440 63444) and many taxi ranks and car-hire firms. Tavernas and bars line the seafront.

Corinth Korinthos

To the north of the small boat harbour: 37°56'.59N 22°56'.26E

Corinth stands at the head of Corinth Bay, in the south-east corner of the Korinthiakos Gulf. For a major city, it is decidedly unremarkable. Centuries of earthquakes have left it devoid of much character, and indeed style, and the city now heaves under a mass of faceless concrete buildings. It lacks the cosmopolitan feel of

Corinth is a working port backed by a mass of faceless buildings

Corfu or the vivacity of Athens and has the air of an industrial town – something you can't forget moored in the small boat harbour amidst the incessant clamour of a working port. It's also a city whose centre is plagued with cars and scooters. The central shopping streets double as the main thoroughfare for much of its traffic and, unlike Patra, you don't seem to be able to get away from it.

Corinth is very much a Greek town and panders little to tourism, despite its proximity to Ancient Corinth. As somewhere to stop while waiting to transit the Corinth Canal it's fine, and as the nearest place to explore Ancient Corinth it suits well, but otherwise I wouldn't recommend it as a destination – although the shelter in the harbour is very good, as are the nearby amenities, I still find it lacks appeal.

NAVIGATION

Charts: Admiralty 1600, SC5771; Imray G13, G14, G1; Hellenic Navy Hydrographic Service 232/2, 232

The approach to Corinth is straightforward, through deep water. From some distance you will be able to identify the city – a large mass of tall buildings – but the harbour itself blends into the cityscape and will not become obvious until closer to. The small boat harbour, which is suitable for boats of up to 50ft (15m), lies immediately to the east of the main commercial harbour, which is usually identified by the large ships berthed alongside. Maintain a good look-out at all times, as craft waiting to transit the Corinth Canal gill around in Corinth Bay. There is also regular movement in the commercial harbour.

If approaching at night, look for the lights at the entrance to the Corinth Canal (Iso G 2s10M and Iso R 2s10M), to the east of the city. They are easier to pick out than the light on the end of the commercial harbour's breakwater (Fl 6 3s3M), which often gets lost against the city lights.

BERTHING

Most yachts can berth in the small boat harbour but bigger vessels should contact the port authorities (VHF Ch12 / Tel: 27410 28888) for a berth in the commercial area. In the small boat harbour, yachts should berth alongside the eastern end of the breakwater or on the hammerhead end of the pontoons, wherever there is room. Most of the stern- and bows-to berths on the pontoons are rigged with lazylines and occupied by local boats, although you might be lucky here. Depths in the harbour are between 3.5-4m and the holding is good on mud. There is good shelter from all directions except the north-east, although there can be swell in a strong northwesterly.

The small boat harbour at Corinth, near the centre of the city

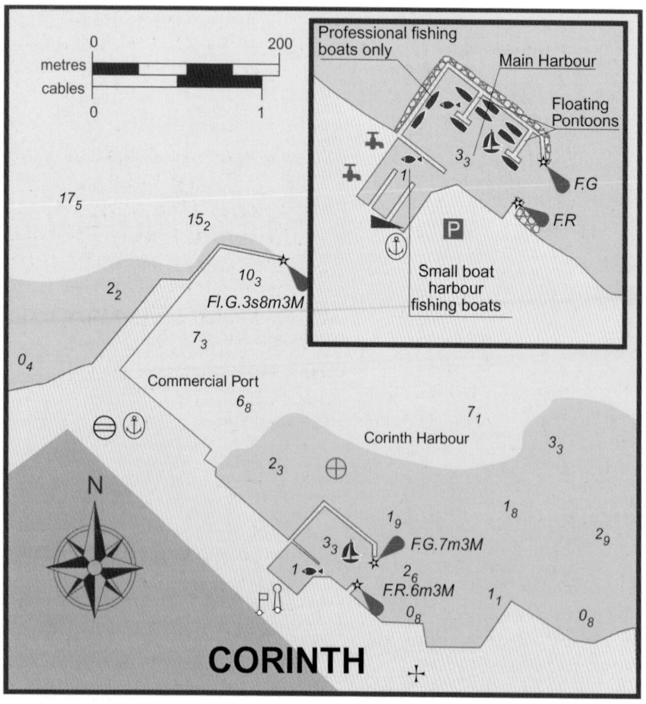

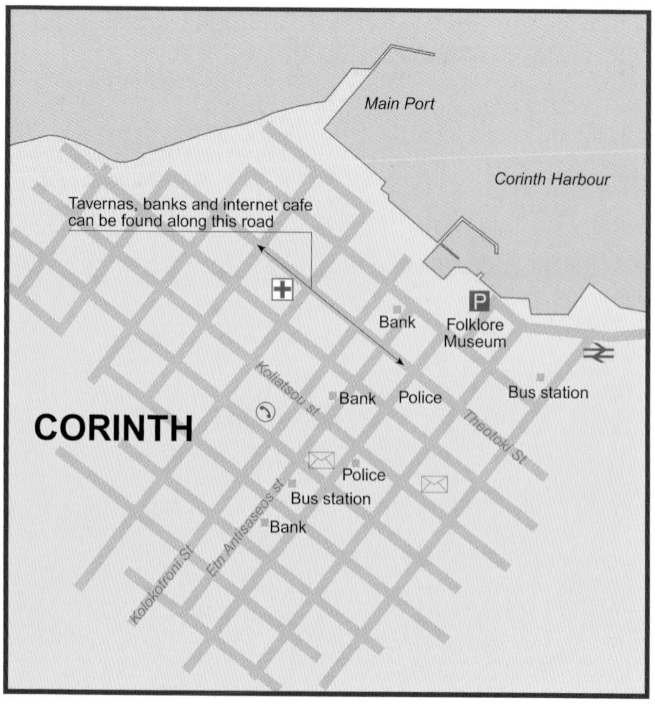

ANCHORING

Corinth Bay is generally too deep. Occasionally yachts anchor off the beach at Loutraki or in Agrilou Bay (Ormos Agriliou), a small cove on the north shore of the bay, 4nm north-west of Loutraki. Both bays are calm-weather, daytime anchorages only and offer no shelter from the prevailing winds. Care should also be taken around Agrilou Bay as there are rocks close inshore.

Useful information – Corinth

FACILITIES

Water: Taps but they do not always work.
Fuel: 24hr Silk Oil mini-tanker (Tel: 27410 24024/24079) will deliver to the harbour.
Ice: Sold at supermarkets.
Gas: Several hardware shops near the centre or try the supermarkets.
Rubbish: Bins to the west of the harbour.
Yacht services/chandlery: No but there are several hardware shops.
Telephone: A couple of phone boxes in the square behind the marina. More on the pedestrianised Theotoki St. Phone cards at kiosks. Mobile reception is good.
Internet café: On Theotoki Street. Rates vary but expect to pay around €6 for 60 minutes.

PROVISIONING

Grocery shops: Several mini-markets on the side-streets off Ethnikis Antistassis. Also a couple of grocery shops. Larger supermarkets on the outskirts.
Bakery: Near the centre.
Butcher: Near the centre.
Banks: The Alpha Bank (Tel: 27410 27163) is the nearest, just behind the harbour. The Emporiki Bank (Tel: 27410 22202), the National Bank of Greece (Tel: 27410 25628) and the Agricultural Bank of Greece (Tel: 27410 26690) are on Ethnikis Antistassis, the main road that runs south from the harbour. Citibank is on Koliatsou St, a side street to the south of Ethnikis Antistassis, and the Piraeus Bank (Tel: 27410 85598) is on Kolokotroni St, parallel to Ethnikis Antistassis, on its south side.
Pharmacy: Several: one on Theotoki Street, the pedestrianised road off Ethnikis Antistassis.
Post: Post office on Adimantou Street, a side street to the north of Ethnikis Antistassis. Open Monday-Friday, 0900-1400. Post box in the square behind the marina. The postal service in Corinth is good. Stamps also sold at kiosks and souvenir shops.
Opening times: Most shops open: 0900-1400 and 1730-2100; cafes and bars may stay open all day.

EATING OUT

You will find plenty of small but busy cafés, creperies and bars on Theotoki St, the pedestrianised street off Ethnikis Antistassis, and a few mediocre tavernas on the road past the harbour. Fast food appears to be the main sustenance in Corinth.

ASHORE

The small Historical & Folklore Museum of Corinth is near the harbour. Open Tuesday-Sunday, 0830-1330, it houses a collection of engravings, tools, pottery and examples of traditional crafts. Admission €2.

If you have a day to spare for some sightseeing, head south to the ancient city of Corinth. It's a fascinating place to explore and is the largest example of a Roman town in Greece. It was established in the Neolithic period (5000-3000BC) and for the Romans its location was highly significant. Even before the canal was built, the narrow strip of land between the Saronic and Corinth gulfs was a major trade route, with goods being transported overland between the two. Any city built on such a route was its linchpin and when the Romans took control of it they also took charge of all trade between the Peloponnese and northern Greece. Although they destroyed the city in 146BC, it was rebuilt under Julius Caesar a century later and prospered as the capital of Greece. Earthquakes in Byzantine times and general abandonment have reduced the city to ruins but subsequent excavations have revealed a massive settlement, dominated by temples, market places and theatres.

What's even more impressive is the fortified acropolis of Acrocorinth, which perches on a mountain, high above Ancient Corinth. At one time it was Greece's most important fortress and has been ruled by each and every one of the country's occupying forces. What's unusual about it is that it bears the hallmarks of all these occupiers – there are the remnants of Roman, Turkish, Venetian, Frankish and Byzantine architecture and the views from the top are astonishing. It's a steep 2½-mile (4km) walk from Ancient Corinth but well worth it.

Ancient Corinth is open Mon-Fri, 0800-1900, in the summer and 0800-1700 in winter. Admission costs €6. There is also a museum on the site, which includes artefacts found during excavation. Buses to Ancient Corinth leave from the centre of Corinth regularly throughout the day in season. Acrocorinth is open year-round; admission is free.

If you've hired a car, then one other site to visit is the Sanctuary of Heraion at Perachora on Melangavi Pt, to the N of Corinth. Founded as a religious centre in around the 8th century, it is open Tues-Sun, 0830-1500; admission is free.

TRANSPORT

Car hire: Travel agents on Enthnikis Antistassis St will organise car hire. Terzis Travel (Tel: 27410 71710) and 24 Hours TEK (Tel: 27410 85908).
Taxis: Often near the commercial port and at the marina end of Ethnikis Antistassis.
Bus: The KTEL bus station (Tel: 27410 25643) is on Koliatsou & Ermou St, a side road to the east of the marina, off Ethnikis Antistassis St. Regular services run between Corinth, Athens and the Peloponnese. You can also catch one to Ancient Corinth or Loutraki. Check with travel agents for times and prices.
Railway: The train station (Tel: 27410 22523) is near the KTEL bus station, to the east of the marina. Daily services to Athens and the Peloponnese.
Ferry: The nearest international ferry port is Patra, on the north-east tip of the Peloponnese. Daily services to Kefalonia, Corfu, Igoumenitsa and Italy. For timetables and tickets, see www.greekferries.gr
Air travel: Athens Airport (Tel: 21035 30000) is a 2-hr drive from Corinth. Regular services to and from the UK and the rest of Europe.

OTHER INFORMATION

Local Tel code: 27410.
Port authority: The Port Police office (Tel: 27410 28888) is near the entrance to the commercial port. Small temporary Port Police office in the fishing boat harbour.
Police: The police station (Tel: 27410 23282) is on a side street off Ethnikis Antistassis.
Doctor: Doctor's surgery on a side road off Theotoki Street, the pedestrianised road off Ethnikis Antistassis.
Dentist: Surgery on a side road off Theotoki Street.
Hospital: Corinth Hospital (Tel: 27410 25711) is to the north of the town.

Corinth Canal

Dhioriga Korinthou

Charts: Admiralty 1600, SC5771; Imray G13, G14, G1; Hellenic Navy Hydrographic Service 232/2, 232

The Corinth Canal slices through near vertical limestone cliffs

The Corinth Canal is a short-cut between the Korinthiakos and the Saronic gulfs. Stretching for 4 miles (6½ km) in a straight line from Corinth to Isthmia, it is a shorter and quicker alternative to reach the Ionian than sailing around the south coast of the Peloponnese. Access is available to all craft with a

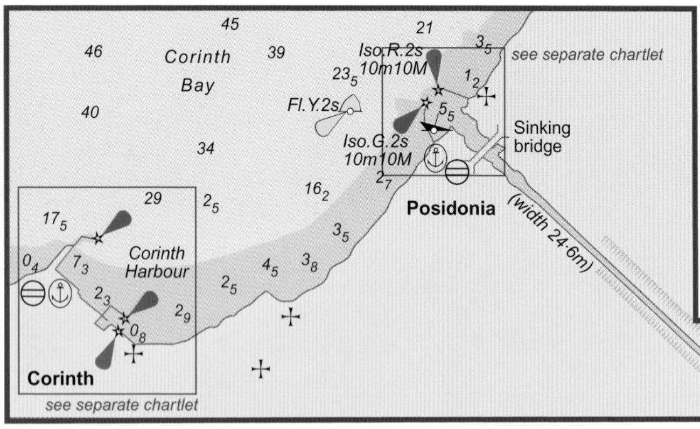

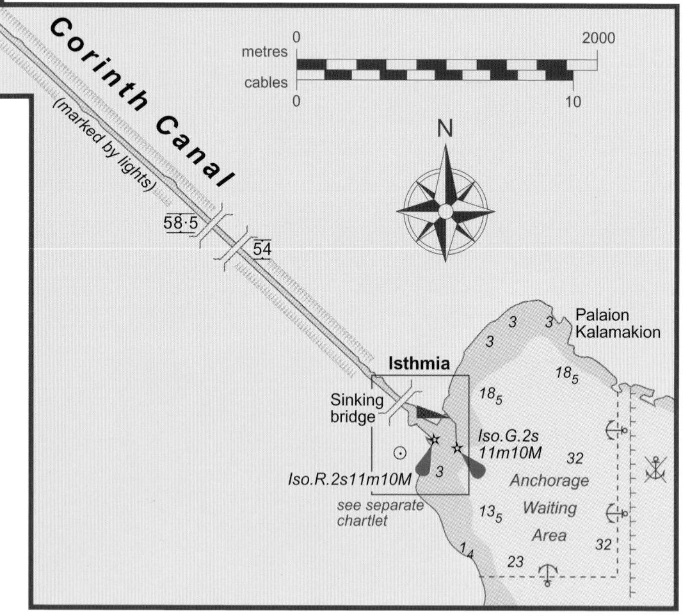

beam of less than 60ft (18.3m) and, although per mile it is one of the most expensive canals in the world, its creation has had a significant impact on trade in the 112 years since it was built. Over 11,000 boats from 50 countries world-wide transit the canal each year.

The canal first opened in 1983, 24 years after the Suez Canal, but the idea dates back centuries. Periander, one of the Seven Sages of Greece, first considered the feasibility of a canal in 602BC, seeing significant benefits for trade if the sea route between east and west Greece was shortened. He is said to have abandoned the plans, though, out of fear of wrath from the Gods.

However, 300 years later, under the command of Demetrios Poliorketes, King of Macedon, the idea surfaced again. This time concern over different sea levels halted the work and it wasn't until 44BC that the feasibility of the canal was reconsidered. In the meantime, however, the short stretch of rocky isthmus separating the two gulfs was still used as a trade route. Trading ships were brought to Poseidonia and Isthmia, unloaded and brought ashore, before being dragged on a wheeled sled along a limestone-paved road (Diolkos) to the other side of the isthmus. They were then relaunched, reloaded and continued on their journey. It involved a massive effort and, although restricted by the size of vessel that could be dragged overland, meant that the time required to transport cargo from the Aegean to the Adriatic was greatly reduced.

Emperor Nero was next to pick up the plans and in 66AD organised thousands of slave Jews and war prisoners to start digging. He succeeded in making a 3,300m trench, but in 68AD was sentenced to death for treason and the project ground to a halt.

The Byzantines and later the Venetians also made attempts to excavate a route through the isthmus, but it wasn't until the 19th century that it was finally done. Since then, it's been in almost constant commission, bar a closure of four years during the Second World War when retreating Germans blew up parts of it and caused landslides.

Cutting a narrow slice through vertical limestone cliffs, it is one of the most impressive canals in the world, recently becoming a popular tourist attraction. Access is available 24 hours a day, seven days a week, although it is shut on Tuesdays for routine maintenance, between 0600-1800.

Poseidonia Posidhonia

Off the entrance to Poseidonia: 37°57'.33N 22°57'.36E

Poseidonia is the western entrance to the Corinth Canal and is situated at the eastern end of the Korinthiakos Gulf, halfway between the towns of Corinth and Loutraki. The approach via Corinth Bay (Ormos Korinthou) is through deep water and at night the lighthouse on Melangavi Pt (Fl 10s58m17M) identifies the northern side of the bay. Lights on the breakwaters at Poseidonia (Iso G 2s10M and Iso R 2s10M) mark the mouth of the canal.

On arrival at the entrance, contact the canal authority on VHF Ch11 for permission to enter. You may have to wait for up to three hours before you can go through, and as there is nowhere to berth or anchor at Poseidonia, you should gill around near the entrance, in Corinth Bay. It is often quite windy here, particularly in a northwesterly, and make sure you maintain a good look-out for other vessels entering or leaving the canal. The canal authority's office is at the Isthmia end, and once you are through it you must berth alongside the quay and pay your transit dues.

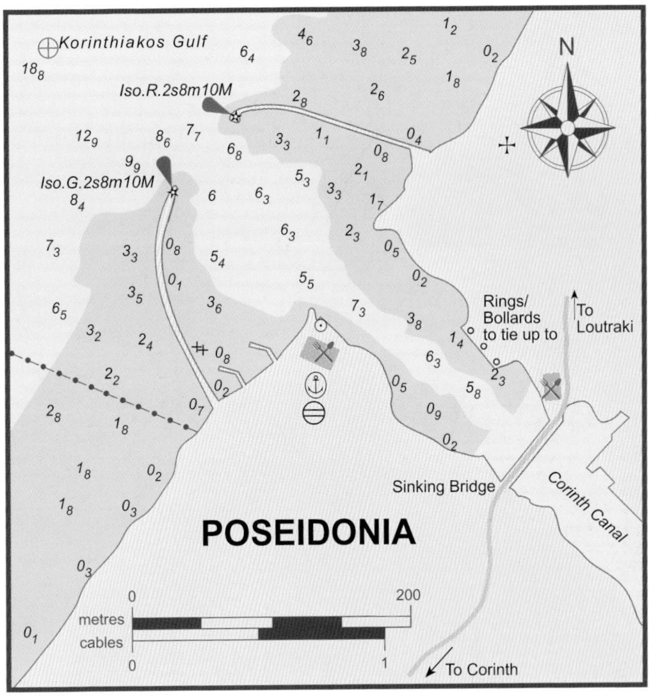

Isthmia

Off entrance to Isthmia: 37°54'.88N 23°00'.86E

Isthmia is the port at the eastern end of the Corinth Canal. Situated in Kalamaki Bay (Ormos Kalamakíou), in the north-east corner of the Saronic Gulf, Isthmia stands on the shores of the Aegean Sea. On approach, head in the general direction of Ag Theodori. There is an oil terminal there and tankers can usually be seen anchored offshore. Isthmia lies 3½nm to the west. Close to, you should be able to identify the canal's breakwaters and the canal office, a tall, aircraft control tower-type building on the western side of the entrance. At night, the breakwaters at the entrance are lit: Iso R 2s10M & Iso G 2s10M.

Immediately to the east of the canal office is a concrete quay. Berth alongside here and go ashore to complete the necessary paperwork and pay your transit dues. Make sure you have plenty of fenders out and

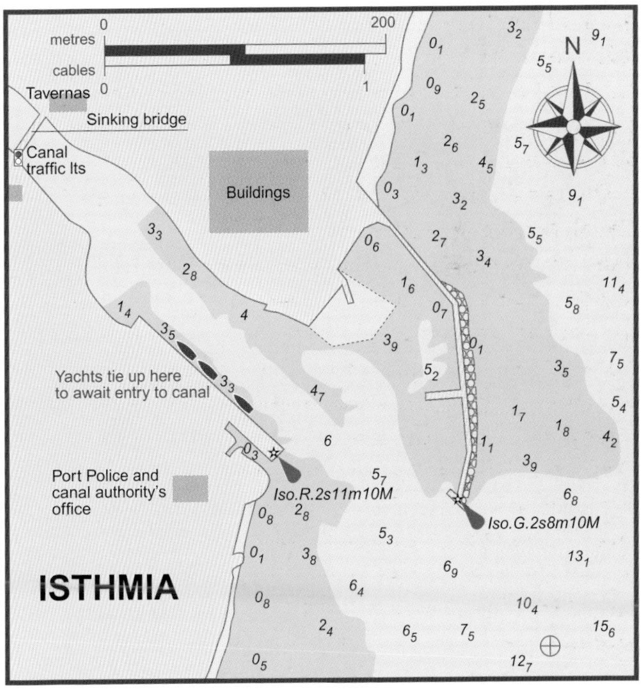

The eastern end of the Corinth Canal at Isthmia

that your lines are secure; if possible, leave someone on board. Big vessels manoeuvring in the entrance can churn up the waters considerably and if you are not careful you may find yourself being bashed against the quay.

If you are over 80ft (24m) and too big for the quay, you should gill around outside the entrance and request that a pilot boat brings the necessary paperwork out to you. The quay on the eastern side of the entrance is not suitable for berthing.

Transiting the canal

Once you have got permission to enter the canal and the signals permitting transit are shown (see opposite), the hydraulic metal road bridges at either end will be lowered and you should proceed. Traffic through the canal travels in one direction at a time and the speed limit is 6 knots. If a big ship is transiting, yachts will usually follow behind the convoy, but don't get too close as wash from the ship's propellers can make the waters quite turbulent at times. There is a current in the canal of between 2.5 and 3 knots and this usually changes direction every six hours, following a short period of slack water. Signals at both ends of the canal indicate the direction of flow. The difference between High and Low Water is minimal at just 60cm (23in).

Signals in the canal

Signal	Day	Night
Entry permitted:	Blue flag	A single white light
Entry prohibited:	Red flag	Two vertical white lights
In the direction of transit:	Two white triangular flags, one above the other	Two vertical lights, red over white
Against the direction of transit:	One triangular flag	Two vertical red lights
Slack water:	No signals	No signals

Paperwork required by the canal office

- Name and nationality of the vessel
- Port of registry and your ship's papers*
- Details of the boat's class or type, including specification (LOA and width)*
- Name of skipper and crew members, and contact details for the owner if not on board
- Details of where you have come from and where you are heading

* Please note that photocopies of ship's papers may not be accepted.

Canal dues

All private cruising boats and non-Greek cruising vessels fall under the canal's Category ST, for which dues are calculated according to overall length. In 2007, they were as follows:

Less than 6m:	**€65.45, including VAT at 19%‡**
6-9m:	**€85.68, including VAT at 19%‡**
Over 9m:	**€72 + €20.10 per extra metre + VAT at 19%‡**

For example, a 36ft (11m) yacht would cost €133.52, inc VAT, and a 45ft (13.7m) yacht would cost €198.10, inc VAT
‡ All fees were correct at the time of going to press

A ship passes through the Corinth Canal

- Assistance from a pilot costs an additional €140 and if you are engineless and require a tow then you will be charged an extra €168. Both the pilot and towing fees are subject to a 25% surcharge for a night-time transit and a 30% surcharge on a Sunday or a national holiday.
- All dues must be paid at the canal office on the Isthmia side of the canal. Payment can be made in cash (Euros, US Dollars, Pounds sterling or Swiss Francs) or by credit card (Visa, Mastercard, American Express).

Useful information

Opening hours: 24/7, except Tuesdays, 0600-1800 when it is closed for maintenance.
Port office: VHF Ch11; Tel: 27410 30880; 27410 30886 (24 hours).
Postal address: Periandros SA, Isthmia Corinth, 200 10 Corinth, Greece.
Website: www.corinthcanal.com

Specifications

Length:	20,820ft (6,346m)
Width at sea level:	80ft 7in (24.6m)
Width at sea bed:	70ft (21.3m)
Depth:	24ft 6in-26ft (7.5-8m)
Maximum air draught (due to height of bridges):	170ft 6in (52m)

Patra Patras

To the north-west of Patra Marina:
38°15'.98N 21°44'.11E

Patra is the third largest city in Greece and a major commercial centre in the Peloponnese. Much of Greece's trade passes through Patra and it's an important port of entry and stopover for yachts heading north and south. The marina offers a reasonable selection of amenities and good shelter from all directions. It's a 10-minute walk from the centre of Patra and highly recommended for victualling.

Patra itself is an energetic city. Of its 250,000 citizens a large number are students, evidenced by the wide variety of trendy shops and cafes. It has a very vibrant atmosphere and, although dominated by big tower blocks, there are areas with pretty architecture and side streets away from the main thoroughfare. Up near the castle, in the old town, you'll find many 19th century houses and neo-classical buildings, and the Roman Odeion is a particularly arresting monument.

NAVIGATION

Charts: Admiralty 2404, 1676, SC5771; Imray G13, G1; Hellenic Navy Hydrographic Service 231/2, 40

Patra is easy to locate from some distance. Lying just to the south-west of the Rio-Antirio suspension bridge, the sprawling mass of city at the foot of a high mountain range is the first harbour you come to on this stretch of coast. It can also be identified from some distance by the large ferries using the commercial dock.

From all directions, head towards the commercial harbour, maintaining a good look-out at all times as the surrounding waters can be very busy. The marina is situated immediately to the north of this harbour, behind a low-lying breakwater, and will become visible close to. Its entrance is at the southern end of this breakwater. On approach to the marina, contact the harbour authorities on VHF Ch 12 or 16 (Tel: 2610 429130) to request a berth.

At night, the harbour lights merge into the city's lights but should become obvious once you get a bit nearer in. Both ends of the marina's breakwaters are marked with lights: the northern end with an FG and

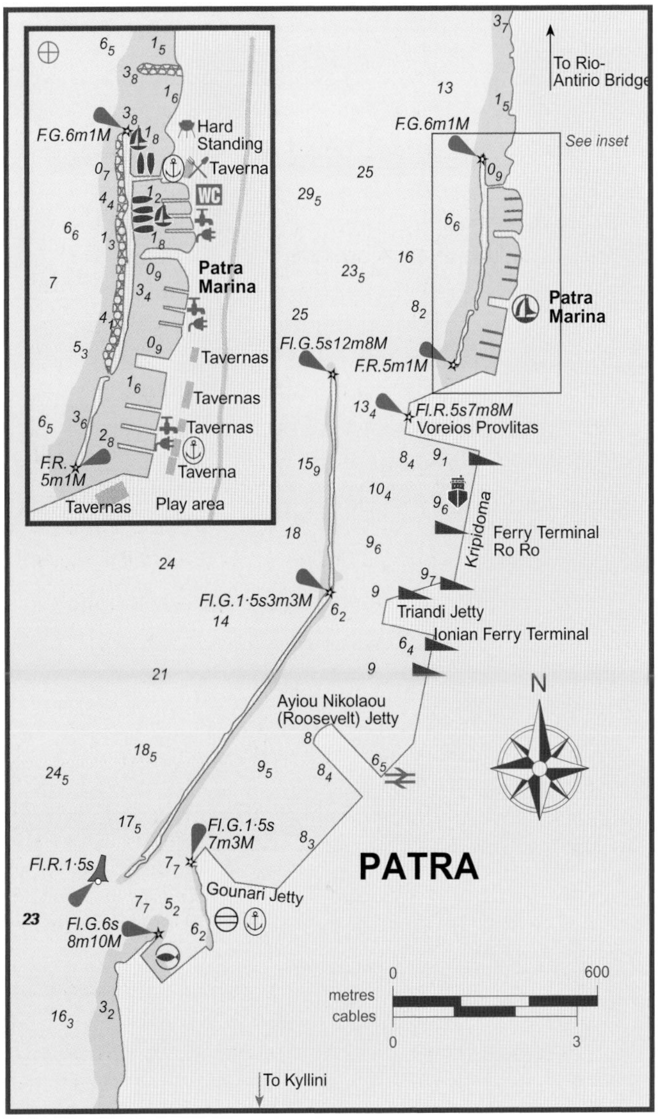

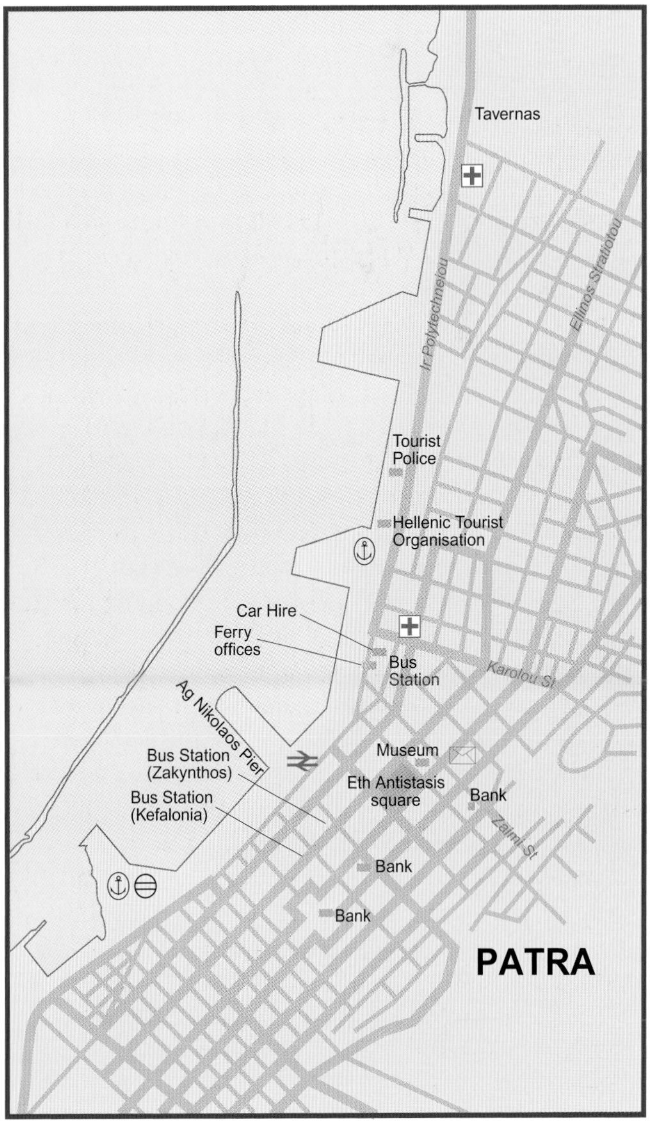

The southern end of the breakwater at the entrance to Patra Marina

the southern end with an FR. South of this you will see Fl G 5s8m8M, which indicates the northern entrance to the commercial harbour and Fl G 1.5s, which identifies its breakwater, one-third of the way along its length. The southern end of the breakwater is marked with a buoy, which is lit Fl R 1.5s, and a light on the quay shows Fl G 6s8m10M.

BERTHING

Patra Marina: Accommodating up to 400 yachts, this is the best place to berth and its entrance lies immediately to the north of the commercial harbour. Lazylines are rigged on all berths and you should go bows- or stern-to wherever directed by the harbour staff. The berths in the northern part of the marina offer the best shelter, but it is shallow off the pontoons so, if possible, berth off the breakwater where depths are around 2m. Deeper draught vessels will need to berth nearer the entrance where there is 3m of water. Shelter here is good, although in a southwesterly the pontoons nearest the entrance are affected by swell.

Berthing fees: You will be charged for a minimum of two nights at Patra Marina, which for an 11m yacht would cost €76.50 (inclusive of water and electricity) during high season.

Commercial harbour: If your vessel is over 20m (66ft) and therefore too big to use the marina, you can occasionally find room in the commercial harbour. Call the harbour authorities on VHF Ch 12 or 16 to request a berth before approach. While the holding here is good, you will be affected by swell from the ferries and ships manoeuvring in and out of the harbour, and it is not an ideal place to berth.

ANCHORING

There is nowhere to anchor within easy reach of Patra.

One of several tavernas at Patra Marina

The marina is a short walk from the centre of Patra. The town is an excellent place to provision

Useful information – Patra

FACILITIES

Water: There are taps on each pontoon.
Fuel: Take jerrycans to the BP and Shell petrol stations on the main road past the marina, or call 6944 528675.
Showers: At the marina; also toilets.
Ice: Ask at the supermarkets.
Laundry: In the centre of Patra, near the Archaeological Museum.
Gas: Bottles sold at larger supermarkets and/or hardware shops.
Shorepower: 220v power points on each pontoon.
Rubbish: Large bins in the marina.
Yacht services/chandlery: Boatyard at the northern end of the marina offers general repairs, including haul-out. Chandler nearby.
Telephone: Several phone boxes on the road past the marina. Phone cards sold at kiosks and the post office. Mobile reception is good.
Internet: Several internet cafes in the centre of Patra.

PROVISIONING

Grocery shops: Large AB supermarket on the main road past the harbour, about 5 minutes away by car. Lots of mini-markets scattered through Patra, also fruit and veg shops.
Bakery: The nearest to the marina is on the main road, on a side road opposite the marina office. Many more bakeries and patisseries in the centre of Patra.
Butcher: Several in Patra, lots on the W side of town.
Banks: Branches of all the major banks here: The National Bank of Greece (Tel: 2610 637280) is on Mezonos St, near the Archaeological Museum; another branch and ATM on Ellinos Stratiotu (Tel: 2610 455305) at the junction with Lemessou St, east of the marina; the Agricultural Bank of Greece (Tel: 2610 277303) is near the Police Station and another on Trion Navrhon, which runs east of the south end of the commercial harbour; Citibank is on Ag Andreou St, which runs parallel to the road past the docks; Emporiki Bank (Tel: 2610 277764) is also on this road and another branch on Ermou St (Tel: 2610 620017), a side road off Ag Andreou St.
Pharmacy: The nearest is on the road behind the marina. More in the centre of Patra.
Post: Post office is to the east of the marina off Ellinos Stratiotou, and another to the east of the main bus station on Zaimi St. The postal service in Patra is good. Stamps are also sold at souvenir shops.
Opening times: Most shops are open 0900-1400 and 1730-2100. Some are open later, as are the tavernas and bars.

EATING OUT

There are several restaurants at the marina, which serve reasonable, if slightly expensive, fare. Others line the road behind the marina. For more choice, head into Patra. Some of the most popular are along Ag Nikolaos, the pedestrianised road to the west of the railway station, about a 5-10-minute walk from the marina. Of these, most serve dishes with an international flavour. Traditional Greek tavernas are less evident in Patra but you may find some in the Old Town, near the castle.

ASHORE

Patra is very good for shopping. As well as several big supermarkets and DIY stores, there are also loads of clothes and shoe shops, book and music stores. For entertainment, there's an eight-screen cinema and a bowling alley near the AB supermarket, on the road past the port. In the summer months plays are put on at the Municipal Theatre, near the centre of Patra. There are also various sites of historic interest: Patra Castle (Tel: 2610 623390), above the city, dates back to the late 6th century and was in almost constant use until the Second World War. It was built on the site of an ancient city and bears the hallmarks of centuries of occupation – Byzantine, Frankish, Venetian and Turkish architecture can all be seen within its walls. It is open to the public six days a week: Tuesday to Friday: 0830-1700; Saturday & Sunday: 0830-1500; admission is free.

Just to the south of the castle is the Roman Odeion (Tel: 2610 276207). It is thought that this was built pre-161, but for centuries it lay buried under a pile of earth. It was rediscovered in 1889 and restored after the Second World War. A beautiful example of Roman architecture, it is occasionally used as a concert and theatre stage during the summer. It is open Tuesday-Sunday, 0830-1500; admission free.

The Archaeological Museum (Tel: 2610 220829), on Mezonos St, houses a number of Roman artefacts found in the Patra area and is open from Tuesday-Sunday, 0830-1500. Admission free.

In February and March, the city comes alive with its annual carnival, a vibrant mix of parades and theatrical displays. Held 10 days before Lent, it is the largest non-profit making carnival in the world. See www.carnivalpatras.gr.

For wine lovers, the Achaia Claus Winery (Tel: 26130 25051), 5 miles (8km) south-east of Patras, may be of interest. Established in 1861, it's one of the largest vintners in Greece. Visitors can take a tour and sample some of its collection. Open daily, 0900-1700.

TRANSPORT

Car hire: Most of the car-hire firms are set back from the commercial docks, near the ferry offices. Hertz (Tel: 2610 220990) is on Karolou St, near the Superfast Ferry Office, open Mon-Sat, 0830-1400 & 1600-2030 and Sun, 0900-1330 & 1730-2030. Avis (Tel: 2610 275547) is nearby and open Mon-Sat, 0900-2100; Sixt (Tel: 2610 275677) on Ag Andreau St, the street behind, open 0800-2100, seven days a week, as is Europcar (Tel: 2610 621360), on the same street (Tel: 2610 273667).
Taxis: Usually some near the commercial port. Others near the main square. Alternatively call Patra Radio on 2610 346700.
Bus: There are three bus stations in Patra, all near the ferry port. The main one is slightly north of the train station on Othonios Amalia. From here you can travel to Athens (3 hours), Kalamata (4 hours) or Corinth (1½ hours). Services to Zakynthos (Tel: 2610 220993) depart from the bus station to the south of the train station, and those to Kefalonia and Lefkada (Tel: 2610 274938) leave from just south of this.
Ferry: From Patra you can travel to Kefalonia, Ithaca, Corfu and Igoumenitsa on inter-island ferries. There are also daily international services to Bari, Brindisi and Arcona in Italy. For booking details and timetables, see www.greekferries.gr. Most of the ferry agents have offices near the port.
Train: From Patra's station, near the ferry port, you can travel to Athens (3½ – 5 hours), Corinth and Kalamata. Timetables on www.ose.gr.
Air travel: The nearest airport is Athens, a 3-hour car journey from Patra. Daily charter and scheduled services to Europe.

OTHER INFORMATION

Local Tel code: 2610.
Port authority: In the main port, near Gate No5. Tel: 2610 341024/341046/341002.
Tourist Police: The police station (Tel: 2610 695000) is on Gounari St, which runs east of the port.
Tourist Office: The Hellenic Tourist Organisation (Tel: 2610 461740) is near Gate 5 of the main port.
Hospital: Tel: 2610 223812/999111/622222/227000).

Chapter six
Kefalonia and Ithaca

The southernmost pair of islands in this part of the Ionian are Kefalonia and Ithaca. Separated by the 2nm-wide Ithaca Strait, they are easy to locate from all directions. They lie due south of Lefkada and to the west of Atokos, a distinctive three-peaked islet that is conspicuous from several miles.

It is generally windier in this part of the Ionian than around Lefkada and the islands to the north-east, but the waters are still reasonably sheltered and offer cracking sailing. Expect the Ithaca Strait and the east coast of Ithaca to be particularly breezy, with gusts whipping off the high mountains and funnelling down between the islands. Don't get too alarmed, though, as it is rarely dangerous.

The main hazard around Kefalonia and Ithaca is commercial shipping. Cargo vessels and ferries on routes between Italy, the north Ionian and the Peloponnese and Eastern Mediterranean pass between Lefkada and Kefalonia and along the east coast of Ithaca. Be vigilant at all times as it is amazing how quickly some of them creep up on you. Wash from the fast-moving craft can also be a problem here.

Kefalonia

Nisos Kefallinia/Cephalonia

Mountainous and densely vegetated, Kefalonia is the largest of the seven major Ionians. Lying immediately to the west of Ithaca, the 350-square-mile (904km²) island is easily recognisable from some distance. Mount Enos, the highest peak in the Ionian, stands on the south-east tip and is conspicuous, as is the mountain range that forms Kefalonia's backbone.

For its size, Kefalonia has comparatively few harbours and anchorages. Its east coast provides most of them and is a popular cruising ground for leisure craft, while the island's ragged western and northern coasts are fairly inhospitable, with long stretches of vertiginous cliffs plunging into deep waters. Yet it's a beautiful island and any forays inland will be very rewarding.

The harbour of Fiskardo, which faces Ithaca on the north-east tip of the island, is a favourite port of call and heaves with yachties in the season. In fact, it's almost reached the stage where you need to get there in the early afternoon to guarantee a berth. Primarily this is because it is the most picturesque place on the island: it's a beautiful and quintessential Greek harbour, although now rather dominated by up-market tavernas and souvenir shops.

Ag Efimia and Sami, to the south, are slightly more traditional, although still revelling in the publicity that came with the filming of Louis de Bernières' *Captain Corelli's Mandolin*. Argostoli, on the south coast, is very much an administrative centre, but with the completion of a new marina near the town should have more to

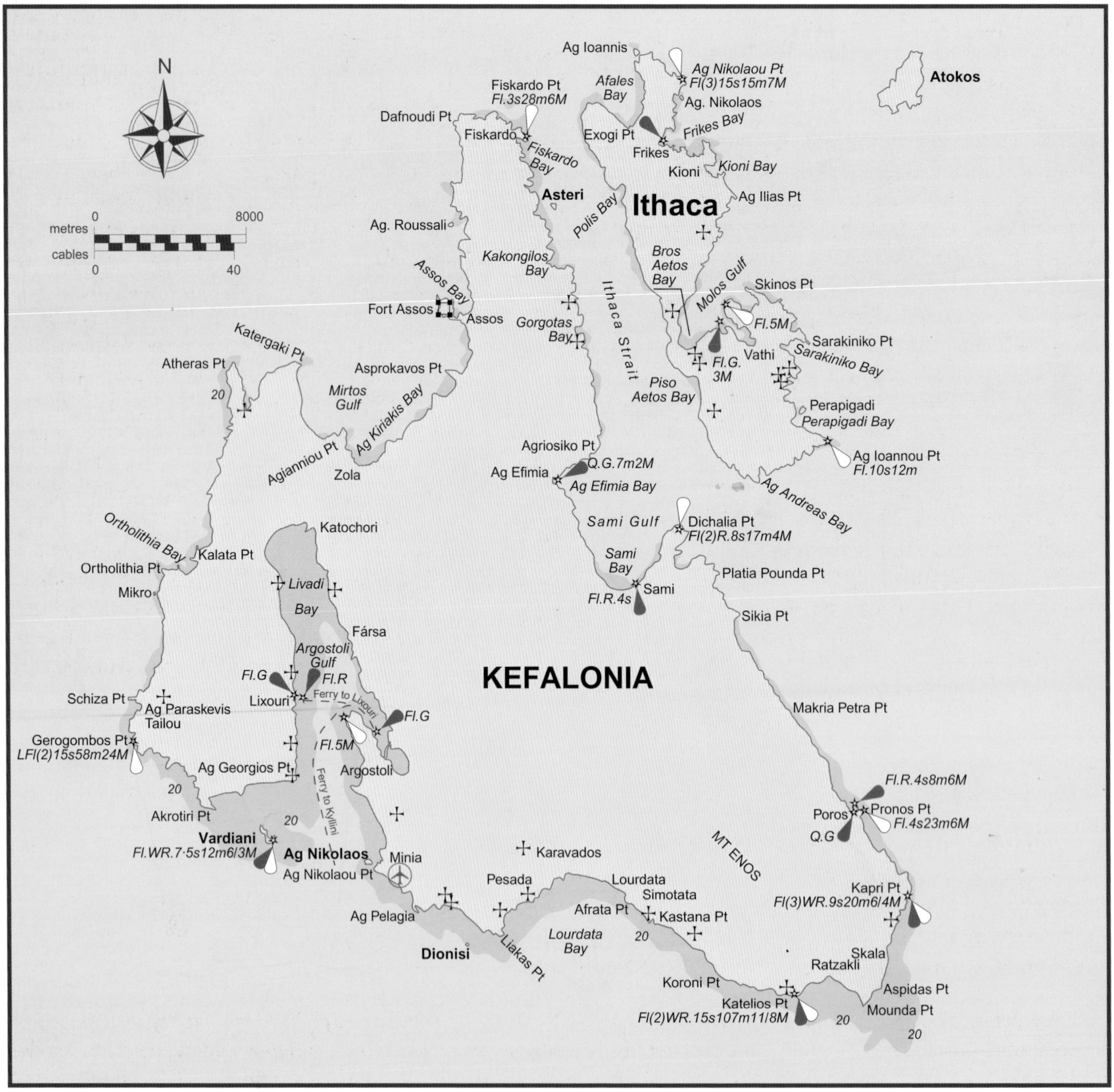

Fiskardo is the prettiest and most traditional village on Kefalonia

offer. Lixouri, on the opposite side of the Argostoli Gulf, is a good, quieter, alternative.

In recent years, Kefalonia has become known for two things: the earthquake of 1953 and the connection with *Captain Corelli's Mandolin*. The film brought with it mass interest in the island, although the Kefalonia it portrays no longer exists. Its Venetian-style architecture and ancient rural villages were destroyed in the 1953 earthquake but rebuilt for the film as a series of sets. These were taken down afterwards and now all that remains is part of a jetty in Gorgotas Bay, on the north-east coast of the island. However, masses of tourists have since visited the island on the Captain Corelli trail, and day-tripper boats are still taking people on special tours.

Of all the islands in this part of the Ionian, Kefalonia was the worst hit in the 1953 earthquake. Measuring 7.3 on the Richter Scale, it razed about 80 per cent of the island and only Fiskardo survived. Most of the major towns and villages have since been rebuilt, but few display their original architecture, which was replaced with low-lying modern buildings. These are beginning to mature now but they still give parts of the island quite a contemporary feel.

Despite this, Kefalonia is thought to be one of the earliest inhabited islands in the Mediterranean. Archaeologists have discovered evidence of human life that dates to 50,000BC and think it has been inhabited since the 11th century BC. Since then, it too has seen a turbulent past. During the Bronze Age the island was divided into four semi-autonomous city-states and saw various allegiances, including those with the Corinthians and the Athenians. Under the Romans, it became a naval base but was later besieged by pirate attack. It flourished under Byzantine and Venetian occupation, and in between was captured by the Normans under the command of Robert Guiscard.

In the 15th century, Kefalonia alternated between Venetian and Turkish rule and started to command an impressive trading position. Indeed between the 17th and 19th centuries it is said to have produced over 10,000 tons of raisins annually. The French and the British have also controlled and influenced the island, but it returned to Greek ownership in 1864.

Kefalonia is now known for its excellent wines and unadulterated countryside of pine-covered mountains, sprawling vineyards and olive groves. It offers a plethora of anchorages and, although parts have been developed to meet the demands of tourism, much is unspoilt, with a quiet and slow pace of life.

Fiskardo

Fiskardho, Fiscardo

Approach to Fiskardo from North: 38°29'.00N 20°35'.58E

Fiskardo Harbour: 38°27'.72N 20°34'.71E

Entrance to Fiskardo Bay: 38°27'.55N 20°34'.96E

Anchorage in cypress-lined bay: 38°27'.18N 20°34'.85E

Architecturally, Fiskardo is the most interesting town on Kefalonia, purely because, unlike the rest of the island, so much of it is original. It is thought to sit on a different type of bedrock, with shock-absorbing qualities that saved it from the devastating effects of the 1953 earthquake, which razed much of the island and

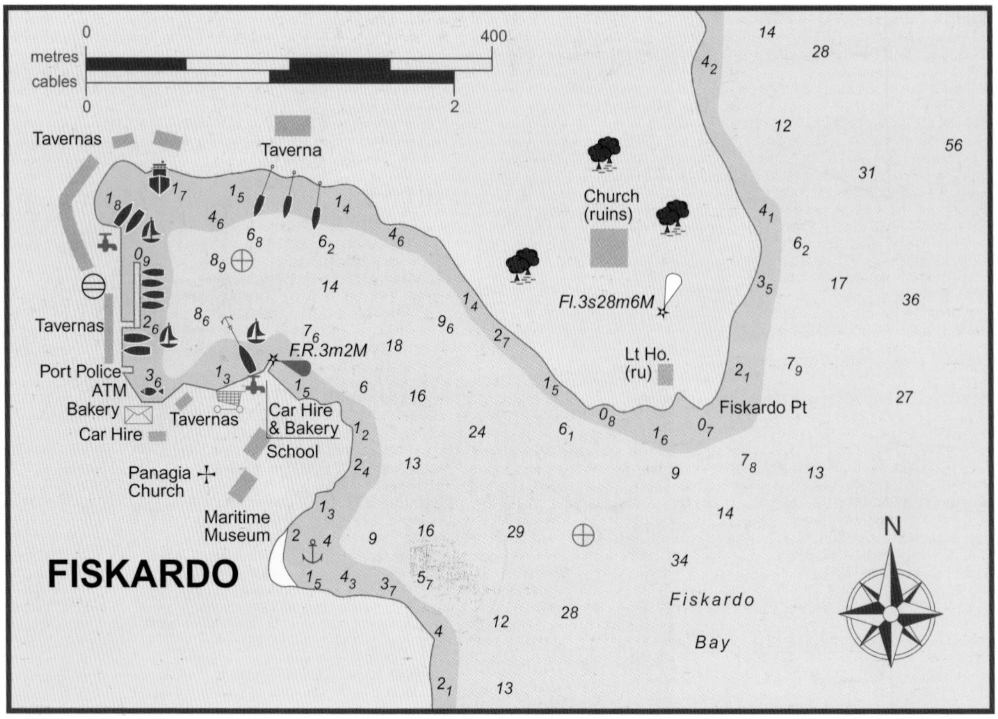

the surrounding area.

Fiskardo's architecture is principally Venetian and similar in style to that of Gaios on Paxos. Its colour-washed houses and wrought-iron balconies draped in swathes of colourful flowers make it a popular and much photographed destination, where prices have escalated. It's not cheap to eat out here and, in season and unlike a lot of other traditional villages in the Ionian, tourists often outnumber locals.

Fiskardo has gained itself an 'upmarket' and cosmopolitan reputation, and in the summer months it can be positively heaving. If you want to spend the night here you need to arrive early in order to guarantee a berth. Yet it's a really lovely place to visit and, with reasonable shelter and all facilities within close reach, plus good transport links around the island and to Lefkada and Ithaca, it's a perfect base from which to explore.

Fiskardo derives its name from the Norman adventurer Robert Guiscard (1015-1085) who campaigned with his brother, Roger I of Sicily, against the Byzantine Greeks in Italy. After capturing Corfu and much of western Greece, it is said he turned his attention to Kefalonia and was so enamoured with Fiskardo that he decided to settle there. Just a year later he died of a fever.

NAVIGATION

Charts: Admiralty 203, 189, SC5771; Imray G121, G12; Hellenic Navy Hydrographic Service 036, 030

Fiskardo is easy to identify from the south: head north up the Ithaca Strait, the channel between Kefalonia and Ithaca, and Fiskardo is the last village you come to before reaching the north coast of the island. On approach from this direction, the harbour and houses of Fiskardo can be seen easily from some distance.

From the north, however, Fiskardo is hard to identify until within close proximity. If approaching from Lefkada or Meganisi, head for the Ithaca Strait or, if you cannot see this, just to the west of Ithaca. You should keep a good look-out when crossing the Kefalonia Strait as it is usually very busy with traffic. This is the main route between Italy and the northern

Fiskardo Bay on the north-east tip of Kefalonia

Yachts berth stern- and bows-to the quay at Fiskardo. Crossed anchors and cramped berths are common features at certain times of the season

Ionian and ports to the south such as Patra and Kyllini, so ferries and cargo ships are constantly plying this channel. It is usually busy with yachts too.

Once level with the top of Ithaca, a group of houses on the north coast of Kefalonia will become obvious. They are visible from all directions and lie just to the north of Fiskardo. Immediately to the south of the houses you'll see a lighthouse (Fl 3s 28m6M) on Fiskardo Pt. The harbour is just to the west of this headland.

It's fairly shallow around Fiskardo Pt, so don't cut in too closely. On entering the bay, watch out for the ferry, *Captain Aristidis*, which turns around in the harbour and uses the quay in the north-west corner.

BERTHING

Space is often at a premium in Fiskardo Harbour, particularly in the summer months; but if you get there early you will probably find somewhere to squeeze in. Most yachts berth either bows- or stern-to the town quay, on the southern and western sides of the harbour and, if there's room, you can also use the floating pontoon. The floating pontoon has the benefit of water and electricity points but the holding off it is not good. The seabed is a mixture of sand, mud and weed, and you should make sure your anchor is well dug in before leaving your boat unattended. It is also in a more exposed position. In a southerly, when the winds funnel up the Ithaca Strait and into Fiskardo Bay, the chop can get quite unpleasant and yachts often drag when berthed here.

If there is any hint of a southerly, particularly a strong one, try to berth on the south side of the harbour and, if this is not possible, consider going elsewhere, maybe

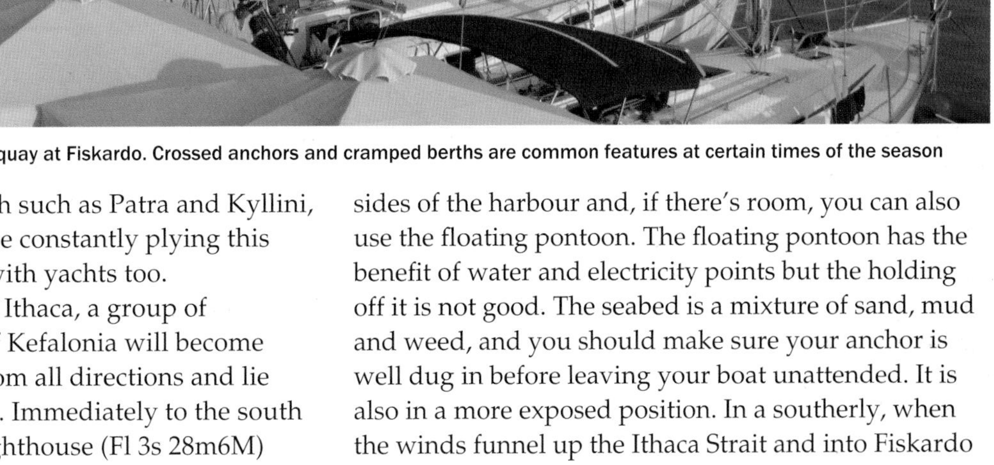

Two lighthouses on Fiskardo Pt help identify the bay

even to one of the bays on the west coast of Ithaca. At the very least, row a kedge out for extra protection.

The south-west corner of the harbour is reserved for local boats, and day-trip boats berth at one end of the floating pontoon, in an area marked with yellow and black stripes. These come and go several times a day, so always keep clear. Crossed anchors can be a problem in Fiskardo, due to the harbour's layout, so check where your neighbour's is before dropping your own.

Berthing fees: A 30ft (9.1m) yacht at Fiskardo costs around €2.93 per night. Pay at the Port Police office.

ANCHORING

When Fiskardo gets really popular in peak season, you will often find yachts anchored off the northern shore of the bay, from just to the east of the ferry quay to Fiskardo Pt. Take a long line ashore to prevent swinging and make sure your anchor digs in well. In a northerly the anchorage is protected, but in a southerly it is exposed and you should consider finding an alternative.

One anchorage close to Fiskardo is in the bay just to the south of the harbour. Although not very sheltered, it's a very pleasant spot for lunch and the bay is within easy walking or dinghying distance of the village.

Immediately to the south of this is a cypress-lined bay with a little beach at its far end. It's about a 30-minute walk to Fiskardo and well protected. There's also a cave in the bay, which you can go into, but don't forget a torch. The water is a beautiful colour as you enter the cave; you can't go in very far but it's worth a visit.

Useful information – Fiskardo

FACILITIES

Water: Several hoses along the waterfront, which reach everywhere. Water points near Captain's Cabin and Tassias taverna. On the floating pontoon it is metered and fees must be paid to either the Port Police or one of the tavernas. There's usually a notice on the pontoon to indicate where to pay. Be aware though that filling up with water here is both expensive and slow.

Fuel: Take jerrycans to the nearby Eko petrol station. If you need 100 litres or more, a local mini-tanker will deliver. Tel: 6972 216 469.

Showers: Several tavernas offer showers for a charge of €4: Theodoras, Tassias and Elli's (on the far side of the bay). Beware of showering on the boat. People have been fined for too much soap polluting the harbour.

Ice: From Theodoras taverna and the supermarkets.

Gas: Gas bottle exchange at the supermarkets.

Shorepower: Metered electricity points on the floating pontoon. Pay either the Port Police or one of the tavernas. A notice on the pontoon indicates where to pay.

Rubbish: Large rubbish bins on the outskirts of the village, up past Pama Travel and past the ferry quay.

Yacht services/chandlery: Marine engineer, Alekos Kavadias (Tel: 26740 41407; VHF Ch72).

Telephone: Several phone boxes on the quay. Phone cards are available at Theodoras and the supermarkets. Mobile reception here is good.

Fax: Ask at Nautilus travel agency, on the quay.

Internet: At Pama Car Hire: 1-10 minutes, €2; 10-25 mins, €3, 25-40 mins, €4.50, 40-60 mins, €6. Minimum charge €2.30c per printed sheet. Nautilus Travel Agency also has internet access.

PROVISIONING

Grocery shops: Three supermarkets in Fiskardo, all well stocked. The one next to Captain's Cabin has fresh meat. Open until late.

Bakery: Two: one next to Pama Travel, another behind Theodora's taverna.

Butcher: No but fresh meat is available from the supermarket next to Captain's Cabin. The other supermarkets have a limited selection.

Banks: A branch of the Alpha Bank (Tel: 26740 41361) and ATM is to the right of Theodora's. Monday-Friday, 0900-1400. There is a second ATM on the side of the supermarket next to Irida's. Travel agencies also offer currency exchange.

Pharmacy: The nearest is in Vasilikiades, about 8 miles S of Fiskardo. However, all supermarkets sell basic first-aid items.

Post: Post Office behind Lagoudera restaurant. Open Mon-Fri, 0800-1400.

Other shops: Several souvenir, trinket and clothes shops along the quay, and peak season there are usually several street stalls along the waterfront. Most are open between 0900-1400 and 1730 until 2200 or later.

EATING OUT

The choice is extensive in Fiskardo. Most of the tavernas and cafés line the harbour, with eating areas overlooking the water; there are also some good places to be found in a quieter setting towards the back of the village, so it pays to wander around before making your decision.

Eating out can be expensive here compared with other villages in the Ionian. It's a very popular destination, and a lovely one, so restaurants can afford to charge what they want and still attract business. Be prepared to pay a little extra.

Captain's Cabin, at the south-east corner of the harbour, is very popular with sailors, particularly flotillas, and is usually bustling until the early hours. Its menu includes several Kefalonian specialities and the food is good. Lagoudera, near the square, can be recommended for its grilled dishes and reasonable prices. Nefeli's restaurant, towards the north of the harbour, is one of the most expensive in the village but its menu is extensive and you are usually guaranteed a delicious meal.

For drinks and lighter snacks, try Café Tselenti, just off the quay, which has a great atmosphere in the evenings and jazz music is regularly played. Theodora's café and cocktail bar is on the W side of the harbour and serves excellent breakfasts and cocktails. Up past Theodora's is a café that sells very exotic, highly recommended ice-creams.

ASHORE

There's a good little museum next to the church. Set up to promote environmental awareness and ecological and marine research, Fiskardo's Nautical & Environmental Club (FNEC) and the Ionian Sea Research Centre are manned by volunteers and involved in a number of studies and research programmes. The museum houses an interesting collection of exhibits relating to the environment and wildlife to be found on and near Kefalonia. Open daily during the summer, 1000-1800. FNEC also runs PADI diving courses. For details, ring 26740 41081.

If you want to stretch your legs, wander around the harbour to Fiskardo Pt and the Venetian lighthouse in front of the present one. There are also ruins of a Norman church on the

Useful information – Fiskardo

headland behind and the views across to Ithaca are lovely.

From Fiskardo you are within easy driving distance of the beautiful port of Assos, on the north-west coast (see p215). You can also visit Mirtos Beach, one of the most famous sandy beaches on Kefalonia, the Drongarati Caves and the Melissani Lake (see p205).

TRANSPORT

Car hire: Pama Travel (Tel: 26740 41033) in the south-east corner of the bay. Prices from €49-€120 per day, depending on size of car. Litsos Car & Motorbike Hire (Tel: 26740 41401), in the centre of Fiskardo. Nautilus Travel Agency on the western side of the harbour can also arrange car hire.

Taxis: In the square in the centre of Fiskardo.

Bus: Bus stop above the town near the car park. Two a day to Argostoli, journey time 1¾ hours.

Ferry: Car and passenger services run daily from Fiskardo to Nidri and Vasiliki on Lefkada and Sami on Ithaca during peak season. Timetables change regularly so check with one of the travel agents in Fiskardo.

Air travel: Kefalonia's airport (Tel: 26710 29900) is 5½ miles (9km) south of Argostoli, about 1½-hours' drive from Fiskardo. Although there is a bus service to Argostoli from Fiskardo there is nothing between Argostoli and the airport, so you will have to arrange a taxi. Daily flights to Athens (journey time 1 hour) and some international services peak season.

OTHER INFORMATION

Local Tel code: 26740.

Port Police: Above Alpha Bank on the waterfront.

Police: In the centre of Fiskardo. Tel: 26740 41400.

Doctor: The nearest is at Vasilikiades, about 8 miles south of Fiskardo.

Dentist: No but several in Argostoli. See p212.

Hospital: The nearest is in Argostoli: Tel: 26710 24641.

If there is no room to berth off the town quay, you can anchor off the rocks in Fiskardo Bay, taking a line ashore

Gorgotas Bay

Ormos Sarakiniko, Captain Corelli's Bay

Entrance to Gorgotas Bay: 38°21'.87N 20°37'.03E

Charts: Admiralty 203, 189, SC5771; Imray G121, G12, G1; Hellenic Navy Hydrographic Service 030, 21

The olive, cypress and oak-lined Gorgotas Bay, on Kefalonia's east coast, 6nm south of Fiskardo, is a charming lunch-time anchorage. Although the beach is just a short sandy strip, it's a good place for a swim or a quiet interlude before heading for your evening port. However, you may not get it to yourself. In recent years, the film of *Captain Corelli's Mandolin* has made this rather unlikely bay a popular spot with day-trippers, who have flocked to see the scant remains of a jetty built for the film, where Nicholas Cage and Penelope Cruz stood wrapped in each other's arms. Nothing else from the film remains on the island, but it is still popular with the tourists.

The jetty in Gorgotas Bay, built for the film of *Captain Corelli's Mandolin*

If you do find yourself alone in the bay, then it's a tranquil spot. However, it offers minimal shelter, so should only be considered in settled conditions and in daytime. Anchor in 8m or less on mud and sand.

Agia Efimia

Ayia Efimia, Agios Eufimia

Off Agia Efimia's outer mole: 38°18'.09N 20°36'.07E
Approach to Agia Efimia: 38°18'.04N 20°37'.43E

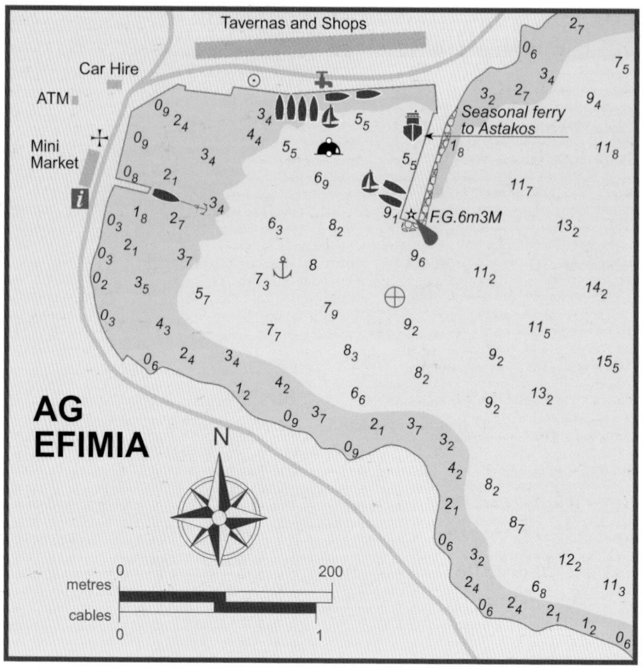

Agia Efimia stands on the north coast of the Sami Gulf, 3½nm north of Sami and level with the south of Ithaca. It's a small, slightly understated little town that was once the major ferry port on Kefalonia. However, the 1953 earthquake demolished much of it, and little was rebuilt after it was decided that Sami would make a better port. Today a decent handful of tavernas and shops line the waterfront and cater for the passing trade. The quay offers reasonable protection, although it can get quite breezy and rolly here, particularly in the late afternoons and when a southerly swell is pushed into the bay.

NAVIGATION

Charts: Admiralty 203, 189, SC5771; Imray G121, G12; Hellenic Navy Hydrographic Service 036, 30

The Sami Gulf is unmistakable from all directions. It's like a large hole in the side of Kefalonia and, lying opposite the southern tip of Ithaca, is easy enough to find. Agia Efimia itself lies tucked up in a bay in the gulf's north-west corner and is hidden on approach from the north but visible once past Agriosiko Pt. Passage through the Ithaca Strait from Fiskardo to Agia Efimia is straightforward, although it can get quite gusty, especially in the afternoons when the wind picks up and is funnelled along the channel.

From Ag Andreas Pt, on the south coast of Ithaca, Agia Efimia couldn't be easier to find. Just head east for about 6nm. From the south coast of Kefalonia, head north up the island's east coast as far as Dichalia Pt. Agia Efimia is about 3½nm east-north-east of this headland.

Strong and gusty northwesterlies often blow directly out of Agia Efimia in the afternoons. If you intend to sail into the bay, be prepared as you may be headed and need to drop sails and motor the last bit.

BERTHING

Yachts should berth on the town quay, on the north coast of Agia Efimia Bay, immediately to the west of the mole. The quay here is very high, so most yachts of less than 40ft (12m) LOA should go bows-to, rather than stern-to, to make getting on and off easier. If the harbour is not too busy, you can go side-to the quay but make sure you leave plenty of fenders out as it can get very choppy when the wind is gusting from the north-west. Occasionally boats berth stern-to the mole, but only do this if there is lots of space available, as it is used by a

Agia Efimia was once the island's main ferry port. It now offers reasonable shelter to passing yachts

ferry and several large day-trip boats. The yellow and black-striped area on the mole is reserved for the Port Police who, if they turn up, will ask you for harbour dues (€2.93 per night for a 30ft yacht).

Strong northwesterly winds often blow across the harbour at Agia Efimia, so lay your anchor upwind and let out plenty of scope. The bottom is weed on mud, so ensure your anchor digs in well. Watch out for crossed anchors, as the bay is deep and diving in to untangle them can be unpleasant.

The quay at Agia Efimia is quite high, so yachts often berth alongside to make getting ashore easier

ANCHORING

If the town quay is full, but you want to take advantage of Agia Efimia's facilities, you can free-swing to your anchor in the middle of the bay, to the south-west of the mole. It's relatively deep here – 5-8m – so let out plenty of scope and dig your anchor in well.

An alternative daytime anchorage lies immediately to the north of Agia Efimia in a small cove just to the south of Agriosiko Pt. Shelter is reasonable here, although not for an overnight stay as it is exposed in a southerly.

Anchoring is prohibited in the bay just to the north of this (38°20′.93N 20°37′.61E) as there are underwater electricity cables.

Useful information – Agia Efimia

FACILITIES

Water: A couple of water points on the quay, plus another on the mole. €5 per fill, which you pay to the woman in the white kiosk half way along the northern quay. She comes round morning and evening to unlock the taps.
Fuel: No but a mini-tanker will deliver from Sami. Tel: 26740 22005; Mobile: 69776 62562. El Petrol & Diesel for boats (Tel: 26710 22282/Mobile: 69727 10800) should also deliver.
Showers: Good showers behind Captain Corelli's restaurant. Open 0800-1200 & 1700-2100, price €2.50. Finikas, to the east, also has showers, as does Kosta's Tourist Shop.
Ice: Ask at the tavernas or in the supermarkets.
Gas: Bottle exchange at the supermarkets.
Shorepower: On the quay.
Rubbish: Bins on the quayside.
Telephone: Several phone boxes on the quay. Phonecards are sold at the kiosk near Captain Corelli's Restaurant and at the newsagent. Mobile reception in Agia Efimia is good.

PROVISIONING

Grocery shops: Well-stocked supermarket at the western end of the bay, near Gialos café-bar. There are a couple of other small mini-markets in the town.
Bakery: On the road off the quay.
Butcher: At the western end of the bay, near the currency exchange shop.
Banks: The nearest bank is at Sami, about 3½nm from Agia Efimia. Currency exchange office on the waterfront near the chemist; Kosta's Tourist Shop also offers currency exchange.
Pharmacy: On the waterfront at the western side of the bay.
Post: Post office next to Captain Corelli's Restaurant. Open 0800-1400. Also has post box. The service on Kefalonia is good.
Other shops: Agia Efimia boasts one of the most impressive tourist gift shops in Europe. Kosta's Tourist Shop sells everything you never knew you wanted and advertises under the slogan, 'Gift shop extraordinaire – If we don't sell it, nobody does!' So if you're looking for a painted pottery seal, flip-flops that don't match or an out-of-date wall calendar, this is the place to visit. There is also a newsagent, a kiosk and several other gift shops in the town.
Opening times: Most shops open between 0900-1400 and 1730-2100.

EATING OUT

Agia Efimia may be a relatively small harbour but the competition between tavernas is fierce and wherever you eat, you'll get a very good meal at a reasonable price. At the western end of the harbour, you'll find Gialos (Tel: 26740 61028), a café-bar. Next door is Captain Corelli's (Tel: 26740 61666), a taverna that was renamed after the making of the film, when many of the cast and crew ate there. Pictures of the film and its stars now adorn the walls. To the east of this, beyond the post office, is Finikas (Tel: 26740 61507), a very good restaurant and café-bar with an extensive international menu for breakfast, lunch and dinner. To Steki (Tel: 26740 61025) is good for fish and To Perasma (Tel: 26740 61990), next door, for grilled foods.

A five-minute walk along the coast from Agia Efimia is the Paradise Beach Taverna (Paradissenia Akti, Tel: 26740 61392), a popular spot with the locals and always very busy.

ASHORE

Agia Efimia is a good place to hire a car in order to explore the rest of the island. The north coast of Kefalonia is within easy driving distance and there

Useful information – Agia Efimia

are some interesting sites within close proximity, such as Assos (see p215), Mirtos beach, the Drongarati Caves and the Melissani Lake (see p205). The north side of the bay is also suitable for swimming, and the Aquatic World Diving Club (Tel: 26740 62006) in the town runs a range of diving courses for all abilities.

TRANSPORT

Car hire: CaRent (Tel: 26740 61591) at the western side of the bay; Scooteraki (Tel: 26740 62003), Gerolimatos Travel (Tel: 26740 61036).
Taxis: Taxi rank on the quay.
Bus: Daily service to Argostoli, Fiskardo and Sami in peak season.
Ferry: In summer there is a daily service from Agia Efimia to Astakos on the mainland. Regular services to Lefkada and Ithaca operate from Fiskardo (see p201) and from Sami (3½nm to the south) you can travel to Argostoli or Vathy on Ithaca.
Air travel: Kefalonia's airport (Tel: 26710 29900) is 5½ miles (9km) south of Argostoli, 1 hour's drive from Agia Efimia. International and domestic services several times a week during peak season.

OTHER INFORMATION

Local Tel code: 26740.
Port authority: There is an office on the quay (Tel: 26740 22456), usually only manned in the summer.
Tourist Information Centre: 26740 61775.
Police: Tel: 26740 61204.
Doctor: No but there is a medical centre in Sami (Tel: 26740 22222).
Dentist: No but several in Argostoli. See p212.
Hospital: The nearest hospital is in Argostoli (Tel: 26710 24641); medical centre in Sami (Tel: 26740 22222).

The town quay is close to tavernas, showers and shops

Sami

Approach to Sami from the N: 38°16'.21N 20°38'.20E
Approach to Sami from Dichalia Point: 38°17'.14N 20°40'.61E
Entrance to Sami Harbour: 38°15'.24N 20°38'.77E

Sami is a fairly nondescript port on Kefalonia's east coast, 3½nm south of Ag Efimia. It's a ferry port, serving Astakos and Kyllini on the mainland and the island of Ithaca, so can get quite busy with tourists passing through. However, the harbour itself remains relatively quiet. Charter flotillas tend to head for Agia Efimia or Fiskardo so there is usually plenty of room in the harbour. It offers reasonable shelter but is exposed if a northwesterly swell builds up.

Ashore you'll find all the amenities you require and some of the island's most interesting tourist sites are within easy reach.

NAVIGATION

Charts: Admiralty 203, 189, SC5771; Imray G121, G12; Hellenic Navy Hydrographic Service 036, 030

Sami is situated in the southern corner of the Sami Gulf. From Fiskardo, head south along the Ithaca Strait for about 13nm. The town and harbour of Sami are conspicuous from this direction and the approach straightforward, although in the afternoons it can get quite windy in the Ithaca Strait.

From the south, Sami remains hidden until you have rounded Dichalia Pt, after which it is easy to spot. Maintain a good look-out within the Sami Gulf as ferries regularly travel between Sami and harbours on Ithaca and mainland Greece.

BERTHING

Local fishing and day-trip boats use the quay on the south-east side of the harbour, so yachts are advised to berth stern- or bows-to the pontoon on the western side. Sami Harbour rarely gets full and not many charter flotillas come in here, so you can sometimes berth alongside the northern breakwater. However, bigger boats tend to use this area, so it is not always possible.

There is usually quite a bit of swell in the harbour, mostly caused by the prevailing northwesterlies which send it across the bay and in through the entrance. Channels cut into the bottom of the pontoon intensify

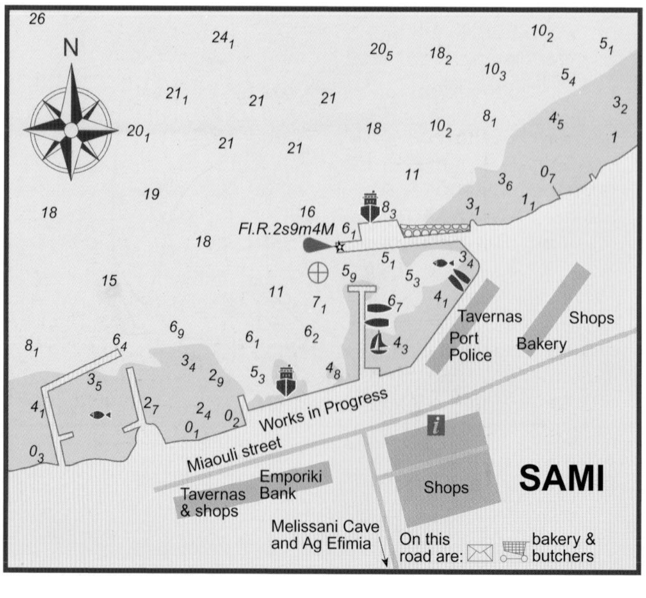

The entrance to Sami's harbour

this as the swell is funnelled through them and into the harbour. At times it can be quite uncomfortable and rolly when berthed on the pontoon, so don't get too close to it and leave plenty of fenders out. If conditions are settled, though, most of this swell will ease in the evening. The holding is generally good, although you should let out plenty of scope to allow for the swell.

Alternatively you may be able to find space in a second harbour that has been built to the west of Sami. This is mainly used by local fishing boats, but yachts under 40ft (12m) in length are able to berth alongside the northern quay. Note that in 2007 work was in progress on the ferry quay between the two harbours.

ANCHORING

The nearest anchorage to Sami is about 4nm away at Andisamos Bay, a large bay to the east of Dichalia Pt (Akra Dhikhália). Shelter here is reasonable from all directions, although occasionally a swell does get pushed in with the prevailing winds.

Agios Andreas Bay, on the south coast of Ithaca, is a good lunch-time anchorage, approximately 4nm from Sami. See p230.

Useful information – Sami

FACILITIES

Water: Tap on the quay near the fishing boats. Water also available in the E harbour, where taps are positioned under manhole covers. Note that not all of them work.
Fuel: Avin fuel station next to Dimoulas supermarket. Fuel can be delivered to the harbour: Elinoil (Tel: 26740 22005/Mobile: 69776 62562); El Petrol & Diesel for Boats (Tel: 26710 22282/Mobile: 69727 10800).
Ice: Ask at the tavernas.
Gas: Bottle exchange at the supermarkets.
Rubbish: Bins on the quay.
Telephone: On the quay.

PROVISIONING

Grocery shops: Several grocery shops and plenty of supermarkets in Sami. You'll find Sami Supermarket near the post office, Dimoulas supermarket near the Avin petrol station and two more along the main road through the town.
Bakery: Two bakeries on main road out of Sami. Another one, Meare di Midi, behind the Port Police.
Butcher: Several in the town. The nearest to the quay is next to Batistatos rent-a-car.
Banks: Emporiki bank and ATM (Tel: 26740 22237) is on Miaouli St, the road past the quay. Eurobank ATM at Marketou Travel (Tel: 26740 22055), on the same road. Several of the travel agents in Sami offer currency exchange.
Pharmacy: On main street, near the post office.
Post: Post office on the main street, near the pharmacy. The postal service on Kefalonia is good.
Opening times: Most shops are open 0900-1400 and 1730-2030, but times vary. The supermarkets are usually open later.

EATING OUT

The majority of the tavernas and cafés in Sami are along the street that runs past the quay. There is nothing particularly memorable but most places serve basic Greek or international cuisine. For light snacks or pizza, try the Riviera Café and Pizzeria (Tel: 26740 23223), Captain Jimmy (Tel: 26740 22059) or Captain Corelli's Café (Tel: 26740 22128). For a larger meal, try the Takatakaman grill-house, the Lighthouse fish restaurant or Dolphins Restaurant (Tel: 26740 22008).

ASHORE

The Melissani Caves, two miles inland of Sami, are worth a visit. They're one of the most spectacular groups of caves in this part of Greece and feature a very impressive subterranean lake. Visit around noon on a sunny day, as the roof of one of the two caves has collapsed, leaving it open to the sky; the colour of the water when the sun hits it is the most incredible shade of ultramarine. There are usually small boats on the lake, with guides who will give you a short tour of the caves (€5 for adults and €2.50 for children between 6-12 years of age). In season, it is open 0900-1900, seven days a week.

The Melissani Caves are part of a larger network extending to the other side of Kefalonia. In 1959, three scientists discovered this when they poured uranine dye in the swallow holes at Katavothres (see p212). Two weeks later, it filtered into the brackish waters of the Melissani Lake.

To the SW of Sami is Drongarati Cave. Stalactites and stalagmites dominate this cave network and the Chamber of Exaltation, a semi-circular cave with good acoustics, is sometimes used as a concert hall for up to 500 people. Open all year round, 0900-2030, entry costs around €4.

Useful information – Sami

TRANSPORT

Car hire: Batistatos Rent a car (Tel: 26740 22631), is opposite the Port Police at the far end of the quay. Island Car Rental (26740 23084) is on Miaouli St, the road past the quay.
Taxis: Taxi rank on the quay and another near the Customs and Port Police.
Bus: Twice daily services between Sami and Argostoli, and in summer between Sami and Fiskardo. The bus station (Tel: 26740 23370) is near the quay.
Ferry: Services from Vathy and Piso Aetos on Ithaca and Astakos, Patra and Kyllini on the mainland call at Sami daily during peak season. Visit www.greekferries.gr for timetables as well as booking details.
Air travel: Kefalonia Airport (Tel: 26710 29900) is 5½ miles (9km) S of Argostoli (a ¾-hour journey from Sami by car). There are services to and from Athens and European countries several times a week in season.

OTHER INFORMATION

Local Tel code: 26740.
Port authority: The Port Police office (Tel: 26740 22031) is situated on the east side of the quay.
Police: The police station (Tel: 26740 22100) is beyond the town hall.
Dentist: Several in Argostoli. See p212.
Hospital: There is a health centre (Tel: 26740 22222/22807) near the town centre and a hospital in Argostoli (Tel: 26710 24641), ¾-hr away by car.

Poros Porou

To the north-east of Poros Harbour:
38°09'.24N 20°48'.16E

Poros, on the south-east coast of Kefalonia, is one of the island's most significant ports. It's the main link between Kefalonia, Ithaca and the mainland and an increasingly popular resort with holidaying tourists. Its location, towards the bottom of the island, means that it is not so popular with cruising yachts, although as somewhere to stop when heading north or south it serves very well. Regular ferry movement during the day does make the harbour fairly noisy and there is often quite a bit of swell around. Nevertheless, it's a good place to victual or to use as a base to explore the rest of the island by car.

The town itself sits in a very picturesque location, surrounded by steep mountainsides and lush vegetation. It is relatively modern, having been substantially rebuilt after the 1953 earthquake. However, it is thought that there has been a settlement here since 10,000BC and that Poros was the main port of Proni, one of Kefalonia's four regions at the time.

NAVIGATION

Charts: Admiralty 203, 189, SC5771; Imray G121, G12, G1; Hellenic Navy Hydrographic Service 036, 030

From the bottom end of the Ithaca Channel, head south-east for about 10nm. Poros town is identifiable from some distance and lies immediately to the west of Pronos Pt (Ak Sarakinato). The harbour is just beyond the town.

If approaching from the south coast of Kefalonia, keep well offshore around Mounda Pt where shallows extend for some distance to the south and east. Poros is hidden until you have rounded Pronos Pt, although there are a few conspicuous houses on this headland. Inside the harbour, watch out for traffic as the ferry quay is just to the south of the breakwater.

BERTHING

Currently, visitors to Poros should berth stern- or bows-to the quay in the south-west corner of Poros harbour, to the south of the ferry terminal, wherever there is room. Although the small inner harbour to the west of the quay is deep enough to take yachts, it is reserved for local fishing boats. Keep well clear of the ferry quay, too, and watch out for a warp that is occasionally run across the harbour from the anchored vessel to a large buoy to the north of the fishing harbour's breakwater.

The harbour offers reasonable shelter from the south but swell from the regular car ferries can be a problem.

Yachts share Poros' harbour with car ferries that travel between Kefalonia and the mainland

Berth well off the quay and leave plenty of fenders out as protection. The holding on mud is good and the depths are between 2-4m.

Works are currently in progress in the harbour, with a second breakwater (possibly for fishing boats) and an extension being added on the SE side. The intention is for this to become the new docking area for the ferry, therefore freeing up the rest of the harbour for more visiting yachts. Work should be completed by the summer of 2007.

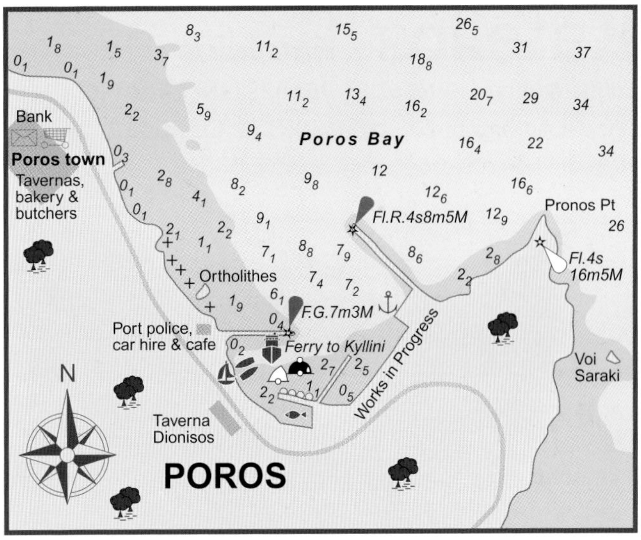

ANCHORING

There is nowhere to anchor near Poros. Either head to Andisamos Bay (see p205), 10nm to the north-west, or Perapigadi (see p230 for details) on the south-east coast of Ithaca.

Useful information – Poros

FACILITIES

Water: Water points and hoses to the east of the ferry quay. Ask at the Port Office for the taps to be unlocked.
Fuel: Take a taxi to the Avin petrol station on the outskirts of town.
Showers: Available at Taverna Dionisos (€2), near the quay.
Ice: Ask at Taverna Dionisos (€1.50). For a delivery, call Tel 26740 72574.
Gas: Taverna Dionisos has a gas bottle exchange: 2kg bottle, €8; 3kg bottle, €11.
Rubbish: Small rubbish bins on the quay.
Telephone: Telephone and fax service at Poros Bay Hotel, behind the quay. Several phone boxes on the quay and a couple more in Poros itself.
Internet: Mythos Internet Café on Poros's main street. €3 per hour.

PROVISIONING

There are some shops near the quay, but most of them are in Poros itself, a 5-minute walk away.
Grocery shops: Taverna Dionisos, behind the quay, sells some groceries. There are three supermarkets on the main road through Poros and a greengrocer nearby.
Bakery: Two on Poros's main street. Taverna Dionisos behind the quay also sells fresh bread.
Butcher: Three in Poros.
Banks: The Alpha Bank (Tel: 26740 72752) is on Papagou St, the main road through Poros. You can also exchange foreign currency at the Poros Bay Hotel, behind the quay.
Pharmacy: On main street.
Post: There is a post box just outside Pithari souvenir shop and the post office is on the main road through Poros. Stamps at souvenir shops. The postal service on Kefalonia is good.
Opening times: Most shops operate to usual opening times: 0900-1400 & 1730-2100.

EATING OUT

There is plenty of choice in Poros, of varying quality. Taverna Dionisos behind the quay is good for seafood and also does takeaway food with discounts for yacht crews. There's a snack bar nearby at the Poros Bay Hotel and Maistrali Café at the north end of the port.
In Poros itself, a short walk from the harbour, Romantsa Taverna (Tel: 26740 72194) is good for fish and Pantelis (Tel: 26740 72484) serves an extensive menu of traditional Kefalonian cuisine.

ASHORE

If you want to stretch your legs, wander up the gorge that cuts through the mountains behind the town. The River Vohinas runs through the 262ft (80m)-deep ravine and there are some good walks nearby. According to legend, the hollows in the rock face are the footsteps of the god Hercules.

Alternatively, drive to the Tzanata Tombs or the Monastery of the Virgin Mary of Altros. The Tzanata Tombs, 2½ (1½km) miles south-west of Poros, feature a large Mycenaen burial chamber. It was excavated in 1991 and relics found at the site are now in the Archaeological Museum in Argostoli (see p212). It is thought to be the tomb of a local chieftain. The Monastery of the Virgin Mary of Altros on Mt Altros, immediately to the north-west of Poros, is the oldest on Kefalonia and part of it dates to the Middle Ages. During its history it has been rebuilt 17 times, after being destroyed by earthquakes and attacks from Saracen pirates. The views from here over Poros and towards Ithaca are stunning.

TRANSPORT

Car hire: Sun Bird car and bike rental (Tel: 26740 72517) is to the west of the Port Police. Open Monday to Saturday, 0830-1430, 1730-2130, Sun Bird prices range between €100-€180 for a three-day hire. Mythos Travel car hire (Tel: 26740 73003) and Makis Rent a Car (Tel: 26740 72365) are in the town. Alternatively, ask at the Tourist Office (Tel: 26740 72000) in Poros.
Taxis: Tel: 26740 72909; 26740 72230. There are often taxis near the ferry quay or ask at one of the travel agents in Poros.
Bus: The bus station (Tel: 26740 72284) is on the outskirts of Poros. Daily services to Argostoli (1 hour away) and Skala (35 minutes) in season.
Ferry: Strintzis Ferries (Tel: 26740 72284) and Ionian Ferries run daily services from the quay at Poros to Kyllini in the Peloponnese. Strintzis Ferries has an office on the quay, or ask at the travel agents for a timetable.
Air travel: Kefalonia airport (Tel: 26710 29900) is 5½ miles (9km) south of Argostoli, a ¾-hour journey from Poros. International and domestic flights to Athens service the airport.

OTHER INFORMATION

Local Tel code: 26740.
Port authority: The Port Office (Tel: 26740 72460) is above the Strintzis Ferries office at the north side of the harbour.
Tourist information: The Tourist Office (Tel: 26740 72000) is on the outskirts of Poros on the road to Sami, near the medical centre.
Police: Tel: 26740 72210.
Doctor: Ask at the Medical Centre (Tel: 26740 72552) on the outskirts of Poros.
Dentist: No but try Argostoli. See p212.
Hospital: Poros Medical Centre (Tel: 26740 72552); Argostoli Hospital (Tel: 26710 24641.

Katelios Kateleios

To the south of Katelios Pt: 38°03'.21N 20°44'.68E
Charts: Admiralty 203, 189, SC5771; Imray G12, G1; Hellenic Navy Hydrographic Service 030, 21

The once small fishing village of Katelios on Kefalonia's south coast is now a thriving mini-resort. In recent years a number of hotels have opened up in the village and a mass of tavernas and bars now line the beach road.

For the yachtsman, Katelios has little attraction on the water. The anchorage and small fishing harbour is strewn with rocks, it's shallow and the prevailing winds often whistle though this area, rendering it rather exposed. Ashore it has a couple of good tavernas and an interesting wildlife centre, but as the anchorage has little to offer it is almost worth leaving your boat at Poros or Sami and visiting Katelios by car.

If you do intend to visit, on approach from Poros, head south down the east coast of Kefalonia. Keep well off the coast near Mounda Pt as a shoal area extends for about 2nm to the south-east. The village of Katelios lies in the western corner of the bay, with the small fishing harbour just below. If you want to anchor here, do so to the east of the breakwater, taking care to maintain a good look-out for rocks, as there are plenty in the vicinity. Only make this approach in calm weather and in daylight, and if there is any hint of a southerly, head for shelter elsewhere as there is no protection here. Anchor in 5m or less on sand.

Anchoring is forbidden close to Katelios Pt as there are underwater submarine cables here.

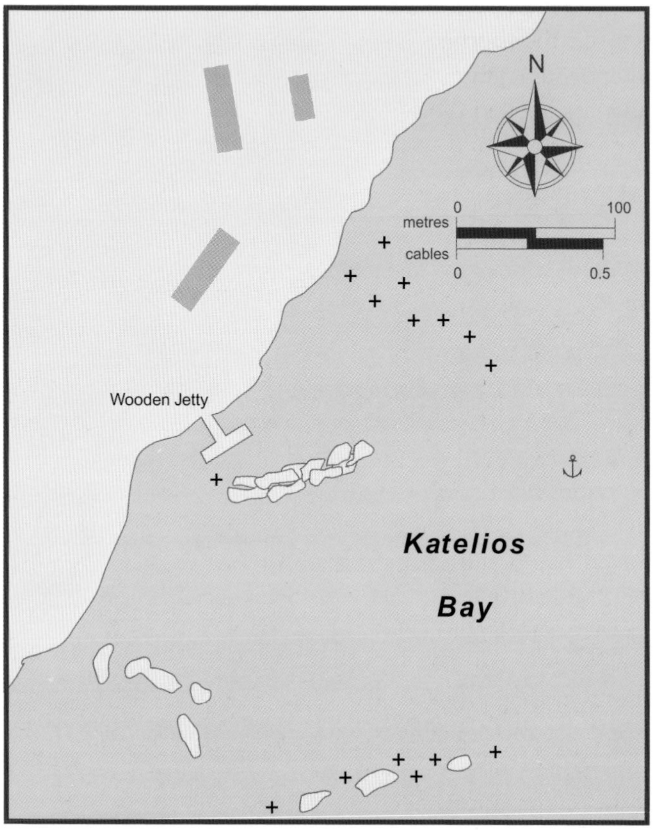

Useful information – Katelios

FACILITIES

Water: Tavernas may fill a jerrycan.
Rubbish: Bins behind the beach.
Telephone: There are a couple of card phones near the beach. Phone cards sold at the souvenir shop. Mobile reception is okay.

PROVISIONING

Grocery shops: Small mini-market on the road out of Katelios.
Bakery: Some fresh bread at the mini-market.
Banks: The nearest banks are at Skala, 5 miles (8km) to the east. Venus Rentals (Tel: 26710 81650) does foreign currency exchange.
Pharmacy: Some basics at the mini-market.
Post: The nearest post office is in Skala.
Opening times: The mini-market and souvenir shop are usually open all day to cater for the tourist trade.

EATING OUT

Katelios is home to about half a dozen beachside tavernas. The food here is moderate, although the Blue Sea taverna is said to have a good reputation.

ASHORE

Here you'll find the Environmental Centre, set up by the Katelios Group (Tel: 26710 81009). This organisation is involved in the protection and research of marine and terrestrial life and is primarily concerned with Loggerhead turtles. Although this is the most common species of turtle in the Mediterranean it is now also one of the most endangered marine species in Europe, under threat from fishermen and their nets, and from the tourist industry, which is developing the beaches where they nest. Associations such as the Katelios Group are now working towards their protection, and its Katelios centre is an interesting place to visit.

There is also a good walk from Katelios to the village of Pastra to the north. It is about 6 miles there and back, through some beautiful countryside.

TRANSPORT

Car hire: Venus Rentals (Tel: 26710 81650), behind the tavernas.
Taxis: Ask at the tavernas.
Ferry: There are various inter-island and international ferries on Kefalonia: from Sami, Poros and Argostoli you can travel to Kyllini on the mainland. Services to Zakynthos run from Pesada. From Fiskardo you can travel to Nidri and Vasiliki on Lefkada and Ithaca. From Sami, ferries run to Vathy on Ithaca and Astakos.
Air travel: Kefalonia Airport (Tel: 26710 29900) is 5½ miles (9km) south of Argostoli (a ¾-hour journey by car from Katelios). Services to Athens and European countries several times a week in season.

OTHER INFORMATION

Local Tel code: 26710.
Hospital: The nearest medical centre is in Skala (Tel: 26710 83222).

Pesada Pessada, Pesadha

To the south of Pesada Harbour, in Lourdata Bay: 38°06'.04N 20°35'.76E

Charts: Admiralty 203, 189, SC5771; Imray G12, G1; Hellenic Navy Hydrographic Service 030, 21

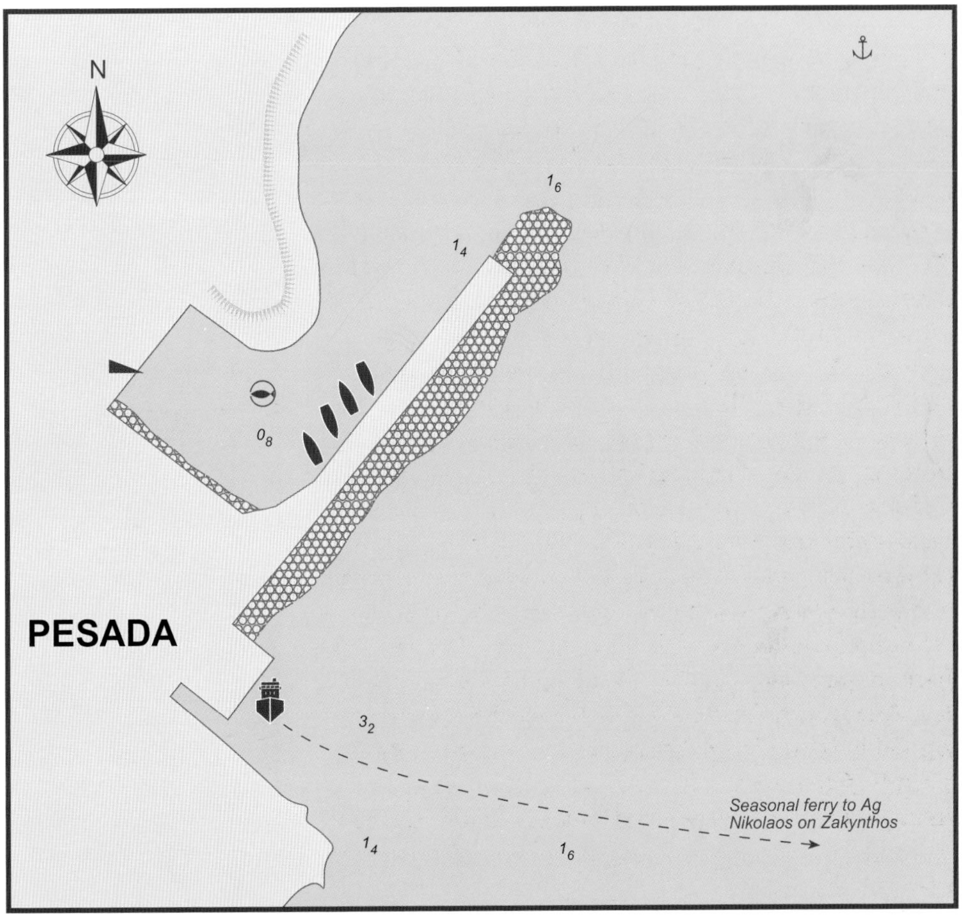

Pesada lies in Lourdata Bay on the south coast of Kefalonia, 8nm west of Katelios and the same distance east of the Argostoli Gulf. Lourdata Bay and the tiny fishing boat harbour at Pesada offer little protection. They are totally exposed to the south, and their rock-strewn coastline would prove a serious hazard in anything but a light breeze. The harbour itself, which is protected by a short breakwater, is too small for most yachts, so Pesada should be considered solely as an anchorage.

Anchor to the east of the harbour in 5m or less on sand and mud. The holding is adequate in calm weather but, being unprotected, it should be used for short-term stops only.

On approach from all directions, watch out for ferry traffic between the bay and Zakynthos. A daily service runs between Pesada and Ag Nikolaos on Zakynthos and leaves from the quay to the south of the harbour breakwater.

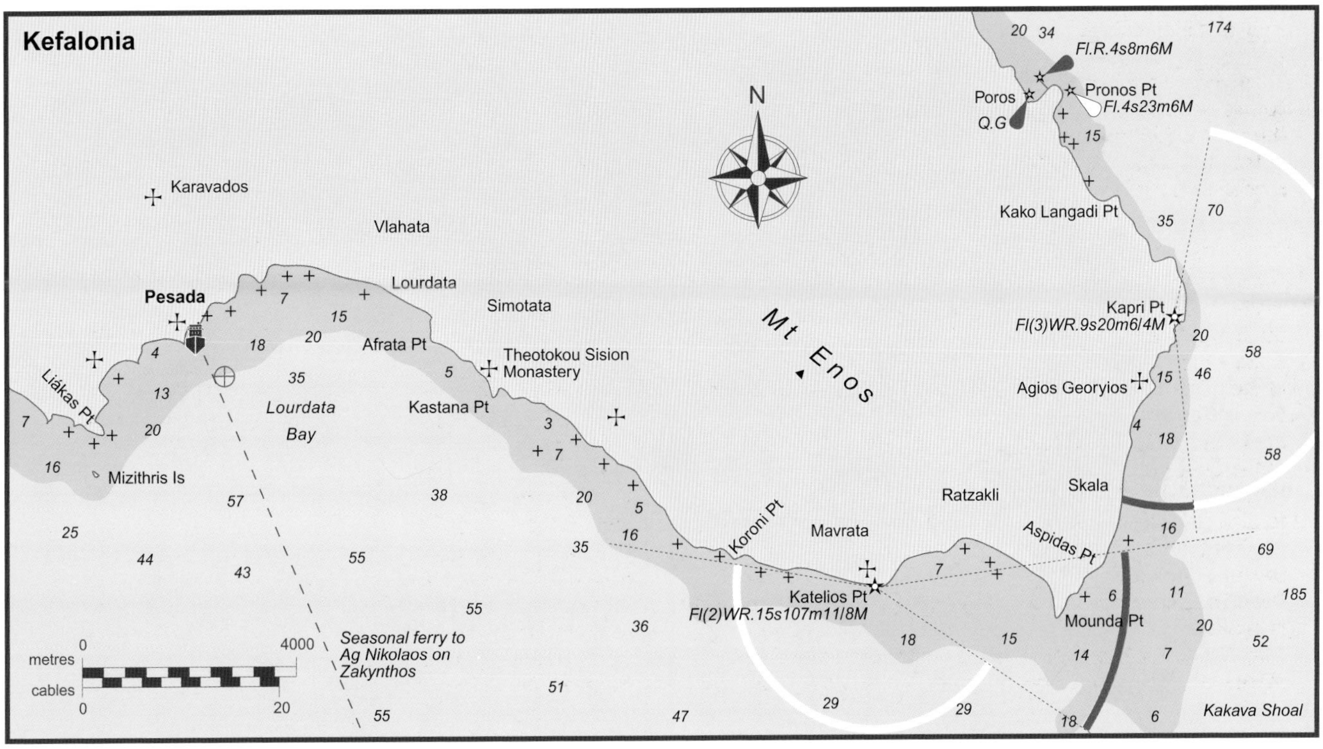

Argostoli Argostolion

Entrance to Argostoli Bay: 38°12'.14N 20°28'.16E
Argostoli Bay: 38°11'.44N 20°29'.16E

Argostoli is the capital and administrative centre of Kefalonia, a role it assumed in 1757 when an earthquake partially destroyed the earlier one at the fortified castle of Agios Georgios. Situated on the western shore of an inlet off the Argostoli Gulf, it lies protected behind a peninsula; while in a strong northwesterly it can be affected by swell, it offers reasonable to good shelter at all times. Recent developments locally have included the building of a new marina, on the bay's eastern shore. This was not complete at the time of going to press, but boats were beginning to use it. This eastern shore is connected to the town via a long, concrete causeway, the Drapano Bridge, which separates the bay from the Koutavos Lagoon. Originally constructed of wood in 1813, it was built when Kefalonia was under British rule and governed by the politician Charles Philippe de Bosset.

For the cruising yachtsman, Argostoli has all the amenities required and is a lively place to spend a couple of days. The palm-fringed quay is fronted by tavernas and used by leisure and commercial craft alike, while the main square has a vibrant atmosphere and bustles with cafés and bars. It doesn't get too busy in mid-season either, despite being so close to the airport and Kefalonia's political and cultural capital. It's well placed as a base to explore the rest of the island, and once the marina is fully functional should offer a great deal to cruisers.

Like the rest of the island, Argostoli was devastated during the 1953 earthquake. Remnants of the original Venetian town still exist but the majority was rebuilt using foreign money. It is relatively modern in style, although still attractive.

A new marina has been built at Argostoli, opposite the town

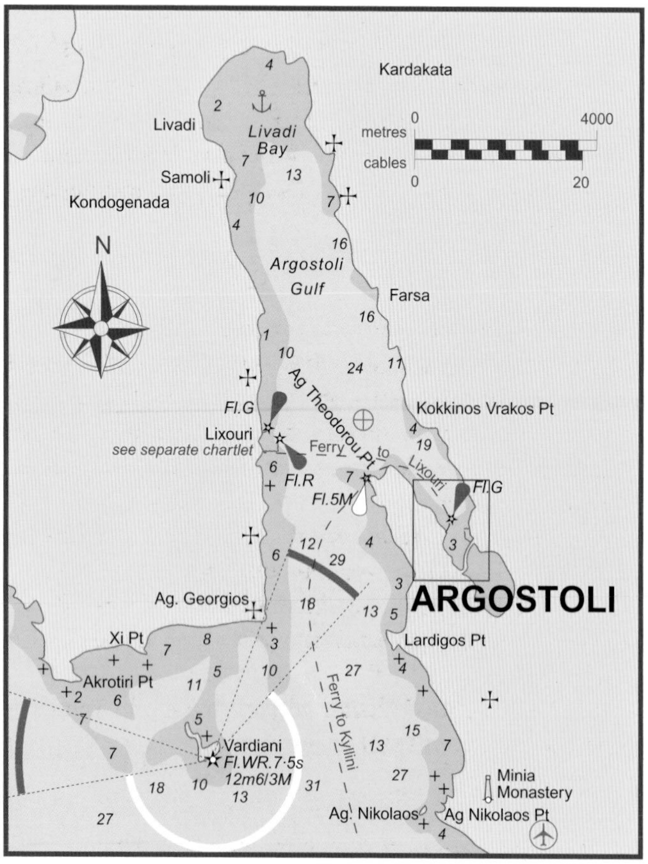

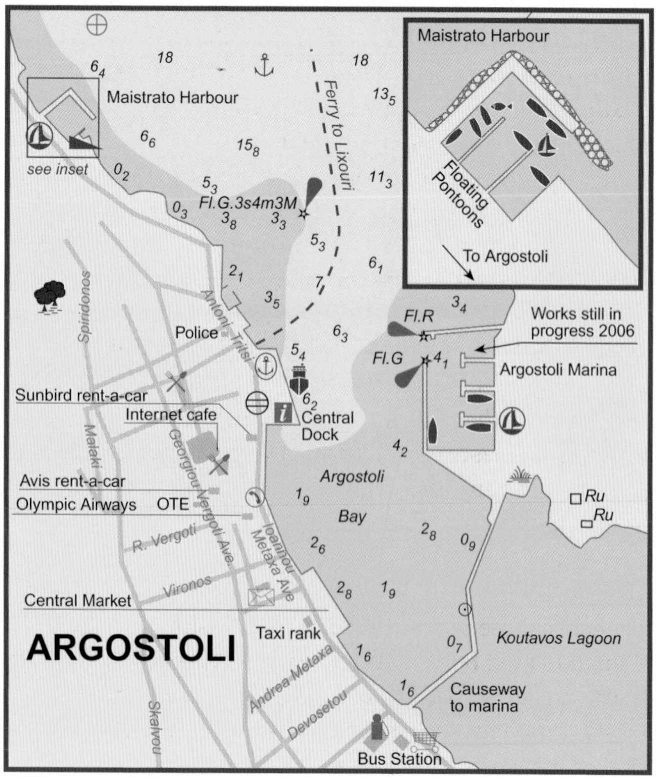

Argostoli's Maistrato harbour, used by fishing *caiques*, is often busy, but small yachts can sometimes squeeze in

NAVIGATION

Charts: Admiralty 2402, 203, 189, SC5771; Imray G12, G1; Hellenic Navy Hydrographic Service 036, 030

The entrance to the Argostoli Gulf, on which Argostoli lies, is on the western end of the south coast of Kefalonia, between Ag Georgios Pt and Lardigos Pt. From the east coast, head west, staying well offshore, particularly between Liakas Pt and Ag Pelagias Pt, where it is very rocky.

On approach from the west, watch out for the rocks between Akrotiri Pt and Xi Pt and the reef around the low-lying island of Vardiani, about 1½-miles south-east of Akrotiri Pt. The reef extends about ½-mile south and ¾-mile west of the island but depths over it range between 5-7m so it is passable by most vessels. It is also possible to sail between the island and the mainland if you stay mid-channel but don't get too close to Ag Georgios Pt, to the north-east of Vardiani, as depths decrease here to less than 3m.

Once inside the entrance, head north for about 2nm. Depths in the middle of the Argostoli Gulf range between 16-27m but decrease to less than 10m at the northern end. You will soon see the town of Lixouri to the west and, directly opposite it, the entrance to Argostoli Bay. A lighthouse (Fl 5M) with Doric-style columns is conspicuous on Ag Theodoron Pt and marks the bay's western headland.

Once round Ag Theodoron Pt, the town will become visible to the south-east. Maistrato Harbour is the first you come to. Just beyond are the ferry and town quays and, to the east, the new marina.

Maintain a good look-out at all times as there is usually quite a bit of traffic in the bay and a regular ferry runs between Lixouri and Argostoli. When approaching the quay or marina, leave the buoy (Fl G) to the south-east of Maistrato Harbour to starboard. It marks a rock and the water between it and the shore is quite shallow.

BERTHING

There are three places to berth at Argostoli: Maistrato, a small fishing boat harbour to the north-west of the town, the quay to the south of the ferry dock and, when complete, the new yacht harbour on the eastern side of the bay.

MAISTRATO

The small harbour of Maistrato is home to fishing boats, although it can also be used by small numbers of visiting yachts under 30ft (9.1m). Sheltered from the swell, the harbour offers good protection but is usually quite busy so space is tight. Berth stern- or bows-to the end of one of the pontoons on the western side of the harbour or off the breakwater. Watch out for fishing boat mooring lines, which may foul your prop.

TOWN QUAY

If possible, tuck yourself in stern- or bows-to the corner of the quay directly to the south of the main commercial dock. It can get very rolly here, particularly with swell generated by the ferries and the prevailing northwesterlies, so keep well off the quay and leave plenty of fenders out. The holding is good and depths range between 2-4m.

ARGOSTOLI MARINA

Work on Argostoli Marina is progressing well, if slowly. In 2007 yachts were beginning to use it but there were no facilities on the site and plans for a lazyline system had yet to be implemented. It's in quite a remote location and a fair distance from the town, but once up and running should provide good facilities.

Until work is complete, berth alongside the breakwater or stern- or bows-to the pontoons. Some small ships were tying up alongside the breakwater in 2007, so keep clear of them when manoeuvring. Once the marina is finished it will have fixed lazylines and offer good all-round shelter, although the prevailing northwesterlies will still create swell.

ANCHORING

Anchoring is not advised in Argostoli Bay. There

is a significant lack of suitable bays. Anchoring is prohibited in the bay immediately inside Ag Theodoron Pt, where there are underwater electricity cables.

If the wind isn't blowing from the south, however, one place you *can* anchor for lunch is at the head of the Argostoli Gulf in Livadi Bay. Depths decrease quite gradually and you can drop your hook in 6m or less. It is exposed, though, so not suitable for an overnight stay.

Useful information – Argostoli

FACILITIES
All the facilities, provisioning and transport details listed below relate to Argostoli town. In 2007 there were no facilities at Argostoli Marina.
Water: Tap situated on the south side of the commercial quay.
Fuel: There are Shell and El Petrol service stations on the outskirts of Argostoli.
Ice: At the supermarkets.
Laundry: Uphill of the main square.
Gas: Bottle exchange at larger supermarkets.
Rubbish: Large bins on the town quay and near Maistrato Harbour.
Yacht services/chandlery: No chandlers in Argostoli, but several ironmongers.
Telephone: Several phone boxes near the quay and in the square. The nearest to Maistrato Harbour is just up the hill, past the taverna. The newsagent in Argostoli and the kiosks sell phone cards. Mobile reception is good.
Internet: Internet café to the west of the square.

PROVISIONING
Grocery shops: There are several supermarkets, mini-markets and grocery shops in the centre of Argostoli, plus a large supermarket at the southern end of the town, near the causeway. There is also a very good market halfway between the Drapano causeway and the commercial quay.
Bakery: A couple in Argostoli, one near the quay.
Butcher: Several within the centre of Argostoli. The large supermarket near the causeway also stocks some meat products.
Banks: The Emporiki Bank (Tel: 26710 22334) is on Vyronos Street, which runs at right angles to the quay, to the north of the market. The National Bank of Greece is on Siteboron St, which runs parallel to the road past the quay, to the south of the market. The Agricultural Bank of Greece (Tel: 26710 22341) is on a side street immediately to the south of the market. Alpha Bank (Tel: 26710 25181) is on Antoni Tritsi Avenue, the road past the quay. Eurobank (Tel: 26710 27161) is on a side street off the quay. Most are open Monday-Friday, 0900-1400.
Pharmacy: On Lithostroto St, the pedestrianised high street.
Post: Post office on Lithostroto St, Monday-Friday, 0800-1400. The postal service on Kefalonia is good.
Opening times: Vary but usually 0900-1400 & 1700-2100.

EATING OUT
Most of the tavernas surround the main square, but you will also find tavernas and cafés along the road past the quay. The Captain's Table (Tel: 26710 27170) near the Port Police is good and the prices very reasonable. There is also a small taverna near Maistrato Harbour and a café-bar behind the marina.

ASHORE
There are several good museums in Argostoli. The Archaeological Museum (Tel: 26710 28300) on G Vergoti St, to the west of the central square, has a collection of Kefalonian antiquities that range from Prehistoric to Roman times and includes a number of finds from the Melissani Caves (see p205). Open Tuesday-Sunday, 0830-1500, entry €3. The Corgialenion Historical & Folk Art Museum (Tel: 26710 28835) is on the ground floor of the Corgialeneion Library on Ilia Zervou Street. Founded in 1962, its aim was to 'preserve the memory of the historical and social conditions that prevailed in Kefalonia before the 1953 earthquake' and it houses a collection of material from the early 15th century to the mid-19th century. Open Mon-Sat, 1000-1500.

The disused waterwheel

On the outskirts of Argostoli are the botanical gardens Cephalonia Botanica (Tel: 26710 26595). Built on the site of an abandoned olive grove, they are relatively new but include a comprehensive collection of native Greek and Mediterranean plants. Open Mon-Sat, 1000-1400 and 1800-2000.

At the north end of the town is the disused water wheel of Katavothres, while nearby at the entrance to Argostoli Bay is the Ag Theodoron lighthouse. Its Doric-style circle of columns make it a distinctive landmark for yachts entering the Argostoli Gulf.

There is also a go-kart track and a paint ball field not far from Argostoli.

TRANSPORT
Car hire: Europcar (Tel: 26710 24634) is on Papandreaou St, the hill behind Argostoli; Sun Bird Car Rental (Tel: 26710 23723) is on Antoni Tritsi Avenue, the road past the quay; Neptune Car & Bike hire (Tel: 26710 23723) is on the same road, opposite the Hellenic Tourist Organisation.
Taxis: The taxi rank is next to the town square.
Bus: Argostoli's bus station (Tel: 26710 22276) is at the south end of the quay, on Antoini Tritsi Avenue. Daily services to Sami, Poros and Fiskardo, among other destinations.
Ferry: A service between Argostoli and Lixouri operates daily every half-hour, 0645-2230. Prices: car, €3.60; person, €1.20; motorbike, €1. Ferries to Kyllini in the north Peloponnese also leave from Argostoli. See www.greekferries.gr for details.
Air travel: Kefalonia's airport (Tel: 26710 29900) is 5½ miles (9km) south of Argostoli. Take a taxi there as there is no bus service linking the airport with the town. Charter flights to most European destinations several times a week. Out of season flights are fewer. Olympic Airways has an office on Vergoti Street (Tel: 26710 28808). Hertz, Europcar and Avis have branches at the airport.

OTHER INFORMATION
Local Tel code: 26710.
Port Police: The Port Police (Tel: 26710 22224) office is next to the cruise-ship quay.
Tourist information: The Tourist Office (Tel: 26710 22248) is near the commercial quay.
Police: Police Station (Tel: 26710 22314) near the commercial quay.
Doctor: Several in the centre of Argostoli.
Dentist: Pollaton Anthiopi (Tel: 26710 27501) is on Lithostroto St; Drakopoulos Ioannis (Tel: 26710 24599) is on Vergoti Street.
Hospital: The hospital (Tel: 26710 24641/23230) is to the south of the town.

Above left: The Doric-style Ag Theodoron lighthouse stands at the entrance to Argostoli Bay. Above: The water surrounding the headland is shallow

Lixouri Lixouriou, Lixourion

Off Lixouri Harbour: 38°11'.94N 20°26'.76E
Harbour entrance: 38°12'.27N 20°26'.48E

Lixouri is Kefalonia's second largest town and stands on the west coast of the Argostoli Gulf, on the Paliki peninsula. It's an unremarkable but pleasant enough place spanning the length of the waterfront and the streets are full of the usual cafés, tavernas and shops, the central focus being Ethnikis Antistasseos Square, immediately behind the quay. The town was built on the site of the ancient city of Pali, one of four main cities on Kefalonia in ancient times. Much of Lixouri was destroyed in the 1953 earthquake, so it is now fairly uniform and modern in style and consequently lacks some of the character of other waterside towns.

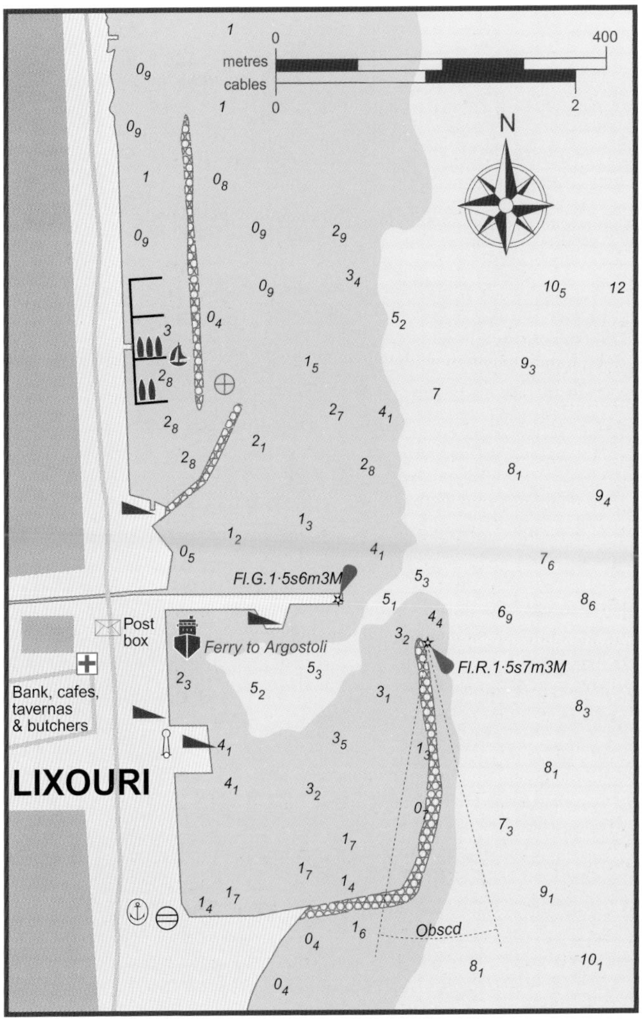

As a cruising destination, however, it has much to offer. It's away from the hustle and bustle of Argostoli, it doesn't get too overrun with tourists peak season and all the amenities you require are near the harbour. Recent developments, such as the addition of pontoons in the small boat harbour, have improved berthing facilities, and it offers reasonable shelter. Only occasionally, if a strong northerly is blowing, will it feel too exposed, although swell generated by the Lixouri-Argostoli ferries can be unpleasant.

NAVIGATION

Charts: Admiralty 2402, 203, 189, SC5771; Imray G12, G1; Hellenic Navy Hydrographic Service 036, 030

The approach to Lixouri is identical to that of Argostoli, except that, instead of heading east into Argostoli Bay, you turn west. The small boat harbour lies just to the north of the ferry quay. Watch out for ferry traffic in this area as a regular service operates between Lixouri and Argostoli and they approach the harbour at speed.

Lixouri's harbour is currently being developed

BERTHING

In previous years, most yachts have berthed to the north and south of the ferry quay, either bows- or stern-to, but recent work here has included the development of a small boat harbour just to the north. Four floating pontoons are in place and there is plenty of room for yachts to berth, stern- or bows-to. The small boat harbour provides good protection, although occasionally swell does get pushed in here. Depths are between 2-3m and the holding on mud is reasonable.

If you'd prefer to be near the ferry quay, tuck yourself in either to the north of it, near the mole, or just to the south. Wash from car ferries can be uncomfortable, particularly if a northwesterly is blowing.

ANCHORING

The coastline near Lixouri is rather exposed and not suitable for anchoring off. However, in settled conditions you can anchor for lunch at the northern end of the Argostoli Gulf in Livadi Bay in less than 6m. It is not recommended for overnight stays.

Useful information – Lixouri

FACILITIES

Water: A water tanker will deliver (Tel: 26710 91605; Mobile: 69447 68765).
Fuel: An Avin petrol station just outside the town.
Showers: Cold water showers on the beach. Public toilets near the ferry quay.
Ice: Try the supermarkets.
Gas: Bottle exchange at the larger supermarkets.
Rubbish: Large bins on the quayside.
Yacht services/chandlery: A1 Yacht Trade Consortium (Tel: 26710 91306/VHF Ch12) will organise a range of services for private yacht clients, including repairs, provisioning and laundry.
Telephone: Several phone boxes near the square in Lixouri. Phone cards sold in the newsagent and kiosks. Mobile reception is good.

PROVISIONING

The main shopping streets in Lixouri run parallel to each other near the town square, Ethnikis Antistasseos Square, which lies to the south of the ferry quay. The square itself has shops, restaurants, tavernas and kiosks around its perimeter.
Grocery shops: Supermarket next to Avin Fuel. There is another on the road off the north-west end of the square and a greengrocer off the southern end. Also a larger supermarket on the outskirts of town.
Bakery: A couple are situated off the square. The supermarkets sell a selection of baked products.
Butcher: On north side of the square.
Banks: All the banks are either near the main square or on the side streets off it. Open Monday-Friday, 0900-1400. All have 24-hour ATMs. Alpha Bank (Tel: 26710 93636); The Agricultural Bank of Greece (Tel: 26710 91225); Emporiki (Tel: 26710 91212); The National Bank of Greece (Tel: 26710 92366). Foreign currency exchange is available at Ertsos World Travel Services (Tel: 26710 92933), near A1 Yacht Services.
Pharmacy: One on the north side of the square and a couple more on side roads off the square.
Post: The post office is opposite the ferry terminal. Post box near the National Bank of Greece. Stamps from kiosks. The postal service on Kefalonia is good.
Opening times: Most shops open between 0900-1400 & 1730-2100. Tavernas and souvenir shops are open until later.

EATING OUT

Like Argostoli, most of the tavernas and cafés in Lixouri are arranged round the main square and waterfront. There's quite a bit of choice and prices tend to be more reasonable than in Argostoli as it isn't such a popular destination. Akrogiali restaurant, behind the quay, seems to be the favourite, particularly with locals, but Archipelagos restaurant is also good. There are numerous cafés and bars nearby.

ASHORE

Lixouri's public museum and library (Tel: 26710 91325) are housed in the Typaldos-Iakovatios building, to the east of the main square. The neoclassical building, which was restored in the 1980s, houses a collection of manuscripts, books and icons. Open Tues-Sun, 0830-1500. There are some good beaches on the Paliki peninsula: Lepeda, Mega Lakos and Xi are all within easy driving distance of Lixouri.

TRANSPORT

Car hire: Perdikis Travel (Tel: 26710 91097) near the ferry quay; Ertsos World Travel Services (Tel: 26710 991306); Rallatos Rent-a-Car (Tel: 26710 92511).
Taxis: Taxi rank near the ferry quay.
Bus: The bus station (Tel: 26710 93200) is behind the quay.
Ferry: A ferry to Argostoli runs every half-hour between 0645-2230. Prices: car, €3.60; person, €1.20; motorbike, €1. Services to Kyllini in the northern Peloponnese run from Argostoli and Poros and services to Astakos on the mainland and the island of Ithaca from Sami. See www.greekferries.gr for timetable or booking details, or visit one of the travel agents.
Air travel: The nearest airport (Tel: 26710 29900) is 5½ (9km) miles from Argostoli. Regular international and domestic services fly into Kefalonia airport peak season. There is no bus service between the airport and Argostoli, so travel by taxi or hire car. The nearest Olympic Airways office (Tel: 26710 28808) is on Vergoti Street in Argostoli.

OTHER INFORMATION

Local Tel code: 26710.
Port Police: The Port Police office (Tel: 26710 94100) is at the S end of the quay.
Police: The police station (Tel: 26710 91207) is near the Port Police office, on GR Lambraki St.
Doctor: Voutsinas Fotis (Tel: 26710 91960), near the National Bank of Greece.
Dentist: Several in Argostoli. See p212.
Hospital: Lixouri Medical Centre (Tel: 26710 91194/94245) is on the outskirts of town.

The main town square stands behind the Argostoli-Lixouri ferry quay

Atheras Bay

Ormos Atheras

Atheras Bay: 38°21'.24N 20°24'.66E

Charts: Admiralty 203, 189, SC5771; Imray G12, G1; Hellenic Navy Hydrographic Service 030, 21

Situated to the west of Assos, Atheras Bay is a little-known but delightful anchorage on the north-west tip of Kefalonia. Rarely visited by cruising yachts due to its location, it is remote and unspoilt and the blueness of its waters stunning. A church, a small taverna and a spattering of buildings are the only evidence of habitation here, and in good weather it's a perfect place to stop for lunch.

However, its situation on Kefalonia's west coast and its orientation towards the north mean that it is exposed in a northwesterly and should only be considered in calm conditions. The small islet of Atheronisi, in the middle of the channel near the head of the bay, provides some protection for the anchorage behind, blocking the wind and waves before the full force hits the shore. It still feels quite exposed though.

On approach from the south, watch out for reefs extending off the west coast of Kefalonia, particularly around Ortholithia Pt and Koukouli Pt and close to Atheras Pt, at the entrance to the bay.

Once inside Atheras Bay, you can pass either side of Atheronisi and then head for a small rocky mole at the head of the bay. Depths off the end of the mole are about 4.5m and you can anchor here quite comfortably – either free-swinging or with a line to the mole; but make sure you avoid the small fishing boats that also use the bay. The holding is reasonable on mud and sand.

Ag Kiriakis Ay Kiriakis

Ag Kiriakis Bay: 38°19'.04N 20°28'.86E

Charts: Admiralty 203, 189, SC5771; Imray G12, G1; Hellenic Navy Hydrographic Service 030, 21

Only small yachts should consider entering the harbour at Ag Kiriakis, in the southern corner of the Mirtos Gulf. Reefs and shoals at its mouth make it a hazardous approach and the shallow waters within its perimeter leave little room for manoeuvring or anchoring. The bay of Ag Kiriakis faces north and, while both breakwaters offer some protection from the prevailing northwesterly winds, it is still exposed and therefore suitable for calm conditions only.

The approach to Ag Kiriakis Bay is straightforward from all directions but, once within close vicinity of the harbour, caution is essential and you should proceed at a slow speed. If there is room within the harbour, anchor off the eastern end of the western mole, leaving plenty of room as there is a lot of underwater debris at its base. Be careful, too, not to snag the buoyed, permanent lines used by the harbour's small fleet of fishing boats. Depths just inside the mole are between 2-3m but it gets very shallow at the eastern and southern sides of the harbour. The holding is moderate on mud and sand.

Ashore you'll find a small taverna.

Assos Asos

Assos Bay: 38°23'.19N 20°32'.56E

Assos is a beautiful little village on the west coast of Kefalonia, tucked into the edge of a short isthmus and protected from the sea by a large peninsula, where a Venetian fortress reigns supreme. Despite being hit by the 1953 earthquake, much of the village's Venetian architecture remains, and Assos, like Fiskardo to the north, is one of the few places on the island that has a very traditional feel to it. It was rebuilt with donations from the city of Paris, and so far has been relatively untouched by tourist development, although holiday apartments are beginning to appear on the surrounding hillsides.

It's a really lovely place to spend the day, and there are some superb walks in the area. However, as a cruising destination it isn't so good as it lacks a decent harbour. There's a short quay off which small boats can anchor, but the bay offers minimal shelter and is very shallow in places. Any swell generated in a northwesterly is quickly swept into the bay, which can make it quite rolly, so it should only be considered in calm weather. Perhaps it is the lack of a secure harbour

Assos is a picture postcard village on the west coast of Kefalonia

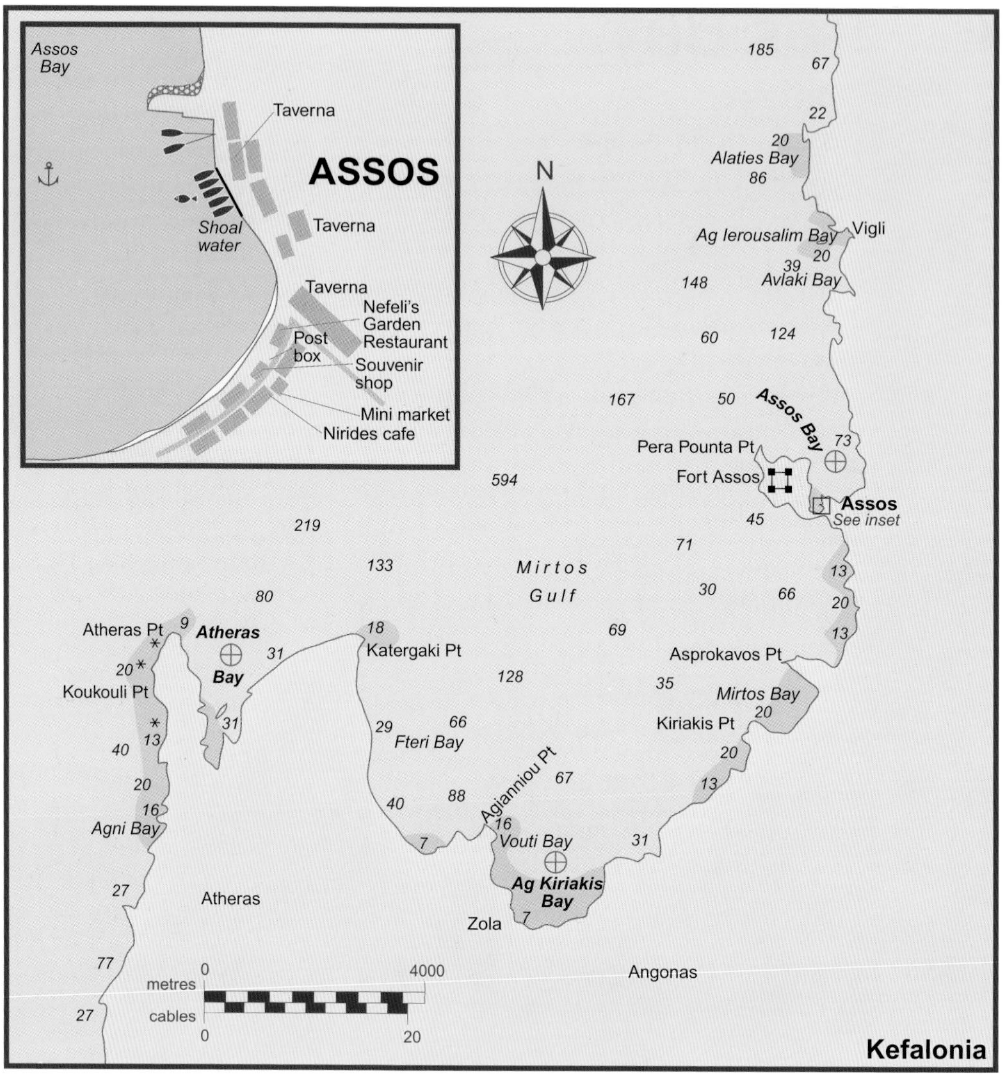

that has so far preserved Assos and prevented it from becoming over-developed. There's no bus service to the village, so visitors can only arrive by car and, while it can get very busy peak season, it is still comparatively unspoilt. If you are passing on a calm day, however, it's well worth a detour.

NAVIGATION

Charts: Admiralty 203, 189, SC5771; Imray G121, G12, G1; Hellenic Navy Hydrographic Service 030, 21

Assos is distinctive and the fort on the high-peaked peninsula, to the west of the town and harbour, is conspicuous from some distance. From the south coast of Kefalonia, follow the west coast of the island north for about 15nm. Stay well offshore as there are shoal patches along the coastline, particularly to the south of Atheras Pt. Assos lies to the north-east of this headland, tucked away in the south-west corner of Assos Bay.

From the north, the fort and the houses on the bay's eastern headland identify the village.

Watch out for swimmers in the bay and check your depth close in, where it is very shallow in places.

BERTHING

Assos is an idyllic little spot but there's not much of a harbour here for yachts and, consequently, room to berth is limited. There's a small length of quay in the north-east corner of the bay, and you can berth off its western tip. However, this area is extremely shallow so proceed with caution and, if possible, check the depths by dropping a lead line from a dinghy before making an approach. There are lots of rocks just under the water, close to the quay, so you can't get too close in either. Anchor bows-to with a kedge off your stern and take a line ashore from your bow.

ANCHORING

It is possible to anchor in the bay to the south-west of the quay, although again this needs care. It gets extremely shallow close to the beach, so anchor in about 4m of water and only in settled conditions. If a strong northwesterly blows in here, the anchorage quickly becomes untenable as the holding is poor.

There is a small quay at Assos, but the surrounding water is shallow

Useful information – Assos

FACILITIES

Water: Tavernas may fill up water containers.
Fuel: The nearest petrol station is 20 minutes away by car.
Rubbish: Bins in the car park at the south end of the harbour.
Telephone: Phone box opposite Nirides Café bar and grill.

PROVISIONING

Grocery shops: The mini-market next to Nirides café sells limited supplies.
Bakery: The mini-market does sell some bread.
Butcher: Some meat products are sold at the mini-market.
Banks: The nearest is at Fiskardo, about 12 miles (19km) away by car.
Pharmacy: The mini-market sells some basics.
Post: No post office but there is a post box next to souvenir shop, where you can also buy stamps. The postal service is OK but post urgent letters in Argostoli.
Other shops: Souvenir shop opposite Nirides café.
Opening times: The shops cater for the tourist trade, so are open from about 0900-1400 & 1800-2030. The cafe is usually open later.

EATING OUT

The village of Assos is tiny but there are several good places to eat. As its main income is from tourists, expect prices to be slightly higher.

The bougainvillaea-strewn Nefeli's Garden Restaurant (Tel: 26740 51347), near the souvenir shop, has stunning views over the bay and is particularly good for seafood. Nirides (Tel: 26740 51467), on the quay, serves an extensive menu of high quality dishes, and Assos taverna (Tel: 26740 51360) is good for traditional Kefalonian cuisine. Platanos café-grill is near Litso's Rent a Car and if you only want a light meal, try the North Snack Bar near the souvenir shop.

ASHORE

There are some fabulous walks around Assos but only if you don't mind steep climbs. From the village, walk over the short isthmus and follow the rough, tree-lined track up the hill to the fortress on the summit of the peninsula. The path zigzags around and is really quite steep in places, but the views across to the village are well worth the effort. The fortress itself was built in the late 16th century by the Venetians as a stronghold to protect the northern part of Kefalonia from pirate attacks. Despite plans to develop it into a permanent city, they never came to fruition and in 1684, when the island of Lefkada was recaptured from the Ottomans by the Venetians, the importance of Assos was diminished.

Until the early 19th century, part of the fortress was used as a prison. Since then, however, earthquakes and general deterioration has reduced a great deal of it to ruins, although much of the 1¼ miles (2km) of wall remains.

If you want to relax on a beach and have hired a car, Mirtos beach, two miles to the south of Assos, is worth a visit. It's the finest beach on Kefalonia and was also where much of *Captain Corelli's Mandolin* was filmed. Be prepared for it to be very busy peak season.

TRANSPORT

Car hire: There is a small branch of Litsos Rent a Car (Tel: 26740 41401) near Platanos café-grill.
Taxis: Ask at Nirides Café.
Ferry: The nearest ferry port is at Fiskardo, from where you can travel to Lefkada and Ithaca, peak season. Services to Astakos leave from Sami, and to Kyllini from Argostoli, Poros, Sami.
Air travel: Kefalonia's airport (Tel: 26710 29900) is 5½ miles (9km) south of Argostoli. Charter and domestic services fly several times a week in season. There's no bus service to the airport.

OTHER INFORMATION

Local Tel code: 26740.
Doctor: The nearest is at Vasilikiades, about 5 miles (8km) north of Assos.
Dentist: There are several in Argostoli. See p212.
Hospital: The nearest is at Argostoli (Tel: 26710 24641) – an hour's drive by car.

The village of Assos was rebuilt with money donated by the city of Paris after the 1953 earthquake

Ithaca
Nisos Ithaki, Ithaka

Everywhere in the Ionian claims to have a connection with Homer's *The Odyssey*, yet Ithaca is universally acknowledged as the likely home of the book's hero Odysseus. Numerous attempts have been made to align the mythological and actual geographies of the area and finds by archaeologists have led many to believe that this is the island of which Odysseus was king, and to which he returned after 10 years away.

The 37-square-mile (96km^2) island nestles next to the north-east coast of Kefalonia, to the south of Lefkada. Mountainous throughout its length, Ithaca looks as if it is formed of two islands, joined at the waist by a narrow isthmus. To my mind, it is one of the prettiest and most appealing of the Ionians. It's a mixture of steep, barren cliffs, lush, green hillsides and traditional rural villages and some of the coastline is particularly dramatic. The Molos Gulf, which almost bisects Ithaca, is fjord-like and one of the most attractive parts of the island. It can be extremely gusty at times but is stunning nevertheless and worth a visit.

Ithaca's heavily indented coastline has numerous anchorages and on the rugged east coast there are also three good harbours. Although affected by heavy swell from passing high-speed ferries, Kioni and Frikes on the north-east tip of the island are delightful. Frikes is nothing more than a hamlet, bordered by beautiful countryside, and the slightly bigger Kioni has excellent amenities for yachtsmen ashore. As the island's capital, Vathi has much to offer too and, despite being flattened by the 1953 earthquake, has been sympathetically restored. Ithaca, like neighbouring Kefalonia, also suffered extensive damage but, amazingly, only one life was lost.

One of the attractions of Ithaca is that there is nowhere on the island that has been over-commercialised. It is wrapped up in the myths surrounding *The Odyssey* but this has not been exploited and, unlike Lefkada, Kefalonia, Zakynthos and Corfu, there are no tacky resorts or glitzy hotels. The three harbours, while popular with yachts in the season, remain very traditional. They're packed with tavernas and cafés and you'll normally stumble across a souvenir shop or two, but they don't feel contrived and the further inland you venture the more rural it gets. This is partly due to the natural geography, which does not lend itself to development but it does make the island rather special.

A view of Ithaca, looking towards Vathi, the island's main harbour

Ithaca, mountainous throughout its length, is a mixture of steep, barren hills and lush greenery

Ithaca shares a similar history to Kefalonia and it is thought that it was first settled around 4000BC. Despite major periods of decline, such as constant attack from pirates during the Byzantine period, and an invasion by the Turks in 1479, Ithaca has also seen incredibly prosperous times. Under the Venetians, in particular, it flourished. They occupied the island almost continuously from the 13th to the 19th century, increasing its population considerably and creating industries that have had a significant impact. As well as the cultivation of olives and grapes, Ithaca became famous for shipbuilding, which helped it become one of the wealthiest islands in the area.

Today it continues to live up to this legacy and, set in arguably the best part of the Ionian, it's a real gem.

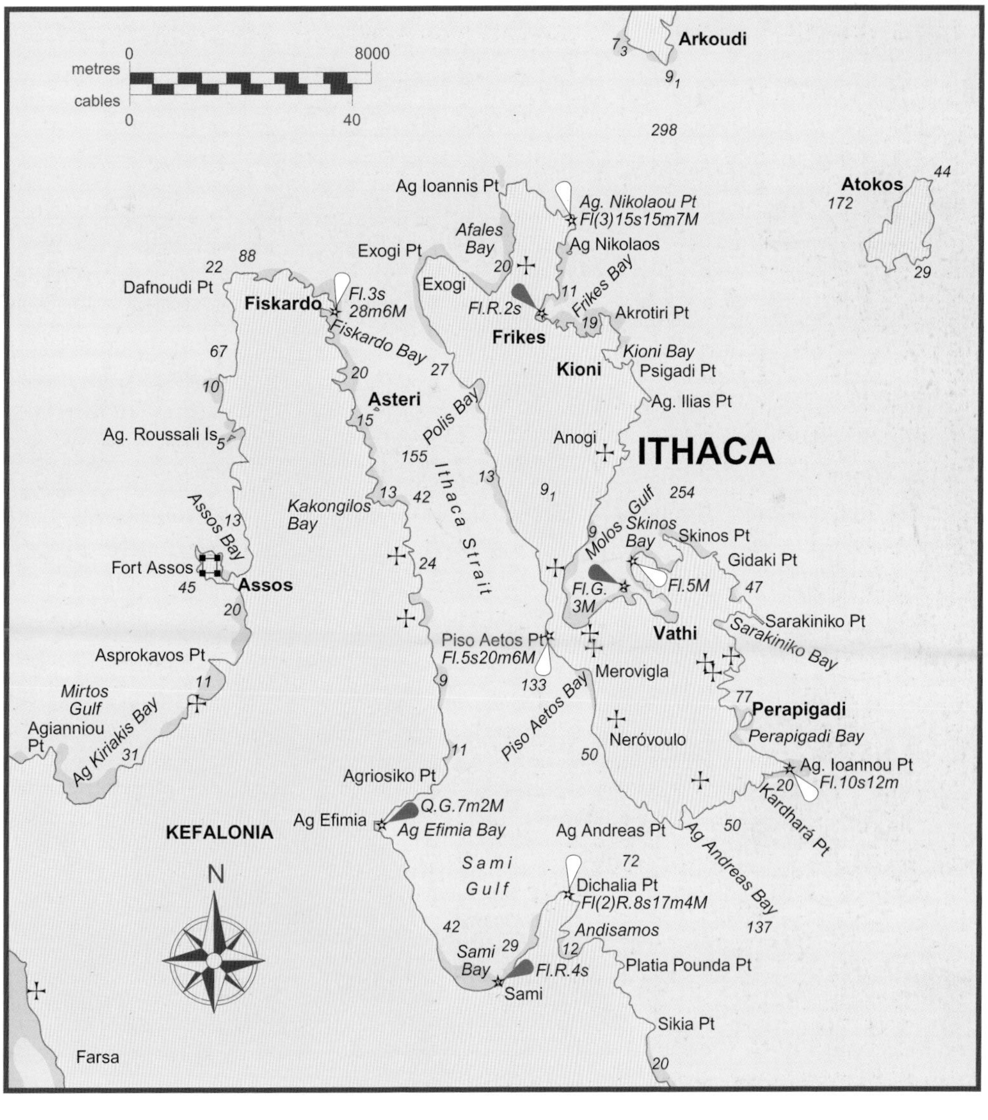

Molos Gulf

Gulf of Molos, Kolpos Aetou Molou

Off Skinos Pt: 38°23'.56N 20°42'.81E

Charts: Admiralty 2402, 203, 189, SC5771; Imray G121, G12, G1; Hellenic Navy Hydrographic Service 036, 030

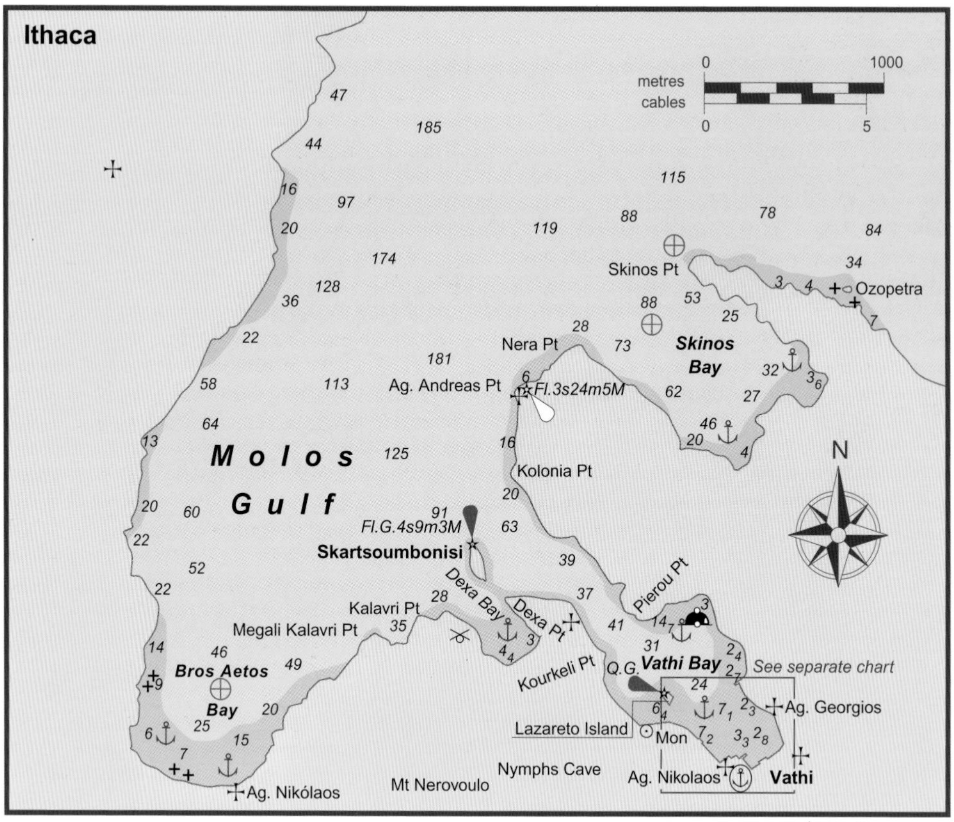

The Molos Gulf, on Ithaca's east coast, almost bisects the island and is recognisable for miles. You can see it from the Meganisi Channel and from Kalamos and Kastos, its steep-sided, fjord-like coastline making it a distinctive landmark. It is very deep, with depths at its centre ranging between 100-150m; it is also said to be one of the 'windiest places in the Ionian', when vicious northwesterly gusts whip down the hills and into the gulf. Potentially good anchorages in coves and inlets on the northern shore get the worst of it, particularly when combined with the swell of passing ferries. Yet despite its windy reputation, some of the island's most beautiful scenery can be found in the Molos Gulf. Its S coast is home to some very good day-time anchorages and to Ithaca's capital town, Vathi.

Skinos Bay

Ormos Skhoinos

To the north of the entrance to Skinos Bay: 38°23'.33N 20°42'.70E

Charts: Admiralty 2402, 203, 189, SC5771; Imray G121, G12, G1; Hellenic Navy Hydrographic Service 036, 030

Skinos Bay is a delightful anchorage to the north-east of Vathi and away from its hustle and bustle. Tucked behind Skinos Pt, on the eastern coast of the island, it is fringed with olive and cypress-covered hills and offers clear, emerald green waters.

Skinos Bay is a lovely place for a lunch-time swim or an evening sojourn. You can anchor in the south-east corner in 5-8m of water, or in the south-west corner which, although much deeper, offers marginally better protection from the prevailing winds. The bay is open to the north, so not suitable in more than a moderate breeze. The holding on sand and mud is reasonable.

Vathi Vathy, Ithaki

Approach to Vathi: 38°22'.89N 20°42'.03E

Off the north quay: 38°22'.34N 20°42'.80E

Vathi Bay: 38°22'.14N 20°42'.84E

Vathi stands on the shores of a large enclosed bay off the Molos Gulf on the east coast of Ithaca. It's been the island's capital and main port since the 17th century and is also one of the windiest places in the Ionian. Vathi is often referred to as Big Vathi, to distinguish

Vathi Bay. The north quay is visible above left

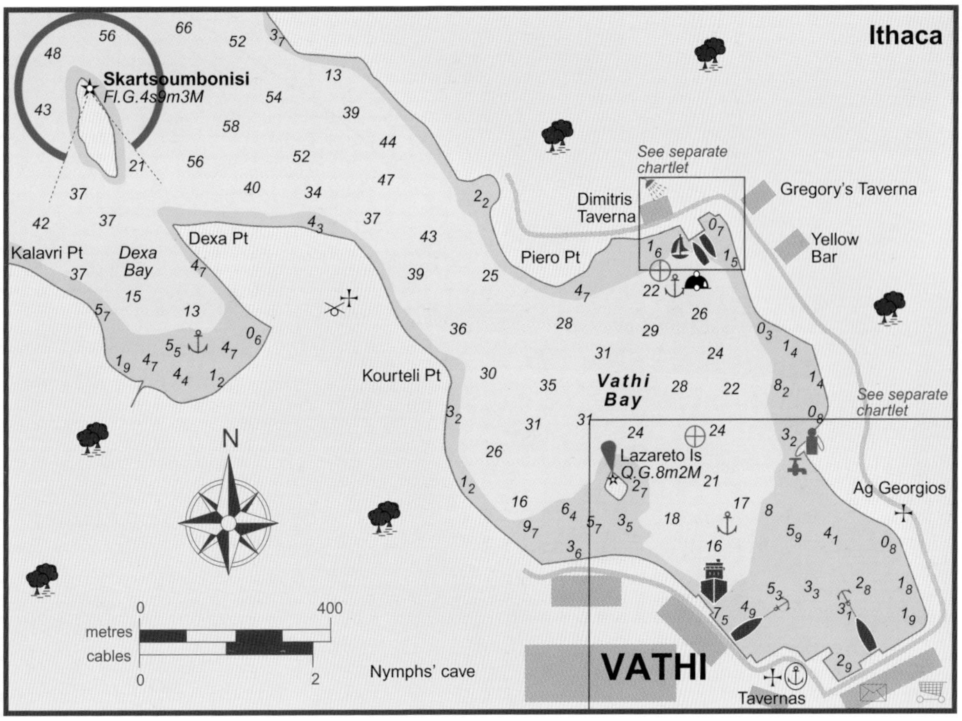

it from Little Vathi on Meganisi, and is a busy port regularly serviced by inter-island ferries and small cargo ships. The town is lively and bustling, particularly during the summer months when charter boats visit and Greek tourists take their holidays here. Yet it is still a charming place to spend a few days or explore ashore. The town is an attractive one that was extensively rebuilt after the 1953 earthquake but which retains much of its old character. It has a good selection of tavernas and cafés and plenty of shops, while most of the amenities that you require are within easy reach. For those seeking a quieter refuge, the north-east side of the bay has much to attract and there are some beautiful walks around the headland.

The small islet of Lazareto (Nisos Loimokathartirio) was once a leper colony. It was later converted into a prison but this was destroyed in 1953 and the rubble from its walls used to build the town quay.

NAVIGATION

Charts: Admiralty 2402, 203, 189, SC5771; Imray G121, G12, G1; Hellenic Navy Hydrographic Service 036, 030

The approach to Vathi is straightforward and through deep water. From the south, follow Ithaca's east coast north until the wide entrance to the Molos Gulf (Kolpos Aetou Molou) becomes visible. Once inside the mouth of the gulf, head south-east past Skinos Bay and Ag Andreas Pt, which at night is lit (Fl 5M). The entrance to Vathi Bay will then become visible, as will the town at its head. At night, the small islet of Skartsoumbonisi, opposite Dexa Bay, is also lit (Fl G 3M).

There is usually a lot of traffic in the bay. Commercial vessels and ferries, in particular, whizz in and out at great speeds, so keep a good look-out and stay well clear of them. In the afternoons, the bay is also affected by severe gusts, which roll off the steep-sided mountains. The Molos Gulf and Vathi Bay are both deep until very close inshore.

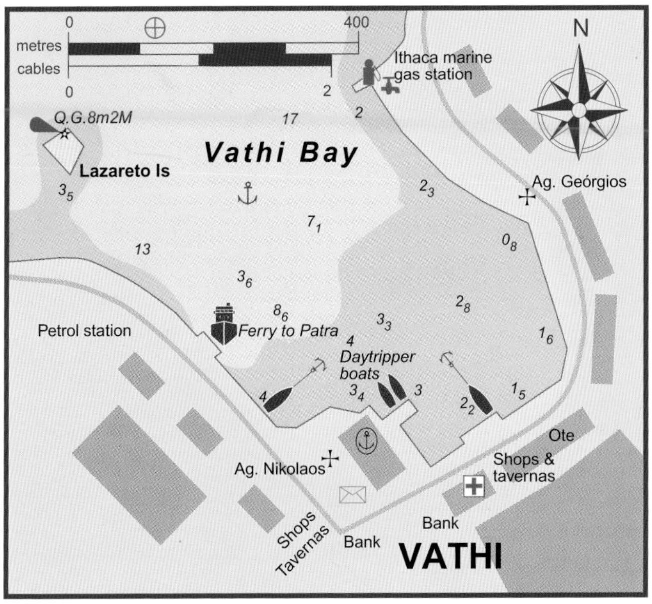

BERTHING

There are two places to berth at Vathi: either on the main quay, in front of the town, or on the quay in the north-east corner of the bay.

Town quay: There is normally plenty of room for yachts to berth stern- or bows-to, or occasionally side-to, along the waterfront to the south-east of the ferry quay.

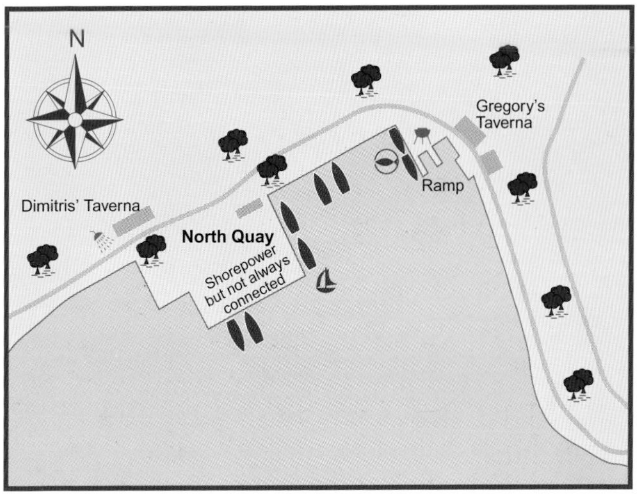

The town flanks the southern end of Vathi Bay and is a pretty mix of architectural styles

Depths here range between 2-2.5m and the holding is reasonable, once your anchor has dug in. However, this quay is very exposed in a northwesterly, so not suitable in strong winds when a northerly swell penetrates the harbour. In these conditions, waves can crash over the quay and strong gusts can cause anchors to drag. Commercial vessels can make Vathi quite noisy at times, although the quay is convenient for the amenities.

North-east quay: This quay is popular with charter flotillas and offers the best protection in Vathi Bay, being less exposed to the prevailing northwesterlies. Berth stern- or bows-to wherever there is room. Smaller boats may prefer to berth bows-to as the quay is quite high. The holding here on mud is reasonable but lay plenty of scope as there is deep water not far off the quay.

ANCHORING

There are several anchorages within the Molos Gulf (see p220). Most of these should be used only for a lunch-time stop, as the steep-sided bay is susceptible to severe gusts from the north-west in the afternoons. In calm, settled weather, though, some may be suitable for overnighting in.

Useful information – Vathi

FACILITIES

Water: Available from Ithaca Marine Gas Station on the eastern side of the bay.

Fuel: Petrol and diesel is sold at the Ithaca Marine Gas Station (Tel: 26740 33316 33317; Mobile: 6977 407388). Also a couple of petrol stations on the outskirts of Vathi.

Ithaca Marine Gas Station sells fuel, water and some provisions

Showers: Available at Dimitris Tsiribis taverna (€3), in the NE corner of the bay.

Ice: Ask at the tavernas.

Gas: Ask at Ithaca Marine Gas Station.

Shorepower: None on the town quay. There are powerpoints on the quay in the NE corner of the bay, but in 2007 these hadn't yet been repaired after a fire in one of the junction boxes.

Rubbish: Bins situated near both quays.

Telephone: Lots of phone boxes in Vathi. Also one on the quay near Dimitris Tsiribis taverna. Phone cards sold at mini-markets and kiosks. The mobile reception here is good.

Internet: Internet café near the south-west corner of the town quay.

PROVISIONING

Grocery shops: Several mini-markets near the quay and main square, which sell a good selection of fresh and packaged products. A limited supply of goods is also available from the Ithaca Marine Gas Station,

Useful information – Vathi

on the eastern side of the bay.
Bakery: Behind the quay.
Butcher: Behind the quay. There is also a fishmonger in the town.
Banks: National Bank of Greece (Tel: 26740 32017) to south-east of the main square. Agricultural Bank of Greece (Tel: 26740 32785) nearby. Both have ATMs.
Pharmacy: A couple on the road past the quay.
Post: Post office and post boxes on the central square, Plateia Efstathiou Drakouli. Open Monday-Friday, 0800-1400. The postal service on Ithaca is fairly slow. Stamps sold at souvenir shops.
Opening times: Most shops open to the hours 0900-1400 and 1730-2100, but during peak season may stay open later.

EATING OUT

North-east corner of the bay: Dimitris Tsiribis taverna (Tel: 69323 42185), near the quay, is a lovely place to spend a lunch-time or evening. Away from the busyness of Vathi, it's a very quiet spot and the tables beneath the eucalyptus trees offer beautiful views across the water. The food is good, too, particularly the fresh fish platter, and its owner, Dimitris, is very knowledgeable about the area and its history. Paliocaravo (Tel: 26740 32573), or Gregory's Taverna as it is also known, is just to the east of Dimitris. It has a good reputation for fish and seafood dishes and the family-produced wine is also very palatable.
Vathi: Numerous tavernas and cafes lie along the waterfront and around the square. Batis Restaurant & Pizzeria (Tel: 26740 33010) serves very good pizzas and Italian and Greek fare, including the island's traditional dish, onion pie. The owners will also provide weather forecasts for cruising yachts. Sirens Yacht Club near the square can equally be recommended.

ASHORE

There are some really lovely walks around Vathi and the Molos Gulf but if you want to indulge in some cultural sightseeing, the Archaeological Museum (Tel: 26740 32200) on Kallinikou Street, two roads behind the quay, is interesting to visit. The museum is open Tue-Sun, 0830-1500, admission free. The Folklore & Nautical Museum near the square may also be of interest. Mon-Sat, 1030-1400. Homer's Cave of the Nymphs (or Marmarospilia) is within walking distance of Vathi. This cave is thought to be where Odysseus hid gifts from the Phaecian king Alcinous, and is a popular site with tourists on *The Odyssey* trail.

TRANSPORT

Car hire: Alpha Bike & Car Hire (Tel: 26740 32850), near the Port Police office, at the south-west corner of the quay, is open 0800-2100, seven days a week. Rent a Scooter (Tel: 26740 32840) is nearby.
Taxis: Taxi rank near the main square, in the south-west corner of the quay.
Bus: Daily between Vathi and Stavros, Frikes and Kioni. Bus stop near the main square.
Ferry: Daily from Patra to Vathy. There is also a ferry from Astakos and other services leave from Piso Aetos, on the west coast of the island. International services to Corfu, Igoumenitsa and Italy leave from Patra. See www.greekferries.gr for timetables and tickets.
Air travel: The nearest airport is 5½ miles (9km) south of Argostoli on Kefalonia. In peak season there are several charter flights a week to the UK and domestic flights to Athens.

OTHER INFORMATION

Local Tel code: 26740.
Port authority: The Port Police office (Tel: 26740 32909) is on the south-east side of the quay.
Police: On Evmeou St, a road off the waterfront. Tel: 26740 32205.
Hospital: 24-hour medical centre (Tel: 26740 32222) on south end of Evmeou St.

Dexa Bay

Ormos Dexia

Dexa Bay: 38°22'.39N 20°41'.96E

Charts: Admiralty 2402, 203, 189, SC5771; Imray G121, G12, G1; Hellenic Navy Hydrographic Service 036, 030

Immediately to the west of Vathi Bay, tucked in behind the islet of Skartsoumbonisi, lies the horseshoe-shaped Dexa Bay. With its pebble beach and olive tree-covered hillsides, it is thought to be Phorcy's cove, named after the Old Man of the Sea in Homer's *Odyssey*, in which a sleeping Odysseus is laid by the Phaeacians following his return to Ithaca.

As an anchorage, Dexa Bay is a very pleasant spot. The holding on mud, in 5-8m of water, is reasonable. However, despite the entrance being guarded by Skartsoumbonisi, the bay is open to the prevailing winds and in unsettled conditions may not offer much shelter. Watch out for motor boats, water-skiers and swimmers, as the beach is used by a watersports company and the surrounding waters can often get quite busy.

The islet of Skartsoumbonisi, with Dexa Bay beyond

Bros Aetos Bay

Aetou Bay

North of Bros Aetos Bay: 38°22'.11N 20°40'.84E

Charts: Admiralty 2402, 203, 189, SC5771; Imray G121, G12, G1; Hellenic Navy Hydrographic Service 036, 030

Bros Aetos Bay, which is open to the north and north-east, and has a good anchorage in its south-west corner, is 1¼nm south-east of Dexa Bay. Anchor in around 5m on mud and sand.

This large bay offers good protection from the south and is not affected too badly by the prevailing winds, although it is exposed if a northeasterly blows up. There are two reefs to watch for when manoeuvring here: one in the eastern corner and another at the south of the bay, immediately to the east of the anchorage.

Kioni

Off Agios Illias Pt, to SE of entrance: 38°26'.03N 20°42'.72E

Off Koutsoumbos Pt: 38°26'.83N 20°42'.37E

Approach to Kioni: 38°26'.92N 20°41'.91E

Approach to Kioni: 38°26'.91N 20°41'.71E

Kioni Harbour: 38°26'.98N 20°41'.50E

Kioni is one of the prettiest villages in the Ionian. Situated on the north-east tip of Ithaca, 4nm north of Vathi, its elegant Venetian-style buildings cluster round the harbour amid a backdrop of thickly wooded olive and cypress-covered hillsides. Kioni was relatively untouched by the 1953 earthquake, compared with similar villages in this part of the Ionian, so has retained a very traditional feel and sustained little architectural loss or damage. It's one of the island's most popular destinations and can get really busy with tourists and yachts in the height of summer. The harbour offers good shelter from all but the south-east and fills up early; but the village has an amazing ability to absorb all its visitors without seeming too crowded. There's always room to squeeze in more boats than you would expect. The quayside tavernas have a vibrant and bustling atmosphere in the evenings and with a couple of well-stocked mini-markets, it's also a good place to top up supplies.

NAVIGATION

Charts: Admiralty 2402, 203, 189, SC5771; Imray G121, G12, G1; Hellenic Navy Hydrographic Service 036, 030

Yachts approaching from all directions should head for the north-east tip of Ithaca. Kioni lies 2nm south of Frikes Bay and 3nm north of the Molos Gulf. Kioni Bay is easily identified by the three windmills on the headland on the southern side of its entrance. On approach from the south you may not see these until near Psigadi Pt but they are conspicuous from all other directions. Once inside the entrance, the buildings around Kioni and the masts of moored yachts will become visible.

The approach from all directions is through deep water and hazard free, although you should maintain a good look-out at all times. The waters off the east coast of Ithaca are often busy with fast-moving ferry traffic and day-tripper boats coming in and out of Kioni between 1000-1600. Yachts arriving in the bay in the afternoon may also experience strong gusts, which skid off the surrounding hillsides.

BERTHING

There are several places to berth in Kioni. The most popular is stern- or bows-to the quay immediately to the west of the short mole. The mole itself is reserved

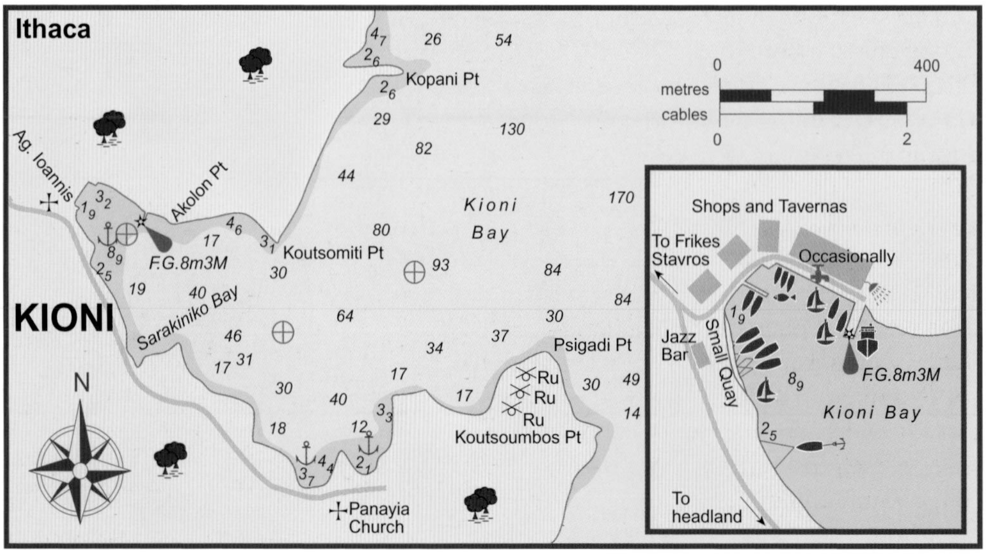

Kioni is a vibrant place that is popular with charter boats and flotillas. Expect the quay to be busy peak season

for day-tripper boats, so you should not berth off it during the day. After 1600, when most day-tripper boats have stopped running, a couple of yachts can berth alongside the mole, or stern-to off its end or outer edge. There are rocks along its outer edge, though, so keep some distance between you and the mole, particularly as this area is affected by swell from passing ferries. Day-tripper boats start running at 1000, so vacate the mole by then.

If the northern part of the quay is full (and it usually fills up very quickly), berth on the western side of the harbour. It is quite shallow close to the quay, so you may need to berth well off and use your dinghy to get ashore.

Kioni Bay is relatively deep so lay lots of chain when setting your anchor. It is also weedy in places, particularly near the mole, so make sure your anchor has dug in well before leaving your boat. The ferry swell that pounds Frikes also affects Kioni, so remember this when berthing. If your boat is pulled well off the quay, your anchor has dug in properly and your rode is taut, you should experience nothing worse than the occasional gentle swell at night. Without these precautions, you may find yourself having to re-lay your anchor in the early hours.

ANCHORING

Occasionally yachts free-swing to their anchors near the quay, but this is not advised. It is deep here (about 15-20m of water) and affected by gusts off the hillsides. A secluded anchorage not too far from the village is off the rocks at the southern end of the harbour. There are rings in the rocks which you can tie a stern line to in order to prevent you from swinging, while steps set into these rocks allow you to get ashore easily.

If you just want to stop for lunch, you can anchor at the southern end of Kioni Bay in one of the little bays to the west of the windmills. These are open to the north and, although not suitable in unsettled conditions, offer reasonable protection from the south. Anchor in 5-8m and check your anchor digs in well as the bottom is fairly weedy.

Kioni Bay is deep and often gusty, but there are couple of places to anchor

Useful information – Kioni

FACILITIES

Water: Water point on the town quay. Ask at the supermarket to use it. A metered water tanker also visits Kioni morning and evening mid-summer.
Fuel: Take a taxi to nearby petrol station.
Showers: At souvenir shop near Café Spavento (around €4) and at Hamilton House near the harbour mole (0800-1000 & 1700-2000).
Ice: Sold at Elpinor mini-market or ask at tavernas.
Gas: At the supermarket.
Rubbish: Bins behind the harbour mole.
Yacht services/chandlery: The nearest chandler is at Frikes, about 3½nm to the north.
Telephone: There are several phone boxes along the road past the quay. Phone cards from mini-markets and the newspaper shop. Mobile phone reception in Kioni is poor.

PROVISIONING

Grocery shops: Elpinor Mini Market & Yacht Supplies (Tel: 26740 31560) stocks a wide range of goods, including bread, dairy products, wine, beer, spirits, ice and toiletries. Open daily. Pantopoleion (Tel: 26740 31464), near Spavento Bar, is also very well-stocked and has a deli counter. Open daily, 0800-2100.
Bakery: Fresh bread is available at Pantopoleion (except on Sun) and Elpinor. Bread is also delivered by van along the quay at about 0900 each day.
Butcher: No but cold meats are sold at Pantopoleion and Elpinor.
Banks: The nearest is in Vathi (see p223).
Pharmacy: No but there is one at Stavros, 5km away.
Post: The nearest post office is in Vathi. Post box next to doctors' surgery. Stamps at the souvenir shops.
The postal service on Ithaca is slow.

EATING OUT

The tavernas and cafés along the waterfront at Kioni offer excellent choice combined with good views across the bay. Calipso (Tel: 26740 31066) serves breakfast, snacks and main meals and has a very good, traditional Greek menu, including the local speciality, onion pie. It is usually one of the busiest in Kioni, so if you want to eat at the water's edge, book in advance. Mythos (Tel: 26740 31122) is very reasonably priced and offers a varied menu of traditional cuisine. Avra (Tel: 26740 31453) is a popular spot with flotillas and specialises in meat dishes cooked over an open grill. There are also several café-bars in the village. One of them, Café Spavento (Tel: 26740 31427), also known as Jenny's Bar, opposite the supermarket, makes superb cocktails and plays jazz from its enormous CD collection.

ASHORE

The villages of Frikes and Stavros are just a short car journey away, or you can walk there. The island's main port of Vathi is also within easy reach. For those who want to stay in Kioni, there is a good walk around the bay to the windmills and a few small pebble beaches to the S of the harbour.

Ruins of three windmills stand at the entrance to Kioni Bay

TRANSPORT

Car hire: Hire car firms in Vathi. See p223.
Taxis: Yiannis Taxi (Tel: 26740 31712); Dymos Taxi (Tel: 26740 31130); Costas Taxi (Tel: 26740 31792); Alekos Taxi (Tel: 69460 96802).
Bus: Daily service between Vathi, Frikes and Kioni.
Ferry: From Frikes and Vathi you can travel to Nidri on Lefkada. From Vathi, you can also travel to Kefalonia, Astakos and Patra on the mainland. Other inter-island and international ferries leave from Poros, Sami and Argostoli on Kefalonia.
Air travel: The nearest airport is on Kefalonia (Tel: 26710 29900), 5½ miles (9km) south of Argostoli. Take a ferry from Frikes to Fiskardo on Kefalonia and then a taxi or hire car to the airport.

OTHER INFORMATION

Local Tel code: 26740.
Doctor: Surgery behind the supermarket on the road to Stavros, near Café Spavento.
Dentist: The nearest is in Vathi.
Hospital: Medical centre in Vathi: Tel: 26740 32222.

Frikes

Entrance to Frikes Bay: 38°27'.78N 20°41'.51E
Approach to Frikes: 38°27'.65N 20°40'.22E
Alongside quay at Frikes: 38°27'.60N 20°39'.81E

Frikes is a small harbour nestled into a wooded valley on the north-east tip of Ithaca, 2½nm north of Kioni. With just a handful of houses and tavernas lining the shore, it's still very traditional and unspoilt by tourism but has enough facilities to make it a good destination for cruising yachts. It's a really lovely place to spend some time: the surrounding countryside has some stunning walks and there's no shortage of choice in the village when looking for somewhere to eat. It does, however, have only limited room to berth and, as a popular destination with flotillas, can get very busy peak season. If you want to stay the night, aim to get here early. Shelter is generally good but the bay is badly affected by swell from passing ferries.

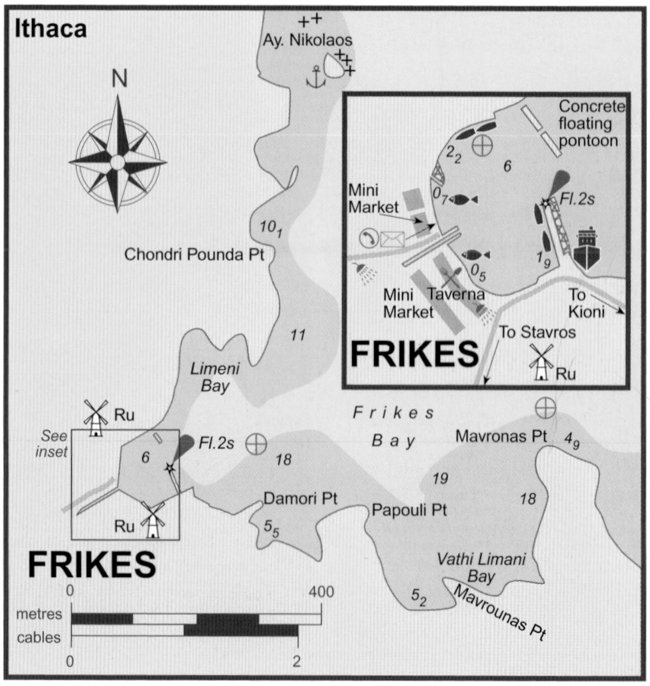

Frikes was first established in the 17th century by families from the nearby villages, who cultivated the surrounding land and started fishing in the bay. Its name, though, is thought to come from the pirate Frikon, who reputedly launched his attacks on passing ships from the bay.

NAVIGATION

Charts: Admiralty 203, 189, SC5771; Imray G121, G12, G1; Hellenic Navy Hydrographic Service 036, 030

From Kioni, follow the coast north for 2nm. Frikes is tucked in the western corner of a large bay and is identifiable from some distance. The approach from all directions is through deep water, although from the north you should take care to the south of Ag Nikolaos Pt as there are a couple of isolated rocks offshore and around the islet of Ag Nikolaos.

Once in Frikes Bay, you will be able to see the white buildings of the village nestled on the shore and a couple of sail-less windmills immediately to the south. Another windmill and the village of Stavros can be seen on the hillside behind Frikes.

By mid-afternoon, the bay can be quite windy as gusts whip off the steep hills and skid across the water, so be prepared to shorten sail. You should also maintain a good look-out at all times as the waters to the north and east of Ithaca are the main shipping channels between the Peloponnese and the north Ionian and Italy.

BERTHING

Frikes is one of the few places in the Ionian where normal practice is to berth alongside. This is due, principally, to the strong, offshore winds that gust out of the village, plus a lot of rubble on the seabed with the potential to snag anchors. The best berth is alongside the breakwater in the south-east corner of the harbour.

Usual practice in Frikes is to berth side-to off the breakwater

It is fairly sheltered here, but this is a very popular spot, particularly with flotillas, so expect to raft up two or three deep. Yachts can also berth alongside the quay in the north-west corner of the bay. However, this quay is affected by swell day and night, so put out all available fenders if you do berth here. The swell from ferry traffic causes a great deal of movement for several minutes, so considerable damage can be done if you haven't enough fenders out or if your warps are too slack.

Berthing alongside the floating concrete pontoon to the east of this quay is not advised. It is badly affected by swell and many boats have been severely damaged when berthed alongside. If you have to berth here, go stern- or bows-to, with your anchor dug in well and the boat pulled as far off the quay as possible. Even with these precautions, though, berthing is not recommended as you will still be affected by swell.

ANCHORING

There are several small inlets around Frikes Bay that provide adequate shelter in most conditions. In calm weather, nearly all are suitable for overnight stops but they are all affected by ferry swell and gusts that roll off the hills. If you do stay overnight, make sure your anchor is dug in well and, if you require extra protection, take a long line ashore. Frikes Bay is generally very deep until close in but is hazard free.

Limeni Bay, to the north-east of Frikes, offers the best all-round shelter of these anchorages, although at times is still affected by offshore gusts. Anchor in 5-6m on mud and weed. The holding is reasonable once your anchor has dug in.

You should only anchor in the eastern corner of the bay to the eastern of Damori Pt, as cables run ashore in the western part. However, the eastern corner offers good shelter and you can anchor in about 7m.

Frikes is little more than a hamlet, but you can guarantee a good meal at one of the many tavernas

To the east of this, between Papouli Pt and Akrotiri Pt, is a twin-headed bay. This offers good shelter from the south but is exposed to all other directions, so should be used in calm weather only. Anchor in around 5m of water on mud and weed.

The islet just to the north of Frikes is Ay Nikolaos. Its northern and eastern shores are lined with reefs, but you can anchor in settled conditions to the west of the islet when approaching from the south. Drop your anchor in depths of 3-6m, where the holding is good. This daytime anchorage provides a pleasant spot for snorkelling.

Useful information – Frikes

FACILITIES

Fuel: Take a taxi to nearby petrol station. The nearest fuel quay is at Vathi, about 9nm to the south.
Showers: At Penelope restaurant (€2), just round the corner from Kiki's Mini Market (€3; 0700-2400), Symposium Taverna (€2).
Ice: At Kiki's Mini Market.
Laundry: Round the corner from Kiki's Mini Market.
Gas: Bottle exchange at Penelope Market.
Rubbish: Bins behind the ferry quay.
Yacht services/chandlery: Small chandler behind the main street.
Telephone: Phone box opposite Penelope Market. Phone cards sold at mini-markets. Mobile reception is okay, although patchy in some of the anchorages. Weather forecast: Ask at Penelope restaurant.

PROVISIONING

Grocery shops: Kiki's Mini Market (Tel: 26740 31762/Fax: 26740 31150) on the waterfront sells Greek, English and Oriental products and a wide range of local goods, such as olives and vinegars. You can fax a shopping list in advance and it will be ready for you to pick up when you arrive. Penelope Market also has a good range of produce and a very good deli.
Bakery: Fresh bread at Penelope's Market and at Kiki's. Bread and pastries sold at Isalos café.
Butcher: No. Some meats at Penelope Market and Kiki's Mini-Market.
Banks: No. Nearest at Vathi, 9nm to the south.
Other shops: Souvenir shop on the waterfront, jewellery shop (Kosmhmata Antikeimeno Tzoylia) on the side road past Symposium.
Pharmacy: No but some pharmaceutical items are sold at Kiki's Mini Market.
Post: No post office. Post box next to Penelope Market. Post is erratic on Ithaca, so post urgent mail on the mainland or on one of the bigger islands.

EATING OUT

The four tavernas along the waterfront, Ulysses (Tel: 26740 31733), Rementzo Café & Restaurant (Tel: 26740 31719), Symposium Taverna (Tel: 26740 31729) and Penelope Restaurant and café-bar (Tel: 26740 31005) are all good, particularly the last two. The menus are extensive and include many island specialities, such as sea urchins' eggs, which are supposed to be aphrodisiacs. All the tavernas are busy during the summer, so if you want to eat right on the water's edge it is worth booking in advance. All serve breakfast, lunch and dinner. There are also a couple of café-bars in the village.

Penelope mini-market

ASHORE

The village of Stavros is a 1¼-mile (2km) walk from Frikes. There are fantastic views from the village – both down the valley towards Frikes and over the west coast of the island. Stavros is also home to a small but fascinating Archaeological Museum (Tel: 26740 32200), open Tuesday-Sunday, 0830-1500.

An alternative walk is along the shore to the east of the harbour. Near the breakwater, a small bronze statue of a mermaid commemorates the valour of local partisans who are said to have used Frikes during World War II as a base from which to attack German landing craft.

TRANSPORT

Car hire: Frikes Bike Rental (Tel: 26740 31021) has a number of scooters for hire. Open seven days a week, 0800 till late.
Taxis: Ask at Penelope Restaurant. Yiannis Taxi (Tel: 26740 31712); Dymos Taxi (Tel: 26740 31130); Costas Taxi (Tel: 26740 31792); Alekos Taxi (Tel: 69460 96802).
Bus: Daily service to Vathi. Bus stop by the ferry quay.
Ferry: Ferry from Nidri on Lefkada to Frikes runs twice daily: 0730 & 1600. The journey takes two hours, via Fiskardo on Kefalonia. From Vathi you can catch a ferry to Lefkada or Astakos and Patra on the mainland.
Air travel: The nearest airport is on Kefalonia (Tel: 26710 29900), 5½ miles (9km) south of Argostoli. Take a ferry from Frikes to Fiskardo on Kefalonia, and then a taxi/hire car to the airport. The airport at Preveza (Tel: 26820 22355) is another option. Take a ferry from Frikes to Nidri and then a taxi/bus to Preveza.

OTHER INFORMATION

Local Tel code: 26740.
Doctor: No. The nearest is in Kioni, 2½ miles (4km) away.
Dentist: In Vathi.
Hospital: Medical centre in Vathi: Tel: 26740 32222.
Weather forecasts: From Penelope taverna.

Polis Bay Ormos Polis

Entrance to Polis Bay: 38°26'.14N 20°38'.06E
Charts: Admiralty 203, 189, SC5771; Imray G121, G12, G1; Hellenic Navy Hydrographic Service 036, 030

Polis Bay lies on Ithaca's north-west coast, opposite the islet of Asteri. A small cove open to the south-west, it offers reasonable protection from the prevailing winds, although it is exposed in a southerly and to any swell generated in a northwesterly. Anchor in less than 5m off the north-west coast of the bay, taking a line ashore. The holding is reasonable, although there is quite a bit of weed on the bottom, so make sure your anchor is dug in well before leaving your boat unattended.

Occasionally shallow-draught yachts anchor off the north-west end of the small breakwater in the eastern corner of the bay, but it is not advised. It is shallow here and the breakwater is used by local fishing boats, so it is best to keep clear. Watch out for their permanent moorings as they are scattered around the bay and may foul your prop.

While Polis Bay offers no amenities, Stavros, a pretty little village perched on the hillside above is just a 1km walk away. This is the largest village in north Ithaca and a good place to stock up. Facilities include a bakery, several mini-markets, fruit and veg shops and tavernas, plus a hardware store and a health centre. A daily bus service runs between Stavros and Vathi, Ithaca's capital (see p220), and there is also a small but fascinating Archaeological Museum (Tel: 26740 32200), open Tuesday-Sunday, 0830-1500.

The museum's collection includes a number of archaeological finds from the area, which is considered to be one of the most important on the island. Ithaca's topography and the discovery of remains of a settlement at Pilikata, just to the north of Stavros, have led historians to believe that this is where Homer set Odysseus' palace. Perched high on the hill, the site has magnificent views of three bays: Polis, to the west, Afales, to the north, and Frikes, to the east. It closely matches the views that Homer describes in *the Odyssey*.

The museum is also home to fragments of several bronze tripods which were found in Loizos Cave at Polis Bay. They are thought to be similar to those given to Odysseus by the Phaecians. Other finds at the cave have included carved inscriptions to the goddesses

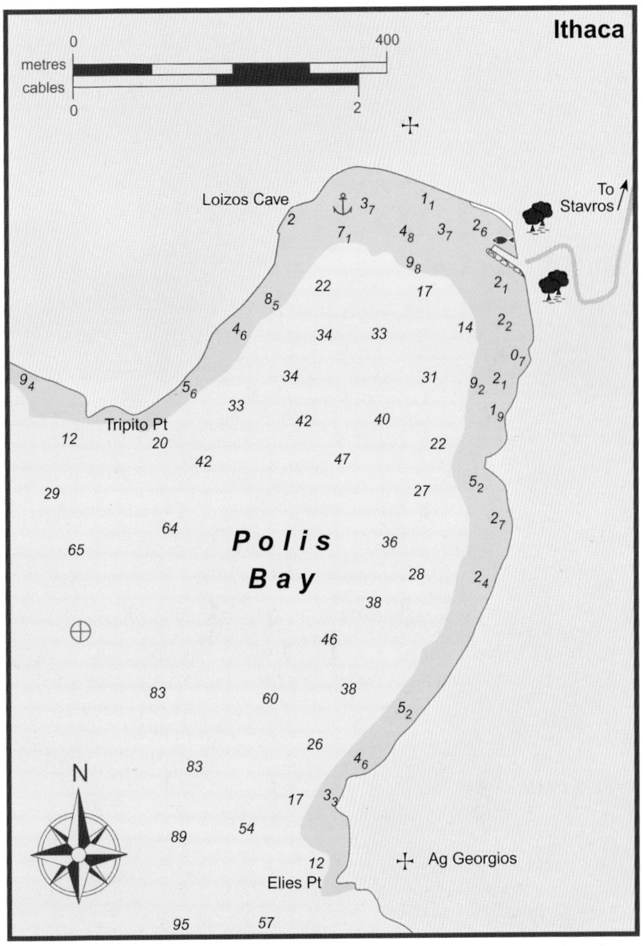

Athena, Hera and Artemis, and it is thought to have been a significant place of worship in ancient times.

Piso Aetos Bay

Pis'Aitou Bay, Ormos Pisaitou, Pisaetos

Entrance to Piso Aetos Bay: 38°20'.80N 20°41'.00E
Charts: Admiralty 203, 189, SC5771; Imray G121, G12, G1; Hellenic Navy Hydrographic Service 036, 030

Piso Aetos Bay is 5½nm south of Polis Bay. The large but fairly shallow indentation on Ithaca's west coast is a good stopping place for a daytime swim but provides no shelter from the prevailing northwesterlies and swell generated in the Ithaca Strait. In a southerly it is also extremely exposed, so the bay should be considered a calm-weather, daytime anchorage only. In season, a regular ferry service runs between Piso Aetos and Sami on Kefalonia and Astakos on the mainland and the ferry quay lies in the eastern corner of the bay. Immediately to the east of this is a tiny fishing harbour, which is usually busy with *caiques* and too shallow for yachts. Anchor off the quay to the north of the ferry quay in 5m or less. The holding on mud and weed is

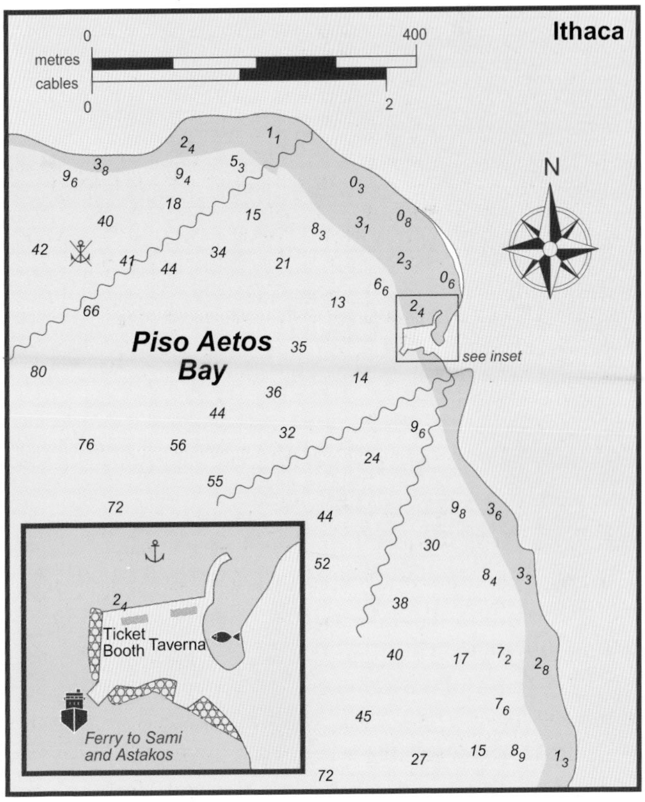

reasonable once your anchor has dug in. Do not anchor near the coast to the north-east of the harbour as there are submerged cables in the area.

There are no facilities at Piso Aetos, apart from a telephone and a small, seasonal café/taverna which caters for the passing ferry trade. However, it's easy to get to if you need to change crew and don't want to go to Sami or Fiskardo on Kefalonia, or Vathi on Ithaca.

Ag Andreas Bay Ormos Ay Andreou

Entrance to Ag Andreas Bay: 38°17'.94N 20°43'.66E

Charts: Admiralty 203, 189, SC5771; Imray G121, G12, G1; Hellenic Navy Hydrographic Service 036, 030

Ag Andreas is a deep but narrow bay on the south coast of Ithaca. Situated 5nm from Perapigadi, Ag Andreas Bay is a good spot for lunch or, in the right conditions, an overnight stay. It is isolated enough not to attract many visitors, and small enough that even if it does, there's not much room for many yachts to anchor.

Although the bay is protected from the prevailing winds, it is open to the south, so should not be considered if there is any hint of a southerly. Wash from passing ferries is also swept into the bay occasionally, and while the holding on sand is reasonably good there are patches of weed, so make sure your anchor is dug in well. The bay is deep until close in but near its head you should be able to anchor in 8m or less.

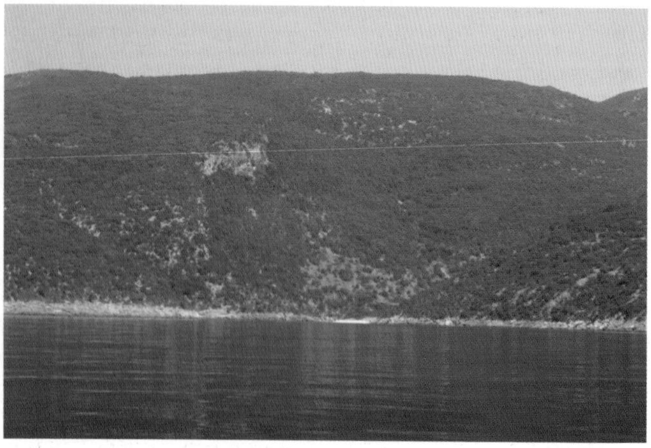

Ag Andreas Bay is deep, but is a good anchorage in settled conditions

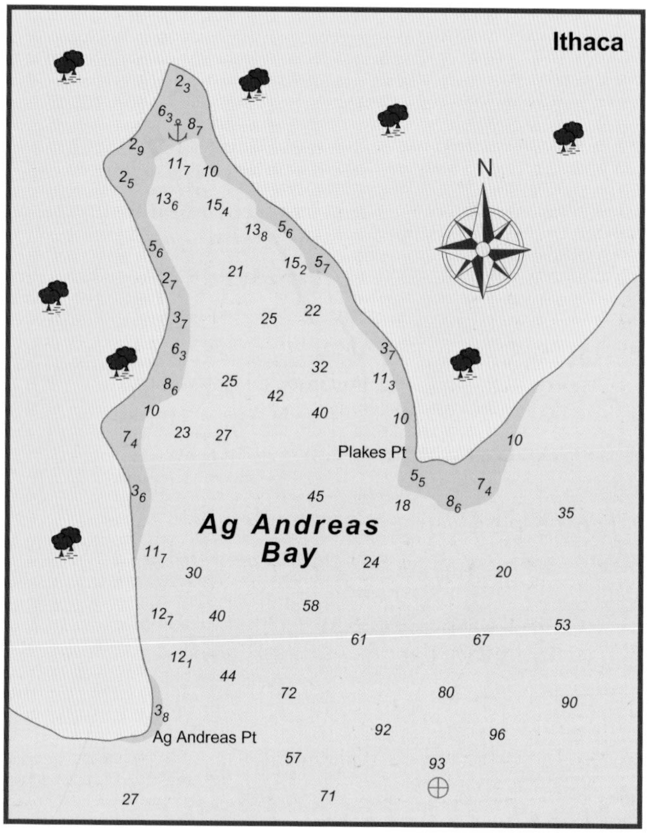

If you are approaching Ag Andreas Bay from the east coast of Ithaca, don't get too close to Ag Ioannou Pt (Fl 10s12m10M), the island's easternmost headland, as a reef extends from it for about a third of a mile.

Perapigadi

Pera Pigadhi, Liquia

East of Perapigadi: 38°20'.42N 20°45'.26E

Off quay: 38°20'.18N 20°44'.83E

Fish farm in bay north of Perapigadi: 38°20'.99N 20°45'.08E

Charts: Admiralty 203, 189, SC5771; Imray G121, G12, G1; Hellenic Navy Hydrographic Service 036, 030

One of the most beautiful anchorages on Ithaca is south of Sarakiniko Bay, off the islet of Perapigadi. Steep-sided, garrigue-covered hillsides, fringed with a thin line of light grey rocks, plunge into incredibly clear turquoise waters.

It's an anchorage that provides probably the best shelter from the prevailing winds along this stretch of coast and, while the southern end of the island can be quite gusty, the small coves to the south give good protection in moderate conditions.

There are several places to anchor near Perapigadi, the first being off a small, L-shaped concrete quay on the islet's west coast. Although Perapigadi is private (it was recently up for sale for £440,000), you can go alongside the quay, or stern- or bows-to at either end. In recent years it has been christened 'Rat Island' due to the influx of rather large rodents that have been spotted in the area. If you do go alongside, don't leave any food out. The holding on sand and shingle is reasonable and, although the quay is exposed to the prevailing winds, you'll find adequate shelter here.

A second anchorage lies in Perapigadi Bay, just to the south. The narrowest part of the channel between the southern end of the islet and Ithaca is quite shallow, at just 3-4m, so stay in the middle and proceed slowly. Both the coves in Perapigadi Bay offer good shelter and you can anchor off either the beach or the rocks on shingly sand, in less than 5m. The holding is generally good, although there are patches of weed, so make sure your anchor digs well in.

From here you can walk up the hill to the Raven's Crag and the Spring of Arethusa. It is thought that this is where the goddess Athena led Odysseus to meet the swineherd Eumaeus in Homer's *Odyssey*, and the spring that he mentions, 'where they (Eumaeus' pigs) find the right fodder to make them fat and healthy, feeding on their favourite acorns and drinking water from deep pools (Chpt 13, 406-411)', still exists under the Raven's Crag. It's a good, but very steep walk, so take great care if you head that way. The views towards Kefalonia and Zakynthos are worth the climb, and just beyond the spring is what is thought to have been Eumaeus' cave.

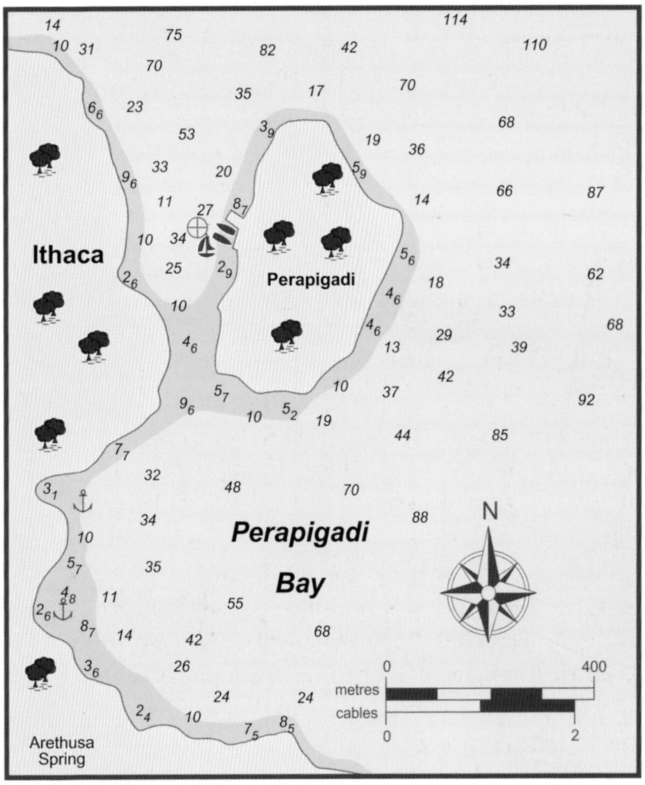

Sarakiniko Bay

East of Sarakiniko Bay: 38°21'.84N 20°44'.66E
Charts: Admiralty 203, 189, SC5771; Imray G121, G12, G1; Hellenic Navy Hydrographic Service 030, 21

Sarakiniko Bay, on the east coast of Ithaca, 4nm south of the Molos Gulf, is a very good anchorage in a northwesterly. Protected by the arm of Sarakiniko Pt (Ak Skotaryia), the bay tucks deep within the island and offers good shelter from all directions apart from the south-east. Anchor in 8m or less on sand and mud. Despite its remote location, this bay is often busy with tourists brought by day-tripper boats from Vathi, and a large desalination plant overlooking the bay also makes incessant noise in an otherwise tranquil anchorage.

Atokos

Lying half way between Ithaca and Kastos is the island of Atokos. A rugged island, formed of chalky white cliffs and garrigue, Atokos is conspicuous from all directions and can be easily identified by its twin, 300m peaks.

It's uninhabited bar an occasionally-used fisherman's cottage on its east coast, but has two good anchorages, and its crystal clear waters are spectacular.

Cliff Bay

West side of Cliff Bay 38°28'.63N 20°48'.58E
East side of Cliff Bay 38°28'.69N 20°48'.80E

Cliff Bay, on the south coast of Atokos, is a stunning anchorage. White, stratified cliffs, streaked with red rust stains plunge into crystal clear waters. Little beaches at the foot of screes disappear into Prussian blue seas tinged with a hint of aquamarine, while up in the trees there's the constant chatter of cicadas mixed with the calling of birds. In the right weather conditions, it's an extremely beautiful and isolated daytime stop. Protected from the north, this is a good anchorage when the prevailing northwesterly winds are blowing, but when the breeze turns to the south it becomes untenable. Steep cliffs fringe the bay, so if you want to go ashore head to One House Bay instead.

NAVIGATION

Charts: Admiralty: 203, SC5771; Imray: G121, G12

All approaches are straightforward and through deep water. However, a good look out should be kept on all passages as a major shipping lane runs between Ithaca's east coast and Atokos. From the Molos Gulf off Ithaca, steer 047°T for about 8nm towards the southern end of Atokos. You will be crossing the shipping lane at right angles, so pay good attention. From the Meganisi

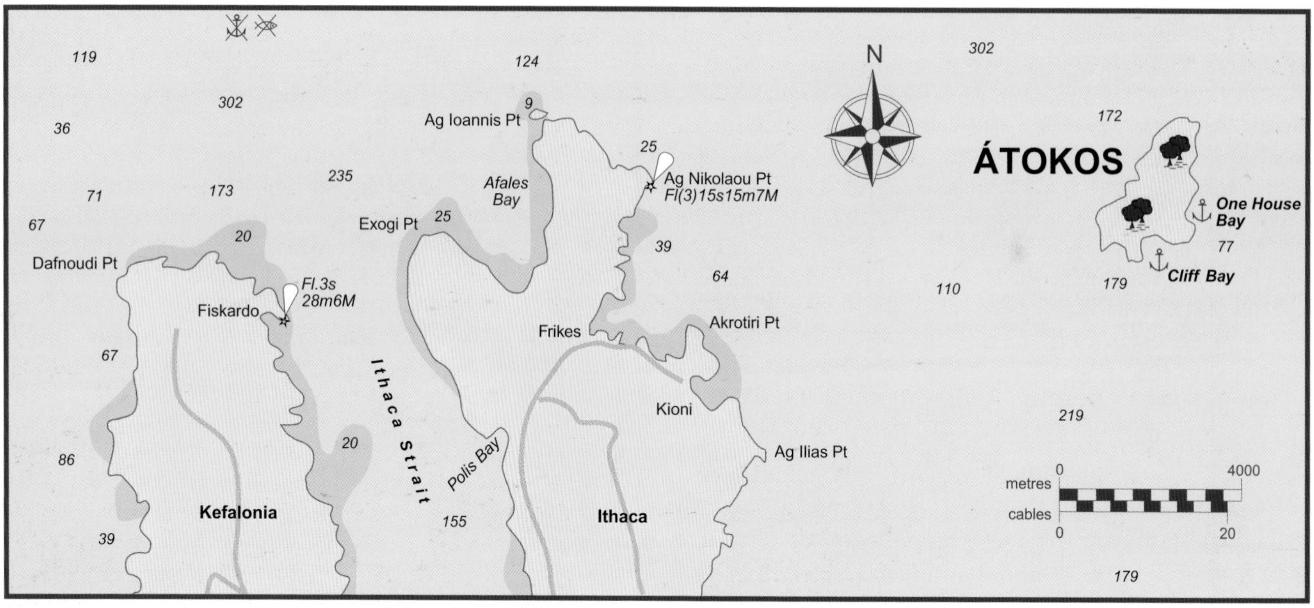

Channel, steer 163°T towards Atokos. On approach from the south, steer 341°T and from the channel between Kalamos and Kastos, to the north-west, head 223°T. From the west and south the white cliffs of Cliff Bay can be easily seen.

ANCHORING

The bay is very deep, so you need to anchor fairly close to shore. On the western side, the deepest part of the bay, there is only room for one yacht to anchor off the small beach, but you can get quite close in and anchor in about 5m of water. The bottom is sand and weed but the holding is good.

It is generally shallower on the eastern side of the bay and there is room for more yachts. Anchor on gravel and weed in less than 8m. This side of the bay is slightly more open to gusts as northerly winds whip round the headland, so if you want more shelter then it is worth trying to squeeze into the western corner.

One House Bay

Entrance to bay: 38°28'.94N 20°49'.40E

One House Bay (5m water): 38°28'.99N 20°49'.25E

This anchorage gets its name from the solitary house that sits on the densely wooded hillside above the bay. Lying on the east shore of Atokos, it is another beautiful inlet with aquamarine waters, sheer white cliffs and a pale pebbly beach. It's a good spot for both lunch-time and overnight stops as it is protected from the prevailing northwesterly winds, but in a strong southerly, it is not advised. The bay's rugged beauty is a great attraction and consequently it is often very busy with yachts. But it is still worth a visit.

NAVIGATION

Charts: Admiralty 203, SC5771; Imray G121, G12

Follow the instructions detailed above for the approach to Cliff Bay. One House Bay lies about a mile north up the coast and is easily identifiable by the conspicuous white house above the beach. Caution should be exercised when crossing the shipping lane off the east coast of Ithaca and if approaching from the north, via the east coast of Meganisi, care should be taken around the Formikoula shoals that lie off the south-west tip of Kalamos.

ANCHORING

The whole bay has a depth of less than 10m so there are plenty of places to anchor. You can anchor quite close in to shore or off the rocks on the north side of the bay, taking a line ashore. If you do go onto the beach, please make sure that you take all your rubbish with you. Atokos is uninhabited and any rubbish you leave will spoil it for the next person to visit the island.

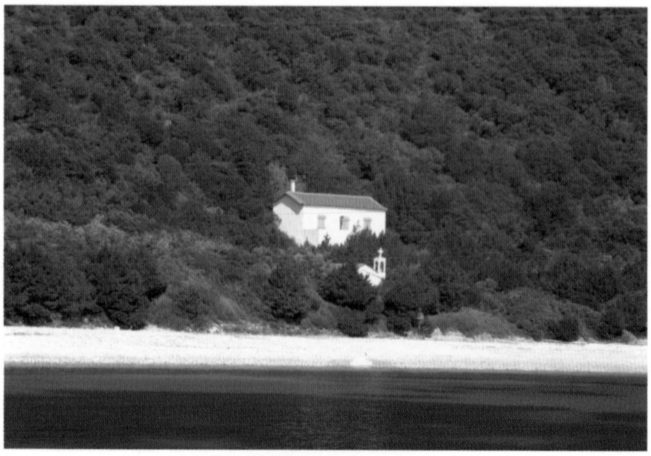

The solitary house after which this bay is named

Chapter seven
Zakynthos & the Peloponnese

The Southern Ionian is a lovely part of Greece but little explored by yachts. Like the Korinthiakos Gulf, it is more an area which people pass through than a destination in its own right, yet there are some idyllic places to visit.

Zakynthos, the southernmost Ionian island, provides a handful of anchorages and though not as well set up for cruising yachts as Lefkada, Kefalonia or Ithaca, it is a beautiful spot nonetheless. The west coast of the Peloponnese, too, offers superb sailing in clear waters, dotted with pretty harbours where shelter is reasonable and amenities good.

Generally, the prevailing winds in this area are from the NW, although the southern tip of the Peloponnese experiences more westerly and southwesterly breezes. As with the waters to the N, the mornings are normally calm with little or no wind; it will usually blow up to a Force 3-5 after lunch, decreasing again in the evening.

Zakynthos
Nisos Zakinthos/Zante

'Zakynthos could make one forget the Elysian Fields,' wrote Dionysis Solomos, poet and author of the Greek National Anthem. Homer, too, referred to it as a 'wooded island' in *The Odyssey*, and it has long been known for its lush, verdant terrain. The Venetians called it the *fiore di Levante* (the flower of the Levant) and agriculture was always vital to the island's economy. It still is, to a certain extent: vines for the Black Corinth grape, or Zante currant, introduced by the Venetians, still extend over much of Zakynthos and are renowned for their succulence and flavour. Olive and wine production is high too, although most of the island's income now stems from tourism.

At 158 square miles (410km^2), Zakynthos is the third

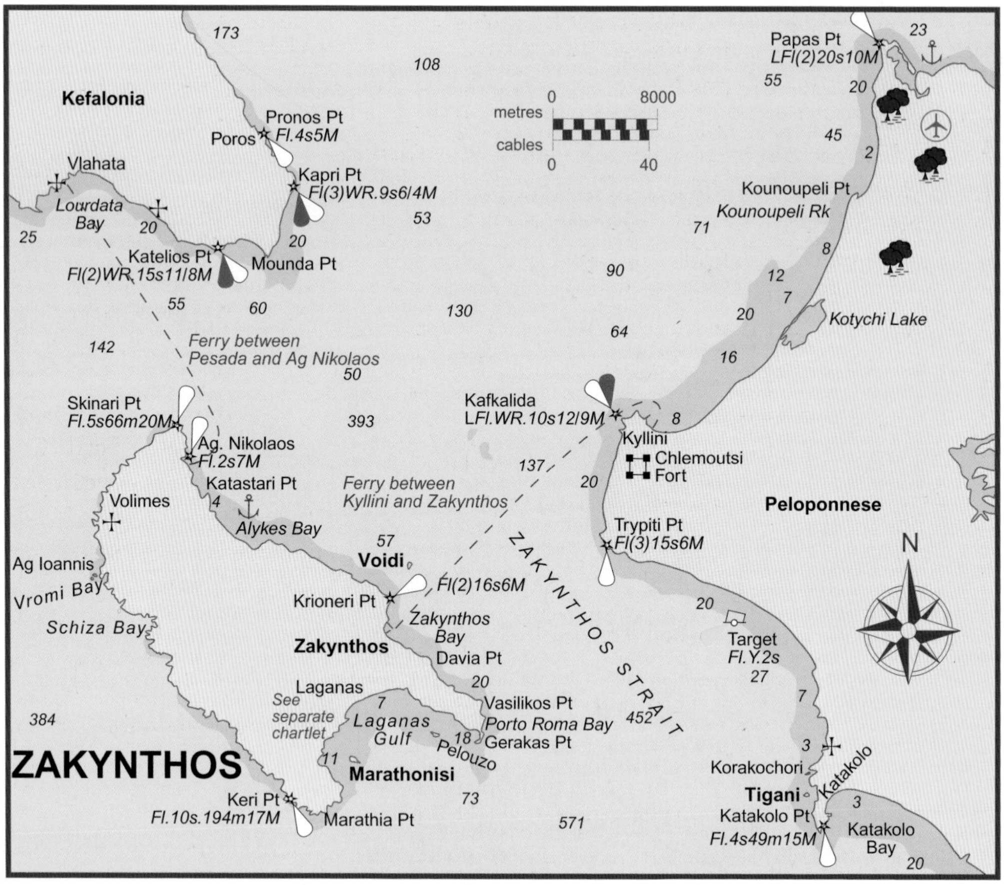

largest Ionian island and the southernmost of the group. It lies off the north-west coast of the Peloponnese, 7nm south of Kefalonia, and is one of Greece's most popular islands, although little explored by cruising yachts.

Package holiday tourists descend in droves but, being slightly off the beaten track and away from the main group of Ionians, it does not attract a regular invasion of yacht-borne visitors. Principally this is because it has only a handful of destinations and just one secure harbour, Zakynthos Town. It's the island's main port and is being developed; but for the moment, despite a fair amount of room and shelter, it cannot compete with the capital towns on the other Ionians. Also, its limited anchorages are only suitable in fair weather.

Most of the island's main resorts are on the Laganas Gulf, on its south coast. It is beautiful here, but boat movements in the area are strictly limited. The beaches are the breeding ground of the endangered loggerhead turtle, *Caretta caretta*, one of the only places in Greece.

It's a shame that there aren't better facilities on Zakynthos as parts of it are really beautiful. Away from the chaos of beach resorts, it has some stunning countryside and, although limited in cultural interest due to the 1953 earthquake, there's still plenty to do.

Zakynthos Town Zante, Zakinthos

Off the entrance to Zakynthos harbour: 37°46'.79N 20°54'.33E

Attractive Zakynthos Town on the east coast is the island's capital and the main port of call for visiting yachts. Backed by high mountains and wooded hills, it has the most usable harbour with good shelter from all directions and it's the best place on the island for provisioning. There have been plans for some years to develop a marina at the southern end of the harbour but in 2007 works were still in progress and no completion date had been set. However, the town quay offers a reasonable berth for a day or two and at either end of the season, when there aren't so many tourists, it is relatively quiet.

The town is Venetian in style, although quite modern in construction. Like Kefalonia, Zakynthos suffered greatly during the 1953 earthquake and much of the town was razed. Unlike Kefalonia's capital, Argostoli, however, the architects here remained true to the old town and have restored much of it sympathetically, reconstructing many of the Venetian elements and retaining its original layout. It's quite a sprawling place compared with the more compact Lefkada and Corfu, but nevertheless attractive and surprisingly untouristy amidst so many major resorts.

As a base for exploring inland, or to reprovision before heading north or south, Zakynthos has much to offer. Lying slightly further away from the main cluster of Ionian islands, it is also less busy with charter boats and flotillas.

NAVIGATION

Charts: Admiralty 2404, 203, 189, SC5771; Imray G12, G1; Hellenic Navy Hydrographic Service 221/1, 22

Zakynthos Town is situated about two-thirds of the way down the east coast of the island. It's the largest town on this stretch of the coast, and indeed the island

and, set against a large hillside, is conspicuous on approach from the south and east. If approaching from the north, the town will be hidden until you have rounded Krioneri Pt, but you should head towards the south-east corner of the island. To the south of the town, Mount Skopos is distinct from some distance.

On approach from the east and south, care should be taken around the reef If Dimitis, just to the east of the harbour entrance, as depths here decrease to less than 3m. A red buoy marks the northern end of the reef and should be left to port. At night, this buoy is lit (Fl R 3s), as are the breakwaters at the entrance to the harbour (Fl R 1.5s & Fl G 1.5s).

Maintain a good look-out at all times as ferry traffic near the harbour entrance is often heavy.

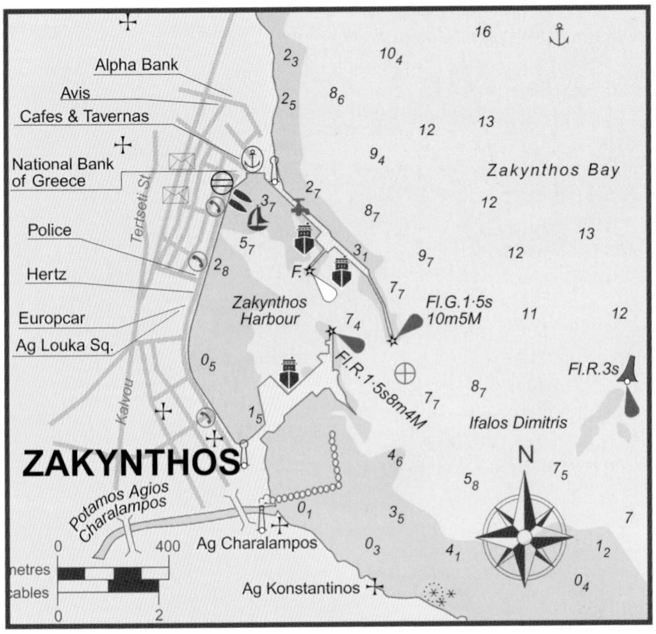

BERTHING

Berth stern- or bows-to the quay in the north-west corner of the harbour, wherever there is room. Occasionally you can also berth stern- or bows-to the western end of the main breakwater but keep clear of the day-tripper boats and ferries. If in doubt, contact the port police on VHF Ch12/Tel: 26950 28117 and ask where to berth. Depths in this part of the harbour range between 2.5-4m, but it gets shallower the further south you head. In the far south-west corner of the harbour there is as little as 0.5m of water. The holding on mud is good.

In 2007, the marina development behind the southern breakwater was not open to visitors. There are plans to install pontoons, lazylines and facilities for yachts but it is unclear when these will be finished.

ANCHORING

There is nowhere to anchor within the immediate vicinity of Zakynthos Town, and care should be taken along the shore to the south of the harbour as there are many shoal areas. The nearest anchorages are either in Alykes Bay (see p240), 9nm to the north of the town, or Porto Roma (see p236), 6nm to the south.

Zakynthos Town. Work is in progress to build a marina in the harbour, but in 2007 it was not open to visitors

Useful information – Zakynthos Town

FACILITIES
Water: Can be found on the northern breakwater.
Fuel: Take jerrycans to a nearby petrol station. There are a couple near the main quay.
Ice: At the supermarkets.
Gas: Ask at the supermarkets or hardware shops.
Shorepower: On the northern breakwater.
Rubbish: Large bins near the quay.
Yacht services/chandlery: A couple of chandlers in Zakynthos, one of them near the quay.
Telephone: Several phone boxes on the road past the quay. More in the centre of Zakynthos. Phonecards sold at kiosks. Mobile reception here is good.

PROVISIONING
Grocery shops: Lots of supermarkets and grocery shops in the town centre. Daily market on Filioti St, one of the roads that runs at 90 degrees to the waterfront.
Bakery: Several in the town centre.
Butcher: Several in the town centre.
Banks: National Bank of Greece (Tel: 26950 22000) branch and ATM near Solomou Square, the main square at the northern end of the harbour; the Agricultural Bank of Greece (Tel: 26950 22772) and the Emporiki Bank (Tel: 26950 22338) are both on El Venizelou St, which runs off the south-west corner of Solomou Square. A branch of the Alpha Bank (Tel: 26950 22336) on Ag Markou Square, to the west of Solomou Square.
Pharmacy: Lots in the centre of Zakynthos.
Post: Post office on Tertseti St, to the west of Alexandrou Roma St. Stamps at souvenir shops; the postal service on Zakynthos is good.
Opening times: 0900-1400 and 1730-2100 but most souvenir shops, tavernas and cafes are open until later.

EATING OUT
There is plenty of choice in Zakynthos Town and you can usually guarantee a decent meal. The tavernas along the waterfront tend to be quite expensive, although Komis has a very good reputation for seafood. The streets near Solomou Square are packed with cafés and can be a really pleasant place to spend the evening. You will also find some pleasant traditional tavernas, such as Arekia (Tel: 26950 26346), to the north of the harbour.

ASHORE
Interesting cultural sites include the Byzantine Museum (Tel: 26950 42714) on Solomou Square, at the northern end of the harbour, which houses a collection of wall paintings and Byzantine icons, as well as artefacts salvaged from the town after the 1953 earthquake. Open Tuesday-Sunday, 0800-1500, admission €3.

Solomou Square is named after the poet Dionysios Solomos (1798-1857). A museum to its west on Ag Markou Square is dedicated to him. Open since 1966, the Museum of Solomos (Tel: 26950 28982) contains his tomb, plus manuscripts, photographs and an extensive library. Open daily, 0900-1400, admission €3.

You will find some stunning views if you wander up the hill to the Castle, at the northern end of Zakynthos Town. Built by the Venetians in 1646, it has been largely destroyed by earthquakes over the years, but there is evidence of churches, a Venetian prison and English barracks. The castle is open Tues-Sun, 0830-1430, admission €3 (Tel: 26950 48099).

TRANSPORT
Car hire: Avis (Tel: 26950 27512) is on Stravopodi St, open daily, 0800-1300 and 1800-2100; Europcar (Tel: 26950 41541) is on Ag Louka Square, towards the south end of the quay; Budget (Tel: 26950 51738) is on Makri St, parallel to El Venizelou St; and Hertz (Tel: 26950 45706) is on Lomvardou St, along the waterfront. There are also several travel agents along here, which can organise car hire.
Taxis: Taxi rank near Solomou Square, at the north end of the harbour.
Bus: The bus station (Tel: 26950 22255) is on Filita St, one road back from the waterfront. Regular daily services to Laganas, Alykes and Kalamaki. Timetable from the travel agents. Also four or five buses a day to Patra and Athens on the mainland.
Ferry: Ferries to Kyllini, on the north-west Peloponnese coast, leave Zakynthos Harbour several times a day. Shipping companies have offices near the harbour. In season, you can travel to Pesada on Kefalonia from Ag Nikolaos, a small harbour on the north-east tip of Zakynthos (see p239).
Air travel: The island's airport is to the south of Zakynthos Town, near Kalamaki on the south coast. There is usually one flight a day to Athens and in season charter flights operate to other European destinations. The Olympic Airways office (Tel: 26950 28611) is at the northern end of Alex Romanou St, three roads back from the waterfront. No bus service between Zakynthos Town and the airport.

OTHER INFORMATION
Local Tel code: 26950.
Port authority: The Port Police office (Tel: 26950 28117) is on the quay.
Police: Tel: 26950 24480/24450. The Tourist Police station (Tel: 26950 24482-4) is on Lombardou St, the road past the waterfront.
Doctor: Several in the town, or try the First-Aid centre (Tel: 26950 23166).
Dentist: Ask for recommendations at the First-Aid centre.
Hospital: Zakynthos Hospital (Tel: 26950 22514/59100) is to the W of the harbour, on the outskirts of town.

Porto Roma

Entrance to Porto Roma Bay: 37°42'.47N 20°59'.61E

Charts: Admiralty 189, SC5771; Imray G12, G1; Hellenic Navy Hydrographic Service 22

About 6nm south of Zakynthos Town, Porto Roma, on the SE tip of the island, is a delightful anchorage in settled conditions, though not suitable in bad weather or for overnight stays. On approach from the north, don't get too close to Vasilikos Pt (Ag Nikolaos Pt) as there are reefs immediately to the south.

Anchor in the bay in 5m or less, keeping a good look-out for swimmers as the beach is popular with tourists. There are a couple of small seasonal tavernas ashore and a narrow strip of pebble and sand beach.

Gerakas Bay

Ag Yerakas, Ormos Yeraki

South of Gerakas Pt: 37°41'.44N 20°59'.26E

Anchoring and all on-the-water activity are prohibited in and around Gerakas Bay, so you should steer clear and anchor elsewhere.

The cove, tucked in the south-east corner of the Laganas Gulf, is part of an area where strict restrictions have been set up in order to protect the endangered loggerhead sea turtle (*Caretta caretta*).

While the beach is a popular destination for tourists, it is also an important nesting ground for these loggerhead turtles, which the authorities are keen to preserve. See under Laganas Gulf below for the full list of restrictions.

Laganas Gulf

Kolpos Lagana

Immediately outside the entrance to the Laganas Gulf: 37°39'.68N 20°56'.21E
Charts: Admiralty 189, SC5771; Imray G12, G1; Hellenic Navy Hydrographic Service 22

The Laganas Gulf, on the south coast of Zakynthos, is one of the most important environmental areas in the Ionian and indeed the Mediterranean. Female loggerheads, an endangered species of sea turtle, come here to nest and lay their eggs, one of the only places in the Ionian they do so. There are six nesting beaches in the Laganas Gulf: Gerakas, Dafni, Sekania, Kalamaki, East Laganas and on the islet of Marthonisi in the western corner of the gulf, and all boating activity is restricted.

The Laganas Gulf has been a National Marine Park since 1999 and the bay is now split into three zones (A, B and C), all of which are governed by certain regulations.

In **Zone A**, which lies between Kalamaki and Gerakas Pt, all boating activity, including access, passage and anchoring, is prohibited.

In **Zone B**, from Laganas to Gerakas Pt, incorporating the islets of Marathonisi and Pelouzo, there is a 6-knot speed limit and all anchoring is forbidden.

In **Zone C**, from Keri Bay to Laganas, the speed limit is again 6 knots.

These restrictions apply during the turtles' nesting season (1 May–31 October) but should be adhered to at all times throughout the year. Failure to do so could result in a hefty fine.

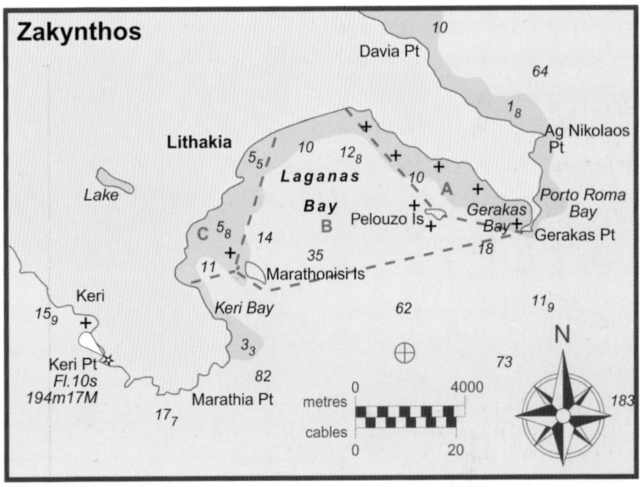

The south coast of Zakynthos. Bays along this coast are used by nesting Loggerhead turtles and so boating activity in this area is restricted

Keri Bay

Ormos Keri, Limni Keri

Keri Bay: 37°41'.18N 20°50'.96E
Charts: Admiralty 189, SC5771; Imray G12, G1; Hellenic Navy Hydrographic Service 22

Keri Bay, in the south-west corner of the Laganas Gulf, is a very pretty spot and the only place in the area where anchoring is allowed, although a speed restriction of 6 knots still applies.

The bay should be approached from the south-east, taking care to avoid the reefs to the north of Marathia Pt and those to the west and north of the islet of Marathonisi. The bay itself is relatively deep until close in. It is a secure anchorage in most conditions but exposed in an easterly. The holding is reasonable on sand but there is weed on the bottom so make sure your anchor digs in well.

Those wanting to use the breakwater should anchor off stern-to wherever there is room and take a long line ashore. Watch out for tripper and fishing boats.

Keri is quieter and more attractive than the tourist resorts of Laganas and Kalamaki to the east. There are a few houses near the harbour, but the main village of Limni Keriou is to the north-west, beyond the lake. South-west of this, on the hillside above Keri Pt, is the village of Keri.

Near the harbour is a small mini-market and several tavernas and cafés. The Diving Centre Turtle Beach (Tel: 26950 49424), among others, operates diving trips from Keri to 15 sites around the island. Costing around €35 per dive, including equipment, the centre also runs five-day PADI courses from €320.

If you're looking for lively nightlife, take a taxi to Laganas and Kalamaki where there are bars and clubs galore. To explore further afield, hire-car firms include Pelargos Tours (Tel: 26950 52017) and Stamatis Rentals (Tel: 26950 52466).

The 3-mile (5km) walk to the village of Keri, on the hillside to the south-east, is a good way to stretch your legs and there are some beautiful views across Zakynthos and the Laganas Gulf from here.

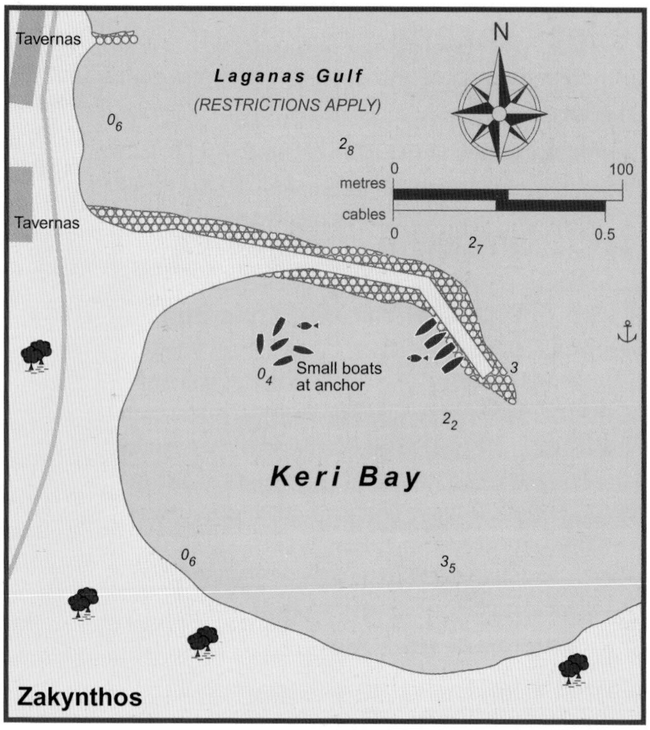

Vromi Bay Ormos Vroma,

Porto Vromi

Entrance to Vromi Bay: 37°48'.83N 20°37'.46E
Charts: Admiralty 203, 189, SC5771; Imray G12, G1; Hellenic Navy Hydrographic Service 22

The west coast of Zakynthos is inhospitable with few secure anchorages. However, an exception, in calm weather, is Vromi Bay, in the north-west corner of the island.

From all directions, the bay should be approached from the south-west. Day-tripper boats use the small channel between the islet of Ag Ioannis and Zakynthos, but this is shallow so yachts approaching Vromi Bay from the north should pass to the west of Ag Ioannis and head into the bay from the south-west.

Anchor in the northern part of the bay in around 8m or less, taking a long line ashore for extra protection; watch out for permanent moorings used by local boats. The bay offers good shelter from all

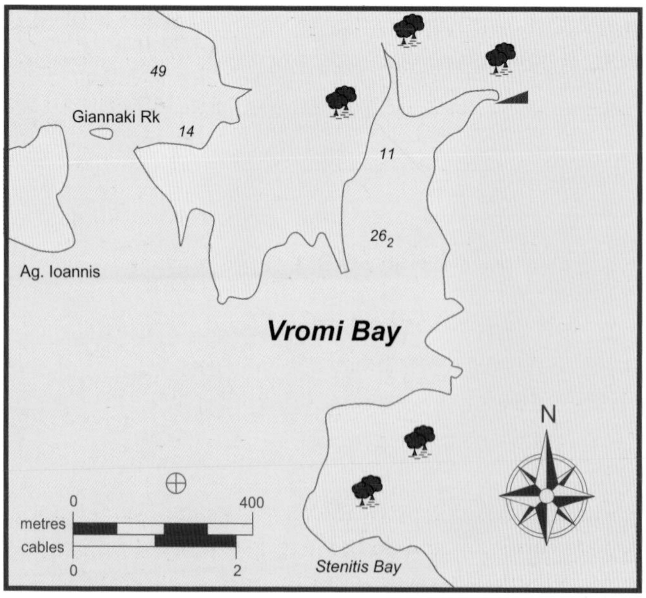

but the south-west. Holding on sand and mud is reasonable, but it is a bit rocky in places.

The bay is often called 'Porto Vromi', meaning 'dirty

port', said to be named after the tarry deposits frequently found on the shoreline.

Most of the boats here are used to take tourists to Navagio Bay, to the north. If you have seen a picture of Zakynthos, it will probably have been an aerial of Navagio Bay (shipwreck bay), with a half-buried coaster stranded in the middle of a beautiful white sandy beach fringed with azure waters. Now a popular tourist attraction, the ship is thought to have been smuggling cigarettes from Turkey to Italy when it was wrecked in bad weather in 1982.

A half-buried coaster lies stranded on the beach in Navagio Bay

Zakynthos's west coast is rocky and unfriendly to yachts, but its limestone cliffs plunge into stunning blue waters

Ag Nikolaos Bay

Ay Nikolaos, Skinari

To south-east of Ag Nikolaos: 37°54'.18N 20°42'.96E
Charts: Admiralty 203, 189, SC5771; Imray G12, G1; Hellenic Navy Hydrographic Service 221/1, 22

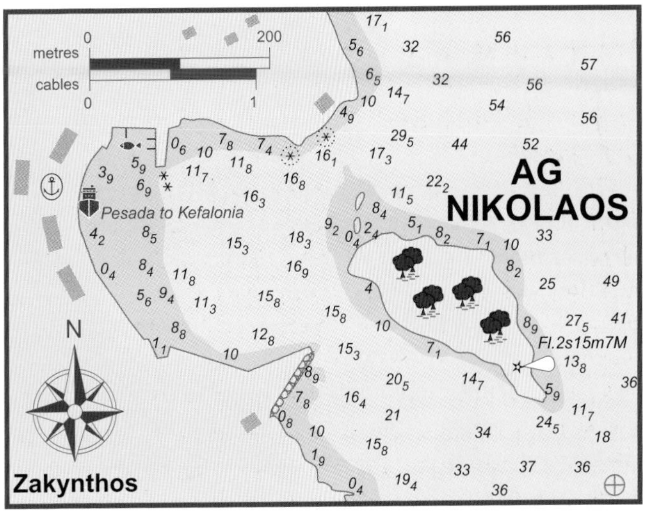

Semicircular Ag Nikolaos Bay, on the north-east coast of Zakynthos, is guarded at its entrance by the islet of Ag Nikolaos. It offers reasonable shelter from the prevailing winds but is exposed in anything with an easterly in it and often affected by swell.

The approach from all directions is straightforward, the main hazard being the day-trip boats and the ferry that links Ag Nikolaos with Pesada on Kefalonia during the summer months. You can pass on either side of the islet of Ag Nikolaos but leave plenty of room round it if approaching via its north coast as a reef extends for some distance offshore.

Visiting yachts usually berth stern- or bows-to the quay in the south-west corner of the bay or anchor in the lee of the islet, off its north-west shore. The holding on mud and sand is reasonable, although it is weedy in places. Day-tripper boats use the quay in the north of the bay, so keep clear. Yachts sometimes anchor off its eastern side and take a line to the breakwater.

Ashore you'll find several tavernas, a mini-market and a petrol station. There have been reports that the harbour is to be developed, but in 2007 it had yet to happen.

Ag Nikolaos's main trade is passing tourists, heading for the Blue Grotto of Korithi, or the Blue Caves, just to the north of the harbour, below Skinari Pt. The caves are an incredible sight, purely because the colour of the water is such a wonderful shade of azure. White limestone cliffs plunge into turquoise waters and on a calm day when the sun is at its highest, the effect is startling. The day-trip boats visit a couple of caves and also the Kamares of Marathia – natural arches in the limestone cliffs.

Ag Nikolaos Bay on the east coast of Zakynthos. During the season a small ferry service runs between here and Pesada on Kefalonia

Alykes Bay Ormos Alikes

Anchorage in Alikes Bay: 37°51'.83N 20°45'.46E
Charts: Admiralty 203, 189, SC5771; Imray G12, G1;
Hellenic Navy Hydrographic Service 22

Five nautical miles south of Ag Nikolaos is Alykes, a large, shallow bay that is home to the first major holiday resort along this stretch of coast. A small harbour in the southern corner is protected by a hook-shaped rocky breakwater, which gives good, all-round shelter

The coastline around Alykes Bay was one of the first parts of Zakynthos to be developed into a tourist resort

and provides space for boats of average size.

The approach from all directions is quite straightforward, although you need to watch out for swimmers and waterskiers in the bay as several watersports companies operate from here. Berth bows-to the breakwater wherever there is room, keeping some distance off it as there is debris at its base. If there isn't room in the harbour, anchor just to the north of it in 5m or less. The holding on mud and sand is reasonable, although the anchorage is slightly more exposed in a northerly.

Ashore you'll find two resorts: Alikana is the one nearest to the harbour while Alykes is slightly to the north. Both offer a wide range of amenities including supermarkets, gift shops, tavernas, bars and travel agents and hire car companies such as Dragon Car Rentals (Tel: 26950 83957). You can even ride on a model train up to the villages of Katastari and Pigadakia and discover 200 years of local history at the Vertgagio Cultural Museum.

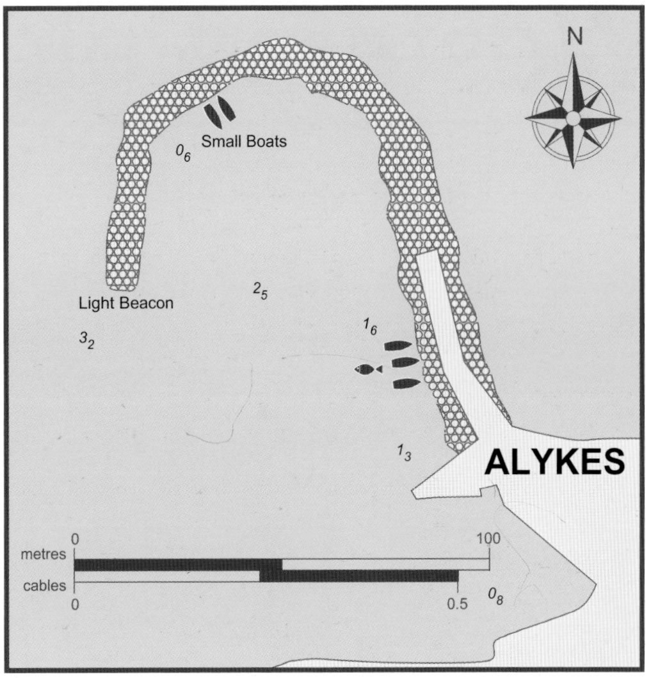

The harbour at Alykes Bay offers good, all-round shelter but is shallow, so should be used with care

Western Peloponnese

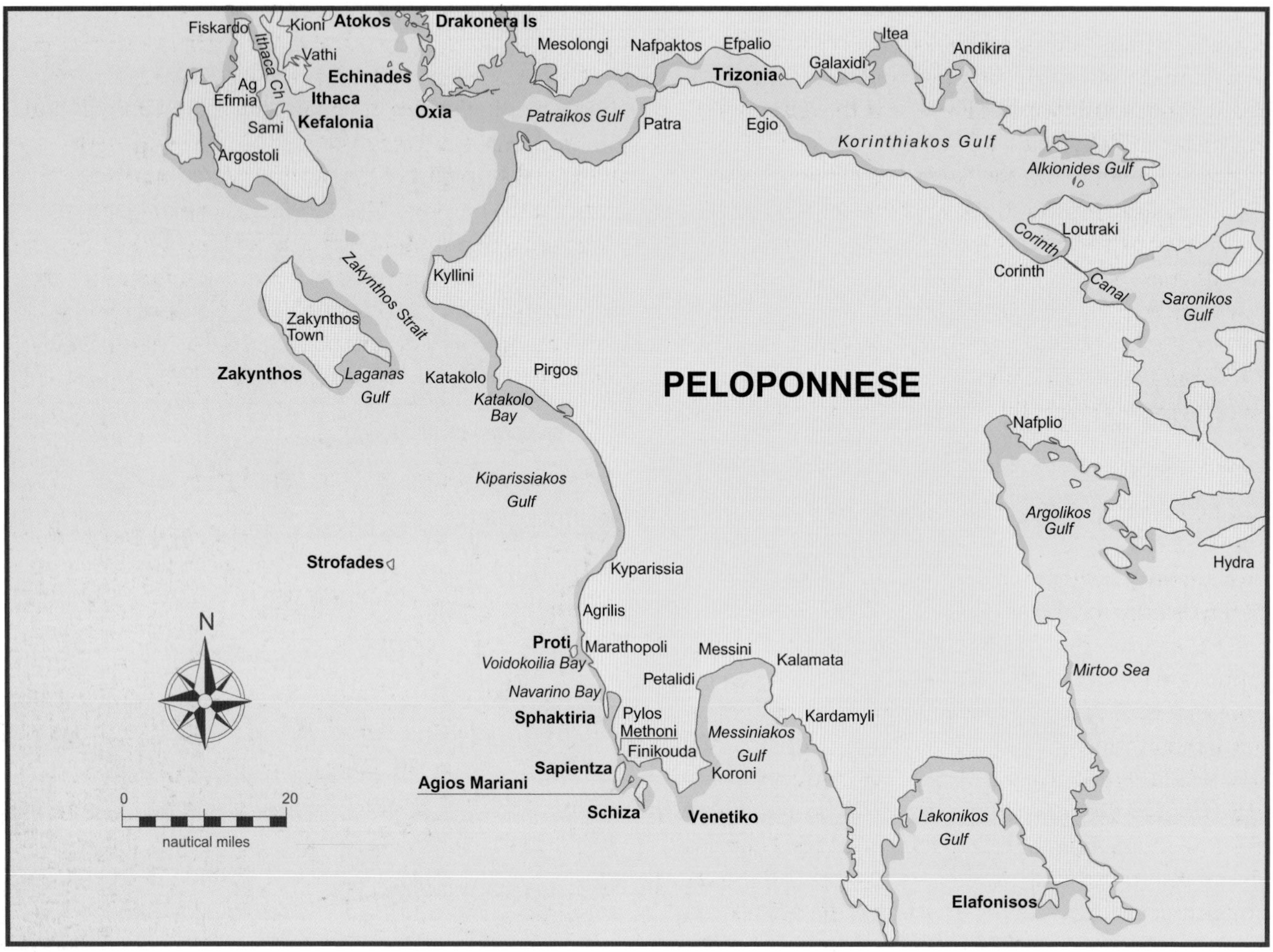

At first glance, the west coast of the Peloponnese looks to have little to recommend it. Not only is it a lee shore, exposed to the prevailing winds, but it lacks the protection of nearby islands, which the Etolo-Akarnanian coast to the north enjoys. Yet in places it is a beautiful coastline and some of the harbours along its shores offer reasonable shelter and good amenities, particularly towards its southwestern tip.

Cruising boats tend to bypass this stretch of coast, but if you get the chance it is well worth spending time here. Navarino Bay is a wonderful natural harbour bordered by the Gialova Lagoon, and the town of Pylos, on its shores, is a delightful place to spend a day or so. Methoni, to the south, is a pretty little anchorage, as is Longo Bay on the east coast of the island of Sapientza. Kalamata, at the northern end of the Messiniakos Gulf, offers first-class marina facilities and good transport links, and Katakolo is a suitable place to leave your boat if you want to go on a cultural day-trip to the ancient site of Olympia.

Like the island of Zakynthos, to the west, the Peloponnese is lush and verdant. Messinia, the south-west region, is considered to be the most fertile area of land in Greece and large quantities of citrus fruits, figs, grapes and almonds have long been produced here; the olives grown around Kalamata are the best in the country. Tourism is starting to take over in many areas but it remains very rural.

The name Peloponnese means 'Pelop's island' and is thought to have been named after Pelops. He was a mythological hero who conquered the region in ancient times and was killed and cooked in a stew by his father as an offering to the gods. It's something of a misnomer to describe this area as an 'island', although strictly speaking it is. Until 1897 its only link with the rest of the Greece was via a narrow isthmus to the east of Corinth. Since the Corinth Canal was dug though, this has been severed, leaving the mountainous 8,276-square-mile region stranded. Now there are just a couple of bridges over the Corinth Canal and the Rio–Antirio Bridge over the Patraikos Gulf.

This area, having seen Roman, Byzantine, Frankish, Turkish, Venetian and Russian occupation, is rich in cultural heritage. It often gets overlooked now even though it is a superb sailing area. It is slightly windier than the northern Ionian, particularly around the Messiniakos Gulf, but nevertheless is well worth the detour.

Kyllini Killini

Off Kyllini: 37°56'.24N 21°09'.66E

Kyllini, a small town on the west coast of the Peloponnese, is a fairly lack-lustre place. Lying about 36nm south-west of Patra, it is the main port for ferries to Zakynthos so, like Igoumenitsa in the northern Ionian, it has the feeling of a staging post, with everyone passing through. The town is tacked on to a ferry quay and lacks the vitality of other harbours on this coast, such as Patra and Kyparissia. As a destination it has little to offer the cruising yachtsman, although it is good for crew changes. There are regular ferry connections to Zakynthos and Kefalonia, and the bus services to Patra, Pyrgos and Athens are good, too.

NAVIGATION

Charts: Admiralty 2404, 1676, 189, SC5771;
Imray G12, G16, G1;
Hellenic Navy Hydrographic Service 061, 40

Kyllini is easy to identify from all directions – just look for the ferries – and the approach is straightforward until close to. Stay well offshore, particularly if coming from the south, as there are rocks and shoals along the coast and around the uninhabited islet of Kafkalida. A lighthouse (LFl WR 10s12/9M) marks the islet at night and, as there is shallow water between it and the mainland, you should pass to the west of it. There are also rocks immediately to the north-west of the harbour, so keep well clear until due north of the breakwater. At night, a lit buoy (Fl G 3s) off the eastern end of the breakwater should be left to starboard. Two flashing yellow lights mark the entrance to the inner harbour.

The main hazard on the approach to Kyllini is ferry traffic, which travels at some speed. Maintain a good look-out at all times when making the approach.

BERTHING

Work has now been completed on the inner harbour, but improvements are still being made to the ferry port. The best place to berth is stern or bows-to the harbour's northeastern breakwater (see chartlet below). The outer half of this breakwater is not equipped with lazylines; however, the further in you go, the more you will find that the berths are reserved for local fishing boats, which take up part of the north-east and north-west sides of the harbour. You are sheltered here from the prevailing winds, although exposed in an easterly. The holding is good in depths of 3-5m, although be aware of ground chains the further into the harbour you go.

If you have any doubts about where to berth, contact the Port Police on VHF Ch12, Tel: 26230 92211.

ANCHORING

There is nowhere to anchor near Kyllini.

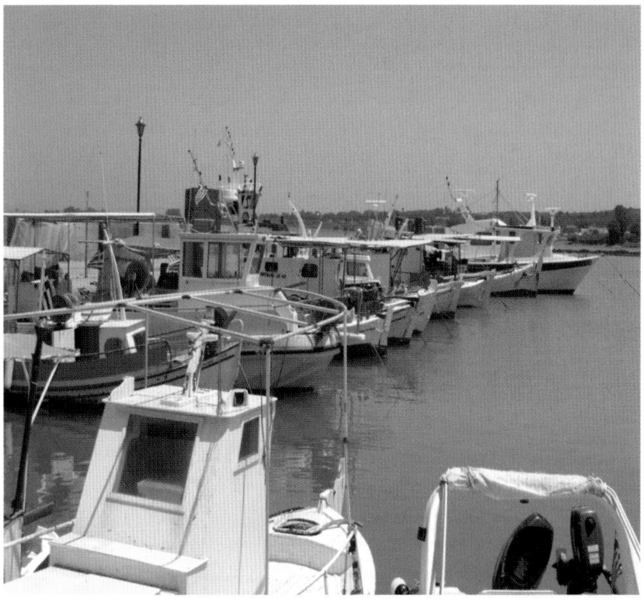

The small harbour at Kyllini is packed with fishing boats

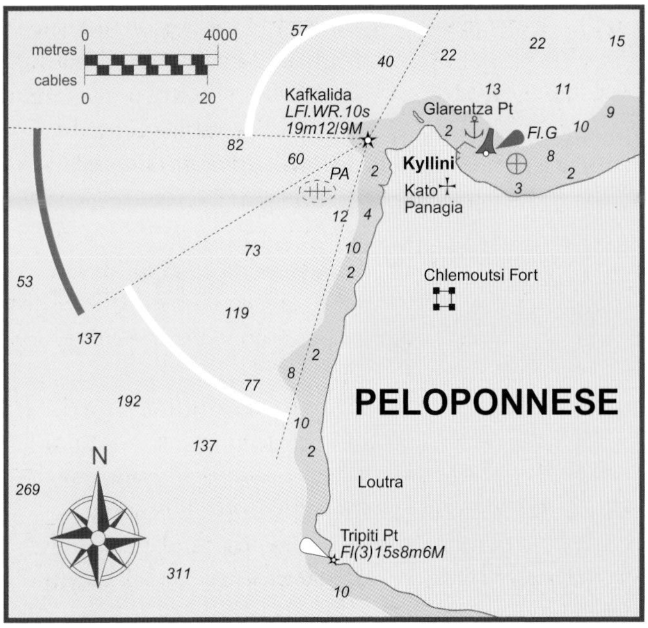

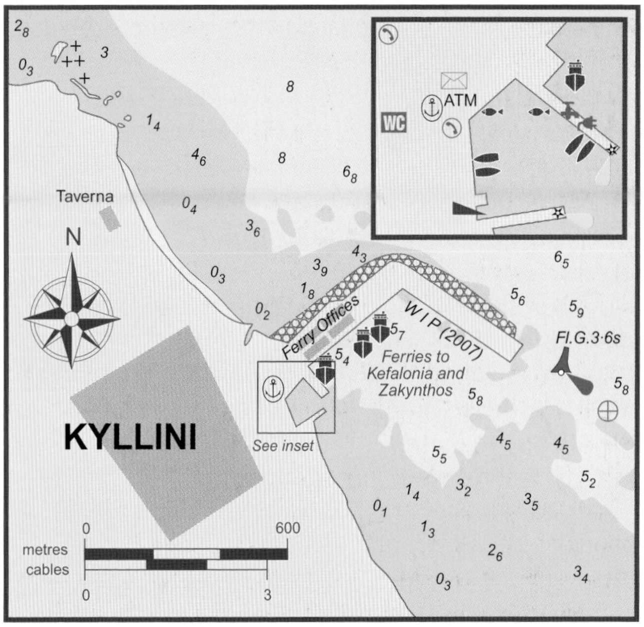

Useful information – Kyllini

FACILITIES

Water: Taps situated on the dockside.
Fuel: Take jerrycans to the petrol station in Kyllini. Two more on the road out of the town.
Shorepower: Power points are intermittently spaced along the inner harbour.
Showers: Open-air showers on the beach. Toilets behind the Customs Office.
Ice: Ask at the tavernas.
Rubbish: Large bins on the quay.
Telephone: Several phone boxes in town, one near the port exit and another near the Customs Office. Phonecards are sold at a nearby kiosk and mobile reception is good.

PROVISIONING

Grocery shops: A couple of mini-markets on the main street.
Bakery: On the main street.
Butcher: On the main street.
Banks: Emporiki ATM at the Robinson Club Hotel (Tel: 26230 22410). Another ATM located in front of the Customs Office.
Pharmacy: Situated on the main street.
Post: Post office in the centre of town. Open Mon-Fri, 0900-1400. The postal service is good.
Opening times: Most of the shops are open throughout the day but close for a siesta in the afternoon, which is usually between 1400-1700.

EATING OUT

Several tavernas and fast-food cafés are situated near the ferry port. By far the best place to eat though is Taverna Anna (Tel: 26230 92416) on the beach to the west of the harbour. The reasonably traditional Greek fare is superb. Set amid olive trees and away from the hubbub of the main port, it's a really pleasant place to spend a few hours and is popular with locals.

ASHORE

The main site of interest ashore is the castle of Chlemoutsi (Tel: 26230 95033), which perches on the hillside above the village of Kastro, about 3½ miles (6km) south of Kyllini. Dating from 1220-1223, the castle is one of the finest examples of Frankish architecture in the Peloponnese and one of the best preserved in Greece. Open Tues-Sun, 0800-1900; Mon, 1200-1900, admission costs €3.

TRANSPORT

Car hire: Ask at tavernas.
Taxis: Taxi rank is situated near the ferry terminal.
Bus: Several a day between Kyllini and Patra and Kyllini and Pyrgos. Also services to Athens.
Ferry: From Kyllini you can travel to Zakynthos Town on Zakynthos (1½ hours), or Poros (1¼ hours) and Argostoli (2¼ hours) on Kefalonia. Several services a day peak season, and fewer in winter. Ionian Ferries, Strintzis Ferries and Katina Ferries all have ticket offices at the port. Timetables and more details can be found at www.greekferries.gr
Air travel: The nearest airport is on Zakynthos (Tel: 26950 28322, 1½ hours away by ferry). International and domestic services fly to the island several times a week. Athens airport (Tel: 21035 30000, 4½ hours away by car) offers more destinations.

OTHER INFORMATION

Local Tel code: 26230.
Port authority: Port Police office (Tel: 26230 92211) behind the ferry terminal.
Police: Police station (Tel: 26230 92202) in the town.
Hospital: Medical centre (Tel: 26230 92222).

Taverna Anna on the beach is recommended for food

Katakolo Katakolon

Off the entrance to the harbour: 37°38'.94N 21°19'.46E

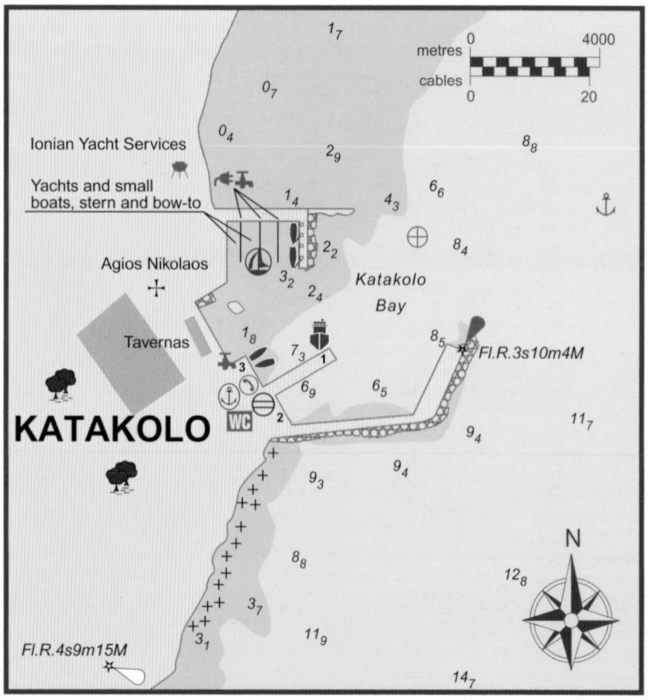

Katakolo, 31nm south of Kyllini, has a chequered reputation. It's a port used as a stop-over by cruise ships and, while it can be hideous when thousands descend, it can also be rather charming. Moreover, as a yachting destination it's really good. The marina is secure and, tucked in behind Katakolo Pt, it's definitely the snuggest harbour along the Peloponnese's west coast. Katakolo is sheltered from all directions, and although a swell kicks up in a strong southeasterly it is rarely untenable. Facilities include shorepower, water and a boatyard at the harbour and, while the town isn't that big, most provisions are available.

For the culturally minded, Katakolo is the best harbour from which to visit Ancient Olympia. The Sanctuary of Olympia, where the Olympic Games were first held in 776BC, is one of Greece's most famous archaeological sites and just 45 minutes' drive from the harbour.

NAVIGATION

Charts: Admiralty 2404, 189, SC5771; Imray G16, G1; Hellenic Navy Hydrographic Service 221/2, 22

Katakolo is on the eastern side of Katakolo Pt and hidden from view on approach from the north until east of this headland. If approaching from the north, stay offshore until well past as there are isolated rocks and shoals all the way along the coastline from Palouki to Katakolo Pt. From the south, the harbour is easier to pinpoint, even from some distance, and the approach via the Kiparissiakos Gulf and Katakolo Bay is through deep water. At night, look for a lighthouse on Katakolo Pt (Fl 4s49m15M), and a light on the end of the harbour breakwater (Fl R 3s10m4M). The marina is immediately to the north of the commercial port.

BERTHING

Berth stern- or bows-to the floating pontoons in the marina. Local fishing boats on lazylines take up much of the space here but there is usually room for visitors to berth. Watch out for the mooring lines, though, when manoeuvring under power. The marina offers good shelter from all directions, although it can sometimes be a bit rolly with swell in a southeasterly.

If you can't find space in the marina, berth stern-to off the quay to the north of the ferry dock, in around 3m. The holding is reasonable but you are near the commercial port so don't expect much peace and quiet. Quite the reverse in fact.

ANCHORING

Just to the north of the marina is a good anchorage that is protected from the prevailing northwesterlies. It is very shallow off the beach, so anchor in about 3.5m off the eastern end of the marina.

Watch out for mooring lines when manoeuvring in the marina

If there's not room in the marina, you can berth stern-to the town quay. Being a commercial port, though, it can be noisy here at times

Useful information – Katakolo

FACILITIES

Water: Taps near the ferry quay.
Fuel: Take a taxi to a nearby petrol station.
Showers: No but there are toilets near the ferry quay.
Ice: Ask at the tavernas.
Gas: Sold at the supermarkets.
Shorepower: Yes.
Rubbish: Bins on the quay.
Yacht services/chandlery: Ionian Yacht Services (Tel: 26210 31353) is a small boatyard on the beach to the north of the marina. It offers routine maintenance, GRP repairs, engineering and electrical work, as well as boat launch and winter storage.
Telephone: Phone boxes on the waterfront and the high street. Phone cards sold at kiosks and souvenir shops. Mobile reception is good.
Internet: Internet cafe on the high street.
Weather forecast: Posted on each pontoon every day.

Ionian Yacht Services' boatyard at Katakolo

PROVISIONING

Grocery shops: There are a couple of small supermarkets on the high street.
Bakery: Near the high street.
Butcher: In the town.
Banks: Emporiki ATM kiosk near the Port Police.
Pharmacy: In the town.
Post: Post office on the high street. Monday-Friday, 0800-1400. The postal service here is good. Stamps are also sold at souvenir shops.
Opening times: Most shops operate to usual Greek opening times, although the more tourist-related shops tend to be open all day to cater for the cruise ships.

EATING OUT

Like Kyllini, much of Katakolo's regular trade is tourists passing through on ferries and cruise ships. However, unlike Kyllini, it has quite a good choice of eating establishments and some of the tavernas and cafés along the waterfront are really rather pleasant for lunch or dinner. The Archipelago Restaurant is good as is the Arte di Venezia café.

ASHORE

The site of Ancient Olympia is about 45 minutes' drive from Katakolo. It's one of the most famous archaeological sites in Greece, and if you can put up with the coachloads of tourists and the tacky souvenir shops it's definitely worth a visit.

The site, at the confluence of the Alphios and Kladeos rivers, was first inhabited in 3,000BC and is one of the most significant sanctuaries in the world. Dedicated to Zeus, the gold and ivory statue to the god that was one of the Seven Wonders of the World stood here before it was removed to Constantinople and destroyed by fire.

Olympia was also the birthplace in 776BC of the Olympic Games. The sporting contests, dedicated to the Olympian gods, were held every four years on the plains at Olympia. The Games began with sprinting tournaments but gradually they grew to include the pentathlon, a gruelling, five-event competition that incorporated running, jumping, the discus, wrestling and boxing. At its height, 40,000 spectators watched the Olympic Games, attracting interest from far and wide. Originally, entry was for Greek nationals only but in 146BC the country became a province of Rome and these restrictions were lifted.

The Games continued for a further 12 centuries until 393 when they were banned by Emperor Theodosius I. The Roman Emperor was a Christian who sought to rid the country of the pagan rituals on which he considered the Olympic Games were based. Earthquakes and the gradual silting of the Alphios River slowly eroded and buried Ancient Olympia and it wasn't until the 1870s that it was rediscovered, following excavation work by German archaeologists.

The Olympic Games were revived in Athens in 1896 and returned to Ancient Olympia for the first time in 2004, when the shot-put was held in the original stadium.

Visitors to the site can see, among other things, the 5th century BC Doric Temple of Zeus; the Temple of Hera, long-suffering wife of Zeus, one of the oldest temples in Greece; the stadium, and the Palaestra, where wrestlers and boxers practised their sport. There's also the fascinating Olympia Archaeological Museum, where exhibits include collection after collection of treasures excavated from the site.

The museum and site are open Tues-Sun, 0800-1900 and Monday 1200-1900. Entry to the museum is €9; archaeological site, €6.

TRANSPORT

Car hire: Europcar branch (Tel: 26210 55153) at Skafidia, a village to the north of Katakolo. Will deliver for a surcharge. Open seven days a week, 0730-2100.
Taxis: Near the ferry quay.
Bus: Ktel services to Kyllini, Athens and Kalamata leave from Pyrgos (Tel: 26210 22592), about 15 miles (24km) east of Katakolo.
Ferry: The nearest ferry port is Kyllini, to the north. Regular daily services to Zakynthos and Kefalonia throughout the year.
Air travel: The nearest airport is on Zakynthos (Tel: 26950 28322). International and domestic flights several times a week. Athens Airport is a 5½-hour drive from Katakolo.

OTHER INFORMATION

Local Tel code: 26210.
Port authority: The Port Police office (Tel: 26210 41206) is near the cruise ship quay.
Police: Tel: 26210 41111.
Doctor: In Pyrgos, 15 miles (24km) to the east.
Dentist: In Pyrgos.
Hospital: In Pyrgos, Tel: 26210 82300.

There are plenty of tavernas along the waterfront

Kyparissia

Kiparissia, Kyparisia

Kyparissia Bay, to the north-west of Kiparissia harbour: 37°16'.41N 21°39'.29E

Kyparissia is one of the prettiest towns along this stretch of coast. It lies at the southern end of the Kiparissiakos Gulf, 28nm south of Katakolo, and on the lower slopes of Mount Kyparissias, in the Egaleo range. It's a small agricultural town which can meet most needs and, if conditions allow a long enough stay, it is a very good place to victual. The harbour itself is disappointing though. It doesn't offer the shelter of Katakolo, to the north, or Pylos, to the south, and is really only suitable in calm weather. Being on a lee shore, it is too exposed in anything else.

The town dates from around 1,500BC and is described in Homer's *The Iliad* as one of the nine largest cities in Nestor's Kingdom. Eleven of its ships are said to have taken part in the Trojan War and when Kyparissia was liberated from the Spartans, rulers since the Peloponnesian Wars, it was one of the most important ports of the area. Evidence of an ancient harbour still remains and a spring nearby, which is protected by carved stones, is said to be the Spring of Dionysus. According to legend it was created when the god hit a rock with his staff.

NAVIGATION

Charts: Admiralty 189, SC5771; Imray G16, G1; Hellenic Navy Hydrographic Service 061, 22

Kyparissia is easy to locate from all directions. It stands on the lower slopes of the distinctive Mount Kyparissias on an otherwise low-lying stretch of coastline. The castle, perched on a rocky outcrop above the town, is conspicuous from some distance.

From Katakolo, head south through the Kiparissiakos Gulf for about 27nm.

If approaching from the Proti Channel to the south, head north up the Peloponnesian coast for about 17nm. Stay well offshore between Kounellos Pt and Kyparissia as there are rocks and shoal patches close inshore.

The harbour is exposed and should only be considered in calm conditions

There are also rocks around the northern tip of the breakwater, so keep clear until well past its end. Then head south for the quay.

The town of Kyparissia lies on the lower slopes of Mount Kyparissias

BERTHING

Work was being carried out in 2007 on the south and south-east sides of the harbour. The small inner harbour on the east side is used by fishing boats and is too shallow for yachts. Berth either bows or stern-to the southern end of the main breakwater to the west or inside the new mole which extends north-west beyond the fishing harbour. Note that the latter option offers the best shelter. Depths are around 3-4m, but the holding is dubious as the seabed is rocky in places and the mud in between is quite hard. Make sure your anchor is dug in well before going ashore.

Berthing here is not recommended in a northerly, especially if it looks set to increase. Head for the more sheltered harbours of Katakolo, 28nm to the north, or Pylos, 25nm to the south.

ANCHORING

There are no safe anchorages within easy reach of Kyparissia.

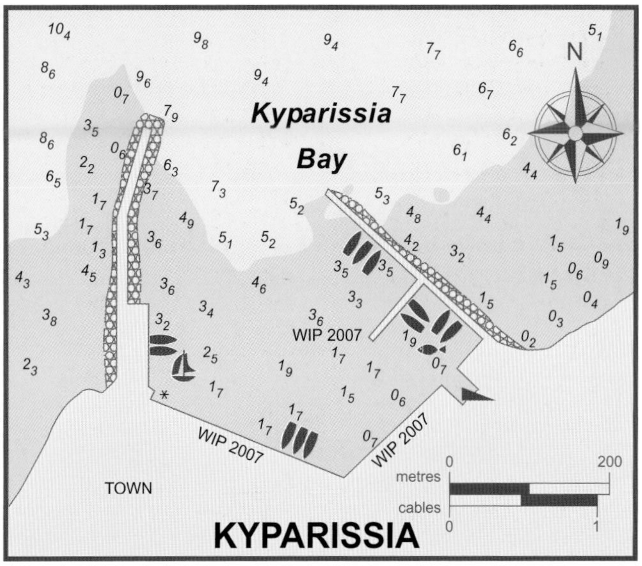

Useful information – Kyparissa

FACILITIES
Fuel: Take jerrycans to local petrol stations, such as BP and Silk in the centre of Kyparissia, near the square.
Ice: At the supermarkets.
Gas: At the supermarkets.
Rubbish: Bins on the quay.
Telephone: Phone box near the harbour; lots in the town centre, near the square. Phone cards sold at kiosks in the square. Mobile reception is good.
Internet: Internet cafe near the fishing boat harbour.

PROVISIONING
Grocery shops: Two large Atlantic supermarkets and several smaller mini-markets and grocery shops in the town centre. Excellent fruit and veg shops uphill from the main square sell really good fresh produce.
Bakery: Lots of bakeries and some patisserie shops. The nearest to the harbour are by the square.
Butcher: Several near the square and a couple of good fishmongers.
Banks: Alpha Bank (Tel: 27610 24384) is on Georgio Kalantzakou Square; The Agricultural Bank of Greece (Tel: 27610 22226) is nearby, as is the National Bank of Greece (Tel: 27610 22903). All are open Monday-Friday, 0900-1400, and have 24hr ATMs.
Pharmacy: Several near the square.
Post: Post office on the main square. Monday-Friday, 0900-1400. Stamps sold at kiosks and souvenir shops; postal service good.
Opening times: Shops here operate to usual hours, 0900-1400 and 1700-2100. Tavernas and souvenir shops are usually open later.

EATING OUT
There are plenty of places to eat in Kyparissia. The most popular with tourists are near the square, but there are some really pleasant little tavernas on the winding roads above the main town. On a clear night, try the café-taverna at the castle, where the views are stunning. The eating area beneath pine trees is a beautiful place to spend the evening. Open from 0900 until late.

ASHORE
If you have a few spare hours, wander up the road past the square towards the castle. The old town is a lovely collection of small winding streets, ramshackle wooden buildings and abandoned houses. The castle itself is Byzantine in origin, built on the site of a Mycenaean citadel. It was extended by the Franks in the 13th century and later modified by the Turks and Venetians during their various occupations. From its position on a rocky outcrop, it watches over the town below and commands fantastic views over the Kiparissiakos Gulf to the north and the plains to the south. Admission is free and it is open throughout the day.

TRANSPORT
Car hire: Travel agents in the town centre can organise this.
Taxis: There are usually taxis near the main square, bus or train stations.
Bus: The bus station (Tel: 27610 22260) is immediately to the north of Georgio Kalantzakou Square, in the town centre. From here you can travel to Pylos (1 hour), Kalamata (2 hours), Patra (2½ hours) and Athens (5½ hours).
Train: Kyparissia's train station (Tel: 27610 22283) is near the bus station. There are up to five services a day between Kyparissia, Patra and Athens and Kyparissia and Kalamata.
Ferry: Services to Zakynthos and Kefalonia leave from Kyllini, situated 58nm to the north, and international and inter-island ferries to Corfu leave from Patra (which is approximately 2½ hours from Kyparissia).
Air travel: The nearest airport is at Kalamata, an hour's drive from Kyparissia. Flights to Athens leave twice a week. Details from the Olympic Airways office at Kalamata (Tel: 27210 22376). Some international flights leave from Zakynthos airport on the island of Zakynthos.

OTHER INFORMATION
Local Tel code: 27610.
Port authority: The Port Police (Tel: 27610 22128) are near Hotel Kanellakis, behind the harbour.
Police: The Police Station (Tel: 27610 22039/62004) is near the square.
Doctor: Near the square.
Dentist: A couple near the internet cafe.
Hospital: Medical Centre (Tel: 27610 22222/24052/24051).

The castle at Kyparissa is Byzantine in origin

Agrilis Agrili

North-west of Agrilis: 37°12'.75N 21°34'.27E
Charts: Admiralty 189, SC5771; Imray G16, G1; Hellenic Navy Hydrographic Service 22

Agrilis is a pretty little harbour on the Peloponnese's low-lying coastline, 4½nm south-west of Kyparissia. It's very shallow and compact, and therefore only suitable for small, shoal-draught yachts. Facilities are scarce, apart from a couple of tavernas, but its real charm lies in the life-sized fairytale castle, just to the south of the harbour.

The tiny harbour at Agrilis is only suitable for shallow-draught boats

Not your usual landmark! The life-sized Disney-style castle at Agrilis comes as something of a surprise when sailing past this stretch of coast

The approach is straightforward from all directions and the harbour easy to identify by the colourful castle that is conspicuous from far off. It is very shallow immediately to the south of the harbour entrance and, this being a lee shore, an approach should only be made in settled conditions.

If there is room, berth alongside the southern breakwater where holding is reasonable, in depths of around 2.5m. However, the entrance is open to the north-west and the swell which is often pushed into the harbour can make the berth untenable. Depths decrease considerably on the eastern side of the harbour, so do not be tempted to berth further in. The shoreline immediately to the north and south of Agrilis is very rocky and inhospitable, so offers no suitable anchorage.

The Castle of Fairytales at Agrilis is a wonderful example of one man's eccentricity. It's an echo of Disneyland's Sleeping Beauty Castle, complete with turrets, battlements and drawbridges, but built entirely of painted concrete. Greek-American doctor Harry Fournier, or Haris Fournakis, returned to Greece from Chicago in the early 1960s and built a scaled-down version of the Eiffel Tower as a present to the town of Filiatra, about three miles to the south of Agrilis. A smaller version of the globe used in the 1964 New York Expo followed, and then, a few years later, came the castle at Agrilis.

The castle is totally incongruous, set amid low-lying agricultural countryside, but it's a magical place. Open seven days a week, 0900-1400 and 1700-2000, admission €1.50.

There's even a massive Trojan horse at the castle!

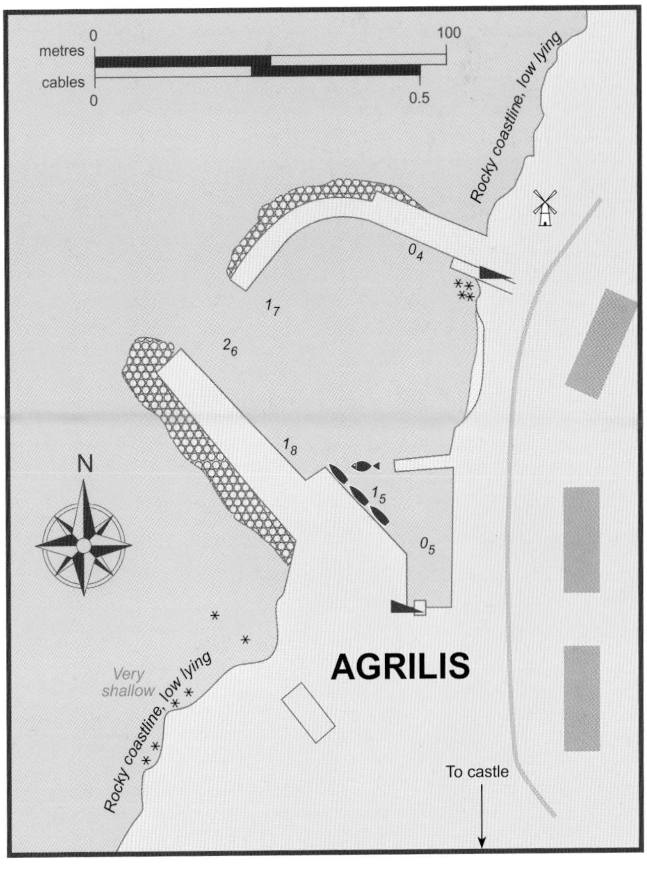

Marathopoli

Marathoupolis

To the north of Marathopoli, in the Proti Channel:
37°04'.14N 21°34'.21E

Marathopoli is a small fishing boat harbour opposite the island of Proti. It is an unremarkable place but pleasant enough, with a handful of shops and tavernas, a couple of hotels and a campsite.

The harbour itself is usually busy with fishing boats, so is of limited use to visiting craft. It is not recommended for boats over 30ft (10m) and even smaller boats may have difficulty finding a space. Shelter in the harbour is reasonable, although it can be quite choppy if a northerly is blowing.

NAVIGATION

Charts: Admiralty 189, SC5771; Imray G16, G1; Hellenic Navy Hydrographic Service 22

From both the north and south, head for the island of Proti, 10nm north of Pylos and Navarino Bay. On approach from the south, stay well offshore as there are reefs and shoal patches along the coast. Care should also be taken around the entrance to Marathopoli, opposite the north-east tip of Proti, as there are reefs on both sides. Watch out for fishing boats coming in and out of the harbour.

Head into the harbour from a northeasterly direction, keeping well clear of the end of the western breakwater, as there is underwater rubble nearby. You should then be able to see fishing boats berthed alongside the southern end of the breakwater and a scruffy beach on the harbour's inner perimeter. There is usually a large number of small fishing boats lying to permanent moorings off the beach.

BERTHING

Quay space for visiting craft is limited at Marathopoli. Fishing boats tend to occupy the quay at the southern end of the western breakwater, so your best option is to berth stern- or bows-to the eastern breakwater. There's around 2.5m of water at its western end and the holding is reasonable but not that satisfactory. Be careful not to snag your anchor or prop on the local boats' permanent moorings.

ANCHORING

The harbour at Marathopoli is so small that there is nowhere for yachts to anchor comfortably. However, there is an anchorage off the east coast of the island of Proti, which is suitable in settled conditions (see p251).

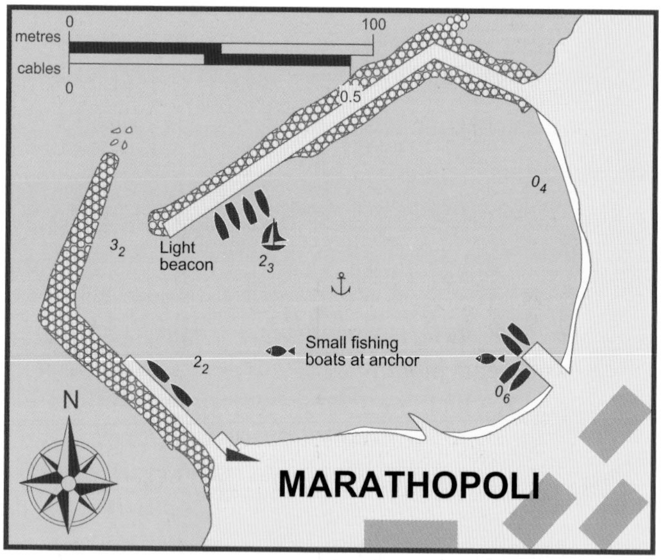

The small fishing boat harbour at Marathopoli

Useful information – Marathopoli

FACILITIES
Fuel: Take a taxi to the petrol station on the main road past Marathopoli.
Ice: Ask at the tavernas.
Rubbish: Bins near the quay.
Yacht services/chandlery: The nearest chandler is in Pylos, 12nm to the south.
Telephone: There are a couple of phone boxes in the village. Mobile reception is good.

PROVISIONING
Grocery shops: Mini-market in the village.
Bakery: In the village.
Butcher: In the village.
Opening times: Most shops open: 0900-1400 and 1800-2000.

EATING OUT
There are a couple of fish tavernas in the village.

ASHORE
During the summer months, a day trip boat runs between Marathopoli and the island of Proti.

TRANSPORT
Taxis: Ask at the tavernas.
Ferry: The nearest terminal is Kyllini, to the north. Services to Zakynthos and Kefalonia leave from Kyllini daily in peak season. For international services, head to Patra, to the north-west. From here you can travel to Corfu, Igoumenitsa and further afield to Ancona, Bari and Brindisi in Italy.
Air travel: Kalamata, on the south coast of the Peloponnese, is the nearest airport to Marathopoli. Two flights a week between Kalamata and Athens airport. Contact Olympic Airways (www.olympic-airways.gr). Athens Airport is a 5-hour drive from Marathopoli.

OTHER INFORMATION
Local Tel code: 27630.

Basic provisions can be found in the village, which flanks the harbour

Proti Island

Nisis Proti

Off the west coast of Proti: 37°02'.94N 21°31'.21E
Off the east coast of Proti: 37°03'.07N 21°33'.68E

Immediately offshore of Marathopoli is the small island of Proti. A former haunt of pirates, the lush green island offers an alternative anchorage if you are too big to get into Marathopoli Harbour. Anchor halfway down its eastern shore in a bay near the monastery. The holding is dodgy and it is also deep here (10-15m), so lay plenty of scope. There is good shelter from the prevailing northwesterlies, but none in a southeasterly. A large bay sits on the opposite side of the island, but it is very exposed and only suitable for short stays in calm weather.

Ashore you'll find the Monastery of Theotokou and the remains of an ancient Mycenaean acropolis.

The Monastery of Theotokou on Proti is a good landmark

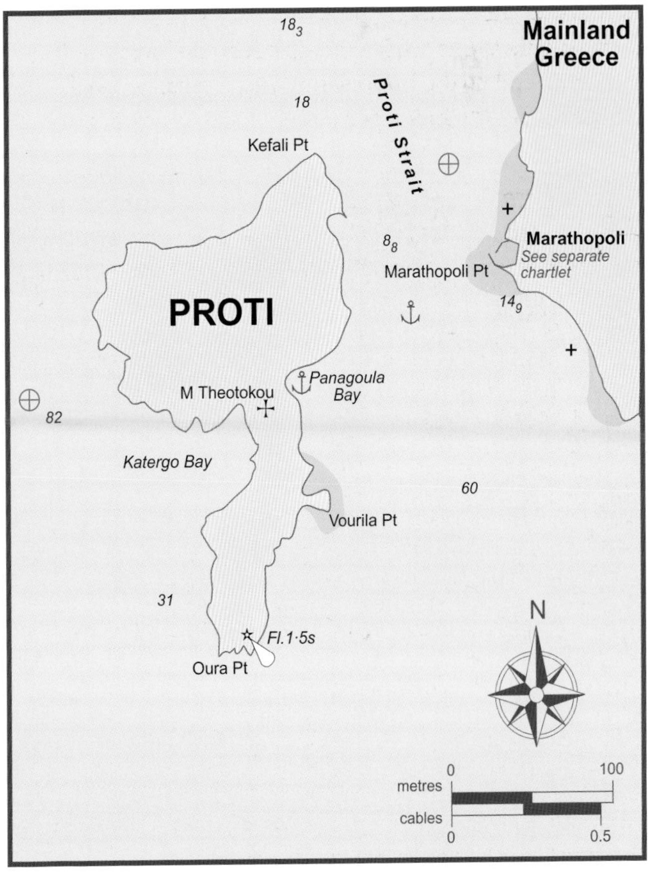

Proti Channel

Steno Protis

Charts: Admiralty 189, 1092, SC5771; Imray G16, G15, G1; Hellenic Navy Hydrographic Service 22

The Proti Channel separates the island of Proti from the Greek mainland. At its narrowest point, off the village of Marathopoli, it measures just ¾nm.

The channel is fairly deep for most of its width (20-30m), although on the western side near the coast, depths decrease to 5m or less and there are isolated rocks just offshore. It is fairly protected and doesn't get too choppy, but watch out for fishing boat traffic in and out of Marathopoli.

The Proti Channel is fairly deep and protected

Vromoneri Bay

Ormos Vromoneri

To the west of Vromoneri Bay :
37°00'.68N 21°35'.96E
Charts: Admiralty 189, 1092, SC5771; Imray G16, G15, G1; Hellenic Navy Hydrographic Service 221/3, 22

Vromoneri Bay lies 3½nm south of Marathopoli, on the west coast of the Peloponnese. It's tiny, with a narrow, rocky entrance and a little sandy beach along its eastern shore.

During the summer, Vromoneri is used by small fishing boats and dories, which anchor or pick up moorings in the north-east corner. Small yachts should anchor on the western side of the bay in about 2.5m, but only in very settled conditions. While the anchorage offers some protection from the prevailing north-westerlies, it is exposed in a southerly and can get quite rolly with swell. Stay in the middle of the channel when entering as there are rocks on both sides. The eastern shore of the bay is also very shallow, so it is best to anchor as close to the entrance as possible. There is a small, seasonal café ashore but, even with the handful of tourists that the beach attracts, it is still fairly secluded.

Vromoneri is Greek for 'dirty water' and this name comes from the nearby sulphurated springs, which have a particularly nasty smell. The springs are said to have healing powers, particularly for arthritis-related diseases.

There are usually seasonal tavernas on the beach at Vromoneri

Small, shallow-draught boats can anchor near the beach

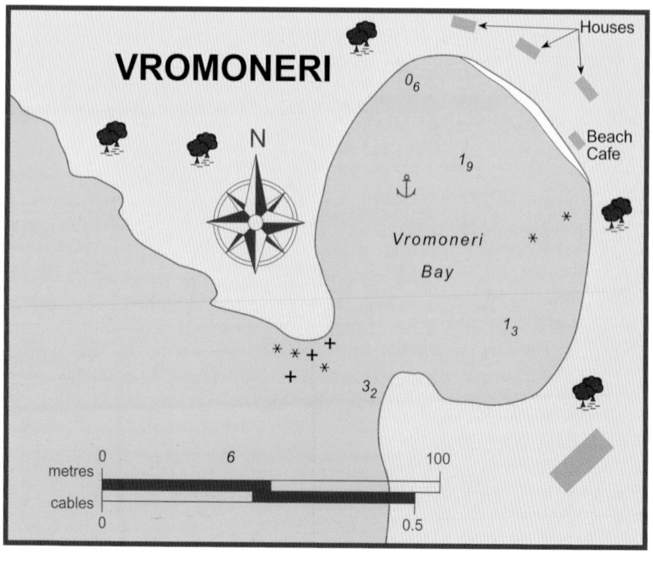

Voidokoilia Bay

Ormos Voidokilias, Voidhokoilia

To the west of the entrance to Voidokoilia Bay: 36°57'.93N 21°38'.46E

Entrance waypoint: 36°57'.86N 21°39'.57E

Charts: Admiralty 2404, 189, 1092, SC5771; Imray G16, G15, G1; Hellenic Navy Hydrographic Service 221/3, 22

Voidokoilia Bay is situated on the west coast of the Peloponnese, 4½nm north of Pylos. The approach is hazard free and through deep water. It is a stunning location: the crescent-shaped bay is fringed by one of the best sandy beaches in the Peloponnese, and has a backdrop of cliff-fronted hills on one side and on the other a low-lying, marshy lagoon, with Navarino Bay beyond. As an anchorage it is only suitable in very calm conditions; once swell generated by the prevailing northwesterlies has built up, the bay quickly becomes very rolly and any protection is lost. If conditions are right, however, it's a beautiful place for lunch or a swim. Anchor close to the bay's northern headland in about 2.5m as it gets very shallow just beyond. The holding on sand is reasonable.

This area is steeped in history and sites of interest. Even if conditions do not allow you to anchor at Voidokoilia Bay, it is worth stopping at Pylos, to the south (see p255), and visiting the area by car.

Just to the east of the bay is the Gialova Lagoon (also known as Yialova and/or Divari). The lagoon has a high biodiversity, and is considered to be one of the most important of its kind in Greece. Over 20,000 birds visit each year, many of them en route to and from Africa, and it is also the only place in Europe where you will find the African chameleon (*Chamaeleo africanus*).

Just to the south of Voidokoilia Bay is an impressive cave. Legend has it that this is Nestor's Cave (*Spilia tou Nestora*), where Hermes, herald of the Olympic gods, hid Apollo's cattle.

Beyond this cave, on the steep hillside overlooking the Gialova Lagoon, and the northern entrance to Navarino Bay, are the ruins of Paleokastro, or Kastro Navarinou. The castle was built by the Franks in the late 13th century on the site of an ancient acropolis. It's impressive and extremely well preserved, and the views from the hill across Navarino Bay are stunning.

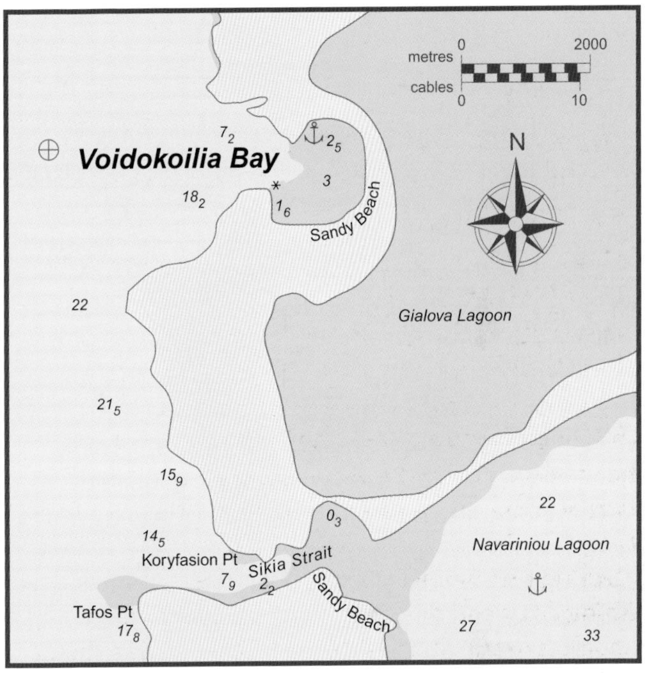

The crescent-shaped Voidokoilia Bay. Gialova Lagoon and Navarino Bay lie beyond

Navarino Bay

Ormos Navarinou

Navarino Bay, to the south of the islet of Chelonisi: 36°55'.83N 21°40'.96E

Navarino Bay is a large, protected bay on the south-west tip of the Peloponnese. Bordering the Gialova Lagoon and with the town of Pylos on its southern shores, it is almost totally enclosed on its western side by the islet of Sphaktiria. It is the largest harbour in the Peloponnese and used regularly as an anchorage by big ships.

It was here, in 1827, that the Battle of Navarino was fought, which resulted in the liberation of the Greek state and was probably the most significant event in the War of Independence.

NAVIGATION

Charts: Admiralty 2404, 189, 1092, SC5771; Imray G16, G15, G1; Hellenic Navy Hydrographic Service 221/3, 22

Navarino Bay is situated approximately 10nm south of Proti Island, its entrance lying just to the west of Pylos. There is an entrance at its northern end but access is prevented by a sandbank with depths of around 0.3m and less across its width.

Enter the bay via the channel between the small, high standing islet of Pylos, just off the southern tip of Sphaktiria, and Neokastron Pt on the mainland, which is identified by its fort that is conspicuous from some distance. At night both the southern end of Pylos (Fl(2)10s36m7M) and Neokastron Pt (Fl G 3s6M) are lit. The approach is hazard free, although a good look-out should be maintained at all times, particularly when big ships are manoeuvring. The west coast of the bay is deep but it is shallower and shelves much more gradually along its eastern shore.

BERTHING

The nearest place to berth is at Pylos, on the southern shore of Navarino Bay. See p255.

ANCHORING

There are several anchorages within Navarino Bay. Deep water flanks the east coast of the rocky islet of Sphaktiria (Nisos Sfaktiria), but off its northern end, near the bay's northern entrance, it is possible to anchor in around 10m. This anchorage is protected from the prevailing northwesterlies, although it can be affected by swell at times.

Avoid dropping your hook in the area to the east, opposite the Gialova Lagoon, as the ground here is foul. In settled conditions when the winds are light you can anchor off the village of Gialova, in the north-east corner of the bay, in 6-8m of water. There is less protection than in the north-west corner but you will find a few tavernas ashore here. The holding on mud and sand is good once your anchor has caught.

Big ships tend to anchor in the lee of the small islet Chelonisi (Nsis Marathonisi or Khelonisi) or in the south-east corner, immediately to the north of Pylos.

ASHORE

Nestor's Cave and the ruins of Paleokastro, a 13th century fortress, can be found on the headland to the north of Navarino Bay, to the south of Voidokoilia Bay. It's a beautiful spot and worth the walk if you want to stretch your legs,. The Gialova Lagoon (see p253) is also interesting to explore. On Chelonisi, the islet in the middle of Navarino Bay, you'll find a monument to the English soldiers lost in the Battle of Navarino and there is a similar one to the Russians on Sphaktiria.

The ship dock at Pylos. The small islets seen beyond guard the entrance to Navarino Bay

Pylos Pilos

To the south-west of the harbour entrance, in the channel between Pylos and Sphaktiria: 36°54'.68N 21°40'.96E
Harbour entrance: 36°55'.15N 21°42'.03E

Pylos stands on the southern shore of Navarino Bay, on the south-west coast of the Peloponnese. A small town, with a commercial port, a decent-sized marina and good shopping, it is a really lovely place to spend a few days and one of the pleasantest harbours along this stretch of coast. The marina offers good, all-round shelter and, although facilities on site are minimal, there are plans for it to be improved at some stage. It's a good alternative to the harbours at Katakolo or Kalamata and quieter too. The natural harbour of Navarino Bay is beautiful and although the various archaeological sites in the area are popular with tourists, Pylos is unspoilt and has retained its natural charm.

NAVIGATION

Charts: Admiralty 2404, 189, 1092, SC5771; Imray G15, G16, G1; Hellenic Navy Hydrographic Service 221/3, 22
From all directions, head for Navarino Bay, which lies 7nm north of the island of Sapientza. The entrance to the bay is located between the Greek mainland and the south-west tip of Sphaktiria, a rocky islet that shelters the bay from the west. The sheer, light-coloured cliffs of the island's south and west coasts are conspicuous from all directions. Closer to, the Neokastro, Pylos's castle, will be seen on Neokastron Pt, a headland on the mainland, directly to the east of Sphaktiria.

Head into the bay, passing to the east of the small islet of Pylos, which sits off the southern coast of Sphaktiria. Once round the wooded Neokastron Pt, you will see the town of Pylos and its commercial harbour. Immediately to the north-east of this, behind a rocky breakwater, is the marina. Its entrance is at the northern end of the breakwater and the approach is through deep water.

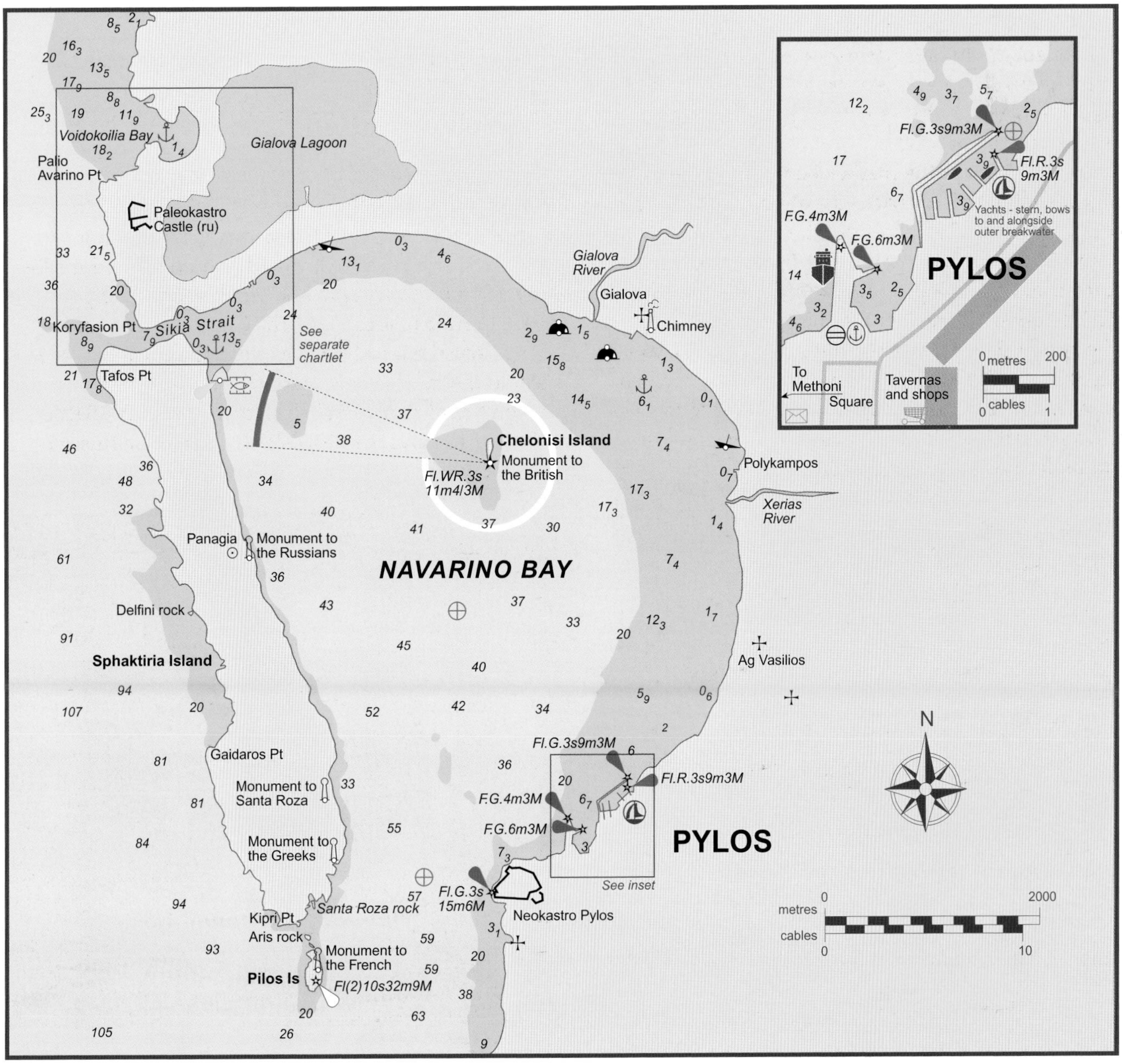

Big ships and day-tripper boats come in and out of Pylos fairly frequently, so maintain a good look-out.

BERTHING
Berth alongside the inner edge of the breakwater or stern- or bows-to one of the pontoons, among the local fishing boats. Depths in the harbour range between 3-4m and the holding is good. Some lazylines had been fitted to the pontoons in 2007, but the rest have yet to be installed.

ANCHORING
There are several anchorages in Navarino Bay, see p254.

The harbour at Pylos. Berth alongside the breakwater where there's room

Useful information – Pylos

FACILITIES
Fuel: By jerrycan: petrol station in the square, another on the outskirts of Pylos.
Ice: Ask at the mini-markets.
Laundry: One to the north-east of the square (Tel: 27230 22502).
Gas: From the supermarket in the square.
Shorepower: There are electricity points but in 2007 these were not connected.
Rubbish: Bins in the marina.
Yacht repairs/services: Pilos Marine (Tel: 27230 22408/ www.pilosmarine.com) specialises in boat and marine accessories and fishing equipment. There is also an Evinrude outboard shop near the post office, while Fotis Seaman chandlery (Tel: 27230 25501) is 100m from the main square.
Telephone: Several phone boxes in the square. Phonecards sold at the kiosks. Mobile reception is good.

PROVISIONING
Grocery shops: Atlantic supermarket on Trion Navarchon, the main square, underneath the Port Police office. Also a well-stocked and very fresh fruit and veg shop on the square, as well as lots of super- and mini-markets dotted around the town.
Bakery: On the square.
Butcher: One near the square and several more in the town. Also a fishmonger.
Banks: Branches of the National Bank of Greece (Tel: 27230 22357), the Agricultural Bank of Greece (Tel: 27230 22201) and Emporiki Bank (Tel: 27230 22398) are all on Trion Navarchon Square.
Pharmacy: On the square, near the off-licence. Another to the west of the square.
Post: The post office is off the south end of the square, on the road to Methoni. Post box on the square. Stamps sold at kiosks and souvenir shops. The postal service from Pylos is good.
Opening times: Most operate to usual working hours: 0900-1400 and 1800-2030, but mini-markets and souvenir shops may stay open later.

EATING OUT
There are a handful of good tavernas in Pylos. The best is Restaurant 1930 (Tel: 27230 22032), just off the main road behind the marina, open 1230-1530 & 1800-0100. The food is superb – mostly traditional Greek, although the menu also includes some delicious international dishes. The view across the harbour from the awning-covered seating area is stunning and the *trompe l'oeil* scenes inside the restaurant are rather fun. Alternatively, try 4 Epohes (Tel: 27230 22739) near the harbour or Ta Aderfia (Tel: 27230 22564), which both serve simple Greek cuisine.

ASHORE
Pylos's castle, Neokastro (Tel: 27230 22897), on the headland to the south of the town, is interesting to visit. Built in 1573, when Pylos was under Turkish rule, it guards the entrance to Navarino Bay and has been a military base for the Turks, Venetians and French, and for the Italians and Germans during the Second World War. A hexagonal fortress at the top of the castle now houses a museum and underwater archaeological research centre and the pretty domed church was originally a mosque. Open Tuesday-Sunday, 0830-1500, admission €3.

Archaeological finds from the Pylos area can be found at the Antonopouleion Museum (Tel: 27230 22448) in Pylos, open Tuesday-Sunday, 0830-1500, admission €2.

A 30-minute car journey away from Pylos is Nestor's Palace, or Ano Englianos, one of the best preserved examples of a Mycenaean palace (Tel: 27630 31437). Discovered in 1939 by the American archaeologist Carl Blegen, the site was fully excavated in 1952 to reveal a large complex of buildings dating to the 13th century BC. It is thought to have been the home of King Nestor, described by Homer in *The Iliad* and *The Odyssey*. The site is open daily, 0830-1500, admission €3.

Some of the earliest Greek script, known as Linear B, has also been found here, and examples of this and other items from the site can be seen at the Archaeological Museum in Hora, a two-mile (4km) drive from the palace (Tel: 27630 31358). Open Tuesday-Sunday, admission €2.

Other sites of interest in the area include the 13th century Paleokastro, on the north shore of Navarino Bay, the Gialova Lagoon and Nestor's Cave (see p253 & p254, for details).

TRANSPORT
Car hire: Pylos Travel Agency (Tel: 27230 22326) or M

There are some really good fruit and veg shops in Pylos

Useful information – Pylos

Travel (Tel: 27230 22696) near the centre of Pylos will organise this, or try Chameleon Trekking (Tel: 27230 28215) in Gialova, a village to the north of Pylos. Alternatively, call Rent-a-car on Tel: 27230 22751 or 69733 15994.
Taxis: Taxis near the square or ask at a taverna.
Bus: Nine services a day between Pylos and Kalamata and one between Pylos and Athens. For more services to Athens, travel to Kalamata. Intermittent services to Methoni, Finikouda and Kyparissia. Bus station in Pylos: Tel: 27230 22230.
Ferry: The nearest ferry port is Kyllini, to the north. From here you can travel to Zakynthos and Kefalonia. Long-distance services to Corfu, Igoumenitsa and Italy leave from Patra, see p194.
Air travel: The nearest airport is at Kalamata. Flights to Athens twice a week. Also a couple of charter flights a week to and from the UK in season. Details from Olympic Airways at Kalamata (Tel: 27210 22376).

OTHER INFORMATION

Local Tel code: 27230.
Port authority: The Port Police office (Tel: 27230 22225/VHF Ch 12) is by the main square.
Police: The police station (Tel: 27230 22100/22316) is situated in the town's main square. The Tourist Police can be contacted on Tel: 27230 23733.
Doctor: Medical centre (Tel: 27230 23777) on the road to Methoni. Follow the signs from the southern end of the square.
Dentist: Several in Pylos: Tel: 27230 22263; 27230 22200.
Hospital: Pylos Hospital (Tel: 27230 22315).
Yacht repairs/services: Pilos Marine (Tel: 27230 22408).

The pretty town of Pylos is a lovely place to spend some time, and there are several interesting places ashore to visit too

Methoni

Methoni Bay, to the east of the breakwater:
36°48'.83N 21°42'.76E

Methoni is a really delightful anchorage on the south coast of the Peloponnese. Tucked into the very south-west tip of the mainland, the bay is protected from seaward by the island of Sapientza and guarded by a distinctive castle that has been of great strategic importance for centuries. The anchorage offers excellent shelter from all but the south-east and, ashore, the town of Methoni has most of the amenities that a cruising yachtsman requires.

Standing at the western gateway to the south coast of the Peloponnese and Eastern Mediterranean, Methoni has played a significant role since ancient times. It is thought that the area was originally colonised by the people of Nafplio and that it was first fortified in around the 4th century BC. Since then, it has been ruled by various occupying forces, including the Franks and the Turks.

However, it was under Venetian rule that it really flourished. The Venetians occupied the town, and the castle that dominates the bay, for 300 years between 1200 and 1500, controlling a vital trade route between the Western and Eastern Mediterranean. Alongside Koroni, on the eastern tip of this finger of the Peloponnese, Methoni was known as the 'eyes of Venice', and watched and dominated shipping here. It became a key trading centre, but in doing so, attracted the Turks, who eventually attacked and won control of the town in 1500. The Venetians regained it in the 17th century, only to lose it once more to the Turks, 30 years later. Following a period of decline, the town, and the rest of the Peloponnese, were finally liberated in 1829.

The pontoon near the breakwater is used by dories and small fishing boats

NAVIGATION

Charts: Admiralty 1683, 189, 1092, SC5771; Imray G16, G15, G1; Hellenic Navy Hydrographic Service 061, 22

The approach to Methoni from all directions is straightforward and through deep water. From the north-west, follow the mainland coast south, past Pylos and

The octagonal Bourtzi is a distinctive landmark that identifies Methoni

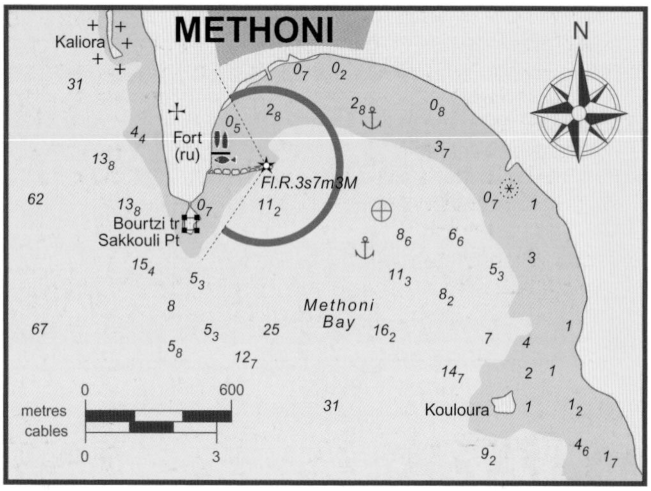

towards the island of Sapientza. From the east, head towards the south-west tip of the mainland. You can pass either side of the islands of Venetiko, Schiza and Sapientza but should stay well offshore around Kolivri Pt, just to the west of Finikouda, as a reef extends off this headland.

The Bourtzi, an octagonal tower built by the Turks, stands on a rocky promontory immediately to the south-west of Methoni and is conspicuous from all directions. If approaching this headland from the north, stay well offshore as there are rocks around it, and the area between it and the breakwater to the east is shallow. The anchorage lies to the north-west of the breakwater. If approaching at night, look out for a red light (Fl R 3M) marking the eastern end of the breakwater.

BERTHING

There is nowhere to berth at Methoni. Occasionally yachts berth stern- or bows-to off a tiny quay in the middle section of the breakwater. However, the breakwater is made of boulders and there is no access ashore, so you may as well free-swing to your anchor.

ANCHORING

Fishing boats lie to moorings in the western corner of Methoni Bay but there is usually room for visiting yachts to anchor to the east of these, off the beach. Anchor in 5m or less. The holding on sand is good and the bay offers shelter from the north-west but not the south.

Useful information – Methoni

FACILITIES

Fuel: No. Fill jerrycans at the petrol station on the main road through Methoni.
Ice: Try the mini-markets.
Gas: Try the supermarket or mini-market.
Showers: No, but toilets are situated on the beach.
Rubbish: Bins are situated near the beach.
Yacht services/chandlery: Pilos Marine (Tel: 27230 22408) in Pylos, 7nm away, is the nearest chandler.
Telephone: Phone box near the beach. Phone cards sold at the nearby kiosk. Mobile reception in Methoni is good.

PROVISIONING

The main part of Methoni is set back from the beach, along two parallel roads.
Grocery shops: Dia discount supermarket on the main road to the beach. Mini-markets on the road behind.
Bakery: In Methoni.
Butcher: In Methoni.
Banks: The National Bank of Greece (Tel: 27230 31320) and the Agricultural Bank of Greece (Tel: 27230 31570) on the main road through Methoni.
Pharmacy: On the main road.
Post: Post office on the main road. Mon-Fri, 0800-1400. Stamps also sold at souvenir shops. The postal service in Methoni is okay.
Opening times: Shops in Methoni operate to usual times: 0900-1400 and 1730-2030, Mon-Sat. Few are open on Sundays.

EATING OUT

There are a couple of tavernas on or near the beach and more in the town. Those near the beach are particularly good on a warm evening as the view over the water towards the castle and Bourtzi is stunning. Restaurant Kali Kardia, Elena, Meltemi and Klimataria in the town can also be recommended.

ASHORE

The castle at Methoni (Tel: 27230 31255) has been fortified since around the 7th century BC and has seen occupation and development by the Byzantines, Franks, Venetians and Turks. It's an impressive, rambling structure and, while little remains inside the castle walls, it's not hard to see what a dominating presence it must have been in its heyday. Evidence of its occupiers remain, with ruins of a Byzantine church, Turkish baths and a church built by the French liberation army. In several places, you'll also see reliefs of the Lion of St Mark, patron saint of Venice. Open daily, 0800-1500, admission free.

Standing on an islet, just to the S of the castle, is the Bourtzi. Built in the 16th century during Turkish occupation, the fortified octagonal tower was used as a prison and as a place of execution. Immediately to the N of this is where the Venetian harbour would have been sited.

TRANSPORT

Car hire: No, but one of the hotels may be able to recommend where to go.
Taxis: Ask at the tavernas.
Bus: Daily bus to Kalamata and Pylos.
Ferry: See Pylos, page 256.
Air travel: See Pylos, page 256.

OTHER INFORMATION

Local Tel code: 27210.
Port authority: Methoni is looked after by the Pylos Port Police: Tel: 27230 22225.
Police: Police station (Tel: 27230 31203) in Methoni.
Doctor: On main road through Methoni, near Hotel Albatross (Tel: 27230 31456), or ask at the pharmacy.
Dentist: No but several in Pylos or Kalamata, see p256 & 258.
Hospital: The nearest is at Pylos (Tel: 27230 22315), but a medical centre can be contacted on 27230 31456.

Sapientza Island

Nisis Sakiotsa

To the north-west of Sapientza Island: 36°48'.43N 21°40'.96E
Anchorage to the east of Longo Bay: 36°45'.48N 21°42'.99E
Charts: Admiralty 189, 1092, SC5771; Imray G16, G15, G1; Hellenic Navy Hydrographic Service 22

Sapientza lies 1nm due south of Methoni, off the south coast of the Peloponnese. It's a steep-sided island, fringed with rocks and covered in wild garrigue and the evergreen strawberry tree *Arbutus unedo*. Measuring 3½ miles (9km^2) in area, it rises to 718ft (219m) above sea level at its highest point, and an impressive stone lighthouse, built in 1885, stands proud at its summit. The island passed from Greek to Venetian hands following the signing of the Sapientza Treaty of 1209, and for a long time was used as a base for ships for both the Venetians and Turks. More recently, in 1825, it was used by the Greek Navy. Unsurprisingly, ships have often fallen victim to its jagged coastline and the wrecks of many of them lie around the island's north coast.

Longo Bay (Porto Longos), on the east coast, is the best anchorage. Tucked behind the islet of Lichnos, it offers shelter from all directions, although it is a bit rolly in an easterly. There are a couple of fish farms in the bay but several yachts can still anchor comfortably with room to swing. Drop your hook in 5m or less on mud, sand and weed.

If you can get ashore, take a wander up the hill to the lighthouse, to the south-west of the bay. The views from the top are spectacular and worth the walk.

Schiza Island Nisis Skhiza

To the south-west of Schiza Bay on Schiza's west coast: 36°42'.18N 21°43'.96E

Charts: Admiralty 189, 1092, SC5771; Imray G16, G15, G1; Hellenic Navy Hydrographic Service 22

Schiza is the biggest island of the three off this part of the south coast of the Peloponnese. Covering 4½ square-miles (12km²), it is lower-lying than Sapientza, but shares the same rocky coastline and scrub-covered landscape.

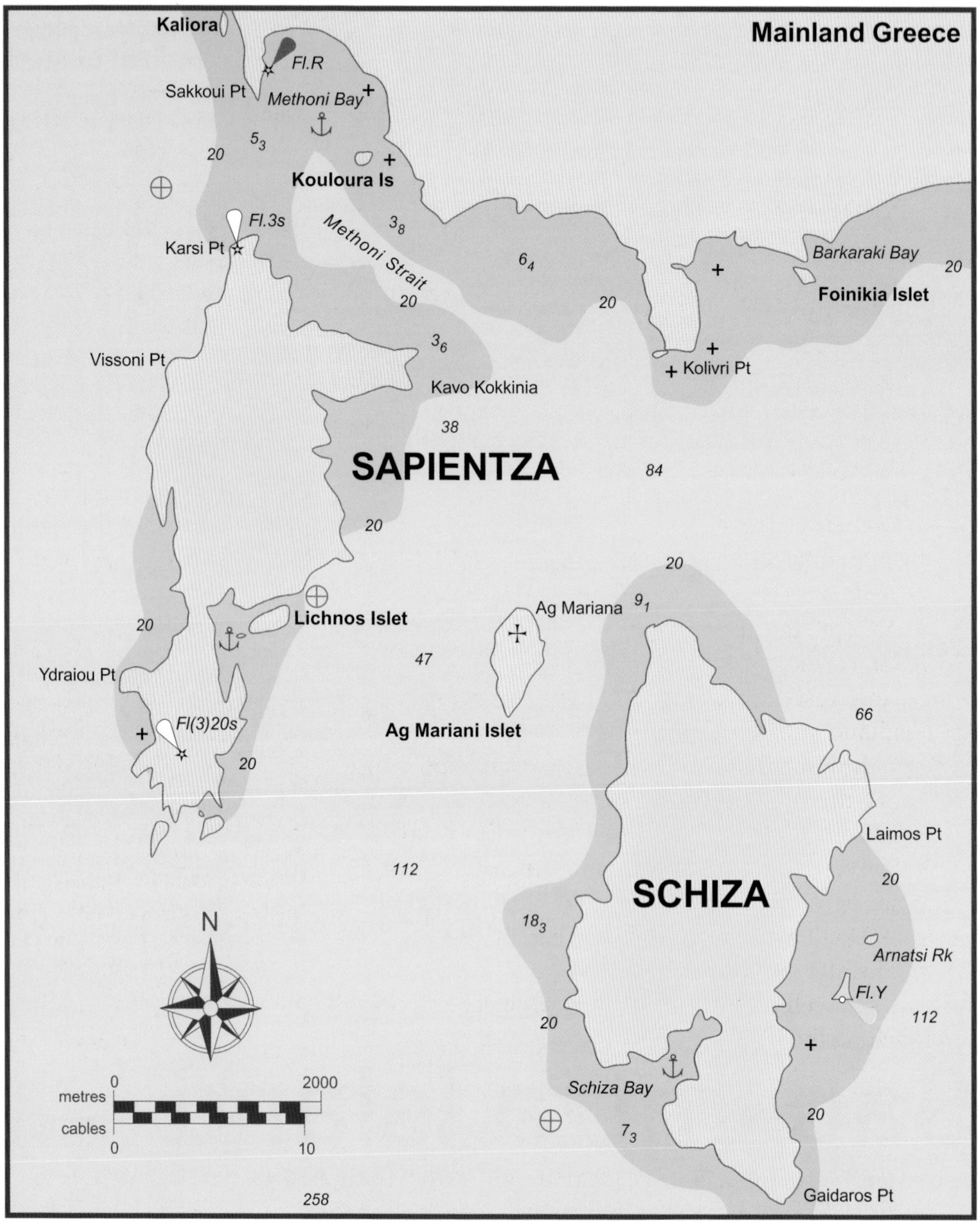

The only possible anchorage is on the south-west coast of the island in Schiza Bay. Although the bay offers good protection from the prevailing northwesterlies it is not considered safe, principally because the island is regularly used as a military firing range. Access to the island is forbidden by the military and, as the risk of being shot at is high, I would not recommend using the anchorage!

The island hit the headlines a few years ago when an international diving team received permission from the Greek authorities to search the surrounding waters for sunken treasure. A hoard of gold coins and jewels, plundered from Greek Jews by the German Max Merten during WWII, are said to have been sunk in a fishing boat off the Peloponnese coast in 1943. As far as I am aware, no treasure has ever been found.

Finikouda

Foinikou, Finikoundha, Finikunda

To the south of the harbour entrance:
36°48'.04N 21°48'.96E

The village of Finikouda lies 5½nm east of Methoni, due north of the island of Schiza (see above). It's a pretty little place, with a small fishing boat harbour and good amenities ashore. With the recent growth in the hotel and tourist industries, fishing and agriculture are less important economically than they used to be. However, it is still a far cry from the over-developed resorts on Zakynthos.

There's been a settlement here since 2500BC, when seafarers from the Eastern Mediterranean used it as a trading base; but it wasn't until the 1840s that the existing village was established.

Although occasionally affected by swell in a southerly, the harbour at Finikouda gives good shelter from all directions and the village has a selection of shops and tavernas.

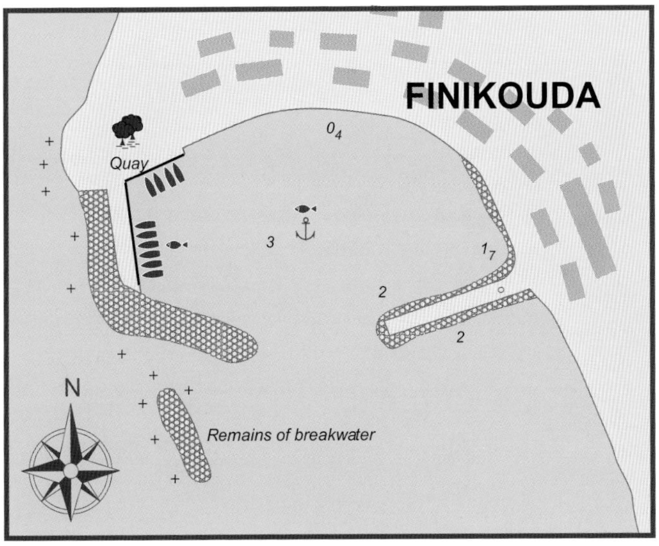

NAVIGATION

Charts: Admiralty 189, 1092, SC5771; Imray G16, G15, G1; Hellenic Navy Hydrographic Service 22

From the west, the approach is straightforward. However, care should be taken around Kolivri Pt, 3nm to the west of Finikouda, as there are rocks off the headland both above and below the water. From the east, the approach is through deep water, and you can pass either side of the islet of Venetiko. Care should be taken from all directions, though, near Finikouda's harbour. On its western side, part of the rocky breakwater has become detached and now lies stranded offshore. Don't attempt to pass between this and the breakwater, as there is a shallow patch here. Instead, sail well past the western breakwater before approaching the harbour from an easterly direction. Depths in the harbour are between 2-3m. An approach at night cannot be recommended as the breakwaters are not lit.

BERTHING

The harbour at Finikouda is small and usually full of fishing boats. If possible, go bows-to off the outer edge of the eastern breakwater. Depths at its tip range between 2.5-3m, but decrease considerably closer in to shore. Leave plenty of room between you and the breakwater to avoid grounding on the rubble at its base. It is also deep enough to berth off the inside edge of the western breakwater but you should check first with the local fishermen as this quay is usually reserved for them. The holding in the harbour is generally good, although there are patches of weed in places.

ANCHORING

You can anchor off the beach to the west of Finikouda in about 5m of water, taking care to avoid the shoal patches off the headland immediately to the west of the harbour. The holding on sand is good but it is totally open to the south, so not suitable in poor conditions.

Finikouda lies on the south coast of the Peloponnese

Useful information – Finikouda

FACILITIES

Water: In the harbour.
Fuel: Fill jerrycans at the petrol station in the village.
Ice: Try the mini-markets or tavernas.
Gas: Try the mini-markets.
Rubbish: Bins situated near the harbour.
Yacht services/chandlery: Pilos Marine (Tel: 27230 22408) in Pylos is closest.
Telephone: Phone boxes in the village. Phone cards sold at kiosks and newsagents. Mobile reception is good.

PROVISIONING

Grocery shops: At least four mini-markets and general grocery shops in the village.
Bakery: A couple near the centre of the village.
Butcher: In the centre.
Banks: No but there are banks in Methoni, to the west, and Koroni, to the east.
Pharmacy: No, the nearest are in Methoni and Koroni.
Post: No, the nearest is in Methoni.
Opening times: Usual hours: 0900-1400 and 1730-2030, Mon-Sat. Few are open on Sundays.

EATING OUT

Several tavernas near the waterfront at Finikouda. Of these, Elena (Tel: 27230 71235), behind the harbour, is particularly good for fish. There are plenty of grill-restaurants in the village too, plus a pizzeria and several cafés.

ASHORE

There are good beaches to the east and west of Finikouda, although inevitably they get very crowded in the summer. Finikouda Bay is also recommended for windsurfing and there are several watersports companies nearby that hire out equipment.

TRANSPORT

Car hire: No car hire but one of the hotels may be able to recommend where to go.
Taxis: In the village.
Bus: Bus stop in the village. Four services a day to Kalamata (Monday-Friday) also call at Methoni and Pylos; three on Saturdays, one on Sundays. Two buses a day to Petalidi, Monday to Friday; none at weekends.
Ferry: The nearest ferry port is Kyllini, to the north, from where you can travel to Zakynthos and Kefalonia. Services to Corfu, Igoumenitsa and Italy leave

Useful information – Finikouda

from Patra on the north-west tip of the Peloponnese. See www.greekferries.gr for booking details.
Air travel: The nearest airport is Kalamata. Two services a week to Athens and weekly charter flights to the UK during the summer. Details from Olympic Airways in Kalamata (Tel: 27210 22376).

OTHER INFORMATION
Local Tel code: 27230.
Doctor: Tel: 27230 71127.
Dentist: In Pylos. See p257.
Hospital: The nearest one is situated in Pylos (Tel: Tel: 27230 22315).
Yacht repairs/services: Pilos Marine (Tel: 27230 22408) in Pylos is the nearest service. Kalamata Marina also offers boat repair work.

Koroni Koronis

Off Livadia Pt: 36°47'.75N 21°58'.91E

Harbour entrance: 36°48'.00N 21°57'.65E

Standing on the eastern shore of the first finger of the Peloponnese, Koroni watches over the entrance to the Messiniakos Gulf. The once significant trading centre is now a modest little town that can be a lovely spot to spend a day or two. Narrow streets, colourful gardens and distinctive Venetian architecture combine with a convivial atmosphere, and the town has much to offer cruising yachtsmen. There are plenty of places to provision and the tavernas overlooking the waterfront serve excellent cuisine at reasonable prices. As a harbour, Koroni offers good shelter from the prevailing northwesterly and southerly winds. However, heavy swell in the bay can be uncomfortable when a strong northerly is blowing.

A settlement known as Koroni has existed here since the 9th century. At this time inhabitants left their ancient city of that name, near the present-day village of Petalidi (see p264), and established a town on the rocky headland of Livadia Pt.

After a short period of Frankish rule, the town was given to the Venetians as part of the Sapientza Treaty of 1209. They built a castle on the headland. For the next 300 years, Koroni flourished, becoming an important commercial centre and another 'eye of Venice' alongside Methoni (see p257). The Turks took over control in the 16th century until 1828 when it was liberated by the French.

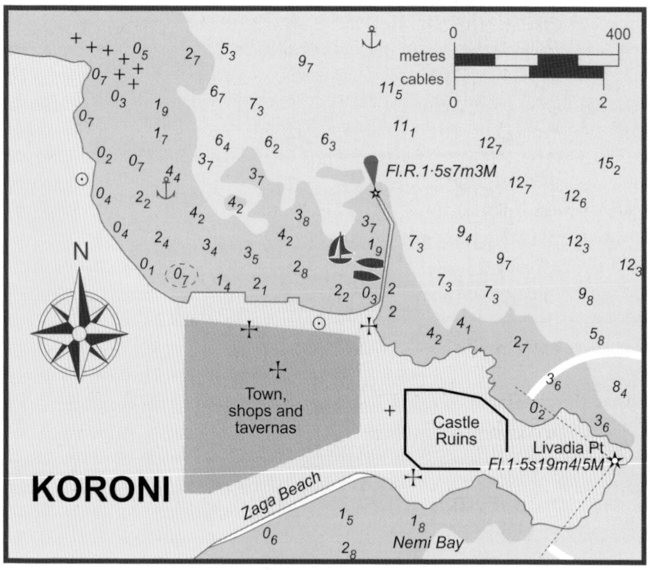

NAVIGATION

Charts: Admiralty 1683, 1092; Imray G16, G15, G1; Hellenic Navy Hydrographic Service 061, 22

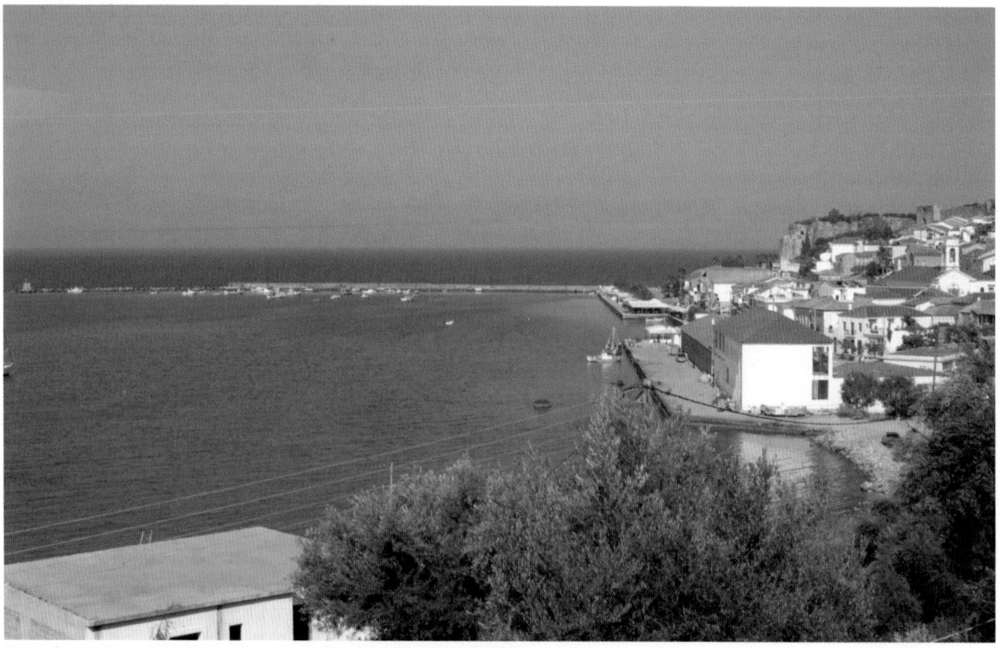

Koroni watches over the entrance to the Messiniakos Gulf

From the west coast of the Peloponnese, head east past the islands of Sapientza, Schiza and Venetiko. Koroni lies on the west coast of the Messiniakos Gulf, guarded from the south by Livadia Pt, which can be identified by the large fort on top. This is conspicuous from some distance and is what you should aim for on approach from both the west and east. The harbour lies immediately to the north of this headland and, along with the town, will

Koroni is a pretty little town. Most provisions can be found here and there are plenty of places to eat at along the waterfront

be hidden from view until you are clear of Livadia Pt. The approach from both the west and east is through deep water.

If coming from the north of the gulf, the town of Koroni is visible from some distance. On entering Koroni Bay, stay well offshore. There are several shoal patches on its western side, so do not be tempted to skirt close inshore.

At night, look for the white light on Livadia Pt (Fl 1.5s). A red light (Fl R 1.5s) marks the end of the harbour breakwater.

BERTHING

The long harbour breakwater provides somewhere to berth at Koroni. Berth stern- or bows-to off its middle section, staying well clear of the local fishing boats. Depths here are around 2m and the holding is reasonable once your anchor has dug in. Take care not to catch the fishing boat moorings. Although it is deeper off the northern end of the breakwater, there is no quay here, which makes landing harder. The southern end of the breakwater and the main town quay are shallow at around 1m, so not suitable for most vessels to berth alongside.

ANCHORING

Two anchorages exist near Koroni: one in the bay itself, to the west of the breakwater, and a second off the beach to the south-west of Livadia Pt. In Koroni Bay, you should anchor in 3-4m to the north of the western end of the quay. Don't come too close inshore, though, as there are several shoal patches nearby. This anchorage is good in calm conditions, but should not be used in a strong northwesterly when it can get quite rolly in the bay.

The bay to the south-west of Livadia Pt is also a calm weather only anchorage. It's a lovely location but totally open to the south and southerlies regularly blow through here.

Useful information – Koroni

FACILITIES

Fuel: Take a taxi to a nearby petrol station. There are several close to Koroni.
Ice: Ask at the supermarket.
Gas: Available from the supermarket or hardware shops.
Rubbish: Bins near the quay.
Yacht services/chandlery: No but there is a tool and hardware shop.
Telephone: Several phone boxes on the quay. Phone cards sold at kiosks. Mobile reception in Koroni is reasonable.

PROVISIONING

Grocery shops: Several supermarkets and greengrocers. Some are near the square, to the west of the quay, and others along the main road through the town.
Bakery: In the centre of Koroni.
Butcher: In the town centre.
Banks: Branches of the Agricultural Bank of Greece

Useful information – Koroni

The Venetian castle at Koroni

(Tel: 27250 22133) and National Bank of Greece (Tel: 27250 22080) and ATMs in the centre of Koroni.
Pharmacy: On a street that runs parallel to the waterfront.
Post: The post office is near Ag Dimitrios Square. Open Monday-Friday, 0800-1400. Stamps also sold at souvenir shops. The postal service in Koroni is okay.
Opening times: Usually 0900-1400 and 1730-2030, although some shops may open for longer. The banks are open 0900-1400, Monday-Friday only, and most shops shut on Sundays.

EATING OUT

Like all the ports along this coast, there is no shortage of places to eat. Tavernas line the waterfront at Koroni and you can usually be sure of a good meal. There are several fish tavernas along the quay and also a couple of pizzerias, which offer a good alternative to seafood. More cafés and tavernas are near the main square.

ASHORE

The castle to the west of Koroni is interesting to visit, if only for its stunning views across Zaga beach and the Messiniakos Gulf. Built on Livadia Pt by the Venetians, the 13th century castle stands on the site of the ancient town of Asine. Now it is home to a collection of houses, a Byzantine church and the Timiou Prodromou convent, established in 1925. It's not as dominant as the castle at Methoni but the location is beautiful and it's a lovely place to wander around. Open daily, admission is free.

Zaga (Zanga) beach, on the opposite side of Livadia Pt to the town, is one of the best beaches in the area. It's long and sandy and a good place to relax for an hour or two.

TRANSPORT

Car hire: A couple of car and scooter-hire offices in the centre of Koroni, a short walk from the quay.
Taxis: Taxi rank near Ag Dimitrios Square, to the west of the harbour.
Bus: Bus stop at Ag Dimitrios Square. You can travel west to Methoni and Pylos or north to Petalidi and Kalamata.
Train: The nearest station is at Kalamata. Daily services to Athens, Patra and Kyparissia. See www.ose.gr.
Ferry: The nearest main ferry ports are Kyllini and Patra on the west coast of the Peloponnese. Services to the Ionian islands and Italy leave from both. From Kalamata, you can travel to Kythira and Crete.
Air travel: Kalamata Airport is 6 miles (10km) north of Kalamata, a large town to the north of Koroni, at the head of the Messiniakos Gulf. Services to Athens and other European destinations fly in and out of Kalamata a couple of times a week. Contact the Olympic Airways office (Tel: 27210 22376) in Kalamata.

OTHER INFORMATION

Local Tel code: 27250.
Port authority: The Port Police office (Tel: 27250 22377) is on the quay.
Police: The Police Station (Tel: 27250 22203) is off the far western end of the quay.
Dentist: Surgery on the waterfront, near the creperie.
Hospital: Medical centre (Tel: 27250 22208) on the outskirts of Koroni.

Petalidi Petalidhi, Petalidhion

Off Petalidi Pt: 36°57'.50N 21°57'.16E

Petalidi is a small town on the north-west shores of the Messiniakos Gulf, about 9nm north of Koroni. It's a pretty little place, surrounded by sandy beaches, and is popular with Greek tourists. The town offers most amenities and, although water and fuel are not available, Kalamata Marina is not far away to the north-east. The harbour has good, all-round shelter but is usually busy with fishing boats, so you can't always guarantee a berth here. However, the anchorage in Petalidi Bay offers a good alternative in all but very rough conditions.

NAVIGATION

Charts: Admiralty 1092; Imray G16, G15, G1; Hellenic Navy Hydrographic Service 22

If you follow the coast north from Koroni you will eventually come to Petalidi in the north-west corner of the Messiniakos Gulf. There are several small towns and villages along this stretch of coast, but after Koroni, Petalidi is the largest and easy to pick out on approach. Look for the distinctive, low-lying Petalidi Pt, which forms the southern headland of Petalidi Bay. An old harbour mole projects off this headland, and just beyond this, to the west, is a rocky breakwater that forms Petalidi's harbour. Don't get too close to either this headland or the old mole as it is shallow for some distance offshore. A night-time approach is not recommended, despite the peninsula (Fl 4s) and the harbour breakwater (Fl G and Fl R) being lit.

BERTHING

Berth stern- or bows-to the end of the breakwater in around 2-2.5m of water. The holding here on sand and mud is reasonable. Space is usually at a premium in

Petalidi, due to the fishing boats, so you may need to make enquiries ashore before berthing. If this is the case, anchor off and take your dinghy.

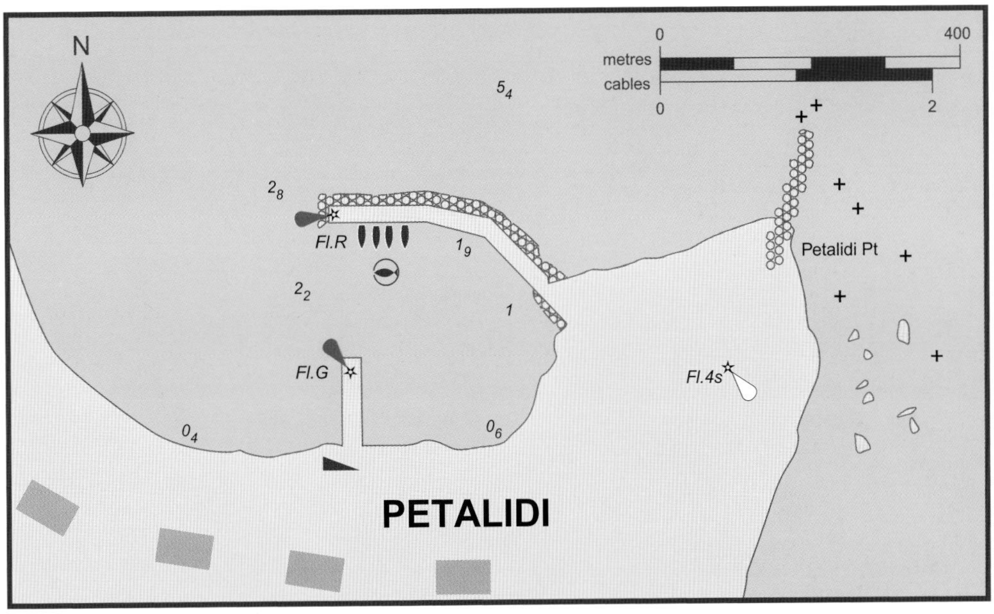

ANCHORING

Yachts can anchor in Petalidi Bay, to the north of the harbour, in 4-5m. Shelter here is good and the holding reasonable, although you should consider heading elsewhere if conditions deteriorate significantly.

Useful information – Petalidi

FACILITIES

Water: Available at Kalamata Marina, to the north-east.
Fuel: Take jerry cans to a nearby petrol station. Kalamata Marina has a fuel pontoon.
Ice: Supermarket in Petalidi.
Gas: Bottle exchange at Kalamata Marina.
Rubbish: Bins near the quay.
Yacht services/chandlery: Services are available at Kalamata Marina.
Telephone: Several phone boxes in Petalidi. Phone cards sold at kiosks and mobile reception here is okay.

PROVISIONING

Grocery shops: Several mini-markets in Petalidi and good grocery shops.
Bakery: In the centre of Petalidi.
Butcher: In the town centre.
Banks: Branch of the Agricultural Bank of Greece (Tel: 27220 31288) near the main square and also an Emporiki Bank ATM kiosk.
Pharmacy: Near the square.
Post: Post Office to the north of the square. Stamps sold at souvenir shops. The postal service here is good.
Opening times: Shops in Petalidi open to usual times: 0900-1400 and 1730-2030, Monday-Friday. Most shut on Sundays, but tavernas are usually open all the time.

EATING OUT

There is a broad selection of tavernas and cafés in Petalidi, most of them near the square, to the north-west of the harbour.

ASHORE

There are several good walks from Petalidi and some of the surrounding countryside yields remnants of an ancient city near the current village. This city was called Koroni, although it was also referred to as Corone or Aipeia, and was founded by the Messenians around 371BC. It predates the current town of Koroni, to the south of Petalidi (see p262), but it is thought that the inhabitants of this ancient city were responsible for establishing the modern town.

TRANSPORT

Taxis: There are often taxis near the square but if not ask for a recommendation at one of the tavernas.
Bus: Buses pass through Petalidi on the way to Kalamata and Pylos, and en route travel to Methoni, Finikouda and Koroni. There are regular services several times a day, Monday-Saturday.
Train: There is a station in Kalamata, from where you can travel to Athens, Patra and Kyparissia, among other destinations. See www.ose.gr for timetable details.
Ferry: Services to Kythira and Crete leave from the commercial harbour at Kalamata. For regular services to the Ionian islands or Italy, travel to Kyllini or Patra on the north-west coast of the Peloponnese.
Air travel: The nearest airport is 6 miles (10km) north of Kalamata. Services to Athens and other European destinations fly in and out of Kalamata a couple of times a week. Contact the Olympic Airways office (Tel: 27210 22376) in Kalamata.

OTHER INFORMATION

Local Tel code: 27220.
Police: Police Station (Tel: 27220 31203) near the square.
Doctor: Ask at the medical centre in Petalidi.
Dentist: On the waterfront in Koroni.
Hospital: Petalidi medical centre (Tel: 27220 31216).
Yacht repairs/services: Kalamata Marina (Tel: 27210 21037) in Kalamata.

Kalamata

Kalamata Marina: 37°01'.39N 22°06'.28E

Kalamata is probably best known for its olives. The plump, almond-shaped, aubergine-coloured olives are sold world-wide and considered to be the finest in Greece for their meaty, rich flavour. But the city, on the north coast of the Messiniakos Gulf, is also the area's capital and the second largest in the Peloponnese. For cruising yachtsmen, Kalamata offers superb facilities and, although rather commercial in places, an ideal place to pause to replenish stocks. Excellent transport links also make it a good location to change crew, and

Kalamata Marina offers the best facilities in this area

the marina, with its dramatic backdrop of Mt Taygetos, is a pleasant enough place to spend a few days. It offers good, all-round shelter and the facilities are the best in the area.

Like many of the towns around the south coast of the Peloponnese, Kalamata has had a chequered history under the rule of various occupiers. Under Turkish rule it flourished as a commercial centre, but it was one of the first to re-establish freedom in 1821 during the Greek War of Independence. Good fortune has been mixed with bad, though, and over 11,000 buildings were destroyed in a major earthquake in 1986. Much of the town has since been rebuilt, and once attractive buildings have been replaced with rather unimaginative structures. However, the Old Town, a 20 to 30-minute walk from the harbour, has still retained some pretty streets and the surrounding hillsides are beautiful.

NAVIGATION

Charts: Admiralty 2404, 1092; Imray G15, G1; Hellenic Navy Hydrographic Service 222/2, 22

The approach to Kalamata from all directions is straightforward and through deep water.

The city lies to the north-east of Koroni, at the head of the Messiniakos Gulf, and can be easily identified from some distance, being the largest mass of buildings on this coast. To the east of it rises a high and very distinctive mountain range. From the mouth of the Messiniakos Gulf, head north towards the western side of the city. The marina is immediately to the west of the commercial harbour, identifiable by its long rocky breakwater. The entrance to the marina is at the western end of this breakwater. Once outside the entrance, contact the marina on VHF Ch69 for berthing instructions.

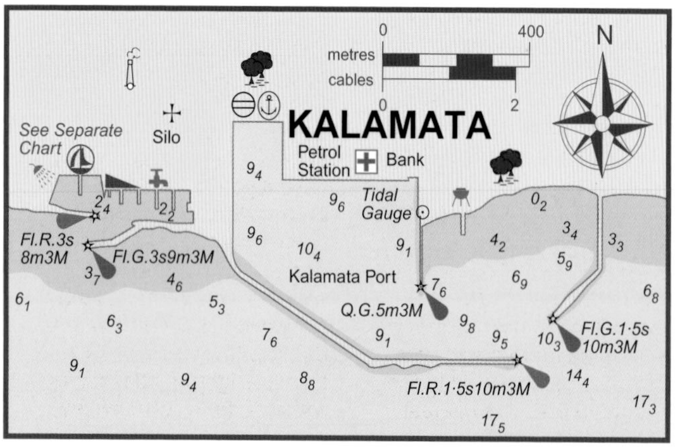

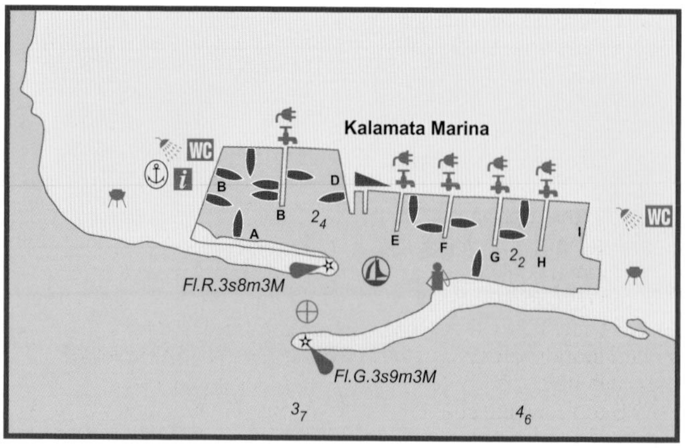

On approach at night, look for the lighthouse on Kitries Pt (Fl(2)12s31m6M), which lies to the south of Kalamata. Lights from the city are conspicuous from some distance and, closer to, you should be able to identify those on either side of the marina entrance (Fl R 3s3M & Fl G 3s3M).

BERTHING

On contacting the marina office you will be told where to berth. Kalamata Marina has room for 250 boats up to 25m (82ft) LOA and 3m (9ft 8in) draught and all the pontoons are rigged with lazylines for stern- or bows-to berthing. There are some alongside spaces available but expect to be charged extra. The marina offers good all-round shelter, with depths between 2.5-3.8m.
Berthing fees: Sample prices for an 11m (36ft) and a 14m (46ft) yacht during high season (1 April–30 September): €24/€33 per day or €290/€390 per month. Low season (1 October–31 March): €15/€19 per day or €197/€242 per month. Fees include 220v electricity. Daily fees are valid from time of arrival until 1400 the next day. Catamarans are charged 50 per cent extra and alongside berthing is plus 80 per cent. Prices may vary.

ANCHORING

Anchoring within the marina or within its vicinity is prohibited except in an emergency. There is nowhere to anchor nearby.

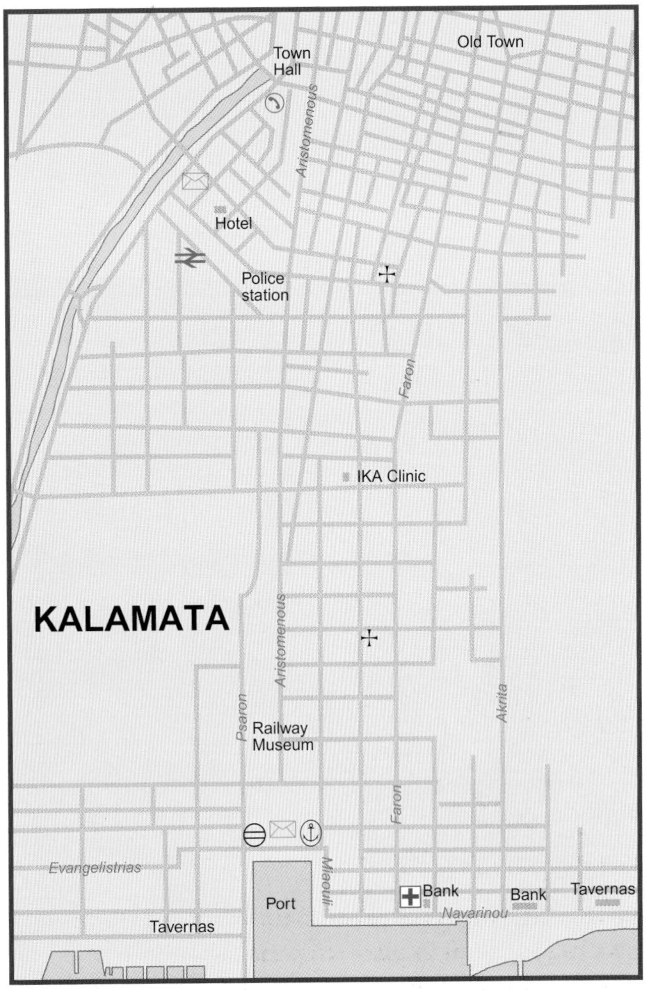

Useful information – Kalamata

FACILITIES

Water: Fresh water at all the berths. Drinking water available on the pontoons and at the fuel quay.
Fuel: Fuel quay at the south end of the marina on Pontoon J.
Showers: Facilities at both ends of the marina. Disabled toilet facilities also available.
Ice: From supermarkets in Kalamata.
Laundry: Self-service laundry near the showers.
Gas: From supermarkets and hardware shops in Kalamata.
Shorepower: Berthing fees include 220v and 380v electricity at all the berths.
Rubbish: Several bins around the marina. Also facilities for biological and non-biological waste disposal.
Yacht services/chandlery: Hard-standing for 150 boats at Kalamata marina and a 65-ton travelhoist and chandler. Sample prices for an 11m (36ft) and 14m (46ft) yacht (prices may vary): crane in/out, €163/€218; pressure wash, €58/€92; crane hire, €95 per ½ hour; sewage pump-out, €0.24/lt. There are also a couple of smaller companies located on the western side of the marina offering maintenance work, including marine electronics.
Telephone: Phone box near the marina office.
Fax: Ask at the marina office for details.
Internet: Kalamata marina is wireless. Ask at the marina office for details.
Weather forecast: Daily reports posted at the marina office.

PROVISIONING

Grocery shops: Supermarket at the marina, plus many more in the centre of Kalamata, near Aristomenous St. More in the Old Town near the castle, plus a daily market, but this is a good 20-minute walk from the harbour.
Bakery: Several in the centre of Kalamata.
Butcher: Lots in the town centre. Supermarkets sell limited goods and there is also a fishmonger.
Banks: Branches of the National Bank (Tel: 27210 88945), Emporiki Bank (Tel: 27210 85108) and the Alpha Bank (Tel: 27210 29286) are on Aristomenous St, which runs north of the port, immediately to the east of the marina. There is also a branch of the Agricultural Bank of Greece (Tel: 27210 22641) nearby. Other branches can be found near the town centre.
Pharmacy: Plenty. One on the road past the port.
Post: Several post boxes within the marina and post can also be delivered to the marina office. The nearest post office is on the road that runs past the port. Stamps are sold at souvenir shops. The postal service in Kalamata is good.
Opening times: Shops operate to usual opening times: 0900-1400 and 1730-2030, Mon-Sat. Tavernas and cafés are open later, as are the larger supermarkets. The post office and banks are open 0900-1400, Mon-Fri only. Most shops shut on Sun.

EATING OUT

Plenty of tavernas and cafés are situated near the marina and more in the centre of Kalamata. The tavernas behind the marina have a good reputation for traditional dishes and those near the commercial port are recommended for seafood. Otherwise, take a wander up to Kalamata's Old Town, where there are some delightful little places, some of them very low key

Useful information – Kalamata

and untouristy. Don't forget to try the local olives.

ASHORE

Kalamata is very much a commercial city but there are still a few interesting places to visit if you have a couple of hours to spare. On Aristomenous St, which runs north of the harbour, is the open-air Railway Museum of Kalamata (Tel: 27210 26404). Located at Kalamata's old station, it contains a large collection of rolling stock, including steam and diesel engines, carriages and various freight trains. A couple of platforms have been restored and there are lots of exhibits relating to the railways. It is open daily.

In the old town, a 20-30-minute walk from the harbour, is the Benakeion Archaeological Museum (Tel: 27210 26209). Housed in a Venetian-style mansion, it stages various exhibitions relating to the Bronze and Roman ages, plus artefacts found at the nearby villages of Petalidi and Koroni. Open Tues-Sun, 0830-1500, admission €2.

Kalamata's castle (**Kastro**), to the north of the old town, dates back to the 13th century. It was built by the Frank prince Geoffroi de Villehardouin on the site of the ancient city of Farai, which Homer mentions in *The Iliad*. The castle has since seen Venetian and Turkish occupation and, although not much remains, it is still an interesting place to wander around. Within its walls are a couple of churches, including a Byzantine one dedicated to the Virgin Mary.

TRANSPORT

Car hire: National Car Rental (Tel: 27210 96262) is near the marina and open daily, 0800-2100; Hertz (Tel: 27210 88628) is on Faron St, which runs north of the harbour. Open daily, 0800-1300 and 1700-2100. Europcar (Tel: 27210 81031) is on Akrita St, parallel to Faron St. Avis (Tel: 27210 28810) is on Kesari St, open Monday-Saturday, 0900-2030. There are also some smaller car and scooter-rental companies near the harbour.

Taxis: Ask at the marina office. There is a taxi rank on Aristomenous St, which runs north of the port.

Bus: Ask at the marina office for details of local services. The main bus station is at the north end of the town, to the west of the castle. From here you can travel to Athens (up to nine services a day, a 4-hour journey), Kyparissia (1½ hours), Patra and Corinth. There are also regular local services to Petalidi, Koroni, Methoni and Pylos.

Train: The station in Kalamata is to the north of the port. Regular services to Athens, Patra and Korinth run daily, see www.ose.gr for the latest information.

Ferry: A weekly service to Crete runs from Kalamata, but for international destinations head to Patra or Kyllini. Services to the Ionian islands and Italy leave from both ports. See p194 and p244 for details.

Air travel: Kalamata Airport is 6 miles (10km) north of the town. From here there are two services a week to Athens (1 hour flight) and usually at least one charter flight to and from other parts of Europe per week. There is an Olympic Airways office (Tel: 27210 22376) in Kalamata, near the OTE building in the Old Town.

OTHER INFORMATION

Local Tel code: 27210.

Port Police: In the Public Services building at the western end of the marina. VHF Ch12/ Tel: 27210 22218.

Kalamata Marina: Kalamata 24100, Peloponnesus, Greece. Tel: 27210 21037/21054; Fax: 27210 26079; Email: kalamata@medmarinas.com; website: www.medmarinas.com

Police: The tourist police station (Tel: 27210 44680) is on Aristomenous St, which runs north of the port.

Doctor: Ask at the marina office for recommendations.

Dentist: Ask at the marina office for details.

Hospital: Kalamata Hospital (Tel: 27210 46000) is near the marina.

Yacht repairs/services: Both available at Kalamata Marina (Tel: 27210 21037).

Kalamata Marina offers the best facilities in this area, but like Corfu and Lefkada marinas, expect to pay premium prices

GREEK PHRASEBOOK

Greetings

Hello	Yasas or yasu
Goodbye	Adío
Good morning	Kali méra
Good afternoon	Kali spéra
Good night	Kali Adío

General expressions

Yes	Né
No	Ohi
Please	Parakaló
Thank you	Efharistó
Excuse me	Signómi
Do you speak English?	Miláte Ang lika?
I don't speak Greek	Then milo Elinika
What time is it?	Ti ora ineh?
What's your name	Pós se léne?
My name is Vanessa	Mé léne Vanessa
Left	Aristerá
Right	Dhexiá
Today	Símera
Tomorrow	Avrio
Yesterday	Khthés
Morning	Proí
Afternoon	Apóyevma
Evening	Vrádhi

Shops & provisioning

Bakery	Foúrnos, psomádhiko
Post Office	Tahydhromío
Stamps	Gramatósima
Bank	Trápeza
Money	Leftá
Petrol station	Venzinadhiko
Toilet	Toualéta
Police	Astynomía
How much?	Póso?
How much does it cost	Póso káni
At what time?	Tí óra

Health

Pharmacy	Farmakio
Doctor	Latros
Hospital	Nosokomío

Transport

Harbour	Limani
Boat	Plío
Car	Aftokínito
Scooter/motorbike	Papáki/Mikhanáki
Bicycle	Podhíkato
Taxi	Taxi
Bus	Leoforío
Bus station	Praktorío leoforíon, KTEL
Train	Tréno
Train station	Sidhirodhro mikós
Aeroplane	Aeropláno

Pilotage terms

Bay	Ormos
Beach	Paralía
Cape	Kávos
Cave	Spiliá
Channel	Porthmos/Dhiávlos
Gulf	Kólpos
Harbour	Limáni
Headland	Akrotiri
Island	Nísos/Nisí
Islet	Nisídha
Point	Poúnda
Reef	Ifalos
Rock	Vráhos
Sea	Thálassa
Strait	Stenó

Numbers

1	énas/éna/mía
2	dhyo
3	trís/tría
4	tésseres/téssera
5	pénde
6	éxi
7	eftá
8	okhtó
9	ennéa/enyá
10	dhéka

Days of the week

Sunday	Kyrakí
Monday	Dheftéra
Tuesday	Triti
Wednesday	Tetárti
Thursday	Pémpti
Friday	Paraskevi
Saturday	Sávato

Food & drink

Menu	Katálogo/lísta
The bill	O logariasmós

Ingredients

Bread	Psomí
Butter	Vootiro
Cheese	Tyrí/Tiri
Eggs	Avgá
Fish	Psári(a)
Honey	Méli
Ice	Pagos
Water	Neró
Yoghurt	Yiaoúti/Yaoorti
Salt	Aláti
Sugar	Záhari
Pasta	Makaronia

Greek dishes

Hortofágos	Vegetarian
Kréas	Meat
Lahaniká	Vegetables
Makaronádha	Pasta dish
Psitó	Roasted
Saganáki	Fried cheese
Skáras	Grilled
Stó foúrno	Baked
Thalasiná	Seafood
Tis óras	Grilled food
Yemistá	Stuffed

Appetisers

Avga meh tiri	Cheese omelette
Dolmádhes/Dolmathakia	Stuffed vine leaves
Domatosaláta	Tomato salad
Kafterí	Cheese and chilli dip
Kopanistí	Spicy cheese dip
Melitzanosaláta	Aubergine dip
Patatasalata	Potato salad
Skordhaliá	Garlic dip
Soúpa	Soup
Taramosaláta	Cod roe paté
Tzatziki	Yoghurt and cucumber dip
Horiátiki saláta	Greek salad – tomatoes, feta and olives
Saláta	Salad

Fruit & vegetables

Angoúri	Cucumber
Bouréki/kolokithakia	Courgette
Domátes	Tomatoes
Fakés	Lentils
Fasolákia	French beans
Karota	Carrots
Kerasia	Cherries
Patátes	Potatoes
Piperiés	Peppers
Ryzi/Piláfi	Rice

Meat & meat dishes

Arni	Lamb
Arni brizoles	Lamb chops
Arnaki meh bami	Lamb and okra stew
Arni meh melitzanes	Lamb with aubergines
Keftédhes	Meatballs
Keftédhes meh saltsa	Meatballs in tomato sauce
Khirino	Pork
Kotópoulo	Chicken
Krehatika	Meat dishes
Melitzanes yemistes meh kima	Aubergines stuffed with minced meat
Moussaká	Aubergine, potato and lamb mince with béchamel sauce
Papoutsákia	Stuffed Aubergine
Soutzoukákia	Minced meat rissoles
Souvlaki	Chicken, lamb, pork, beef or fish kebab
Spetzofáï	Sausage and pepper stew
Stifádho	Meat stew with tomatoes and onions
Vothino	Beef

Fish

Astakos	Lobster
Bakaliáros	Cod or hake
Barbóuni	Red mullet
Garídhes	Shrimps or prawns
Glóssa	Sole
Kalamaria	Squid
Koli	Mackerel
Mydhia/Mithia	Mussels
Psari/Psaria	Fish

Drinks

Boukáli	Bottle
Byra	Beer
Frapeh	Iced coffee
Gála	Milk
Kafés	Coffee
Khimos frooton	Fruit juice
Aspro krasi	White wine
Kókkino krasi	Red wine
Nero	Water
Nescafe	Instant coffee
Portokalatha	Orange juice
Potíri	Glass
Tsáï	Tea